TED BUNDY. DAVID "SON OF SAM" BERKOWITZ. JOHN WAYNE GACEY. JUAN CORONA.

These are today's convicted serial murderers, men whose crimes are grisly, shocking, and terrifying. But there was another serial murderer whose crimes were more macabre, more horrible—and even more numerous. His name was Herman W. Mudgett, alias H. H. Holmes. He lived—and killed—in America at the turn of the century. He admitted from 27 to 133 murders, although the actual total may have topped 200. His case, notorious in the annals of crime, is called "The Holmes Case." And now award-winning author Allan W. Eckert brings us this chilling story...a true tale of evil incarnate...a nightmare of torture, cruelty and death in...

THE SCARLET MANSION

Bantam Books by Allan W. Eckert
Ask your bookseller for the books you have missed

The Narratives of America Series
  The Frontiersmen
  Wilderness Empire
  The Conquerors
  The Wilderness War
  Gateway to Empire

The Scarlet Mansion

The Scarlet Mansion

Allan W. Eckert

BANTAM BOOKS

TORONTO · NEW YORK · LONDON · SYDNEY · AUCKLAND

THE SCARLET MANSION
*A Bantam Book / published by arrangement with
Little, Brown & Company*

PRINTING HISTORY
*Little, Brown edition published June 1985
Bantam edition / September 1986*

*Bantam Books are published by Bantam Books, Inc. Its trade-
mark, consisting of the words "Bantam Books" and the por-
trayal of a rooster, is Registered in U.S. Patent and Trademark
Office and in other countries. Marca Registrada. Bantam
Books, Inc., 666 Fifth Avenue, New York, New York 10103.*

PRINTED IN THE UNITED STATES OF AMERICA

KR   0 9 8 7 6 5 4 3 2 1

for
ARTHUR E. OSTERGARD, M.D.

. . .with unlimited appreciation for favors past
and—most of all—for the wonderful
and treasured gift of friendship.

The Scarlet Mansion

Prologue

August 1871

The two boys snickered nervously, each unobtrusively trying to maneuver himself so that the other would be first to enter Old Man Gant's farmhouse. They'd seen the ramshackle place often, but only from a distance. This was their first attempt at penetration and what was initiated as a lark had now become a matter of courage and honor, neither wanting to lose face by backing down, yet each wishing desperately he were anywhere else.

The abandoned house crouched far from the road on the outskirts of Gilmanton, New Hampshire. There were stories about the queer old man who had lived here years ago; many years before either of these eleven-year-olds was born. Strange lights had been seen, odd sounds heard, and maniacal laughter—not always attributed only to Gant—occasionally floated eerily across the small valley, mostly at night but sometimes even on gloomy days when tendrils of mist enshrouded the unkempt fields. It was a decrepit old house even when Old Man Gant lived there. No one could recall a time when both the man and the house were not old and strange. Crudely lettered signs warning would-be visitors to stay away were rendered redundant by the several brutish mongrel dogs, gaunt and perpetually suspicious, that were Gant's only known companions.

The old man's eventual death, undiscovered until long after the fact, was always linked to the dogs in one of two prevalent tales. Human bones, allegedly his, were found scattered about the interior of the house. One story had it that his canine companions, deliberately maintained in a state of near starvation, had finally turned on him, brought him down and devoured him, then fled, never again to be seen. The other version was kinder, perhaps, having the food-deprived dogs wait for some time after he had died—whatever the cause of death—before being driven by hunger to consume him. In either case, the grisly tales ordinarily sufficed to keep the curious away. There were no known heirs and the land, pimpled by rocks, was sterile and mean, covered by no one. And so the ramshackle old house had remained untouched through these years. The windowpanes were lost early on, shattered by rocks bearing the courage of boys whose bravery ended precisely a stone's throw from the structure. Walls and floors became banquets for termites and carpenter bees, padded furniture and cornhusk mattresses served as bedding for mice and rats, while layers of reeking guano built up beneath rafters that had become diurnal roosts of ugly little brown bats. The passing seasons took frightful due and gradually Old Man Gant's house disintegrated, each year its siding boards more warped and sprung, its shaked roof more sagged and holey.

This was the house upon whose threshold the two boys were now poised.

For six years—more than half their lives—Tom Eschler and Herman Mudgett had been closest of friends. Tom was a big, muscular boy who usually led the way in whatever enterprise they embarked upon. Herman was shorter, thin to the point of scrawniness and much more hyperactive. But he was certainly brighter by far, considered by his teachers to be one of the better students they'd ever had, and it was he who usually came up with the novel ideas of what they would do next. However apparently mismatched, Tom and Herman thoroughly enjoyed each other's company, experiencing together the varied delights and miseries of boyhood and competing with one another in every undertaking.

More often than not, when what the boys engaged in was an indoor pursuit, it was carried out in Tom's house. His parents were warm, friendly, interested and interesting—a far cry from Herman's. The smaller boy's mother was a cold, harsh woman, blond, blue-eyed and more than moderately attractive, yet unbending in discipline and incapable of showing affection. At no time in his memory had she ever hugged or kissed him and once, when he impulsively hugged her while she was ironing, she had deliberately jammed the heavy flatiron against his bare arm, giving him a severe burn. He never forgot it and, deep inside, he never forgave. His father was friendlier, yet more to be avoided because of his mercurial temperament. In seconds he could change from a reasonably pleasant individual to a raging tyrant. Once he struck Herman with a rake and broke the boy's thumb. Another time, when the boy had complained of a toothache, his father had dragged him wailing with fear to the toolshed, forced him to lie on a bench, pushed a greasy pliers into his mouth and pulled out the molar by brute strength; but it had been the wrong tooth, so he pulled the correct one as well. And when Herman's screaming annoyed him, he poured kerosene on a cloth and held it over the boy's nose and mouth until he fell unconscious.

Herman Mudgett feared and hated his parents.

In Tom Eschler he had found more or less an equal, with whom he could be himself without fear. There was nothing of his that he would not give to—or at least share with—this best friend. And what they shared, even more than material things and experiences, were their confidences, their dreams, their innermost hopes and fears.

In summer Tom Eschler and Herman Mudgett were inseparable, planning their forays most often at Tom's house, since even the larger boy had learned that Herman's father was too quick to see or imagine minor infractions and lay on with an axe handle. They skinny-dipped together in the creek, with diving contests from a great leaning tree overhanging the swimming hole. They roamed the maple forest, fighting Mohawks and Mohegans or testing their stealth against one another. In winter they trailed rabbits together, used streams of urine to sign their names on fresh snow in yellow-edged script and held distance-pissing competitions.

Not many months ago the pair had even masturbated together once in the Mudgetts' hayloft, sniggering over the way they were tempting terrible fate with their flagrant transgression, each flaying himself vigorously in concerted effort to be first to transform his penis from utilitarian to creative, to reach that point when "it" happened—that elusive "it" the older boys discussed that left a body weak and trembly. Though the marvelous awakening had never before happened to either, they had pulled and jerked with the greatest of expectation. But for these two it hadn't yet been time for that giant step through the threshold of puberty. Respectively turgid members withstood as much punishment as they could bear and then finally betrayed aching loins by returning to frustrating flaccidity. The intense mortification was mitigated only by each boy's overwhelming relief that even though he had not climaxed, neither had his companion.

Now this different challenge lay before them. The front door of Old Man Gant's house, long ago having fallen from rotted hinge holes, lay amid shards of glass on the porch and the portal yawned vacantly. The boys became silent and dared not look at one another, lest their expressions exhibit traces of weakness or fear. They crunched slowly forward over the debris and entered the house reasonably abreast, too proud to hold hands or grip one another's arms, but comforted by pressing close together.

The interior of the old structure was lighter than they had expected, largely due to a multitude of holes in the roof and upper story as well as from the gaping trapeziums that once had been windows. Being inside was not so scary after all and their nervous laughter returned. True grit now demanded that they separate and embark on independent explorations, no longer concerned with the racket of broken glass and plaster continuing to grit and crackle beneath their feet. In mutually unspoken I-won't-mention-it-if-you-don't-mention-it, both pretended not to notice the dark and narrow open doorway leading downward to what had evidently been a fruit cellar.

Tom made his exploratory decision first, inching his way cautiously toward the remains of the kitchen. Herman, with Hobson's choice, moved to a solid stairway, remarkably intact except for a broken balustrade, and edged carefully upward. He wisely clung close to the wall, testing each step with gradual pressure of one foot before placing his weight on it and moving up one more level. The musty, acrid stench of bat urine became stronger as he ascended and his nose wrinkled in distaste. He found the upstairs hallway still reasonably intact but the remainder of the upper story an absolute shambles. Decades of termitic assault had exacted its toll and the floors of the bedrooms were largely gone, having caved in and dumped themselves into pick-straw piles of debris in the rooms below. What little flooring remained sagged and creaked menacingly at the boy's weight and, except close to the load-bearing walls, was treacherously unstable.

His progress thwarted, Herman was about to return downstairs when he saw Tom almost directly below him in the kitchen, stooped over and peering hesitantly into a battered cabinet. A euphoric sense of power blossomed; a giddy feeling, never before experienced, of having dominance over another human being: *I could piss all over him from up here. I could all of a sudden scream and scare the living shit out of him. I could jump down and land right into the middle of his back. I could drop that board, broken end first, smack-dab on his head.*

Tom straightened from his fruitless inspection and took a step toward the sink, then yelped as his foot crashed calf-deep through decayed floor planking. He fell and jerked his leg free, faintly moaning as he rubbed a wounded shin. An object in the hole caught his attention and the minor injury was forgotten as he peered more closely. His mouth pursed with silent wonderment as he reached into the cavity and extracted an old tobacco tin. The flat metal container bore the residue of a rust-speckled painted green label and the hinged lid at one end had rusted shut. The tin's heaviness prompted him to shake it and, at the faint sound of heavy coins inside, his mouth spread into a grin that exposed somewhat bucked teeth. He glanced around but not upward and, seeing no one, furtively thrust the tin inside his shirt, wedging it under the pressure of his belt. He looked into the recess again but nothing else was there.

"Hey, Herm," he yelled toward the stairway, wincing a little as he straightened. "Let's go. Ain't nothing worthwhile here. Just an old falling-down dump of a place. I gotta get home anyhow."

Herman drew back out of sight, making no reply until he had tiptoed to the head of the stairs. "Yeah," he said then. "Sure. Coming." He clumped downward and met Tom at the bottom. "Find anything?"

"Nope. How 'bout you?"

Herman shook his head. "You didn't find *anything?*"

"No. I told you no. C'mon, let's go."

Tom Eschler turned away toward the front doorway. He did not see or hear Herman snatch up a three-foot length of broken two-by-four, neither heard nor saw the makeshift weapon swung in a savage arc. His only sound was a stifled inhalation following the thud of impact as a rusted joiner spike projecting from wood drove through his temple and fully two inches into his brain. The wood was yanked from Herman's grip as Tom fell on his side atop a pile of broken wood from the collapsed floor above. His tensed form relaxed and lay still, eyes half-open, the death weapon wedged beneath his head.

Without expression, Herman looked down at the body. For a moment his consciousness turned inward, expecting to encounter a burst of remorse, fear, panic. None was there, only enhanced euphoria. He was, at this wonderfully exhilarating moment, omnipotent. And, simultaneously, he experienced a powerful erection. The faintest suggestion of a smile twitched his mouth corners.

He stooped and pulled the hidden tin from Tom's waist and thrust it into his own pocket. His gaze moved around and upward, then turned back to the stairs. He climbed them again and moved cautiously into the front bedroom, edging along the wall toward the hole beneath which lay Tom. With outstretched foot he pressed tentatively against the broken edge of the flooring. It creaked and groaned. A single board fell and came to rest across Tom's legs. He put on more pressure and the planking splintered and broke as a table-sized section of the floor split, hung pendulous for a fragile moment, then snapped free and crashed onto the form below.

Much later—after Tom had been reported missing, after searchers had finally located the body at the close of their second day of searching, after the Belknap County sheriff had reconstructed to his own satisfaction how the boy had entered the house, gone upstairs and fallen through the floor, after a coroner's inquest had pronounced it death by accident, after a funeral service had been held in Gilmanton's First Methodist Church—Herman W. Mudgett stood at the graveside behind the church and wept along with Tom's parents. And as he wept, he considered what he might buy with the six tarnished silver dollars the tin had contained.

One

*A*t the far end of Michigan's New Haven station house, twenty-four-year-old Robert Leacock sat scrunched down under the sun canopy of the buggy, vainly endeavoring to make his two-hundred-sixty-pound bulk look smaller. The heat was all but intolerable, yet he wore a black rainslicker with the collar turned up and a floppy fishing hat with the brim turned down to help hide his features. He wiped his face frequently with a limp cloth. Fortunately, the only person on the platform was the stationmaster, battered mail pouch looped over one arm and rheumy eyes fixed on the watch cupped in his palm.

A big thunderhead was looming in the northwest when the six-car Grand Trunk Western train rumbled in, wheezing and hissing, passing the stationary buggy and causing Leacock's horse to shy in its traces. The engine stopped beyond the far end of the platform and a conductor alighted from the third car. He positioned a portable step on the planking, then assisted an elderly woman and little girl in alighting. Leacock watched from under his hat brim, expecting Herman to be next off.

"Hello, Bob."

The voice coming from directly behind and below caused him to start violently. Herman Mudgett, a derby perched jauntily on his head, grinned and winked at him, stepped around behind the rig, and climbed up next to him. His only piece of baggage was a smart valise of quality suede. He spoke through the grin. "Come on, Bob, you didn't expect me to get off in front of God and everybody, did you?"

"I don't like this one bit, Herman," Leacock growled without greeting.

"Relax, Bob, relax. And it's not Herman anymore. It's Holmes. Henry H. Holmes."

Ignoring the reply, Leacock snapped the reins and put the horse into a brisk trot. Neither man spoke again until they were outside town on the road leading southward to New Baltimore. Then it was the driver who spoke again, repeating himself. "I don't like this one bit! I'm getting established here, sharing my father's practice. Something like this, if it ever got out . . . Dammit, Mudgett, I wish I'd never gotten involved in it. I wish—"

"You can wish in one hand and shit in the other and see which gets filled first. Grow up, Bob. And I'll tell you one last time: Holmes, not Mudgett." There was quiet menace in his tone, but then he shrugged and became placating. "You're here, aren't you, Bob? No one made you come. Is it that you don't want me to have my share? Bear in mind, I've taken all the major risks and even lost my identity in the process. Nevertheless, I can't force you to give me the money. If you feel so strongly about it, just turn around and take me back to the station."

Dr. Robert Leacock's jaw clamped shut. *Damn you, Mudgett. Damn you clear to hell and back. Always so cocksure of yourself. And of me. And everybody else.* His heavy lips protruded petulantly, but he made no effort to turn the rig back. Nor was he able to maintain his silence. "I just don't see why we have to go through all this rigamarole about the boat. Why not split it right here and now and be done with it? For God's sake, Herm—I mean Henry—there's no one around."

"Can you guarantee there's no one in that grove over there, watching us? What about this farmhouse? Isn't that someone in the upper window? No, I guess not. But, Bob, we've done it right so far and we're not going to start acting stupidly now. Did you burn the letters?"

The letters. The planning and confirming of this idiocy. "Yes, of course. Yes." *Leacock, stop repeating yourself.*

"Anyone see you leave home in this rig?"

"No, only in the boat a few hours ago. I took the buggy out to Crane's old barn—the one I wrote you about. He's gone for the summer. I took it there after dark last night and walked home."

"That's where the boat is too, at Crane's?"

Leacock nodded. "Rickety old dock, but serviceable. Far enough away from town, at least, that you can't even see another house till you're out a half a mile."

"How long till we're there?"

"Half an hour, maybe a little more."

"Fine. Wake me when we get there." He folded his arms across his chest and leaned back with eyes closed. Almost immediately he was asleep.

Leacock grimaced, wondering how his companion could actually fall asleep at such a time, when his own nervousness was all but tangible. Nothing had changed. Mudgett—no, Holmes now—had been a cool-head from their very first meeting at Ann Arbor five years ago come September. That had occurred in the admissions office at the University of Michigan medical school. That time, Leacock, lubricating his own rotundity with ample perspiration from every pore, found himself seated on a hard chair between opposites: to his left an engaging young fellow, self-assured, nattily dressed and quite handsome—Herman Mudgett; to his right, a freckled, red-mopped, animated fencepost, all knots and knees and nerves with frazzled ends—Chester Fish. An unlikely trio for companionship, yet close companions they had become, each contributing through their association to the overall betterment of scholastic standing on the one hand and the thrill of nonconformity on the other.

Chester's contribution in academics was an amazingly photographic memory. On his brain cells became embedded the most important passages of their texts, the most pertinent utterances of their professors, and the full scope of anatomical schematics that he could sketch at will with phenomenal accuracy. It was in the *application* of his stored wealth of medical knowledge that Chester failed . . . and Robert Leacock excelled. A born diagnostician, his knack of correctly attributing even the most obscure of symptoms was uncanny, but no less so than his general excellence in all studies relating to the field of medical art, excepting only surgery and pharmacology . . . the very two fields of utmost fascination to Herman Mudgett. A scalpel in his hand was akin to the brush of a Vandyke or chisel of a Michelangelo; his dissection of cadavers was masterful and held forth as examples to fellow students; his grasp of chemical compounds and their value or detriment to the human system far more than merely impres-

sive. Combining their talents over those years saw all three
graduated together, if not with honors, then certainly in the
upper echelon of their class.

It was Herman who had assumed leadership of their
little clique from the beginning. His two fellows were constantly
flabbergasted at the casual way in which he perpetrated
anything from minor infractions of rules to outright frauds.
That very day of admissions he boldly circumvented having to
pay nonresident tuition fees by claiming he was from Maple
Rapids, Michigan, and showing forged documentation to prove
it, all of which were accepted without question. He involved
his two friends in frauds pulled off with consummate skill,
such as bilking fellow students of their allowances or material
goods in such slick manner that they blamed their losses on
fate and were not even aware that they were victims of
swindles.

It had taken Leacock over a year to acquire a glimmering
of understanding about how Herman used people. In addition to being extremely personable and an individual with
whom one felt incomprehensibly impelled to open up, he had
about him a mesmerizing intensity that seemed to nudge
other people into telling him things far better left unsaid.
And, once having uncovered indiscretions, Herman then
used them as levers to make them do other things, perhaps
more indiscreet or even felonious. Chester Fish fell into this
trap early on and was soon engaged in a strange business with
Herman, obtaining unclaimed cadavers allegedly from morgues
in Detroit, Jackson, Flint and Lansing and selling them to the
university's medical school at Ann Arbor. When Leacock once
asked Chester exactly where and how they procured the
bodies, the nervous young redhead became pale and a haunted expression filled his eyes.

"I . . . don't get them," he had muttered. "Herman does.
I just help transport and deliver them."

It hadn't explained much, especially Fish's evident apprehension, but Leacock had not pressed for more information. He had begun to feel it would be better if he didn't
know. He and Fish roomed together in a fraternity house but
they dined frequently and very well at the Mudgetts' sumptuous rental house not far from the campus. Herman always
did things in a first-class manner, and the meals at his fine
house were always repasts far more elegant than either of
them could have afforded. Little by little the pair pieced

together bits of information that showed Herman was attending school and living in such lavish style on money he had gotten from his wife—money that had resulted from an inheritance of her parents' estate and as beneficiary of their life insurance policies.

The thought of the Mudgetts' first residence in Ann Arbor brought with it thoughts of Clara, and Leacock shook his head, rousing briefly from his reverie. His companion was still asleep in the seat beside him and Leacock felt a surge of the old anger. *God, I loved her. No, love her. And she never knew. And never will. And this bastard beside me just threw her away. Why did I ever have anything to do with him? Why am I meeting with him now? I don't know, but it's the last time. I swear it. The last.*

The shabby way Herman had treated Clara galled Leacock. The Mudgetts' baby, a boy they named Theodore, had been born that first January at Ann Arbor and after that Herman had shamefully neglected them both. It was as if they no longer existed in his eyes, tolerated in the household only because it was expedient that she continue to see to his needs. He spent their money with abandon, while keeping her in a state of near poverty, and what sexual gratification he needed he acquired elsewhere. Mudgett's contempt for Clara had become most manifest in one particular activity in which he engaged. Without concern that Clara was nursing their own infant son, on four separate occasions he dissected with meticulous obsession on the kitchen table. When the revulsed Clara asked where the tiny bodies had come from, he told her they were from the university's dissection lab. Neither Leacock nor Fish had had the nerve to tell her that this was impossible; adult cadavers were difficult enough to get and those of children were extremely rare. They had no idea where he procured the bodies and could not bring themselves to ask. They were in awe of how he somehow always managed to get what he wanted.

Leacock and Fish had also marveled together at the facility with which Mudgett found all the women he wanted. Not sluts preying on the allowances of first-time-away-from-home students with superheated loins. No, these were classy ladies, almost always blond, blue-eyed and beautiful, upon whom he lavished gifts and whom he took to the most expensive places. Even though he got money from some, his outlay of funds was considerably greater than his income.

Clara's inheritance from her father's business, which should have been at least half again as much as they needed to see him through the four years at UM, had become disturbingly depleted by spring of his junior year. With careful budgeting they might have eked through to graduation on what remained, but then a breach of promise suit had been brought against Herman by a widowed hairdresser from St. Louis, Michigan, who had moved to Ann Arbor. What remained of the funds was used to hush the matter and settle out of court. That was when the Mudgetts had given up the fine house and moved into a cheap flat. Herman was out of money, but not out of ideas for getting more.

And that was when Leacock had been sucked into this present scheme, after Herman had properly primed him with such a volume of whiskey that kidnapping President Arthur and holding him for ransom would have seemed plausible.

"It's so simple, Bob." Herman's eyes had sparkled with his enthusiasm. "I've got it all figured out, right down to the last detail, which I'll tell you later. In a nutshell, it's this: We insure your life for forty thousand dollars and you name me as beneficiary. I pay the premiums. We wait a respectable time and then I start looking for a suitable cadaver. Soon as I locate it—and I will—you go into hiding for a while. I destroy the features, dress it in your clothes, plant your identification on it and identify the body as yours. Then I collect the insurance money and we split it. Think of the practice you can start— that we *both* can start—on twenty thousand apiece!" His excitement was contagious, and as he went into the finer details of the plan, it *did* seem easy.

Jesus, Leacock thought, how could I have gotten myself involved in this thing? Why didn't I just walk away? But I didn't. He made it sound so damned easy and I, God help me, went along with it. Well, I went along with the second version of it. I have to give myself credit for that.

The second version. The one they agreed on the following September—when Leacock had gotten cold feet with the first. Before that, Leacock had gone home to New Baltimore for the summer last year, believing that Mudgett had stayed in Ann Arbor. But as their senior year began last September, they were reunited and Herman, in fine new clothing and flush with money, took his two companions out for a night on the town. Normally he drank very little, but that night, in a secluded back booth of a tavern near the campus, he had become very drunk, flashed his considerable roll of bills with abandon and was more garrulous than they had ever known him to be, dominating a conversation that had begun with Leacock's casual inquiry as to the health of Clara and little Teddy.

"How the hell should I know?" Herman's words were slurred and he occasionally squinched his eyes, as if having trouble focusing.

"Well, for God's sakes, Herm," Fish interjected, "they're your wife and son, aren't they?"

"Not any more, Chester, m'boy. I sent 'em packing. Dead weight. No room for dead weight."

"When?" Leacock asked quickly. "Where are they now?"

"Right after school was finished last June. And s'far as I know, Bob, ol' frien', they're back in Tilton in..." he hiccoughed and then giggled, "... in the family mansion." He blinked at Leacock and frowned. "Why, Bobby-boy? Something there I don' know about?"

"No. No, of course not." Leacock was immediately flustered and then blurted, as if it were important to the subject at hand, "But what'd *you* do all summer? Where'd you get all the money? Last I saw, you were broke."

"Ups and downs. Ups and downs. Life's jus' full of ups and downs. You're right, Bobby, abs'lutely right. I *was* down, but at the risk of being banal, you can't keep a good man down, so it was time I got up. Gen'lemen," he raised his glass, "a toast t'me. You sit tonight in the company of a 'complished crim'nal. I'm happy to inform you that two very willing sources contributed to my reversal from misfortune." He paused to drink the remainder in his glass and poured the tumbler half full again. "Never having been to Chicago, I decided to see what fertile fields it had to offer a bright and ambitious young man. Ever hear of Dearborn Publishing Comp'ny?" Both Fish and Leacock shook their heads. "Well, thass all right, 'cause they never heard of Franklin Pratt, either. Thass me, y'see. Franklin L. Pratt. L. for Larcenous. An' Lecherous." He giggled again. "The Dearborn Comp'ny, gen'lemen, publishes textbooks and they have a great many 'counts outstanding. They hired me to visit these people and collect. So I did. In Milwaukee, Minneapolis, Dubuque, Wichita, all over. By the time I got t'Kirkwood—thass in Missouri, near St. Louis, 'case you nontrav'lers don' know—I had twen'y-three hunnert dollars. Seemed a shame t'hav'ta share it with good ol' Dearborn Comp'ny, so I decided not to. 'Course, part of the reason I didn' go back t'Chicago was 'cause I met Frances in Kirkwood. Won'erful lady. Very well off, too. Fell in love, we did, she a li'l more than me, but thass all right. August two, gen'lemen. Thass the day Frances Teller became Mrs. Franklin L. Pratt."

"Jesus Christ!" The words exploded from Chester and his mouth hung open.

"Herman, you can't do that." Leacock was shaking his head in stunned disbelief. "My God, man, you're married to Clara."

"Oh, no!" Herman shook his head and took another swallow from his glass. "Herman Mudgett's married to Clara. It's Franklin Pratt who's married to sweet li'l ol' Franny."

"Dammit, Herman, that makes you a bigamist."

"Bigamist figamist! How c'n I be a bigamist if there's no such person as Franklin Pratt?"

"What a shitty thing to do." Chester had finally found his tongue again and he was thoroughly disgusted. "What are you planning to do, give her and Clara alternating weekends? Jesus, Herman!"

"You don' un'erstan', Shester. Franny 'sisted I take her savings and invest 'em for her. Honest. Was all her idea, not mine. So I took it. What else could I do? I took it an' lef' for California an' she won't see Franklin Pratt anymore. Ever. 'Cause Franklin Pratt doesn't exist."

"You really are a bastard, Herman," Leacock said, but Mudgett didn't hear him, since he'd passed out.

They didn't know where he was living then, so they took him to the fraternity house and dumped him into Chester's bed. Chester took the sofa. In the morning Herman had the worst hangover he'd ever endured and vowed he would never in his life get drunk again—and Mudgett never vowed lightly. When, in private, Leacock reminded him of what he had told them, he denied everything, but he was obviously furious and disgusted with himself.

"I don't believe you now, Herman." Leacock was scornful. "I did last night, but not now. Count me out. I'm not going through with the insurance thing."

"Bob, be reasonable. How can you turn your back on twenty thousand dollars?"

The fat man shook his head. "Do you really think I

believe I'd ever see you again, once you got your hands on the forty thousand?"

"Then, goddamnit, Bob, *you* make the split. I trust you."

"What a wonderful idea. Why didn't I think of that? We just fake my death and then I walk in and say, 'Well, here I am, fellows, come to collect on my policy.' Christ, Herman, I wasn't born yesterday.'"

Mudgett slammed his fist to the table. "Wake up! Forget the policy on you. We'll just let it lapse. We'll take one out on me. Now. Today. You'll be beneficiary. I'll disappear and you'll identify the body and collect on the policy. And we'll arrange where and when you'll make the split with me.'"

So that was the second plan. Everything in him screamed at Leacock not to do it, but the twenty-thousand-dollar temptation was too much and he agreed. The new policy on Herman, drawn on another insurance company, was taken out that very day and the remainder of the school year was taken up with refining the plan. A cadaver, similar in height and build to Herman, was stolen from the dissecting room at the university the day following graduation. The theft was laughed off as a student prank and everyone was sure the body would turn up shortly. It did, but no one recognized it as such. It was dressed in Herman Mudgett's clothes and carried his identification. In an alleyway behind the very tavern where Herman had become drunk, he had positioned the body late at night and then rolled over it with a heavily loaded dray, crushing the head beyond recognition. The body was discovered the following morning and the rest had worked out precisely as planned. And now, here they were, turning off the New Baltimore road into the long lane that led to the Crane farm on the shore of Anchor Bay, the northernmost bulge of Lake St. Clair.

"We're there, I take it." Herman straightened in the seat.

Leacock nodded, his heavy jowls jiggling as he did so. He wiped his face again with the damp cloth and his initial words were muffled. "Mr. Crane and his wife and son went to Tennessee. They won't be back for several weeks yet. Fred Folson, his cousin, comes out from town once a week to check the place. He was here day before yesterday, so we're all right."

The house was old and needed painting, but was in otherwise good condition. Most of the acreage of the small farm seemed to be in apple and peach orchards. A small barn, not much more than an oversized shed, stood sixty feet from the house and a path between the structures led down to the dilapidated pier where a cumbersome wooden rowboat was tied. It was thumping gently against the pilings with the action of small waves. Leacock pulled around to the lake side of the house and left the horse and buggy under an aged, gnarled oak. Together, Leacock taking a black leather medical satchel from beneath the seat and Herman carrying his valise, they walked out on the pier, moving carefully past loose boards. Despite his obesity, Leacock was quite agile and stepped into his boat with practiced ease. Herman followed and untied the rope as his companion fitted oars to the oarlocks. A cane pole with hook, line and cork bobber was in the boat, as well as a small tackle box and, in the shade under the middle bench seat, a squat bucket containing dirt and earthworms.

"Been ages since I've been in a boat," Herman said, face splitting in a wide grin. "Makes me feel like a kid again. Mind if I row?"

Leacock shrugged. "If you want." Relievedly he took off the raincoat and folded it into a square, placed it in the middle of the rear seat and sat on it. He was saturated with sweat. The satchel he placed between his feet, partially under the seat. Herman sat in the middle seat, his valise on the floor behind him. He gripped the oars and rowed out into the open waters of Anchor Bay until they were a quarter-mile from shore, chatting about nonessentials all the while. A herring gull approached, coasting on the light offshore breeze. It circled the boat several times, saluted them with a blob of excrement, then flew on.

"This is probably far enough," Herman said, shipping the oars. "I take it you have the money in there?"

Leacock nodded. "Eight packets, five thousand each. I've had it in there ever since I got it, and I have to tell you it makes me nervous to walk around with that much cash." He opened the satchel, pushed aside the instruments, bandages and medications, and exposed the packets in a layer on the bottom.

Herman's eyes glittered and he chuckled. "Now there's a pretty sight if I ever saw one. Makes all the trouble we went to worthwhile, doesn't it, Bob? I think—" He broke off and his eyes widened.

Leacock was instantly concerned. "What's wrong?"

"Don't move. There's a big rat under the seat near your foot. It looks rabid. Sit still, I'll get him." He continued staring at a point beneath Leacock's seat and reached out slowly for an oar.

The rotund physician remained frozen in place, wide eyes and a sheen of sweat on his cheeks betraying his apprehension. He watched as Herman lifted the oar from its socket and carefully turned it around so he was gripping the narrow part of the shaft just above the blade, with the butt end poised as a ram.

"Steady, Bob," he murmured, taking aim. "Steady."

"Don't miss!" Leacock hissed, lips barely moving. "For God's sake, don't miss!"

Herman aimed an instant longer and then thrust the makeshift weapon forward very hard. But as he thrust, he raised his point of aim and the butt slammed with great force into Leacock's solar plexus. The doctor doubled over on the seat, mouth agape as he strove to draw air into his lungs. Immediately Herman dropped the oar and grasped Leacock's ankles. He jerked them upward and his companion somersaulted backward over the transom and into the water with a heavy splash. Leacock struggled to the surface, fighting the dual peril of a partial paralysis and lungs demanding air. He began to sink and was a foot beneath the surface when the paralysis relaxed and he inhaled automatically. But it was water, not air, that filled the trachea.

Herman watched, the excitement building in him as unconsciousness closed over Leacock and the man sank slowly out of sight. His hand went to his front and he gripped his turgid penis through the fabric of his trousers and felt the familiar explosion of ejaculation and the warmth of the semen that bathed his crotch. After a few minutes the excitement abated and he methodically transferred the eight thick packets of hundred-dollar bills from the satchel to his own valise. He closed and latched the satchel and slid it back under the rear seat, then rowed directly to Crane's pier with steady strokes. There he dug into the bait bucket, threw several handfuls of dirt overboard and selected a fat earthworm, which he threaded on the hook. He then dropped the pole in the bottom of the boat and set his satchel on the pier. Sitting beside it with his feet on the transom, he shoved hard and the clumsy boat moved away with diminishing speed until it was drifting outward only with the slight force of the offshore breeze.

Herman watched until the boat was thirty feet away and the gap gradually widening. Then he picked up his valise and walked back toward the horse and buggy. The body of Robert Leacock, he knew, would rise to the surface in two or three days and subsequently be found. He was equally confident that it would be ruled an accidental drowning. As soon as that occurred, he would appear at the office of the insurance company to collect his due as beneficiary of the $40,000 life policy on Robert Leacock which he had not, after all, let lapse.

It would be his final act under his true identity as Herman W. Mudgett. From that time on, he would be Henry H. Holmes . . . or whatever other name he chose to use.

The Etude Music Shop was located two doors south of the corner of Washington and Marquette in Minneapolis. It was owned by Melvin Gregory, a five-foot gnome of a man with a fringe of grizzled hair and a physique most reminiscent of a gourd. Over these past three years, however, he only rarely appeared on the premises. That was when he had found a most engaging and knowledgeable young woman of eighteen, just out of high school, to be his clerk. Her love of music, combined with an intuitive sense of what might appeal to any given customer, steadily increased the shop's clientele.

Myrta Belknap, now twenty-one and a willowy, slightly sharp-faced blond, was a moderately gifted pianist whose musical tastes ranged from plebeian to the esoteric. She frequently sang as she worked, although what she sang were most often merely melodic sounds rather than words, rendered in clear soprano tones that floated through the shop as pleasingly as the trails of birds on a still forest morn. Occasionally, if customers were absent and work was caught up, she would sit at the Chickering and accompany herself with delicate touch, the wedded sounds in perfect complement.

She was so engaged late on this crisp October afternoon when a gentleman in an immaculate dove gray suit and matching derby entered the shop unheard by her. He closed the door quietly behind him and stood just inside for a long moment, absently stroking his full, neatly trimmed beard, listening to her play and enchanted by the vocal counterpart.

Of average height and medium build, he wore a gleaming, baroque pearl stickpin just above his waistcoat on the broadly knotted maroon cravat.

Still unheard, he stepped up quietly behind her, admiring the thick upswept hair piled into a bun atop her head, catching the elusive scent of carnation cologne. Her floor-length Blackwatch plaid skirt was only faintly bustled, reflecting the modern trend away from that style, while her tight Prussian blue basque was fastened with almost a score of embossed brass buttons from high on her neck to below the hourglass waist. The new style of low-cut shoe adorned her feet, slipperlike and trim, with higher heel than the button or flap shoes. Still unaware of his presence she played on, and he watched her hands moving effortlessly across the keys. Strong, sure, graceful.

"From *Die Fledermaus* by Johann Strauss," he said.

She started and turned her head sharply to see him, but continued playing. "You read it there," she said, dipping her head at the sheets open on the Chickering's music desk.

"Actually, no. It's a piece I've admired ever since it was first presented by Strauss."

"When?"

"In 'seventy-four. April, I think."

Her mouth quirked. "Where?"

"At Vienna's Theater-an-der-Wien."

"Bravo! You *do* know." She stopped playing, swiveled about on the stool and came to her feet facing him. Their eyes met and held, blue locked to gray, and a magical something, undefinable by either, passed between them. She felt her cheeks tinge. "Excuse me, sir. May I help you?"

"At the moment," he replied, smiling, "you could help me most by continuing to play. You have a very nice touch."

She looked at him speculatively and then nodded and resumed her place at the piano. She thought a moment and then began to play, long fingers authoritative on the keys. He listened carefully for several bars and then shook his head. "Tchaikovsky certainly, but I'm not sure what. *The Maid of Orleans*, perhaps?"

"Bravo again. That's fairly new." A mischievous light glinted in her eye. "Try this one." She added her voice to the keys, matching tone for tone in a smoothly lilting piece with oriental touch. When his brow puckered and he finally shook his head, she laughed aloud. "Not really fair of me," she said.

"It's just come out. I'll give you a hint. Lyrics by William, music by Arthur."

"Gilbert and Sullivan?"

She nodded. "From their new light opera introduced at the Savoy in London last March. It's called *The Town of Titipu* or *The Mikado*. It has some delightful pieces. Very clearly Gilbert and Sullivan, though. I think I like it even better than *H.M.S. Pinafore*. All right, one more." Again the mischievous look.

She had hardly begun to play when his rich baritone voice filled in the words of the Malloy and Bingham song that had become so popular last year. In a moment she added her voice in "Love's Old Sweet Song," this time with words rather than sounds.

> *"Just a song at twilight,*
> *When the lights are low,*
> *And the evening shadows*
> *Softly come and go . . ."*

They laughed together at the conclusion of their impromptu duet and it was as if they were old friends who had met again after a long absence. They strolled to the counter together and she spoke more seriously past the lingering merriment in her eyes. "Now, what may I help you with, sir?"

He glanced at a small upright wooden placard with engraved name. *Myrta Z. Belknap*. He indicated it with his thumb. "That's you?"

"It is."

"What's the Z for?"

"Not very original of you. Everyone asks that."

"Well?"

"Zeldora."

"I never heard it before."

"Mother wanted Zelda. Dad wanted Dorothy. They compromised."

"Dora. I like that."

She shook her head. "No one calls me Dora."

"I do. I can hardly call you Miss Belknap if I'm taking you out to dinner." The blue eyes twinkled and a grin framed even white teeth in sharp contrast to the darkness of his beard.

She smiled at his audacity, felt her own pulse quicken and hoped it was not noticeable. *He's the handsomest man I've ever met. I wonder if he's married.*

"Are you married?"

Her directness amused him. "Nope. Are you?"

"Nope," she mimicked. "But about dinner—I don't dine with men whose names I don't even know."

"That's reasonable. Forgive me. It's Holmes. H. H. Holmes."

"H. H.?"

"Henry Howard."

"Alliterative, if not imaginative." The mischief had returned with a sidelong glance. "I'll call you Holmes." She looked at the Seth Thomas pendulum clock over the counter. "It's closing time. What are we waiting for, Holmes? The Chelsea's only three blocks away and I'm starved."

They learned a great deal about one another over dinner in the plush hotel dining room. In the preliminaries he told her he was a pharmacist, graduated from the University of Michigan, temporarily clerking in Collier's Drug Store only two blocks from the Etude Music Shop and living in a boardinghouse less than a mile from where she had lived all her life. He neglected to tell her that the name he went under at both drugstore and boardinghouse was Herbert A. Henderson.

"What about your family?" she asked. "Parents alive? Brothers or sisters?"

He shrugged and the lie came easily. "They're gone. I'm the last of our line. My parents died the same year—'eighty-one—while I was at UM. My mother got sick from some disease the doctors never had time to diagnose. She died too fast, hastened along by pneumonia. Eight months later my father followed her. Stepped on a nail, let it go too long and it turned into blood poisoning. My older brother and sister both died—from diphtheria, I think it was—when I was little. What about you? You mentioned your mother and father; I take it they're still living?"

"Yes. Mother's name is Lucy and she's sort of quiet. Not like me, mouthy and ambitious." She laughed. "But then I'm not like Dad, either. His name is Jonathan and he works in the Chicago and Great Western Railroad office here. Also at home there's my brother John—he's sixteen—and my great-uncle Jonathan, after whom Dad was named."

"Two Jonathans and a John in the same household? Sounds confusing."

"At times."

"You said you were ambitious. Ambitious how?"

She shrugged. "Just about every way imaginable, I guess. I want lots of money, power, fame, you name it. Fame's the least on the list. I can do without that. But money and power . . . indeed!"

"Power doesn't come too often to women, Dora," he observed.

"Maybe. Maybe not. Maybe we just don't always recognize it when it's there. Maybe we're a little too wrapped up in preconceived ideas of poor little defenseless ladies . . ." she put on a cat smile, ". . . which itself can be turned into an asset in this man's world, if one learns to use it rather than be stifled by it. Or intimidated." Her gray eyes bored into his and then her smile became more genuine. "This is when you're supposed to run. Most men do. Or else they become defensively belligerent. What's your choice?"

He chuckled. "Do you always make a conscious effort to frighten would-be suitors?"

"Always. I like to uncover weaknesses early. It simplifies matters."

"What about your own?"

"Weaknesses?" She shook her head. "I discover, not divulge." She paused a moment to sip her wine, and he refilled her glass. "All right, Holmes, you've neither panicked nor fought back. We'll return to ambitions and philosophies later. On to phase two. Tastes."

Dora, as he continued to call her, was the most intelligent and enchanting young woman in his experience. Holmes, as she continued to call him, was the most intelligent and enchanting young man in *her* experience. They examined their commonality of interests in art, music, literature and theater with the enthusiasm of explorers forging through uncharted territory and delighting in their discoveries. It was Dora who launched the ship of their dual expedition.

"You like music, that's obvious. What about theater?"

"Yes, definitely. It's not possible for me to tire of Shakespeare. Ibsen is wonderful. Belasco's a rough-cut gem." He became rueful. "I don't get to attend as often as I'd like."

"Nor I. Minneapolis is not high on the list for touring companies. Especially in winter."

Holmes touched a finger to his glass, drawing a short line through the condensation. He looked at her steadily. "Let me see if I can divine your tastes in art. You're definitely not traditional. Renaissance? Unlikely. Impressionistic? Aha, yes. But who? Seurat? Gauguin? Degas? Cézanne? Renoir? No, I think something bolder, more defiant. Toulouse-Lautrec, perhaps, or Manet."

"Perceptive, Holmes. Very perceptive."

He acknowledged the accolade with a mock toast. "On to literature. What do you like to read? What are you reading now?"

"My tastes are varied. Certain of the classics, of course, but new literature as well. I'm amused and sometimes touched by Twain—Clemens, if you prefer. This past summer I read *The Adventures of Huckleberry Finn*. I almost didn't. It's been out for a year but I was avoiding it because so many people were saying it's a young people's adventure book. That's really an injustice. There's substance there. He's saying things far beyond the story itself. I think it's a book that will live. And Clemens...I think he's one of the few truly literary figures this country has produced."

"I'd have to agree with that. Have you read his *Life on the Mississippi?* Now there's a work that appeals to me."

"Of course. And I'll bet," she touched the back of his hand impulsively, then drew back quickly at her own forwardness, "...I'll bet I know something about that book that you don't."

"Apart from the fact," he interjected with exaggerated innocence, "that it was the first book manuscript written on one of those typewriter machines?"

She rolled her eyes and grimaced and they burst into laughter, enjoying the sparring. *I like this man. I really like him.* "What about you," she said at last. "What are you reading?"

"H. Rider Haggard."

"Not *King Solomon's Mines?*"

"As a matter of fact, yes."

"Kindred souls, Holmes. I'm reading it, too, along with Meredith's *Diana of the Crossroads*. Meredith's all right, but he's no Haggard."

Holmes nodded, though he hadn't read anything by George Meredith. "Most often I read on the train. It's really about the only chance I have."

"I don't get to travel that much," she admitted. "The last time was when I went to New York two years ago. I didn't want to take anything heavy, so I settled on Stevenson's book that had just been published, *Treasure Island*. A young people's book, yes, but what an absolute delight to read. I not only read it on the way there, I read it a second time on the way back. Now there's a book that is definitely a classic."

"I have to admit," Holmes said, "I haven't read it. I'll rectify that. Why did you go to New York?"

"For one of the greatest moments of my life." Her eyes were glowing. "The opening of the New York Metropolitan Opera House."

"You went to *that?* I'm envious."

"It was wonderful. Nothing I'd say could describe it adequately. Thirty-seven hundred seats and the most marvelous acoustics conceivable. They did Gounod's *Faust*."

"In German?"

"No, Italian. Christine Nilsson was Marguerite and she was at her best. I'll never forget it."

"Perhaps one day we can attend the opera together," Holmes ventured.

"Perhaps," she said. *Oh, we will, we will. You're going to marry me, Mr. H. H. Holmes.*

In the several times he had been out with her thus far, Holmes had not mentioned to Dora that, under the name of Herbert A. Henderson, he was concurrently courting a somewhat older woman across the Mississippi in the twin city of St. Paul. Actually, he had met her several weeks before meeting Dora when she had come into Collier's Drug Store to have a prescription filled. Holmes sized her up while waiting on her, noting that she was a well-dressed lady ornamented with some very fine jewelry. When he finished her order and she paid the charge of $3.25, it was with a fifty-dollar bill taken from a very fat money purse in her handbag. There had not been enough money in the cash drawer to make change, so Holmes had gone to Mr. Collier with it.

The fusty proprietor of the store glanced over his glasses at the lady waiting at the counter and nodded. "Oh, of course, Herbert," he said, "that's Mrs. Duncan, one of our regular customers. She usually stops in here on her way home from visiting her sister. Very pleasant widow lady, but I'm always having to change big bills for her. I do wish just once she'd give us the correct amount for her purchase."

It had been no great trick after that to engage her in conversation and impress her with his charm, good looks and gracious manners. He immediately made high marks with her, not only listening carefully to what she said but making it seem important and interesting. It was something few people did, since she was garrulous to an extreme. As his lunch hour was at hand, he invited her to join him at a nearby restaurant and they chatted—actually, she chatted while he listened— for the full hour. Nancy Duncan was thirty years old and quite plump, her round features painted with a perpetual smile. Her husband, Claude, a mining man, had been killed in a cave-in several years previously, and she had inherited his considerable wealth. Now she lived by herself and staved off loneliness with her weekly visits across the river to visit Mildred, her sister. The lunch together was a thorough delight for her and, though she objected, he gallantly paid the bill, even though it left him very short of funds. She left with a glow on her cheeks, having already decided that Herbert A. Henderson was one of the most enchanting persons she had ever met.

It became a weekly event for them after that to have lunch or dinner together, and on the fifth such occasion she invited him to her house—a huge estate hidden behind a spiked iron fence and dense shrubbery in the outskirts of St. Paul. On the third visit he stayed all night. If it was not a fact before then, it was immediately after—Nancy Duncan was hopelessly in love with the young man whose life up to the present, she decided, had been one of absolute purity; a young man she was now calling "My Herbie."

Holmes rocked back and forth with the laughter that belched uncontrollably from him. He could remember no time in his life when he had laughed this hard and it was minutes before he could recover himself enough to reply to the suggestion from Dora that had set him off. All the while she was watching him closely, a tentative smile on her lips, waiting patiently and with utmost confidence. Other diners in the restaurant were staring at him.

He wiped his eyes with a clean kerchief yanked from his

pocket, burst into another gale of laughter that he muffled into the cloth, then dried his streaming eyes a second time. "Ohhh," he gasped. "Ohhh, Dora, God love you, you told me in the beginning you were ambitious. What an understatement! I wouldn't have believed it if I hadn't sat here listening to every word."

The suggestion that had brought this all about came as they finished the final bites of their latest dinner together. It was the sixth time in a month that they had met to dine and there was a decided eagerness in the steps that brought them both from different directions to the Chelsea Hotel dining room where they had gone that first evening. Over these weeks they had learned a great deal more about one another and what they learned had only enhanced the initial impressions. There had been no sex involved in this togetherness, which rather surprised Holmes, since it didn't seem necessary, as it always had been before. It was her company that fascinated him, not a potential conquest.

Though not sexually intimate, they had become very intimate in their conversation, revealing things to one another of an extremely personal nature. To a point. Never had Holmes been so open about himself as he was with her, though he still told her nothing of his marriages to Clara, Fanny or Jenny—the latter being Jenny Moeller of Mooers, New York, whom he had married not long after his killing of Bob Leacock and whom he had deserted only a few weeks after their wedding. Nor did he mention having killed Jacob Renswyck, father of Cat—short for Catherine—for the money the old man had hidden. He'd become engaged to Cat but she'd been terribly demanding and when she discovered he was simultaneously engaged to Jenny Moeller, she had threatened to expose him, so he had killed her, too. These things he did not mention, nor did he tell her about his current engagement to Nancy Duncan. But he did tell her of defrauding the book company and of a stolen goods operation he had established in Chicago. Much of what he told her during this interval of their association was not true, or only partially true, or altered to suit his own purposes.

Dora knew his stories were distorted and had anticipated it. Rather than considering it a failing on his part and being offended, she was amused. She was also shrewd enough, intuitive enough, to sift through the distortions and fill in many of the gaps with an accuracy that, to Holmes, was both disconcerting and endearing. What intrigued him most was her failure to become shocked or judgmental at whatever he revealed. Instead, she was quick to applaud the bold deceptions he had perpetrated and suggest ways in which he might have emerged from a particular situation with greater advantage to himself.

When he became encouraged by her interest in his less-than-honest enterprises and realized she was not going to thrust him aside for this reason or contemplate reporting him to the authorities, he took the plunge and told her how, while at the University of Michigan, he and a fellow student— whom he called Tom Lambert—had successfully pulled off the life insurance swindle. He detailed the faking of his own death through theft of a cadaver from the dissecting laboratory and then disfiguring it so it was unidentifiable except by the apparel and contents of the pockets. He did not mention the subsequent death of his cohort in the swindle. She was fascinated and delighted until he told her of losing the insurance money and having to flee when the police came to his house, which was how he had wound up in Mooers, New York. She actually chided him at that point, listing several mistakes he had made, the most grievous of which, in her opinion, was leaving the money where it was not safe.

"Now if we had been associated at that time," she said seriously, "the wise thing would have been for you to place the money in my keeping. I, as an acquaintance totally unconnected to the matter, would have been free of any suspicion. In such an instance, even if you had been caught, as you nearly were, the money would have been safe and waiting for you upon your release from custody. What you need, Holmes, is a manager, to keep you from making mistakes that could be disastrous. And I know exactly who that manager should be."

"You?"

"Absolutely. What a team we could make!" She hadn't been so enthusiastic about anything since relating her attendance at the opening of the Met in New York. "Think about it."

"What I'm thinking," Holmes reached out impulsively and placed his fingertips under the chin, "is that you should become my wife."

"Of course I will," she was matter-of-fact about it, "but not quite yet. First we need to establish our relationship on a very solid footing. I will not be party to an association riddled by mistakes. Initially this means we must plan together carefully, consider all implications of a given project and eliminate every possible element of danger to ourselves. We can't eliminate all risk, I know, but we can reduce it to a minimum. This *has* to be the foundation of our association, if there is to be any association at all. That's the first matter." She paused for only a heartbeat and then went on, watching him intently. "Secondly, a separation from your wife is not enough—you must get a divorce before I will marry you."

His jaw dropped and for one of the few times in his life he was entirely nonplussed. She was smiling faintly, his reaction having lived up to her expectations. At last he managed to blurt, "How did you know?"

The smile broadened. "I didn't. *You* just told me. I only made an educated guess based on certain things you've said. You see, I listen very closely. And analyze. Holmes, I'm going to be very frank with you. This may be that moment when you decide to run, as we discussed that first evening. I do not intend to skirt issues, and if that bothers you, then indeed you should leave."

With composure restored, he regarded her with a pleasantly set expression that masked his thoughts. *Lord, what a woman. She's incredible. And I will damned well marry her, come what may.* "I have no intention of running, either now or later. Admittedly, you shocked me once this evening. You won't again."

"Good, since we're only at the threshold. Actually, *who* your wife is and *where* she is at this moment concerns me not at all. The fact that you are not with her indicates to me not so much your lack of concern for her—I presume you deserted her—but rather her inability to interest you enough to hold you. My guess would be that she was probably a high school or early college sweetheart, that she was almost surely your introduction to sex and that your entire relationship was on that physical basis, which was not sufficiently stimulating to a man of your mentality to establish solid bonds. All that's unimportant. Even bigamy does not disturb me if it's advantageous to a particular goal. What *is* important to me is that I do not intend to be involved in a marriage where I am not your only *legal* wife."

"I'll take care of it," he said, thinking fleetingly of Nancy

Duncan and determined not to mention her to Dora, despite their growing involvement.

"I was sure you would. All right, considering the nature of the insurance fraud you perpetrated with Mr. Lambert, I take it you are a reasonably accomplished natural actor?"

"I suppose you could say that," he replied. *You should have seen my act at Tom Eschler's funeral. Or the one in the boat with Bob Leacock. Girl, I'm a far better actor than you imagine. But I haven't been acting with you. I don't think I'd get away with it.*

"Are you," she continued, swallowing the bite she had been chewing and dabbing her lips with a napkin, "open to a suggestion at this time in regard to a project that might be mutually beneficial?"

"I'll certainly listen. *Damned right I am!*

"Good enough. We both know your present employment as a pharmacist is no more than a stop-gap job. How much working capital do you have available?"

Her propensity for changing pace was disconcerting but he answered without hesitation. "Around three thousand dollars." He did not include the total of over a thousand dollars he had already sent to Jenny to hold for them in Mooers.

"For what I have in mind," she said, "you'll have to risk it. I've saved two thousand dollars, which I'll contribute. There's a very nice restaurant at the corner of Washington and Central, a block from Milwaukee Station. That restaurant is going into bankruptcy very soon. Don't ask me how I know, it's unimportant. The fact of it is enough. The business has been badly mismanaged, but it's exceptionally well located and valuable. Even as is, it's worth in the neighborhood of thirty-five thousand dollars. When it goes into receivership, you, as a gainfully employed and respectable citizen of this city, will apply immediately to become receiver, putting ten percent down, with the remainder payable in full at the end of six months. You will then use the remaining fifteen hundred dollars in two ways: first, to improve the interior with quality furnishings, equipment and fixtures, as well as to stock up with a full supply of whatever staples are requisite for the operation of such an establishment. All these items you will purchase primarily on credit, using as little cash for down payment as possible. Next, you will hire the best available workmen to redecorate and put the restaurant in

operating condition as soon as possible. At that stage it will
be worth approximately sixty thousand dollars."

She paused to nod at a couple who recognized her with
smiles and little waves as they moved toward the exit.
Holmes, though his expression had not changed, hardly
believed what he was hearing, simultaneously impressed at
her grasp of business and the extent of her imagination. *How
can this innocent-looking young woman be sitting here outlining
to me a proposed fraud of such magnitude? She's fantastic.*

He dipped his head toward her when she looked back at
him, as much in respect as to indicate she might continue. "I
take it," he murmured, "you're not finished."

"No. I will then, through very subtly dropped hints,
steer your way a number of businessmen of substantial wealth,
with whom I have become acquainted over the past three
years in the Etude Shop. That gentleman who just left with
his wife is one such. These men will individually approach
you in the belief that you own the restaurant free and clear of
all encumbrance. They will believe that you have been
notified of an inheritance in England—an estate valued at
several million pounds sterling—but one which, in accord-
ance to British law, you can collect only by taking up residency there and renouncing your American citizenship in favor of
becoming a British subject. It has therefore not only become
necessary for you to sell your restaurant business here in
Minneapolis and go to England, but you must do so quickly,
since there is an inflexible time limit involved in your claiming
the inheritance. This, they will believe, has placed you in the
unenviable position of having to sell in a hurry, for somewhat
less than you could get had you the time to sell at your
leisure. After some discussion, you will reluctantly admit this
is true, but at the same time you will make it known that
because you are leaving the country permanently, you must
have the full sale amount—forty thousand dollars—in cash
only."

"Question." He put up a finger. "If it is worth upwards of
sixty thousand dollars, then why don't we set the sale price at
that amount?"

"We do, but what you will eventually *sell* it for, having
been placed in the position of no recourse but sacrifice, is
forty thousand dollars. *Cash.* You will then, upon receiving
the money, deliver three-fourths of it to me, which I will
keep for the subsequent establishment of our own home. You,

with the remaining quarter, will immediately disappear, going
elsewhere, preferably to a large city—I suggest Chicago—
where you will establish yourself solidly. When your divorce
decree becomes final—and you *show* it to me—we will then
get married and establish our household in the better area of
whatever city you've chosen. So that's the plan. What do you
think of it?"

It was at this point that Holmes had burst into great
guffaws while Dora waited patiently. When he had regained
his composure, she leaned toward him and spoke very softly.
"We have now reached the moment of your third and final
opportunity. Tell me, Holmes, do you run? Or are we partners?"

Holmes picked up his wineglass and lifted it to eye level
in a toast. "To the future Mrs. H. H. Holmes."

On the day following his sale of the restaurant, which
was accomplished according to Dora's plan without hitch,
Holmes got married for the fourth time, but not to Myrta
Zeldora Belknap. He met with her early this morning and
they divided the proceeds of the restaurant sale strictly along
the lines of their agreement. Then, with a final fervent kiss,
he left her, also according to their plan, to catch his train to
Chicago.

Holmes did not, however, go immediately to the Minneapolis railroad station. An hour later he and Nancy Duncan
were married by a justice of the peace and, following a quick
stop at the First National Bank of St. Paul, took a carriage to
Milwaukee Station and boarded a train for Toronto.

Had it not been that the restaurant swindle was already
in progress when he learned of Nancy's financial setup, his
plans would have been significantly different. Only when the
fish was nibbling the bait in the restaurant operation did he
learn that according to the will of her late husband, Nancy
Duncan did not have free access to her inheritance. Aware
that his wife was a financial incompetent, the wise Mr.
Claude Duncan had drawn up his will in such manner that
the cash assets and income therefrom were held in trust for
her, from which she could draw at will . . . but only up to a
maximum of $25,000 in any one calendar year. That, he knew,
along with the palatial home and servants, would keep her
quite well in the manner to which she had become accustomed as his wife.

It was time for quick thought on Holmes's part. He formulated his own revised plan and presented it to Nancy so deftly that she was convinced it was basically her own idea. A fantastic business opportunity presented itself—the chance to buy a rapidly growing pharmaceutical company in Toronto. For $120,000—only ten percent of which was needed as cash down payment and the remainder in ten years at an interest rate of six percent—he could buy the firm. As president of the company, with his drive and imagination, Herbert A. Henderson could turn it into one of North America's largest and most successful pharmaceutical laboratories. The plan that Nancy Duncan was under the impression she devised, was for her and Herbie to get married, withdraw the necessary $12,000 and take a honeymoon trip to Toronto, during which the pharmaceutical house could be purchased.

And so they had gotten married and boarded the train for Toronto, snug and happy in their own private compartment. Less than a minute before the train was to leave, he excused himself to go order a special wedding lunch to be brought to them in an hour. As the train began to roll, he stepped off the rear platform with his black satchel containing Nancy's $12,000 in cash. He threw a casual salute after the train and then walked across the terminal and boarded the Chicago-bound train with five minutes to spare before its scheduled departure.

If there was ever any activity that inspired a sense of anxiety in H. H. Holmes, no matter how well he kept it hidden, it was having any dealings whatever with the law. Therefore, he was especially nervous when he entered the Superior Court of Cook County in Chicago as Herman W. Mudgett and filed a libel in divorce against Clara A. Mudgett *née* Lovering of Tilton, New Hampshire. It did not help his composure to be so acutely aware that a wallet in his breast pocket contained almost $22,000—the $12,000 that he had gotten from Nancy and $10,000 from Dora.

He need not have been concerned. The entire session was very brief, handled by bored county officials whose chief aim in life seemed to be to perform all duties by rote, utilizing only the barest modicum of intelligence to process legal paperwork in which they were not in the least interested. There was not even the lifting of an eyebrow when this particular document charged the former Miss Lovering with desertion and infidelity. His fear that he might be recognized— he had shaved off his beard, though not his mustache, since coming to Chicago—no longer seemed justified.

Immediately following the session, a copy of the action was entombed in the Cook County records buildings, tabbed for automatic review after five years if not deliberately called for prior to that time. The other two copies were given to the complainant, one to retain in his own files; the other to be forwarded to the party against whom the divorce libel was filed.

Holmes walked several blocks north, one hand holding his derby against the cold wind that whipped his overcoat about his legs. A promise of snow was in the air and those who had to be outside hurried on their own missions with scarcely a glance left or right. The water of the Chicago River was murky and hostile beneath him as he paused midway across the Dearborn Street bridge. Jamming his hat tight upon his head, he reached into his inside pocket and extracted one of the two copies of his petition. Six times he tore it in half, then extended his arm and the wind swept the roughly inch-square pieces from his hand in a whirling cascade.

Clara would never see the copy meant for her, but that was of little moment. The important thing was that Myrta Zeldora Belknap would very definitely see his copy, with its official signatures and the seal of the Superior Court of Cook County.

Holmes smiled as he read the small advertisement in the classified section of the *Chicago Times-Herald:*

WANTED: QUALIFIED PHARMACIST in south suburban drug store. Must be experienced. One letter of recommendation required. Inquire in person. E. S. Holton, cor 63d and Wallace. Englewood.

Holmes tore out the ad and began framing in his mind the letter of reference he would write for himself on the letterhead stationery he had taken from Collier's Drug Store in Minneapolis. It was going to be a very high recommendation, signed in an excellent forgery of the hand of Mr. Collier himself.

* * *

Jenny Moeller Holmes tore open the package that had just been handed to her by the Mooers postmaster. Though it bore no return address, it had been postmarked in Chicago and the handwriting was familiar enough that she knew it was from Henry. She gasped when she opened the small box and saw the money. The note inside was brutally brief: *Hold this for us. H.*

The $5,000 in hundred-dollar bills would go into hiding with the other money he had sent her—the whole of it now totalling $8,300—but it gave her little satisfaction. She was crying as she left the post office, the tiny note gripped in her hand.

We've been apart for a year and this is what you write to me? You could have started it with Dear Jenny. You could have ended it with Love, Henry. You could have said when you were coming for me. You could have written. Really written. *Oh, Henry . . . Henry . . .*

"And how long was it you worked for . . . um . . ." Everett Holton glanced at the top of the sheet of paper he was holding, ". . . Collier's Drug Store in Minneapolis?"

"A full year, Mr. Holton," Holmes replied, his grin ingenuous. "I think it says that in the letter there from Mr. Collier."

Holton was a dour individual who looked to be well over fifty years old. His downturned mustache, full and unkempt, was grayed with age and yellowed from years of pipe smoking. He cleared his throat frequently with deep rasping sounds that were highly disconcerting. The bushy white brows were drawn down in a frown when he glanced over his spectacles at the young man.

"Hrrragggggh!" The nauseousness of his throat-clearing was compounded when he noisily spat a great glob of phlegm into a filthy porcelain spittoon. A surrounding ring of stains attested to his imperfect aim. He tapped the paper in his hand with a stubby forefinger. "Well, it's a good enough recommendation, but it doesn't tell *why* you left."

"Excuse me, sir, but I believe it does." *You miserable old son of a bitch.* "Toward the end there. Doesn't Mr. Collier mention that his son had just graduated from pharmaceutical college?"

"What's that to do with your leaving?"

"I had taken the job, Mr. Holton," *you crotchety old bastard,* "with the understanding that when Mr. Collier's son returned from college to enter partnership with him, I'd have to leave. I wasn't fired or anything like that. It was all prearranged. I also worked as pharmacist at City Pharmacy in Philadelphia for nearly a year, but it burned down one night and Mr. Walling—he was the owner—died of a heart attack the next day and so I was never able to get a letter of reference from there."

"Well," the druggist grumbled, refolding the letter and stuffing it into a pocket too small to hold it properly, "'spect I'll take you on, on a trial basis, anyway. I got to have someone to help around here. I been poorly lately and me and the missus can't do it all by ourselves no more."

"I'm sorry to learn you haven't been well, Mr. Holton," Holmes said courteously. *But don't worry about it,* he added mentally, *I'll soon be giving you a permanent cure.* "This is a very nice store, sir. I'll be proud to work here." *And I'll own it before the summer is out.* "When did you wish me to start?"

"In the morning, of course." Holton glared at him. "When did you think? Six o'clock every morning except the Sabbath. We close at nine in the evening. You get eighteen dollars and fifty cents a week to start. If you last out six months, you get twenty dollars. Take it or leave it."

"I'll take it. Thank you, Mr. Holton. I'll be here at six."

Holmes had not acted haphazardly in selecting the Chicago suburb of Englewood as a place to establish himself on a more permanent basis. The foremost qualification for his purposes was that it had to have direct, immediate and convenient access to a railroad station where more than an occasional local train would stop. That qualification alone sharply limited the possibilities. For those that remained he procured copies of brochures published by enterprising chambers of commerce interested in attracting new business and residents. One of these was the *Englewood Directory.*

The initial paragraphs were flagrantly commercial, striving to reach every social stratum and boasting of attributes in purple prose capable of turning the stomach of all but the most gullible.

When first established, the promotional piece claimed, Englewood was merely a junction point of three railroad routes. In fact, as a bare settlement—just prior to the Civil War—it was very simply called The Junction or, in an effort to give it more dignity and because it was situated in a forest of magnificent oaks, Junction Grove. By 1868, when the population had zoomed all the way to twenty families, the town leaders met and decided it was time to give their community a more fitting name.

Their final agreement on the name Englewood was arrived at by a rather roundabout route. One settler proudly claimed direct descent from an individual named Adam Bell, who had gained notoriety in early England under the name Clym of the Clough. Along with a companion, William Cloudsley, Bell operated as a sort of benevolent outlaw—long before Robin Hood—out of the huge oak forest of Englewood, England. The story did not lodge overlong in the minds of most of the inhabitants, but the name Englewood stuck.

While it no longer had the dense oak forest it once boasted, there were still plenty of beautiful trees in Englewood and it was one of the few suburbs of Chicago with street lighting. Adequately spaced ten-foot iron poles each had a lamp mounted on top, with jets supplied from the city gasworks. Every evening as twilight deepened, six lamplighters on bicycles went their rounds, each carrying a little ladder and a pole with a slot in one end in which a lighted match could be raised to ignite the gas in the lamp. The warm glow of the gaslights gave the suburb a distinct night-time charm.

The *Directory* Holmes had studied pointed proudly to the fact that Englewood was a wonderful site for professional man and laborer alike to put down roots, extolling the grandeur of rather ostentatious estates of doctors, lawyers and industrial magnates along the avenues named Wentworth and Yale, Harvard and Ross. At the same time it lauded the cosmopolitan charm of Englewood's polygot middle-class neighborhoods, which consisted of a multitude of brick or frame bungalows—the homes of Polish, Negro, Irish, German and other ethnic families that had abandoned the inner city following the great Chicago fire of 1871. In the fifteen years since that conflagration, Englewood's population had blossomed and now exceeded thirty-three thousand. As the *Directory* put it:

> Located twelve feet above the level of the lake, with a perfect water, sewerage and gas system, and an excellent police and fire department, Englewood combines all of the conveniences of the city, with the fresh, healthful air of the country. We have more enterprising men and less 'dead-beats' than any other suburb in the country.

But the lines that caught Holmes's attention most pertinently and clinched him on Englewood as being the ideal place for him dealt with rail transportation. In addition to a network of street-car lines connecting with other suburbs and the inner city, it said:

> Englewood also enjoys advantages as an accessible point which none of her sister suburbs can claim. Nine leading lines of railway furnish 108 trains daily. Every single one of these trains must stop at Englewood. These magnificent facilities give us advantages possessed by no other suburb of Chicago, the majority of which are mere flag stations, dependent upon one or two dummy trains a day, while the regular trains whiz through the town unmindful of its interests.

It was after reading this that Holmes had torn from the newspaper the advertisement he saw seeking a pharmacist in Englewood. The E. S. Holton Drug Store was situated on the northeast corner of Sixty-third and Wallace and he had been infinitely pleased at discovering that this very intersection was the nucleus of Englewood's business district. It was hardly a block from here that the Western Indiana Railroad Station was located, with tracks that crossed the busy Sixty-third Street thoroughfare at ground level.

The first twenty-four days he worked as pharmacist for the Holtons was a most unpleasant time for Holmes. He swiftly developed a consuming hatred not only for the vitriolic druggist but also for his equally caustic and irascible wife, Claire. The only thing that made the unpleasant association bearable was the sure knowledge that this drugstore would soon be his; that and the joy of planning how Everett Holton would die.

There were complications to Holmes's planning that made this matter one of particular challenge. The principal obstacle was that Holton and wife were inseparable, sharing the same bed at night in the large flat directly over the store, occupying the pharmacy together during the days and rarely out of sight of one another. That they had never held any employee for long, whether pharmacist, clerk or janitor, was clearly understandable. Even though Holmes did his work well and was obviously competent as a pharmacist and an asset to the operation, the Holtons seemed to delight in teaming up to expend their bile on the new employee, badgering, browbeating, carping and often blaming him for their own errors or shortcomings.

Compounding the situation was a seventeen-year-old daughter named Naomi who, when not in school, was also a permanent fixture in the store. A short, chunky, dark-haired girl, she duplicated her mother in temperament, with the added charm of a mean streak that frequently saw her deliberately cause problems that could be blamed on the young pharmacist.

Holmes rented a room in a nearby boardinghouse and spent his evenings either planning how he could eliminate Everett Holton with no risk to himself or in writing lengthy letters—partially, or sometimes wholly, in cipher—to Dora in Minneapolis. The cipher was one they had devised prior to his departure from there. It was a complex combination of letters and numerals that enabled them to discuss matters that could have been incriminating. It was in one such encoded missive he had received from Dora that she made it quite clear she had no objection to anything he might do—*anything!*—that would provide them with the sort of life-style they desired . . . so long as no evidence could directly link her to the crime.

Pondering the possibilities for murdering Holton was a knotty matter. With the wife and daughter already so suspicious of anything he did, pulling this off while at the same time avoiding being accused of it seemed at first an impossible hurdle. And perhaps it might have remained such, had not nature taken a hand.

Three weeks and three days after Holmes had begun working there, he was busy behind the prescription counter and the owners were at the front of the store when Everett Holton gasped and sank to his knees, gripping his chest. He tried to speak as Claire rushed to him, but could not. He toppled to his side and rolled onto his back as Claire screeched with alarm. "Mr. Holmes! Quickly!"

Holmes dropped what he was doing and ran to them. He found Holton conscious but moaning, gasping jagged words about terrible pains in his chest, back and jaw. In these few moments his face had become slick with profuse perspiration. His skin was cool and clammy under Holmes's professional touch, and his lips were turning blue, the facial skin pale lavender.

"Get some blankets," Holmes ordered. His eyes flicked up to Claire, who was gnawing at the fingers of her right hand and showing no sign of having heard him. "Dammit, woman, he's having a heart attack and going into shock. Get some blankets—three of them. Hurry!"

Claire Holton nodded and raced off and he heard her clumping up the stairs to the flat. By the time she returned with three folded blankets, Holton's extreme pain seemed to have eased somewhat and his eyes focused on his wife. "I'm . . . I'm dying, Claire. Get . . . Doc Pettit."

She moaned in rising panic and Holmes, kneeling beside the stricken man, snatched the blankets from her. Two he left folded, placing one under the lower legs, the other under the buttocks. The third he opened and spread over the man's body, neck to ankles. Immediately, Holton's color began improving and his breathing became more normal. As Holmes worked he spoke softly but in a commanding voice. "Don't talk anymore, Mr. Holton. Mrs. Holton, how far away is this Dr. Pettit?"

"Two . . . two doors away."

"Then go get him. Tell him it's severe and to hurry."

He watched until she left and then turned his attention back to the druggist. The man's color was quite improved and the pulse was steadier. He was sure the attack was only moderate and full recovery was likely. Nevertheless, Holmes smiled faintly at him and said, "You're right, Mr. Holton, you are dying.'

He leaned over the druggist, putting his leg across Holton's near arm and reaching across to pin the other arm to the floor. With his free hand he lifted the edge of the blanket under Holton's chin and pulled it across his nose and mouth and then applied pressure. Holton's eyes widened as he realized what was happening and he tried unsuccessfully to move his head away. The pinned arms tried weakly to break the restraint, but could not. Before long he stopped struggling. Holmes maintained the position until he heard the approach of excited voices and then straightened and pulled the blanket back under the chin. He was taking the druggist's pulse when Claire Holton and Dr. J. Wendell Pettit rushed in.

"You're Dr. Pettit?" Holmes asked.

"I am."

"Good. We have extreme myocardial infarction along with shock. Diaphoretic. Central and peripheral cyanosis. Probable pulmonary edema. Respiration irregular and pulse thready at first, now with primary ventricular fibrillation."

Dr. Pettit took in the elevated extremeties and blanket-covered body at a glance, but frowned when he saw the patient's face. "You may have saved his life, young man," he murmured, kneeling at Holton's other side. He felt for a pulse and, finding none, threw back the blanket and tore open Holton's vest and shirt. He placed his ear on the chest, then placed the flat of his palm slightly left of the sternum and thumped again. He jerked his glasses off and held one lens at Holton's mouth, pinching the nostrils closed. After a moment of staring at the lens, he put the glasses back on and exhaled deeply. He rose and stepped to the woman's side, taking her arm.

"I'm sorry, Mrs. Holton. He's gone."

By the time Holmes was through cleaning himself up in the Holton flat, the sun was rising and people were moving about outside on Sixty-third Street. He moved with the pedestrian flow to a restaurant near the railroad station where he ate a substantial breakfast. On his way back to the store he stopped off at a shop called Concord Sign Painting, at the corner of Stewart Avenue.

"Good morning," he greeted the clerk cheerfully. "My name is Holmes. I have a store sign I wish to have taken down, repainted to new specifications and replaced. Can you do it?"

"I'm sure we can, Mr. Holmes. Where is the sign now and how do you want it changed?"

"Are you familiar with the E. S. Holton Drug Store at Sixty-third and Wallace?"

"Certainly. I knew Everett Holton for years. Saw him the day before he died, in fact."

"Well, that's the sign. I've just bought the business from Mrs. Holton."

"Really? I'd heard she was thinking of selling but didn't think she'd do it so soon. What's she going to do now?"

"I'm afraid I have no idea. She merely said she and her daughter were going to California. They left yesterday."

"Well, fancy that. All right, how do you want the new sign to be painted?"

"Black letters on a yellow background. Designed like this." He took a piece of paper from his pocket and handed it to the clerk. On it was boldly lettered:

ENGLEWOOD PHARMACY

Drugs • Paints • Oils • Toiletries
Our motto: *"Friendly service and quality merchandise"*
H. H. HOLMES, Prop.

Returning toward the drugstore, Holmes crossed over to the east side of Sixty-third Street. On the southwest corner at Wallace he looked at the property for sale diagonally across the intersection from the drugstore. It was a good-sized lot, its frontage on Wallace running south for one hundred twenty-five feet to an alley, its frontage on busy Sixty-third fifty feet. In the middle of the lot was a large old frame house in run-down condition. The price was very high when one considered that a brand-new six-room suburban cottage was selling for $3,200. This property, including the house, was for sale for $17,500, which was not surprising, considering the location. It was the lot that was valuable, not the house. Holmes meant to have it.

From the very first day he had begun work at the drugstore, he knew he would own this large property eventually and that he would build here a storefront mansion that, on the outside, would be one of the most eye-catching buildings on Sixty-third Street. On the inside, it would have very specially designed rooms to serve all the needs he had in mind. All of them.

He crossed to the drugstore and disappeared inside.

Within moments a "Closed Today" sign was hanging in the front window. He emerged, locked the door and, hardly looking like a man who just passed an extremely busy night without sleep, walked off at a jaunty pace toward the office of the realty firm handling the property across the street.

It was January 28, 1887, and at two o'clock in the afternoon on this bright, clear, extremely cold Friday, Myrta Zeldora Belknap became the wife of Henry H. Holmes.

The wedding took place in the chambers of Judge William Anderson and the witnesses included the bride's parents and brother. The judge thought it was the first marriage for both bride and groom. Jonathan and Lucy Belknap and their son, John, knew it was the bride's first wedding and were quite sure it was also the first for the groom. The bride knew, or thought she did, it was Henry's second marriage, but that he had divorced his first wife and that she, Myrta Z. Holmes, was now his legal—and only—wife. Only the groom himself knew that Dora was his fifth wife and that he had never been divorced from any of them.

The former Clara Lovering was still in Tilton, New Hampshire, with their son, Theodore, awaiting the return of her husband, Herman W. Mudgett.

The former Frances Teller was still in Kirkwood, Missouri, awaiting the return of her husband, Franklin Pratt.

The former Jenny Moeller was still in Mooers, New York, awaiting the return of her husband, Henry H. Holmes.

The former Nancy Duncan was, so far as he knew, right across the river in St. Paul, awaiting the return of her husband, Herbert A. Henderson.

When this present ceremony was over, the bride's family returned home while the newlyweds took their first trip together. It could hardly have been construed as a honeymoon, but it was all that either of them wanted. They climbed into a chauffeured sleigh, snuggled together beneath a cheery plaid blanket and drank champagne to the accompaniment of a sharply snapping buggy whip and the jingle of harness bells over the muffled thud of hooves in ankle-deep snow. The wedding trip was brief, out Hennepin Boulevard to Loring Park, where the sleigh made a delightful figure eight around the twin lakes—pausing only briefly to watch the skaters skimming over the smooth ice—and then back downtown again to the Chelsea where Holmes had checked in last night.

They dined in the same gracious room where they had first discussed marriage and then retired to the bridal suite to spend their first night together as a married couple. They were both keenly aware it would be for this one night only; he was going back to Chicago on an early train tomorrow and she would not be able to join him there for a long while, until he found a suitable place for them to live. He did not like the idea of seeing her so briefly, but he liked taking chances even less and so he was relieved when he finally closed the door of their suite and locked the world away. Minneapolis was assuredly not a healthy city for him to be seen in; a warrant was still enforceable here for his arrest under the name of Herbert A. Henderson on a charge of swindling in the restaurant scheme. And even though it had amused him to be married in city hall, he had felt the danger uncomfortably close. The exhilaration of flaunting his presence in the very nest of the law would hardly be compensation for being apprehended. Then, too, he thought, what if I'd been recognized by one of Nancy's friends?

"You're suddenly very quiet, Holmes," she said, sitting on the edge of the bed. She reached behind her neck and opened the clasp of the gold necklace he had given her—the one that had belonged to Martha Meigs Gilbert—and pulled its heavy, sinuous length through her fingers before placing it on the bedside table. The matching earrings followed. "We've hardly had a chance to talk. I mean *really* talk."

"Who, in his right mind," he replied with a mock leer, "wants to *really* talk on his wedding day? Or night?"

"We do, whether you know it or not." She smiled and patted the bed. "Come over here and sit down. We'll compromise."

He hung his three-quarter-length suit coat over the back of a chair and sat beside her. She began to unbutton his vest, but when he reached toward the front of her exquisite multi-buttoned ivory silk dress to do the same, she caught his hands momentarily. "It's a compromise, remember? We talk at the same time. You never told me," she added with exaggerated petulance, while continuing to unbutton, "that your real name was Herman Mudgett. I had to find it out yesterday from the documents you gave me."

He shook his head, his story well prepared for this

moment. "My real name was Holmes when we met. You saw the legal name-change granted by the court three years ago." It was a document he had neatly forged less than a month ago—the only way to account for the Mudgett name on his libel in divorce document from the Cook County Superior Court. "I always hated it. Who could go through life with a name like Herman Mudgett?"

"Holmes is definitely an improvement. Henry, too." The outer corners of her eyes crinkled. "There is no possibility that I could love a man named Herman Mudgett." She had unbuttoned his shirt as well as the vest and, at her nudging, he moved so she could pull off both garments simultaneously, tossing them to the floor. She helped him take off her dress, which, along with a milk-white camisole, joined his clothes on the floor as she continued. "I'm glad you had it legally changed. Glad, too, that you were granted the divorce."

Holmes nodded. "Strictly formality. I knew Clara would never contest it." He had paid a Cook County records clerk a stiff bribe to provide him with a copy of a divorce decree which he had painstakingly copied two weeks ago. In the proper places he had inserted the names of Clara and Herman Mudgett and then, at the bottom, skillfully forged the signature of the judge who had signed the original libel in divorce. He pulled off Dora's low boots and stockings and kissed her ankles in turn, running his lips lightly up one shin to her knee.

"And the Holtons—they're gone?" Her voice had lowered.

He brought his eyes up to a level with hers and they kissed gently first, then with greater need. "Gone," he echoed when they pulled apart.

"He . . . died?" She removed his footwear.

He looked at her directly. "In a manner of speaking, yes."

"And the woman? And girl?" Her hands were busy at his trousers and soon they were on the floor. He raised himself to assist in removal of his undergarments and then she did the same. They had worked slowly with the disrobing but, even so, it was completed far in advance of the talking.

"Gone also." He leaned over and touched the tip of his tongue to her nipple and felt her grip reflexively tighten on him. She brought up her hands and pressed his head more firmly against her breast. She bent and kissed the top of his head, and her voice was small in his hair.

"Permanently?"

His gentle nibbling stopped and he tilted his head back to look at her. His expression was no different than it had been, yet there had come into his eyes now a fathomless depth. "Yes." He rolled away and lay on his back, head deeply cupped in the down pillow.

She leaned over him, loosened hair cascading on both sides, enclosing their faces in a diaphanous cage, and the clear gray eyes held his unwaveringly as she whispered to him, momentarily more serious. "There are some things it would be better I didn't know. What I don't know could never be extracted from me."

"I agree. There are such things. However," a tone of merriment came into his voice, "I strongly suspect a thousand bull elephants couldn't extract from you a single thing you didn't care to reveal. Remember, it was you who said 'I discover, not divulge.' Now sit up straight. I feel a strong need to look at my wife."

They had made love often before but never so openly, so enjoyably, with such mutual satisfaction as now. There was an element of the first time on this occasion, yet better than a first time, perhaps because of the lack of haste, a greater opportunity to appreciate, to comment, even to joke about minor imperfections. Hers was hardly the most beautiful body he had ever seen; thin enough that her ribs clearly showed, elbows and knees knobby and a greater inclination toward gangliness than grace. Her breasts were not truly symmetrical, one slightly smaller than the other, and a large birthmark, vaguely hourglass in shape and violently magenta, began between those breasts and extended downward onto her stomach. Though his physique was reasonably good—not overdeveloped, yet smoothly muscled—he, too, had flaws that had become emphasized with nakedness. Everything about him was a trifle out of line, his right ear and eye just slightly higher than the left and his left nipple lower than the right, as if somehow in the process of birth his body had been wrenched on one side. A remarkable mat of swirly hair covered his chest, arrowing down his stomach and blossoming at the pubes into a dense shrub. It formed a dark nest for a penis that seemed not only slightly smaller than it should have been but was somewhat inclined to the left. He sat up, too, and they pointed and they laughed, touching one another's imperfections, fondling them, admiring, kissing, finding them adorable rather than unattractive. And they continued talking through the night, neither inclined to sleep, their conversation lagging only briefly on the several occasions of most intense passion.

He told her of packing up and dropping in the outside poor box of a distant church the clothing and personal items the Holtons had forgotten and left in their flat after their departure; and of his unfeigned delight at unexpectedly finding in the flat a metal box containing just over $8,000 in cash. He told her of using the money toward the purchase price of the large piece of property diagonally across Sixty-third Street from the Englewood Pharmacy and immediately renewing, in his own name, the existing fire insurance policy on the old building located there; and of how a witness—whom, incidentally, Holmes had given $300 as a gift—testified to police that he had seen smoke coming from the old house and had entered to find three small boys who had accidentally set the place on fire while playing with the big sulfur stick matches called lucifers, and though they had run away, this man had himself rushed out and given the alarm. The house was engulfed in flame by the time the fire department got there and it was totally destroyed. He told her of how, after a brief investigation, the insurance company had paid Holmes the $5,000 for which the house was insured. At that point there was nothing to do but hire workmen to scrape the lot bare to prepare for the construction of a very large storefront mansion that Holmes had designed... and work on the new building was moving along very well, thank you.

Dora had done more listening than talking, occasionally interjecting question or comment but mainly content at lying partially atop him, stroking him in a manner ranging from casually pleasurable to intense, shifting position occasionally for the mutual exploration of new areas. She missed no word or nuance of his narration, impressed and delighted at his accomplishments, confident she had at last found the man to give her what she wanted—which was everything—and in no measure concerned with how he got it.

She mentioned one matter, however, that initially bothered him. It was at a lull in their conversation, while she lay with her head across his loins, his penis quiescent within her mouth, that she startled him, speaking around the obstruction. "I've told my family about you."

He was silent, confused at first. *What the hell are you*

talking about, Dora? Of course you've told them about me. They were there at the wedding. And then he suddenly knew what she meant and he jerked upright, gripping her hair and twisting it until she was facing him. "You *what?*"

The grip hurt but it was an oddly pleasing pain and she grinned. "You should be more careful, Holmes. You could lose a substantial chunk of your manhood doing that."

He released his grip but was not amused. "What, exactly, have you told them? And for God's sakes, *why?*" *Jesus, Dora,* he thought, *how could you be so goddamned stupid?*

"It wasn't so dumb, Holmes," she said, reading him perfectly. "You don't know them yet. They've been involved in some strange things over these years. Mother and Dad . . . well, she's a lot like me in some ways. And Dad's in some ways like you." He tried to speak but she reached up and put her hand across his mouth. "Now, listen to me! I've been listening to you all night, so now it's your turn. Don't get impatient. Dad's been systematically stealing from Great Western for nearly twenty years. He's clever. They've never even suspected. And Mother's established the contacts. I think she could get rid of a locomotive if Dad filched one. My God, how do you think we got the house we live in? On a railroad clerk's salary? And I'm no different. I've been stealing Melvin Gregory blind at the Etude Shop ever since I started there. He's making half again as much money as he was when he ran the shop by himself, which suits him just fine. But he doesn't know I've increased the profits over three hundred percent. Where do you think the remainder is going that Gregory doesn't get? You bet! How do you think I got to go to the opening of the Met, in one of the best seats in the house? Where do you think these beautiful clothes I wear— which you like so much—come from? So quit looking so upset. Mother and Dad don't know *everything.* Only the swindles, which they think are masterful. They know nothing about anyone who might have . . . gone away. Nor will they. Not from me. And you know I mean it."

The silence was heavy when she finished, broken only by her heavy breathing from the passionate outpouring. The set expression remained on his face a moment more and then it softened. He reached out and gripped her hair again, more gently this time, and leaned down and kissed her, pulling her up to him and wrapping his arms around her in an embrace that lasted a long while.

"Amazing, Dora, that's what you are. Absolutely amazing. I love you."

"Of course you do. You'd be insane not to. And I love you, too. I'll never betray you, never deliberately hurt you in any way. You can rely on that. I'll give you my support and I'll always be truthful with you. I don't care what *you* do, ever. If you want to go out and behead ten people, I don't care. Just don't tell me about it. The only thing I'll ever ask of you is loyalty. I don't mean loyal in the matter of sex, either. If you want other women, for fun or profit, then have at it. Just don't flaunt it at me. I'll be the one you can come home to, no matter what. By loyalty, I want you to want *me* to rely on, the one you *want* to come home to, always. And I want to be the one you support in the manner in which I want to be supported."

"You have my word," he told her. "I'll be as loyal as you ask and I'll never involve you or hurt you in any way."

It was the first time he ever said that or felt it . . . or meant it.

Two

Construction of the mansion Holmes had designed began in April upon the lot on the southwest corner of Wallace and Sixty-third being cleared of the debris from the old house that had burned. It was the strangest, most frustrating and aggravating work that any of the workmen had been engaged in, involving more workmen than construction projects of infinitely greater scope and expansiveness. The reason was that Holmes acted not only as architect but as general contractor and straw boss over the entire project. It was rare indeed that any single gang of laborers worked on more than one room of the edifice, or that any individual remained on the job for more than six weeks. Quite a few lasted only one or two days. He used in excess of eight hundred men, drawn from every part of Chicago and its suburbs . . . except Englewood. On a job that could have been completed by a maximum of two-dozen skilled workmen, in less than four months. And the work not yet finished.

The amazing turnover of construction workers was all part of a clever plan by Holmes to keep everyone in the dark. Whenever a subcontractor or his workers would begin asking questions about what they were building, Holmes would quickly find some sort of excuse—usually claiming shoddy workmanship—to fire them. This served the dual purpose of not only preventing them from getting a clear picture of exactly what it was they were building, but providing him with a basis for not paying for the work they had done. Often the anger of the men was intense at being cheated out of their wages for infractions they did not consider themselves guilty of committing, but they had little recourse. Those who tried to sue found themselves ensnarled in costly and unproductive litigation which they almost universally lost if and when it came to trial. Those who tried to become physically abusive and wring the money out of this difficult young man found to their dismay that he now carried a revolver in his pocket which he was not loath to brandish. The combination of looking directly into the barrel of a deadly weapon and into the equally lethal eyes of the individual holding it—and recognizing there a sure intent to kill—reasonably enough turned their insides to jelly and encouraged them to back off in haste. By far the greater number simply accepted their loss of time and labor and left the premises in disgust, vowing never to come back, which was precisely what Holmes had in mind.

Since no setback restrictions existed, the plans Holmes had sketched utilized every inch of the 50-by-125-foot lot for the outer walls of the mansion. He originally planned only a full basement and two stories, but added a third floor when he realized the initial plan would not suffice for his needs. Including the nine huge rooms in the basement, the mansion had a total of one hundred and five rooms, comprising well over twenty-five thousand square feet, the excess due to stolen space above ground and below.

Holmes was omnipresent on the construction site, organizing, overseeing, directing, coaxing, revising, ordering construction materials and supplies, tongue-lashing, wheedling, arguing, coordinating, unfailingly getting his own way in every matter. Frequently he dressed in old clothes and worked late into the night by himself in the rising building. And day by day the incredible structure took shape.

The basement was first, of course, and where other basements were usually between six and seven feet from floor to ceiling, this one was twelve feet, divided into its nine rooms by rough stone partitions. Three of these rooms were hidden. The floor was hard-packed earth and the foundation walls were bricked. Yet, unsatisfied by the limitations of his own property lines, Holmes had the alley behind the building undermined to form a room twenty-two feet long by nine feet wide. In this room was built a double-walled tank within a tank. In the smaller interior tank, made of zinc, was a virulent and highly combustible mixture of his own concoction; in the larger exterior tank, a volatile mixture of kerosene and heavy oils of various types in different proportions. These were so designed that when the proper valves were turned, a prescribed mixture of the two tanks would flow from a pipe in a noxious fluid. When the tank was finished and filled and the outlet pipes run underground to emerge elsewhere in the basement, the entry to the room was bricked over so that it appeared to be nothing more than the continuous brick wall of the basement.

As soon as the city gas and water lines were officially connected by city employees and capped, ready for installation throughout the structure when the building was completed, another passageway of significant proportions was dug. This one went outward from the basement on the front side of the building, well beyond the sidewalk and beneath Sixty-third Street. Here the city gas mains and water lines were illegally tapped for future projects Holmes had in mind. The illegal lines were run underground to a secret room behind a huge coal bin, providing ready access free of charge whenever desired.

A final excavation was made near the southwest corner of the basement—a pit seven feet deep, eight feet wide and twelve feet long. It was securely lined with foot-thick concrete and capped with a wooden platform containing a trapdoor four feet square. The pit was filled with five feet of quicklime, which could eat a body away to its skeleton very quickly and then, in time, dissolve even the bones. The platform, with the exception of the slightly raised trapdoor, was re-covered with earth.

There were three open stairways leading down to the basement, plus two hidden entrances accessible from above through cleverly concealed trapdoors and secret stairways. Finally, along the west wall was a six-foot-square shaft running without impediment from roof to basement floor.

The first floor of the mansion, at ground level, had twenty-four rooms and was comprised principally of five storefronts. Two of the shops, including the fancy new drugstore on the corner, faced onto Sixty-third Street, the other three onto Wallace. Those other shops—each divided into several large rooms for customer business, shop storage and shop workspace—included a permanent restaurant, barbershop, jewelry store and, next to the alley on Wallace, a blacksmith. These streetfront shops were designed to create a most favorable impression in the community. They had large plate-glass windows instead of the usual multi-square divided windowpanes and excellent workmanship went into the facades. The corner drugstore was especially attractive, with a large mortar and pestle overhanging the semihexagonal entry. A large pillar topped with an elaborately carved Corinthian capital was in the midpoint of the entryway with an open arch of stained glass fanning out on either side and a catherine-wheel design in relief on the entry ceiling. Inside the store were color-tinted frescoed walls and a floor of gleaming black and white ceramic tiles laid diagonally. Through a doorway at the back end of the drugstore, and reachable also by an outer door at that point, was a winding stairwell that went all the way up to the third floor.

It was not until the outer brick walls of the second and third floor were erected that the residents began calling the place Holmes Castle or just the Castle. The reason for this was that six large turretlike battlements started at the base of the building and went all the way to the roof where they terminated in raised sections, imparting the castlelike aspect. The largest such turret, on the corner, had four large curved-glass bay windows on second and third floors. The other turrets, including the one for the winding stairway, were squared and had four flat-pane windows for each floor.

The second floor was Holmes's masterwork. There were thirty-five rooms, some with doors opening inward, others outward, none with transoms. Some of these rooms were to be utilized as flats for employees, some as rental flats and some as offices. Narrow, zigzagging, frequently intersecting hallways, dimly lighted with far-spaced gas jets, separated all the flats. A number of the interior walls were very thick, hiding secret passageways or long storage closets with entry through sliding wood panels or hinged sections of plastered wall. Other walls were stuffed with mica, ostensibly as fireproofing but equally to act as soundproofing. Some of the closets had doors on opposing walls, so he could enter one and exit from the other. Rooms in the center of the building were windowless and became airtight with the doors closed. Some had asbestos-covered sheet metal walls, to withstand high heats. Most of these rooms could be peeped into through spyholes and all had gas jets for light, with the individual gas pipes that fed them converging to a closet in Holmes's own private corner apartment above the drugstore, where each could be controlled by its own valve. In this same closet, rigged by means of a self-contained electrical unit, a bell would ring when any door on the second floor was opened or when anyone used the stairs. Under a rug beside the bathtub in Holmes's bathroom was a trapdoor through which, by descending a steep stairway, he could emerge through a very narrow secret door into the principal entry foyer facing on Wallace, but there was no way to open it from the foyer. In a back room near the southwest corner was a four-foot-square trapdoor directly below a wall mirror. It was cleverly concealed by a piece of carpeting that overlapped on all sides but which was nailed to the floor at the baseboard. The trap could be sprung by triggering a small concealed lever that was part of the molding of the doorjamb. Anyone standing on the carpet would, when the trap was sprung, plummet straight down to the basement and, if the trapdoor there had been opened first, directly into the quicklime pit. Other rooms had trapdoors similar to the one in Holmes's bathroom, with ladders beneath them leading to hidden escape avenues on the first floor.

The third floor, with thirty-seven rooms, was comprised largely of one- or two-room flats bisected by another network of winding, angled hallways and hidden passages. The principal exceptions here were the front rooms overlooking Sixty-third Street and one adjoining them on the Wallace side. The large bright room with the curved-window bay two floors above the drugstore and one floor above Holmes's apartment was his private office, to which no one else had access. In one of its adjoining rooms was a locked door for which, again, only Holmes had a key. When opened, it led into the top of the six-foot-square shaft with a straight drop to the basement. In this room as well was a trapdoor with a ladder leading down into a clothes closet in his apartment. In the large office itself, a huge floor-to-ceiling Diebold vault of the walk-in type occupied one corner of the room, having been built in during the construction. The outer door of thick iron with a combination lock opened to a narrow inner chamber, the opposite wall of which had a door of tungsten steel openable only with a key Holmes kept in his pocket. Beyond the second door was a completely steel-lined room with built-in shelves and boxes for storage of valuable goods and papers. It was a very expensive vault which Holmes had purchased with as small a down payment as possible. When he ignored duns for missed installment payments, a crew was sent to the Castle to collect the money or repossess. He led the men up to his office and pointed at it.

"I have no money, so there it is. Go ahead and take it back. But I warn you," he pulled the pistol from his pocket and that strange, flat look came into his eyes, "do not mar this building in the slightest."

The men held a brief huddled conference and then left without the safe. Holmes smiled and put the gun away, knowing the company would continue trying to collect but would, as other creditors had already done, finally chalk the whole matter off as a bad debt.

During construction of the outer walls, Holmes looked up one day to see his recently acquired brother-in-law, John Belknap, grinning at him. The eighteen-year-old was extending an envelope with the single word "Holmes" written across the face. The handwriting was distinctively Dora's. He took it wordlessly and tore it open.

> HOLMES: *I know you're not fond of John but we're hoping that with all the construction you have going on down there you'll find some work for him to do. A month ago he announced he was dropping out of high school (his grades this year have been absolutely atrocious) and he has been driving us all crazy ever since, with nothing to do. He has given his promise that he'll work hard and at least it's worth a try. Please? If it gets too tough on you, ship him back and we'll try to work something out. We're all greatly impressed with your progress. Mother and Dad send love, but hardly as much as I do.—Dora.*

The week that followed was more than mildly trying for Holmes. John was very quickly poking his nose into everything and not only drawing conclusions uncomfortably close to the truth but becoming vocal about it. On three different occasions Holmes caught him talking with workers, casually discussing trapdoors and secret passages and rooms he was describing as death traps. On the first occasion Holmes dragged him away and, in private, savagely warned him to keep his mouth shut. On the second occasion, two days later, he struck him on the jaw, knocking him to the ground, fired the three watching workers for idling and later seriously threatened John should he ever become loose-mouthed again. He did, in just two more days. Again he fired the worker John had been talking with and then drove John into the alley with a series of well-placed kicks. When they got there he beat him. The boy tried to defend himself and even took the offensive a time or two, but he was no match for Holmes, who pummeled him until he was bloody.

"That's the final warning," Holmes said, standing over him. "Now you pick up a hod and get busy carrying bricks as you're supposed to be doing."

He watched the dazed boy do as he was bade and then returned to the construction. George Bowman, an apprentice bricklayer whom Holmes had hired only a couple of days ago, had watched what was happening from his scaffold. As Holmes began passing below, Bowman laughed aloud.

"Finally got the kid's attention, did you?"

Holmes looked up at him, eyes cold. He seemed about to say something, but then he suddenly climbed up the scaffolding and joined the bricklayer. He pointed at the hodful of bricks beside the man.

"Don't you find it pretty hard work to lay bricks?"

Bowman shrugged. "Hard enough." He laughed again. "I guess if I didn't need the money I wouldn't be doing it."

"What am I paying you a week? Nine dollars? Ten?"

The man shook his head. "Five. I'm still apprenticing."

"How'd you like to earn a lot more money than that"

"Sure. How much?"

"Ten weeks' worth in less than a minute. Fifty dollars."

"Whew, you bet! Who do you want me to kill?" Bowman was joking.

"Him." Holmes indicated John moving about below them. He was not joking. "All you have to do is accidentally drop one of those oversized capstones on his head."

Bowman was taken aback and then became frightened at what he saw in Holmes's face. He stammered a reply. "I...I...I'll have to...uh...can I have some time to think about it?"

Holmes considered this. "All right. Overnight. Come see me first thing in the morning."

Bowman nodded, but he knew he would never show up at this construction site again.

"Mr. Holmes?"

Pausing with his foot on the bottom step as he was on his way upstairs to check the progress of workmen in the upper floors, Holmes turned to look at the middle-aged man who had just entered the door from Wallace Street. "Yes?"

"You wrote to me in regard to certain very specific needs you have for a furnace in your basement. I am Wade Warner."

Holmes shook the man's hand with genuine enthusiasm. "Good to see you, Mr. Warner. I rather expected one of your employees would come."

"On a, uh, shall we say, normal job, that would have been the case but, as you know, what you've specified is most unusual. Most."

"When I heard about your process, Mr. Warner, I became intrigued. Glass bending is nothing new, of course. All the front windows of this structure are, as you may have noticed, curved glass."

Warner smiled but there was an underlying shrewdness in his eyes. "I prefer not playing games when involved in business, Mr. Holmes. You know, as do I—else I would not be here—that the Warner Glass Bending Process I've patented is far superior to any similar process in the world today. We are not speaking of rolling curved-glass sheets, sir. Nor of glassblowing techniques. We are speaking in terms of bar stock of virtually any thickness which can be bent— distortion free, I say!—to preconceived requirements within one five-hundredths of an inch. The applications are numerous and of extreme value and the patents I've taken out cannot be contested or infringed upon. Why don't we go down and take a look at the furnace our firm installed for you?"

Holmes led the way and they continued talking while descending. "I don't really have much doubt adaptation can be made in the model we installed for you," Warner continued, "although it would have been easier had we known in the beginning. You must have known, since you had the tanks installed in preparation."

"Well, at that time," Holmes replied, lighting the lantern he had removed from its peg, "the need I foresaw was merely my own proposed invention of a furnace capable of totally incinerating refuse." He continued leading the way to the larger of two furnaces that had been installed several weeks ago by the Warner Company. "That was before I heard of your process or that an incinerating adaptation of your patent might be for sale."

"Yes, yes, of course." Warner cleared his throat and sniffed. They passed the smaller furnace—a standard heating unit—and continued to the larger device thirty feet distant. "Please understand, Mr. Holmes, that the amount of heat required for burning refuse is considerably less than that required for the Warner Process. We shall have to see if the jets in this model can be adapted to the high-pressure atomizers. The tank valves are connected now?"

"Yes."

"Fine, let's have a look." He took the lantern from Holmes and inspected the fittings connecting the pipes to the furnace from the distant hidden tanks, then opened the huge furnace door and crawled partially within to check the dozen compression nozzles on each side. He hummed in an annoying, tuneless manner and moved this way and that, reminiscent of a bird inspecting the nest it has just built.

The furnace was an odd-looking device not unlike a modified version of a locomotive boiler. Made of quarter-inch steel, it was nine feet long and four feet in height and width, held two feet off the ground on a solid firebrick platform. The entire four-foot-square end opened on a well-balanced cast-iron quadruple hinge arrangement. Inside, it was fully lined with more firebrick and had a three-by-eight-foot rectangular pedestal of the same material. The fuel jets were positioned in such manner that live flame sprayed every inch of the pedestal's surface. Gases formed in the chamber by burning matter escaped through vents in the firebrick and struck baffles which turned them back into the flame for recombustion. An oxygen flow for continued combustion was provided for by four inch-wide slots near the base on either side of the furnace cylinder. Chimney piping, six inches in diameter and wrapped along its whole length by double-layered asbestos, protruded from the back, opposite the door. A foot from the furnace this pipe turned upward at a right angle and went straight to the roof. Any faint trace of odor remaining from whatever was burned was carried off by the breeze above the roof.

"I take it," Warner said, backing out and closing the

door, "the self-starting pilot has not malfunctioned and you've had no complaints from neighbors about smells?"

"No, none. Everything's been perfect."

"Fine, fine. That was our guarantee, provided the required twenty-eight hundred degrees Fahrenheit was achieved. Evidently it was." He pulled a kerchief from his pocket, wiped off his hands and swatted it at his trouser knees. He appeared pleased with himself. "I can, if you wish, make the adaptation to atomizer nozzles the day after tomorrow. Maximum temperature will thereby be raised to the full three thousand Fahrenheit required for the Warner Process. The adaptation charge of three hundred dollars is in addition to the thirty-thousand-dollar purchase price of the incinerator adaptive patent. You're still in agreement?"

"I am. A check will be acceptable?"

"Quite. Made out, if you please, to the Warner Furnace Company."

"I'll have it ready."

"Excellent. I'll bring the final papers with me. Oh, yes, lest I forget, it will be required as a condition of the sale that the name Warner Process be retained as shown on the patent."

Holmes nodded and the two men shook hands.

It took Wade Warner over six hours to convert the high-pressure nozzles in the Castle furnace to atomizer jets. Holmes watched, held lanterns and handed tools into the furnace to Warner the whole while. The official transfer of patent title papers, fully executed and making Holmes sole owner of the Warner Process Refuse Incinerator, were on a nearby table, as was the satchel containing the cash payment Warner would take with him. As usual, Warner talked incessantly as he worked.

"Bear in mind, Mr. Holmes," the voice came hollowly from within the furnace, "that you must not keep anything flammable within three feet of the furnace. The outer shell will become extremely hot, turning a dull red, but this is normal. Allow about two hours for complete cool-down after the furnace is shut off. What ash results from refuse incineration, including even bone matter, should be minimal, light gray and very powdery. It can be removed whenever necessary simply by pulling out the removable ash basin in the bottom. All right, it's all set. If you'll take these things from me, I'll come out and we can give it a test."

Warner handed out tools and lantern but, as he turned around to back out, Holmes swung shut the heavy iron door with a deep clanging sound. The immediate frenzied shouting from inside was barely audible. Holmes turned a small valve and lighted the pilot. He then opened the main valve controlling the flow of the fuel mixture from the hidden tanks. Immediately there was a dull whump as atomized fluid from the twenty-four new feeder jets ignited. One brief cry came from inside and then there was no other sound than the continuing muffled roar of the intense flames.

A few hours later Holmes returned and shut the furnace down and two hours after that he returned and opened the door. In the light of the lantern a whitish, powdery residue on the firebrick pedestal was all that remained of Wade Warner. Holmes was extremely pleased.

The measure of Wharton Plummer's success as a lawyer was reflected in the location of his legal offices. Downtown Chicago's new Chamber of Commerce Building, among the first to be electrically lighted in Chicago, was being touted as the finest commercial structure in the world and certainly one of the country's grandest office buildings. It was an accolade well deserved. Thirteen stories high and containing five hundred offices, it was a city within itself, with more people doing business here than might be found in many a prosperous town. Plummer's suite of offices was not only in this magnificent building, but in one of its choicest locations—the twelfth floor, directly overlooking the prestigious corner of Washington Boulevard and La Salle Street.

On this first working day of 1888—a bright, snappy morning with the temperature just below freezing—three handsomely dressed businessmen heading for Plummer's domain entered the building together. They passed beneath an entry arch with ceiling work of intricate colorful mosaics and strode along a broad hallway. Their heels clicked on a floor comprised of beautifully fitted mosaic tiles, carrying them to a grand inner vastness at the center of the structure, the like of which had never before been seen in any building.

The three were heading for one of their regular meetings

with Plummer but, as on previous visits, they briefly succumbed to the impulse to stop at the base of a great centrally located fountain to survey the overpowering grandeur surrounding them. Thirteen stories straight above was the world's largest skylight—a plate-glass arch thirty-five feet wide, one hundred and eight feet long and supported by an iron-trussed bronzed copper framework—allowing daylight's brilliance to illuminate the whole interior expanse. Circumnavigating the inside walls from skylight downward were twelve balconies with rails of gleaming brass, each balcony free of pillars or other obstructions and seemingly unsupported as they jutted on cantilever principle from the interior walls. The walls themselves, top to bottom, were masterfully matched slabs of Italian marble polished to mirror finish in Belgium.

The men resumed walking, threading their way through the bustle of people to a bank of ten elevators with scrollwork gratings in engraved copper and bronze. The ride to the twelfth floor, including seven stops en route, took just over one minute. They followed the balcony to its northwest corner and entered Suite 1218 at exactly 10 A.M.

The receptionist, a handsome woman of about thirty, was expecting them. She delivered their coats and hats to a young woman assistant and showed them into Mr. Plummer's richly appointed private office. Thick carpeting cushioned their feet and two of the walls were a composite of built-in bookcases filled with fine leather-and-gold volumes, tastefully framed pictures and neatly shelved *objets d'art*. The other two walls were dominated by four drapery-flanked oversized windows with a spectacular view of the Chicago skyline, two looking north, two facing west. The furnishings were few and placed at a diagonal to take advantage of the windows; Plummer's massive mahogany desk angled between the north and west windows, while four large, very comfortable leather chairs fanned out in a moderate arc facing the desk.

Wharton Plummer rose as they entered, moving with fluid grace despite the fact he was a very big man, over six feet tall and just this side of obese. He was forty-five, with thin brown hair meticulously combed in transverse strands over a shiny scalp striving to become bald. Tiny ears lay tight to his head and, though his face was etched with jollity, his features gave the impression of being bunched too closely together.

"Gentlemen, welcome! Right on time. I appreciate that." It was a hearty courtroom voice and he shook hands firmly with each, murmuring, "Mr. Woodbury, Mr. Holmes, Mr. Blackman," as he did so. He waved them into chairs before resuming his own seat.

Their conversation was initially of a chatty nature, touching on items that concerned them but not really getting into particulars to any extent. Holmes smiled at Plummer, silently approving of the way his attorney dominated and knowing it wasn't just because this was his office. Wharton always dominates, he thought, no matter where he is. I made a good choice in selecting him.

In the year since Holmes had retained Plummer, their association had proved fruitful for both. In addition to being a far better than average lawyer, Plummer was an excellent actor when acting was required. During their association, it had been called for several times. He was sharp in matters of law, brilliant in recognizing opportunity and uncommonly shrewd in sensing vulnerability, whether in court or in business dealings. As these offices suggested, his tastes were expensive and making money was his most joyous pursuit. He preferred doing so within the guidelines of legality but was by no means averse to stepping considerably beyond, though always with infinite care to avoid detection. The two men had sized up one another with remarkable acuity in their first meeting. By the time they parted they had become undeclared partners in nonviolent crime and Holmes had retained Plummer on an annual basis. Since that day scores of minor swindles had been perpetrated by Holmes with Plummer's assistance and counsel, the proceeds always scrupulously divided between them.

The association Holmes had with the other two men had come shortly after his meeting with Plummer, since the attorney had introduced him to both. Fitzallen Woodbury was an attorney in his own right who, some years ago—on his fiftieth birthday—had abandoned his practice in favor of becoming involved in real estate speculation and moneylending, at both of which he was markedly successful. Tall and conservatively dressed, he was normally reserved in nature, speaking little and content to listen carefully to a great many people, analyze developing opportunities from all possible perspectives and then act decisively. His reputation for astuteness was well deserved and recently he had established a real estate consulting service on a percentage basis. It was largely through him that, even while engaged in the exhausting effort of getting the Castle built, Holmes was able to buy and sell—at considerable profit to them both—eight different business and residential properties in Englewood. Holmes still owned two houses there—one on Sixty-seventh and another on Honore Street—as well as a confectionary shop on Milwaukee Avenue on Chicago's northwest side, under the name of Frank Wilde. Most of the properties remained in his possession only a month or two before being resold, and in every case Woodbury's advice had been sound. He had also been Holmes's legal counsel in matters concerning the Castle, almost since its inception, and had smoothed many difficulties for him. Occasionally he even loaned money to Holmes, which was always repaid in full and on time. His only shortcoming, so far as Holmes was concerned, was his scrupulous honesty.

Frank E. Blackman was only thirty-three but he was a minor financial genius. For six years he had been connected with the New York Stock Exchange and had earned enough to break away and leave New York City, which he despised, in favor of Chicago, which he very much liked. Now, as a Chicago broker on his own, he had a very limited clientele, including Holmes, whose funds he invested quite wisely. Part of his value where Holmes was concerned lay in his ready availability to receive, in person or by telegraph, large sums of money that might unexpectedly accrue or, if necessary, to give or send money to Holmes that might be needed immediately. He also frequently acted as a money handler apart from brokerage functions, relaying substantial funds to Myrta Holmes in an untraceable manner. Blackman was vaguely aware that a preponderance of the sums Holmes passed on to him to invest or relay were illegally obtained but he neither cared nor asked questions. For his advice and services, Blackman charged four percent of the monies handled.

The conversation to this point in Plummer's office had concerned Holmes little and he had not given it his full attention, but now Woodbury addressed him.

"Henry, I have been growing a little edgy about your purchase of some of these properties I've recommended."

"How so?"

"I've been hearing rumors that you buy them—some of them, at any rate—under assumed names and that you then take out a mortgage on the property, also under the assumed name. That you then pocket the money you've mortgaged the property for and sell it to someone else without letting him know there is an existing lien. Is this correct?"

Holmes shot a look at Plummer, who was involved with him in some of these deals, but Plummer merely returned the look expressionlessly. Holmes answered cautiously. "Fitz, if that were true, I certainly wouldn't own up to it."

"No, I suppose you wouldn't. I hope it isn't true. I feel honor bound to advise you that if I encounter evidence you've been so engaged, our association will terminate. I'd hate to see that happen."

"So would I, Fitz, so would I."

"I'm glad we understand one another. Now," he took them all in with a glance, "I do have some potential projects to lay before you gentlemen, but none that might not benefit by holding off till our next meeting. Since I do have another appointment before noon, may I ask that we conclude my part in the transactions here so I can go on?"

"The same goes for me," Blackman spoke up. He opened his briefcase and removed three sets of papers, which he distributed to the others. "These are reports on the financial transactions since our last meeting. We've made some profits, but nothing really significant. Fitz, here's a check for you for the amount due on the Clement property sale. You were right; it was a good move." He shut the briefcase and closed the snaps.

Holmes and Plummer had similar checks to give to Woodbury as his percentage on property sale profits, which they went over quickly. Then the broker and real estate man left.

"Fitz is getting suspicious," Plummer told Holmes. "He'll drop us one of these days when he puts things together."

"No doubt," Holmes agreed. "He's a wonder, but I could wish he were a little less righteous."

"Well, he's not and we are." Plummer dismissed the topic with a flick of his hand, as if brushing away a fly. "What's been happening with our little joint ventures? Anyone currently after your scalp?"

"Morrison, Plummer."

The lawyer winced. "I wish," he said wryly, "you would not defraud people who share my name. Makes me uncomfortable." Morrison, Plummer and Company were Chicago wholesale druggists, but the Plummer of that firm was no relation to Wharton Plummer. "Same action or a new filing?"

"Same one."

"Nothing to worry about, then. We can keep that tied up in litigation for years. They'll eventually drop it."

Holmes nodded, certain they would. Last June 12 he purchased from them a selection of $2,500 worth of drugs to stock the new corner pharmacy in the Castle. Following the scheme outlined to him by Wharton, he'd given them a mortgage on the Castle in payment but asked them to wait a few days before recording it, which they agreed to do. The next day he had deeded the Castle property to Dora's mother. When the company got around to trying to record the mortgage they were holding, signed by Holmes, they found the building had changed ownership in the interval and the new owner was one Lucy Belknap in Minneapolis. The mortgage held by Morrison, Plummer and Company was worthless. They tried to collect from Holmes at the Castle but he merely shrugged and walked away. They'd sued, of course, but Wharton Plummer was throwing all sorts of roadblocks in the way and, as had happened with similar deals he and Holmes had worked out, it would eventually wither away.

Wharton Plummer turned in his chair to look out the window. A cloud bank was rolling in over Lake Michigan, changing the blue to white-capped gray. "We'll get some snow from that one," he commented. He turned back to look at Holmes. "What about the Jones thing? Anything new on that?"

Holmes shook his head. "No. I don't think we'll ever see him again."

A. L. Jones, a happy-go-lucky, mild-mannered young man, had come to Chicago from northern Michigan with his entire savings, looking for a business opportunity. He heard the Castle Pharmacy was for sale and came to look it over. Holmes had just finished putting in a beautiful $1,500 soda fountain and the place looked as if it had real promise. He offered Holmes his $8,500 savings for the store and they closed their deal on Saturday evening, with Jones to take possession on Monday morning. On Sunday, Holmes hired some men to carry everything out of the drugstore to an upstairs room—furnishings, cases, stock and equipment—leaving behind only the new soda fountain. When Jones came on Monday and saw everything gone, he was understandably upset and confronted Holmes.

"You got what you paid for, Mr. Jones," Holmes told him. "I sold you the store. You're in it. Nothing was said about equipment, furnishings or the stock of goods. You surely didn't think all that was included for just eighty-five hundred, did you?"

"Well," he looked confused, "yes, I guess I sorta did, Mr. Holmes."

"How sad," Holmes said. He smiled and then walked off.

Three days later, Jones was still wandering around at intervals in his store when a crew of men showed up and took the soda fountain away. Holmes had laid only $150 down for it and they were repossessing. Jones continued to show up every now and then for the next week. When a man stopped in and offered him $2,500 for the premises as is, he was glad enough to sell and immediately transferred the place over to him, took his money and left. The man immediately signed the ownership papers back to Holmes, who had hired him, and got $100 for his trouble. The next day Holmes had all the drugstore equipment brought back down and put into place, then went out and bought another fancy soda fountain . . . on time.

He pulled the same sort of fraud with his restaurant, which fronted on Sixty-third Street next to the drugstore, selling it fully equipped to Walker L. Phillips of Aurora, Illinois, for $1,900 down. Within weeks all the furnishings and equipment were repossessed by the dealers who had sold them to Holmes on time and had never been paid. And he did the same with the barbershop. And the blacksmith shop. And the jewelry store. Quite often he rented the shops or ran them himself, with hired help. The turnover of personnel was great, since he usually found ways of cheating workers out of part or all of their just wages. Yet Holmes was an anomaly. Some of the people he employed were paid more than they expected and he was unusually generous, even lavish, with gifts to those he liked, especially females. Now and then he would depart and be gone for two or three days at a time, yet

leave quite large sums—up to $2,500—in the cash drawers
for his hired store personnel or Castle housekeepers or
janitors to use.

Holmes remained obsessed with swindling, irrespective
of how great or small the profits. It was the game that
counted most. When a customer in the drugstore selected a
bottle of patent medicine, Holmes would always offer to open
the deeply seated cork. He would take the bottle back of the
prescription counter, ostensibly for that purpose, but instead
would substitute a bottle already made up with what seemed
to be the same medicine, but which was actually cut three to
one with water. After the customer left, the genuine bottle
with cork intact would be replaced on the shelf.

There were times when Holmes took out legitimate
loans, sometimes from Fitzallen Woodbury, often from Frank
Blackman, occasionally from important Chicago moneylend-
ers such as John L. Du Breuil—from whom he borrowed as
much as $4,000 on several instances—but such loans were
always repaid without stint.

It took an enormous amount of goods and services to
finish and furnish the interior of the Castle and its shops.
Sometimes he actually spent large amounts of cash in such
matters, but far more often Holmes resorted to swindles,
working them in every area of Chicago and its suburbs,
buying and reselling goods, buying and reselling properties,
sometimes using his own name, often using aliases. Angry
creditors threatened him with physical violence. Suit after
suit was filed against him by merchants. Subcontractors took
out mechanics liens against him. And it was always the skillful
Wharton Plummer who fended them off. Only rarely did any
of the merchants ever get their goods back or recompense for
them.

One of the better swindling schemes, worked over and
over, was suggested by Plummer and refined through use by
Holmes. He would purchase building supplies or goods or
furniture under his own name, but ostensibly as agent for
Hiram S. Campbell, fictitious owner of the Castle building.
Oh, Mr. Campbell's personal authorization is needed?...
Of course, you'll have it tomorrow.... Well, I'm back and
here's the authorization you asked for.... What? Verification
of the signature is needed? Well, unfortunately, Mr. Campbell
has become ill and is confined to bed, but his attorney can

verify his signature. So messengers are sent to the resplend-ent Chamber of Commerce Building and ushered into the elegant suite of the reputable attorney Mr. Wharton Plummer, who takes one look at the authorization and laughs and says of course it is the signature of Hiram Campbell, which he knows very well, And, later, when payment is not made and irate merchants wish to see Mr. Campbell, well, that's a shame. You see, he's gone out of the country on an extended trip, but certainly he'll take care of the matter as soon as he returns.

The variations of the merchandise and real estate swin-dles were endless. But these schemes were not where the *big* money was. And, more than almost anything else, H. H. Holmes was interested in *very* big money.

"Y'see, 'cording to my wife," the man's words becoming slurred now, "my problem is labels."

"Labels?" Holmes frowned, not understanding.

"*Whiskey* labels, thass what! An' Carrie says th'only way I k'n read 'em is from inside the bottle." His giggle terminat-ed in a hiccough as he dangled the half-empty bottle in front of Holmes's face. "See. I'll be able t'read this one pretty soon." He uncorked it and refilled the shot glass on the table.

"Toas' t'you, frien'." He threw it down and immediately refilled the glass, then focused with some difficulty on the neatly dressed man across from him. "I been doin' all the talkin'. Your turn. Sus...supposin' you tell me why you bought me outta that jam?"

Holmes did not answer immediately. He was thinking of how this had all come about so suddenly. He'd been down-town having a brief meeting with Wharton Plummer when the big attorney said he had to leave, as he was due in court. Much to Plummer's aggravation, he'd been appointed *pro bono* by the court to defend a man who could not afford to hire an attorney. The man in question, Benjamin Fuller Pitezel, was thirty-four and, according to Plummer, a ne'er-do-well. He had a record of arrests for minor crimes ranging from public drunkenness and petty theft to extortion and bribery. On most of the charges he had not been convicted, but he had served time briefly in Fort Wayne for assault and battery and in Detroit for shoplifting. In the present case, to which Plummer had been appointed defense counsel, he was charged with forgery.

Holmes was not quite sure what prompted his reaction at that point, but he persuaded Plummer to take him along to court. Pitezel, so the charges went, had stolen a blank check from a West Side grocer's desk while the man was busy with a customer. The accused had made a quick copy of the owner's signature from a letter, also on the desk, and then slipped away undetected. Later that same day he had made out the check to himself in the amount of $100, clumsily forging the groceryman's signature at the bottom. His arrest had come about when he attempted to cash the check at a downtown bank, far from the grocer's neighborhood, only to discover later he'd had the misfortune of selecting a teller who was the victim's younger brother. The teller, a timid man, had become suspicious and followed Pitezel to where he was staying, then quickly visited his brother and found that the check was indeed fraudulent. In the morning the two men had then gone to the police and reported the crime. Pitezel was arrested, but the money was not recovered.

On being questioned in court, Pitezel, having waived trial by jury, told a straightforward story of having a wife and four children to support, that they were hungry and his wife was sick, that he had seriously looked for a good job and, finding none, had become desperate. The money, he swore, had not gone to buy liquor; he had used it all to purchase food and medicine and to pay the long overdue bill of the doctor who had been treating his wife.

Six feet tall, Pitezel was dark-haired and good looking, a pleasantly rough-hewn man who exuded an aura of being able to handle himself well in a fight, an aspect enhanced by a once-broken nose that did not detract from his good looks at all. His features were squared and craggy, complemented by a neatly trimmed dark reddish-brown mustache. On the back of his neck at collar level he had a granular wart as large as a good-sized pea. His suit was shabby but he stood straight and proud, exhibiting no overt signs of fear for what lay ahead.

It had been at this point that Holmes had slipped a note to Plummer, who, after a moment's hesitation, requested a five-minute recess. The court had granted ten, during which Holmes and Plummer held a whispered conference. When court had reconvened, Plummer addressed the judge.

"Your Honor, there happens to be in this courtroom a respected businessman from Englewood who has been touched by the plight of the defendant. He has asked me to appeal to the Court in this present matter. If the Court will release the prisoner into his custody, he will make full restitution to the plaintiff and will provide Mr. Pitezel with employment."

The judge asked for the identity of the businessman and then questioned Holmes briefly, evidently impressed with his appearance and intelligence. The prosecutor was asked if he would be agreeable to dropping the charge if restitution were made. With some reluctance, the prosecutor agreed and Holmes had immediately paid the $100 plus court costs. The judge dismissed the case but warned that he would hold Holmes responsible for Pitezel's future conduct and would be harsh if the man were to appear before him again.

Outside the courthouse, Plummer had left the two men after telling Holmes he thought this was all a mistake. That was when Holmes and Pitezel, at the former's suggestion, had come to this tavern on South Wabash. Over the first hour or more, Pitezel had drunk steadily from the bottle Holmes bought him, becoming progressively more loquacious, as Holmes had suspected he would.

Pitezel, he quickly learned, was originally from Galesburg, Illinois, close to two hundred miles west and a little south of Chicago. He'd had a girlfriend—Carrie Canning, in the nearby Henry County town of Galva—who had borne his child out of wedlock late in 1877 when she was eighteen and he was twenty-three and, though he might have merely disappeared, he'd felt the weight of his responsibility and married her two months later, early in 1878. The child was a girl whom they'd named Jeanette Deressa, the middle name after Carrie's grandmother and the one most often used, though shortened to Dessa or Dessie. Three other children had followed: Alice Rose, born in 1879, Nellie in 1881—she had slightly deformed feet, which did not hamper her walking— and Howard in 1883. A good worker when sober, Pitezel lost job after job as a result of his drinking and so he and his family had moved around considerably. He'd been hired as roustabout for a circus in Wheeling, West Virginia, but was fired in Grinnell, Iowa, where he found new employment in a lumberyard. When that didn't work out they'd moved on to

Topeka. There he'd had to flee to avoid being arrested for stealing a horse and wound up in Fort Collins, Colorado, where he sold the horse and used the money to bring his family out there. That was about four years ago. He got a job in railroad construction, using an alias, but within five months had to flee again for what was evidently a much more serious crime related to his job. The family was reunited a month or so later in Detroit, but Pitezel was soon jailed there for six months. He had badly beaten a man in a tavern brawl that turned into a near riot. When a squad of policemen had tried to stop the fight, he had assaulted them as well, sending two to the hospital. That was when he had suffered his broken nose. He had then compounded his difficulties by trying to bribe a jailer to let him go. Less than a year later he'd been arrested in Pittsburgh on a charge of extortion. He was released on bail but jumped bond and drifted to Chicago. Since then he'd been doing his best to stay out of trouble and make a better life for Carrie and the children by greatly moderating his drinking and hiring himself out as a handyman on a per-job basis wherever possible. But Carrie had been ailing these past few months and he hadn't been able to resist temptation at the unexpected opportunity in the grocery store.

"You gonna answer me, Holmes?"

Holmes returned his attention to Pitezel and nodded. "Yes, excuse me. My thoughts were wandering. I was quite serious when I told the judge I had a job for you in Englewood. I want you to work for me on a permanent basis as a handyman and will pay you no less than twenty dollars weekly." It was a fair wage for such a job.

Pitezel pursed his lips and shook his head slowly. He seemed not quite so influenced by the alcohol as he had been a short time ago. "There's more to it than that."

Holmes smiled approvingly. "You're right. There could be considerably more, depending upon the job involved. I'll be very frank with you, Mr. Pitezel..."

"Jus' call me Ben."

"All right, thank you, Ben. The nature of my business has resulted in my having occasional disagreements with certain people, some of whom become upset enough to wish me bodily harm. I carry a gun," he parted his coat pocket, "but I really have no wish to shoot anyone over a simple dispute. What I need is someone to help discourage people from rash acts against me should they begin to lose control."

"You mean you want a bodyguard." It was not a question.

"Yes, at times."

"In addition t' the handyman work."

"Yes. Could you handle that?"

"Well enough, but thass not 'nough pay for both."

Holmes nodded. "I agree. I said no less than twenty dollars weekly. That's for the ordinary upkeep work you'd be doing for me. For any instance where you have to seriously discourage someone, there'll be a bonus of five dollars."

"Good 'nough." He looked at Holmes speculatively. "You got more'n that on your mind."

Holmes laughed aloud. "Very good, Ben, you're vindicating my judgment. I take it, considering your past record, you would not be averse to making substantially larger sums of money on occasion? In tasks that might be considered by some as...uh...shall we say, extralegal?"

"I don' wanna go t'jail again, Holmes."

"I assure you, Ben, the very greatest of pains would be taken to avoid that. I have essentially worked alone in my operations in the past, but there are often times when the services of another person could be particularly useful to me. I don't intend going into any specifics at this time, but I have need for someone who could do as directed, yet have intelligence enough to improvise if necessary. Someone I could trust implicitly in matters where discretion is absolutely essential. Someone who might eventually become more than merely an employee."

Pitezel looked steadily at Holmes for a long moment. He reached for the whiskey bottle and uncorked it, then picked up the shot glass and poured his drink back into the bottle. Not a drop spilled. "I'm your man."

Holmes masked his pleasure and regarded the older man no less steadily. "Perhaps. We'll see."

William Pinkerton, general superintendent of the home office of Pinkerton's National Detective Agency on Fifth Avenue in Chicago, had promised results in less than a fortnight and he had been true to his word. The confidential report handed to H. H. Holmes was succinct:

Our agent in Denver reports that in March, 1884, one Robert Jones was hired as tie-layer by the Colorado and Western Railroad in laying a new line from Fort Collins to Laramie, Wyoming. On April 14 of said year, Jones and a fellow laborer, Wilton Crawford (also called Willie Cash), engaged in a dispute over division of goods allegedly stolen by them from a U.S. mail car temporarily sided on a spur for repairs. In course of said dispute, Jones was witnessed to have struck Crawford a severe head blow with a tie pick, causing immediate death. Jones fled the scene before officials arrived. Subsequent investigation indicated Robert Jones was an assumed name, but no positive identification has been made. Following inquest, a warrant was issued for Jones on a charge of murder. A Federal warrant was also issued for his arrest on charge of mail theft. No apprehension was ever made. If the party for whom this investigation has been pursued has any knowledge as to the present whereabouts of said Jones, he is urged to contact his nearest U.S. Marshall to provide details.

Holmes refolded the report and tucked it into his inner breast pocket. He was smiling.

Wilmette, the pleasant upper-class suburb north of Chicago, was in the midst of an especially beautiful May when Holmes had finally found the house he wanted for Dora and himself. It was located on John Street between Central and Lake Avenues. A discreet FOR SALE sign in front asked interested parties to contact realtor Horace Drury at 107 Central Avenue, which Holmes did at once. Drury, a bluff, good-natured man, was not only a very successful realtor, he was president of the village board and delighted to interrupt what he was doing and show Holmes the property.

The lot on which the house was situated, next to the Congregational Church of Wilmette, was very large and studded with gigantic elms whose towering canopies provided cooling shade over most of the grounds. The comfortable, well-built frame house had been painted a deep red and was largely hidden from view of the street by a heavy screen of shrubbery in front.

"How much?" Holmes asked.

"Sixteen thousand dollars, Mr. Holmes, which is quite a good price considering its location and the size of the lot."

"I'll buy it."

"Excellent!" Drury was very pleased. Not too often was a sale so quickly made. "Would you like to go see the owner and complete the deal right now?"

Holmes agreed and they went at once to a large house on Chestnut Avenue. Drury tapped the ornate knocker and the door was opened by a grizzled man in his early sixties.

"Ah, Mr. Dingee, so glad to find you home. I have a party who wishes to buy your property on John Street. This is—"

"Holmes, by God!" Dingee's interruption exploded as he looked past Drury at the prospective buyer. He looked back at Drury. "Get that thief off my porch." The fierce glare returned to Holmes. "Damn you, I wouldn't sell you a cup of water if you were dying of thirst and offered me a thousand dollars."

The door slammed violently shut in their faces. Drury was completely nonplussed. Holmes shrugged ruefully. "Had no idea he was the owner. We had a business deal at one time that fell through. He lost some money. Obviously, he blames me for that."

"Well," Drury was very disappointed, "it's a shame he won't sell to you, since you were so taken with the place."

Holmes nodded, but thought, Oh, I'll have that house, Drury. One way or another, I'll have it.

"All right," Dora said, rolling over so her face was only inches from her husband's, "we've gone over everything you've found out about Dingee and it seems to me there's only one way to do it."

Holmes made a noncommittal sound and waited. I assumed you'd come up with something, Dora. You always do. He let his fingertip trail down her shoulder and arm and then trace the curve of her hip. It was good to be with her again. Minneapolis was a long way from Chicago and their weekends together were all too few. He was tired of it and that was one of the reasons he'd been so eager to get the Wilmette house.

"Look," she reached down and placed her hand on his, holding it firmly against her thigh, "you say he's a widower and the only family he has left is that married daughter who lives a block away with her husband. What's her name? Louise?"

"Yes. Louise Fearoin."

"How old?"

"I don't know. Twenty-five, maybe. Twenty-six."

"Attractive?"

"Not really. Sort of plain."

"And her husband's a doctor?"

Holmes kissed the end of her nose and chuckled. "Where the devil are you going with all this?"

"Is he?"

"Yes, a surgeon. Very successful. Dr. Edward H. Fearoin."

"And you say Dingee dotes on her?"

"He seems to."

She was silent and he leaned forward and kissed her neck, feeling the vibration in her throat as she purred in response. He kissed the bare shoulder and let his lips slide to the hollow of her throat and then down until his face was buried in the soft warmth between her breasts. She stroked his hair and spoke in a dreamy voice. "Let's say Mother and Dad make an offer on the property, as you suggest, and get it. We give them about five thousand to put down on the place. Now all of a sudden old Mr. Dingee dies..."

"From incurable meanness," Holmes interrupted.

"...and Louise Fearoin inherits his estate, including the mortgage on the John Street house."

Holmes raised his head. "So? We wind up—or your folks do—making the rest of the mortgage payments to her."

"But do we?" Dora's eyes bored into his. "Let's take a closer look at Mrs. Fearoin. She's a plain woman with a well-to-do husband who obviously provides for her extremely well. But, like any successful doctor, he's not home a lot. How long has it been since she's had anything really exciting happen in his life? If ever. She's lonely and bored, maybe without even realizing she is. Now supposing a handsome, charming man came briefly into her life and ignited a spark of romance that's been missing lately? What if Louise Fearoin subsequently committed a very serious indiscretion which, if it ever came to light, could seriously endanger her marriage and the wonderful wealthy life she's become so accustomed to? What might she not give up to prevent her husband from ever finding out?"

The slow smile that had been stretching Holmes's lips split into a wide grin and Dora rumpled his hair and joined him in his rapidly expanding laughter.

Louise Fearoin stood in the open doorway, embarrassed, acutely conscious of the three buttons of her dress open at the neck. She had thought it would be Jean Courtley come to call and talk, not a well-groomed gentleman, a doctor, calling for Edward. Almost unconsciously her hand moved to her throat and covered the unseemly gap.

She shook her head in puzzlement. "I just can't understand why my husband would have asked you to come out to the house to see him today, Dr. Holmes, when he knew he was going to be in surgery all day."

"Well," Holmes sighed, his smile boyish, ingenuous. "I guess I owe you an apology, madam. Looks like I've gone and done it again. Got my dates mixed up, I mean. Please forgive the intrusion." He turned to leave and then turned back, looking directly into her eyes. "That July sun's very hot, Mrs. Fearoin, and I wonder if I might trouble you for a small drink of water."

"Oh, dear," she gasped, "where are my manners? Please, do step in. Water will never do. We have some nice cold lemonade in the icebox. If you'll have a seat, I'll get some."

"You're very kind."

Those eyes again. So disconcerting. She put a hand to her hair and turned away toward the kitchen. In front of the icebox she paused and brought up her hands to button the dress at her throat, but then made a small exasperated sound and dropped them to the icebox and opened the door. The quart-sized pitcher was on the top shelf and she gripped it by the handle, bumped the door closed with her knee and turned. She gasped and jerked violently when she nearly ran into him. A wave of lemonade slopped from the pitcher and splattered on the floor.

"Oh...oh, I'm...sorry. You...startled me. I didn't expect..." She set the pitcher down on the table, snatched a dishtowel from its holder and squatted to wipe up the mess.

"No," he squatted beside her and covered her hand with his, "it was my fault. Please," his voice was gentle, persuading, "let me clean it up."

She felt him take the towel but his eyes never left hers and she realized she was holding her breath. He wore a whimsical expression and for a moment neither of them moved. A hand came up, his, and fingertips touched her cheek, burning her skin, and she thought, My God, what's happening here? I've got to get up. I've got to run. I've got to do *something!*, but she remained rooted, impaled by his eyes while his voice, soft, oh so very soft, caressed her ears.

"Listen. Don't say anything yet, please. Just listen. I know you don't remember me, but there were so many there that night. We weren't even introduced, but I saw you. I saw you, Louise, and then there was no one else I *could* see, only you."

Her throat was dry and the words emerged scratched. "The ball? You were at the ball? But I didn't see—"

The fingers moved from her cheek to her lips, staunching the flow. "No, let me say what I have to. There may never be another chance. I watched you dance, turning, flowing. It was as if you were a part of the music, as if it had been composed only for you. Someone said something and you laughed and I watched your head go back and your neck..." he touched her throat "...became long and smooth and the sound bubbled out, sweeter by far than the music..." His face moved closer, only inches from hers, and she felt her heart beating wildly, painfully. Move away, she told herself. This is crazy. It can't be happening. It can't! "...and I yearned to come closer, but didn't dare, *couldn't* dare. But I knew I'd see you again, *had* to see you again... somehow... somewhere."

His lips touched hers with exquisite gentleness, and for a heartbeat she responded. My God, no. *No!* She jerked back, trying to scramble away, but he caught and held her, pulling her to him and kissing her fully with a passionate, frightening, fierceness. She struggled to break free, jerking her head back and forth to dislodge his punishing mouth. They toppled to the floor together and she struck at him with weak fists, hurting herself, not him.

"Don't," she cried. "Don't do this. Please, don't…don't…"

She strained and pushed even harder, but he was too strong, too overpowering. She heard the string of buttons on the front of her dress pop in staccato burst from neck to waist, heard one of them hit the wall and others rolling on the floor. I'm being raped. This is real, I'm not dreaming. I'm actually being raped. Her struggling became even more frenzied and she opened her mouth to scream but he closed it again with his own, pinning her, holding her. He forced her onto her back, his weight crushing. Her hands became claws, digging at the back of his neck, snatching his hair and pulling at it. She inhaled the animal scent of him, sickened by it, frightened by it and, in a recess of her mind, excited by it and shocked at what it was eliciting within her—the vulvate burst of wet warmth in her own loins—and she moaned, now as much in fear of herself as of him.

The strength went out of her and she fell back, sobbing, eyes closed, resigned to endure. She felt the torn dress pulled away, more gently now that she was no longer struggling. The weight left her fleetingly and she heard and felt the whisper and brush of his clothing. Now! her mind shrieked at her. Now! Leap up! Run! Get away! The will was too weak. His weight was upon her again, warm skin against her own, her legs being parted by his, not roughly but insistently. And then penetration, movement, response. *Response!* Her hands in his hair, gripping, not pulling. Pelvic thrusts, hers, meeting his.

It isn't happening. I can't be doing this. I can't.

But she was.

No one at the Wilmette meeting, least of all Dr. Edward Fearoin, could understand why Louise had done it. He couldn't believe it was, as she claimed, her father's wish. But if not that, then what?

He was disappointed in the first place when his father-in-law sold the Jones Street house, having hoped someday it would have been inherited by Louise. If only he could have held off for three weeks more! But the irascible old man sold it to that middle-aged Minneapolis couple—the Belknaps—for $5,000 down and the remainder on a ten-year mortgage which Dingee had agreed to carry. And three weeks later he was gone, his body discovered two days dead at the foot of the stairs. There were injuries, the inquest showed, but no more than could be attributed to the fall. The conclusion was that he had probably become dizzy or suffered some sort of seizure at the head of the stairs and tumbled all the way down into a broken heap at the bottom. Accidental, so it was ruled.

Instead of the house on John Street, Louise had inherited a mortgage and now, today, unfathomably, she had deeded the property free of any encumbrance to the Belknaps.

"Why, Lou?" he demanded on the way home. "Why would your father have made you promise to do that if he died? It doesn't make any sense."

Louise Fearoin shook her head, thinking of the hot July day that Dr. Holmes had first visited her, thinking of the second visit, shortly after, and then that terrible third visit, following her father's death—the one in which he instructed her in what she had to do unless she wished to risk losing all she had. He said he would never bother her again if she faithfully followed the instructions.

She turned and looked at her husband. "I just don't know, Edward. I don't think we'll ever know. But I promised him and I could not renege."

She turned her eyes forward, thinking again of that first day . . . and the second.

A ripple of fear swept across the United States in December as major newspapers picked up a grisly story that originated in London and continued for several weeks. Three ladies of the night in that city's East End—Mary Ann Nicholls, Annie Chapman and Elizabeth Stride—along with two of their less professional neighbors, Catherine Eddowes and Mary Kelly—had been murdered in identical fashion. The unknown killer had first fed the women poisoned grapes and then, while they were incapacitated but still alive, disemboweled them. Imaginative reporters had dubbed the assailant with the colorfully descriptive name of Jack the Ripper and the whole world was shocked at such hideous atrocities. And those who read the banner-headlined accounts of it in the *Chicago Tribune*, the *Chicago Daily News* and the *Chicago Times-Herald* shook their heads and shuddered and thanked

Providence that there was no such monster as that in their area.

Chicago was suffering growing pains, its inner city becoming much too crowded. Stretching its developing muscles, the city reached out in May of 1889 and embraced the suburbs called Hyde Park, Lake, Jefferson, Lake View, Cicero and Englewood and absorbed them in its mighty maw in a devouring process called annexation. But even though they became part of an expanding Chicago and lost their status as individual cities and towns, these former suburbs continued to be called by their former names by residents. So even though the postal address was now Chicago, if a resident were asked if he lived in Chicago, he would be apt to nod and then add, ". . . in the Englewood district."

With the annexation came growth even greater than previously. The turnover of Holmes's employees and tenants at the Castle at 701–703 Sixty-third Street was amazing. Many came and stayed only a few days before leaving, having heard and seen things in and about the huge, mysterious building that elicited suspicions all was not as it should be and they'd better go while they could. Others came and stayed longer and, of these, some eventually packed up and left hurriedly in an aura of fear; others simply vanished and, to anyone who asked questions of their whereabouts, the story was given that they had "gone to California" . . . or Kansas . . . or Texas . . . or elsewhere. Then there were the select few who stayed on for much longer tenures and who became the "family" of the Castle.

Ethel Loomis was one of these—a dumpy, strident woman of about forty-five with hair the color of yellow pond scum. She had been one of a score of women who had answered Holmes's advertisement for a housekeeper at the Castle and who turned out so well that she was quickly made head housekeeper, with the vested power of being able to hire or fire housekeeping help. Her staff consisted of six or seven other women whom she ruled inflexibly and who were mortally afraid of her.

Mrs. Beverly Dietz was another who stayed on longer than others, though not under the thumb of Mrs. Loomis. Beverly was the twenty-four-year-old daughter of Dr. J. Wendel Pettit whose office was across Sixty-third Street from the Castle—the same doctor who had been summoned when druggist Everett Holton was stricken with a fatal heart attack.

She was hired first as bookkeeper in the Castle jewelry shop and soon expanded her duties to a certain amount of general secretarial work for Holmes. She was a plain woman, unimaginative and steady, though not markedly competent.

S. H. Byins and James McFarland were among the first permanent renters of office space in the Castle—taking a room on the second floor overlooking Wallace Street from which to operate a real estate and loan office. They were more often away than in the office, which suited Holmes quite well, and they also eased a burden for the Castle owner by assuming the duties—in exchange for reduced rent—of collecting rents each month from other tenants in the Castle, both individual and business.

Ann Cobb—better known as Auntie Ann—was an enormous black woman hired initially as temporary kitchen help in the Castle restaurant. She quickly proved herself so skilled and dependable that she was elevated to the post of chief cook and head of the restaurant staff. Less strident than Ethel Loomis, she was no less domineering in her operation of the restaurant. Her only permanent underling—there were many transient workers—was Selene Knotts Morton, a sharp-faced woman of about twenty-four who served as head waitress and cashier.

Clarence E. Davis took over management of the Castle jewelry store. An incredibly neat and efficient man of twenty-five, he always wore a suit, high-collared shirt with wide cravat and, when outside, a derby hat. A round-faced man of pleasant disposition, he had a very full and always neatly trimmed handlebar mustache. His dense, wavy hair was parted in the middle and, constant exasperation to him, had cowlicks fore and aft. He enjoyed talking, especially about bizarre subjects, among which was not infrequently engaging in conversations with Holmes about such matters as poisons and the effects of corrosive chemicals on human tissue, which the dapper Davis considered as exercises in speculation. Holmes did not.

Ian MacDougall and Henry Owens were at the nether end of the list of permanent Castle employees. MacDougall, better known as Mac, was an odd-job employee hired to do any heavy lifting and maintenance work around the Castle. A Goliath of a man, he quickly proved his usefulness by single-handedly carrying up to the second and third floors of the Castle a total of seventeen iron bathtubs, each weighing over two hundred and fifty pounds. Owens, always cheerful and accommodating, was a black man who was hired as a porter and did most of the dirty work around the Castle that no one else cared to do. The combined IQ of these two men was somewhere in the vicinity of their body temperature.

Benjamin F. Pitezel had no title but he was equivalent to chief of staff. In a remarkably short time Holmes had come to rely on him very heavily, and their association, initially business, bloomed into a friendship closer than any that Holmes had ever allowed himself to enjoy. Ben's loyalty was absolute; there was virtually nothing he would not do for Holmes and similarly, Holmes for the first time did not view a fellow man as a possible victim for swindle or insurance claim. Their only contention came when Pitezel refused to wear a tie, but as soon as he explained his reason, Holmes gave in; the wart at the back of Pitezel's neck quickly became aggravated by the friction of a collar held snug against it with a tie worn more than merely occasionally.

Every employee—with the single exception of Pitezel— was required by Holmes to take out a $5,000 life insurance policy for which Holmes paid the premiums and in which he was listed as sole beneficiary. No one questioned this unusual arrangement.

There was one other employee—hired late in September of 1889—who became as important to Holmes as Pitezel and was no less dependable and loyal. An Irishman of medium height, slight build and receding sandy hair, he had answered Holmes's advertisement for a janitor at the Castle. He had so quickly proved his worth that he was placed third in charge of the operation, following Holmes and Pitezel. Thirty-five years old when hired, Patrick Quinlan was a nervous, wiry man who smoked a pipe so constantly that there were those who wondered if it was permanently anchored to the corner of his mouth beneath the scraggly reddish mustache.

Pat was the youngest of three boys and a girl born to Doyal and Mary Quinlan on their farm near Nottingham, Ohio. On his twenty-first birthday he had left home for good and became a hired hand on various farms in Lake County, Ohio, east of Cleveland in the vicinity of Willoughby. A frugal, serious and shrewd young man, he saved his money to eventually realize his dream—having a fine farm of his own. When he was twenty-five, he had married Ella Hitt of Willoughby, a mousy but hot-tempered young woman who

promptly made his dream hers. Together, she working as a
domestic and he continuing with farm work, they had lived in
the poorest imaginable conditions, saving practically every
penny earned. To compound their financial situation, their
daughter Cora was born in 1886. Late the next year, after the
passage of nine full years of such self-imposed privation, they
had enough money saved to buy a fine eighty-acre fruit farm
in Michigan. They had paid for it in cash, fearful of having a
mortgage overhanging them, but they had failed to make sure
the title was clear. It was not. They thought the law would
protect them when a claim was made against the farm but it
hadn't, and within six months they had lost the farm and their
entire investment. Bitter and disillusioned, Pat sent Ella back
to her parents in Willoughby until he could become solvent
enough again for her to join him. No longer harboring much
respect for the law, he migrated to Chicago, willing to do just
about anything to make money. It was not long afterward that
Pat had answered Holmes's ad and was hired. He accepted
without argument the matter of having his life insured with
Holmes as beneficiary. After all, he reasoned, his new employer was paying the premiums, so why shouldn't he be
named beneficiary?

For long months Quinlan helped with the extensive
remodeling being done on Holmes's Wilmette house, proving
his value over and again, since he was a wizard at working
with his hands. Holmes was there, too, almost daily, overseeing the work. Once it was finished, however, he was rarely
there on weekdays, his attentions returning to the Castle and
the multifarious businesses conducted there. On weekends,
providing his specific attentions were not required in
Englewood, he would go home to be with Dora, not only
merely for her company but equally to discuss future projects. Included among these was coordinating the moves of
Grand-uncle Jonathan, who was flitting about in a wide arc
around Chicago, visiting suburb after suburb and taking out
mortgages against either the Castle in Englewood or the
house in Wilmette. He was getting old and tired and so the
plan was for him to get as many of these as possible, divide
the substantial proceeds that resulted and then retire incogni-
to to some remote place to live the remainder of his life in
easy comfort.

A busy man—and Holmes was indeed that—needs occasionally to relax with an absorbing hobby. If such a hobby can

also result in a profit, so much the better. Holmes's principal hobby, established during those early days of medical school in the University of Michigan, was human dissection. He still pursued that peculiar endeavor whenever possible, and, though never so frequently as he wished, with considerable variation. In his always enterprising manner, he often managed to make his hobby become income-producing. Chicago was home to a number of medical colleges, some well established and highly respected, others of a more temporal foundation. Such institutions were unceasingly desirous of obtaining whole cadavers for medical study and were quite willing to buy from the well-dressed gentleman with papers identifying him as an official of the city morgue in charge of unclaimed, unidentified bodies scheduled to be buried in Potter's Field. For such cadavers, delivered in long narrow boxes constructed by Quinlan and Pitezel, they were willing to pay from $25 to $50 each. Of course, selling the bodies whole deprived Holmes of the joy of dissection and so, in his wonderfully equipped basement laboratory—to which no one else had access—he engaged in the practice when haste was not essential. Disposal of the residue was no problem. The fleshy parts were reduced to ash in the Warner Process furnace. And the bones...ah! Never one to let opportunity pass him by, he cleaned them with various acids and caustic agents. Then, as if working on a jigsaw puzzle, he carefully articulated the skeletons and sold them to medical students—these for prices as high as $125 to $200 apiece. There were even several occasions when Holmes, representing himself as a butcher, sold kegs of fatty tissues labeled *Animal Fat* to a soap manufacturer whose factory fronted on the Chicago River.

Holmes rarely had any real difficulty finding the raw material for pursuing his hobby. One was Dr. Russell Casper of Medford, Oregon, who had rented a room for two weeks. At the end of that time there was a controversy between him and Holmes over the rent, when Holmes demanded twice as much as he had quoted at the time Dr. Casper took the room. Casper at last gave in and disgustedly paid the higher rate with bills peeled off a thick roll. He threw them on the floor and turned away and so he missed seeing the blow coming when Holmes struck him savagely on the head with a heavy wooden stool, killing him. The wad of bills amounted to $430 and Casper's body wound up on the dissection table at Cardiff Medical College.

Then there was Miss Jennie Thompson of the tiny southern Illinois town of Eldorado, come to the big city in April to make her fortune. An ingenuous, lovely girl of seventeen with sea-blue eyes and long honey-toned hair, she was not well endowed with intelligence and made a series of mistakes above and beyond accepting employment in the Castle. One of these was taking lodging in a room of the Castle. Another was confiding in that nice Mr. Holmes that her entire life savings of $114 was rolled up and tucked into the toe of her Sunday shoes. A third was telling Mr. Holmes that she hadn't written home yet to tell them about her wonderful new job and, my, wouldn't they be surprised to find out she was in Chicago instead of New York, where everyone thought she'd been heading. When he'd asked her to accompany him to his third-floor office, she considered it an employer-to-employee directive and did so. When he told her to remove her clothing, she decided this was definitely not the type of work she had applied for and told him so in blunt, unflattering terms.

Holmes merely smiled and said he was testing her, as he could not have ladies of that caliber working for him. She was very pleased and proud that she had passed the test so admirably. He sat down at his desk and excused her and then, as an afterthought, asked if she would please get the large brown ledger out of the vault for him. She walked through the massive outer door, which was open, and pushed against the iron inner door, which didn't budge. Holmes apologized and got up, saying the outer door had to be closed before the lock on the inner door would disengage. But when he swung the outer door closed and twirled the handle, the inner door hadn't opened at all. The space between the doors was very dark, very narrow, and with an extremely limited air supply, much of it used in a short while by Jennie Thompson taking great gasping breaths and shrieking for someone to open the door. Outside, standing quietly with his ear close to the vault door, Holmes could barely hear her cries. Having an interval of time to expend, he went to her room and found the roll of bills in the toe of her shoe. He pocketed it and then carried all her meager belongings to his office where he burned them in the barrel-sized oil stove.

When he opened the vault door an hour later, Miss Thompson was dead. He undressed her and availed himself at various orifices earlier denied him, after which he unlocked a door and dropped her limp form into the six-foot-square shaft to the basement. Two days later Mrs. Loomis sought Holmes out and reported that the new girl had skipped out. A week later, her neatly articulated skeleton was the proud possession of a third-year medical student at the University of Illinois.

Hardly a week after that, one of the better rooms was rented to Mrs. Pansy Lee of New Orleans. A widow, she was obviously quite well off. Watch as he might, Holmes could not discover where her money was kept, so he tried a different tack. He so charmed her with attentions and gifts that she became smitten and finally let it slip that most of her money was in the bank in Louisiana, but that she did have some $4,000 with her. Holmes expressed grave concern that it would be stolen and urged her to place it in his vault for safekeeping. She refused, saying she'd been traveling all over with it in the false bottom of her trunk without any problem and there was no reason to change now. But there was. Since Holmes was pressed for time, he simply cremated her remains.

There were others, quite a few in fact, but Holmes was sure he had not yet reached his stride.

The measure of Holmes's feelings for Pat Quinlan and his trust in the man was evident in the fact that he had allowed Pat's life insurance policy to lapse and had no intention of renewing it. And when, only a few days after Mrs. Pansy Lee had "checked out," as Holmes put it, Pat Quinlan came to him, obviously distressed, Holmes was concerned. They repaired to the third-floor office and Holmes poured him a drink but Quinlan ignored it.

Holmes raised an eyebrow. "You're more upset than I thought. What's wrong?"

"Do you know Lizzie Knotts?"

Holmes's brow furrowed. "Seems to me I've heard the name. Can't remember where."

"You do know Selene Morton." It was more a statement than a question.

"Our restaurant cashier? Of course. Good worker. She rents rooms in the building here. What's she have to do with this?" The sharp-faced Selene was a widow, her husband having been killed in a railway accident only a few months after their marriage over a year ago. She had been working at the Castle restaurant for ten or eleven months at this point.

Quinlan shuffled his feet uneasily and sucked at his empty pipe. "Lizzie Knotts is her sister. She's eighteen. I met her in the restaurant when she came to see Selene one day. That was only a week or so after I started here. She was . . . well, damn it all, Holmes, she was the prettiest thing I'd ever seen. We started talking and one thing led to another and we started going out together."

Holmes cleared his throat to cover a smile and said, "Evidently you didn't tell her you're married."

Quinlan shook his head. "She got in the family way right off. The baby's due in a couple of months—July. And then I . . . I don't know how it happened, but I promised I'd marry her."

"Has she told Selene?"

"About the baby or about me?"

"Both."

"She says no, but I think she has because of the way Selene's been looking at me lately. Lizzie's moving in with her tomorrow."

Holmes rubbed his chin. "There's more. What?"

Quinlan sighed and was quiet for some time, staring at his hands. Holmes waited patiently. At last the janitor looked up. "I was really going to do it, I guess. But she's been having some second thoughts. About marrying me, I mean. She wants to have the baby and wants me to take care of all the medical expenses and so forth, but once the baby's born, she says, she'll take it and go away and not bother me. Provided I pay her three hundred dollars."

"And you don't have that much?"

"Hell no! I don't even have enough to pay medical expenses. Everything extra I've earned I've sent to Ella in Ohio."

"What can I do to help?"

"You said you'd delivered babies before. Well, I'd like it if you'd deliver Lizzie's baby, so no one else will be brought in on it. Then, if you feel you can trust me enough, I'd like you to advance me the three hundred she wants, so she can go away. I don't know when Ella's going to join me here in Chicago for sure, but she swore she wouldn't stay apart from me for over a year. I'd sure like to have Lizzie gone before Ella gets here."

Holmes stood up and Pat came to his feet, too. Holmes clapped a hand to his shoulder. "Pat, don't worry about a thing. I'll take care of it. You have my word."

Three

*I*t was exactly six o'clock in the evening and Pat Quinlan's color had still not returned when he reached the third floor and knocked on Holmes's office door—three raps, three raps, one rap.

"Pat?" The voice from inside was cautious.

"Yes. I have to see you right away."

The door opened and Holmes, in shirtsleeves, let him in. He closed the door immediately and locked it. One look at Quinlan was enough to dispense with inconsequentials. "Talk."

"Take a look at this wire." Pat's voice was strained. He pulled a folded yellow paper from his pocket and extended it toward Holmes, his hands shaking. "It was handed to me in the restaurant a few minutes ago."

Holmes unfolded the telegram and his eyes flicked across the page.

PAT STOP ARRIVING 1 PM AUG 14 UNION STATION
CHICAGO STOP MEET ME STOP YOUR WIFE STOP ELLA

"You didn't know she was coming?"

"God, no. Of course not. Didn't expect her for another three weeks. Selene saw me reading it and sneaked up and read it over my shoulder. I thought she was going to kill me. I've never seen her so mad. She ripped off her apron and threw it in my face and ran upstairs to tell Lizzie. I followed her."

"And what was Lizzie's reaction?"

"Even worse. She's mad. No, not just mad. Holmes,

she's furious. Gave me an ultimatum. Now she wants five hundred, not three hundred. Says she'll take Billy and leave if I give her the money by nine o'clock in the morning."

"And if you don't?"

"Then Selene'll go to Union Station, too, and tell Ella everything."

Holme handed the telegram back to Quinlan and walked to his large rolltop desk. He opened a wide drawer and took out a board on which there were at least fifty keys on hooks. He looked them over and then selected one and handed it to Quinlan. "You realize there's no choice now?"

Quinlan nodded, looking at the key. Without a word he turned and left the room. The hallway was dimly lighted with gas jets and he became a shadow moving quietly to the stairs and descending to the second floor. Beads of perspiration slid down his cheeks as he tiptoed along close to the wall. The room where Lizzie and Selene were staying now was Number 221, one of the interior rooms, to which Holmes had ordered they be moved a few days after he had delivered the baby three weeks ago, telling them it was better insulated and therefore the crying of the infant would not disturb other guests. Since he was giving it to them without charge they really couldn't object very much, but it was a dismal room, located halfway across the building from the nearest tenant. There was little chance of Billy's crying creating a disturbance for anyone and the windowless room was always so stuffy they usually kept the door ajar. Without the benefit of daylight filtering in, several gas jets were lighted all the time and the approaching Quinlan saw a trapezoid of the diffuse yellow gaslight stretched across the gloomy hallway from the partially open door.

Quinlan paused in the shadows outside the room and listened, his hands clammy and the key he held slippery with perspiration. He could faintly hear Lizzie and Selene conversing, but could not make out their words. He reached out and soundlessly pulled the heavy door closed, turning the knob so there would be no click. There were two keyholes in the door, above and below the knob. The one below was for the key Selene had; the one above for the key in Quinlan's hand. He tried to lock the door silently but the bolt fell into place with a metallic clunk and he withdrew the key hurriedly. Almost at once the doorknob was turned from the other side and there were faint shrill shouts and soft thuds on the inside of the door. With shaking hands he quickly tore two small strips from a kerchief and stuffed them into the keyholes. Then he spun away and raced back toward the stairs, pausing a moment to listen as he reached them. He thought he could hear barely audible thumps and cries but they were so muffled it could have been his imagination.

Returning to the third floor he found Holmes waiting in the doorway to the office and he walked past him wordlessly, pale and trembling. Holmes shut the outer door and indicated with a jerk of his head for Quinlan to follow, leading the way through two rooms and then to a closet he had to unlock. There were a dozen or more brass valves inside the closet, each connected to its own pipe, each with a number painted on it in black.

Quinlan looked at Holmes with a sick expression and Holmes stared back with that weird, penetrating, disconcerting gaze he sometimes affected. Holmes's voice was flat. "I shut the ceiling vent while you were downstairs. The rest is yours."

Quinlan licked his lips and his Adam's apple bobbed. He was shaking badly as he reached out and gripped the open valve bearing the painted number 221. He closed his eyes a moment and stood there, then opened them and with sudden resolve sharply turned the valve ninety degrees, shutting off the flow of gas. In his mind's eye he could see the gas flames in the room downstairs quickly diminish and go out, plunging the room into darkness. His lower lip quivered. Do they realize yet exactly what's happening? Do they know I'm behind it? What are they doing now? Screaming? Crying? He continued to stand there, white-knuckled hand locked to the valve, for fully two minutes; plenty of time for all residue of gas in the pipe to have burned off and the flame to be gone.

"Now," Holmes said. *"Now!"*

Quinlan turned the valve back to where it had been and heard the venomous hiss as the gaseous flow resumed. His hand dropped and he stumbled backwards until stopped by the doorjamb where he stood shivering violently.

It was three hours later when the two men went together to the third-floor closet above Room 221. There was, in one corner, a six-inch stovepipe emerging from the floor and disappearing into the ceiling and out the roof. Just above floor level was a damper, closed, and immediately above that a rotary fan device with two wires connected to a large battery on the floor. Holmes opened the damper and then pulled the short chain switch on the fan. Immediately they could hear the blades inside the pipe begin to turn, the revolutions increasing until the individual pingings merged into a continuous noisy hum.

"Go open their door, Pat," Holmes said. "It's all over. And make sure your pipe is completely out. Sooner or later someone's going to ask about them, so be prepared: Selene quit and went with Lizzie and the baby to live with relatives in Omaha."

Quinlan walked off as if somnambulant and Holmes watched him go, his expression not changing but feeling very pleased; if Quinlan's loyalty had not been assured before, it was now—every bit as much as Ben Pitezel's.

Cosgrove W. Arnold—known as C.W.—was a gangling individual, his long face appearing morose to those who did not look deeply enough to see the humor lurking in his eyes or stay around long enough to hear his great honking laughter. His eyebrows were thick and curly, his ears overlarge and projecting outward in a manner that made him look almost doltish, but he was far from being stupid. His business sense was sharp and his willingness to become involved in carefully calculated risks was what had attracted Holmes's interest in him from the beginning.

The two had become relatively close friends over the past couple of years, a friendship based on mutual contribution and mutual gain. Arnold was, in fact, the only person in Chicago who knew Holmes's real name was Herman Mudgett. He had learned this when Holmes, after sizing him up for some time and recognizing the incipient larceny in his soul, opened up enough to tell him of the initial life insurance fraud he and a fellow student had pulled off during his days at Ann Arbor; not the whole thing, of course, but of his faking his own death and then assuming a new identity. Arnold had been intrigued and, as Holmes had known would happen, it unleashed that larceny to the extent that the pair had become partners of a sort.

At the moment, Arnold was expounding on the future of life insurance. He sat close to the warmth generated by the oil stove in the third-floor Castle office. It had snowed again last night and occasionally he glanced through the huge floor-to-ceiling bowed windows of this turret room to the busy intersection of Sixty-third and Wallace directly below, where horses and humans stamped through the late February deposit.

". . . and I'm telling you, Holmes," he went on, "one of these days—and not too many years off, either—you're going to see tremendous consolidations take place. Everything's fragmented now. There must be thousands, maybe tens of thousands, of little storefront insurance companies around the country today. Look at right here in Chicago. How many would you guess there are? Fifty? A hundred? Jesus, Holmes, there are three hundred and seventy-six. Think of it, three hundred and seventy-six of 'em and that's just right here in Chicago. It's the same everywhere—New York, Philadelphia, St. Louis, Denver, San Francisco, Detroit, Cincinnati, all the big cities. Even a lot of the small ones."

"So? What's your point, C.W.?" Holmes leaned forward over the small table separating them and poured from a sterling silver pot with long narrow spout and ceramic handle. Arnold paused to pick up the delicate china cup from the saucer before him and carefully sip at the steaming coffee.

"Um, that's good." His cup made a musical clink as he set it down. "The point is, one of these days the more successful and aggressive companies are going to start gobbling up the smaller ones. You watch. Companies like Hartford and Liberty Mutual and Prudential and others—they're going to be corporate giants. And they're not going to get there by paying off every claim made without a lot of investigation. And those investigations are going to be done by men trained for just that purpose, not by independent underwriters like me who are called on to, quote, look into things, unquote, when there's a claim. So, a word to the wise—make hay while the sun shines."

"I've hardly stinted in that respect," Holmes murmured over his cup. "How many policies have I had you take out over the past couple of years?"

"Sixty-seven," Arnold replied promptly, "including the

three on yourself. No two with the same company, and of which, thus far, you've collected on eleven. You've made one hell of a lot of money."

Holmes put his own cup down and looked intently at his guest. "*We've* made a lot of money, C.W., not just I. Twenty percent of a paid claim is rather a good return for the little work—or risk—you take. Are you leading up to telling me it's not enough?"

"Oh, damn, is *that* what you think? Absolutely not. All I'm saying is that before very much longer it's going to get too risky to pull off such frauds. I give it maybe five years before the risks outweigh the potential. After that you'd be crazy to do it anymore."

"I'll bear it in mind."

"Well, here's another thing to consider for the future. We're going to have an influx of people into this area beyond anything you could imagine."

"Oh?" A spark of interest came to life in Holmes's eyes. "How so?"

"You haven't read today's paper?"

"No. What's happened?"

Arnold got up and went over to his overcoat hanging on a clothes-tree. He pulled a folded newspaper from the pocket and came back to the table. "The city's going wild about this. Read." He tapped the article in question as he handed the paper to Holmes, who read:

CHICAGO NAMED SITE OF
WORLD'S COLUMBIAN EXPOSITION

In a vote held by Congress yesterday, Chicago emerged victorious as the United States city slated to host the World's Fair in 1892, culminating two years of fierce inter-city contention.

At the time the final voting occurred, only four cities remained in the running: Chicago, New York, Washington and St. Louis. A majority of 154 votes was required for victory. In the first balloting the results were as follows: Chicago, 115; New York, 70; St. Louis, 61; Washington, 58. (The final vote of the 305 was cast by a wag who opted for Cumberland Gap, Kentucky.) Six more ballots in succession were taken, with Chicago steadily climbing on each, the

7th ballot resulting in Chicago having 152, only 2
below the requirement. Opponents at that point
made a last ditch effort to stall passage by making a
motion for adjournment, but that motion was easily
defeated. In the 8th ballot, Chicago received 157
votes, three over the mark.

"The best part's in another story," Arnold said as Holmes
looked up. "They're expecting over twenty million people to
attend. And here's the ace: the fairground's going to be built
at Jackson Park, eight blocks from here."

"Twenty million people," Holmes echoed.

"With lots of money," Arnold grinned.

"And needing accommodations," Holmes added.

"A fantastic opportunity for an individual with an enterprising bent," Arnold pointed out.

"Indeed," Holmes murmured. "Indeed."

The combination graduation and going-away party held
September 18 at the ostentatious Vanderhorn mansion was
being given in honor of Minnie Williams, the last significant social function she would attend before her departure. At twenty-three, she had recently been graduated
from the Boston Conservatory following completion of a
three-year course of study in music and elocution. Though
moderately gifted as a pianist, she was perversely less
interested in following a musical career than in becoming
an actress, at which her talent was not so pronounced.
She would soon be heading for a visit to her maternal
uncle in Jackson, Mississippi, and from there to Denver to
invest a substantial portion of her inheritance in a theater
production.

Minnie was by no means a raving beauty—at five feet
three inches and one hundred fifty pounds, she had unkindly
been referred to more than once as being pleasingly plump—
but she did have a very pretty face. Her hair was blond and
curly, cut quite short because she felt it would deemphasize
her weight problem, but than she negated whatever benefits
so derived by wearing necklaces more in the nature of
chokers than the elongated looped or pendant varieties. The
one she was wearing tonight was a simple strand of perfectly
matched pearls, well chosen to complement her gown—a

stunning and daring off-the-shoulder diaphanous creation, sublimely tinted the same pale powdery green of a newly emerged luna moth.

Two-score guests or more moved about in their finery, clustering here and there in conversational coveys, some of the ladies with sherry in stemmed crystal, some of the men holding small glasses of Scotch whiskey. The hum of their conviviality rose to a pervading drone interspersed with small bursts of polite laughter. Minnie Williams, during a lull in her particular group's discussion, let her gaze wander across the crowd until suddenly her attention became riveted to an individual across the large room.

"Who," she breathed, "is that absolutely *beautiful* man?"

Claudia Copley Vanderhorn, standing beside her, raised a bejeweled lorgnette from the bosom of her exquisite peach jacquard gown and peered through the lenses in the direction her guest was staring. A pair of gentlemen just entering the room swam into focus and the hostess was immediately quite certain the one she knew was not the one referred to by Miss Williams.

"My, my," she said in glottal contralto, "he is rather dashing, isn't he? Chester mentioned he'd be bringing a friend, but I must admit, I haven't the foggiest notion who he is." Her proper Bostonian accent was very pronounced. "However, my dear, since they're headed this way, I'm sure we'll soon find out."

The two men smoothly threaded their way through the milling guests and approached them, smiling, the taller of the pair in the lead. He was a thin man in his late twenties with carrot-colored hair and multitudinous freckles of very nearly the same color. Neatly dressed in black cutaway suit and fine white linen shirt with broadly knotted crimson ascot, he appeared quite fashionably dressed until one compared him to his companion.

The second man was also dressed in a black evening cutaway, but one tailored so exceptionally well that no inappropriate wrinkle or fold appeared anywhere on the fabric. His immaculate white silk shirt was discreetly frilled at collar and cuffs and punctuated with iridescent buttons of most delicate nacre. His tie was black and much smaller than his companion's, perfectly complementing his broad scarlet cummerbund. It was his raiment that had first caught Minnie's attention but now, as they neared, her gaze locked on his face—the strong square chin and jawline, the dense, neatly trimmed mustache that upturned just slightly at the ends, the broad forehead beneath thick, lustrous dark hair, the wide, sensual mouth with lips just short of being too full, the aristocratic nose with nostrils flared nearly to the point of arrogance, and the eyes—*the eyes!*—disturbingly compelling, deeply blue as a perfect October sky, so disconcertingly penetrating as they fell full upon her that she felt as if she had been struck and she nearly gasped aloud. In that instant, though she would not admit it, Minnie Williams fell in love.

"Chester, how good of you to come," Claudia said, surrendering her hand to both of his and amused at the wetness of his lips as he kissed it.

"Mrs. Vanderhorn, what a wonderful honor to be included as a guest in your lovely home. Allow me, please, to compliment you on one of the most strikingly beautiful gowns I have ever seen."

"Still full of the old blarney, I see, Chester dear." The crinkled eyes softened the sting of her words. "Allow me to present Miss Minnie Williams of Fort Worth, our honored guest. Minnie, this incandescent young gentleman is Dr. Chester Fish, who belies the time-honored concept that to be a good physician one must be pedantic, paunchy and not far short of septuagenarian."

"Indeed a pleasure, ma'am," said Chester, bowing and kissing her hand as well. "May I present to you both an old friend of mine from Chicago, Mr. Harry Gordon."

The second man bowed in courtly manner and addressed them in a rich baritone. "Mrs. Vanderhorn, Miss Williams. I hardly expected to encounter the setting sun and rising moon in the same room." His direct gaze took in the beautiful floor-length peach-colored gown of their hostess and he nodded. "At the risk of equally being accused of engaging in blarney, I must second Chester's opinion of your gown, madam. It is exquisite." His eyes rolled toward the younger woman. "And yours, Miss Williams, is positively dazzling. I don't recall ever having seen so delicate a fabric."

She colored faintly but did not lower her gaze. "Thank you, Mr. Gordon. It is a relatively new material from France, called chiffon."

The four chatted together a while longer until muted xylophonic tones instigated a general movement of the guests toward the resplendent triple-chandeliered dining room. The Vanderhorns took their places at the center of the enormous U-shaped table, with Minnie Williams to the left of the hostess. Near one end of the table the two young gentlemen found the place card on which was lettered in fine flowing script: *Dr. C. Fish and Guest*. And, far apart though they were, the eyes of Harry Gordon and Minnie Williams met and briefly held a score of times during the course of the meal.

"What do you know about her?" Gordon murmured as they dined.

"Who?" Fish asked, "Mrs. Vanderhorn? Well, she's a member of one of Boston's first families and—"

"Not her, you ass! The Williams girl."

"Nothing. How would I know? Christ, Holmes, we were introduced to her at the same time."

"Not Holmes!" His whisper was intense, harsh. "Here I'm Harry Gordon. Period. Don't you forget it again, Fish."

Fish looked disgruntled. "How the hell do I keep up, *Mister* Gordon?" he complained. "Every time I see you you've got a different name. I suppose when I move my practice to New York City next month and you visit there, if you ever do, you'll have yet another name."

"Altogether possible, Chester, old friend, altogether possible." The harshness was gone, replaced by mild smiling sarcasm. "But, I have great faith in your ability to keep pace. And you *will* be seeing me in New York, I promise you, for the same reason I came to see you here."

"Damn it, Hol——Harry!" Fish spoke in a rasping whisper. "I have a medical practice. I don't operate a morgue. I told you there was no way I could supply you with cadavers from here in Boston and there won't be any way I can supply them from New York. That's final!"

Holmes merely looked at him until Fish self-consciously dropped his eyes. Then he reached out and patted the redhead's arm. "Sure there is, Chester. I have the greatest faith that somehow you'll find a way." He spoke so softly that his words could be heard by no one but Fish. "I find that a man can accomplish remarkable things if he has great enough impetus. I'm not unreasonable. I know it'll be difficult. But I suspect it would be far more difficult for you if someone were ever to suggest, anonymously of course, to the Ann Arbor police that a certain highly respected physician in New York City might be able to shed light on the unsolved disappearance of some residents of their fair city, including a couple of children. Yes, that could make matters far more difficult for you." Fish paled, his freckles appearing to have been amateurishly painted on his face. Holmes chuckled and continued. "So, there, that's settled. You'll be making contacts in New York soon and I know you'll find it in the goodness of your heart to aid me." His voice became a razor slicing through taut fabric. "You *will* see to it, Chester, won't you?"

The redhead chewed at his lower lip for a long moment before replying. "I'll . . . do my best."

"Good, good!" Holmes spoke aloud, wrapping his arm around Fish and patting his shoulder. "It's so great to have reliable friends."

The two spoke to one another little after that, Holmes concentrating on catching Minnie Williams's eye every now and again, Fish picking halfheartedly at his serving of roast squab and heavily overcooked vegetables.

Following dinner, the guests moved to the ballroom and waltzed to the triple-time strains of a twenty-piece orchestra. For the first few waltzes the man who was known tonight as Harry Gordon danced with Minnie Williams, but the couple soon strolled out onto the terrace and chatted under a beautifully balmy night sky.

Minnie Williams was lost in a haze of romanticism. She had had escorts before and once had nearly become engaged, but never before had she been so smitten by any man. She mentally berated herself for an inability to stop talking but he didn't mind at all and, though once or twice she tried to curtail her outpourings, he always encouraged her to go on. No one had ever before listened to her so closely, so gratifyingly, nor found what she had to say so interesting. It was in fair measure because he was such a good listener, she thought him to be the most fascinating and profound man she'd ever met. When he kissed her, as he did before they left the terrace and strolled out through the fragrant gardens, it was the first time she had ever allowed a man to do so on such short acquaintance and she thought she would swoon in his arms. Not until later did she realize and feel mortified at the fact that she had told him things about herself that she had never told anyone, yet she hardly knew anything about him except superficialities: He was extremely good looking, debonair, charming, a gifted conversationalist and a cultured man of considerable polish. She deduced that he was not only highly intelligent but evidently extremely wealthy. She had no conception that the conversation had gone precisely as the man called Harry Gordon had wanted.

For Holmes, the evening was enormously exciting because the more he talked with this slightly frenetic young woman—or, more accurately, encouraged her with adroitly placed comments or questions to talk to him—the more he became convinced he could well be on the threshold of something uncommonly profitable. By the time the evening ended, he knew quite a lot about her, but he was eager to learn more. And so he did. During the remaining ten days left to Minnie in Boston, Holmes saw her every day. They strolled the Common and Public Garden together, visited art galleries and the library, climbed to the tower window of the Old North Church, had their pictures taken together, attended the theater and concerts. At the end of these days he could have written an accurate encapsulated biography of her.

Minnie Randall Williams, he learned, was the eldest of four children. Her father, as an enterprising young man, had made a sizable fortune in railroads during the Civil War and then increased his net worth substantially through sagacious stock market investments. Within a month after Lee's surrender to Grant at Appomattox, Clarence Williams had wed Mary Black of Jackson, Mississippi. In that same city just a year later—in 1866—Minnie had been born and shortly afterwards the little family moved to Fort Worth, Texas. Three other children had followed, the secondborn being another daughter, Ina Anne, whose name underwent a process of evolution, from Ina to Inie to Annie and finally to Nannie. She was two years younger than Minnie. Eighteen months later their brother Baldwin Heath was born and, two years after that, William Robert, who was called Billy Bob. In 1875 her father had been killed in a railroad accident and her mother died within a year following. The children had at that point become wards of two different uncles. Minnie went to live with their paternal uncle, Calvin Williams, also of Fort Worth, and also quite wealthy. Nannie, Baldwin and Billy Bob had gone to live with their maternal uncle, the Reverend

Will C. Black, first in New Orleans and then in Jackson, Mississippi. Following primary and secondary education, Minnie—who, Holmes discovered, had inherited the bulk of her parents' wealth in real estate and a trust fund—came east to attend the Boston Conservatory. Nannie, following high school graduation in Jackson, returned to Texas and was currently attending teacher's college there. Baldwin, who had always been weak and sickly, was presently vegetating in Fort Worth, while Billy Bob, newly graduated from a Jackson high school, had recently taken a job with the Arkansas Smelter Yards in Leadville, Colorado, determined to learn the business from the ground up.

It took some clever maneuvering on Holmes's part to extract the information from Minnie that interested him most, but he succeeded in the main. From the trust fund her father had set up for her, Minnie received $30,000 annually in perpetuity. The younger siblings each received half that amount. Minnie's guardian, Uncle Calvin, had some large real estate holdings—one of the properties, in downtown Fort Worth, a vacant lot valued at about $80,000—as well as a considerable amount in liquid assets. The bulk of his estate was willed to his favorite niece, Minnie Williams. Of course, if Minnie happened to die before Uncle Cal, then his estate would be divided evenly among Nannie, Baldwin and Billy Bob. If any of them died, his share would be divided among the survivors.

When the time came for them to part, Minnie boarded her train for the South in tears, promising to keep in touch with Harry and to visit him in Chicago after the theatrical project in Denver was finished. With each of their meetings, Minnie had fallen more in love with Harry Gordon. By the time her train pulled out and he headed for the ticket office, he had all but perfected in his own mind a decidedly grandiose plan. That it was far-fetched, illogical and the product of a very sick mind never occurred to him.

Calvin Williams, a distinguished, white-haired man of medium height, no sooner stepped out onto the sidewalk from his downtown Fort Worth office building on October 7 than he collided with a passerby. Both men were rocked by the encounter but the passerby seemed to fare worst. He caromed into a lamppost, derby knocked off in one direction and briefcase spilling open in another. The man himself very nearly fell to the pavement.

"Terribly sorry, sir," Williams apologized, reaching for the few scattered papers and briefcase as the younger man retrieved his hat. "I'm afraid I wasn't paying attention. I hope you're not hurt?" He appeared to be about fifty and spoke with the warm soft drawl of a native Texan.

"Not at all," the man said, brushing some dust from his hat, "how about yourself?"

"I'm fine, fine. You sure you're all right?"

"Thank you, yes." He replaced his derby on his head, the hat looking somewhat out of place amid all the high, wide-brimmed Stetson hats worn by the men walking past along the busy thoroughfare. He reached for the briefcase and papers Williams was still holding, saying, "Thanks again."

Williams surrendered the items without looking at them, until one of the papers fluttered free again as the younger man took them. Williams stooped to get it—a portrait photograph of this stranger with a woman—and then froze with it in his hand, his mouth falling open. "Why, that's Minnie!" he exclaimed.

"You *know* Minnie Williams?" the younger man said incredulously.

"Know her? *Know her?*" The older man threw back his head and laughed so unrestrainedly that passersby turned to look and grinned in response. "Lord God A'mighty, man, Minnie's my niece." He looked at the picture again and then back at the younger man. "This is you in the picture, I see, but *who* are you?"

"Gordon's the name," said Holmes, extending his hand and smiling broadly. "Harry Gordon."

"If that don't beat all," Williams chortled, pumping Holmes's hand. "Minnie mentioned you in a letter I got from her just last week from Boston. Said she'd met this fine upstandin' young feller and—" He broke off and took a new tack. "Listen, I'm just on my way to get a bite of lunch. I'd be right proud to have you join me, if you can spare the time."

"Well," Holmes was momentarily dubious. "I do have something planned." He paused and then spoke more jauntily. "Why not? That can wait. I'd be pleased to join you."

They strolled to a nearby restaurant and had an animated conversation over lunch. Holmes said he remembered Minnie had mentioned having an uncle in Fort Worth but, regretfully, had not elaborated. Minnie was now, so far as he knew, in Mississippi.

"What brings you to Fort Worth, Mr. Gordon, if I may ask?" Williams said as they were finishing.

"No secret," Holmes replied. "I've come to look at some properties which I might add to my holdings."

"Well," Williams said expansively, "I do have a certain limited experience in Fort Worth real estate, Mr. Gordon. If you'd care to consider it, I'd be glad to go with you and look over whatever properties you have in mind and maybe provide a bit of insight regarding investment or development potential."

"Agreed," Holmes said promptly. "I'd very much appreciate that. And please, call me Harry."

"Be glad to, Harry, an' you call me Cal. Maybe you'd like to see the building I'm putting up, too. Actually, I was planning on dropping by there after lunch anyway."

"Certainly, I'd like to see it. Why don't we go there first? I think my schedule's probably more flexible than yours."

The building under construction was four blocks distant and as they walked, Cal Williams explained there had been a temporary work stoppage due to a contractual dispute but that the matter was nearly settled and he expected work to begin again within the next few days. His planned visit was for the purpose of inspection in case there was any matter about the construction under progress that needed to be settled before the new agreement was signed. The building was to be ten stories high, of which eight floors were thus far partially completed. They inspected each floor in turn, climbing stairs connecting the first six floors and ladders to the upper two. On the eighth floor, at the edge of a centrally located three-bank elevator shaft that had been formed in, Williams paused to look down at the jumble of broken concrete and other rubble at the bottom.

"These'll be the fastest, smoothest elevators in all of Fort Worth when finished," he commented.

"That's wonderful, Cal," Holmes said from behind him. He placed his hand in the center of the older man's back and gave a sharp shove. He expected Williams to scream as he plummeted, but except for an immediate sharp gasp there was no sound at all until the meaty thud as he struck bottom. Holmes opened his fly and masturbated into the shaft.

No one had paid any particular attention to the two men

when they entered the construction site and now no one at all saw Holmes leave. Less than one hour later he was on a train headed for Chicago.

"The least you could have done, Henry, was be here for the birth of your daughter."

The measure of Dora's anger was reflected in her use of his first name. At other times she called him Holmes. Her expression was set in hard lines that softened only when she glanced down at the infant lying beside her, suckling contentedly at her engorged breast.

"Dora, if I could have been, I would have been. It just wasn't possible."

His sincerity was evident and she stopped stroking the baby's head to glance back at him, the line of her lips less stern. "She was born on Monday at two-thirty in the afternoon. Where were you at that time?"

"On the eighth floor of a building under construction in Fort Worth, Texas."

"Fort Worth?" Her eyebrows went up in surprise. "I thought you were in Boston."

"I was, just prior to that. The Texas matter was directly related to the Boston matter."

A crafty look entered her eyes. "Do I detect the sweet scent of money?"

"You do. Big money, Dora. Very big."

"Do I want to know the details?" She kissed the top of her daughter's head.

"You do not."

"Do I want to know how much?"

Holmes smiled. "I think it might amuse you."

"All right, then, how much?"

"In excess, I think, of one hundred thousand dollars."

Her mouth turned into an *O* and then she bent her head and kissed the nursing infant again. "Lucy," she murmured, "you want to know something? Your daddy's very sorry he wasn't here to greet you when you arrived, but he's going to make it up to you. He's going to make you a very rich little girl."

Exuberant greetings were not uncommon at the redbrick Jackson Railroad Station, but the shrieks and squeals that split the air on the arrival of Minnie Williams a week ago today had been a bit more than might have been anticipated. The joy that had filled Minnie at seeing Uncle Will again was considerably more than doubled when it turned out that Nannie, taking advantage of a mid-semester break, was also at the terminal to greet her.

Uncle Will—the Reverend W. C. Black—still bore a marked resemblance to his sister, Mary, the girls' mother. But the passage of time had caused a certain deterioration. At sixty-two he was showing his years, his stature less than ramrod straight, hair pure white rather than the salt-and-pepper it had been ever since Minnie could remember, speech slightly more fumbling than it had always been. But there was still that fire in his eye and that righteous thunder in his voice when he preached his Sunday sermons; and his pen was no less incisive than it had always been. He was still editor of the *Methodist Christian Advocate*, as he had been for more than two decades.

Uncle Will lived alone now, since the passing of Aunt Sally Bea, and the arrival of his talkative nieces had loosed the wellspring of his own garrulousness. How any thoughts could have been imparted one to another during that drive from the station to the stately old manse where he still lived was moot, since the three talked in simultaneous nonstop concert all the way there. No one seemed to mind.

The Reverend Black's interest lay in his flock, his words dripping benevolence for the devout and suffering, spouting brimstone for the backsliders. He and God had long had an agreement: the Lord could provide the written Word but it was the whiplash tongue of the Reverend Black that would send it snapping and crackling over the congregation's collective head in perpetual reminder of the eternal horrors that transgressors would eventually reap. Yet, one with an acute ear and perspicacious eye might have surmised with certain justification that he took a particular vicarious enjoyment in recounting the details of those sins that brought about such multiple damnations.

At twenty-one, Nannie was a little shorter and a little darker than Minnie, and, though overweight, not quite so plump. She laughed a great deal, a rich, rolling laughter that seemed to tumble upward and outward from some inexhaustible resource deep within. She was, at the moment, very full of herself and her accomplishments at East Texas State Teachers College at Commerce. Her grades were most respectable and there was a good chance that after graduation she could get a job teaching at Midlothian, only twenty miles southeast of Fort Worth. She had not yet plighted her troth but there was one young man in whom she was showing more than mere mild interest.

Minnie, at first, could talk of nothing but the wonderful, marvelous, intelligent, talented, charming, wealthy, debonair, generous, kind, successful, witty and totally virile man she had met at the Vanderhorn estate in Boston. She proudly displayed pictures of him alone and of the two of them together. In a remarkably short time she became a total bore.

"He must be a ghost," Nannie said seriously, her eyes dancing.

"Whyever would you say that?" Minnie asked, missing the masked amusement and frowning.

"Because you've told us everything about him, silly, except his name. If he doesn't have a name he must be a spirit figure."

Minnie laughed along with the others. "All right," she said, "all right. Give me a chance. First I had to tell you about him. His name is Harry Gordon."

"Gordon?" echoed Nannie.

"Harry?" put in Uncle Will.

"With the buildup you gave him," Nannie continued, "I expected at least a name like Sebastian Courtright the third or Beauregard Q. Wellington, senior. But Harry Gordon!"

"I think it's possible we might now talk about something else," Uncle Will suggested, eyes twinkling, "since Minnie's used every complimentary adjective immediately recallable to describe this young man."

"Oh, come on now, that's not fair," Minnie pouted. No one spoke for the space of several breaths and then Minnie added, "Besides, above and beyond everything else, he's got the most gorgeous blue eyes!"

All three burst into howls of laughter, rocking back and forth, holding their sides, trying to talk but only increasing the merriment with choked and garbled words. Thus was the pattern set for those first seven wonderful days.

Then a Western Union telegram was delivered by a teenaged boy riding a bicycle with a front wheel nearly five feet in diameter and a rear wheel hardly a sixth that size. It was for Minnie from Uncle Calvin's attorney and friend, Mossie H. Watt, whom she had always called Mr. Mossie.

MISS MINNIE R WILLIAMS STOP REGRET INFORM YOU CALVIN WILLIAMS ACCIDENTALLY KILLED IN FALL MON OCT 7 STOP NOT FOUND TILL WED OCT 9 FUNERAL 3 PM SAT OCT 12 STOP YOUR PRESENCE WITH NANNIE URGENT STOP MOSSIE

There were those who considered Julia Louise Conner— the former Julia Smythe—the most handsome female they had ever encountered. Not the most beautiful, perhaps, because the sense of physical prettiness was not exactly the emphasis at first encounter. But striking, yes. A woman with inherent grace, definitely. Classically featured, assuredly. She was uncommonly tall—an inch short of six feet—and superbly proportioned. Statuesque was the term used by many. Shoulder-length hair of deep rich chestnut was usually pulled back in an upswept bun high at the back of her head, exposing a smooth cameo neck. The guileless green eyes were large and widely set, in harmony with high cheekbones and delicate nose and a pair of generous lips that seemed poised to trigger into a smile.

Men tended to stare slack-jawed when they saw Julia, instantly affected by the magnetism that was so integral a part of her physical being. Some even turned to follow her, not to accost, merely to *look* upon her even more. Oddly enough, women were not ordinarily jealous; to the contrary, they wanted to be close to her, to become a part of her, as if by so doing they might absorb unto themselves some of this mysterious, not quite definable quality that made her something very special. Nor was this attraction she held for men and women alike based simply on physical attributes. She was uncommonly intelligent, yet did not wear that intelligence as a badge of accomplishment to be lorded over others, nor use it as a means to intimidate those around her. She was a voracious reader, as much enthralled by the classics as with modern works. Poetry in particular moved her and she wrote sensitive lines kept hidden in a box within the closet.

To all who knew her, it was a mystery why she had ever married Icilus T. Conner—better known as Ned—who had no vestige of those elements of class with which she was so amply endowed. Essentially he was a nondescript namby-pamby: average height, average build, average intelligence, average appearance; a man who, in a single word, might best be described as rumpled, physically and mentally. His drab brown hair was receding and his mustache, grown too long, was always unkempt, his clothing somehow always slightly seedy. Worst of all, perhaps, he was almost wholly lacking in ambition. Julia alone was aware of why she had married him. In the optimism of youth—she was only eighteen years old when they wed—she felt she could impart some of her ambition to him, that she could bolster his own self-image and fire him to move on to bigger and better things and, in the process, remove her from the stultifying existence that she hated. Anything seemed better, at the time, than continuing to be the youngest of seven daughters of a Davenport, Iowa, grocer, for whom she was a skilled but greatly underpaid bookkeeper.

So Julia Smythe, in marrying jeweler Ned Conner of Muscatine, Iowa, in 1880, found she had merely traded one life of boredom and frustration for another. For the first three years—until the stillbirth of a daughter who was to be named Pearl—they existed in Ned's lackluster jewelry shop in Muscatine. After that she demanded they move on, look for opportunities elsewhere and, grudgingly, simply to keep peace, he agreed, but hardly with foresight in the forefront.

Ned Conner's first venture in the great world beyond Muscatine was the purchase of a jewelry shop even worse than the first, located in Columbus Junction, Iowa. The world did not beat a path to their door and she finally convinced him to sell out—at a loss—and at least try his hand in another state. So he did, moving his despairing wife to a store he bought, no better than the first two, in tiny Bradford, Illinois. Ned was not noted for thinking big.

He soon lost the Bradford business, too, through timidity and mismanagement. Considerably poorer and progressively angrier over his own ineptitude, he blamed the failures on her. As outlet for his increasing fright and sense of being threatened by her independent, free-thinking manner, he began beating her and, even worse, deliberately thwarting her ambitions and squashing her innovative ideas at utterance. In pointless rebellion he burned all her poetry and, without her knowledge, used the remainder of their savings to put a down payment on the very store he had owned when they first met. Despite her objections, he moved her back to Muscatine in time for the birth of another child—this time a healthy daughter—whom Ned insisted on naming Gertrude after his thirteen-year-old sister. Julia, who liked her young sister-in-law well enough, despised the name Gertrude and called the child by the name she had favored from the beginning—Pearl. After a while, even Ned gave in and called her Pearl, too.

They eked out a bare existence for several years more, barely able to meet their mortgage, and finally, with ruin crouched on the horizon, he sold out again. At that point he acquiesced to Julia's demands that they use what meager funds were left to go to a big city where opportunity would surely be better and where Pearl, now five years old and soon to start school, might get a better education. Chicago was the choice and at their arrival on October 14 they carefully scanned the help wanted ads in the newspapers and found one that seemed ideal—a businessman in the Englewood district of the city advertising for an experienced jeweler, with skill in jewelry repair and design, to take over management of his shop.

In the morning Ned left their shoddy hotel room in the near downtown area and took the streetcar all the way out to Englewood to apply for the position. Julia dressed Pearl in her best clothes and put on her own threadbare coat and the two went out to explore this great metropolis.

It was such a big, lusty, brawling city, abustle with life and strength and activity, filled with people who had great goals and stunning dreams and wondrous ambitions; a city where people made things happen and where a woman might become more than merely a drudge and bearer of children; the city where a young woman named Jane Addams was capturing national attention by initiating significant social reforms; the city where eleven years before Frances Willard had established the now nationally powerful Women's Christian Temperance Union; where women of wealth, such as Mrs. Potter Palmer and Mrs. A. Montgomery Ward, were using their social positions to help improve the human condition.

Julia and little Pearl strolled the great thoroughfares, overwhelmed at such a flux of people and traffic. They craned their necks to see the tops of tall buildings, appropriately being called skyscrapers, and they entered the marvelous mercantile world of Marshall Field where, for the first time in any business, the customer was always right. They walked until Pearl's legs gave out and then Julia carried her back to their decrepit quarters, convinced more than ever that this was the city of opportunity. She was still in a glow when, four hours after leaving, Ned returned, bearing a small bouquet and whistling.

"Ned, you got the job!"

"I did," he told her proudly. "You are looking at the new manager of the Englewood Jewelry Company. How could Mr. Holmes resist when I turned on the charm and told him of my vast experience?"

"Oh, that's wonderful. I'm so proud of you. Pearl," she said, stooping and hugging the pretty little girl, "your daddy has a new job and things are going to be ever so much better for us now."

Pearl clung to her mother's arm. "Ith Daddy going to get a whole thouthand dollarth?" she lisped, naming the largest figure she could conjure.

"Well, maybe, sweetheart, sometime." She kissed Pearl's shiny pink cheek and looked up at Ned. "How much is this Mr. Holmes paying you?"

Some of the excitement in his attitude dwindled. "Well, it's not a lot, but it includes our own three-room flat in his building, right where the store is located."

"How much?"

"Twelve dollars a week."

"Oh, Ned," she was shocked. "You should be getting more than twice that!"

"Yes, but with our lodging included, it's . . . it's . . ." The words dwindled off.

"It's still not enough," she finished, but then smiled and reached out and squeezed his hand. "But it's a start. We're in Chicago and it's a great city and who knows what the future holds? I'm sure this is going to turn out to be the most momentous step we've ever taken."

From that incredible first instant he saw her, the day after hiring Ned Conner, Holmes knew he must have Julia Conner. He was entranced by her, dumbfounded at the powerful surge of pure lust that overtook him as they were introduced and all but tongue tied in his response. He covered his stunned fascination by turning his attention to the little girl.

"You must be Pearl," he said, cursing his own inanity.

"Yeth," she said. She held her hand high toward him. "Would you like to thee my ring?"

Grateful for the opportunity to collect himself, Holmes bent over the tiny hand, supposedly inspecting the ring. *How the hell can she affect me like this? I've never even seen her before. But she's . . . magnificent!* "Is that a real diamond?" he asked, referring to the infinitesimal chip of glitter set on the narrow gold band.

"Oh, yeth, thir. My daddy made it. An' he made thith, too." She dug into a small pocket and extracted a minute gold watch.

"Looks as if I've hired the right man," he said to Conner, after inspecting it and handing it back to the girl. "Very nice work. Do you, also," he asked, turning to Julia, "have special examples of your husband's craftsmanship?"

"I'm afraid not, Mr. Holmes. Over the years he's made me some things that were very nice, but somehow they've always wound up being sold to an admiring customer." She flicked a meaningful glance at Ned, who refused to meet her eye.

"A shame," Holmes said softly, "but perhaps for the better—one should never attempt to gild a lily."

For one fleeting, fractional instant Julia's eyes met Holmes's and in that moment he knew—and knew that *she* knew—he would have her.

For the first few weeks after the Conners' arrival, while he and Ben Pitezel were engrossed in a special project in the cellar, he saw little more of her than to offer an occasional "Good morning" or nod in passing. And though he appeared not to notice, he saw that her eyes surreptitiously followed him whenever he appeared. He also quickly saw that not only did precious little love exist between Ned and Julia, there was rarely even cordiality. Ned seemed to delight in belittling her at every opportunity and to make derogatory remarks about her in the guise of humor. For her own part, Julia felt if she heard him say, "Just joking, honey," one more time she would either kill him or quietly go mad.

At the moment, Holmes had no time for the Conners. The project in the basement was one that he had long been planning, even since before building the Castle, but he had not the mechanical skills required. Pitezel did and Ben was delighted with the entire scheme when Holmes explained it. The first task had been for Ben and Quinlan to build four wooden walls to enclose the principal staircase to the cellar. A secret panel permitted access to the remainder of the basement, but was virtually invisible from inside the room when closed. The floor was of heavy planking covered with unbroken linoleum. The twelve-foot-square room thus formed appeared to be all there was of a basement to this building and was not only the terminus of the stairway but was also large enough to hold a simple but peculiar device Pitezel constructed to Holmes's specifications.

The contrivance stood in the open on four decorative legs of intertwined wrought iron, each leg three feet high and welded to a two-foot-square sheet metal tank a foot in depth. The top of the tank contained a screw-in cap four inches in diameter. This cap had a length of pipe running through it, open on the bottom side, which would be inside the tank when the cap was in place, the top expanded into a bulbed chamber and, above that, a funnel arrangement. The only other appurtenance to the tank was a pipe extending from one end for about a foot and then turned upward in an L-joint, ending in a nozzle with brass shut-off valve.

It was Holmes himself, clad in a conservative suit, who led the delegation of three newspaper reporters and seven businessmen to the basement room as the decade of the 1890s was still in its first month. Two of the businessmen were from the Englewood Gasworks, one from the City of Chicago Gas Company, two from the Canadian Natural Gas Company of Toronto, and two from the Metropolitan Buffalo Gas Company. Half a dozen lamps turned up full made the room cheery and bright. On a nearby table were four quart-sized Ball-Mason jars. Three contained powders, the fourth a clear liquid. A red line had been painted around the jar containing the liquid at about the midpoint. Beside the jars was a two-tablespoon measuring cup and a bowl.

"Gentlemen," Holmes began, "I do not intend going into lengthy explanations over how I invented my process or developed the Holmes Gas Generator. Suffice to say that many years of trial and failure went into finding the proper chemicals and blending them into the correct mixtures for the chemical reaction desired. Once that was successfully accomplished, development of the Holmes Gas Generator was swift. This model you see here," he patted the tank, which made an empty booming sound, "is very small and for demonstration purposes only. Generation of gas for a town or city would, of course, necessitate construction of much larger tanks with thicker walls to contain the enormous pressures that are created."

"Excuse me for interrupting, Mr. Holmes," said Lowell Trafford, Canadian Natural Gas Company executive, "but before any sort of demonstration is made, I, for one, would appreciate the opportunity to inspect your invention." The others nodded in agreement.

"Of course," Holmes said. He rapped the tank with his knuckles. "This tank is the generation chamber." He unscrewed and removed the peculiar cap. "It is empty now, but please feel free to look inside and also sniff the opening to satisfy yourself that nothing is inside."

"Safe to light a match?" asked Edgar Zholesczk of the Englewood Gasworks. When Holmes indicated it was, he struck a lucifer and held it to the opening, squinting at the flickering illuminated interior. "Nothing inside that I can see," he said, sniffing, "or smell."

The others made their own examinations until all were satisfied it was exactly as Holmes had represented it to be, an empty tank. They also inspected the strangely constructed cap, the intertwined wrought-iron legs, the pipe extending from the end of the tank, the nozzle and valve. Each turned the valve on and off, sniffing at the nozzle until confident nothing was there.

"The formulae for the composition and ratio of the chemicals I have blended must, for now, remain secret," Holmes went on, indicating the three jars containing powders, "for obvious reasons. This jar," he picked up the one containing clear liquid, "contains nothing more than ordinary water." He put it to his lips and drank several swallows of it.

The others, in turn, inspected the liquid, holding it up to the light and looking through it and sniffing it. Three of them, including one of the reporters, took tentative sips. All agreed it was nothing but water.

"All right, gentlemen, enough said. It is time for action to supplant words. Observe." Holmes tipped the water-filled jar over the bowl and spilled it out carefully until the level was exactly to the red line. He then picked up the two-tablespoon measuring cup and scooped up one of the powders, leveling it with the edge of his finger. This he sprinkled into the water jar and swirled until it had entirely dissolved. A similar measure from the second powder-filled jar was dumped into the empty tank and the tank lid then screwed firmly into place. A scoop of powder from the third jar was then dumped into the funnel top of the cap device. Holmes held up the water jar with dramatic flair and poured it into the cap funnel. As he finished, the jar slipped from his grip. He tried to catch it but only succeeded in thrusting it away so it hit the floor with a thud and rolled into the wall.

On the other side of the wall, listening carefully for precisely that sound, as they had rehearsed, Ben Pitezel straightened and opened the valve of the pipe that disappeared under the new floor. The other end of the pipe was connected to the illegal tapping Holmes had made of the Englewood gas mains at the time the building was constructed. From the valve opened by Pitezel, the high-pressure gas followed the pipe under the flooring and up through one of the intertwined legs of the table which, instead of wrought iron like the rest, was copper tubing painted black to match the rest. This led into the pipe which emerged from the tank.

Inside the small room, Holmes was shaking his head over the dropped jar. "Clumsy of me. No matter, it didn't break. All right now, allow me to explain. The powder, dissolved in ordinary water, encountered the second powder here," he pointed at the bulbous expansion on the pipe, "initiating the first chemical reaction. If you listen, you can hear the liquid draining at a prescribed flow into the tank." It was true. The gurgle of the liquid dribbling into the tank could clearly be heard. "Now, as it encounters the chemical mixture I placed in the tank, another reaction occurs. Tremendous energy is released and the fluid begins vaporizing, creating great pressure. The reaction is virtually instantaneous. Now, may I ask the gentleman with the matches to please step to the generator, open the valve and light the fumes that issue."

The individual who had looked into the tank under the light of a match now hesitantly opened the valve about halfway. Immediately there was a hissing sound. He scratched his match on the tank and held the flame to the nozzle. Instantly the escaping gas burst into a three-inch flame, intense blue at the base, yellow at the top. There were exclamations from all present.

"That's not all, gentlemen," Holmes said, stepping up to join him. "When we turn the valve to full force, you can see the result." He opened it all the way and the flame jetted out twice its previous distance and turned wholly blue. It made the sound of a blowtorch. "And," Holmes added, "when the pressure is diminished," he turned the valve to less than a quarter open and the flame reduced, turning to bright yellow, "you see we have an illuminating fuel every bit as bright as that presently used by our gas companies, but produced at approximately one-thousandth of the cost of natural gas."

Holmes turned it up all the way again until it was hissing loudly. He was smiling contentedly as he looked up at them. "The cubic capacity of this tank, gentlemen, as is obvious, is very small. The amount of chemicals—and even water— introduced was negligible. Yet, the volume of gas produced by that small amount will keep this flame burning at its highest pitch for three hundred and sixty hours. Five times that long if used for illuminating purposes. Think of it! Gas, gentlemen, at almost no cost. Gas not only for lighting but for heat, for cooking, for industry! Anything else I would say at this point would be superfluous. The formulae and the plans for the Holmes Gas Generator, along with full instructions for proper insertion levels into the tank, will be sold as a single unit. I will accept sealed bids for the next ten days. At the end of that period the bids will be opened and the entire process and generator plans sold to the individual or corporation making the highest bid."

Beginning on the day after the demonstration and continuing for several days afterward, the newspapers had carried explosively exciting stories about Holmes's amazing invention, claiming the Holmes Gas Generator would not only revolutionize industry but greatly improve the quality of life for every American. On the fifth day after the demonstration a sealed bid arrived from the Englewood Gasworks. Holmes opened it immediately, of course. It was for $7,500. The next day came one from the Metropolitan Buffalo Gas Company for $6,000. And on the first day of February the Canadian Natural Gas Company of Toronto bid came for $9,250. No bid was received from the Chicago Gas Company. Holmes was ready. A letter of acceptance was sent to each of the three bidders, with congratulations on having made the successful bid. The other firms, it was stated, were being notified that they had been outbid. As soon as a certified check for the offered amount was received, the chemical formulae, proper mixture procedures and plans for the Gas Generator would be sent. The checks, totaling $22,750, came by return mail and the plans, formulae and instructions, such as they were, were sent at once.

"Anything else up your sleeve like this, Holmes?" Wharton Plummer chortled when Holmes today handed him his check for $5,687.50, representing twenty-five percent of the proceeds.

"I don't see why you're so opposed to doing it again, Wharton," Holmes grumbled. "It worked perfectly."

"Until they try to use the process, at which time they'll start screaming, loud and long. You, as we agreed, will have to maintain that their chemicals are impure or improperly mixed or the machine incorrectly constructed, or a combination of all these. They'll go to court but they'll have a hard time proving the fraud. Give it a year or so of litigation and delays and they'll just chalk it off and fire the individuals who made the deal. As for doing the same thing again, that would be stupidity. If you try, I promise you, I'll take no part in it. Penitentiaries are full of those who outsmarted themselves. I won't—" He broke off as a discreet tapping came on his office door and it opened.

"Excuse me, Mr. Plummer," his secretary said, "but Mr. Woodbury's here and insists on seeing you immediately."

"It's all right, Edna, show him in."

Fitzallen Woodbury did not look at all pleased when he entered. His eyes narrowed when he saw Holmes was there, but he said nothing until Miss Jessup closed the door, leaving the three men alone.

"Hello, Fitz," Holmes said.

"Well, Fitz, I didn't expect to see you today," Plummer came to his feet, hand extended.

Woodbury ignored him for the moment, his gaze locked on the owner of the Castle. "Holmes," he said, "I've given you a couple of warnings, and you, Wharton," his head swung toward the big attorney, "I've told you a half-dozen times. No more." He looked back at Holmes. "That monstrosity of a building you have down there in Englewood. It seems to be at the foundation of all the trouble that keeps popping up. Now it's that ridiculous gas machine of yours. I'm weary of people concluding that because I've been in association with you two, I am engaged in nefarious practices. I won't have it. I've done some figuring, Holmes. I know that at this point you can sell the building and pay off all your indebtedness—which is substantial—and emerge with approximately sixteen thousand dollars intact. I want you to give me the go-ahead today, right now, to sell it."

"I can't do that, Fitz," Holmes said.

"You *can*, by heaven!"

"Let me rephrase. I won't. I have no intention of selling it."

"Then our association is ended, as of here and now." Woodbury strode to the door and opened it, then turned and looked back at Plummer. He shook his head sadly. "And ours, too, Wharton." He looked at both men a final moment and walked away. In a moment Miss Jessup discreetly shut the office door.

"We knew it was going to happen sooner or later," the attorney said glumly.

Holmes nodded. "I wish it had been later. We've made a lot of money on his advice."

When Holmes, in casual conversation with the Conners, learned that Julia had been bookkeeper for her father's grocery business in Davenport for over two years and that she was skilled not only with figures but in typing general correspondence and other secretarial tasks, he wasted no time in firing Beverly Dietz. The daughter of Dr. Pettit from across the street was not only lazy, she was not especially bright and recurrently made mistakes that were at least irritating and often cost time or money to correct. Besides, even had Beverly been better than average, he would have let her go in favor of Julia.

Holmes was wise enough, however, to go to Ned Conner with his proposal that Julia work for him as his private secretary and Ned, though disinclined to give in to something that would increase Julia's independence, nevertheless decided it would be politic to do so. He balked, however, at the matter of life insurance when it was broached. It was not so much that he was suspicious of Holmes's being beneficiary—after all, his employer would be paying the premiums, wouldn't he?—but rather that he had always considered life insurance a gamble he could neither understand nor condone. His reasoning was that the insurance company was betting he wouldn't die and he was in the position of betting he would, which he figured was basically stupid.

Julia had no troubles with it, perfectly willing to sign policies taken out on both herself and Pearl, and she even added her efforts to persuade Ned to get a policy, but he resisted. C. W. Arnold also tried his best to convince Ned that he should have the insurance, but he fared no better than Holmes or Julia. Finally he put it on a quota basis, telling Ned that his company paid the agent a bonus dollar for every application written up and he really wanted that dollar. Conner merely stared at him a moment and then reached into his pocket and took out a bill.

"If it's the dollar you want for turning in the policy application, then here, take this one, but don't bother me ever again about taking out a policy on my life. I won't have one."

Holmes ensconced Julia as his new secretary in a small outer office connected to his third-floor office. Future visitors were now directed to enter her office first, where she could screen them and attempt to turn away bill collectors, process servers and others Holmes considered undesirable and announce those that he might wish to see. Not only did she serve well in her capacities as receptionist, stenographer and typewriter—as general secretaries were termed—but she was also admirably closemouthed about his business and did not snoop into matters that did not concern her.

Holmes had a very difficult time keeping his eyes off her. The lust that had sparked in him at their first meeting had grown geometrically over these weeks and now was so strong he was all but dizzied by it when in her proximity. The promise of something inevitable was in the glances they exchanged but that something had not yet taken form, mainly because of two things: Ned was always just below in the jewelry store and Pearl was practically never away from underfoot. The first hurdle was overcome without difficulty, simply by Holmes's assigning to Ned tasks that involved considerable amounts of work to be done in a short time, such as taking inventory of the entire stock. The second obstacle involved a little more difficulty but was solved by placing Pearl, during Julia's working hours, in the care of an older couple, John and Sylvia Crowe, who were tenants on the second floor just around the corridor corner from the Conners' flat.

On March 2, Holmes entered the outer office from the corridor and found Julia on a three-step ladder reaching far out to arrange books on the upper shelf of a built-in bookcase. She was wearing a deep gray merino dress with a raised black soutache braid running from high neckline to hem. He clicked the locking latch at the same time he closed the door and then walked to the ladder.

"You're apt to tip the ladder and fall, stretching out like that," he said. "Let me brace it for you."

"Oh, thank you, Mr. Holmes." She flashed him that wonderful smile.

He bent over ostensibly to reach for the top step of the ladder but instead his hands slid beneath the hem of her dress and closed about her ankles. He felt her momentarily stiffen and was sure he heard a faint gasp, but she continued what she was doing without pause or turning around. For him, the contact with her skin was electric and he experienced an immediate erection. He moved his hands an inch or so upward, to the bottom of her calves, and now she did cease what she was doing and stood quietly facing the shelves. His hands moved higher, to the center of her calves, and he became tremendously excited by the satin swell of them beneath his touch, the soft hairs caressing his palms as he moved.

She had said nothing more and she said nothing now, but she turned to face him and his hands slid to opposite legs with the turning, moving now to the inward curve of the upper calves just beneath her knees. Again he thought he heard a faint hissing intake of breath. His head was on a level with her hips and as he moved his hands to the swell of her knees he felt her hands come to his head and stroke his hair, then move to his nape and pull him forward against her, his face lost in the heavy folds of her dress.

Elusive as the breeze from a butterfly's wing, a faintly musky scent touched his nostrils, so delicate it seemed more imagined than real. With the movement of his hands upward her legs had become exposed, shapely, lovely. He abruptly stooped more, pressing his lips to her knees in turn, allowing the gathered folds of dress and petticoat to fall behind his head and down his back. Her legs were close together and his lips touched lightly across the front of her knees and his hands rose more, encountering the legs of her underpants halfway down the thighs, slipped beneath the elastic and rose higher yet to the firm and marvelous swell of her buttocks, cupping and then gripping, yet unable to cup or grip enough.

He tilted his head upward, forward in the tent of her dress that was at this moment his only world. In the facilitative mode of the day, her underpants had no material covering the crotch and his face became nested in her. And now he did hear her, a moaning inhalation that increased as it issued. She lifted one foot from the ladder and raised it over the crook of his arm. The inner ankle touched his forearm, slid to his upper arm and upward still, then downward on his back until her knee was hooked over his shoulder. The scent was stronger now, enveloping him, the open taste of her faintly acrid but not offensive, only exciting—overwhelmingly exciting.

He lifted her from the ladder and eased her to the floor and they lay together, touching, exploring, murmuring. They undressed one another and his previous mental images of her unclothed paled before the breathtaking reality. He sat up and let his eyes devour this virtually perfect female form. And then he caressed her with the awe of one who beholds a sculpted masterpiece and is so moved he cannot resist the need to trace with his palms the curve and swell of the creation.

Julia seemed equally enthralled and they lay together for a very long time, both knowing without saying so that this was only the beginning of a long, very close relationship.

Relations between Julia and Ned Conner steadily degenerated while those between Julia and Holmes remained at a very high level. In late March Ned accused her of infidelity, which was momentarily startling to both Holmes and Julia until they realized it was no more than an unfounded shot in the dark fired merely as a distraction from his own torrid affair with a waitress he had met in a Halsted Street restaurant a mile or so from the Castle.

Ned became progressively more abusive in his treatment of Julia and Holmes seriously considered killing him but decided against it as an unnecessary risk with little to gain, since there was still no policy on his life that named Holmes as beneficiary. So Holmes, while covertly exacerbating the volatile situation, overtly acted as peacemaker instead, inveigling himself between them in their quarrels, soothing and conciliatory, turning aside anger where possible. All the while he and Julia continued their own passionate affair and, not unexpectedly, she fell very much in love with him, aware of certain of his minor shortcomings but adoring him despite them. She was certain that one day she and Ned would separate permanently and then the road would be clear for her to marry Holmes. Along with most of those who knew him at the Castle, she thought he was a bachelor.

Dora—now often being addressed by Holmes as Mama in view of her role at home with Lucy—almost never came to the Castle. On rare occasions, long prior to Julia's employment, she had walked into Holmes's flat on the second floor unannounced. To avoid this, as well as to avoid the risk of Ned similarly walking in and catching him and Julia in their compromised positions, he put new locks on the doors and also rigged another battery-operated bell to sound when anyone approached to within twenty feet of either his office or flat. More than once he sent Julia scurrying up the secret stairs to the office from his flat, or through the trapdoor in his office down to his flat. As it turned out, in no case had it been necessary, but Holmes rarely left things to chance.

Ben Pitezel and Pat Quinlan were the only people in the Castle with any idea of what Holmes was doing and neither would mention it to anyone, primarily because of their unswerving loyalty to him, but also because the information he had about them could, if revealed, at the very least result in their going to prison. So useful had Ben become to Holmes, so close a companion and so reliable a confederate in swindles and other crimes as well as legitimate business matters, that Holmes one day in a surge of gratitude presented him with a deed which transferred one-third ownership of the Castle to him. Ben, extremely moved, became even more devoted and never for a moment doubted the legitimacy of his title, unaware that ownership of the Castle was no longer in Holmes's name.

In June, Holmes was introduced to Frederick George Nind, an enterprising businessman of about thirty who was looking for an investor in a potentially lucrative field. While in London early last spring, Nind, a very serious-minded individual, had discovered a patent for sale on an innovative copying device. He borrowed several thousand dollars from a moderately successful businessman of his acquaintance named

Thomas H. Bryan, bought American rights to the patent and returned with it to Chicago. Bryan had no real interest in the device and had loaned Nind the money only because he knew him to be an honest and deserving young man. Nind let him take the patent as security, with the understanding that as soon as Nind could find someone to buy the patent he would repay Bryan's loan and release him from any connection with the business. An office was opened on Dearborn Street in downtown Chicago as the home office of the ABC Copier Company and production of the machine was begun. Its reception in the business community had been slow at first but now it was catching on and business was picking up substantially. Holmes viewed the machine and immediately recognized its potential, not only as a profit-making device in its own right, but as one that could well be used to perpetrate remunerative swindles.

The purchase price of Bryan's share was $9,000 and Holmes gave him a note for that amount. The individual copier was an expensive device to buy but when businessmen saw how it could save them not only money but much valuable time in copying and reproducing letters and other documents, they began to respond. By the end of July the ABC Copier Company had become such a success that Nind, leaving Holmes in charge of the home office, took a trip to New York City to establish an office there for that city's potentially very lucrative market. He did his work very well, finding two New York investors—Henry Bainbridge and F. W. Devoe—to become the legitimate eastern counterparts of Holmes.

An official of the Pullman Palace Car Company south of Chicago dropped in and was very taken with the device and ordered two dozen of the machines at the price of $900 each—a total of $21,600. He gave Holmes twenty percent down—$4,320—and Holmes promised delivery within one month, while never having any intention of filling the order at all.

Some of the bad-debt chickens began coming home to roost by the time Nind returned. The young man was dismayed to find that the Chicago end of the business was in trouble and the debts had become very large. Holmes suggested they look for an attorney to represent them and Nind thought this a good idea; did Holmes know of any good lawyers? Well, Holmes said, he had heard of a very powerful lawyer named

Wharton Plummer, who was evidently among the best in the city, and if one were going to get a lawyer, he might as well get the best, right? Nind thought that a fine idea. A few days later Plummer entered the Dearborn Street office and went over the books with a lot of head-shaking and tsk-tsking. When finished, he morosely informed Nind that bankruptcy was looming as a very real threat, but that if he and Holmes would appear at his office in exactly a week, he might have a solution to offer.

Precisely at 9:00 A.M. seven days later, Holmes and Nind were ushered into the august chambers. Awed to begin with by these prestigious offices occupied by Plummer in the Chamber of Commerce Building, Nind decided anything the attorney had to say was undoubtedly gospel.

"I have given a great deal of attention to your firm's present indebtedness, Mr. Nind," Plummer said, voice low and expression grave, "and I see only one possible hope in your present predicament."

"Yes, sir, anything!" Nind was close to tears.

"I have, as it turns out, some parties from Pittsburgh who are willing to buy the patents and assume the indebtedness and also give you and Mr. Holmes each five thousand dollars cash."

Though Nind had upwards of $20,000 invested already, it seemed a real blessing to him to be able to salvage anything at this stage. "What must we do in return, Mr. Plummer?" he asked.

"You two gentlemen will have to sign over total ownership of the business, including the New York office. These businessmen have given me power of attorney to act for them in this matter and if you and Mr. Holmes are agreeable, you will each sign your own individual sale papers, which I have prepared here according to their wishes. They are made out to myself and your signing of them will turn ownership of the firm over to the parties in Pittsburgh. However, they wish you, Mr. Nind, to stay on as manager of the firm and Mr. Holmes as assistant manager. If you agree, both of you will be salaried employees, your wages to be paid quarterly by the Pittsburgh firm. I have been empowered to serve as Chicago middle agent between yourselves and the Pittsburgh people, so all of the firm's affairs will have to be transacted through me."

Nind sent a stricken look toward the obviously downcast Holmes, who shrugged and then said bitterly, "What other choice do we have? It's either sign the papers and get *something* in return, or lose everything. I'll sign."

He took the proffered papers from Plummer and signed them. Nind watched, a muscle twitching in his jaw, and then he, too, signed his copies of the papers. The two men left. Later in the afternoon Holmes returned to Plummer's office and together they burned the bill of sale that Holmes had signed. The latter reached into his inner pocket and withdrew a copy of an advertising circular.

"I've hired some people to distribute over a thousand of these in the business community," Holmes said.

Plummer read it quickly. It was a nice piece of advertising, extolling the wonders of the new ABC Copier and including a sweeping endorsement by the Chicago, Burlington & Quincy Railroad Company.

"This is wonderful," Plummer said. "How'd you ever get them to give their imprimatur?"

"So far as I know," Holmes replied seriously, "they've never even heard of the ABC Copier. What're they going to do, demand a retraction?"

The two men looked at one another and then the office resounded with their laughter. Plummer slapped Holmes on the back in warm approval, shaking his head in wonder at the man's continued audacity.

Holmes grinned. "Congratulations, partner," he said, shaking the big lawyer's hand. "We now own the ABC Copier Company."

Since that time matters had progressed smoothly with the ABC Copier Company. Through dint of a great deal of hard work on Frederick Nind's part, the company was now on a more even keel and substantial profits were rolling in. The product was a good one and Nind, who had predicted it had a grand future, kept reminding Holmes of the fact. "I just wish," he said rather wistfully, "that the Pittsburgh people would hurry up and give us each our five thousand dollars."

"Oh, I'm sure they will," Holmes told him, "very soon."

With Nind back at the helm and in managerial control, Holmes spent considerably less time there. Matters at the Castle required his attention, one of which was the business of incorporating the Englewood Jewelry Company to better avoid suits being brought against it. A meeting of the alleged board of directors was held and C. W. Arnold, having no connection whatever with the store except for insuring its employees, was elected president. Kit Durkee, a friend of Dora's in Omaha and an alleged stockholder, was represented by Holmes and elected, in absentia, chairman of the board. Julia Conner was elected secretary and treasurer and new board members included Benjamin F. Pitezel, Patrick Quinlan and Joe Owens, who had become Quinlan's chief assistant janitor. Any process server would now have a very difficult time locating the proper person on whom to serve papers.

There was also the irritating matter of the continuing strife between Ned and Julia Conner. While Holmes was downtown, Julia had taken a couple of weeks of vacation to pay a visit to her family and friends in Davenport. She was in no hurry to get back to Ned, and when she wired and asked Holmes if she might extend her vacation into a leave of absence for a few months, to return right after Christmas, Holmes wired back his approval. He missed her, missed that unbelievable body of hers, and might have insisted she return except that not only was he busy downtown, other matters intervened: Minnie Williams arrived in Chicago for a brief stay.

Holmes became aware of Minnie's arrival when Frank Blackman dropped in at the office of the ABC Copier Company and held a murmured conversation with him out of earshot of Frederick Nind.

"She's here. In my office."

"Who?" For a moment Holmes thought he was talking about Julia and he couldn't imagine why she had gone to see Blackman.

"The one who's been writing all those letters to Harry Gordon from Denver. Minnie Williams."

"Well, fancy that!" Holmes ignored the faint note of disapproval he detected in Blackman's voice. "She wrote she might stop off in Chicago on her way back to Boston. I'll go back to your office with you."

The reunion with Minnie was pleasant, though Holmes was relieved to learn she was only here for three days. She had taken a room in the Palmer House and they went there first for lunch during which Minnie filled him in on the details of matters she had only touched upon in her letters. Only two of the matters were of any real significance to Holmes. The first was the tragic death of her Uncle Cal, who had accidentally fallen down an elevator shaft while inspecting a building of his under construction in Fort Worth.

"Oh, Harry, it was so sad," she said, squeezing his hand. "Nannie and I got word of it while we were visiting Uncle Will in Jackson and we left for Fort Worth right away. We managed to get back in time for the funeral and all I could do for days was cry. He was such a wonderful man and I really loved him. I guess what bothered me a lot was the casual way we had said good-bye the last time I saw him. I kept wishing there had been time for a more...a more...Well, I don't know. A more meaningful farewell, I guess. A chance to take one last look at him. It's such a void, knowing he's gone and I'll never see him again. Then, after the funeral, there was all the details of settling his estate—the reading of the will and all that—and it was all so...so *ghoulish!* I hated it. I didn't *want* his money and property. I wanted *him*. I guess I just thought he'd be around forever."

Holmes patted her hand. "You said you didn't want his money and property. Surely he left some of it to Nannie. And what about Billy Bob and Baldwin?"

She shook her head. "No, he left it all to me. I guess because I was the one he raised after Mama and Daddy died. Remember, Nannie and Billy Bob and Baldwin all went to live with Uncle Will. But Uncle Cal didn't forget them entirely. He suggested in the will that I make out my own will so that if anything ever happened to me, the estate I inherited from him would be divided evenly among them."

"I didn't think you could do that in a will," Holmes said, frowning. "I mean what he did. How can he, after he wills you something, then state what you have to do with it?"

"It wasn't a *have* to, Harry. It was just a suggestion. Mr. Mossie—that's Mossie Watt, who was executor, and he's still administrator, of Daddy's estate—he told me I couldn't be forced to do that, but I thought it was a good idea, so I had my will made out for them to get everything equally if I died first, just as Uncle Cal suggested."

"Well, the whole thing must have been a very bad time for you," Holmes sympathized, inwardly cursing this stroke of bad luck. Already he was mentally revising this long-evolving scheme concerning Minnie. It would be nice to figure out a means by which he could get her money, but looming far more importantly to him at this stage was getting ownership of the very valuable property in downtown Fort Worth. He saw she was looking at him questioningly and he shook his head. "Wish I'd been there to help you through it."

He sighed. "Let's get on to a happier subject. Tell me about the theatrical company in Denver."

Now it was her turn to frown. "Not all that happy," she said. "I had such high hopes, Harry. With what I'd learned in the Conservatory and all, I thought it would be a snap. It wasn't. Everything went wrong."

"But you said in that one letter that you'd set the company up and everything looked good."

"It did, right at the beginning, but then things just sort of fell apart. The director wasn't very good and he ran off with one of the actresses halfway through. And the actors and actresses weren't very good, either. Or the musicians. Everybody was blaming everybody else and everything seemed to go wrong. Then, when we finally opened, it was just awful. Would you believe, Harry, people actually got up and walked out? I thought I'd die. After all that work and then to have everything just fall apart. So we closed and the company was dissolved and here I am, heading back to the Conservatory in Boston to try to learn what I did wrong."

"What *you* did wrong? Minnie, it wasn't you, it was all those other people involved."

"Not really, Harry. I was behind it all. I should've relied on more experienced people instead of doing it my way. It was an expensive way to learn a lesson."

"Did you lose very much?"

She colored. "Uh huh. 'Fraid so. Fifteen thousand dollars."

"Oh, what a shame." *Damn, damn, damn! What a stupid waste!*

"It wasn't really a waste, though, Harry," she added, as if reading his thoughts. "It was good experience for me and there are a lot of mistakes made that I won't make again. And next time—if there is a next time—maybe I'll get less involved behind the scenes and just get into the acting. I think I'd like that. It's why most of the courses I'm going to take now are in elocution."

"What about Nannie? What's she doing now? When am I going to meet her?"

"She's dying to meet you! I've told her all about you and she thinks you must be just about the most wonderful person in the world. It doesn't look like you'll see her for a while yet, though. Things have been going so well for her and she's happier than I've ever known her to be. She got her teaching certificate in June and now she's managed to get that teaching job she wanted so much in Midlothian."

"Good for her. What about Baldwin and Billy Bob?"

"Not much changed there. Billy Bob's still working at that awful smelter place in Leadville and Baldwin's still ailing in Fort Worth. The doctor says his health might improve if he went to the mountains for a while. I tried to get him to come to Denver while I was there, but he didn't make it. Says he's still considering it, though. I wish he would. It'd do him a world of good, I'm sure. It's so nice there."

They continued talking animatedly over their lunch and then Holmes took her out to see the sights of Chicago as he had long ago promised to do, a project that kept them engrossed over the next three days. Harry Gordon continued to be the perfect gentleman, very attentive to her, yet making no effort whatever to seduce her, even though he was quite sure she would now be more than amenable to an attempt. That wasn't part of his plan. Not yet. And when he finally saw her off at Union Station, she cried and vowed to come back to him just as soon as her courses in Boston were finished.

Though Holmes did not know what sparked it, Julia seemed more intent when she returned, more desirous of establishing exactly what their relationship was. She was even more affectionate than before. Yet, what she said as they lay together that first night of her return made him wonder if she had begun to suspect the existence of Dora or Minnie.

"Henry," she said, "I'm concerned about us—about where we are and where we're going."

He opened his mouth to speak but she covered it gently with her hand. "No, give me a moment. I want you to listen to what I have to say. I know I don't have any real claim on you, but we've got something very good going between us. I don't know that we can put the label of love on it, but we do like one another a great deal and we're good for one another, good together. I've helped you some and I'll help you a lot more. I'm quite well aware Ned and I are still married—if you can call it a marriage—but there's nothing there. I feel much closer to you than I ever felt to him. Ever. I dislike being near him. When he touches me my skin crawls and I feel dirtied, as if I've been unfaithful to you. And, my God, *he's* my husband, not you. What kind of crazy twisting of values is that? I don't know. All I know is that I want to be with you, no matter how. And in being with you, I have every intention of being true to you."

She paused, then hurried on. "I don't expect you to feel **as** I do. I don't even expect you to be faithful to me when I'm away for long periods, like this one just past, but I do expect it when we're together. I can't bear the idea of you running from me directly into the arms of another woman, or," a small shudder shook her, "or coming to me fresh from a visit with somebody else. Henry," she slid her hand away from his mouth and touched her fingertips to his cheek, her voice taking on a wistful quality, "I've given you all of me. Please, give me at least that much of you?"

His nod was all but imperceptible. "All right, Julia, I will."

Oddly enough, he meant it.

Four

I agree with you, Mr. Holmes." Melvin Jonas pulled on his cigar and blew a plume of smoke into the air of the Castle office. "I'd be last to disagree with you in your belief that Englewood has an excellent future, especially with the World's Fair in the offing. But ten thousand dollars is a lot of money and I want to be very sure of my investment before I make it. I'm sure you, as a businessman, can understand that."

"Of course I can, Mr. Jonas. But the price I'm asking for the Castle Pharmacy, which includes all stock and fixtures, is eminently fair. Perhaps in Peoria you do business a different way." He held out a hand, palm up, in a supplicating gesture. "What would you have me do to prove to you the value of the place? I'm perfectly open to any suggestion you might have."

Jonas let his lip curl in a mirthless smile. "In Peoria," he said, "we usually know the person we're dealing with. The fact is, I really don't know you at all. Now that," he added hastily, "is not to say I don't trust you. It's just that I'd like to satisfy myself that I'm not buying a pig in a poke. Here's what I'd like to do. You let me put one of my top Peoria clerks in your store for ten days to see what kind of business you do. If his report is good, I'll meet your price. Deal?" He stuck out his hand.

"That's a deal, Mr. Jonas." He shook the man's hand heartily.

"All right, this is January ninth. I'll have my man here on Monday, the twelfth. I'll be back here first thing a week from the following Friday. Let's see, that would be on . . ." he glanced at a calendar on the wall, ". . . yes, Friday the twenty-

129

third. If my man has a good report, we'll sign the papers right then and there."

"Fine. But remember, cash only. I have my suspicions, too, Mr. Jonas. I've been stung in the past. I never will be again in the future. I deal in cash only."

"Agreed," Jonas said. "Good day."

The ten days were busy ones. As soon as the Peoria clerk had been installed to work beside Harry Walker as an observer, Holmes put his prearranged program into execution. A steady flow of customers entered the store making all kinds of purchases and the Peoria clerk had no way of knowing that these "customers" included not only every employee of the Holmes Castle, who were provided with money to go into the pharmacy and make purchases, it even included passersby recruited by Pitezel and Quinlan. They were given money to go in and buy whatever they wanted with it, so long as they didn't say where they had gotten the money or why they happened to patronize this particular store. The purchases made by Castle employees were taken to a back room upstairs in the Castle and stored there. The money to passersby was lost, but Holmes considered it a good investment.

"Mr. Jonas," the Peoria clerk told his employer enthusiastically, "this store is a gold mine. I've never seen anything like it. They do more business here in a day than our downtown Peoria store does in a week. And it's been like that every day. Every single day!"

"All right, that's what I wanted to know." Jonas turned and called to the store's manager. "Mr. Walker, is Mr. Holmes in?"

"I don't know, sir," Harry Walker shook his head. "But if he's not, I'm sure he will be soon. Excuse me, Mr. Jonas, I have a customer."

Jonas hesitated, then went upstairs to Holmes's office. Holmes was there alone and Jonas opened his briefcase and removed from it two packets, each containing fifty hundred-dollar bills. He tossed them on the desk. "You've got a deal," he said.

Holmes smiled and took the title out of the drawer, preparing to sign it over to Jonas. "Would you mind," he said, as he brought out the ink pot and a pen, "placing the money on a shelf in the vault there and then closing the door? I get nervous with that much cash around."

"Certainly," Jonas said. He walked to the partially opened vault door Holmes indicated and in a moment his voice came from inside. "The inner door seems to be locked, Mr. Holmes."

"Oh, I forgot," Holmes said. "Just a moment, I'll bring you the key." He got up and strode to the thick outer door and slammed it closed, twirling the combination dial. Without even pausing he snatched up his hat and overcoat and left the office, donning them as he went downstairs. He emerged from the Wallace Street door and paused only long enough to scoop up a handful of snow from a windowsill and scrub his cheeks with it vigorously. Then he walked directly to the corner and entered the front door of the drugstore, his cheeks as red as if he had been outside for quite some time.

"I'm back, Harry," he called to his own clerk. He sniffled, as from the cold. "I'll have to admit it," he added with a short laugh, "there are some wonderfully modern buildings in downtown Chicago, but somehow I always feel better when I get back here to Englewood. I think I may be a little late. Is Mr. Jonas here yet, or his clerk?"

"I'm here, Mr. Holmes," said Jonas's man, coming from behind a counter.

"Ah, good. I hope I haven't kept you waiting." He looked around curiously. "Evidently Mr. Jonas hasn't arrived yet?"

"Yes sir. he has. He was here just a moment ago, no more'n two or three minutes."

"Excellent. I presume you told him what a bustling little business we have here?"

"It's a whole lot busier than I would've thought and I told him that, Mr. Holmes."

"Good, good! Am I correct than in assuming he told you he was going to follow through with his offer to buy?"

"Well," the man hesitated, "as a matter of fact, he didn't say that. He didn't really say anything. He just listened to what I said and then walked out the back door. I thought he was heading up to your office to see you."

"Fine. Why don't you come along with me and we'll see if he's there."

They climbed the steps to the third floor and walked down the corridor toward the office. The door was open. "We're here, Mr. Jonas," Holmes said loudly as they approached the door. "I must apologize for keeping you—" He broke off as he and the clerk entered and saw the room was empty. "Well, that's odd," Holmes said, steering the man back into the corridor and walking toward the stairs. "I thought you said he was up here."

"Well, no, not exactly, sir. I said I *thought* he came up here. Evidently I was wrong. I can't imagine where he's got to."

"Nor I," Holmes said, as they started down the stairs. "I must say I'm disappointed. I really thought he'd be anxious to buy the store."

"I don't know, Mr. Holmes. I guess you'll just have to ask him when he comes back from wherever he went."

"All right. As soon as he comes in, please tell him I'm over in the restaurant. I want to get a bite to eat."

There was a desultory investigation of sorts when Melvin Jonas never appeared again, anywhere. Both the missing man's clerk and Harry Walker gave an accurate account of what had occurred so far as they knew and innocently diverted any suspicion from falling on Holmes, since the time element obviously precluded any opportunity for foul play on his part. The body of course, had been cremated in the Warner Process furnace long before the investigation even began. The $10,000 Holmes had delivered to Frank Blackman, half for investment and half to relay to Dora.

Ned Conner, more than just a little drunk and a quart bottle of whiskey in his hand, returned to the flat just after midnight. He found it empty. Pearl was being cared for by the Crowes and Julia was with Holmes in his apartment. The longer he waited, the more furious he became. When finally she returned to her apartment at seven in the morning, Ned was reeling in the corridor outside their room. As she neared him, he lurched and struck her full in the mouth with his fist, splitting her upper and lower lips and knocking her down. Her scream brought other tenants into the hall where they stood petrified at what was occurring.

"Bitch! Filthy sow! You've been fucking them, haven't you? *All* of them. That goddamned barber, Vogel, and the salesman, Warden. And what about Holmes? You're fucking him, too, aren't you? Answer me, whore! *Aren't* you?" He aimed a kick at her but she rolled out of his reach and came to her feet. Losing balance with his momentum he fell against the wall with a crash, caught himself and faced her in a half-crouch.

Holmes suddenly appeared descending the stairs and running down the corridor toward them. "Stop!" His cry was thunderous, authoritative, and both stared at him. "Ned, stop it! What the hell's wrong with you, anyway?"

Ned Conner stared at him, blinking to bring him into focus. "You rotten son of a bitch," he snarled. "You're the one who started all this. Well, I'm getting t'hell out of here. For good! Away from you and away from this . . . this . . . *slut!*"

He lurched away, shoving Holmes as he passed, slamming into the wall twice before reaching the stairs. He almost fell as he clattered down. And Holmes helped Julia into her flat, slamming the door behind them.

The Castle was considerably quieter these days.

No one had seen Ned Conner in the nine weeks since his precipitous departure. Julia was gone, too, with Pearl, having returned to Davenport for another visit, promising Holmes she'd be back in a few weeks.

Since there was no indication Ned would ever return, Holmes had placed the Castle jewelry store under the supervision of Harry Walker. As good a worker as Walker was, he had two serious faults, so far as Holmes was concerned. He was not only intensely curious over everything that occurred in and about the Castle, he was an inveterate gossip. A short man of medium build, he had come to Chicago a year ago from Greencastle, Indiana. He had quite readily agreed to sign up for the life insurance he'd been told was a requirement for the job. The policy was for $15,000 with a double indemnity clause for accidental death. Walker was initially taken aback when Holmes said that it was customary, since he was paying the premiums, that he be named beneficiary. Walker had wanted very much to name as beneficiary his sister, in Reading, Pennsylvania.

"Nothing to worry about in that respect, Mr. Walker," Holmes told him. "If you should die, God forbid, as soon as I get the insurance payment I'll make sure two-thirds of it goes to your sister."

Walker decided that was just fine, but insisted they draw up a contract to that effect and send a copy to his sister. Holmes agreed and wrote out the contract in duplicate, keeping a copy himself and placing the other copy in an envelope, which Walker addressed to his sister.

"Patrick," Holmes had called, and at once Quinlan came to him. "Take this letter to the post office immediately and mail it."

"Yes, sir, Mr. Holmes." Pat took it from Walker and left. Since Holmes had addressed him as Patrick, he knew exactly what to do. He went immediately to his own quarters and burned the envelope.

Now, almost a year since the policy was written, Harry Walker was preparing to go home to Greencastle for a week's vacation and invited Holmes to join him, saying the rest would do him good and he'd very much like Holmes to meet his parents. Holmes agreed and this evening they caught a late train. Walker chattered incessantly until finally, at about the midpoint of their journey, Holmes yawned and shook his head.

"I'm getting a little drowsy," he said, "and I really don't want to go to sleep. Maybe I'm just hungry. Tell you what, let me take a few minutes of air on the platform between cars and then you join me and we'll go on to the dining car and have a bite to eat."

"Suits me," Harry said. "Go ahead and I'll be along shortly."

Holmes walked to the forward end of the car and stepped through onto the dark, noisy platform. Immediately he stooped and pulled up his trouser leg. Three short lengths of cord held a heavy sixteen-inch construction bolt to the inside of his calf. He untied it, tossed the cords into the night and then stood at the outside edge of the platform, the air tugging at his clothing. In less than five minutes Walker appeared, shutting the door behind him.

"Ah, there you are." He spoke loudly to be heard above the noise of the train and rushing wind.

"Something very curious over here, Harry," Holmes said. "Lots of sparks showering out of the firebox. Come take a look and see if you think we ought to report it."

He stepped aside so Walker could pass him and as the man did so, swung the bolt and struck him heavily across the back of the neck. Walker's knees buckled and he slumped, semiconscious, against the guardrail. Holmes caught him and braced him there while he struck him again, even harder, on the back of the head. Holmes tossed the bolt far out in the darkness and then gripped Walker by the seat of the pants and an ankle and upended him over the guardrail. The man's body struck crosswise on the track and instantly disappeared beneath the train. Holmes straightened his own clothing and walked briskly through three more cars to the diner and took a place at a table.

He called for two menus and two cups of coffee, saying his friend would be along in a moment. Fifteen minutes later, having finished his own coffee, he flagged down the porter and handed him a dollar. "My friend was supposed to join me here, but I suspect he might have fallen asleep. Would you be so good as to check and see?" He told the man where they were sitting and added, "If he's awake, tell him his coffee's getting cold and I would like to order some food. If he's asleep, just let him be and let me know and I'll dine alone."

In a few minutes the porter was back saying the man wasn't in his seat and no one was in the lavatories between there and the dining car. He'd even checked the rear platform and no one was there, but the people in the seats behind had seen him get up about five minutes after Holmes left and head toward the front. Holmes frowned. "Now that's peculiar," he said. "Where in the world could he have gotten to on a train?"

"Maybe he's visiting someone he knows in a compartment, sir."

"I hardly think that's likely, and I certainly can't go around opening compartment doors. Summon the conductor, will you please?"

Holmes was more concerned than ever when the porter returned with the conductor. Aided by the porter, Holmes told his story and a search was made from one end of the six-car train to the other, the conductor checking each compartment they passed. Harry Walker was nowhere to be found and now Holmes was getting very upset.

"What is this?" he asked. "A man can't just disappear while walking through a few cars."

It was nearly midnight when the train rolled into Greencastle and railroad authorities were notified. Holmes was beside himself with fear and worry and paced about in the station all night. In the morning he very nearly collapsed

with grief when word was brought the mangled body of
Harry Walker was found on the trackbed. An investigation
was made and only three theories could be advanced: That he
was robbed and thrown from the train; that he committed
suicide; that he somehow, perhaps from illness, became dizzy
and fell while passing between cars. The first possibility was
ruled out because his gold watch and a fair amount of money
were still on his body when he was found. The second
possibility was ruled out when Holmes asserted—and was
backed up by family members—that so far as he knew Walker
was not depressed and had never seemed to be the sort of
man who would take his own life and, besides, there was no
suicide note. The death was ruled an accident and a telegram
was sent immediately to the Capital Insurance Company.

Two weeks later Holmes received his $30,000 double
indemnity payment of the claim. He paid $10,000 of it in
back fees to Wharton Plummer and sent $10,000 more of it to
Dora via Frank Blackman, giving Blackman another $5,000
for investment and fees. The remainder he held on to for
expenses.

Holmes, carrying a large Marshall Field & Company
brown paper bag, stopped off at 6232 Carpenter Street. A
knee-high iron paling fence provided dubious protection for
the table-sized patch of earth in front where scrawny plants
were making a valiant effort to flower. The front of the
two-story house was faced with a particularly ugly species of
tarpaper designed to look like yellow brick but which had
never fooled anyone, even when brand new. It was streaked
with filthy stains of rain runoff as well as being broken and
curled here and there in scabrous patches. The front door,
evidently once painted white, was a blistered, sooty gray and
flecks broke free and fell when Holmes knocked. It was
opened by Ben Pitezel, who greeted him with a warm
handshake and showed him into the squalid interior. A greasy
overstuffed chair was suffering from partial disembowelment
and an equally grimy sofa was punctured and pitted and
protuberant with wayward springs. A fly-specked calendar on
the patchy wall still showed June.

"Carrie!" Ben's voice was faintly slurred. "If you're not at
it yet, get dinner started. Henry's here." He waved his guest

to a seat on the sofa and plopped down himself in the tired chair.

Carrie Pitezel appeared in the doorway leading to the kitchen, dressed as she was every time Holmes had ever seen her, in a drab and not terribly clean gray dress that ended at her ankles. Her feet were bare and dirty and her hair, bearing no resemblance to any sort of coiffure he had ever seen, straggled from an unkempt cluster atop her head.

"'Lo, Henry," she said, mustering up a dreary half-smile. "Benny said you was comin' by t'day. Figgered you'd be here a little later."

"Good afternoon, Carrie." Holmes flashed a smile. "I hope I haven't inconvenienced you. I finished my business downtown sooner than expected. Where are the children?"

Her face tightened and her answer was short. "Ain't back yet from school." She disappeared back into the kitchen.

Ben scowled and then leaned toward Holmes in a conspiratorial way. "She's sort of put out. We both are, I guess. Found out today she's gonna have another baby. We figured since it's been so long since Howard was born—he's just turned eight, you know—that she wouldn't have any more. We sure didn't *want* any more, I can tell you that."

There didn't seem to be anything to say to that, so Holmes merely reached into his pocket and extracted an envelope. He handed it to Pitezel. "A thousand dollars, Ben. Your pay, plus. You need some chairs and a better desk in that patent office you've opened in the Castle. And get out of this place. No offense meant, but you and Carrie really ought to have something better than this. There are a couple of places, furnished and unfurnished, within a block or two of the Castle. Get one. Get Carrie and the kids some new clothes." He indicated the three-quarters-empty whiskey bottle on the floor beside the chair. "And Ben, it's not for booze. I mean it. I've got some plans in mind for us to work together on and we—"

He broke off as the door flew open and three children entered, arguing. Howard was first and, though youngest, was in the process of sharply teasing Nellie and Alice, who were ten and twelve. They stopped short when they saw Holmes.

"Uncle Henry!" The boy, a handsome youngster, ran to where Holmes was sitting and grabbed his hand and danced about holding it. Nellie and Alice came up on opposite sides and each kissed a cheek simultaneously as he hugged them about the waist.

"What's in the bag, Uncle Henry?" Howard cried, grabbing at it. Holmes was quicker and snatched it out of his reach. He tousled the boy's hair.

"Something for each of you," Holmes said, adding with mock gruffness, "but not until Dessie gets here."

"I'm here, Uncle Henry." Dessie was just entering the door, a parcel of strapped-together books dangling from one hand. The fourteen-year-old came to him and kissed him on the forehead.

All four of the children were remarkably similar in looks and favored Ben far more than Carrie—the same oval-shaped face with high foreheads and nicely molded features and Ben's kind, deepset eyes. Their lips were full and smiled easily and their hair was deep chestnut in color, slightly more reddish than Ben's. All three of the girls showed distinct promise of becoming very attractive young women and already Dessie had filled out with surprisingly large breasts for her age. Even Alice's chest was beginning to bud.

"C'mon, Uncle Henry," Howard pleaded, climbing up on the sofa beside him, "c'mon. What's in the bag, huh?"

Ben leaned back in his chair, grinning, pleased at the way his children doted on Holmes. And why shouldn't they, he thought, as good as Holmes has been to them from the beginning. By God, there aren't many people I've come across who're so good with kids right from the very beginning. And not many, either, who can figure out so well just what each kid wants most. A thousand bucks! Jesus Christ, I haven't seen that much money in five years. But he damn sure doesn't have to give me any trouble about my drinking! Ben stretched out his hand for the bottle beside his chair, pulled the cork and took a long swig.

Holmes had reached into the bag and was feeling around the interior. He gave a satisfied little grunt and withdrew a bright red cast-iron streetcar complete with a pair of horses in front. A metal key was included to wind a square gear rod running through both horses. He handed the toy to Howard, who yelled with delight and instantly sprawled on the bare floor, wound it up and set the horses' feet in motion.

Alice received the sort of gift that always made her happiest—a book of lavishly illustrated fairy stories by the brothers Grimm. She hugged it to her chest and her eyes glowed. Nellie's present was a coloring book and a tin compartmentalized box of watercolor paints with two brushes. She squealed with pure pleasure.

Dessie's eyes widened and her cheeks flushed with pleasure when she opened the soft tissue-wrapped package Uncle Henry handed her. It was a very pretty pale yellow voile blouse with a large satin bow at the neck. "Oh, it's so beautiful, Uncle Henry. Thank you. Thank you!" She rushed from the room to try it on.

While the children were busy with their gifts, Holmes and Ben strolled out through the kitchen heading for the back stoop. He paused as they passed Carrie working at the stove and slipped a folded piece of paper into her apron pocket. "That's for you to use on *you*," he told her, "not on anyone else." He smiled and continued with Ben toward the back door. She reached into her pocket and took the paper out and unfolded it. It was a check made out to her in the amount of $50.

The badly warped boards groaned menacingly under the weight of the men as they walked across them and down three steps into a cluttered, weedy back yard. Dingy gray sheets and clothes hung limply from a clothesline. The late afternoon air hung as heavily around them.

"Ben," Holmes said, stopping and facing his friend and partner, "as I started to tell you before the kids got home, I have some things in mind that I'm going to need your help with. How good are you at pretending to be someone else?"

"Playacting? Good enough. I've done some a few times. I've been a banker and a messenger and a preacher at different times without anyone catching on." He shrugged. "Depends on what I've got to do."

"What could you do if the stake—your share of it— turned out to be somewhere around fifty thousand dollars?"

"Fifty *thousand!* Christ, Holmes, that's more'n most men make in their lifetime." Holmes said nothing. Ben shook his head. "Shitfire, there's just about nothing I wouldn't do for that, short of murder."

Holmes's steady gaze held him and his voice was dead flat. "No, Ben, not *short* of murder."

Pitezel recoiled. "You're not serious!"

"I am."

"I couldn't do that, Holmes."

"You not only could, Ben, you did. Remember Willie

Crawford? Some people called him Willie Cash. Remember how you robbed a mail car with him? Remember how you hit him in the head with a railroad pick and killed him?"

Pitezel looked stricken. "How . . . how did you . . . ?"

"Doesn't matter, Ben. And no one else knows where you are. The point is, what I have in mind is a lot easier and a lot safer. But there's plenty of time to talk about it, Ben. Plenty of time to think about it, too. We're going to be doing some traveling, you and I. Some of it together, some alone."

"Where?" Still stunned, Pitezel let the word croak from suddenly dried lips, unable to think of anything else to say.

"Texas. Colorado. The East. Plenty of time to get into all the details. Maybe a year or two. But there's one thing you've got to do, Ben. The one thing I'm going to insist on more than anything else. And you've got to do it first."

"What?" He was quaking inside.

"Dry out. You've got to take the cure, Ben. You're turning into a lush. We can't have that."

"Now listen, Holmes, you've got no right—"

Holmes held up a hand. "Spare me. I don't need to hear it. All you have to think about is fifty thousand dollars. Maybe even more."

"God, Holmes, I don't know."

"You don't have to know anything yet. Ever hear of a place called the Keeley Institute?"

Pitezel shook his head.

Holmes let a small smile tilt his mouth corners. "You will," he said.

It was by sheer happenstance, while she was shopping in downtown Chicago, that Julia Conner saw Holmes and Dora together. She had no idea who the woman was, only that the closeness of their association was clearly apparent in their looks at one another, in the way their hands touched, in the familiarity with which they treated each other. The fury that rose in her was all but overpowering; a jealousy previously unknown to her. She wanted to strike back, to hurt him somehow, as she was being hurt.

She did not confront him until the next day, in the privacy of his office, and even then she made no mention of having seen him with another woman. Her attack was more devious, striking at him in ways she knew would hurt him most. She launched her onslaught by telling him that they were through, that she had a new lover and that she and he had been seeing each other for two months, since early October.

Holmes was stunned by the unexpected revelation but his expression remained steady and he did not change position in his desk chair. The only clue to the extent of his present agitation was manifested in the twitching of his jaw muscle. "Who's the man?" he asked quietly.

Julia remained standing before him with a sense of defiance in her posture, her feet slightly apart and firmly planted, her arms folded across her chest. "It makes no difference who he is," she said evenly, "because it's no business of yours."

"It's my business when you and I are romantically involved," Holmes pointed out.

"Romantically? Romantically?" She tossed her head and a brief burst of laughter devoid of mirth sprang from her. "You forget, I know you too well for that, Henry. Romantically, indeed! The only romance in our relationship, as you put it, was mine . . . initially. I've finally progressed beyond that adolescent romantic idiocy where you're concerned. Whatever involvement you and I have left has nothing whatever to do with romance."

"I still want to know who he is," he insisted.

"And I damned well refuse to tell you."

Holmes was silent a moment. "Are you going to marry him?"

Again she barked the short hollow laugh. "Marry him? Hell no! With Ned, I had all the marriage I could ever stomach." She laughed again, more genuinely, at the unintended double entendre, but the sound became harsh. "You want to know what I've learned about men? I'll tell you. They're bastards, that's what, and you lead the procession, Henry. They're out to get only one thing from any woman they meet and they don't much care how they get it."

"If you're not going to get married, how are you going to support yourself? You must realize I won't keep you on here in the present circumstances."

She dropped her arms to her sides and the hands became tightly clenched fists as she leaned toward him. "You have no choice in the matter, Henry," she said coldly, "none at all. I intend to stay here with my daughter just as long as I care to, and Pearl and I won't have any worries about support because you're going to support us, starting right now. You needn't send your rent collectors around anymore because from today on, we're here rent free, for so long as we care to stay. Not only that, you're tripling my salary as of today. I may even keep on doing the work for you that I've been doing, but I'll work or not as I see fit, not as you direct. And if and when I quit and Pearl and I go elsewhere, you'll still pay, just as if I were here."

Holmes's eyes narrowed. "By what stretch of the imagination do you assume I would agree to anything even remotely like that?"

This was the moment she had been waiting for, the time when she could fire the second and, she knew, far more devastating volley in her limited arsenal, one based on bits and pieces of evidence she had picked up and fitted together to her own satisfaction over these many months of their being so close.

"You don't have to agree. You'll just do it. Period." She shook her head and straightened. "I don't intend beating around the bush, Henry, so here it is straight out. You're a thief, a swindler, and a forger. Your mistake has been to involve me in so many of your schemes. You could be put away for a very long time with what I know about them. But that's not all of it. You're a murderer, too, Henry."

"You have no proof of that," he said, coming to his feet.

"Is that what you think?" She shrugged. "I used to believe you were very shrewd, but you're really not so clever. Maybe I have proof of your committing murder, maybe I don't. That doesn't matter. Without one speck of proof, I could start the police investigating you so fast and in so many directions at once that you'd be behind bars the rest of your life. Or hanged. So don't try to tell me you're not going to support Pearl and me. You are. For just as long as I say." She walked to the door and then turned back to face him, her hand on the knob. "Look at it this way, Henry. I'm not asking much and I have no intention of increasing the demands. You'll pay because what I'm asking is the cheapest way out for you."

She closed the door quietly behind her.

The sense of panic that momentarily gripped Holmes very nearly caused him to retch. She knew so much! He was certain she had no real proof of his killing anyone and knew next to nothing of the life insurance money he'd collected from so many firms, but he was a man whose habits could not stand close scrutiny and if she instigated an investigation in that direction, circumstantial evidence alone would be damning. As always occurred in periods of great danger, he was able to thrust the panic aside and put his mind to work at overcoming the problem. He sat very still for a long while, brow furrowed as he thought, and gradually his knotted stomach muscles relaxed and the lingering trace of fear in his eyes vanished.

Abruptly he came to his feet and left the third-floor office, only to return in five minutes with a nervous Pat Quinlan in tow, the Irishman only too well aware that Holmes would not have brought him up here like this unless something drastic was afoot. Quinlan took the chair Holmes indicated and his eyes stayed on Holmes as the latter pulled up another chair and sat so close in front of him that their knees were almost touching.

"Pat," Holmes began, speaking just above a whisper, "you remember when you started here, we took out an insurance policy on your life?"

Quinlan swallowed. "Yes."

"That policy lapsed a long time ago and I never renewed it. But you remember we also took out policies on your wife and daughter when they came here the day after—"

"I remember," the janitor interrupted, not wanting to hear him even mention Selene Morton and Lizzie Knotts and little Billy.

Holmes nodded, understanding, and went on. "You remember, we took individual ten-thousand-dollar life policies out on them, with you named as beneficiary and with me paying the premiums in the understanding that should something ever happen to either, we would share the money equally?"

A faint sheen of perspiration had appeared on Quinlan's brow and the ticking of the clock on the wall was suddenly very loud as he nodded and licked lips that had gone dry.

"We're going to collect on Cora's policy, Pat."

"No!" Quinlan shot to his feet, his face gone gray.

Holmes had risen too and he gripped the janitor's shoulders tightly, his agate eyes boring into Quinlan's. "Shut up and listen!" he hissed. "I didn't say Cora was going to die. I

said we were going to collect on her policy. Now sit down and
listen to me."

Quinlan sat down slowly, a pulse throbbing at his temple. Again Holmes sat facing him. "Your parents still own that
farm of theirs?"

"They do." His voice was a croak.

"You're going to send Cora there—not immediately, but
very soon—without anyone knowing about it except you and
Ella."

Quinlan shook his head. "Ella won't want to do that. I
don't know what you've got in mind, but I don't want to do it
either."

"It's not a question of want, Pat. It's a question of
have-to." He told him Julia Conner had threatened to call in
the police to investigate murder. He did not name a victim.
Not yet. "There's no choice," he added.

"I don't understand."

"Of course you don't. That's why I brought you up here
to lay it out to you. You're going to quietly send Cora to her
grandparents on the train and they're going to have to keep
her more or less out of sight for a long while. As soon as she's
gone, we're going to substitute the body of an accident victim
dressed in her clothes and you and Ella are going to identify
the body as Cora's. With all the appropriate grief, of course."

"We won't do it, Holmes." Quinlan was shaking his head
and his jaw had become set.

"You will. You have to. As I said, there's no choice."

"What the hell are you getting at, anyway? How could
you possibly come up with the dead body of a little girl Cora's
age? Jesus, Holmes!"

"That's no problem. The substitution will be Pearl Conner."

Quinlan's jaw dropped and his words were a stunned
whisper. "Holy shit."

Holmes watched Quinlan without expression, holding
inside the tugging of an elated smile at the inexpressible joy
of manipulation, the sense of power at being in control, of
being wholly invulnerable. God, what a wonderful feeling!
The silence stretched out until finally Quinlan broke it.

"What . . ." He broke off, then began again. "What about
the kid's mother? Julia. What about Julia? She couldn't be in
on something like this."

Holmes grunted. "You're right about that. We have to
kill her first, Pat."

Quinlan was shaking his head in amazed disbelief. "I can't believe you're seriously saying all this. I just can't believe it. I owe you a lot, Holmes, but not this much. Not to deliberately do something like this."

"You're not listening, Pat. I'll say it one more time: There's no choice. I mean it. This isn't a favor you have to do me. This is something we have to do because we've been forced into it. Julia came to me a little while ago and left with me agreeing to pay her blackmail. I don't know how she found out about it, but she came in and threatened to expose me as the murderer of Lizzie Knotts and her baby—your son—and Selene Morton." Quinlan looked even more stricken, but Holmes went on without pause. "I agreed to pay what she's asking, not only to protect myself but to protect you, too, Pat. You've got to remember it was you who killed them, not me. I was accessory to it, I agree, but it was you who had the motive and who actually did it. If it comes out, I'll not be hanged for it. I'd have to protect myself by turning state's evidence against you. I don't want to have to do that, Pat, but I can't afford to pay the blackmail for very long. That leaves only one answer and you know what it is. We have to get rid of her before she can tell the police anything. Which means that we also have to get rid of Pearl. If we have to do that, we might as well make it worth our while. Pearl and Cora are just about the same age and general description. Ten thousand dollars makes it worthwhile, Pat."

"Jesus," Quinlan muttered, "how could all this happen? Holmes, for God's sake, you can't turn against me."

"I have no intention of turning against you, Pat, unless you force me to. That's why we have no choice. We *have* to do it."

Quinlan reached out and gripped Holmes's hand. "How . . . how do I explain it—this thing about Cora—to Ella? I mean without her learning about the Lizzie thing?"

For the first time Holmes let a small smile play at his lips. "I've given that some thought, Pat, and there's a way. You'll agree Ella likes money? She'd like to have a *lot* of money?" When Quinlan nodded, he continued. "Okay. She knows about the policies. You tell her I know of a little girl Cora's age who is in an orphanage and dying from a disease. Say that I've taken a shine to the child and have agreed to see that she is properly buried when she dies. Tell her to sew a name tag inside one of Cora's dresses and you bring it to me, along with a pair of Cora's shoes, coat and mittens. I'll dress the body in the outfit and take her out and make the death look like an accident, where the child's face is so disfigured that only the parents can identify her. Then, when the body's found, you and she become the bereaved parents, identify her and get her buried. I'll pay the burial expenses. Then you apply for payment of the life insurance. We split it. Five thousand dollars ought to be enough to make her agree it's worthwhile to send Cora to live with her grandparents for a while. What do you say?"

Quinlan didn't speak at once, digesting what Holmes proposed, but at length he began to nod. "It might work," he said, the nodding continuing as he spoke. "It just might work."

"Not might, Pat," Holmes corrected. "Will."

Once again he felt the satisfaction of having the pieces he'd carved fit together with admirable precision. And he was intrigued by the craving that rose in him to be audacious, to pull off the act in such a way that it was fraught with peril, confident that he could play a dangerous game with the police and get away with it because of his superior intellect. He shook his head, trying to force the thoughts away, realizing the ridiculousness of such reasoning, the insanity of it. And yet . . .

Ben, as usual, took ever more frequent refuge in his bottle and was almost never entirely sober. Though he remained easygoing almost to a fault with the children, occasionally he relieved his own frustrations by beating Carrie, which subsequently caused him to plunge even deeper into his enveloping depression. The only productive thing he'd done during the past year was to open an office in the Holmes Castle where he advertised himself as a buyer and seller of patents. As a result of that advertisement he was visited by a young man who had invented a device that fed prespecified amounts of coal into a furnace. But the novice inventor had become discouraged when, in what he considered to be a reasonable length of time, he had been unable to interest anyone in the device. In a rare moment of lucidity, Ben saw its potential and had bought all rights to the patents the young man had taken out. Within a few months he had turned his office in the Castle into a relatively successful patent coal-bin business. With proper promotion it could have been the foundation of a legitimate fortune, but the alcohol interfered and business began to suffer, as did the work he was doing with and for Holmes. Now, in mid-December, Holmes had had enough and summoned Pitezel to his office. As sober as he ever managed to be these days, Pitezel had entered and slumped in the chair before Holmes's desk. He hadn't shaved for several days, his hair was in disarray and his clothing rumpled. Holmes had looked at him with distaste and spoke harshly.

"Ben, you're a goddamned mess. And you're making a bloody mess of your life. We've been friends for a long while now and I've overlooked a lot, but I can't do that anymore. I'll be honest with you. I've been seriously considering severing our relationship." Pitezel's expression had become taut, but Holmes went on without pause. "There are important things ahead that require clear thinking. Obviously, you can't think clearly with your head stuck in a bottle, that's all there is to it. You're an alcoholic, Ben. A drunk. I won't tolerate that in our association any longer. There's too much at stake. You've got to make a choice, today. Now. This minute."

"What choice, Holmes?" The voice was hollow, fearful.

"Either dry out or get out."

Tears of self-pity sprang into Pitezel's eyes. "I've tried, Holmes, honest. It's just that . . . I . . . I'm . . ."

"You're a drunk, period, and you're beyond the point of pulling yourself out of it without help. I told you about the Keeley Institute last summer but you ignored it." Holmes's gaze was hard and his voice became implacable. "I don't intend for you to ignore it any longer."

"Holmes, listen." A too-familiar whine had entered his voice. "I'd do it but I can't afford—"

"To pay for it?" Holmes interrupted. "Let me tell you something, my friend, at this point you can't afford *not* to go. Don't worry about the money. I'll take care of all the bills for now and I'll see that Carrie and the kids have whatever they need while you're gone."

Pitezel shook his head and grasped at a final straw. "You've already given us too much."

"It's no gift, Ben, believe me. You'll pay me back later, every cent of it. With interest."

"Interest?"

"That's right, but not the kind you're thinking of. The only kind of interest I want from you is guaranteed dependability. So now it's on the line. Yes or no?"

Pitezel's response had been barely audible. "Yes."

He had watched as Holmes withdrew a sheet of letterhead from his desk drawer and wrote a letter to the Keeley Institute, making application on Pitezel's behalf in a bold swift hand. He paused only once to look up. "I don't want you to use your own name there," he said. He tapped the letter with a forefinger. "Your name in the application is Robert E. Phelps. That's who you'll be while you're there." He bent to writing again. With the letter completed, he had written a check, addressed an envelope and enclosed the check with the letter. Sealing and stamping the envelope, he had handed it to Pitezel.

"Mail this right now, Ben." He'd looked at his friend then with a faint smile, but there was a quality in his voice as he spoke again that caused a chill to touch the small of Pitezel's back. "Do not make the mistake of losing it."

Julia Conner opened the window and a gust of bitter cold air whirled into the room, causing her to gasp. Six-year-old Pearl, seated at the scarred breakfast table, protested.

"Mama, I'm cold!"

"I know, honey. I'll have it shut in a moment. I have to get the milk." She reached out and grasped the neck of the quart bottle nestled in three inches of new snow on the windowsill and pulled it inside, slamming the window closed at once. She was smiling as she turned around. "Look, Pearl, Jack Frost made some natural ice cream for you last night."

Pearl clapped her hands when she saw how the cream had risen in a frozen cylinder two inches above the bottle neck, the circular cardboard cap resting on top. She watched closely as her mother scooped out the slushy cream into a bowl and set it before her, along with a spoon.

"Well," Julia said when Pearl merely sat there, "aren't you going to eat it?"

Pearl shook her head vigorously. "I want the cabin, too."

Julia sighed. "Now you know I don't approve of that, Pearl." She paused and then broke into a bright smile. "But it *is* Christmas morning, isn't it? I guess we can put the rules aside for something special on this special morning." She stepped to the cupboard and returned unscrewing the cap of a tin in the shape of Abraham Lincoln's boyhood home. The cap was representative of the cabin's chimney. She poured about a half ounce of the rich brown fluid contents over the cream and made a small disparaging sound.

"Ugh," she said. "Who in his right mind wants Log Cabin Syrup over frozen cream?"

"I do! I do!" shrilled Pearl and immediately attacked it with the spoon, rolling her eyes in delight as she took her first bite. "Yummy!"

"Excuse me if I don't watch," Julia said. "I can't take it this early in the morning."

She turned to the sideboard and began wiping the remainder of the silverware she had just finished washing. It was a set of flatware she had borrowed from Mrs. Crowe and she was getting it ready to return before Pearl and she left for Davenport later in the week. She smiled to herself in recollection of the pleasant Christmas Eve they'd just had with the Crowes.

John and Mabel Crowe had been tenants in the Castle for over eighteen months and Julia had come to like them quite a bit, especially since they were always so good to Pearl. She wished she had had something better to give them as gifts last evening, rather than merely the new bandanna handkerchief for him and a pretty teacup for her, but they had acted as if those were the best gifts they'd ever received. And they had made it a very special Christmas Eve for Pearl, letting her help decorate their little Christmas tree and then presenting her with gift-wrapped boxes that turned out to contain a doll, a coloring book and a nice warm snowsuit. To Julia they had given a cotton chenille bathrobe and a pair of warm fluffy mules that made it appear she had comically over-large feet. She was wearing both the robe and slippers now.

The Crowes had insisted on exchanging gifts Christmas Eve instead of Christmas Day, since they were going to her sister's house in the inner city early this morning and did not expect to be home until late tonight. But at least Julia knew there would be a chance to see them again before she and Pearl caught the train for Davenport to be on hand for the wedding of Julia's older spinster sister, Mary, on December 29. Mary was being wed to a railroad man named George

Saddles, who was going to send them free railroad passes for the trip.

Julia was just finishing drying the flatware when there came a rapid-fire tapping on the door. She frowned. "Now who in the world could that be so early on a Christmas morning?" she murmured.

"Open the door and thee, Mama," Pearl lisped, still at work on her treat, though no longer with the vigor initially exhibited.

"Out of the mouths..." Julia said.

She pulled the collar of her robe closer together and snugged the belt, then opened the door, half expecting to see Mabel Crowe despite knowing they were gone. She was taken aback at finding the caller was an obviously agitated Pat Quinlan.

"Beg pardon, Mrs. Conner," Quinlan's words tumbled out, "but I came to you 'cause I didn't know who else might help. It's Mr. Holmes. He's upstairs in his office. On the floor. I think he's had a heart attack. Can you see to him, please, while I go try to find a doctor to come here?"

"Of course. You hurry on. I'll go upstairs right away. Pearl," she turned back to her daughter who had stopped eating and was staring at them, "you finish up and then you can play with your new doll or coloring book, okay? Mama'll be back in just a little while."

She returned to the corridor. Quinlan was gone and she shut the door and walked swiftly to the front stairs. She was breathing heavily when she reached the third-floor office, where the door was ajar. She pushed it open and stepped in and was startled when she saw no one on the floor. As she began to turn around, Holmes stepped from behind the door and gripped her tightly with one arm while forcing a saturated cloth against her nose and mouth. She tried to scream but no sound emerged. She struggled violently to get free and, because she was such an athletically large woman, she seemed to be making headway at first, but he clung tenaciously. As she breathed, her inhalation brought air through the cloth and, with it, a rush of chloroform fumes into her lungs. She blacked out quickly, slumping in his grasp, and he lowered her to the floor, continuing to hold the cloth over her face. He stretched out a leg to kick the door shut.

After a minute he took the cloth away and his expert fingers felt for a pulse in the carotid artery. He could detect none. He opened the belt of her robe and threw the cloth wide, exposing her bare form. A quirked smile came to his lips and the familiar excitement already filling him increased. He felt wonderful—a sense of domination, total control and absolute invincibility. He thumbed striped blue-and-white suspenders from his shoulders and unbuttoned the front of his pants, letting them fall to his ankles. He wore long underwear and made no attempt to remove it, only opened the front to free the painful bulge of tumescense.

"For old time's sake, Julia," he whispered, spreading her legs apart and kneeling between them. He thrust his penis partially into her, lifting her legs with both arms under her knees to facilitate entry, but it was still very difficult to obtain full penetration. The friction was intense and he ejaculated quickly, then was finally able to plunge to full depth in the slick of seminal lubrication.

He lay upon her panting with decreasing rapidity and then finally pushed up from her and returned to a kneeling position. He looked at her a long moment, reached out and cupped both breasts in his palms and touched the flaccid nipples with the tips of index fingers, caressing them gently, a vague regret in him that they would never again become taut with sexual arousal.

He stood up, rebuttoned and hitched up his trousers and then squatted near her head and once again felt her throat for a pulse. There was none. "Pity," he said. "Truly a pity. But then, things never do stay the same, do they, Julia?"

He took off her robe and placed his hands under her armpits and backed up, dragging her into the next room to the locked door facing onto a cubicle of wall in one outer corner of the room. Returning to his desk, he got the key. The sound of Quinlan's code knock came lightly on the outer door and he opened it.

"Did you . . . ?" The janitor left the sentence unfinished.

"Done," Holmes said. "Close the door and follow me." He led the man into the other room and took a grim satisfaction at Quinlan's low gasp when he saw the nude body. Holmes unlocked the cubicle door. It opened into a dark, dank-smelling nothingness—the upper portion of the six-foot-square shaft from cellar to roof. As Quinlan watched, mouth slack, Holmes slid Julia's body to the opening and pulled her into a lolled sitting position, her back to the edge. He kissed her cheek, allowed his hand to linger for a moment on her left breast and then shoved against her chest. She tumbled backward into the darkness and a moment later there was a heavy deadweight thud as her body struck the hardpacked earth at the bottom.

"I'll see to her later," he said, shutting the door and relocking it.

"What about the kid?" There was a quaver in Quinlan's voice as they returned to the main office room.

"Go down and get her. Tell her her mother sent you to get her so she'll come along without a fuss. We'll keep her in three-seventeen until we're ready. Take her right there." The 317 designation was that of a centrally located soundproofed room on the third floor. It was a bare, unpleasant cell of a room with only a small table, two chairs, a cot and, in a partitioned alcove, a sink and toilet.

"How long do we keep her there? I mean," Quinlan added hastily, almost apologetically, "I'll need to know when to put Cora on the train."

"Ella's not had any second thoughts since you finally got her to agree, has she, Pat?"

"No. No, she's . . . fine. She says she'll visit Cora—my folks, rather—every now and then until it's safe for the three of us to be together again."

"Excellent. Dress Cora like a boy and put her on the train tonight. Wire your parents when to meet the train and pick up the parcel. Remind them that when they receive the parcel they will be paid for its storage and are to keep it out of general circulation until further orders."

Quinlan nodded. "When can we . . . ah . . . Ella and me . . . expect to be notified to identify the body?"

"Sometime tomorrow morning, probably. Since the name tag's on the clothes, you'll be located fairly quickly, I should think."

"That's it, then?"

"That's it."

Quinlan turned and walked to the door but before he could open it to leave, Holmes spoke again.

"Pat."

"Yes?"

"Remember, when they find the body, it's Cora, your daughter. Your only child. You and Ella be convincing."

* * *

Holmes checked the time on his heavy gold pocket watch, saw it was nearly 10 P.M. and donned his overcoat. He went to Room 317 of the Castle, awakened Pearl and dressed her in the clothes Quinlan had delivered to him several hours earlier—clothes belonging to Cora.

"I'm taking you to your mama now, Pearl," he told her, smiling pleasantly.

The smile had little effect. Pearl had cried herself to sleep and now burst into tears again, wailing forlornly, not understanding what was happening and very frightened. The loud crying had subsided to convulsive sobbing by the time he carried her out into the hall and to the stairs. It was on the dimly gas-lighted second-floor landing that, with total unexpectedness, he encountered a familiar figure, tall and lean.

"Russler!" Holmes gasped, greatly taken aback. "What are *you* doing here?"

Dr. Eric Russler was equally startled. "I've been working late, Holmes. I just left my office and I'm heading home. I've been—" He broke off as a shuddering sob erupted from Pearl and he frowned. "Where in God's name are you taking Mrs. Conner's little girl at this time of night?"

Considering the abruptness of the situation, the lie came out with remarkable smoothness. "She fell out of bed and I think she's broken her leg. I'm taking her to the hospital."

"Without even splinting it first? My God, man, what's wrong with you? Bring her into my office and we'll put one on." Without waiting for a reply, he led the way down the deeply shadowed hallway toward his office. Holmes followed with Pearl in one arm, his free hand moving into his deep overcoat pocket. They stopped in front of Russler's office door. As the tenant physician bent over, fumbling with his keys at the lock, Holmes brought out his heavy folding knife with five-inch blade. It made a distinctive click as it snicked open and Russler began to straighten.

With tremendous power, Holmes drove the knifeblade to the hilt into his back. Russler grunted and strove to straighten, but could not. He fell to his knees and stayed that way a moment, eyes fixed on the dark door before him, mouth opening and closing soundlessly, then toppled onto his side. The blade had driven into his heart.

A cry rising to a scream came from Pearl, but Holmes clapped a hand over her nose and mouth and cut off the sound aborning. He held her so, oblivious to her struggles, as he pulled the keys from Russler's grasp and managed to get the door unlocked and opened it, leaving the key ring hanging from the lock. Still holding the child, he grasped the back of Russler's coat collar and dragged him into the office. Pearl's struggling was weaker but he ignored her and felt Russler's throat just below the jaw. There was no pulse, and he relaxed somewhat. With some effort he pulled the knife from Russler's back, wiped it on the man's coat, refolded it and dropped it into his own pocket.

Pearl had stopped struggling and was limp in his arms, having fallen unconscious. He bent and turned Russler over, fingers once again exploring the throat. There was still no pulse and the physician's eyes were open but already glazing in the dimness of the low-turned sconced gaslight. Holmes nodded and checked his watch once more and was immediately concerned, as time was now running very short. He stepped out into the hall again with Pearl, pulling the door closed behind him and locking it. A moment later he had resumed his movement downstairs with her and then was outside, striding rapidly along the Sixty-third Street sidewalk. A few carriages passed, slopping through the slushy street, apparently unheeding of anything except their destination. If anyone in them saw him, he appeared to be nothing more than a caring father carrying his sleeping child home.

Within fifteen minutes he was waiting in deep shadows at the railroad tracks within a block of where the Quinlans lived and within a few hundred yards of the Englewood Station. The wait was not long. The last passenger train of the night, outbound from Chicago, whooshed and wheezed into the station and stopped with steaming impatience. Ahead, at the station platform, Pat Quinlan was delivering his daughter— dressed as a small boy and referred to as Carl—into the hands of the conductor on the Chesapeake & Ohio train, to be turned over to his parents, who would meet the train at Nottingham, Ohio. And while this was occurring, Holmes darted from hiding and lay the unconscious Pearl down so that her head was wedged face first between curve of heavy steel wheel and track. Then he stepped back into the shadows. In less than a minute the whistle tooted and the snorting train lurched forward.

The following morning, Patrick and Ella Quinlan had been extremely convincing in their grief as they identified the remains. A fortnight later Columbia Life Casualty Company paid off the $10,000 claim and Pat Quinlan, in turn, gave Holmes his half-share.

"Too bad," Holmes murmured, "we didn't think at the time to ask for a double indemnity clause."

There was an atmosphere of sadness among the Castle employees and tenants with the beginning of 1892. Julia and Pearl were well liked by everyone and it was difficult to understand why they should suddenly have left without a word to anyone and why, having determined to leave, they should have gone away and left everything they owned in their apartment. Added to that was the tragic death of Cora, the little daughter of chief janitor Pat Quinlan. And, though of less importance, there was the peculiar disappearance of Dr. Eric Russler, a physician who lived in the neighborhood of the Holmes Castle and who had rented an office in that building only a month ago.

The tenants and employees asked questions of each other and of Holmes and the rumor circulated that Julia had been offered new employment in St. Louis and had gone there. Some of the tenants—the Crowes, for example—found this inexplicable, but did not know what else to believe. And so, though answers of a sort were given, they were essentially unsatisfactory and somewhat conflicting and, for a while, a sadness prevailed, edged with an unease that no one could quite fathom.

For Benjamin Pitezel these past six months had become little more than a blur. Though he didn't much care on any given night whether or not he ever saw another sunrise, life seemed to be sweeping him along inexorably. His drinking had increased to such a degree that days when he was lucid were becoming rare. The more he drank, the more depressed he became, the downward spiral such that now he felt he was balanced on the thin edge of self-destruction. It was an ambivalent sensation, the prospect simultaneously welcome and sickening.

Inclined as he had always been to periods of shallow introspection, it was easy for him to pinpoint the cause of his own state of mind. It had come as a devastating blow to both himself and Carrie last summer when, eight years after the birth of their fourth child, Howard, she had found herself pregnant again. It had exacerbated problems already existing between them and even had a detrimental effect on the children. In Carrie's case, she had become bitterly accusative and, though never having been particularly careful about her appearance, had let herself go to the point where describing her as a sloven might have been construed as being excessively generous. Her prevalent irascibility had increased to the point where these days she rarely spoke except to whine or nag or blame. More than ever she ignored her obligations as wife and mother, becoming reclusive and even withdrawn from her own family. All sexual activity between her and Ben had ceased to exist from the day she had learned of her new pregnancy and even the prosaic chores of running their little household fell to Dessie, who was not quite fifteen. And Dessie, too early hardened with adult responsibilities, tyrannized twelve-year-old Alice and ten-year-old Nellie, who constantly bickered among themselves and found common purpose only in fending off the malicious teasing of little Howard.

Now, on this fourth day of the new year, Pitezel had once again been summoned to Holmes's office. He found him reading a letter. Several other letters were on the desk, some of which had already been opened and others which remained to be read. Holmes waved him to a seat and continued reading. When he finished, he refolded it and put it back into its envelope.

"From Minnie Williams," he said conversationally. "She's out in Denver again, this time with her sister, Nannie. Wants me to come out there for a few weeks. Believe I'll go."

Pitezel nodded but said nothing, knowing Holmes would soon come to the point of his sending for him.

"In the same mail," Holmes went on, picking up one of the already opened letters and handing it to Pitezel, "was this one from the Keeley Institute. They have quite a waiting list of prospective patients, so they can't take you immediately. But they have accepted the application and you're scheduled to arrive there on the eighteenth of this month. Obviously, if I'm out in Denver I'm not going to be able to nudge you into going, so you're going to have to see to it on your own hook. I've put some cash in the envelope for your round trip fare, as well as for your meals and incidental expenses."

The blue eyes narrowed and became hard as Holmes lowered his voice and continued in measured words. "I'm relying on you to go there and take the cure. Don't fail me, Ben."

"I suppose the next time I see you will be in Chicago, Harry." There was a catch in Minnie's voice and the grip of her gloved hand had tightened on his sleeve.

Holmes nodded, expression sad. "Somehow it seems we're always saying goodbye."

The snow on the Denver sidewalk crunched and squeaked beneath their feet and small plumes of condensation appeared and dissipated regularly from their exhalations. It was very cold—ten degrees below zero—and yet nowhere near so unbearable as the same temperature would have been in Chicago. He mentioned this to Minnie and she agreed.

"No doubt," she added, "it's because of the dryness of the air here. Maybe it will help B.H. I hope so. He's so uncomfortable."

He made no response to this and after they had walked another dozen yards or so she spoke again. "I'm glad we decided to walk to the station together this morning." She smiled at him, looking especially charming, her cheeks rosy and her face prettily framed by the parka. Flakes of new snow were clinging to the fur and a few had settled on her eyelashes. She tilted her head as she so often did when amused. "It's good you finally had a chance to meet Nannie, Harry. She's heard me carry on so much about you and for so long without ever seeing you that she was beginning to tease me, saying Harry Gordon was a figment of my imagination." She giggled. "Now she's met you and I knew she'd love you, just as I do."

"She's a lovely girl, Minnie," Holmes said. "I like her a lot. I expected to," he added, "but somehow I liked her even more than I expected and I think that's nice. I'm surprised how much you two look alike." Except, he thought, she's not as fat as you and certainly better looking. He saw her looking at him and smiled. "I was just thinking that I wish we'd all had more time together."

"I know. I do, too." Her voice became wistful. "I wish *we*—just the two of us—had had more time together. Three weeks seems like a long time when it's ahead, but in retrospect it's almost nothing."

Holmes nodded and again they lapsed into silence. He thought of his arrival here and of Minnie and Nannie meeting him in the station. He had kissed them both and from that moment on they had been almost constant companions. The sleigh that had carried them away from the railroad station had deposited them at the new four-story apartment house called The Devonshire, where Minnie had gotten him a room on the second floor some distance from theirs. It was Room 200, close to the front stairway. She and Nannie were staying together in Room 210, next door to Room 212, where Baldwin was lodged. From the first Nannie had looked at him practically as adoringly as Minnie always did and he was almost certain that, had she been invited to, Nannie might very willingly have accompanied Minnie in her surreptitious nightly visits to his room and bed.

Holmes had arrived in Denver in time to escort Nannie to the final two performances of the play in which Minnie had a secondary role. It had been in production for three weeks. He was surprised at how skilled she had become in her acting, impressed at how well she projected to her audience, amused at the irony of the fact that the play in which she was appearing was Charles Reade's *Dora*, intrigued by the way Nannie squeezed his hand at intervals during the performance, when the house lights were down.

They had introduced him to their twenty-two-year-old brother, Baldwin, whom they had brought to Denver from Fort Worth right after Christmas, hoping the altitude and dryness of the air would be of benefit to him. He was an intense, thin young man, obviously unwell, even though Nannie had whispered, "I think he's been helped by being here, Harry. He looks better now than he has for years."

It was without difficulty that Holmes had lifted the key to the young man's room from Minnie's purse, long enough for him to make a wax impression. Before the end of the first week he had had a key made from the impression and, while Baldwin was taking a bath down the hall, tried it out on the door and discovered to his satisfaction that it worked perfectly. The other Williams brother, Billy Bob, he learned, was still working in Leadville and doing very well for himself.

Often with Nannie in tow and sometimes alone, Holmes and Minnie dined together at the finest restaurants, at one of which they were introduced to a flamboyant long-haired, full-bearded man whose image was quite familiar from the many posters seen of him in the past—William F. Cody, better known as Buffalo Bill. They went to the opera and the theater and attended parties given by her friends, who were among the upper crust of Denver society. Everyone they met could see that Minnie Williams and Harry Gordon were deeply in love with one another.

On the final night of his stay, Nannie had elected to stay home with Baldwin and let Minnie and Harry have this time with one another. They had dined elegantly at the sumptuous Brown Palace Hotel, which had opened less than a year ago and had already achieved considerable fame. While there, Minnie had suddenly squealed and waved, then scrambled to her feet, drawing Holmes with her and towing him to an exceptionally attractive couple who had just entered. The man was about fifty years old, the woman closer to forty.

"Oh, Emily, Edward," Minnie bubbled, "it's so *good* to see you again!" She kissed them both. "Allow me to present my fiancé, Mr. Harry Gordon of Chicago. Harry, these are my friends of the theater, Mr. and Mrs. Edward Langtry."

Holmes shook hands with Langtry and kissed his wife's hand gallantly. "A pleasure to meet you both," he said. His gaze rested on the woman. "And you are, of course—"

"Wait, Harry," Minnie interrupted. She giggled as she put her hand on the woman's arm. "Let me see if I can remember it all correctly, Emily. Harry, this is Mrs. Emily Charlotte Le Breton Langtry."

"*Brava!*" cried the woman. "You *do* remember it, Minnie. I must say I'm impressed! Mr. Gordon, it's truly a delight to meet you. Minnie told us all about you a year or so ago in Boston and what a handsome man you were. I thought she might have been exaggerating, but it seems she was dealing in understatement."

"A pleasure, madam," Holmes said. "Thank you." He tilted his head. "I'm honored to meet so lovely a lady but," he directed his remark at Edward Langtry, "if you'll permit me to say so, sir," he turned again to the woman, "I am appalled that however lovely they have been, no picture of you I have ever seen has done you justice."

Her mouth quirked with amused pleasure. "I'm flattered, sir. I take it you recognize me, then?"

"Indeed, yes," he said. He glanced at Minnie and spoke

with mock accusation. "Minnie, you never told me you knew the famous Miss Lillie Langtry." He turned back and continued with a smile. "Or should I say the Jersey Lilly? Sir John, for all his artistic talent, madam, was also unable to capture what the eye beholds."

Emily Langtry rolled her eyes. "Now I'm even more impressed." She laughed lightly and spoke to her friend. "Minnie, if you don't marry this wonderful man very soon, I may have to divorce Edward here and marry him myself." They all laughed and she went on. "I must say, there are few I meet who are aware that I posed for Sir John Everett Millais."

"And got your soubriquet from the title of his painting," Minnie pointed out. She looked at her escort proudly. "Harry, you continue to amaze me."

"May it ever be so," he chuckled, then turned his attention to the other couple again. "Mr. Langtry," he said, "Minnie and I would be honored if you and Mrs. Langtry would join us at our table."

"You're very kind, Mr. Gordon, and under any other circumstances we would gladly do so. Unfortunately, we are meeting several other couples here for dinner. Perhaps another time."

"Of course," Holmes said. He shook Langtry's hand again and bowed to his actress wife. "A distinct pleasure to have met you both."

Minnie kissed the couple again and then took Holmes's arm and let him lead her back to their table. As they walked, Holmes murmured, "Well, that was quite a surprise, Miss Williams. What other little secrets like this have you been keeping from me?"

She laughed, tickled with herself. "You've only begun to tap the vast reservoir of surprises I have in store for you, Mr. Gordon. You'll just have to stick around and find out."

It had been a pleasant conclusion to their stay together and now, walking with her toward the station in the knife-sharp morning, Holmes genuinely wished he could stay longer. Just before he boarded the train he embraced her warmly.

"I love you, Minnie," he said. "I'll miss you."

"And I love you, Harry. More than ever. We'll be together again before long. I promise."

A short while later, Holmes sat alone on a deep velvet

plush window seat in his luxuriously appointed Pullman Palace Car sleeper suite and watched the pristine snowy landscape streak by. After a while he sipped a fine Napoleon brandy from cut crystal and congratulated himself on a most successful trip.

The intensely cold morning of January 18 had been brittle and bright when Benjamin Pitezel arrived at the Keeley Institute. The scattering of typically institutional-looking buildings was located on the southern edge of the Illinois prairie town of Dwight, about seventy-five miles southwest of downtown Chicago. The institute had been established in 1880 by Dr. Leslie Keeley. A graduate of the Rush Medical School in Chicago, Dr. Keeley harbored a novel belief that alcoholism was a disease, not a vice, and that, as such, it was curable. The preliminary research he had done prior to founding the institute was tested on a select group of volunteers as soon as construction of the alcoholic rehabilitation center here was completed. The treatments he prescribed, the injections he gave and the regimen he demanded that his patients follow had had startling results. Soon Dr. Keeley was publicly proclaiming that within two days the patient had lost all desire to drink and by the end of a month the cure was complete, no matter how inveterate a drinker he had been.

Now, on the threshold of its thirteenth year of operation, the institute had gained wide renown and was drawing clientele from all over the nation, though by far the majority were Chicagoans. Dr. Keeley's cure consisted of having his patients commit themselves to a four-week stay at the institute, during which time they were fed a well-balanced diet and given regular injections of double chloride of gold. The program was not inexpensive. The cost, which included room but not food, was $100 for the four weeks. This was close to seven times more than an average worker's weekly salary, so initially the clientele was most often restricted to the reasonably wealthy.

From the beginning there had been a good deal of opposition to Keeley's so-called gold cure claims, especially in medical circles, where there were strong objections to his flagrant commercialism, strong reservations in respect to his methods and strong assaults on his claims of success, those attacks based on the fact that a rather high percentage of his allegedly cured patients reverted to alcoholism within a few months. Keeley, reasonably enough, countered with the assertion that this was a failure not of the institute and its treatment, but of the patient himself.

The storm of controversy was still raging when Benjamin Pitezel arrived to check in under his new identity as Robert E. Phelps. His life was changed shortly after he entered the doors, not so much by the treatment he underwent as by an individual he encountered. She was Dr. Keeley's personal stenographer—a twenty-year-old Indiana girl who was unquestionably the loveliest woman Benjamin Pitezel had ever beheld. He was by no means alone in that evaluation. An accurate painting of her might well have been considered idealistic because of its flawlessness. Taller than average, she was mantled with long, naturally wavy pale blond hair and her large blue-green eyes were breathtaking. Her figure was remarkable, her features exquisite. A sort of intuitive grace attended her carriage and gestures and, to top it all, she was witty and quite intelligent. In short, Emeline Cigrand was positively stunning.

During his month as a patient at the Keeley Institute, the changes wrought in the man known as Robert Phelps were significant. He regained a sense of pride in his appearance. He began wearing fresh clothing daily, something he had never before done. He even wore neckties day after day, despite the discomfort they caused him. His posture improved significantly. He ceased his chain-smoking of Duke cigarettes and returned to occasionally smoking an aromatic blend in his pipe. He lost the slight potbelly he had been developing and his skin tone improved. He shaved away the ridiculous goatee he had sported for the past three years and both shortened and neatly trimmed a moustache that had become long and scraggly. He became—with etched lines of maturity on his face—even more handsome than he had been in his twenties. He stopped drinking. He fell in love with Emeline Cigrand. And, despite the fact that he was eighteen years her senior, Emeline fell in love with him. Rather, she fell in love with the man she knew as Robert E. Phelps who, by his own admission, was a bachelor—rich, well traveled and the manager of a very successful Chicago firm called the ABC Copier Company; a man whose drinking problem was, so he said, the result of business pressures. He expressed a determination to no longer allow those pressures to affect him so.

Considering her beauty, it was not unexpected that Emeline had been courted with varying degrees of seriousness by quite a few men her own age or slightly older during the past few years, but she had never allowed herself to be seduced. It was to the man called Phelps—who, within a week of their meeting, promised he was going to marry her—that she finally surrendered her virginity. And Pitezel, deprived of sex with Carrie for many months, had not made the promise lightly.

When the time had come, during the third week of February, for Mr. Phelps to be discharged from the Keeley Institute, it was as traumatic for him to leave as it was for Emeline to see him go. When he had suggested that his employer, Mr. Holmes, might have a job for her at a higher wage than she was receiving at the institute, she was immediately eager for him to check further into the matter. He left with the promise fresh in her ears that she would hear from him very soon.

Pitezel was very upset when he returned to Chicago and found Holmes gone and no one, not even Pat Quinlan, knowing when he would return. Finally, after eight excruciating days, the owner of the Castle returned and Pitezel immediately called on him. And now, once again face to face with Holmes in the third-floor office of the Castle, Pitezel found his employer very impressed with the great changes that had taken place in him. Without offering any explanation for his absence, which was not at all unusual, Holmes listened to Pitezel's account of his stay at the Keeley Institute and his infatuation with Emeline Cigrand. He reserved comment until Pitezel had run down and then, as he spoke, Pitezel was less than pleased at his lack of enthusiasm in respect to offering Emeline employment.

"I don't think it's a very good idea to bring her here, Ben," Holmes said seriously. "You're married, don't forget."

Pitezel grunted a sour reply. "You mean what's good for you is bad for me? You're married to Dora, Holmes, but you've had at least a couple dozen women since I've known you, including some on a long-term basis. Julia Conner, for instance. So where's the difference?"

Holmes shook his head, not deigning to comment on that. Instead, he tried another tack. "How serious are you about this girl? Are you planning on divorcing Carrie and marrying her? Or running off with her?"

"No."

"You just want to continue fucking her, eh?"

An angry glint flickered to life in Pitezel's eyes. "I wouldn't put it quite that way."

"But that's what you mean, right?" Holmes sighed. "Ben, I'm not in favor of it but I can tell you're not going to be much good to me until you get this out of your system. All right, I'll write and offer her possible employment. Maybe she can fill Lucy's job here as my personal secretary."

"What about Lucy?"

"I haven't had a chance to tell you about that. She quit a couple of weeks ago to go to New York. Decided she wants a career in acting."

There was no hint in Holmes's expression that what he had just said was anything but the truth. It was an absolute lie. Lucy Burbank had been hired to take Julia Conner's place shortly after the latter's disappearance. Pitezel had seen her once or twice but knew her only to be a recent widow from Cleveland who was without kin. Less than a week ago, instead of having gone to New York as Holmes said, she had taken up permanent residence in the closet of a third-year student at La Salle Medical School as a newly acquired skeleton. Her possessions had been disposed of by Holmes except for some identification papers and a First National Bank savings account book discovered in her purse. The bankbook had shown a balance of $1,450, which Holmes meant to have, but he had been too shrewd to run the risk of trying to withdraw it immediately. Instead, he had made good use of the leverage he now wielded over Ella Quinlan because of the life insurance scheme successfully pulled off with her daughter, Cora. It had not been difficult to convince her to go to the bank and, carrying Lucy's identity papers, make a deposit of several hundred dollars in the account. Ella had been both wise enough and fearful enough to follow his orders and not ask questions. At Holmes's insistence she had also quickly learned to forge Lucy's signature. Holmes planned to continue having her deposit money in the account until, over a period of time, she had become thoroughly recognizable to the tellers as Lucy Burbank. This, in case of emergency, would give him one more source of easily accessible money, for by then Ella would be able to withdraw all the money and close the account without arousing suspicion.

Delighted that the job opening was available for Emeline, Pitezel had not given a second thought to the matter of Lucy Burbank's alleged departure for Broadway. "You'll write to Emeline, then?" he pressed. "Right away?"

"Yes, but I won't promise her work here. Only a job interview, assuming she wants to come for it."

"Hah!" Pitezel said. "She'll come, all right, I guarantee that. She'll be on the first train to Chicago after receiving your letter. And I'll be at the station to meet her."

"No," contradicted Holmes, "as a matter of fact, you won't. You'll be in Denver."

As Pitezel stared at him uncomprehendingly, Holmes reached into his center desk drawer and extracted a skeleton key and a sealed envelope. He extended them toward Pitezel, who took them, frowning.

"The key," Holmes said, interlocking his fingers and cupping his nape as he leaned back in his chair, "is for room number two-twelve in The Devonshire. That's an apartment house at fourteen twenty-five Logan Avenue in Denver. The envelope contains a round trip ticket to Denver, which you will utilize tomorrow morning. In Room Two-twelve there is a young gentleman who has come to that city for his health. He is weak and has trouble breathing. Unfortunately, his particular brand of asthma is fatal. He does not know that. In fact, no one but you and I know that. It gives you the opportunity to be the only one to bid him *adieu* from this life before an inability to breathe causes him to pass away. Since it would be uncomfortable for you to witness the grief of others there who might be close to him—in the room next door, as a matter of fact—it would undoubtedly be wise for you to make your call very late at night. In the morning they will find him and though they will grieve, they will be comforted by the knowledge that he died painlessly, in his sleep."

Pitezel's mouth had become dry and a burning bubble of acid had formed in his stomach. He stared dumbly at the key and envelope in his hand and then slowly lifted his gaze to meet Holmes's. The latter smiled faintly.

"A final thought you might bear in mind," he said. "Since you are still wanted in Colorado on a charge of murdering one Wilton Crawford, alias Willie Cash, I would suggest you not prolong your stay there." He chuckled. "Of course you wouldn't anyway, knowing your Miss Cigrand was here waiting for you."

Pitezel still seemed to be having trouble speaking. His mouth opened and closed several times before the words came. "Who..." he said, "...who... is the young gentleman in Room Two-twelve?"

"Williams," Holmes said, smiling, his eyes half closed. "His friends and relatives often call him B.H. That stands for Baldwin Heath. Baldwin Heath Williams. Have a nice trip, Ben. I'll look forward to seeing you in, oh, about a week, I would guess."

It was a dismissal.

As Ben Pitezel had told Holmes she would, Emeline Cigrand caught the very first train to Chicago after receiving Holmes's letter. He had written that Mr. Phelps was on a business trip and probably would not be back for a week or more, so did not really expect her to come until then. The initiative and enthusiasm she showed, however, not only in setting out from Dwight immediately on the Chicago & Alton Railroad but in finding her way to his third-floor Castle office for the job interview, impressed Holmes, though hardly so much as did sight of the young woman herself. The effect she had upon him, though not quite so strong as Pitezel had felt it, was nevertheless considerable. Her beauty had taken his breath away and it was easy for him to see why Pitezel had been captivated.

Holmes admitted that, yes, he was the owner of the ABC Copier Company—among numerous other enterprises— and that Robert E. Phelps was not only manager of that firm, but one of his best and most trusted employees and a good friend besides. Her eyes widened when he told her that Phelps was also one-third owner of this massive building in which she presently sat. There was no doubt in Holmes's mind, from that first moment of their meeting, that he would hire her.

"I should like to learn your qualifications for the job I have in mind," Holmes told her, "but I must mind my manners as well. This is your first trip to Chicago, is it not?"

"Yes sir," she replied, flashing her dazzling smile, "and I'm quite excited by it. I caught a glimpse of some of the large buildings—the ones they call... uh..."

"Skyscrapers?" His grin was infectious.

"Yes, thank you, that's it. Skyscrapers. I glimpsed some of them and even though I didn't see them very well, I couldn't believe such huge buildings really existed. I hope to see a lot of this city..." she paused and colored faintly, "...assuming I would be staying here to work, of course." She suddenly felt flustered and lowered her eyes. He's so handsome, she thought, almost classically pretty, rather than merely ruggedly good-looking in a manly way, like Robert.

"Exactly what I was getting to," Holmes said. "It is late in the morning and I think it would make our little interview much more pleasant if you would allow me to take you downtown for lunch, during which we can discuss our business, and afterwards I could give you a tour of some of the points of interest in the inner city."

"I really don't want to inconvenience you, Mr. Holmes, but actually, yes, I'd be ever so grateful for such an opportunity."

"Excellent!" He beamed. "No sooner said than begun. Shall we go?"

They dined in Henrici's, a splendid restaurant whose interior boasted much more than its unprepossessing exterior promised. Front doors of highly polished brass and heavy panes of leaded glass opened into what appeared to be, and actually was, a bakery. The heady aroma of newly baked sweet pastries and a variety of wonderful breads filled their nostrils as they walked on a floor of closely fitted hexagonal white tiles past the long glass counter flanked by a waist-high gleaming brass rail. Large milkglass globe lights hung from the ceiling, shedding ample illumination without glare. At the rear of the bakery, just before reaching the two dining rooms, was an area where there were seven or eight tables primarily for those who had come in just for pastries and coffee. Beyond was a huge carpeted room in which were numerous tables covered with fresh white linen tablecloths and upon which were place settings of pure white china, shiny silverware, heavy cut-glass goblets and linen napkins. Through an archway to the left was another room similar to this but even larger, its walls paneled in richly finished walnut and holding virtually a gallery of ornately framed paintings.

The place was filled with diners and there was an overriding low hum of conversation. It seemed all the tables were taken, but Holmes momentarily excused himself from

Emeline and approached the headwaiter. They conversed in a low tone and though at first the headwaiter shook his head, he suddenly brightened and nodded as Holmes slipped a discreetly folded bill into his hand. Emeline's escort then returned for her and they were shown through the archway into the larger dining room and to a table of their own. Conversation was more subdued here than in the other section.

With Emeline's acquiescence Holmes ordered for her. The first course was a wonderful chicken salad—pieces of white meat arrayed on a bed of lettuce, surrounded by wedges of hard-cooked eggs, short lengths of celery and bright curls of carrot. With each serving came a marvelously delicate dressing in individual side dishes. Henrici's was one of the only restaurants serving fresh salad greens at this time of year, shipped on ice to Chicago by rail from California.

The second course was planked whitefish cooked to perfection and served on individual trays of very dark oak, each also with an individual side dish of a light, very smooth tartar sauce. This course was accompanied by large, newly baked and perfectly browned dinner rolls, with heavy sweet butter.

It was more than enough for Emeline and she laughingly protested when Holmes signaled the waiter for the final course, but he ordered anyway—a Napoleon pastry lightly iced on top and with alternating layers of fluffy crust, filled with cream and custard. Freshly brewed coffee complemented the dessert.

Holmes noted with masked delight that heads had turned their way ever since their entrance. The male diners visually feasting on her beauty could not be sated and female diners, of which there were but few, viewed her with expressions ranging from highly admiring to resentful.

"Now tell me," Holmes had begun almost immediately after ordering, "how long have you worked for the Keeley Institute and in what capacity?"

"I've been there just a little over a year, Mr. Holmes. Stenographic work, mostly, in which I've been well trained, although some secretarial duties as well." A holdover of her high school girlishness revealed itself as she went on. "I suppose it would not be amiss for me to tell you that I was valedictorian of my graduating class. I have brought along a letter of recommendation from Dr. Keeley himself, for whom I've worked exclusively over these past five months."

"Very good. That was your first job upon graduating from high school in . . . Lafayette, was it?"

"Yes sir. Lafayette High School. But, no, it wasn't my first job. After graduation I was employed in the Tippecanoe County Recorder's office, but I remained there for only seven months and resigned to take advantage of the better opportunity available at the Keeley Institute."

"You live alone?"

"I have, Mr. Holmes, since leaving Lafayette. That is, I've been living in a boardinghouse in Dwight."

Holmes swallowed the bit of salad he was chewing. "Do you have a large family at home?"

"Well, not large, really. There's Daddy—who is with the Lafayette Fire Department—ane Mom and my sister, Philomena, who's two years younger than I. She's a senior this year."

Holmes was staring at her, entranced not only by her looks, but also by the quality of her voice, the whole of her personality. He caught himself with a start. "Forgive me," he said hastily, "I'm being very thoughtless. You've hardly had a chance to eat a bite yet. Please, do go ahead and eat and we'll continue the discussion as we get near the end."

She nodded and began and he noted that her manners were very refined. She murmured appreciatively over the quality of the food and, as she continued to eat, he talked about Chicago, its theaters and opera, its parks and business establishments, its leadership in modern architecture and educational facilities. It was as she was just finishing her whitefish that she became especially attentive when he mentioned the high regard in which she was held by Robert Phelps. Holmes also said with pointed casualness how busy Mr. Phelps's work for the ABC Copier Company kept him and how often he had to make extended trips out of town.

Emeline was evidently just a little disappointed to discover Robert was not at the office every day. "Well," she said lightly, "at least if I get the job I'll get to see him on those days when he is in."

Holmes shook his head slowly. "I'm sure you'll see a great deal of him, Miss Cigrand, but it won't be at the ABC office. You see, no position is currently open there. The job I have to offer is as my personal secretary, in the office where we met."

"Oh!" she said, momentarily crestfallen. She brightened and added, "Oh, that's quite all right. I think I'd like that a great deal."

"Part of your duties would be handling finances to a certain extent," he added. "Making out the payroll checks for my signature, paying bills, keeping the books. Do you think you could handle that?"

"Certainly. I mean, I'm sure I could, Mr. Holmes. I'm good with figures and I manage my own finances quite well."

Holmes was silent a moment, his lips slightly pursed. "I don't mean to pry," he said, "but it does have a bearing on what we're discussing. How well have you done in saving money from your pay?"

She was not offended. "Oh, that's all right," she said. "I don't mind telling you. I guess I'm rather proud of it. Since graduating from high school, I've saved eight hundred dollars."

Holmes was more than mildly impressed. "I don't know what you've earned, but I'd say that's quite an achievement. You must live on nothing but birdseed and water."

She laughed aloud, a bright tinkling laughter that brought smiles to the faces of nearby diners. "Not quite," she said, "but I do admit to being frugal."

"Then I think my question has been answered," Holmes told her.

"May I . . ." Her cheeks became tinged with pink again. ". . . may I ask what my salary might be, Mr. Holmes?"

"How much," he countered, "have you been earning?"

"Well, at the County Recorder's office I got only eight dollars per week. At the Keeley institute I started at eleven dollars weekly for the first three months and then that was raised to twelve dollars. When Dr. Keeley caught wind of the fact that I might be considering leaving, he raised my salary to thirteen fifty a week."

Holmes nodded and touched his napkin to his lips. "I am prepared," he said, signaling the waiter to clear away prior to bringing dessert, "to hire you at a starting salary of eighteen dollars weekly. At the end of the first year, assuming everything works out satisfactorily, that figure will be raised to twenty-two dollars. The job is yours if you want it."

"Oh, Mr. Holmes, yes! Thank you. It's much more than I anticipated."

"Then we're even," he grinned, his features taking on that boyishness that women seemed to find especially appealing, "because I think in you I'll be getting much more than I anticipated, too. Welcome to my employ, Miss Cigrand. You start next Monday."

Though he had arrived in Denver four days ago, Benjamin Pitezel, now using the alias of Richard French, had spent most of the time in his seedy hotel room. He ventured out in daylight hours only when he took his meals at a nearby low-class saloon restaurant, steeling himself each time against the array of bottles in clear view. He felt a distinct pride in having resisted such temptation but the urge to have a drink was powerful and he always wolfed his food and left the establishment quickly, lest his resolve be lost.

At night he stood for hours outside The Devonshire at 1425 Logan Avenue, studying the frequency with which people entered or left the building. Several times he saw Minnie Williams and kept out of sight on the off chance she might recognize him. With malicious perversity he wished he could see her with a man so he could tell Holmes about it and watch his reaction, but she was always alone or with another woman who looked considerably like her. No doubt the sister called Nannie that Holmes had mentioned.

In the early evening hours there was a fair amount of traffic in and out of the place. By 11 P.M. only a few people were about. Occasionally one or two of the tenants was seen entering the building around midnight, evidently after a late night out. Once a man entered the building at 1:15 A.M. Between the hours of 2 A.M. and 4 A.M., however, there had been no sighting of anyone, not even passersby.

Now, standing in the deepest dark between buildings on the opposite side of the street, Pitezel stamped his feet as quietly as possible against the penetrating cold and blew warming breath into his cupped hands. He had been standing here for nearly half an hour and there had been no sign of anyone. He figured it must be close to 3 A.M. For perhaps the sixth time he reached into his pocket to reassure himself the key was still there. It was. He looked carefully in both directions and then emerged from the shadows and walked casually across the street, not concerned that the glow of the gas streetlight fell upon him fully. He entered the front door of The Devonshire as if he belonged there. Only then did he become furtive.

The stairs were to his right and he went up them quietly, clinging close to the wall. Only one stair creaked and that not loudly enough for concern. On the second floor he walked on the balls of his feet only, keeping to the runner carpet. Five widely spaced gaslights provided illumination enough to see the room numbers. The first door he passed was 200, the second 202. He counted off four more doors on that side of the corridor without pausing to check their numbers and stopped before the fifth. It was 212.

Gently, ever so gently, cursing hands that were still stiff with cold, he slipped the skeleton key into the lock and turned it. There was friction at first, but then it unlocked with a faint click. He paused and listened. Nothing, inside the room or out. He wondered fleetingly what he would do if a deadbolt was closed from the inside, but he needn't have worried, there was none. The knob turned smoothly in his grasp and the door swung inward quietly.

The gaslight inside was turned low but there was still light enough to show the form of a person in the bed, lying at full length under a thick down comforter. The sleeper was breathing heavily, air rasping and wheezing in and out with regular cadence. Closing the door as silently as it had opened and then moving soundlessly to the side of the bed, Pitezel looked down at the figure of B. H. Williams. The young man lay on his back, head turned to the right on his pillow. A second pillow lay against the headboard beside him, unused. Pitezel reached across for the pillow but had no more than grasped it in both hands when Williams's eyes popped open. An instant of confusion was replaced by alarm and he opened his mouth.

"Wha——" he began, but Pitezel jammed the pillow over his face, pressing it tightly against mouth and nostrils, at the same time throwing a leg over the figure and sitting upon him. Williams bucked and jerked and flailed, struggling to get free, but, weak as he was, there was no chance. In less than a minute the struggles had ceased but Pitezel kept the pillow in place for fully two minutes beyond that. Then he pulled it away and felt for the man's pulse, first on his wrist, then at his throat. There was none.

Pitezel stood up. B.H.'s eyes were partially open, sightless. Pitezel gently closed them with thumb and middle finger of one hand and then replaced the pillow he had used, smoothing away the faint wrinkles. He straightened the somewhat disturbed covers, checked the throat pulse one final time and, satisfied, returned to the door. He opened it again, very quietly, and peered cautiously out into the corridor. No one was there. The key was still in the lock and he stepped out, turned the doorknob fully to one side and pulled the door closed without sound. Locking it and removing the key caused again only the faintest of clicks.

He left the building as he had entered it, less furtively but no less soundlessly. Outside he bent his head and stepped away quickly into the darkness. Throughout the affair he had been totally calm and self-assured. Now he stopped and abruptly found himself wracked by a great trembling. He leaned against a tree and vomited into the snow.

"Holmes," he muttered as he straightened, wiping his mouth on his sleeve, "you are a son of a bitch!"

He returned to his own hotel room and tried to sleep, but could not. At 6 A.M. he was aboard the first eastbound train out of Denver. Fifteen minutes later he stepped to the rear of the train and stood on the platform, exulting in the purging rip of frigid wind tearing at him. He reached into his pocket and extracted the key to Room 212 and threw it as far as he could into the deep snow beyond the trackbed.

And at this same moment, about a thousand miles away in Chicago, Carrie Pitezel had just given birth to a son.

Five

Not since his first meeting with Julia Conner had Henry H. Holmes so anticipated the prospect of having sex as he envisioned it now with Emeline Cigrand. He felt certain it would eventually occur, though it might take longer than he was accustomed to waiting, once he'd set his mind on making a conquest. Part of the reason for the delay was the necessity of not alienating Ben Pitezel in the process, but an even more pertinent reason was the fact that he had never been busier nor more fragmented in his activities than he had been thus far this year. Even during the initial building of this so-called Castle at Sixty-third and Wallace, there had not been such a frenetic sense of disparate activity. At least then there had been a degree of organization, a semblance of logical progression. Little of that existed now. Everything seemed intermingled in a haphazard, catch-as-catch-can composite.

There was no mystery about what had inspired it: This was the year of preparation for the World's Columbian Exposition; the year when Holmes intended turning what he could of the Castle into a World's Fair hotel catering to the overflow of visitors requiring a place to stay and not having reserved accommodations elsewhere. With twenty million people expected to pour into Chicago beginning next spring, the potential for making enormous profits in any number of ways was extensive.

The first matter of concern was to get more fire insurance on the building. Even though extensive remodeling was currently under way, Holmes had been experiencing a growing conviction that this Castle of his in Chicago had nearly outlived its usefulness. Increasingly he had been catching wind of rumors and suspicions circulating in the Englewood area that dark and perhaps deadly things were occurring in the huge building. Sooner or later, he knew, someone would begin to take action on such suspicions. Thus, he could clearly foresee a time ahead when, to avoid possible prosecution, he might have to burn the whole place down. The thought of that, which might have distressed him severely in the past, was not so difficult to adjust to now, due to his long-range plan for bilking Minnie Williams out of her downtown Fort Worth property and building upon it a bigger and better version of the Castle . . . and for the same purposes. For now, the Chicago Castle was still to be used to lure transients who might be disposed of quickly and profitably. But if it came to pass that burning the place down was the wisest course to take, Holmes intended profiting from it. He called in Cosgrove Arnold and had the agent write out fire insurance policies on the Castle with four companies: $5,000 each with Girard Insurance, Queen Fire Insurance and London, Liverpool & Globe Insurance Company, plus a $3,000 policy with North American Underwriters. Arnold was glad enough to get more business from his most important customer but Holmes detected a sense of dejection in his manner.

"What's bothering you today, Cos?" he asked. "You're acting as if you've lost your best friend."

Arnold snorted. "Ironic that you should put it that way, Holmes."

"What the hell is that supposed to mean?"

"You've met Hattie."

"You know I have." Hattie Arnold, the agent's brittle wife, was a shrewish, beaver-faced woman of forty who hated Holmes with unbridled passion. Often she would cross Sixty-third Street a block away from the Castle so she could avoid encountering Holmes on the off chance that he would emerge from the building as she walked past it. He knew of no real foundation for her hatred of him, only that it existed and that she railed at Arnold constantly for having anything to do with him or anything with which he was even remotely connected. "What about her?"

"She left me yesterday."

"Permanently?"

"Permanently."

"Should I cry or cheer?"

Arnold shrugged. "Hell, I don't know. That's what I've been asking myself. I guess I should feel like cheering, but still, there's a sort of gap all of a sudden. Know what I mean?"

Holmes chose his words carefully, not really wanting to offend the man. "Put it this way, Cos, I understand what you're saying. It's just that I'm not entirely sure I sympathize with it. What happened?" He wasn't really interested but knew Arnold expected him to ask.

"She thinks I'm a shiftless bum. Hates what I do and hates it when I do any business with you. Says everything wrong about me stems from associating with you. She claims you're going to lead me to the gallows some day."

Holmes raised an eyebrow. "And you believe that?"

"Not really. You might swing, but not me." He chuckled with his little joke. "Anyway, she started in on me when your message arrived yesterday asking me to come today and write some more insurance. Told me if I was to go, it was quits between us. I'll tell you, Holmes, I'd had all I could take of that kind of shit from her. I blew up and told her she didn't have to wait around to find out, that I was damned well going to do it and she could just damned well pack her bag and get her ass out right now." He shrugged and grinned lopsidedly. "Damned if she didn't do it. Like I say, it leaves a kind of gap, but you know what? I think I'll get used to the idea fast." He picked up his papers, gave a half-wave to Holmes and was still grinning when he left.

Holmes had no time to dwell on it. He had all sorts of appointments to keep with merchants and manufacturers throughout the city. Title to the Castle had changed many times but it was currently owned by Dora's grand-uncle Jonathan Belknap on one title and the fictitious Campbell-Yates Manufacturing Company on another. Once again he was buying large quantities of goods on credit, usually with the smallest down payment possible and having the contracts signed by the rich but nonexistent Hiram S. Campbell. As before, anyone questioning the reliability of the purchasing firm was referred to Wharton Plummer in his regal offices in the Chamber of Commerce Building in downtown Chicago. In recent weeks Holmes had bought barrelsful of all kinds of crockery, along with flatware, kitchenware, silent butlers, new beds, chairs, sofas and settees and other overstuffed furniture, dressers, mirrors, lighting equipment, sinks, bathtubs, toilets, stoves, linens, draperies, carpeting, lumber, fixtures, bricks and a multitude of other items. It was easier to buy in great bulk than in small quantity and so, while only mere hundreds of dollars in down payment had been paid— in worthless checks wherever possible—thousands upon thousands of dollars' worth of such goods had been contracted for, far more than he could possibly use at the Castle. Day after day deliverymen were arriving in wagons, carriages and vans with the purchases, and all available hands in the Holmes Castle were kept busy stowing the goods or, after dark, transshipping them away for resale in other cities. Quinlan and Pitezel were directing operations, while the muscle required was being furnished by Joe Owens, Pete Verrett, Sam Butler, Paddy Doyle, and whatever itinerant workmen could be plucked off the streets who wished to make a quick dollar or two. The goods being kept at the Castle were not stored in extra rooms or storage closets. The false walls erected when the Castle was built were being opened and the hidden spaces inside used to stack boxes and bales and barrels of goods, scores of tables and chairs and other furnishings, even pianos and bicycles—all the things Holmes anticipated might be of some use in turning the Castle into a World's Fair hotel, or items of use to guests who might be staying here. As soon as any one such given space was filled, it was walled up again and repapered or repainted until virtually indistinguishable from other walls, thus thwarting the possibility of repossession by force or more traditional legal recovery through writ of replevin. Whole sections of the Castle were sealed away by building false walls across the meandering corridors, with access to the hidden area usually through a secret door or sliding panel in a closet in one of the adjoining rooms.

Electricians were called in to bring electric lighting to the majority of the rooms in the Castle, then to install fixtures, ceiling fans, lamps and light bulbs. Painters were hired, plasterers, carpenters, plumbers, wallpaper hangers, masons, glaziers. Once again workers were not paid and quit in disgust or were fired. Merchants brought lawsuits by the score against Hiram S. Campbell, Kit Durkee, Julia Conner, Henry Holmes, Pat Quinlan, Ben Pitezel and even poor simple Joe Owens—anyone they could even remotely point a finger toward who had, or who they *thought* had, anything whatever to do with the fraudulent purchase of goods or services. All papers served on them were relayed to Wharton Plummer—whom Holmes had recently given a $5,000 bonus—and immediately thereupon snarled in a mass of red tape that would require months or years to unravel, if ever.

Occasionally there were snoopers who poked into places they shouldn't have gone or employees who became greedy and attempted blackmail. Pete Verrett, often called Frenchy because of his heritage, decided some of the merchants and manufacturers might make it worth his while to learn of the goods stored behind false walls in the Castle, but he made the mistake of telling his idea to Joe Owens. Thinking it no more than a joke of some kind that he didn't wish to admit he couldn't understand, Owens repeated it to Quinlan. Pat hastened to Holmes. In turn, Holmes burst into Verrett's miserable quarters and found him packing up his few possessions. He shoved the barrel of his pistol into the man's ear and gave the Frenchman a choice of having his brains scattered about the room then and there or coming along quietly. Verrett elected to let himself be prodded to the dark cellar, his eyes rolling back and forth as he frantically sought some avenue of escape. Before he could find it, his throat was slit with a straight razor. He stood for a horrified moment with his hands clasped to his throat, watching the brilliant gush of his own life squirting through his fingers. He collapsed quickly and nearly as quickly bled to death.

Mandy Strothers, a huge black woman who did the laundry for Castle tenants, chose this inappropriate day to somehow find one of the trapdoors. It was late in the evening and she decided to explore. She inadvertently triggered a panel that closed and locked behind her. At once she became lost in the progressively darker passages. She went up a few short flights of stairs and down a few flights that were longer, feeling her way with outstretched hands and teetering on the edge of panic. At last she almost fainted with relief at seeing a light ahead and Holmes busy at work in its glow and she raced toward him, wailing "Mist' Holmes! Mist' Holmes!" She stopped a few feet short when she saw, too late, that Mist' Holmes was engrossed in the dissection of one Pete Verrett. Her eyes became great bulging marbles streaked with veins and her mouth an open cavern primed to scream, but the sound never came and the eyes had seen all they would ever see. The heavy cleaver that struck the top of her head did not stop until its leading edge reached the bridge of her nose. She was so large that Holmes could not lift her alone and he had to amputate successively her legs, arms and head before finally being able to lift her barrel-sized torso to the platform in the Warner Process furnace. Holmes was clinically surprised when it took less time to reduce her remains to ash than it had with many of the thinner bodies he had cremated here and he attributed this to her abundance of more combustible fatty tissue.

Gradually the interior of the Castle was being transformed into a very adequate World's Fair hotel. Dora often asked about the progress being made in the remodeling of the Castle and, though she listened with interest to his accounts, she never seemed inclined to go see for herself. Now a very wealthy woman, due to the enormous amount of money Holmes had given her over these years, she was usually disinclined to leave her pleasant existence in Wilmette for anything. She was perfectly content to spend her days taking care of their daughter and directing the activities of the domestics she had hired to keep house and grounds spotless. She had reached the plateau she had always so ambitiously sought and was pleased with her lot. There was no longer even any problem with her brother, John, who had finally learned to bridle his tongue. The freight business they'd launched him in with two wagons had now grown to a fleet of eight vans and was called the Belknap Cartage Company. There were not so many outside customers, but the wagons were always kept very busy carting away from the Holmes Castle the excess furnishings, equipment and accessories Holmes obtained fraudulently. These items were carted to various railroad stations within a fifty-mile radius and then shipped by rail to distant points where they could be resold at discount prices by dealers who, because of the profits they were making, asked no questions regarding the origin of the goods. It was a very lucrative enterprise, with the profits split three ways between John, Dora and Holmes.

The matter with Ben Pitezel and Emeline Cigrand was a growing concern for Holmes. Pitezel was beside himself in love with her and wracked with indecision. It took all of Holmes's ingenuity to make him see the sense of being extremely discreet about seeing her, and he got Pitezel to agree only by first reminding him of what her reaction might be at learning he was not the wealthy bachelor businessman, Robert Phelps, and then by promising him gratis use of one of the most pleasant of the Castle's new guest rooms one day each week. Under this arrangement, Emeline was led to believe his work schedule was such that the set-aside day was the only day of the week he had free, at least for a while. On the morning of that day each week, Pitezel would meet her at some prearranged downtown rendezvous and they would have an enjoyable day together, culminating in a return after dark to the Castle, where they would retire to the room Holmes had provided and not emerge again until morning.

Fortunately, Emeline was not living in the Castle. Holmes had insisted she stay at a boardinghouse and she found one nearby without difficulty, at Sixty-third Court and Sherman Street, where room and board were two dollars weekly. That lasted until the owner of the place, Mrs. Louise Hunt, began to comment suspiciously, not only about Emeline's overnight absences once each week but also about the attentions being paid her by Holmes himself, who brought her flowers and took her out until very late hours at least two or three times each week. When she commented about it to Emeline and warned her that Holmes was a married man, the young woman told him about it.

Holmes was upset and at once had her move to another boardinghouse. "From now on," he told her, "I'm going to have to insist that you stay no longer than two weeks at any one place."

Emeline was flabbergasted. "For heaven's sake, Mr. Holmes, why not?"

"It's very involved, my dear," he told her, "and I really can't go into it all right now. As you continue working for me, you'll find out. You see, the business world can be very vicious and a man cannot really succeed in it without making enemies along the way—usually people who are jealous of his success. I'm afraid I have all too many enemies who would like to see me destroyed and would do anything—even make up stories about your relationship with me—if they thought it could harm me. As well it might. Therefore, I really feel it would be best if we do not fall into a pattern of movements that might simplify things for those enemies."

She smiled to disguise her confusion and nodded. "Of course, Mr. Holmes, whatever you say. But I can't imagine anyone deliberately wanting to harm as nice a gentleman as yourself."

Pitezel was not particularly pleased at Holmes's increased attentions to Emeline after working hours. He mentally gnashed his teeth when she innocently told him of Holmes's buying her flowers, candy, jewelry and other gifts, including even a bicycle so they could take evening rides together in the parks. But when Emeline told him that Holmes had promised to take her to Europe with him when next he went there to see into his foreign enterprises, his fury became vocal as he immediately confronted Holmes.

"I want to know just what the hell you're up to, Holmes. Did you think Emeline would try to keep those things from me? Dammit, man, I thought we were friends. Friends! What bullshit! Admit it—you're as much in love with her as I am and you're trying to take her away from me."

They were walking along Halsted Street, having met at the corner of Sixty-third in response to a message Pitezel had sent him. Now, having made his accusation, Pitezel stared at Holmes, prepared for his anger, but hardly for the chuckle that rumbled from the man.

"Ben," he said lightly, "you're simply not using your head. You know she's in love with you, so why would you think I could lure her away from you no matter what I did? The gifts I've given her, the time we've spent together—it's all for very good reason. The more that people believe she's going with me, the less apt they'll be to associate her with you and the less likely that Carrie'll get wind of anything between you two.

"Listen to me, Ben." Holmes abruptly became more serious. "There's a lot at stake here for me. Too damned much for me to jeopardize it in so stupid a manner. You've known me a long time. When was the last time—or the only time—you ever saw me doing something stupidly or without thought? I've counted on you for a lot in the past and I'm counting on you for even more in the future. Have you forgotten the Texas deal that's been shaping up for so long now? The one that'll probably bring in fifty thousand dollars or more for your share alone? And what about our friendship? Do you think I'm going to jeopardize that, or my share in the Williams matter by causing friction between us? Or by letting you become useless to me because of disruption in your personal life? I want you to trust me, Ben, just as I trust you.

And after the excellent job you did in Denver, there's no one I've ever trusted more." Holmes smiled as he thought of the note he'd received from Minnie sadly reporting that poor Baldwin had died in his sleep and that she and Nannie had taken their brother's body back to Fort Worth for burial.

Pitezel was mollified for the time being. "I guess you're right, Holmes," he said. "I just don't know what the hell's the matter with me lately. When I'm with Emeline, I feel like I'm in the clouds. The rest of the time I'm in a pit. And ninety-nine percent of the time I want a drink so goddamned bad that I think it would be easier to blow my own head off than go another day without having one."

"Hang on, Ben," Holmes said sympathetically, squeezing his shoulder. "I know it's tough, but I also know you can do it."

"But what am I going to do, Holmes?" There was a note of desperation in his voice. "I love Emeline so much I'm going crazy with it. But I love the kids, too, and I don't want to lose them. And now Carrie's got the new baby, Wharton, and I can't just turn my back and walk away. Jesus, what a life!"

"It'll work out, Ben," Holmes told him. "That's not much help, but believe me, it will work out. Just try to take every day as it comes. You won't always be so torn, I promise you."

They shook hands and went their separate ways, Pitezel very nearly maudlin in his appreciation at having so good a friend, Holmes considering how best to end all this nonsense without losing Ben and idly wondering if he would be able to seduce Emeline before matters came to a head and he had to kill her.

Emeline was an exceptionally good worker and very intelligent when it came to her job. That intelligence, however, failed significantly when it came to matters affecting her personal life. She did not fully understand what was going on in regard to either her having to switch lodgings so frequently or her association with Robert Phelps, but she agreed readily enough to all the suggestions Holmes made. After all, he was the man paying her salary—and a very good salary at that. Besides, she adored the attention her employer was paying to her, finding him exciting, interesting and immensely cultured. And she was certain she was going to emerge from this stage of her life not only the wife of the rich Robert Phelps, but quite wealthy in her own right thanks to the investments Henry Holmes was making for her.

She had quickly seen what an opportunity it was for her when Holmes suggested that, if she agreed to it, he would pay her room and board wherever she stayed while working for him and, instead of paying her the weekly sum he had agreed to, he would turn it over to his broker, Frank Blackman, and have him invest it for her in what Holmes termed "gilt-edged stocks having surefire futures." Against her initial better judgment, she had gambled that he knew what he was talking about and agreed on a trial basis. When, by the end of the first two months of working for him, he showed her an account book which indicated that her invested salary money had already more than doubled, she was enormously pleased. She wished she had invested her savings as wisely. As if reading her mind, he further suggested that she give him the $800 she had saved from her other employment, so he could invest that for her as well. She turned it over to him eagerly.

"First of all," Holmes said as they walked toward the Terre Haute railroad station, "I find it hard to believe you'd leave like you did without letting me know where you were going or when you'd be back."

Pitezel grimaced and his reply was mumbled. "I told Emeline I'd only be gone for a week at the most and I told her to tell you."

"It's not the same, Ben, and you know it. Besides, you didn't tell her where you were going, so how was I to know?"

There was misery in Pitezel's eyes and his response was, in its own way, an appeal for understanding. "Dammit, Holmes, can't you see I didn't want you to know? If I'd wanted you to know, I'd've told you myself. I . . . just wanted to do something on my own again."

"In view of what's happened, it wasn't the best idea you've ever had. What I'd like, Ben, is for you to explain to me why you did it." Holmes was curbing his agitation but it was nevertheless apparent. "What could have prompted you to jeopardize all our plans by pulling a fool stunt like this? If you needed more money, why didn't you just come to me?"

"Not *our* plans, Holmes. Yours. Always yours. And I did it because I'm sick and tired of you practically running my life. I can do things for myself."

"Just like you did this, right?" Holmes's sarcasm was heavy.

Pítezel's resentment faded as rapidly as it had bloomed and he let his hands fall to his sides helplessly. The pair fell silent, walking side by side with measured pace, and Holmes corked the anger surging in him, its focus not on Pitezel but on Emeline. Everything that went wrong these days seemed traceable to her and the idiotic thing about it was that she was still totally unaware of it. He'd hidden his dismay a fortnight ago when Emeline innocently said, "Robert told me to let you know he was going out of town and would be in touch as soon as he got back."

"Where?" Holmes had asked, keeping his tone casual, "and for how long?"

She hunched one shoulder, a habit of hers he found irritating. "He didn't tell me where he was going. I just assumed you'd know. He said he'd be gone for a week at most. Probably less."

That was all she could tell him and he'd learned nothing else until eight more days had passed and Carrie Pitezel showed up one morning at his Castle office. Ironically, it was Emeline who entered Holmes's inner chamber and said, "There's a Mrs. Pitezel here who wants to see you right away. She says it's important. She's carrying a baby."

Holmes felt a jab of fear but no indication of it appeared in his voice. "Show her in, please."

In the street below one of the new horse-drawn street-cars went by, its noisy bell clanging as it crossed the train tracks running parallel to Wallace Street. Emeline was hesi-tating and Holmes sighed. "Nothing you need to be con-cerned about. Her husband owes me money and she's proba-bly come to ask for another extension." He smiled wryly. "And I'll probably give it to her. But let me speak to her alone. She's poor but very proud. I don't want to embarrass her."

As soon as Emeline followed instructions and left the office, shutting the door after her, Carrie, with Wharton in her arms, had burst into tears. Amidst her sobbing, sniffing, nose-blowing and near incoherency, he'd been able to ascer-tain that Ben had been arrested in Terre Haute, charged with the very same offense he'd been in jail for when he and Holmes first met—forging checks. Holmes gave her some money and sent her home, saying he'd do what he could. A flurry of telegrams resulted in his arriving in Terre Haute yesterday and arranging for Pitezel's bail of $300.

Holmes broke their silence as they entered the station. "You realize, Ben, your leaving the state of Indiana now is a felony and I lose the three hundred dollars. They'll undoubtedly issue a warrant for your arrest. You'll probably be safe enough if you don't get picked up by the police somewhere else for something. If you ever come back to Indiana and they get their hands on you, you'll be sent away for a long time."

Pitezel stopped Holmes among the milling people, his mien contrite. "I guess I owe you an apology," he said. "It was stupid and I admit it. I'll pay you back the three hundred dollars as soon as possible. I thought I could make it. You know, come into town, write a bunch of checks and cash 'em and then get out. It was just bad luck I was caught."

"Like last time, Ben?" Holmes spoke softly, the words barely audible above the station din, his hand on Pitezel's sleeve. "Don't go getting mad on me now. Just listen. If we had talked, this wouldn't've happened. You got caught because you didn't think ahead. You got careless. It's disappointing because I thought you'd gotten over that kind of stupidity. Ben, you're the closest friend I've ever had, but I won't let that sway me anymore. This is final. If anything even remotely like this happens again—whether or not you get caught—and I find out about it, we're finished. Stick with me and we'll make a fortune together, but as I call it, not you. All I want to hear from you right now is whether you're with me or on your own."

Pitezel had started nodding before Holmes was finished speaking. "With you," he said. "I'll do what you say. From now on you're the boss, all the way."

Holmes suddenly grinned. He took Pitezel's proffered hand and the two men shook warmly, moving again toward the ticket cages. Holmes indicated a bench nearby. "Go have a seat," he said. "I'll get the tickets and be with you in a minute."

It took a little longer than that, but he soon returned with the tickets. Pitezel took the ones he was offered without even looking at them. He still felt a need to reassure Holmes that he had learned his lesson. "I meant what I said, Holmes. When we get to Chicago, I'll do just what you say and I won't do anything on my own."

"That's fine, Ben. Glad to hear it. Only you're not going

to Chicago with me right now. You're going back out to Colorado for a little while. Not Denver this time. Leadville. There's a man working out there for a company called the Arkansas Smelter Yards. It's a dangerous job, very dangerous, and this man doesn't know it yet but he's going to have a fatal accident."

Pitezel's expression tightened and he answered tiredly. "What's his name?"

"Williams. Just like the one in Denver. Isn't that a coincidence? Only this time it's a different given name. William. Better known as Billy Bob."

Pitezel stared at the tickets in his hand, as if by looking he could make them go away. When he looked up at Holmes again, his eyes were hollow. "What about Carrie . . . the kids?"

"Nothing to worry about. They'll be fine, I'll see to that. I've given her some money already and I'll give her plenty more before you get back, since you'll be gone for quite a while. This is October twenty-sixth. You'll be five or six weeks, I'd guess. That'll put you back in Chicago around the first week in December."

Pitezel was shaking his head. "I don't understand."

Holmes took an envelope from his pocket and handed it to him. "Money. All you'll need. You're going to Texas as well as Colorado. From Leadville you go to Fort Worth. Use the name Lyman. Benton T. Lyman. I want you to check the county and city records. Look up the land titles on anything held by Minnie Williams. I want accurate copies of everything you find. Everything. When you've got it all, wire me before leaving. Stay there until I wire back with instructions. Clear?"

"I guess. What . . . what about Emeline?"

"I'll take care of her," Holmes promised.

Had the two letters that arrived on November 9 not come in the same mail, Emeline Cigrand probably would not have drawn any connection between them, but the bold handwriting was so distinctive that she laid them side by side on her desk and compared them. The first, addressed to her, bore a postmark from Fort Worth, Texas, and a return address that said: *Robert E. Phelps, c/o Hotel Mariposa, Fort Worth, Texas.* The second, addressed to Henry H. Holmes and marked *Personal,* was unmistakably in the same hand as the first. The odd thing was that the name of the sender in the upper left-hand corner was shown as *Benton T. Lyman*, but without return address, yet it was postmarked in Leadville, Colorado.

She carefully slit open the envelope addressed to her and unfolded the several pages. Five once-folded twenty-dollar bills fell to the desktop. She picked them up and stared at them wonderingly. She slipped them into her pocket and returned to the letter. A warm glow suffused her as she read the pages swiftly, then went back to the beginning and read it again more slowly. The smile that had come to her face in the first reading remained implanted through the second reading and beyond. In fact, a quarter-hour later when Holmes came in, she had just finished reading the letter a third time and the smile remained, the muscles of her face aching pleasantly as a result of it, but she couldn't seem to stop.

Emeline followed Holmes into his office, carrying the day's stack of mail, but her excitement was such that even as she placed it on his desk, the words blurted from her.

"We're getting married, Mr. Holmes, Robert and I, just as soon as he gets back."

Holmes, who had just sat down, straightened in his seat and looked at her sharply. "You what?"

"We're getting married. Isn't it wonderful? Robert says he doesn't expect to be back until around the tenth or twelfth of December, but he says I should get ready because we'll be married right away when he returns. He sent me money to get my wedding dress made. He says he's going to buy me a complete new wardrobe before we go to England. That's where he says we're going on our honeymoon." Laughter rippled from her unbidden and she stifled it with an effort. "I'm sorry," she said, "but I'm just so excited I can't help it. There's so much to do to get ready! Do you suppose it would be all right if I took the rest of the day off? I mean, if nothing's really pressing? I have to get measured for my wedding dress and start getting the things packed up to send home that I won't be needing anymore. And so many other things to do."

The rage churning within Holmes was all but physical pain and it was a tribute to his self-control that he was able to mask it. He even summoned up a smile to accompany his reply. "That's wonderful news, Emeline," he said. "Of course you can have the rest of the day off. I suppose you and Philomena will go shopping together again downtown?"

"Why, no. Don't you remember? She left for home yesterday. Oh, I wish she'd been here just one more day so I could tell her about this in person. She'd've been so excited! Thank you so much. I'll be in first thing in the morning." She turned and walked to the open doorway, but paused there and turned back. "I almost forgot to tell you, Mr. Holmes, there's a personal letter for you from Robert, too." A fleeting frown crossed her features, disappearing almost as quickly as it came. "I suppose it's none of my business, but he put his name on the envelope as Benton Lyman. Why do you suppose he would do that? And it came from Colorado. I had no idea he'd even gone there. Well," the smile was back, "it's probably something he thought he had to do for business reasons and, like I said, none of my business. 'Bye."

Holmes continued staring at the door that had closed behind her. A moment later he heard the outer office door close as well. On his desktop was a heavy copper letter opener, shaped like a dagger, its blade and haft intricately engraved and the hilt knobbed with a beautifully rendered sterling silver representation of an Indian's head in full feather dress. He picked it up and then, in a burst of savagery, drove the point deep into the polished wooden surface. His face was contorted and his eyes staring, locked on the pile of correspondence Emeline had placed there. Though the windows were closed, the faint sounds of traffic filtered into the silent office from below. A short train passed on the tracks adjacent to Wallace Street, while wagon and carriage traffic rumbled and squeaked and horses whinnied. A streetcar rattled past, pausing at the grade crossing and clanging its bell impatiently to be aided across the tracks by the two large white horses kept harnessed and waiting there for just that purpose. The gravelly cries of the driver became audible as the streetcar was lurchingly pulled across the grade. Through all this Holmes sat silently, his hand still grasping the haft of the letter opener, his anger gradually dissolving as he arranged his thoughts.

He had to push and pull the letter opener several times in order to extract it from where it was embedded. The blade was bent, but he set the implement aside, uncaring. He sifted through the pile of mail and plucked out the envelope bearing the Colorado postmark, tore off one end and extracted the paper inside. There was no message, only a folded piece of newsprint. He unfolded it and read the news story that had been preserved.

SMELTER WORKER FATALLY INJURED

William Robert Williams, 20, assistant foreman of line production at the Arkansas Smelter Yards here at Leadville, died yesterday as a result of injuries suffered when he fell into an ore crusher. It was the first fatal accident at the firm in 8 years. J. H. Weddie, plant manager, was at a loss to explain how the unfortunate accident had occurred. Though no one witnessed the incident, Williams, known as Billy Bob to fellow workers, had been inspecting the ore crushing operation and evidently slipped on loose gravel and plunged into the machinery. His body was discovered when the machinery was stopped and inspected after blood was observed seeping from the hopper. There was no evidence of foul play.

Williams, a native of Fort Worth, Texas, had been working for the firm since his graduation from high school and was well liked and considered by officials and fellow workers to be a young man with great promise. It is said that he was soon to be promoted to line foreman. Plant officials stated that the young man's older sisters, Minnie and Nannie Williams, who live in Texas, were notified of the tragedy and have wired in return that they are coming to Leadville to identify the body and return it to Fort Worth for burial. J. M. Maxwell, local attorney, has been appointed administrator of young Mr. Williams's estate and will meet with the sisters when they arrive later today. A brief memorial service will be held at Hillside Chapel tomorrow at 10 A.M.

Emeline went from the Holmes Castle directly to her latest boardinghouse, Mrs. Marietta Knight's place a couple of blocks away at 620 Sixty-second Street. She babbled cheerfully to Mrs. Knight and several of the boarders there about her forthcoming marriage and the need to pack up her things. Then, excusing herself, she retired to her room and began sorting things, putting aside the objects and items of clothing she intended to discard. She came across a framed photograph of her sister and, grinning, hugged it to her breast.

"I wish you were still here, Phil," she murmured. "Why is it we're always apart when something special happens?" She thought fondly of her sister, remembering with pleasure the ten-day visit just concluded. It was the first time they'd seen one another in months and they had immensely enjoyed being together again. Twice Emeline had brought her sister to the Castle and both times they had chatted at length with Holmes, who had suggested Emeline take a full day off to spend with her sister. She had thanked Holmes profusely and the very next day she and Philomena had gone downtown. They spent a wonderful day shopping and having lunch at the place Holmes had first taken her, Henrici's. It was there, over marvelously aromatic coffee, that Emeline finally told her about the wealthy Robert Phelps, bubbling on at great length about him, telling her how they had met at the Keeley Institute and how he had gotten her the job with Mr. Holmes. She was sorry that he was out of town and her sister couldn't meet him.

"Are you getting serious about him, Em?"

Emeline hesitated and then nodded. "I'm going to marry him."

"He's asked you?" Philomena, surprised, had paused with a bite of chocolate eclair poised on her fork. "Em, that's fantastic news! Why didn't you tell me right away?"

Emeline shook her head. "Actually, we've been keeping it a secret from everybody because we haven't been able to set a date yet. He thinks maybe when he gets back from this trip we can make definite plans. I'm hoping things work out so we can come to Lafayette and get married at home."

"And I can be maid of honor?" Philomena's eyes were dancing.

"Of course, silly! Why do you think I'm telling you? But you've got to keep it secret until we set the date. Robert insists on that."

Philomena tossed her head. "Well, I don't see why. How come you haven't pinned him down for a definite date?"

"Phil, he's a businessman. He has things to take care of before he takes a step like that. Give the man a chance. After all, I've only known him since January and he travels so much for Mr. Holmes that we really haven't seen all that much of one another."

"I don't like that man," Philomena said. She put the bite in her mouth and lowered her eyes as she chewed.

"Phil!" Emeline gasped. "How can you say such a thing? You haven't even met him."

"I'm not talking about Robert." She lifted her eyes and met her sister's gaze. "I'm talking about your boss, Mr. Holmes. I don't like him."

"For heaven's sake, why in the world not? You only just met him and he's been nice as apple pie to you. Why would you say such a thing as that?"

"It's a feeling, Em. I can't put my finger on it, but there's something bad there, something wrong. Something in his eyes that makes me think he's not honest. I feel like there's trouble ahead for you because of him."

"Philomena! That's unfair. It's an awful thing to say. And it certainly indicates you don't trust my good judgment. Do you think I'd stay working for him for one moment if I didn't think everything was right and honest?"

Despite that protest, Emeline's own doubts about him had been growing. She was keenly aware of the lawsuits constantly being filed against the Campbell-Yates Company and the lesser number being filed against Holmes in particular. She had questioned him and he had laughed them off as merely one of the occupational hazards of being in business and directed her to relay the papers to his attorney, Mr. Plummer, but she had wondered about it then. And she wondered about it even more later on, in view of Philomena's premonition.

Now, sitting in her room thinking of that lunch, she found her happy mood beginning to fade and couldn't understand why. "I think I've got to get out of here and do something else," she muttered. She shrugged into her coat and left the room hurriedly, pausing downstairs only long enough to ask Mrs. Knight if she knew of a good dressmaker anywhere nearby.

"Mrs. Bailey," the woman said promptly. "She's the best. Everybody goes to her. She's so busy she's got three seamstresses working for her now, so I'm told."

"Where do I find her?"

"In the sixty-four-hundred block of Honore. You'll see her sign out front."

Emeline took the streetcar on Sixty-third west to Honore and then walked south. In just over a block she found a house numbered 6412 with a small sign saying *Dressmaking* attached to the porch rail. The exterior of the place was nicely kept up, which pleased her. She climbed the steps and turned the bell knob, hearing the loud dinging it made inside. The door was opened by an extraordinarily thin redheaded woman of about forty who greeted her, introduced herself as Mrs. Bailey and invited her inside. It was a residence whose front rooms downstairs had been turned into a shop. Bolts of material were stacked on a table against one wall. Four women, rather than the three Mrs. Knight had indicated, were asynchronously busy at foot treadle sewing machines.

"How long would it take to have a wedding dress made?" Emeline raised her voice above the clatter of the machines. "I mean," she added, "if it were needed quickly."

Mrs. Bailey cocked an eyebrow. "My girls are busy, but I suppose I could get Mrs. Augustine to fit it in as soon as she finishes what she's doing." A middle-aged mousy-appearing woman behind one of the machines looked up at mention of her name and smiled briefly, then returned to her work as Mrs. Bailey continued. "A formal wedding? Church?"

"No. No, I don't think so. Probably in my parents' house in Lafayette, Indiana, but I'm not sure yet."

"Floor length, then. All right, I'd say four days. It's for you?"

"Yes. My fiancé, Mr. Phelps, he sent the money and told me to order one made for when he gets back from . . ." She paused, realizing she was talking too much. "Yes," she repeated, nodding, "for me."

"White satin and lace?"

Emeline hesitated and then shook her head. She felt her cheeks growing hot and was angry at herself. "No." She stepped to the fabric table and touched a bolt of satin. "This grayish-yellow color would be perfect."

"I see." Mrs. Bailey sniffed and became more brisk. "That's ecru. I would say full sleeved and with padded buttons and loops close together down the full front, with an ivory lace-edged jabot. Perhaps an under-the-chin lace collar."

"That sounds wonderful, Mrs. Bailey. How much will it cost?"

"Thirty-eight fifty. And you'd better make that five days. Now let's get your measurements."

The fifth day of December was dismally gray in portent of the bitter season presently stalking Chicago. Holmes sat behind his desk waiting. He glanced at the clock and saw it was still twenty minutes before she was due to arrive. And she would be here right on time, he knew. Emeline Cigrand was always on time.

He looked down at the partially opened center desk drawer. The three letters were there, as yet unfolded, dated for tomorrow and ready to be mailed first thing in the morning. He was no typewriter and it had taken him the better part of this past week to carefully compose them. They were typed on the Campbell-Yates letterhead in just the way Emeline usually typed her letters and it hadn't even been necessary for him to forge her signature, since more often than not she merely typed her name at the bottom. One was to Emeline's parents and sister in Lafayette; another to Mary Thomas, who was a close friend of hers at the Keeley Institute, with whom she'd kept in touch; the third to her cousin, Philip Cigrand, a dentist on Chicago's North Side, whom she'd been helping lately in his attempts to trace their family's genealogy. These were the only three who required an explanation of any kind. The rest of those whose names he had found in her address book, as well as the few friends she'd made here—such as Dr. Lawrence and his wife, who lived downstairs—would learn about it in another way.

He reached out and took an apple from among the several in the small wicker basket on one side of his desk and bit into it. Juice squirted and he wiped up the droplets on the desktop as he chewed. His hand ran across the deep gouge made by the letter opener in the center of the polished wooden surface and he grunted faintly, disturbed that he had lost his temper to such extent. There were few times in his life that he'd ever lost control that way and it bothered him, indicating weakness, lack of self-possession. That wouldn't have happened a year or so ago, he thought. What's the matter with me? He quickly moved away from the thought, as if afraid to linger for fear of what he might discover in that

direction, considering instead one other letter in the drawer—
the one he'd received from Ben yesterday. Holmes had
earlier written to Pitezel at the Mariposa in Fort Worth,
ordering him to stay in Texas for at least another month and
promising to join him there immediately after Christmas, but
he'd been sure Ben would object. He was correct. The letter
he'd received was a single page, filed with cramped pencilings—
polite, respectful, indiscreetly direct:

DEAR HOLMES:

> The matter about WRW was taken care of with-
out difficulty, as you saw from the clipping I sent
you from L. The big surprise was the money he had
hidden in a box in his room. He must never have
spent anything he earned. I have it and will need it
for what is ahead. Since getting here I have got
almost everything you asked for about Minnie Williams
real estate holdings and they are substantial. Well
over $150,000, half more than you thought. A few
odds and ends to clear up and the job is done. Now
Holmes I dont want to upset you. I know well
enough of all you done for me and what I promised
in Terre Haute. But I have thought about it all and
just cant see how I can do what you asked in your
letter. You cant really be serious about wanting me
to stay here in FW another month. Surely Emeline
told you about my letter to her? She still thinks I am
Robert Phelps and rich and manage ABC Co. and
I'll keep it that way, as I know you would want. But
I am going to marry her under the Phelps name and
go away with her. It is my chance to start a new life
and I am going to take it. Later on maybe I will tell
her some about me but I wont drag you into it. I
dont know yet what I will do about Carrie and the
children. We been married a long time and I cant
just leave her without nothing and five mouths to
feed so I will send her some of this WRW money and
more whenever I can. I will miss the kids and even
her some ways but I got to do this thing with
Emeline. I will be back on December 12 to give you
the papers I copied here. Then I will take Emeline
and go to England and I dont guess we will ever
come back. I hope you can understand and not be

*very mad at me as I would not be very mad at you if
our places were changed around. I will always think
of you as my friend and hope I am yours.*

BENJ. PITEZEL

Holmes smiled reflectively. Poor Ben, thinking all he
had to do was write a letter in order to start a new life by
running off with Emeline. The smile became rueful as Holmes
remembered only too well his own error last week. He could
easily have raped Emeline then instead of attempting peaceful seduction, but he'd been reasonably sure he would be
able to overcome her expected resistance. Was it perhaps
another sign that he was slipping, to have so badly misinter-
preted her admiration for him that she had so often expressed?
Instead of soon surrendering herself to his advances, she'd
been shocked and upset. She had jerked herself away from
him with an expression of utter loathing and a barrage of
condemnation that made it quite clear she wanted no part of
sexual intimacy with him ever and that she intended telling
Robert Phelps how she'd been so despicably insulted. She
had resigned instantly and demanded the money he owed
her—not only all the $700 in back wages he was supposed to
have invested for her, but the $800 savings she had initially
given him. When he hesitated, she had threatened him with
arrest if he did not give it to her at once. He'd feigned
concern and told her he had no intention of keeping it, but
that it would take him a while to have his broker, Frank
Blackman, make the proper transactions to free the cash.
That was when he had told her to come back today, at 10
A.M., and he would have the full amount ready for her. She
had reluctantly agreed and since then he'd been perfecting
his plan. The letter he'd received from Pitezel had unexpectedly
simplified matters.

Mere seconds after the wall clock bonged the hour, a
discreet knocking came on the inner office door. Holmes slid
the center drawer closed but remained seated. "Come in,
Emeline," he called.

She entered hesitantly and stood fearfully near the open
door, obviously ready to dart away if he started to get
up. Beyond her, the door to the outer office was open
as well. She was taking no chances. Her features were

drawn and she looked as if she had had a difficult week. She spoke without greeting, coldly. "You have my money, Mr. Holmes?"

"I have," he told her. He smiled crookedly. "First, I want to apologize for what happened last week. I was only—"

"I really don't care to hear it, Mr. Holmes," she said. "Nothing you could say at this point would make any difference at all. If you'll just give me my money, I'll be on my way."

"I'd like you to write a letter before you go, Emeline. It's—"

"I don't believe you're actually saying that," she interrupted a second time. "I don't work for you anymore, Mr. Holmes. Why on earth would you think I would write a letter for you? Please," her voice became even icier, "just give me my money."

"I want you to write a letter to your fiancé before you leave," he said, ignoring her demand.

"To Robert? Whyever would I do that now?"

"Because I want you to explain to him that it was your own decision to leave, so I won't have to put up with his chasing after you to Lafayette or Dwight or wherever it is you're planning to go."

She was clearly confused. "He won't have to chase *after* me, Mr. Holmes. He's going *with* me. Have you forgotten we're getting married as soon as he gets back?"

"I rather doubt that, Emeline." He opened the desk drawer and extracted the letter from Pitezel. He removed it from the envelope, unfolded it and leaned forward, placing it on the desk corner nearest her. He then hitched his chair back a few feet, out of reach. He indicated the missive with repeated jabs of an index finger. "I received that the other day from him. Since it concerns you, I think you'd better read it."

Her fear became more clearly pronounced at having to come any closer to Holmes, but curiosity prevailed. Watching him closely, she moved toward the desk and stopped far enough away that she had to stretch out her hand to take it. She moved back to the doorway with it and stopped there, facing him. The handwriting was immediately recognizable as Robert's but her eyes widened as they flicked down to the signature.

"Benjamin Pitezel?" Her brow furrowed. "Why does he sign it like that?"

"Because there is no Robert Phelps, Emeline." The words were harsh, grating. "No Phelps, no Benton Lyman. Only Ben Pitezel. Read it. *Read it!*"

She read and her features froze in an expression of disbelief. When she finished, the page slipped from her hand and fluttered to the floor. Her words were barely audible. "Just give me my money and I'll leave."

Holmes shook his head. "Write the letter first. I don't intend to be in the middle here. Just tell him whatever you want to say. Then you'll get your money. And don't type it. It has to be in your own hand so he has no doubt it is from you."

As if in a daze, Emeline moved to her own desk in the outer office and sat down. She buried her face in her hands and her shoulders shook, but there was no sound. After a few minutes she straightened determinedly and wiped her eyes with the back of one hand. She took a sheet of the company letterhead from the drawer and for several minutes the only sounds were the ticking of the clock and furious scratching of her pen. She paused once to wipe her eyes again, then completed the letter, blotted it, folded the page in thirds and slid it into an envelope. She scribbled a name across the face of the envelope and left it on her desk, then returned to the doorway. Holmes regarded her calmly, appearing not to have moved.

"All right," he said, dipping his head toward the vault, its thick door half open, "your money's in the safe in a brown package. Third shelf. On the left. Your name's on it."

Emeline strode to the vault and walked inside. Immediately he leaped from his chair. She heard him coming and turned, shrinking away, half crouching with her back to the inner door, hands raised and fingers curled into claws to protect herself.

"Keep away!" she cried. "Don't you dare touch me. I'll scream!"

He had not intention of touching her. He struck the massive door in full stride and thrust against it mightily. Before she could grasp the significance of what was occurring, the door had swung shut with a deep thud and he spun the latch wheel.

Only then did the screams erupt, but they were barely audible.

Holmes paid no attention. He went to the outer office and picked up the envelope from Emeline's desk. On the face was written *Mr. Pitezel*. He turned it over and was pleased to find it unsealed. The letter was brief and he was grinning when he finished reading it and slid it into the inside breast pocket of his suitcoat. He closed and locked the inner office door, then stepped out into the hall and locked the outer door as well.

In a moment he emerged from the Castle and crossed the busy intersection. Two doors from the corner, at 706 Sixty-third Street, he entered the South Side Printing House. Its owner, John Honeycutt, was an affable, angular Tennesseean who had recently left employment as printer and pressman with Rand & McNally in downtown Chicago to open his own shop. Honeycutt listened carefully and jotted down a few things.

A few minutes later Holmes emerged from the shop with jaunty step, whistling a snatch of "La donna è mobile" from Verdi's *Rigoletto*.

Henry H. Holmes sat in the deep leather chair beside his handsome polished ebony desk. Earlier, the faint sounds of carolers had filtered into the elegantly furnished study when Dora, with Lucy in her arms, had opened the front door to listen and thank the Wilmette singers and wish them well. But that was hours ago and now the house was pleasantly quiet, the only sound an occasional popping from the fireplace. He had made a special effort to make this Lucy's day, and an exceptionally busy day it had been for the three-year-old, beginning with the early morning discovery of a multitude of presents under the tree. Lucy's excited opening of them was followed by a long period of helping Daddy play with her new toys. And at intervals throughout the day— before and after the traditional feast of roast goose and candied yams, plum pudding and hot mince pie—they had gorged themselves on prodigious amounts of fruitcake and Christmas cookies and peppermint candy canes. The little girl had finally fallen asleep several hours ago on the warm carpeting between fireplace and beautifully ornamented and tinseled Christmas tree. She had been put to bed by Dora and then it had become a different sort of Christmas celebration. Holmes drew the draperies and then he and Dora had cuddled together on the sofa, sipping brandy and occasionally conversing, but most of all merely watching the gradual diminishing of the flames licking over the Yule logs.

They had waited until this time, when they were alone, to exchange gifts. With girlish excitement she accepted and opened the oblong red velvet box and was stunned at the incredible beauty of the necklace. From an intricately linked solid gold chain depended a solitary pear-shaped diamond of at least nine carats, set in the center of a lacy gold filigree which was itself aglitter with a sprinkling of over two dozen matched diamonds, of one carat each. He had bought it at Tiffany's during his quick trip to New York to see Chester Fish and, though he did not tell her, it had cost $72,000, which he had paid in cash.

In turn, Dora had given him a new gold watch, very large and heavy, with exquisite engraving covering both lids. It opened into three compartments; one which exposed wonderfully crafted jeweled workings; another which showed the face of the watch—pure ivory beneath heavy polished crystal, the hands of gleaming gold, the hour numerals indicated by brilliant diamonds except for the hours of 3, 6, 9 and 12, which were rubies; the third compartment bearing a photograph of Dora and Lucy and a flowing engraved inscription: *To our Beloved Husband and Father, Henry H. Holmes, with all Our Love. Dora and Lucy. Christmas—1892.*

They undressed one another and made love on the floor before the fireplace. Later on he had carried her upstairs and placed her on the bed, smiling at her drowsily murmured endearments and staying with her until she had fallen deeply asleep. He covered her gently and returned downstairs. In the study, he poured himself three fingers of Napoleon brandy from a cut-crystal decanter and sank into the comfort of the leather chair, bathed in the soft yellow glow of his desk lamp.

He thought of the lovemaking with Dora and smiled, the image of her face filling his mind's eye, but then altering, melding, shifting, changing to that of the younger and far more delicate features of Emeline Cigrand. As he had known he eventually would, he had finally made love to her, too. There, on the floor of the vault in the office, when at last he returned on that fatal day, he had disrobed both her and himself, fondled and nibbled the cool, firm breasts and pushed open her eyelids so the blue-green eyes, now glazed and unseeing, could stare into his own. He lay atop the unresisting form and thrust himself into her deeply, climaxing several times before ending his obsessive necrophilic interlude.

He had not slept at all that night, those hours spent locked in the hidden laboratory of the cellar as he engaged in the most carefully precise and loving dissection he had ever performed. There was unparalleled satisfaction in meticulously parting the tissues of so perfect a specimen, of realizing that probably never again would a cadaver so flawless be subject to his skill with a scalpel. Before dawn the fleshy portions had all been stacked in neat array upon the platform of the Warner Process furnace and the pressurized gas fumes ignited to reduce the remains to gray ash. The disjointed skeletal remains were carefully, lovingly, lowered piece by piece into a barrel three-quarters filled with a special caustic solution of his own concoction. In three days no trace remained of any fleshy tissue or ligature as he fished out the bones and washed away all residue of the highly corrosive liquid. He dried them with care on a broad tray in the carefully modu-lated oven and then came the most gratifying time of all—the articulating of these perfect, nearly milk-white bones into the most magnificent skeleton he had ever seen. He was sorely tempted to keep it himself, but common sense ultimately prevailed and so he packed it neatly into a long, narrow, sturdy wooden crate lined with soft cloth and filled with spirals of wood shavings to act as protection against possible rough handling. And, reluctantly, finally shipped this *magnum opus* on December 10 as a Christmas gift to Dr. Chester E. Fish in New York City, labeling the crate: *UPRIGHT LONG-BASE CLOCK. FRAGILE. THIS END UP. HANDLE WITH GREAT CARE.*

Two days later, as the letter had promised he would, Ben Pitezel had returned and stormed into Holmes's office, livid with barely constrained rage.

"God damn you, Holmes, where is she? Where's Emeline?"

Holmes was well prepared. He withdrew an envelope from his desk drawer and extended it to his friend. "She wrote this for you. Sit down and read it and then we'll talk. *I said sit down!*"

So rarely had Holmes ever spoken this commandingly to him that Pitezel, for all his fury, was taken aback. He took the envelope and sat down as Holmes directed before looking at it. When he saw to whom it was addressed in Emeline's unmistakable hand, his anger drained away as if a plug had been pulled, leaving him ashen and trembling. He opened the envelope and quickly read the single page:

MR. PITEZEL:

You lied to me, from the very beginning. I loved you but our whole relationship, based on your lies, was a farce, wasn't it? You are married and have five children. How despicable you are! I wish never ever to see you again. Do not follow me or bother me or I will go to the police. I may go see your wife, too. I feel sorry for her. How could you do this to her? How could you do this to me when I loved you so much?

EMELINE

"How . . ." Pitezel's words were anguished. ". . . how did she find out?"

"I have no idea, Ben," Holmes lied. "She just burst in here and made her accusations about you, about me and about us."

"Us?"

Holmes nodded. "We let her get too close to us, Ben. She put things together. Went through papers and records and put things together." His voice, at first sympathetic, became hard. "She found out you were wanted for murder in Colorado. She found out about Minnie Williams and her brothers. She mentioned insurance swindles. God knows what else she found out."

Pitezel groaned and there was panic in his voice when he spoke again. "Christ, Holmes, what're we going to do? She threatened to go to Carrie. Hell, she might even go to the police. We've got to do something!"

"Those were my reactions precisely. Obviously, she'd gathered enough evidence to send us both to jail for a long time. If not to the gallows."

"But where did she go?" Pitezel persisted. "We've got to stop her."

"I did. You don't have to worry about it, Ben. I killed her."

Pitezel's eyes widened and his mouth worked soundlessly. Holmes anticipated what he was trying to get out. "No, she won't be found. There's no chance of that. And I've taken care of everything else. So far as anyone is concerned who might ask, she got married to a man named Robert Phelps and they went to Europe together. Permanently. That's all we know."

Holmes stood up and came around his desk to place a hand on Ben's shoulder. He was sympathetic. "It's all over, Ben. Nothing to worry about. But it was a good object lesson for us both. We've got to be damned careful from here on out. Go home now. Go see Carrie and the kids. Take it easy for a few days and then come back and see me and we'll decide where we go from here. We're on the verge of making a small fortune in property from the Williams thing. Let's not ruin it now."

Pitezel came dazedly to his feet and Holmes walked to the door with him. They shook hands warmly and Pitezel left. He went home to Carrie and the children, but not right away. First he stopped off at a tavern.

Holmes, remembering all this, chuckled and sipped at his brandy. It had been the biggest hurdle to overcome and it had gone very smoothly. The rest had been simplicity itself. The closest people to Emeline here had been Dr. and Mrs. Lawrence. In a few days they had stopped Holmes in the corridor and asked where Emeline was.

"We're very worried about her," Mrs. Lawrence said. "She used to come to our rooms several times a day to sit and chat and have coffee with us. Now she's disappeared and no one seems to know where she's gone."

Holmes looked abashed. "Forgive me," he said. "It's my fault you've been worried. I've been rather caught up in my own end-of-the-year business matters and I'm sure you know how bothersome and time-consuming that can be. Then, too, since you were rather friendly with Emeline, I just assumed you would have known." He reached into an inside pocket and took out an envelope. "You remember Robert Phelps, of course."

Dr. Lawrence shook his head. "We never met him. We heard her talk about him a lot and were looking forward to meeting him, but never did."

"What a shame. I thought you had. Nice chap. A traveling man. Seems he had a wonderful career opportunity come up in Europe and had to go there immediately. A time element involved in his accepting or rejecting the offer. He didn't know how long he'd be gone, so he and Emeline decided to get married immediately and go together. They said they might be back in a few months, but I really rather doubt it. Everything was in a rush and she gave me this to give to you."

Mrs. Lawrence took two cards out of the envelope. They were simple in the extreme, printed on a cheap and very plain heavy white stock in ordinary type rather than engraved:

****

```
*            ROBERT E. PHELPS              *

*         MISS EMELINE G. CIGRAND          *

*                MARRIED                   *

*         WEDNESDAY, DEC. 7, 1892          *

*                CHICAGO                   *
```

****

The second was plain white, the size of a business card, centered on which were the words:

MR. AND MRS. ROBERT E. PHELPS

Mrs. Lawrence looked at the envelope again. "It isn't even addressed to us," she lamented. "Nor does it give an address where we can write to them."

"I expect they didn't really know yet. I'm sure as soon as they get settled wherever it is they'll be, you'll hear from them."

The Lawrences went away, disturbed at the fact that Emeline was gone, but their early concerns over her "disappearance" were eased. Holmes gave the same cards to everyone in the vicinity who had known her. He also mailed copies to every person listed in her address book.

Before the problem erupted, Holmes knew, Emeline had sent home to Lafayette her trunk containing almost all of her personal items and clothes, saying in the brief note that accompanied them that she was soon to marry Robert Phelps and that he was buying her all new clothes, so Philomena was welcome to those she was sending home. The typewritten letter Holmes had sent to them, allegedly from her, along with the two cards, contained essentially the same explanation, saying she was married to Robert Phelps and going to Europe to live and hinting that she had begun to learn that her new husband was a drunk, a gambler and rather a bad man and they were already beginning to have some problems.

Holmes finished off the residue of his brandy and moved to the chair at his desk. A letter was there from Minnie Williams, detailing the sad fact of her brother, Billy Bob, having been killed in an accident in Leadville. She said she and Nannie had gone there and identified the body and brought it back to Fort Worth, where it was buried beside Baldwin. They knew he had saved all his money, she said, but it was not found and they suspected he had buried it somewhere and the secret of its location had died with him. She ended on an upnote:

> *Now for the good news, Harry. Feeling the way we do about one another, it's just ridiculous for us to always be so far apart. Until now I've always more or less put you off on your proposal of marriage, but now I see how foolish that has been. I want to be with you more than anything else, so I am making plans to come to Chicago within the next few weeks so we can be married and really begin our lives together. I do love you so much, dear man.*
>
> YOUR OWN MINNIE

Holmes smiled. It was working out perfectly. He'd shown the letter to Dora and she'd been happy too, commenting that it was about time, since this was probably the most involved and lengthy project he had ever set up.

"And," he had pointed out to her, "potentially the most profitable."

"Why else," she replied, "do you think I'd hold still for the absence from home your marriage to her is going to entail? I just hope you'll get the whole matter concluded rapidly."

"Oh, I will," Holmes had assured her. "As rapidly as possible."

If there was one thing Henry H. Holmes was particular about, it was making sure all loose ends were tied up. The

only other matter requiring such attention now, at the close of
1892, was a follow-up on the Julia Conner matter of a year
ago. There was not only the possibility an investigation might
yet be begun into her disappearance, but he still held the
insurance policy on her life and Pearl's. There had been no
possibility of collecting immediately after their deaths, since
there were no bodies to prove death. Earlier this month he
had written to the insurance company and asked if he were
required to continue paying on the policies, since the two
had disappeared a year ago and people were beginning to
wonder if they were dead. The insurance company had
replied that he could cease making payments but that the
policy could not be paid until the prescribed passage of time
had occurred for the two to be declared legally dead by the
courts.

Shortly before that Holmes had written to Julia's parents, Mr. and Mrs. Andrew Smythe of Davenport, Iowa.
Holmes had complimented himself on having composed a
very clever first letter on the Campbell-Yates stationery:

DEAR MR. AND MRS. SMYTHE:
   *Will you kindly communicate with Mrs. Conner
and say to her for me that it is absolutely necessary
for us to hear from her with regard to the suit in
which she is interested as a witness. She need have
no fear in communicating with us either directly or
indirectly on Mr. Conner's account. And if it is that
she does not desire to come here, we want arrangements made for having her deposition taken wherever she resides. Furthermore, if she does not wish to
make known her place of residence, money will be
furnished her to go to some other place than where
she resides for the taking of this deposition. There
are at least two thousand dollars ($2,000) depending
on her testimony, and it will be very much to her
interest to take a part in this. Kindly let me hear
from you as soon as possible in regard to this matter.*
                         MOST RESPECTFULLY,
                         H. H. HOLMES
                         701-03 SIXTY-THIRD STREET

P.S. I wish personally to have you make known to

Mrs. Conner that although she may have thought my sympathies favored Mr. Conner, from the fact that I remained wholly neutral in their difficulties, I never had, and certainly do not at this time have, any feeling contrary to her interest, and both herself and child are entitled to and will always receive my sympathies and protections. HHH

A reply had come from Julia's mother immediately—the letter in a pained hand now on the desk before Holmes and he read it again:

Davenport, Iowa
December 22, 1892

MR. H. H. HOLMES:

Yours of December 20 to hand and contents carefully noted, and it astonishes us very much that you wrote to us making inquiry about our daughter, Julia L. Conner. We thought you knew all about her whereabouts and were now thinking of writing to you to know where she was. We have never heard from her since last December. She then wrote us she was going away from Englewood on account of Conner making threats that he would take his child away. He said he would take her (Pearl) by fair means or foul means. Mr. Holmes, we were in hopes all the time that you were in communication with her, and if anything was wrong we would hear from her through you. By your letter we are thoroughly astonished, as we know nothing of her whereabouts. We know not that she is dead or alive. Your letter makes us very unhappy. Mr. Holmes, if you should hear anything of her, please let us know and relieve this present unhappiness of an old father and mother.

RESPECTFULLY,
(MRS.) A. SMYTHE

Holmes laughed aloud at this, remembering the typewritten letter he had forged in Julia's style of writing and sent to her parents a few days after he had killed her. It had obviously been accepted without question as having come from her and had had precisely the effect he had planned.
Holmes slid the letter aside on the polished surface and

opened the upper right drawer. He took out a fresh sheet of Campbell-Yates letterhead and wrote a reply with swift sure hand:

Dec. 25, 1892

Mrs. A. Smythe
Davenport, Iowa

Dear Madam:
Your letter dated Dec. 22 in answer to my recent communication to you was received yesterday and I hardly know how to answer it. We have felt sure that you knew where Mrs. Conner was and that she was displeased with us on account of our taking a neutral stand in her difficulty with her husband. If you do not know where she is (and your letter convinces me that you do not), we are certainly worried in regard to her welfare. Two letters were received from her after she left Chicago and both dated St. Louis. She told me the day she went away, as well as Mr. Belknap, an old man with whom she was very well acquainted, that she was going to St. Louis to remain with an aunt, or at least a relative, and she left here with the understanding that she should communicate with us at any time relative to certain low matters in which she was a witness. She was given to understand that she would be paid for her trouble, and if she was compelled to come here, her expenses would be met. There were some debts which she was owing and unable to meet, but these need not have caused her to stay away, much less kept her from communicating with either you or ourselves.

Very truly yours,
H. H. Holmes

Holmes blotted the ink and leaned back in his chair with a smug expression. The ball he had started rolling was picking up momentum. It had a long way to roll, of course, but Holmes was a very patient man.

The accommodations Holmes had gotten for them at Chicago's Plaza Hotel across from Lincoln Park were the best

available and Minnie could not have been more pleased.
With one exception they had hardly shown their faces outside
the rooms for the past forty-eight hours; nor had they done
much sleeping. Even their meals had been brought to them
on wheeled carts. The single exception to the isolation was
when they had strolled through the park for an hour yesterday, reveling in the unseasonable warmth of this March,
delighting in the scores of crocuses with swollen heads that
had poked into view and promised to punctuate the winter-
weary ground with exclamations of yellow and lavender and
white.

"You're sure you don't want to take a walk downtown
with me, Minnie?" he said, shrugging into his overcoat.
"Looks like it's going to be as nice a day as yesterday was. We
could have lunch out for a change."

She looked up from her writing and smiled. Her sleek
dressing gown of pale blue silk with alençon lace at the
cuffs and collar could not quite hide the chunkiness of her
frame. Her eyes were filled with love for him, but she
shook her head and the smile became mischievous. "You
look as if you could stand a reprieve. And after two full
days of your attentions, I *know* I could. You're such a
wild man!" She giggled and reached out to grip his sleeve
and pull him close for a hug. "Oh, I do love you so
much!"

"And I love you, too, Minnie." He leaned over to kiss the
top of her head, the tight curls cushioning his face in a
springy mat. "What I can't understand is why we didn't do
this a long time ago."

"I've been wondering that myself. Doesn't seem to make
much sense now, does it?" She pulled free of him. "Go on,
get out of here or first thing you know the reprieve will be
revoked. Take your time. I'm writing to Nannie and I've got
an awful lot to tell her, as you might surmise."

He grinned and squeezed her shoulder and strode to the
door. Halfway out he stopped and looked back. "Don't forget
to tell her what I suggested," he said.

She nodded and he winked at her and shut the door, his
cheeks puffing out in a silent exhalation. He needed the
reprieve far more than she knew. He felt unsteady, dissociat-
ed and sometimes confused. He was finally at a plateau with
Minnie it had taken some two and a half years to reach, with
the corpses of Uncle Calvin and brothers Billy Bob and

Baldwin in his wake and now, at times, it was as if he didn't know *why* he was at this point, or why he was continuing to drag out the complex scheme. He shrugged the disconcerting thoughts away and his pace became brisk now as he walked downtown. Occasionally he tipped his derby to fashionably dressed ladies who passed. Though he had no real destination, there was no air of insouciance about him, rather a sense of frustrated restraint. So many projects were looming, so many things to be done and yet, for the time being, all attention had to be centered on this present complicated project involving Minnie. The sidewalks were crowded downtown and the late morning air filled with the continuous din of traffic. He paused to watch two city employees with shovels and a two-wheeled barrel as they moved in desultory manner from pile to pile of horse manure, scooping it up and tossing it into the barrel. "There's something to be said for the simple life," he murmured, then chuckled, "but I've never been able to figure out exactly what."

His pace slowed and he glanced in the windows of the various stores as he passed. He stopped for a cup of coffee in a tea room but drank only half before pushing it aside and resuming his aimless meandering along State Street. As he passed the store of Siegel, Cooper & Company, he suddenly entered on an impulse. The store was crowded with shoppers and he felt more relaxed becoming part of the anonymity of the crowd, but it didn't last. At a leathergoods counter he jolted to a stop, taken by the appearance of the clerk—a petite blond young woman with ready smile and pleasantly efficient manner in serving customers. As yet unseen, he watched her for a short distance, increasingly impressed, though not really certain why. She was not particularly pretty, her face a bit too long and angular, her eyes somewhat oversized and her nose slightly beaked, yet there was about her an aspect he found uncommonly compelling. Perhaps it was the ready smile that fetchingly played at her lips, or maybe it was the pert manner in which she tossed her head. More likely it was a combination of these things in just the correct proportions to make her immensely appealing to him. He was at once determined to meet her and considered several approaches before finally deciding on the most direct.

"Good morning," he said, stopping before her.

"Good morning, sir." She smiled brightly, liking the

appearance of this good-looking man in expensive clothing. "May I help you?"

"Indeed. You can agree to take lunch with me."

"I beg your pardon?"

"The dining room in the Palmer House is exceptionally nice. Or Henrici's, if you prefer."

She was flustered. "But I don't know you, sir."

"Aha! We will remove that obstacle at once. Allow me to introduce myself." He swept off his hat and bowed and she stifled her smile as other customers passed with amused expressions. "My name is Henry Mansfield Howard. I'm very wealthy and I usually get my way."

"More often than not, I should judge," she replied. "You're very forward."

"Not always a fault," he said quickly. "Quite often I've found it simplifies things. As now. I have a ready rebuttal prepared for any excuse you might offer for not accepting my invitation and since I refuse to take no for an answer, we can greatly conserve on time and energy by your giving me a simple yes."

"Yes, Mr. Howard."

Now it was his turn to be momentarily taken aback and then he burst into laughter. "When does your lunch hour begin, Miss . . . ?"

"Yoke. Georgiana Yoke." She glanced at a clock on one of the massive square pillars. "As a matter of fact, it's time now. And since the Palmer House is closer, let's go there." She turned away to tell another saleswoman at the end of the long counter that she was leaving, glad the man could not detect how her heart was hammering and how nervous she was. Her own reply had stunned her.

They learned much about one another as they dined on baked onion soup and salmon hollandaise. She was twenty-three and had been born and raised in the town of Franklin, some thirty miles south of Indianapolis. Two years after graduation from high school, she had come to Chicago to attend the wedding of her best friend, Mary Ellen Blye, to a hardware salesman named Tom Ladd. Mary Ellen, who had been working at Siegel, Cooper & Company, managed to get her a job there and, much to the displeasure of her mother in Franklin, Georgiana had stayed on. She'd been there for over two years.

Holmes's story was a little more colorful. "My name is

actually Holmes," he told her. "Henry Howard Holmes. I was orphaned at age six and went to live with my uncle, Henry Mansfield Howard, in Denver. It was after him that I'd been given my middle name. He was very wealthy and owned a number of business properties and ranches in the West, as well as extensive financial interests in Germany—primarily Berlin. Well, he had never married and yet always regretted he didn't have a son, so he adopted me and legally changed my name to Henry Mansfield Howard the second. When I came of age, I set out on my own with his blessings to—as the saying goes—make my fortune. I think he was convinced I'd fail. Actually, I didn't. Using my old name of Holmes, I got a number of jobs, each better than the last, invested well and wound up reasonably well-to-do in my own right. I own the ABC Copier Company a few blocks from here, which you may have seen..."

"Oh, I have!" she interjected, very impressed.

"... plus some real estate holdings of significance in the Englewood section, the most important of which is at Sixty-third and Wallace, just a couple of blocks from the Timmerman Opera House. When Uncle Henry died last year, I discovered I was his sole heir. Since then I've been trying to sort out what it is I *do* own now and what to do with it. I haven't been to Berlin yet, though I'll have to go there before very long, and I haven't been to all the ranches. However, I did inspect the holdings in Fort Worth and I'm planning on raising some office buildings there next year."

Before their lunch was finished, Georgiana Yoke was deeply smitten by Holmes. Accustomed to being escorted, on those rare occasions when she did go out, by young men approximately her own age, she found in the thirty-three-year-old Holmes a greater maturity than previously encountered. She liked his directness, his manner of looking into her eyes as he spoke, his way of telling her about himself in a straightforward manner, with neither self-effaciveness nor excessive pride. He had about him such an aura of inherent competence and honesty that she found herself trusting him implicitly. Thus, though earlier she would not even have considered the possibility of doing so, it amused her now to be able to tell him that she, too, would soon come into an inheritance.

"Nothing like yours," she told him, "but fifty thousand dollars is certainly nice to look forward to. From my grandmother. She got it from my grandfather, who died before I was even born. She and my mother had some kind of a falling out years ago, but I was always her favorite. We never even realized she had so much money, but when she died recently and the will was read, the whole thing was left to me. The rub is, I can't inherit until I reach age twenty-five. That won't be until a year from next October seventeenth, so I've got a while to go. In the meantime, it's in escrow in Indianapolis and I enjoy living in Chicago and working at Siegel, Cooper." An expression of consternation crossed her features. "Speaking of which, I'm late. I have to go."

Holmes walked back to the store with her and on the way they made plans to go out together next Saturday. And both, for significantly differing reasons, had the feeling that this might be the start of something very important in their lives.

At the same moment some block away Minnie was reading over the letter she had just finished:

> *Plaza Hotel, Chicago*
> *Tuesday, March 28, 1893*
>
> *Dear Nannie,*
>
> *Guess what? I'M MARRIED! Harry and I tied the knot in a civil ceremony late Saturday afternoon. I know, I know, we always said you'd be my maid of honor when I got married but honestly, Nannie, it just happened and there wasn't time. I knew you couldn't get away from your teaching at Midlothian until school was finished and once Harry and I made the decision, there was no putting it off. I didn't really want to put it off, and you already know how headstrong Harry Gordon is. So here we are and it's really happened. I'm Mrs. Harry Gordon and we're soooo HAPPY! I'll get at writing other letters one of these days, but for now, you can pass the news along to family and friends. Now, let me back up and tell you how it all happened.*
>
> *When I stopped by Chicago for just a brief visit with Harry, I really was planning on continuing to Boston for postgraduate studies in a day or two. But then Harry and I got to talking about how long we have known one another and wasn't it silly to keep going on this way when we knew that sooner*

*or later we were going to be married anyway, so I
canceled my plans. Harry's secretary had recently
left him and he was in need of someone to fill in and
so I volunteered. Remember how awful I told you
that big building of his was on the South Side? The
one they call the Castle? (Actually it's the Holmes
Castle. Harry goes by the name of Henry Holmes in
this particular business endeavor, although I'm still
not quite sure why. He's explained it but I still don't
really understand. Something to do with business
enemies and incorporation papers and such. It really doesn't make any difference.) The important thing
is that he's done a phenomenal job of remodeling on
it and while I still find it in many ways a very
strange place, it's much better than it was. He's
turned in into a World's Fair hotel in anticipation of
the great influx of people who will soon be here and
is convinced he's going to make a great deal of
money in that endeavor between May and October.
And I'll be helping him. As soon as that is finished
we may come to Texas for a month or so and then
head for Europe. Or maybe we'll go to Europe first.
Nothing's definite yet.*

*I stayed at the boarding house operated by
Mrs. Moss at 613 Sixty-fifty Street first, but she was
such a busybody that I followed Holmes's advice
and moved out after only a couple of weeks. The
second place, at 6235 S. Morgan, wasn't much of an
improvement and I probably wouldn't have stayed
there very long except that Harry and his right-
hand man, Ben Pitezel, had to go on a trip South to
do something. (Some kind of lumber business, I
gather.) This man Pitezel is about five or six years
older than Harry and is a very pleasant man. He's
quite handsome (but he drinks much more than he
should!) and while they were down South he got
sick and nearly died and Harry nursed him back to
health but came back by himself while Mr. Pitezel
was still recuperating. Harry says Mr. Pitezel admitted to him that he had some kind of sickness and
that he is afraid he is going to die from it and he's
been very depressed about it.*

Anyway, I'm getting off the track. Harry was

*very pleased when he came back and saw how I'd
taken care of things and when I told him I didn't
like the boarding house where I was staying, he
said, "Then, damn it, Minnie, let's stop this nonsense and get married and we can live together right
here in my apartment over the drugstore." (On the
second floor, directly under his office, so that makes
it very convenient.) Well, that's what we've gone
and done. Got married, I mean, although we're not
going to stay in the Castle apartment like he suggested.
He knew I wasn't crazy about the idea, so he has
rented us a house of our own at 1220 Wrightwood
Avenue. It is on the North Side not too terribly far
from this hotel, but it's a long way from the Castle.
He doesn't care about that and, knowing Harry, he
only wants what I'll be happiest with. He's such a
dear! (He's not here at the moment. I could tell he
was getting restless at being cooped up and so I
shooed him out, partly because I thought it would
do him good to have some time by himself and
partly because I wanted to have this chance to get a
long overdue letter off to you.) I was starting this
letter when he left and the last thing he said before
going out was "Don't forget to tell Nannie what I
suggested." Well, what he suggested is something
you're going to love!*

*Here it is: We know you can't leave Midlothian
until the school term ends in June, but when it does,
we want you to come for an extended visit. Two
months from right now the World's Fair begins (they
call it the World's Columbian Exposition here) and
it is going to be the most remarkable one that's ever
been held. Harry and I have seen the buildings
they've constructed for it and it is as if one has been
transported to ancient Greece. Such magnificent
architecture! (How I wish Billy Bob and Baldwin
could have seen it.) So far as Harry and I are
concerned, we'll certainly be going to the Fair before you get here, but that's all to the good because
then when you come we can go together and only go
to the very best parts of it instead of wasting time
on things that are not spectacular. It will be such
fun! Please write back right away and please-please-*

PLEASE tell me for sure you will be here. Pack a trunk and plan to stay for a long while, not only for visiting the Fair, but for something else Harry has mentioned which he wants to tell you about himself. He swore me to secrecy, so I can't even give you a hint except to say it is wonderful and you will love it.

I do have to end this. It's well after noon now and Harry will probably be back soon and I am still sitting here in my wrapper, so I'd better make myself a little more presentable. Write soon!

YOUR LOVING SISTER,
MINNIE

Six

$\mathcal{H}$enry Holmes had been waiting for this day, waiting for the proper time to do what he had known all along he would eventually do, once conditions were to his suiting. He hadn't known it would be July 7, only that a certain day would come that would be right. Now it was Nannie who had finally provided the impetus. He refolded the letter she had written and returned it to its envelope, then touched a bit of mucilage to the flap and carefully resealed it. He placed the square envelope in the righthand pocket of his coat and walked from the kitchen into the parlor where Minnie and Nannie were still looking through the photo album.

"Hey, you two," he said, "I've decided you're right. It *is* too beautiful a day to work. C'mon. I'm taking you to the Fair."

The sisters were surprised but delighted. Earlier Harry had adamantly turned aside their cajoling that he take the day off and spend it with them again. Minnie closed the album with a snap and got to her feet. "Don't ask me to explain why he's changed his mind, Nannie," she told her sister, making an exaggerated shrug. "Let's just take advantage of it and get going before he changes it again." She looked back at her husband. "Give us two minutes and we can leave."

"Sure," he replied. As they started up the stairs, he added, "One proviso only. I have to stop by my building and pick up some papers. Which will work out just fine, since Nannie's been wanting to see the place and we can do that today without our having to make a special trip of it."

The girls chattered almost incessantly en route to the Castle, but Holmes was quiet, relieved that it was all coming to an end now, thinking about the events that had brought them to this point.

Because Minnie was so desperately in love with him, Holmes had had little difficulty, in the weeks following their wedding, convincing Minnie to put into his name virtually all of her holdings that were assignable, including not only reasonably large cash reserves but, most importantly, numerous parcels of Texas property. Since her husband was a businessman of considerable experience and ability, it had seemed to Minnie only a logical step to let him handle the matters of her estate. Such details had always been a bane to her and it had come as a relief to let someone else worry about her holdings, especially the properties. Among the largest of these was the one that had interested Holmes most of all from the beginning—a quarter of a block in the center of Fort Worth, Texas; the property that had inspired him at the outset to embark on this elaborate scheme that had evolved into such an obsession.

The moment she legally signed ownership of the properties over to him before a notary public, Holmes sent copies to Texas to be legally recorded there. Once that was accomplished, no time would be wasted in getting construction under way with many refinements the Englewood Castle did not have. It would, for example, be entirely electrified from the beginning instead of having the maze of piping for gas lighting, and its labyrinth of hidden passages, trapdoors, secret elevators and improved cremating furnaces would allow him to continue to pursue his methods with considerably less risk. None of that could be done until the official transfer of the deed was recorded, which would probably take several months. In that interval there were important things to be done here. Every day Holmes became more convinced that the Englewood Castle had outlived its usefulness. He had originally planned on waiting until the great World's Fair was finally closed, at the end of October, before destroying the building, but now he knew he would see to it well before the summer was out. He could not have explained his reasoning at arriving at this conclusion and that bothered him because always before the steps he took were pragmatic, logical. Why was that missing now? Why was he forging ahead to become even more entangled in a complex web that increasingly seemed to be without purpose? He wasn't sure, but one thing was very clear to him now: These past first two months of the

World's Columbian Exposition had made it abundantly clear that the building at Sixty-third and Wallace was simply not equipped to handle the multitude of victims he was now bringing to it.

Though he spent as much time as he could spare with Minnie, taking her out to the Fair on several occasions and occasionally going horseback riding with her or for boat rides in the thirty-six-foot sailboat she had bought him as a wedding gift, most often what he called "the press of business" kept him separated from her. While she occupied her time reading at home or riding in Lincoln Park, he had become an habitué of the World's Fair. He had an uncanny knack for finding exactly the sort of person of most value to him—a visitor who had come to the Fair unaccompanied, who had money in abundance and who was looking for accommodations close to the Fair. Those he considered the most attractive targets were young, lonely, well-to-do widows on their own for perhaps the first time in their lives. But occasionally men became victims, too, and sometimes married couples with children. Anyone who was uncircumspect enough to flash within his view a large amount of money was courting disaster.

With tens of thousands of potential victims from whom to choose, Holmes had no great difficulty finding the subjects he wanted throughout May and June. Laughingly describing his outings to Pat Quinlan and Benjamin Pitezel as "hunting expeditions," he nearly always embarked on them with one or more of the Pitezel children in tow. Being accompanied by a child gave Holmes the camouflage of a respectable family man, which resulted in potential victims tending to trust him far more than they would have had he been alone. Most frequently he took ten-year-old Howard, who, unlike his older sisters, was less curious about why "Uncle Henry" was doing this and more inclined to enjoy the fun-filled outings without question. He also liked the toys Holmes bought him each time they went, though his favorites remained the spinning top and a little tin man he'd selected on their first visit.

By the end of June, Holmes had lured more than one hundred "customers" from the exposition to what he told them was his World's Fair hotel. Of these, fifty-five had disappeared forever. A number beyond that became articulated skeletons for medical students, but there was really little time for such work now. Most candidates merely became "donors" of the wealth they had brought with them and wound up dissolving in the quick-lime pit or becoming small piles of gray ash residue in the Warner Process furnace. Even those methods of disposal had their shortcomings, taking many hours to provide the desired result. The difficulty was alleviated when Holmes hit on the idea of taking individual guests out for a sail in his new boat, usually to see the Chicago skyline after dark. Invariably he returned alone, the guest having been poisoned, chloroformed or bludgeoned before being dumped overboard with a heavy weight wired to the ankles. Old iron flywheels and window sash weights bought at junkyards by Pitezel and stowed aboard the boat were especially favored as weights for sinking the victims.

Nannie had finally arrived in Chicago on June 14, and from the time he and Minnie met her at the train station, they had treated her regally. At twenty-five, she still bore a marked resemblance to her sister. They were both pretty girls and—attesting to their mutual fondness for candies— both of them plump, Nannie now weighing only ten pounds less than Minnie's hefty one hundred fifty. They gave her two rooms of her own in the Wrightwood Avenue house and spent the first week introducing her to the city. During those days when he told them he had to be away at work, Minnie and Nannie occupied themselves with a favorite pastime—shopping at Marshall Field's and the Fair Store and other emporia. When the three were together, however, they spent the days riding or sailing and in the evenings they dined at fine restaurants and attended the theater or opera.

And, of course, they finally went to the Fair.

The World's Columbian Exposition could only be described as stupendous. Together they strolled the midway, Minnie on one side of him, Nannie on the other, the women clinging to his arms and exclaiming over the marvels of architecture and displays of culture as well as reveling in the carnival atmosphere. They walked and viewed and participated to the point of exhaustion at the most wondrous World's Fair ever presented. It was impossible to see it all—there were over sixty-five thousand individual exhibits in the pavilions alone, to say nothing of the attractions of the midway— but they made a good stab at it, returning on three successive days until so weary they could take no more.

"Oh, Harry, Minnie, it's all so fantastic!" Nannie exclaimed shortly after they entered the grounds on the first day. "I've never seen anything like it."

Holmes rolled his eyes toward Minnie and the two laughed. "You've hardly seen anything yet, Nannie," Minnie chortled. "Come on. We're going to have the time of our lives."

And so they did. The technological exhibitions were marvels of progress and a foretaste of tremendous things ahead for civilization. Yet, not unexpectedly, both young women were more inclined to the multitude of cultural attractions and most intrigued of all by the Fine Arts Palace, an incredibly beautiful domed edifice where over nine thousand of the world's finest paintings, drawings, engravings and sculptures were on display. They could have spent days in this one building alone without becoming sated.

As the delighted three exulted in the sublime exhibitions, so too did they enjoy the ridiculous. From viewing marvels of art, they followed the milling throng into the midway to gape and gaze at things they'd never imagined. They stared open-mouthed at a fifteen-hundred-pound Venus de Milo sculpted in New York... entirely of chocolate, and, as if they were a trio of hungry mice, they nibbled on pieces carved from a single twenty-two-thousand-pound block of cheddar cheese from Ontario. They saw Chicago transportation mogul Charles Yerkes's marvelous telescope and viewed with awe a remarkable device called a kinetograph, invented by Thomas Edison, which made pictures of people walk and run... and even talk, when used in conjunction with his amazing cylindrical phonograph.

They viewed with pleasure and even a little embarrassment the suggestive gyrations of Egyptian and Persian belly dancers, pausing to listen to the enraged outpourings of a seventy-three-year-old feminist, Susan B. Anthony, and then wandered on to see more. In the area of the Irish Museum they stopped and paid their dimes to kiss a chunk of the Blarney Stone brought over from Ireland and were chagrined later to learn that the stone they had pressed their lips to was nothing more than a chunk of Chicago sidewalk. They strolled with interest through the ethnic pavilions—African and Chinese villages, Tunisian towns, German beer gardens and Austrian coffeeshops, Persian bazaars and a Moorish palace. Agape with amazement, they walked through "The Streets of Cairo" and listened to exotic music, rode camels and donkeys, visited a Moslem mosque and sixty shops crammed with Egyptian goods.

They climbed the huge flight of stairs that gave them access to an exact replica of the battleship *Illinois* manned by five hundred uniformed sailors. Only minutes later they gazed at what was billed as the largest painting in the world—a canvas sixty-five feet high and five hundred feet long—accurately depicting a panorama of the Swiss Alps. They scaled a replica of the Eiffel Tower and murmured with appreciation as they moved through another replica, St. Peter's Cathedral in Rome. They even walked with the rest of the crowd along the rim of a Hawaiian volcano and into a Colorado gold mine.

They watched demonstrations of spinning and glassblowing and other skills. At the African ostrich farm they ate servings of ostrich-egg omelet—one egg serving thirty-five people—and bought huge fluffy plumes. They watched with great interest as a robust, jolly black woman, a fifty-nine-year-old former Kentucky slave named Nancy Green, stood in the midst of a twenty-four-foot-high flour barrel and demonstrated how water could be added to a flour mix just developed by her employer, R. T. Davis, and the resultant batter, poured in small measures in a hot skillet, became pancakes. And Davis, selling the ready-mix in paper bags, was billing her with a name selected after the name of the daughter of Kentucky's famous frontiersman, Daniel Boone, calling her "Aunt Jemima."

They paused and listened enrapt to a thirty-four-year-old black man playing a wonderful new syncopated music he'd introduced only four years earlier. He called his piano music ragtime and his name was Scott Joplin. And only a short distance from him, they sipped at samples of a score of different beers from around the world that were being judged for excellence. The first-place winner was a Milwaukee-brewed beer called Pabst, which, the delighted owner of the firm declared, would henceforth be called Pabst *Blue Ribbon* Beer.

Nannie and Minnie gasped and clung to Harry Gordon even more tightly when he took them on one of the more significant rides of the Fair—a huge balloon filled with hydrogen gas, tethered with great ropes to a mooring station, but lifting them in its huge swaying basket some fifteen hundred feet above the great Fair and letting them see the whole scope of Chicago stretching beneath them along the great arc of Lake Michigan's southwestern shoreline.

The single most spectacular and breathtaking attraction at the Fair was an enormous device designed and constructed by a bridge builder from Pittsburgh, George Washington Gale Ferris. It was a great double framework iron wheel with a diameter of two hundred sixty-four feet, its forty-five-foot-long and three-foot-thick axle the largest single piece of steel ever forged. The two outer wheels supported between them thirty-six gigantic cars in which people could ride—each of the cars large as a railway Pullman car and each capable of holding sixty people. Powered by a two-thousand-horsepower engine, the Ferris wheel lifted its simultaneously frightened and exhilarated total of 2,160 people per ride to the height of a twenty-five-story building, completing one full revolution every ten minutes.

Just three days ago, on July 4, after another exciting day at the Fair, Nannie retired to her room to write to her old maid aunt, Elizabeth Black, the only person older than Minnie to whom Nannie wrote regularly. Sister of their maternal uncle, the Reverend Will Black, Aunt Elizabeth had lived in Jackson, Mississippi, all her life and had often cared for Nannie when Uncle Will had to go out of town. For that reason, Nannie knew her far better than Minnie did and kept in close touch. The words that flowed from Nannie's pen imparted the excitement that was filling her:

> *I can't remember any time when so many wonderful things have happened in so short a space of time. I had thought I would come to Chicago and see the Fair with Minnie and her new husband and that would be that; after a while I would pack up my things and return to Midlothian to continue teaching. So much for my prophetic abilities! It isn't going to be that way at all. I won't be going back to Midlothian nor, I'm sorry to say, coming to visit you on my return. You see, Brother Harry had a big surprise for me. He and Minnie have invited me to go to Europe with them. Very soon! I never dreamed I'd ever get a chance to go there and I'm beside myself with excitement. Brother Harry has all sorts of business interests over there and he is going to pay for everything. It started out with them just*

asking me to go on a tour of Europe with them, but now they've said if I like it there, I can stay and study art wherever I choose. Paris, here I come! It's all so wonderful and so exciting. We'll probably be going within a few weeks. I wish you could get to know Brother Harry better. He's a wonderful man and Minnie's very lucky to have found him.

She had placed the letter in an envelope and addressed it to her aunt, but then put it in her purse and promptly forgot about it. She was angry with herself when she came across it this morning and prevailed upon her brother-in-law to mail it on his way to the office. Holmes, taking advantage of their preoccupation over the photo albums, had taken it into the kitchen and carefully steamed open the flap over the spout of the already boiling teakettle.

At the downtown train station he paused at the mailbox and held up the envelope Nannie had given to him to mail. "You see," he told her, slipping it into the slot, "I didn't forget."

"You never cease to amaze me, Harry," Nannie said. "Don't you ever forget *anything*?" She grinned at her sister. "It's a good thing you married him, Minnie. If you hadn't, I think I'd've snatched him up."

"Too late, little sister," Minnie laughed. "He's all mine."

They were still talking and laughing together as they climbed the stairs to Holmes's third-floor office some forty minutes later; still talking and laughing as they took seats in the office and selected a bonbon each from the small fancy box Holmes extended. The laughter and chatter ended abruptly as almost simultaneously they were stricken by sodium cyanide poisoning and fell writhing and gasping to the floor. It was Nannie who went first, stiffening into a convulsive backward-bent spasm before abruptly relaxing in death. A short while later Minnie also expired.

Holmes returned the box of candy to the desk drawer and locked it. He stepped to the closet and twice pressed a button set in a recess of the inside wall. In less than a minute Pat Quinlan's distinctive knock came on the outer office door. Holmes opened it a crack, saw the chief janitor was alone and admitted him.

"Is Ben Pitezel in the building?"

Quinlan nodded nervously. "In his office downstairs."

"Good. Go get him. The two of you bring two trunks up here. We have some material to pack. We'll be taking them to the boat this evening for disposal."

Quinlan bobbed his head and disappeared out the door. Holmes sat down in his desk chair and looked at the bodies, feeling nothing more toward them than if they were two bundles of old clothes. He had no insurance policies on them so there was no need to present any evidence of death. Eventually Minnie would be declared legally dead and at that time, since her brothers and sister were dead, he would be the legal inheritor of her cash estate. That was a minor matter so far as Holmes was concerned. The important thing was the properties, and those were already locked into Holmes's ownership. His eyes glinted as he thought of the Fort Worth Castle he would soon be building . . . and the Castle in which he sat, that he would soon be destroying. Unbidden, a weird high-pitched giggle erupted from him, filling the fatal room with the melody of madness.

As a rule of thumb, Holmes rarely allowed himself to become friends with anyone. Those few times in the past when he had done so, the friend—irrespective of whether male or female—almost invariably was a disappointment or in some way failed him. When that happened, one of two things occurred: Either the person got out of Holmes' life very rapidly and very quietly on his own, which happened only infrequently, or he was neatly and most unexpectedly eliminated by Holmes and wound up as a small mound of ashes following painstaking dissection, an indistinguishable residue in quicklime, a skeleton in a medical student's closet, a corpse bound to the bottom of Lake Michigan or a corpse used in the collection of fraudulent life insurance claims, most often disfigured and essentially unidentifiable.

Only three people had ever penetrated the barriers Holmes had established and become close friends; close enough to know he was a compulsive murderer; close enough to become involved, voluntarily or through blackmail, in his murderous schemes and share in the often highly profitable proceeds; close enough to feel so secure in the friendship as to be beyond worry that such association betokened eventual candidacy for the man's grotesque pastime. These three were

Benjamin F. Pitezel, Patrick Quinlan, and the fourth of his so-far six wives, Myrta "Dora" Belknap Holmes.

Lately, Holmes had become very concerned about Pitezel. Ever since the Emeline Cigrand episode he had become more an automaton programmed by Holmes than an incisively valuable associate. His drinking habit was now every bit as bad as it had ever been, if not worse. Often Holmes was amazed that the man could function at all when his system was so saturated with alcohol, yet somehow Pitezel did function as required and remained surprisingly dependable.

Two other matters were eating away at Ben of late, resulting in erratic behavior, excessive nervousness, apparent fright and, less apparent but no less mentally debilitating, an overwhelming depression. The first of these—and most responsible for the depressed state of mind—was his own health, which, Pitezel felt certain, was deteriorating at an alarming rate, instilling in him not only a great and growing fear that he was going to die from the illness but, paradoxically, making him actively consider self-destruction during nadiral extremes. The other matter that had begun plaguing him was his inauguration as a very active accessory—sometimes before, occasionally during and most often after the fact—in Holmes's greatly increased rate of murders this year, culminating most recently in the virtually simultaneous demise of Minnie and Nannie Williams.

It was during one of Ben's rare sober periods that Holmes sat with him in the Castle office and broached a subject in as sorrowful a tone as Pitezel had ever heard him use.

"Ben," he said, "I don't think we can put off the inevitable any longer. I want you and Carrie to plan on moving to St. Louis in a few months, say around the middle of November. Between now and then you're going to have to stay fairly flexible. We're going to burn this place down. What I need from you right now is the name of a good arsonist I can use."

Pitezel was not surprised. They had talked around this eventuality a number of times before. He thought a moment and then replied, "The only one I know here who's not serving time at the moment—and he's just about the best you could get—is Barney Zeigle. Last week he had a room at the Monroe Hotel on Madison near Damen. Whether or not he'll still be there, I don't know."

"He knows you?"

"Sure. We served a little time together once."

"All right, I want you to go there with me next Friday morning. That's August fourth. Be sure you're sober."

—

Barney Zeigle turned out to be a slim, rat-faced man of about thirty who was wearing baggy trousers and a badly torn collarless shirt. His initial suspicion of Holmes had been eliminated by Pitezel's recommendation, and Holmes wasted no time in outlining the arson he wanted perpetrated on the Castle.

"Building empty or occupied?" Zeigle said, his voice a raspy whisper punctuated by dry hacking coughs.

"Occupied."

Zeigle shook his head. "Not good. Someone gets killed and its murder."

"They'll get out okay," Holmes assured him.

"I've heard that before. I'm not convinced. I'll still do it, but it'll cost more than if the place was empty. And when I'm finished, no one'll know it wasn't accidental."

"How much?" Holmes asked.

"How much insurance on the place?" Zeigle countered. "And don't lie to me. I can check."

"Four different policies totaling eighteen thousand dollars."

"My price is five thousand."

Holmes frowned. "That's a hell of a lot for just a few hours' work on one night."

Zeigle stared at him, his nostrils flaring. "It's not a lot when you consider the risk, Holmes. It's my price. Take it or leave it."

Holmes was silent a moment. "Suppose I offer you six thousand, payable when I collect on the insurance?"

"Nope. That's a fool's game. Five thousand bucks in advance. Period."

"It's too much." Holmes was disgusted. "I'll do it myself before I'll pay a price like that."

Zeigle sent him a baleful look and then shifted his gaze to the third man. "Get this tight bastard out of here, Pitezel. We got nothing more to talk about. He's going to get himself caught and I don't want any part of it."

—

The Holmes Castle fire was both a boon and a disaster for its owner and Holmes was irritated, since there needn't have been any element of disaster to it if Pat Quinlan had used some common sense. It had also required some revision of plans.

Quinlan had proven himself to be very dependable at doing a job as directed, but what Holmes had not considered well enough was that the janitor was also very unimaginative. When, last Wednesday night, Holmes had met with Quinlan in the third-floor office and given him instructions for setting fire to the Castle, he told him generally what he wanted done. Now that it was too late, he realized he should have been considerably more specific. He had assumed Pat would show a little initiative, but the man had merely interpreted the instructions in his own way and then followed them to the letter. It hadn't been enough.

"I want the fire to take place late Saturday night," Holmes had told him. "I'm most concerned that nothing is left of this entire third floor. There are still a number of things there that belonged to Minnie and Nannie that I want to be totally destroyed. Tomorrow I'm going to call on the tenants and collect whatever rents are still due for August. Then, for all intents and purposes, I will be gone, out of town. Friday night I'll have the body ready for you. Just before the fire you can put it in the third-floor front hall. I won't be here. As I said, I intend being out of town when the fire occurs. I'll be up in Wilmette with Dora and ostensibly won't know anything about it until the morning after, when Ben Pitezel will send me the emergency telegram." Holmes had stopped and looked around the office. He sighed. "Look at those fine fancy doorknobs and fittings we've put in, Pat. What a shame to have to lose them all. And the new tubs and sinks and fixtures. Well, I guess there's no help for it."

The body he had spoken of to Quinlan was not yet actually a body. It was Catherine Wilkes, a living, walking, talking thirty-two-year-old recent divorcée who met the physical requirements he was looking for and who he stalked for an hour at the Fair before "accidentally" meeting her in the Fine Arts Palace. Since whether or not she had any money was not a criterion for selection, he had not inquired into that aspect. Over lunch they discussed art and literature and she was enthralled with his obvious gentlemanly demeanor, his pronounced culture and his exceptionally good looks. She said she was staying at the Sherman House Hotel downtown but found it rather inconvenient because of its distance from the Fair, and with that opening he suggested she might like to rent a room at the Castle. Although not committing herself, she agreed to take a look.

That had turned out to be her last look at anything. Her final chloroform-saturated breath was taken in the newly remodeled room she was considering renting. His medical training had made him acutely aware that the body of a person killed by fire commonly drew up into a pugilistic attitude and so this was how he positioned her fresh corpse for the onset of rigor mortis, complimenting himself on such a nice little touch. Any investigator would have no doubt whatever—unless an autopsy was performed—that hers was definitely the corpse of a woman who had died as the result of fire. There would be, on the face of it, no call for an autopsy to be ordered.

According to his plan, Holmes collected his rents and made a special point of telling his tenants he was going to be out of town for a while. Late in the afternoon numerous boxes of material from his private files were loaded into a wagon by Quinlan, Pitezel and Owens and sent out to the house in Wilmette and stored there in a shed in such a way that the little building could quickly be burned down, along with all its contents, if such became necessary. As usual, Holmes left almost nothing to chance.

According to instructions, Quinlan made certain the third floor was destroyed. Close to midnight on Saturday night, August 12, he quietly placed the corpse of Mrs. Wilkes in the corridor and then liberally spread coal oil all over the third floor. But that was the only place he spread the volatile fluid and that's where he ignited it, instead of starting the fire in the basement or on the first floor, so the whole building would quickly have been engulfed in the rising flames. The first alarm was received by the fire department just after midnight. By the time the fire company arrived, the entire top floor was engulfed in flames and the blaze was fought doggedly throughout the night. The third floor was destroyed, but the second floor suffered only moderate damage and the first floor was so unharmed that within two days it was business as usual in the Castle shops facing on Sixty-third Street and on Wallace.

Holmes received his emergency telegram from Pitezel early Sunday morning and arrived on the scene of the fire by

THE SCARLET MANSION 229

10 A.M. Having expected entire destruction of the building, Holmes was less than pleased with what he found. Nevertheless, he became the perfect example of a man who had just suffered a severe loss. He conferred at once with fire officials and helped them by positively identifying the single fatality as one of his employees, a Miss Joan Carter. He said she had first been hired by him a year ago as a waitress and had recently become an assistant cook. He added that she had just returned from vacation, making no mention of the fact that the real Joan Carter had left his employ for California a month before, at which time he had told the other employees only that he had given her some time off for a vacation and that she would be returning before long.

The newspapers carried stories of the fire and gave special emphasis to the single fatality having been a female employee, which was precisely what Holmes had hoped for. He bought a dozen copies. The more damaged areas of the second floor were sealed off immediately, and, while normal conditions more or less resumed in the undamaged areas there and on the first floor, no plans were made to do any repairs at all to the gutted upper portion. That it was a distinct eyesore in the neighborhood concerned Holmes not at all.

His first task on Monday morning was to put in fire loss claims with the insurance companies, fully expecting to collect. That was when another major flaw in the scheme manifested itself. Holmes had anticipated that C. W. Arnold would be named—as he had been in the past—as investigator of the fire claims, since he had written the policies. It was only then he discovered that Arnold, whom he hadn't seen in many weeks, had quit his work as insurance agent and moved to Minnesota. An investigator was assigned whom Holmes didn't know and he took his work very seriously.

After filing the fire claims, Holmes paid a visit to a printer who had previously done work for him of questionable legality. To him he delivered the copies of the newspapers he had bought, along with special instructions. He provided the printer with the names and background details of seven different women who had worked for him over the past two years. So far as anyone at the Castle knew, these women had simply quit their jobs and left of their own accord for distant places at varying intervals after being hired. Actually, all seven had been killed by Holmes who, after having sexual intercourse with their corpses, had cremated three and articulated the skeletons of the other four and sold them. The printer's instructions were to make seven exact copies of the newspaper pages on which the fire accounts were given, but in each case, changing the name and description of the victim of the blaze to a different one of the seven women. Holmes offered to pay the printer fifty dollars apiece for these altered papers, then added that if he could get all seven of them finished in a single day, he'd give him a flat five hundred dollars. By nightfall, Holmes had the papers.

All eight of the supposed victims, including Joan Carter, had taken out the standard life insurance policies Holmes insisted on, with him paying the premiums and named as beneficiary. The individual $5,000 policies were with eight different companies against whom he had never filed a claim and each contained a double indemnity clause payable in the event of accidental death. When, toward the end of the week, Holmes personally filed the first of these claims, he entered the insurance office affecting a hesitant air, as if unsure of himself.

"My name is Holmes, Mr. Devlett," he told the company official. "Henry H. Holmes. I'm afraid I don't know much about these things and perhaps you can help me. My office building burned last weekend and one of my employees, Miss Joan Carter, was killed. Tragic," he said tragically, "so very tragic. The account of it is right here." He handed the newspaper to Devlett almost apologetically and pointed out the fire story which described her as the victim.

Devlett read the piece quickly and turned his expressionless gaze back on the man before him, who was clenching his derby hat nervously to his chest. "Very sad," he said. "A shame. How may I help you?"

"Well you see, we just learned that Miss Carter had her life insured here. Evidently," he reached into his breast pocket and extracted a folded packet of papers and handed them to Devlett, "she named me as beneficiary of this policy."

Devlett opened the policy and skimmed through it quickly, satisfying himself that it was a legitimate policy with his firm, had been written up by one of their better independent agents, Cosgrove Arnold, that it was for $5,000 and—he felt his stomach muscles tighten—it carried a double indemnity clause. He looked back at Holmes. "It seems to be in order," he said, "but you realize we'll have to make an investigation, especially since it involves accidental—"

"Oh, my," Holmes interrupted, "how stupid of me! You'll have to forgive me. I have no experience at all in insurance matters. I thought I could merely come in here, hand you this original policy, collect a check for five thousand dollars and leave. Well, I'll just take the policy back and have my attorney look through it while you do your investigation." He laughed nervously. "Actually, he's out of town and I thought I could get this all taken care of without involving him. Shows how much I know, doesn't it? If you'll forgive me?" He reached out and plucked the policy from the man's hand and began walking toward the door.

"Uh . . . Mr. Holmes?" Holmes stopped and looked back and Devlett smiled. "Why don't you let me see that policy again for a moment. Everything seemed to be in order and I could check with our president, Mr. Thurston, to see if perhaps this matter could be expedited for you."

"Oh?" Holmes smiled happily. "That would be so nice."

Devlett asked him to have a seat and disappeared with the policy into another office. Some ten minutes later he returned without the policy but with two pieces of paper. "Wonderful news for you, Mr. Holmes," he said jovially. "Mr. Thurston saw no reason to inconvenience you in settling this claim. I have here a check made out to you in the amount of five thousand dollars and also a release form that will require your signature. Then you can be on your way."

"Release form?" Holmes looked confused. "What sort of release form?"

Devlett's tongue flicked across his lips and he spoke casually. "Just the usual, Mr. Holmes. It states that in return for surrendering to us the original policy you have received five thousand dollars in full settlement and that you will have no further claims against this company in the matter of Miss Carter's death."

"Oh, certainly," Holmes said, bobbing his head. "Glad to sign it." He did so, accepted the check and left. Devlett immediately returned to his superior and handed him the release Holmes had signed, extremely pleased with himself in having saved the company from having to pay twice the amount, for double indemnity.

By the end of the week this same scenario, or slight variations of it, had been accomplished with the other seven firms who had underwritten double indemnity life policies on the seven other missing Holmes employees. A total of $40,000 had been paid out and everybody was very happy.

Especially Holmes. He passed all but $5,000 of it to Frank Blackman, instructing him to give $25,000 to Dora and invest the remainder for him, less Blackman's commission.

Where the Castle's fire insurance was concerned, however, Holmes's good luck failed to continue. The investigator, prowling through the ruined and damaged areas of the building, found a number of matters that were very puzzling. There was evidence that quite a few plumbing fixtures had been removed just prior to the fire, as well as some marble slabs, a number of fancy doorknobs and other items. Further, the remains of file cabinets showed them to have been all but empty at the time of the fire. Finally, there was clear evidence in three different places where wood and plaster was badly scorched in a pattern that bore the earmarks of flames having followed the path of a seeping inflammable fluid, burning that fluid and the wood beneath it without having ignited adjoining areas. The preliminary report he turned in bore a significant comment: *In this investigator's opinion, evidence at the fire scene indicates a possibility of arson. Further investigation recommended.*

Instead of receiving settlements this morning of August 25 as anticipated, Holmes was presented with a copy of the preliminary report by a hard-eyed official representing the joint insurance companies carrying his fire insurance. He was informed only that the investigation was continuing and that he would be hearing from them very soon.

That was enough. Danger flags unfurled. Holmes immediately summoned Pitezel and Quinlan to his second-floor Castle apartment, which had suffered some water and smoke damage, but nothing irreparable. As they entered he handed them $1,000 apiece and spoke seriously.

"I'm not going to stay in this building after today," he told them. "If you need me, I'll be in that flat I've rented at Garfield and Fifty-fifth. I'm there under the name of Henry Howard. If anyone is looking for me, you have no idea where I am or when I'm coming back. Ben, you and I have a number of projects we'll be working on together in the months ahead, most important of which is getting construction going as soon as we can arrange it on that Fort Worth building.

"Pat," he continued, turning to face the Irishman, "I'm leaving you in charge here. I want you to collect the rents and continue to take care of whatever maintenance is needed, but we're not going to make any repairs. Ben and I are going to be doing a lot of traveling. If we're not here and you need to get in touch with us, tell Ben's wife and she'll let us know. If you get letters or wires from Benton C. Lyman or D. T. Pratt, those are the names we'll be using again, but don't mention that to anyone else. And Pat," a wisp of a smile touched his lips, "the next time I ask you to burn a place down, would you, for Christ's sake, please try to remember to start the fire at the bottom?"

From the doorway where he was standing, Holmes saw Pitezel emerge from the offices of the Fidelity Mutual Life Association and fell in beside him.

"How'd it go?"

Ben gave him a sidelong glance. "Just as you figured. No difficulty at all." He reached into his pocket. "Here it is."

Holmes took the policy and looked it over with a skilled eye. It was dated today, November 9, 1893, and showed that the life of Benjamin Fuller Pitezel, age thirty-nine, had been insured for $10,000, with his wife, Carrie Alice Pitezel, as sole beneficiary. The policy had been written up for the premiums to be paid on a semiannual basis, the first of these having been paid today. Holmes gave a small sound of approval and handed it back to his partner.

"Tell Carrie to keep it in a very safe place, Ben, but if you leave town, take it with you. Let's you and I get a bite to eat. You look like you could stand something."

Actually, Benjamin Pitezel looked better than he had for several months, probably because he was not drunk. His sobriety was not a matter of personal choice. Holmes had insisted on it and, not trusting Pitezel to stick to his promise, had spent the last three days with him, keeping him away from the bottle. Now, as they settled down at a table in the Gorman Bavarian Inn on Adams Street, Holmes relented enough to order a large stein of beer for his friend. The look of appreciation Pitezel gave him was all but pathetic.

"All right, we have the policy on you now," Holmes said. "I think we should plan on putting things in motion along about next August. You'll have to tell Carrie about this right away. You don't need to go into details. Just a rough idea of the general plan."

"She won't like it, Holmes."

Holmes shrugged. "She'll like it well enough when she finds out how much you and she are going to be making on it. She's tired of living at a poverty level, Ben. When are you and she and the kids leaving for St. Louis?"

"Day after tomorrow," Pitezel said, having drained half the stein in the first draught. He wiped foam from his mustache. "The furniture's going into storage tomorrow. I don't know how long we're going to have to keep it there. I thought you were going to get us an unfurnished house."

Holmes shrugged. "Best I could do in the limited time I had," he said. "Count your blessings. You're getting a furnished house at what you thought an unfurnished one would cost. That's neither here nor there. The reason I asked is because we not only have to set up when we're going to do this but *where*. Have you given it any thought?"

"What's wrong with right in St. Louis? Fidelity Mutual has a branch office there."

Holmes was shaking his head. "Nope. Not there and not here. Let me see that policy again."

Pitezel gave it to him and Holmes put his finger on the firm's name and address. "Home offices in Philadelphia. We may as well do it there. We'll probably get the whole thing processed faster there than anywhere else. That suit you?"

"Sure," Pitezel said, finishing his beer and signaling for another, "why not?"

"Good. We'll work out the fine points of the details when I get to St. Louis, but for now, this is roughly how we'll work it." He paused as a waiter brought another stein of beer and took their order. They decided on thuringer and sauerkraut. As soon as he left, Holmes continued. "You'll go to Philadelphia and rent a house that you can also use as an office. Establish yourself there as a buyer and seller of patents. Get known around the neighborhood where you'll be."

"I told you I don't want to use my own name, Holmes."

"You really should. It'd simplify things."

"No, damnit! It's easy for you to say, because," he lowered his voice, "you don't have felony warrants out on you in two states. Look, I admit it, I get drunk a lot. Suppose I'm there under my own name, get loaded and somehow get into trouble and get arrested. They run a check and find out I'm wanted for forgery and bail-jumping in Indiana and I'm sunk. From there it's only a step till they nail me for murder in Colorado. I won't do it, Holmes, not under my own name."

Holmes held up a hand, warding off any further gush of words. "All right, all right. So you'll use another name. Let's settle that matter right now. Who will you be?"

Pitezel picked up the policy lying on the table and started to fold it to put it back in his pocket. He stopped, his glance falling on the name of one of the company officers, O. LaForest Perry. "There," he said. "That's who. Perry. I'll be B. F. Perry."

"Good enough. Get yourself established there under that name. While you're doing that, I'll get Chester Fish in New York to find us a cadaver that matches you well enough. When we get it, I'll deliver it to you in a trunk. You arrange it where you want it to be found. Fill your pipe with tobacco and put it in his mouth. You'll have a mixture of a highly flammable fluid I'll give you. Pour it on his face and chest. Stand back and toss a lighted match on it. It'll explode and pretty much burn away the facial features. So far as anyone'll be able to tell, it'll look as if you were handling the fluid— somebody's invention, probably—and it ignited when you lighted your pipe. That's when you leave the body there and disappear. It'll be found sooner or later. The longer it takes, the more decomposition and the easier it'll be to claim it's you. Carrie'll make the identification, saying it's you, and collect the insurance. We'll set up details of where we'll meet you later."

"Sounds complicated," Pitezel said dubiously. "I'm not sure I like it."

"It's not all that complicated and it'll work perfectly. Dammit, Ben, trust me. I've done this dozens of times. There won't be any question at all."

"Well, I guess. But what about my kids? Do we let them know I'm okay?"

Holmes shook his head. "Absolutely not! Their thinking you're dead is what's going to help put this whole thing across. They'll find out soon enough you're alive and you and Carrie'll be able to live very nicely for a long time on what you make out of it."

The waiter brought the lunch then and they fell to eating, Pitezel ordering another stein of beer to wash it down. They talked little as they ate and, after Holmes paid the bill, they walked to the station where Pitezel caught the train just leaving for Englewood and Holmes left to pick up Georgiana Yoke, to whom, as Henry Mansfield Howard, he had become engaged a month ago today.

Half an hour later Pitezel stepped from the train in Englewood, but it was over three hours after that before he entered his own dilapidated house. He was drunk and Carrie stood out of reach and watched him fearfully, trying to analyze his mood as he lurched into his chair at the kitchen table. When he was like this there was no telling what he'd do. At times, she knew, he became affable and then sexually stimulated and they wound up in bed together where he would plunge into her body almost savagely until he exploded in spasmodic ejaculation. Most often he passed out immediately afterward. But there were other times when his drunkenness turned him surly and those were the times when he invariably struck out at her. If she avoided the blows he became even angrier but if he hit her he became almost instantly contrite. She had become skillful at timing her moves so that if he raised his hand at her, she could step into the blow before it reached full strength, then stumble away, pretending greater hurt than had been suffered.

This time was different. Though drunk, he was in greater control of himself and became neither maudlin nor ugly. He pointed at the chair across the table. "Sit down, Carrie. Got to talk to you."

She lowered herself hesitantly into the chair, tensed for whatever unknown thing was in the offing. "Can I get something for you, Benny?" she asked tentatively.

He shook his head and his gaze became more focused on her. "No. Just listen." He studied her a long moment, seeing more clearly than usual the threadbare clothing, the workworn hands, the ingrained fatigue. A welling of guilt filled him. "You haven't had it easy, Carrie. That's going to change soon. The St. Louis move is only temporary. And it's only the beginning. We're going to have lots of money. We'll have our own house, somewhere we've never been before, where we can start fresh. And you're going to have nice clothes and things and maybe even someone to come in and help out once in a while."

"How, Ben? How is all this going to happen?" A pleading note entered her voice. "You aren't going to do something wrong, are you? You're not going to get into trouble again?"

He reached into his pocket and tossed the Fidelity Mutual policy on the table before her. "Got my life insured today. Ten thousand bucks. You're going to collect."

Her eyes widened with the stab of fear. "Benny, no! I want you, not the money."

He giggled. "Both," he told her. "You get both. Me an' half the money."

"Half?"

"Half. Holmes is getting the other half. He's setting it up. He's got a doctor friend in New York who can get him a body that looks like me. We dress it up in my clothes and you come and identify it as me and collect. After a while I send for you and we start a new life."

"Oh, Benny, don't do this, please."

He waved aside her concern. "Get used to the idea. We're going to do it, Carrie. And for the first time, you're going to have plenty of money. With that and my half interest in the new Castle we're going to build in Fort Worth, we got a whole new life ahead. All you got to do is follow directions."

"Benny, you don't understand. I don't want—"

"Shut up!" He lurched to his feet, overturning his chair, glaring down at her. "You'll do what you're told, understand?"

She quailed beneath his dominance and nodded, becoming conciliatory. "Whatever you say, Benny. Whatever you say."

He looked at her a moment longer and then turned and left the house without another word. Halfway down the block toward the tavern he encountered his eldest daughter.

"Papa," she said, recognizing his condition and taking his arm, "come on home with me. Please, Papa."

"Not as drunk as you think I am, Dessie," he told her. He cupped her face in his hands and smiled. "Pretty girl," he said. "So pretty. Need pretty clothes to go along with pretty you. Got to . . . tell you something."

The sixteen-year-old put her hands over his and squeezed them. "I love you, too, Papa. Come on. Come home with me."

"No. No. Want you to listen a minute. Going to get you lots of nice things. Don't want you upset, though."

"What are you trying to say, Papa? I don't understand."

"Dessie, listen. Sometime . . . sometime before long, maybe, I don't want you to worry if you see in the paper that I'm dead. I won't be dead, Dessie. It won't be true, so don't worry. If I'm not alive, you'll know it, but I'll be alive, Dessie. I'll be alive even if it says I'm dead, so don't you worry."

"What do you mean, Papa? Tell me!"

But Ben Pitezel had pulled away from her and was heading toward the tavern, listing only a little.

"Happy?" Georgiana, snuggling next to Holmes in the sleigh, looked up at him adoringly, her face framed by the lynx fur parka. The driver of the sleigh, much higher than they on his raised seat, looked steadfastly forward.

"Never happier," Holmes replied, "and I've never seen you look so radiant." He meant it. He had never really considered Georgiana a handsome woman, but on this subzero Denver morning, her cheeks tinged pink by the bite of the bitterly cold air and her expression filled with the excitement of the moment, she truly was radiant. And the wonderful, unidentifiable quality that had attracted him to her in the first place was still most definitely there.

"I always assumed, Mr. Howard," she said, "that I'd be getting married someday." She broke into a lilting little laugh. "I even assumed it would be to a very rich, wonderfully intelligent and exceptionally handsome man."

"I sense a 'but' coming," Holmes said, keeping a straight face with an effort.

"You're right." Her delight increased and she went on. "But!—never ever in my wildest dreams did I imagine that I would be getting married in Denver, Colorado."

He joined her laughter and then leaned to kiss her on the forehead, on each eye in turn, on the tip of her nose and then on the lips. Her tongue touched his, dartingly, and she murmured "Mmmmmmm" as she let it explore first his upper teeth, then the lower, before pressing it again with warm pressure against his. They moved their tongues back and forth in brief oral mating and Holmes felt the surge of blood to his penis creating a painfully pleasurable erection, bent by the stricture of his trousers. He pulled his head back.

"Enough!" he breathed. "Any more of that and you'll be experiencing something else you never dreamed of."

"Such as?" she teased.

"Such as being sexually assaulted in the middle of a snowdrift."

They laughed together again and fell comfortably silent, he pressing toward her and she clinging with mittened hands to his upper arm. He vaguely wondered why he was on the brink of marrying her. She had nothing of material value that he wanted except, perhaps, her forthcoming property inheritance in Indiana, but it would be no great trick to separate her from that in time without marrying her. Actually, as lavish as he had been with gifts to her—to say nothing of his taking her so often to the theater and opera and superb restaurants— he'd probably already spent more on her than he could reasonably hope to recoup. So what was the attraction? Why was he marrying her? He'd never analyzed the matter so closely before and, thinking about it now, realized almost with shock that it was because he found her so sexually satisfying. Of itself this was strange. Certainly she was no more skilled at lovemaking than Dora, nor more enthusiastic at it than Minnie had been, nor gave and received pleasure in any more satisfying a manner than Julia had, or Cat or Jenny. What was it, then? He had no idea, only knew that it intrigued him, had become all but addictive to him. Would it pass? Probably, sooner or later. Would he then kill her, as he'd killed Minnie and Julia? Possibly, if that became the simplest resolution. But for now he was satisfied and had no qualms about entering into matrimony once again—the seventh time without benefit of divorce.

The turn of thoughts made him think fleetingly of the others: Clara, Franny, Jenny, Nancy, Dora, Minnie. Why, with the single exception of Minnie, hadn't he killed them? He wasn't sure . . . only that they had somehow become a part of him—paradoxically vital and unimportant—during their relationship, an adjunct to the being that was himself, and he had experienced no *desire* to kill them. Minnie, of course, had been another matter. Their marriage had had virtually no sexual impetus so far as he had been concerned. Becoming married had been for the sole purpose of having her transfer ownership in the Fort Worth properties to him. Killing her was necessary to have her out of the way when he did what he was presently engaged in doing with those properties.

"What?" he asked, aware that Georgiana had just asked him a question.

"Pay attention, day-dreamer. I asked if this was Minnie Williams's first time in Denver."

"No," he said, momentarily taken aback that she should

pose a question about Minnie at the moment he was thinking of her. "No, she's been out here several times before. Matter of fact, she was in theater here for a while."

"Before she became your secretary, of course," Georgiana said. "Funny she should go from being an aspiring actress to becoming your private secretary. Did she think it strange when you wired her to come out here just to be a witness at our wedding?"

"She didn't say so when I met her train last night," Holmes said. "But it was more than just being a witness for us. She brought along those business papers I needed for the Fort Worth matter, which saved us having to make a rather inconvenient side trip back to Chicago before going on to Fort Worth."

"Well, whatever the reason, I'm looking forward to meeting her. It's nice she's here and can be a witness for us instead of our just having strangers present."

"Yes," Holmes said, "it is."

Again they fell silent, Georgiana lost in her own thoughts, Holmes recalling the wire he had sent to Pat Quinlan two days ago, telling him it was urgent that he locate a specific packet of papers in Holmes's desk and have his wife hand-carry that packet to him at once in Denver. Quinlan had sent him a confirming wire, saying he had located the packet and that Ella had it in her possession and would be arriving by train in Denver at 10:20 P.M., January 16. He had met the train, not only to get the papers from her but to get her checked into the hotel under the identity she would assume while here—that of Minnie Williams. Before leaving Chicago, Holmes had learned that someone—a man whose description matched no one he knew—had been asking questions in respect to the whereabouts of Minnie Williams. Assuming that this was either one of Minnie's kin or perhaps a detective hired by her Texas relatives to investigate her evident disappearance, it seemed wise to establish that as recently as January 17, 1894, Minnie Williams had been in Denver, Colorado, where she had been witness to this wedding. This would prove not only that Minnie was alive and well at this time, but that even though he and Minnie had gotten divorced—so he would allege—they had parted ways amicably. It would negate his plan to claim inheritance on the remainder of her estate but, more important, it would serve to prevent his being accused of having murdered her when she abruptly disappeared from Chicago last July.

The reasoning, illogical though it was, seemed perfectly sound to him and he was greatly buoyed, as often before, by belief in his own invulnerability, by an unshakable confidence that he was of such superior intellect that there was no possibility that the law would ever suspect him of criminal activities. In a way, he thought, that was a shame. How much more exciting it could be if there was more of an element of danger. How much more interesting to dangle tantalizing tidbits of evidence before the noses of the authorities and then stay one step ahead of them as they strove to track him down. What a fulfillment to toy with them, to cleverly outmaneuver them. His blood surged at the thought. *One of these days, perhaps I'll give them a game to play, after the new Castle is completed.*

Henry Holmes was very satisfied with the way matters were going of late. The period immediately following the partial burning of the Castle—despite his having eight times collected life insurance on one person—had been a risky and exciting time because of the fire insurance investigation. The possibility of his being arrested and prosecuted, at least for insurance fraud and arson and possibly even manslaughter, had died away now and he could look back and grin, congratulating himself on one more game successfully played to its conclusion. And now his more complex game involving the Fort Worth property was going exceptionally well. There was an immense sense of satisfaction in outwitting supposedly shrewd police investigators, but a different and equally gratifying sensation that resulted from manipulating and besting more highly educated bankers, realtors and lawyers; of walking off with tens of thousands of their dollars and leaving them without even a reasonable clue as to the true identity of the perpetrator. For Holmes, these games were almost as satisfying as selecting, stalking and killing people and then finding different ways of disposing of the remains.

In December he had learned that all the papers transferring Minnie's Fort Worth property rights to him had been legally recorded in both Chicago and Fort Worth. It was what he had been waiting for and it triggered an immediate response. He and Pitezel, under their own names, had paid a quick visit to Fort Worth to inspect the properties together in order to make their plans. There had been only one little snag; an incident that could have been disastrous but turned out to be merely amusing. Very nearly out of touch with reality, Holmes jeopardized the whole Texas plan by engaging in a stupid little crime of which he thought practically nothing—a theft. He and Pitezel had laughed over the ludicrousness of it until they abruptly and quite shockingly found the police close on their trail and were forced to flee the state. Fortunately, the Fort Worth scheme was being perpetrated under their aliases and so returning in that guise was safe enough. That theft was the first stupidity, but a far greater one was Holmes's failure to learn from it that he was not so invulnerable as he believed. He totally ignored the danger signs that had always before been so scrupulously studied. Holmes blamed only bad luck and hardly gave the matter a second thought on returning to Chicago. Less than a month later, early this month, the two were back in Texas, operating under their aliases of Pratt and Lyman, this time with Georgiana in tow. Holmes set Pitezel to work on getting the Castle blueprints redrawn on a larger scale—the Fort Worth Castle to have a frontage of 190 feet as opposed to the Chicago edifice's 125 feet—as well as lining up building material suppliers and contractors and starting to apply for the necessary permits. Reasonably enough, Georgiana had become just a little curious.

"Henry," she had asked, when first they got their Fort Worth hotel room, "why in the world did you register us here as Mr. and Mrs. Frank Pratt?"

"I didn't want to cause you concern," he had replied, "but perhaps you ought to know." He had taken her hands in his and explained with the greatest sincerity he could muster that the reason for this was twofold: first, because squatters had taken possession of the ranch outside Fort Worth that his uncle had willed to him. "You have to realize," he told her, "that squatters' rights are more recognized here in Texas than they are in the North. If the squatters had any inkling that Henry Mansfield Howard had come to town, they would think I was here to take charge of my ranch and evict them in the process, and it's altogether possible they would kill me to prevent that. Second, due to business complications and delays and arrangements with various business associates here in Fort Worth in regard to my properties, I simply feel it's unwise to use my own name. In business, you'll find, it's very common to use a pseudonym." Georgiana, who had virtually no business background, had nodded knowingly and accepted his explanation without further question.

After a week in Fort Worth, Holmes left Pitezel there and he and Georgiana took the train to Leadville, where he told her he also had business. He registered them at the Vendome Hotel as H. H. Holmes and wife. While she waited for him in their room, he went to the law offices of J. M. Maxwell, the administrator of Billy Bob Williams's estate. Holmes produced for the attorney's inspection letters of authorization and power of attorney from both Minnie and Nannie Williams. He then demanded the life insurance money due on Billy Bob's death, which Maxwell had placed in escrow. The crusty old attorney was suspicious and refused to surrender the insurance money to anyone other than Minnie herself. Holmes then produced a note issued in favor of himself by Minnie Williams for $600 and demanded payment of that under threat of lawsuit. Maxwell relented enough to give Holmes a check for that amount but remained adamant against releasing the insurance money to him. Holmes left, not entirely satisfied but pleased that he had collected at least something.

The next morning Holmes and Georgiana had taken the train to Denver and this is where they had been ever since. He had at first thought they would remain here for a couple of weeks after the wedding for their honeymoon, but that was before the incident of last Thursday. Holmes, striding through the lobby—fortunately alone—was suddenly jolted to a halt by a voice shrill with delight.

"Harry! Harry Gordon! Imagine seeing you here again!"

He had turned to find two couples he had met almost exactly two years ago—friends of Minnie's from her theatrical group. He managed to regain his composure while shaking hands heartily with the gentlemen and accepting cheek kisses from the ladies.

"Where in the world have you and Minnie been keeping yourselves?" one of the women asked. "Last we heard there were wedding bells in the future for you two and Minnie was on her way to Chicago."

He looked somewhat abashed. "I think," he told her, "you may have read more into that than was actually the case. We were very close friends—still are, for that matter—and I have to admit, I did at one time think we might get married. Maybe Minnie did, too, for all I know. But when she came to

Chicago she met an Englishman at the World's Fair and fell madly in love with him."

"No!" said the woman, clasping her hands beneath a double chin. "Who?"

"Meacham, I believe his name was. Milton Meacham."

"Oh, God," said one of the women, "Minnie Meacham. Couldn't she have picked someone with a less sickening name?"

"Well, I think it's marvelous!" exclaimed the other woman. "What happened then?"

"Just what you might expect," Holmes said. "After the Fair ended, they got married and Minnie moved to India with him. I've only heard from her once since then—a letter from Calcutta—but I presume she's still there."

"Imagine that," said one of the gentlemen.

"Leave it to Minnie!" said the other.

They chatted a little longer until Holmes excused himself, saying he was on a business trip and did have an appointment and could not afford to be late. They bade him good-bye and went on their way, laughing and chattering, while Holmes returned to the room and remained there for the rest of the day, even to the point of sending out to have dinner brought up. He told Georgiana he had received a communication from Benton Lyman which necessitated a change of plans; instead of honeymooning here in Denver, they would return to Fort Worth immediately following the wedding.

Now, in retrospect, he smiled. When such unexpected encounters as that occurred, they were nerve-wracking and required both quick thinking and consummate acting. Afterwards, when the danger had been safely bypassed through extemporaneous skill, there was always a feeling of great achievement; an exhilaration which he thought must be closely allied to what a stage actor experienced following a performance which brought him accolades.

"My goodness," Georgiana said, nudging him with mock crossness, "I wish you'd stop thinking about business affairs on your wedding day. We're here, Henry. This is your last chance to run. Either do that or help your wife-to-be into the presence of the preacher."

The driver had stopped in front of the white clapboard building that was the First Methodist Church. Holmes kissed her a quick peck and then climbed down and helped her out of the sleigh. They entered the building arm in arm and found awaiting them not only the Reverend Mr. Elmer Wilcox and his wife, but Ella Quinlan—known to those present only as Minnie Williams—and a matronly member of the minister's congregation who had volunteered to play the piano on this occasion. In just over a quarter-hour the crucial moment had arrived.

"Do you, Henry Mansfield Howard, take this woman to be your lawfully wedded wife?"

"I do," said Holmes in a strong voice.

"And do you," the Reverend Mr. Wilcox continued, "Georgiana, take this man to be your lawfully wedded husband?"

"Yes," Georgiana said, "I do!"

"Then by the power vested in me, I hereby pronounce you husband and wife."

Georgiana Yoke was now Mrs. Henry Mansfield Howard— seventh wife of Herman W. Mudgett, alias Henry H. Holmes.

What had made the planned destruction of the Englewood Castle reasonably acceptable to Holmes had been the knowledge that he would soon have a bigger, better and far more efficient facility of the same nature in Fort Worth. Since last August, when largely forced to curtail his murders in Chicago, he had missed that pursuit more than anticipated and looked forward to resuming and increasing his activities along these lines as soon as the Fort Worth Castle was operational. Now it was mid-May and he had been forced to the conclusion that the latter structure would never be used as intended.

It had not been a sudden decision; rather, one that he had gradually come to because of a growing conviction that if he ignored the danger signals any longer and tried to follow through with his original plans, he would have severe difficulties with the law. Texas, he had discovered, was simply not a healthy place to be engaged in criminal activities. A phenomenal degree of cooperation existed between law enforcement agencies, from local town constables through municipal police departments and county sheriff offices all the way to the state police. Not only was considerable effort expended to track down and apprehend lawbreakers, the penalties levied by courts—which were prejudicial against those accused of crimes— were frighteningly stiff. Merely stealing a horse, for instance, could result in a sentence of twenty years and, though not recently, occasionally even in the death penalty. And so, after due consideration, Holmes had decided that the smartest thing for him to do was profit by the properties as much as possible, in the shortest time possible, and then get out of the state permanently.

It was a shame, really, since things had been going so well. In much the manner that the first Castle had been constructed, this one in Fort Worth was being built on small down payments and empty promises. It was located at the corner of Second and Russell Streets and the early work was accomplished swiftly and with considerably more craftsmanship than had been exhibited in Chicago seven years earlier. Holmes, as D. T. Pratt and representing himself only as the agent of the owner of the property, Benton T. Lyman, presented the plans for the massive three-story, 152-room structure to half a dozen banks and found them eager to loan him the money he requested—$10,000 each—at eight percent interest. With a small portion of the money thus obtained, he liquidated all the workmen's bills already run up and set the same workmen and half again as many others to working even harder. Materials creditors were paid just enough to momentarily assuage their growing concern over nonpayment of bills and encourage them to extend credit twice as far as previously.

The two largest individual swindles netted them $26,000. The first was a loan of $10,000 borrowed from the Farmers' and Mechanics' National Bank, which was secured by a trust deed on the property given by Pitezel under the guise of Benton Lyman. The second was more involved. On April 26, Holmes, as Pratt, approached the prominent Fort Worth businessman R. B. Samuels, whose offices were in the towering Hendricks Building. Representing himself as agent of the owner, Benton Lyman, Holmes told Samuels and his lawyer son who was present, Sidney L. Samuels, that he wished to borrow $16,000, for four months at ten percent per annum interest plus ten percent of interest and principal for attorney's fees. For this he offered to give, in Benton Lyman's name, a mortgage on the nearly completed structure at Second and Russell Streets. The elder Samuels was clearly interested and, advised by his son, took the necessary steps to execute the matter. Not until all the preliminaries were accomplished and Samuels was ready to have the contract signed did Holmes casually mention that he was unable to fulfill his part of it, saying that Benton Lyman had received a power of attorney from a man named C. T. Klut of Fort Worth, giving Lyman the sole authority to negotiate the loan and fix the mortgage on all the property. Naturally, Klut did not even exist, but Holmes apologized and told them he would take steps at once to eliminate the minor obstacle and return as soon as possible.

Holmes deliberately let them stew for longer than was necessary and then finally returned for another meeting with the two men the day before yesterday. Holmes appeared both apologetic and ingratiating. "I can't tell you how sincerely sorry I am that there has been such a delay," he said. "Unfortunately, work has been halted on construction with the work ninety percent completed, since we are out of funds and can do nothing else without more money. Are you in a position now to say whether or not the loan can be negotiated? I hasten to add that Mr. Lyman is presently in Denver and I can send the papers there immediately if the loan can be negotiated."

The elder Samuels considered this and then dipped his head in a single curt movement. "We have done some checking on our own, Mr. Pratt," he said, "and, if certain mechanics liens existing on the building can be recovered, I see no objection to making the sixteen-thousand-dollar loan, inasmuch as the property alone in its present state, even unfinished, seems to be more than ample security."

The old man swung his gaze to his son, who sat in a deep leather chair to one side. "Sidney, draw up the note for Mr. Pratt to deliver to Mr. Lyman for his signature."

Sidney Samuels drew up the paper on a Promissory Note blank of the Fort Worth National Bank and gave it to Holmes, who shook hands with both.

"Uh, one other matter," Holmes said as an afterthought, "if it will not inconvenience you. Mr. Lyman insists on the loan being made in cash so as to avoid the delays required for a check to clear. Meaning no disrespect to you gentlemen, of course."

"I'm sure we can see our way clear to do that," Samuels said, "assuming all is as represented."

Holmes smiled, bowed slightly and left at once. This morning, two days having passed, he returned to the Hendricks Building and handed a note to R. B. Samuels.

"I'm afraid I owe you one more apology, sir," he told the man, smiling self-consciously. "The note drawn up by your son was somehow lost or misplaced before I could take it to Denver. How this occurred, I do not know. Several secretaries handled it and suddenly it was nowhere to be found. Rather than cause another delay, I took the liberty of substituting another note in place of the first. This new note, so far as I was able to make it be, is, as you'll see by looking it over, practically identical to the first. Along with the bad luck," he grinned ingenuously, "we also had some good luck. This past weekend Mr. Lyman passed through Fort Worth very briefly and I was able to get the new Promissory Note signed by him before he left. You'll note that the only significant difference is that this new note is drawn on a blank from the First National Bank of Fort Worth rather than on one from the Fort Worth National Bank. I don't suppose that makes any real difference?"

"No, I'm sure not," Samuels said. He raised a bushy white brow. "However, Mr. Pratt, I'll read it through if you don't mind."

"Please do, Mr. Samuels."

The note was clearly stated:

$16,000

Fort Worth, Tex.
May 16th, 1894

On or before September 16th, after date, I, we, or either of us promise to pay to the order of R. B. Samuels, Sixteen thousand ($16,000.00 & 00/000) Dollars for value received at the First National Bank of Fort Worth, with interest from date at the rate of ten percent per annum and ten percent of principal and interest for attorneys fees if placed in the hands of an attorney for collection.

Benton T. Lyman

Due Sept. 16th
No.   P.O.

"Sidney," said the elder Samuels, looking up, "please give the money to Mr. Pratt."

The attorney left the room and returned in less than one minute with the cash in an envelope. He counted it out before Holmes and Holmes accepted it. "Gentlemen, on behalf of Mr. Lyman and myself, I thank you. It has been a pleasure doing business with you."

Outside the Hendricks Building, Holmes exhaled deeply and hastened toward the hotel. In his pocket was the original Promissory Note which he had said was lost or misplaced. In Pitezel's hand it was signed Benton T. Lyman. The note Samuels had was not only a forgery of the Lyman signature, but two words had been eliminated that had been in the original note and, as Holmes had suspected would happen, Samuels hadn't noticed. In the original, the due date of payment was followed by *1894, fixed*. In the copy in Samuel's possession, those two words were missing, making the note uncollectible.

Holmes smiled and patted his breast pocket. He could destroy the original now if he wished, but he had no such desire. He still had plans for that note.

Pitezel was waiting on the sidewalk outside his hotel. "You got it?" he whispered.

Holmes nodded and handed Pitezel $500 he had separated from the packet. "Here's enough to tide you over for the Philadelphia deal. I'm going to have to spend the rest of the day settling up with the contractors and suppliers so we can get the Castle finished. That'll take close to fifteen thousand dollars, but we'll have our new headquarters. Right now we still have to be careful. Don't show yourself anymore in the daylight. Catch tonight's ten o'clock train to St. Louis. Georgiana and I will follow on the one that leaves at midnight. We won't be coming back here again until after we finish the insurance job in Pennsylvania."

They shook hands and parted, Holmes wondering what Pitezel's reaction would have been if he'd had any inkling that they were finished in Fort Worth permanently and the $500 he'd just received was all he would ever realize from this project.

An hour and a half later, Mr. and Mrs. Henry M. Howard caught the 1:15 P.M. train for St. Louis while Pitezel sat in his dingy hotel room waiting for nightfall.

When Holmes emerged from the St. Louis City Jail, Georgiana was waiting for him. She ran to him and they embraced, but while there was relief in her expression, there was also curiosity and fear and even a degree of anger.

"Henry," she said, as they walked toward Union Station, "you've got to tell me just what's going on. I've been frantic. I don't understand any of this."

"It's been difficult for you, I know." His arm about her waist tightened in a hug. "I'm sorry it had to happen, but it's nothing to be terribly concerned about. I've told you more than once that I have a lot of enemies. And enemies in the business world sometimes mean trouble. What's happened has been inconvenient, but it's nothing of any major consequence and it'll all blow over quickly, I promise you."

"But what's it all about?" she insisted. "How could they just come and arrest you like that? And for me to actually have to bail you out of jail! I've never been so mortified!"

"Georgiana, listen. It's all very involved and I'll explain it to you fully one of these days, but not now. Suffice to say I was set up for all this, but now that I'm onto them, I'll take care of it quickly. I haven't done anything wrong and all this will blow over. You'll just have to trust me for the time being."

She looked shocked. "Why, Henry, how could you think I *wouldn't* trust you? Of course I do. It's just that I don't understand any of this. You're such a fine man, so how could anyone be so mean as to cause trouble like this for you?"

His short laugh carried no humor. "That's business for you. The important thing is that you've come through for me just wonderfully and now that I'm out and know what they're doing, I can make my counterattack."

He continued talking in circles all the way to the station. The fact of the matter was that he had been arrested because of his own carelessness and it bothered him far more than he was letting on. He continued to believe that he was far too intelligent to be caught in perpetration of his frauds and that his arrest had been the result of plain bad luck—something he would take steps to see would never happen again. The baggage was already at the station and he was solicitous as he put Georgiana on the train for Franklin, Indiana. "You have a nice visit with your mother," he said. "You're staying there for . . . what? Two days? Three?"

"Four. Then I'll go on to Chicago. Mary Ellen said I should wire when I'm to arrive and she'll meet me at the station. I'll stay with her until I hear from you." Mary Ellen Ladd was living at Lake Bluff, a northern suburb of Chicago.

"Fine," Holmes said. "It may be a week after you get

there before you hear from me, maybe even longer. As you know, I've got a fight on my hands here, and as soon as I get it settled, I'm going to have to go to New York, which is where all this trouble originates. I'll wire you when I'm ready to leave there for Philadelphia on the ABC Copier project and let you know where we'll meet."

She had been listening carefully, concern growing more apparent. "But I really ought to stay with you," she protested. "I'll be so worried! What if—"

He cut off the words by kissing her, "No 'what ifs,'" he said as he pulled away. He reeked confidence and his grin was reassuring. "So far as my enemies are concerned, I know their game now and I'll be all right. It's just going to take some time. I'll be all right, I promise you."

The voice of the conductor shouting "Boaaarrrrd!" came to them and he kissed her again and stepped away. "You say hello to your mother and Mary Ellen for me," he called back over his shoulder. By the time he got to the platform she had opened her window and was leaning out. The train started to roll and he could see she was crying as she called, "Wire me soon, Henry. I love you!"

He blew her a kiss and watched until he could see her no more, then turned and headed for the Commercial Building where Jeptha Howe had his law offices. He walked briskly, a crooked grin twisting his lips as he thought of how all this had occurred and how he had so neatly turned a nasty situation to his advantage.

Within a week after he and Georgiana arrived here from Fort Worth and checked into their hotel as Mr. and Mrs. Henry M. Howard, Holmes had located a pharmacy for sale, the Regency Drug Store. The druggist, Edgar Felton, was still paying off a mortgage on the place to the Merrill Drug Company. In his usual method, Holmes gave him a small down payment, with the remainder of the purchase price to be paid in one month. During that interval, Holmes sold the entire stock of the drugstore and then drew up a bill of sale on the empty store itself, which he made out to a Mr. George Browne. He had Pitezel sign as Browne. When Felton came to collect the remainder of his money so he could pay off the mortgage, Holmes blandly told him he had sold the place and Felton would have to collect from Mr. Browne. The mysterious Mr. Browne had, of course, vanished.

This was where things had gone awry. Unlike others

whom Holmes had swindled in this way, Felton refused to slink away finally in defeat. He appealed to the Merrill Drug Company for help and within a few days Holmes, as Henry M. Howard, was arrested for fraud and booked into the St. Louis City Jail. His cellmate had turned out to be none other than one of the few people Holmes had always admired—a flamboyant and very notorious train robber by the name of Marion Hedgepath. Hardly anyone had not heard of the man's exploits. Head of a small gang called the Hedgepath Four, he and his men had successfully robbed a dozen trains in Illinois, Iowa and Missouri before he was caught and tried in 1892. For weeks the papers had been filled with accounts of the daring robberies and the arrest and trial.

Hedgepath, at twenty-six, was a very handsome man with uncommonly romantic notions about crime. Evidently influenced by both Robin Hood and Jesse James, he often gave away much of the money he stole and, during the robberies, made it a point to kiss the prettiest ladies and refuse to take their money or valuables. His downfall two years ago had come following his successful robbery of a train stopped by his gang not far from Glendale, Missouri. A small girl happened to witness where the men hid their guns and the $50,000 they had stolen in this robbery. She told the authorities, who concealed themselves in the vicinity until the robbers returned for their loot, then arrested them. The subsequent trial had become a national sensation and Hedgepath became a sort of folk hero with a great following of women admirers who sent him so many bouquets that the flowers virtually filled his jail cell. But he did go to jail.

In the three days that followed Holmes's incarceration, Hedgepath and the man he knew as Howard came to know one another reasonably well. Hedgepath admitted he had been working on a deal to buy his way to freedom. Everything was set up for it except that to grease the correct palms would cost $500, which he didn't have. Holmes, on the other hand, told him how he had often swindled life insurance companies and of his current plan to defraud one in Philadelphia out of $10,000 by substituting a facially mutilated body for that of his insured partner. What he needed most at this time, Holmes said, was the assistance of a crooked lawyer in pulling off this particular job, since his own lawyer in Chicago, Wharton Plummer, refused to get involved in it.

"Tell you what, Howard," Hedgepath told Holmes, "I

know the perfect lawyer for you. I'll send word for him to come and see me and roughly fill him in on what you're planning. If he's interested, he can talk to you further himself. If you two agree to work together, then you'll give me the five hundred dollars I need to get out of this place."

Holmes thought briefly about such a symbiotic deal and then nodded. "All right, but the five hundred dollars for you is payable only if we're successful in collecting the insurance."

The deal agreed upon between them, Hedgepath contacted his lawyer, Jeptha Howe, who immediately visited him and listened with interest to the plan. A fat man in his midtwenties, Howe then met with Holmes and became enthusiastic as he heard more of the finer details of the proposed swindle. "Damn!" he said, slapping his knee and rising. "That's one of the slickest schemes I've ever encountered. All right, I'm in. Come to my office as soon as you get out of here. I'm in the Commercial Building—junior partner in my father's practice."

So now, having seen Georgiana off for Indiana and walked to the Commercial Building, Holmes entered the office of Howe, MacDonald & Howe. The elder Howe was out of town for an extended period, but Jeptha took Holmes into MacDonald's office. "Marshall," Howe said, "I'd like you to meet Mr. Henry M. Howard, the man I mentioned to you earlier. Mr. Howard, this is my father's senior partner, Marshall MacDonald. Mr. MacDonald is a former district attorney of St. Louis."

The two men shook hands and MacDonald asked him to have a seat. "Mr. Howard, Jeptha has told me only a little of what you have in mind, but from what I've heard I'm not sure it's something I'd recommend he get involved in. Suppose you fill in a few more details?"

Holmes outlined the plan, finishing with why he felt he needed a lawyer's help with this particular swindle. "Pitezel's going into hiding as soon as the body's fixed up to be mistaken as him. If I need to get in touch with him, I'll put a personal in the *New York Times* and *Chicago Tribune* addressed to L. T. Benton. The original idea was to get his wife, Carrie, to Philadelphia to identify the phony body as her husband." He grimaced. "The problem is, she's not terribly bright and I really doubt she can act well enough to handle it convincingly. That's why I'll work it out so I'm on hand to give a positive identification. I was going under the name of Henry Holmes when Pitezel and I were partners in Chicago, so I'll be using the same name for the Philadelphia job, when I go to identify the body. Now then, one of the kids can help with that, but they're all minors and can't collect the money. That's where Mr. Howe comes in. As representative of Mrs. Pitezel, with power of attorney from her, he can collect the insurance payment on her behalf immediately after identification is made."

MacDonald considered this, his expression sour. "I don't like it," he told the young lawyer. "If it were me, I wouldn't touch it. However, since you've obviously decided to go ahead with it, I'll give you a letter of introduction to Bob Linden—that's Captain R. J. Linden, chief of police in Philly. I've known him for quite a few years. Maybe it'll help smooth the way a little for you." His eyes narrowed. "Beyond that, I'll do nothing. I don't intend to get involved. And, Jeptha, if you get into trouble on this, don't call on me."

Howe nodded and turned to Holmes. "Mr. Howard, do Pitezel and his wife know you've contacted me?"

"No."

"Good. Keep them in the dark about it for now. I don't think you need to tell him at all. As for her, you bring her to see me as soon as she gets word that the body has been found."

"All right. Pitezel's leaving for Philadelphia within the next few days to establish himself there as a businessman—a patent buyer. I'll be leaving soon after that for New York to get the cadaver lined up from my contact there. You probably won't see me again until I come here with Mrs. Pitezel."

As he left the law offices, Holmes was amused that no mention had been made regarding how much Howe was going to get out of this, though Holmes was quite sure the young lawyer was laboring under the impression that he would wind up with about half the insurance payment. Then there was Ben Pitezel, Holmes knew, who was certain at this point that he and Carrie were going to get the whole $10,000.

Holmes chuckled as he walked. Actually, the way he was setting it up, there was only one person who was going to make a lot of money on this swindle: Henry H. Holmes.

Seven

Union Depot in St. Louis was crowded this hot evening of July 21 and very noisy, with locomotives steaming and hissing impatiently while the buzzing throng of people milled, most of them either heading for their trains or, having just arrived, leaving the cavernous building. At a whispered word from Ben, Carrie Pitezel put two-year-old Wharton in Dessie's charge and moved with her husband away from the bench to a spot where they could be reasonably alone near the wall. Behind them they could hear Wharton wailing as he attempted to follow and was restrained by his seventeen-year-old sister.

"Well," Pitezel said, "I guess this is it, Carrie. I wish I could say for sure when I'll see you again, but I just don't know. Couple of months anyway. Maybe more, depending on how things go."

Carrie's eyes filled and she shook her head, trying to force the tears back, determined she was not going to cry and speaking with her face turned from him. "I wish you weren't going, Ben. I don't like this. The whole thing is crazy. Just crazy. I don't want you to wind up in jail again. That's what I'm sure is going to happen. I've got a bad feeling about the whole thing. I'm scared. I don't want you going to jail."

He put a hand to her chin and turned her head to face him. "I'm not going to jail, Carrie, believe me. We've got— Holmes and I, I mean—we've got this thing figured down to the last detail. Nothing's going to go wrong. This is the last scheme I'm getting involved in, honest. I told Holmes that. I'm tired of it all. I told him all I want is to be able to live in peace with my family. So that's what this is all about. This last one is for us. And once it's over, honey, we're finally going to have the money to live a better life and maybe do some of the things we've always wanted to do and couldn't."

"Do you really think so? Oh, I hope so, Ben. I really do. You *are* going to write to us, aren't you?"

He nodded. "I'll probably be at a boardinghouse at first. Soon as I find the place where I can set up the patent office as B. F. Perry I'll send you the address. And when you write, remember, it's to B. F. Perry, even inside the letter. Be sure," he lowered his voice, "if you have to tell me anything nobody else should see, you write it in cipher. The one Holmes worked out."

"Why is he doing this, Benny? I mean, why did he change his mind? Why is he working it out so we get the whole settlement? What does he get out of it? You know as well as I do that everything he touches always turns to gold . . . for *him.* So why not this time? How can we be sure we can trust him?"

"Hey, be fair! I know you've never liked him all that much, but he's been damned good to us, Carrie. You forget, he's the one who got me off on that forgery charge when we first met. And what about how he's always buying things for the kids? And the way he slips you money now and then when we're hard up? And how he bailed me out in Terre Haute? He lost three hundred dollars right there. So how can you think bad of him now, after all that? It was his idea to do it this way, Carrie, not mine. He knows how strapped we are. Sure he's always come out with a lot of money on the other deals we've worked on. Why not? They've been his ideas. I guess he figured this time, instead of just paying me a set amount for a job, the whole thing should be ours. Especially since we're going to have to pull up stakes from here and establish our new identities."

"Where? Where are we going from here?"

He shrugged. "Texas, I suppose. We'll be Mr. and Mrs. Benton T. Lyman, half owners in the new Castle. Maybe we'll just take one of the nicer apartments in the building for us. And this time, what with rents from tenants and all, we shouldn't ever have to worry again. Oh, speaking of that, I almost forgot something. That note I signed for sixteen thousand dollars under the Lyman name? That'll be coming due on September sixteenth. Holmes has to pay half, plus the three thousand he owes me for the job, so that's eleven thousand dollars. That leaves only five thousand dollars for us to pay. There's a grace period if it's not paid on time, but it's not very long, so as soon as you get the insurance money, you be sure to get that payment off to Texas. Holmes'll help you on that."

"All right, Ben, I'll take care of it. Don't worry."

"I know you will, Carrie. Now listen, anybody wants to know where I am, you just tell 'em I've gone to Chicago. Say it's got something to do with some lumber I had shipped up there from the South, that I had to dispose of."

"What if..." She stopped and began again. "What if something happens after you've disappeared and I have to get in touch with you? I mean suppose one of the children gets sick or hurt or something. An emergency. Where are you going to be? How can I get word to you?"

"I'm not sure where I'll be. All I can tell you is that I'll be using a turn-around of that new name. I'll be Lyman T. Benton. Even Holmes won't know for sure where I am until I contact him. But if there's an emergency, tell him. He'll get ahold of me somehow." He glanced up at the big clock suspended over the hall. "Getting late," he said. "Let's get back to Dessie."

He put his arm about her waist and she leaned her head against him as they walked back to the bench. Wharton saw them coming and toddled toward them in an unstable run. Pitezel scooped him up and held him high, kissed him on the cheek and then handed him to Carrie. He walked to Dessie who was standing by the benches and placed his arm around her shoulder.

"Have to go now, Baby. You be a good girl, hear?"

Dessie nodded, not far from tears. It was the first time in years he had called her by the nickname he had once always used. "I will, Papa. I'll write to you while you're gone." She pointed to his necktie. "And don't forget to bring this tie back. You promised me I could have it, remember." It was a blue tie she had wanted to use in a crazy quilt she was making.

"I'll bring it back to you," he said. "You know how much I hate wearing them anyway. Now, if you *do* write to me, you be sure to use the cipher I taught you and the others. Tell them, too. That's important."

"All right, Papa."

He hugged her closer to him, kissing the top of her head. "I'll be away for a good while. You take care of Mama while I'm gone. Help her with the others. It's a big job taking care of all the kids, you know."

"Alice and Nellie aren't any problem, or even Wharton. Howard's the one who's just gotten impossible lately."

"Now, Dessie," he chided mildly, "have patience. He's only eleven and he's a boy. What do you expect?"

He kissed her again, this time a peck on the lips, and then went back to his wife. "You been wanting to go visit your folks in Galva for a long time, Carrie. I promise you, you're going to go there this year." He kissed her and, without a backward glance, picked up his scuffed valise from the floor beside the bench and strode off toward his train.

Nattily clad in a new light blue-gray suit with matching derby, Holmes entered New York City's Pennsylvania Station and bought his ticket to Philadelphia. He checked the railroad's system schedule and jotted down a number. Then, with twenty minutes remaining before the train was scheduled to leave, he strode directly to the station's Western Union office prior to catching his train and sent Georgiana a wire:

PENN STA BRANCH CXBRT NYC TTRXTYCXS 9 AM AUG 4
1894 GEORGIANA HOWARD STOP CARE OF THOMAS
LADD STOP 423 OAK ST STOP LAKE BLUFF ILLINOIS

DEAREST STOP TAKE PULLMAN SLEEPER PENN RR TRAIN
2 WHICH LEAVES UNION STATION CHICAGO 5 PM AUG 4
ARRIVES BROAD STREET STATION PHILADELPHIA AT 6
PM AUG 5 STOP WILL MEET YOU STOP MISS YOU STOP
LOVE STOP HENRY

A short time later he settled himself in the plush Palace Car of the train and reviewed the situation as it had developed since he left St. Louis on July 23. His first stop had been Chicago where, disguised in heavily padded clothing and with a heavy false beard and spectacles, he first met with Pat Quinlan in a room of the fire-damaged Castle and gave him two primary instructions: to wire him if any investigators began asking his whereabouts; to burn down the Castle completely if any search of the premises was begun by authorities. His next stop had been a brief visit with Frank

Blackman to go over finances and instruct him to give Dora whatever funds she needed, whenever she asked. He also told Blackman to expect to receive money from him, perhaps in large amounts, sent by telegraph, along with instructions on what to do with it.

Just over three hours later, having stopped off to change clothes and have a light lunch at the Chicago Club, of which he was a member, Holmes entered the front door of his own house in Wilmette, feeling the same pleasant aura of comfort and security wash over him as always happened when he came home. Fine Persian carpets, crystal chandeliers, the most expensive furnishings, valuable artwork and statuary—all these and more made the place reek with elegance.

There was a shriek of "Daddy! Daddy!" and five-year-old Lucy came flying down the stairs, giggling and squirming when he picked her up and hugged her close. She wrapped her arms around his neck and looked him full in the face. "Are you home now forever?"

"Not forever," he laughed, "but for a nice visit."

Dora had followed her daughter downstairs, beaming, and slipped into his embrace. "Welcome back, Holmes," she said.

He spent two days with them, resting, eating well, letting his mind relax from the rigors of the months past, spending pleasant hours in bed with Dora, instructing her that any money she needed could be gotten from Blackman and, finally, telling her most of what had transpired during his absence and his plans for the weeks ahead. He did not tell her he had married Georgiana, nor that his new wife was at this moment only twenty-two miles north of them at Lake Bluff. But neither did he make any effort to go there to see Georgiana.

The planned insurance swindle in Philadelphia involving substituting a cadaver to be identified as the body of Ben Pitezel bothered Dora considerably and she was vocal about it.

"You've always done these things essentially alone and in as simple a way as possible," she pointed out. "Now all of a sudden you're involving a convicted bank robber, a shyster lawyer you don't even know, a New York doctor, Ben, his wife, maybe one of his children and God knows who else, and you're doing it in a city you're not terribly familiar with. Worst by far is that instead of doing it simply, you're making it very complicated and thus increasing the risks. Why are you doing this, Holmes? I don't like it."

He stared at her a moment, nostrils faintly flared, then shook his head. "I've managed to pull off these insurance frauds for years without anyone telling me how it should or shouldn't be done. I don't intend to start taking gratuitous advice now. The trouble with you, Dora," he added, "is you think only of the end result—the money. You don't understand the exhilaration of the *game*. You don't understand the gratification that comes from outthinking the best they can pit against you. Tell you what—I won't tell you what to do with the money you get out of it, and you don't tell me how to do what I do better than anyone."

It was the first time he'd ever left Dora with a sense of chill existing between them. The day before yesterday, on his way to New York, he had stopped in Philadelphia only long enough to establish in his own mind where the boarding-house was located that Pitezel was staying in, as B. F. Perry, and to locate one for himself and Georgiana not too far distant. Though it was early morning, Pitezel had already been drinking but he was still reasonably sober.

"I think I've found the ideal place for our project, Holmes," he said, his pipe bobbing as he spoke. "It's a few block away, on Callowhill Street. Let me take you over there and show it to you."

"No, I'll see it when I get back. Right now I want to get to New York and see the man who's going to supply us with your body."

"Uh, Holmes . . ." Pitezel hesitated, sucked on the pipe-stem, removed it from his mouth and then plunged on. "I've got to have some money. I mean, that's why I haven't rented the Callowhill place yet."

Holmes's eyes narrowed. "Would you like to tell me where the five hundred dollars is that I gave you in Fort Worth?"

"Christ, Holmes, that was almost three months ago." He became defensive. "I had to leave most of it for Carrie and the kids to live on. And then there was the train fare. And living costs after I got here. Nothing's free, you know."

"Especially the booze?"

"Aw, Holmes, have a heart. Sure I have a drink now and then, but not all that much." He chomped down on the pipestem.

Holmes looked at him with set features. "How much is the rent?"

"Forty dollars a month. Unfurnished."

Holmes reached into his pocket and extracted his wallet. "Here," he said, handing him $50. "Rent the place. I'll go with you to get the furnishings when I get back." He gripped Pitezel's wrist and his final words were flat, thick with menace. "Ben, don't drink it up or it's all over between us." He released his grip and walked away.

You son of a bitch, Holmes, Pitezel raged inwardly, staring after him. You miserable son of a bitch. One of these days *I'll* be in the driver's seat!

First thing in the morning yesterday, Holmes called on Malcolm Rolfe, the skilled tailor who had served him several times in the past. Formerly head of the custom tailoring department of Brooks Brothers on Broadway, Rolfe agreed to have his people set aside everything else they were doing and go to work immediately on making the suit for Holmes... receiving in exchange for this courtesy triple what the expensive suit would normally have cost. In midafternoon it was ready and delivered to the hotel room.

A discreet bronze plaque beside the front door of the fine brownstone located on Central Park West bore only the words *Dr. Chester Fish, M.D.* When Holmes entered the tastefully elegant outer office, he walked past the several waiting patients without a glance and stopped before the receptionist's desk.

"I'd like to see Dr. Fish, please," he said.

The efficient-appearing middle-aged woman looked up at him, two small wrinkles forming above the bridge of her nose. She was unimpressed by his look of wealth; virtually all of the doctor's patients had this look.

"I'm sorry, sir," she told him, exhibiting no trace of sorrow, "but Dr. Fish sees no one without an appointment."

He leaned over the desk, face close to hers, eyes suddenly frightening, and spoke softly. "One last time. Go tell him I want to speak to him. Now."

The receptionist paled and leaned back from him. "Your... name, please?"

"Tell him it's Herman Mudgett."

She very nearly scrambled in her haste to reach the closed door on the opposite side of the room and disappeared through it. Seconds later it reopened and Chester Fish looked out. The sight of his visitor caused him to pale.

"It's all right, Miss Galen," he said. "You may return to your desk. I'll let you know when I've finished." He beckoned and Holmes nodded pleasantly as he passed Miss Galen and followed the doctor down a hall past several examination rooms. He noted that Chester was no longer so thin and knobby, no longer imbued with that frightened-rabbit-ready-to-flee aspect that had been his trademark.

"Dammit, Holmes," he rasped when they were in his private office with the door closed, "you didn't have to alarm my receptionist." His natural color had not yet returned and the prominent freckles made him appear poxed.

"I wasn't inclined to stand and argue, Chester," Holmes answered mildly. Then he smiled. "I got her attention, didn't I?"

"Attention! Jesus Jumping Christ, you scared the shit out of her."

"Good. Maybe next time she'll remember."

"I can guarantee that." Fish suddenly looked at him more intently. "What do you mean, next time?"

Holmes did not reply at once, letting his gaze move across the office. It stopped on the skeleton on a special stand in one corner. He tilted his head toward it. "That the one I sent you?"

"Yes."

"Thought so." The ghost of a smile touched his lips. *Nice to see you, Emeline. You're looking wonderful.* He turned back to Fish. "I need a fresh cadaver."

A pulse began to throb noticeably at the doctor's temple and his spread fingers combed through the thatch of red hair. "Right to the point, Herman. Like old times. When and what kind?"

"You were right when you called me Holmes. Not Herman. That was just to get your attention." The doctor said nothing, and after a moment Holmes answered his question. "I want it about the end of this month. Male. Pushing forty. Around six feet tall."

Fish was making notes. "What about eye color? Distinguishing marks or scars? Abnormalities? Healed fractures? Lost digits? Condition of teeth?"

A note of uncertainty was in Holmes's response. "Blue eyes, that I know for sure. He has a small pedunculated wart on the back of his neck. No abnormalities or past fractures that I know of. No lost digits. Teeth not in the best condition. Alcoholic, so the liver's probably sclerotic."

Fish threw down his pencil. "It's pointless. I can't do this on a verbal description. Evidently you're trying to match someone presently living?"

"Yes."

"Any chance of getting him in here for visual examination? Without it, I can't guarantee even coming close. Too many intangibles."

"I think so. Sure. Monday?"

"The sixth? Can't do it. How about Tuesday? First thing?"

"All right. When? Eight o'clock?"

"God, Holmes, 'first thing' in civilized America doesn't mean dawn. I get to the office at ten. Be here with him." He held up a hand, checking himself and momentarily warding off Holmes's response. "No," he said, "change that. Nine o'clock. And not here. This . . . man, he doesn't know me, does he?"

"No."

"Keep it that way. Get a hotel room. Let me know where. I'll come there. Don't speak my name. Tuesday, nine in the morning."

Holmes stood up and started toward the door. "Anything you say, Chester. We'll be there. I can tell you the place now. In the Manhattan, registered as B. F. Perry."

"Holmes!"

He stopped with his hand on the knob. Fish's narrowed eyes were nearly closed, his face resembling a death mask. "No more," he said. "This is the last time, Herman,"—he used the name deliberately—"*ever!* I used to envy you—your dash, your way with women, your I-don't-give-a-damn nature, the way anything you did turned out right for you."

"And now you don't anymore." It wasn't a question.

"That's too mild. I loathe you. You represent everything I consider despicable. I'm horrified that I ever considered *anything* about you as admirable. I'll help you this last time, as best I can, but only if you give me your solemn word that it *is* the last time. And only if you promise never to reveal to anyone I've ever had anything to do with your schemes."

"Sure, Chester." Holmes wore a crooked grin. "Why not?"

"Don't treat it lightly," Fish warned. "I've never been

more serious. If you involve me, jeopardize what I've built up here, I swear, Holmes, I'll take you down with me. *And you know I can*. After this one, you leave me alone, I'll leave you alone. *Fini*. Agreed?"

Holmes opened the door and stepped through it, starting to close it behind him, but then he stopped and thrust his head back at an angle around the door. "You know, Chester, you always were a lot brighter than you looked. Agreed."

He winked and then he was gone.

"Philadelphia next!" the conductor bawled. Holmes stirred from his reverie and watched out the window as the station approached and engulfed them. He walked through the terminal without pause. Nineteen blocks from downtown he stepped off the streetcar and, carrying his medium-sized black leather valise, walked a block east to the Alcorn Boardinghouse at 1905 N. Eleventh Street. A cadaverous man of about sixty answered his knock. "Yes?"

"My name is Howell. I've come to see about renting rooms for my wife and me."

The man passed his badly arthritic hand across a shiny dome rimmed by a horseshoe of sparse hair. His Adam's apple bobbed markedly. "Well, now," he said in a scratchy falsetto, "Mrs. Dr. Alcorn, she's gone off to the shore as usual an' won't be t'home till late this afternoon."

Holmes was amused. "Mrs. Doctor Alcorn? Is her first name Doctor, or is her husband a doctor?"

"Neither." The man cackled an explosively grating laugh. "*She's* the doctor. Or was. Dr. Adella Alcorn. Widder lady. Never did meet her husband. Poor soul died of some kind of aggravated itch 'long 'bout ten-twelve years ago. She got dog-tired of doctorin' an' retired an' opened this here place. Says she wishes she'd a done it long before. Says she was—"

"*Are* there rooms available, Mr. . . . ?"

"Grammer. Grammer's the name. John Grammer. I'm Mrs. Dr. Alcorn's oldest tenant. Come her, oh, eight-nine years ago an'—"

"The room?" Holmes was no longer amused.

"Right. The room. 'Course they's rooms. Ain't that what the sign out t'front says? Come on. I'll show you."

Walking with fragile unsteadiness, he led Holmes down a shadowed hallway poorly lighted with bracketed gas jets on the walls. At the rear of the house a narrow flight of stairs took them to the third floor where there was a three-room apartment with two dormered bedrooms and a parlor with worn carpeting, but with relatively new sofa, overstuffed chairs and lantern-equipped escritoire. The rooms had been newly wallpapered in a jolly pattern of large brown-eyed Susans on a pale yellow background and the place had its own tiny bathroom with sink and half-tub. It was hardly the sort of interior he would have selected, but for his purposes, it would suffice.

"How much, Mr. Grammer?"

"Three-fifty a week with just the rooms. Two dollars and two-bits extra a week per person for food, if you're boardin'."

Holmes nodded. He handed Grammer eight dollars. The man cackled again for no apparent reason, folded the bills in half and stuffed them into his shirt pocket. He handed Holmes a skeleton key. "Where is she?"

"Who?" Holmes asked. "Oh, you mean my wife? She won't be here till six o'clock. I'm meeting her at the Broad Street Station. She's getting in from Chicago and I know she'll be tired, so I'd like to bring her right here and have dinner and then probably get some sleep."

"Nothin' wrong with that," Grammer said, bobbing his head and cackling again. "They's four other boarders 'sides me an' we don't eat till seven o'clock, so you'll be able t'make it fine. An' then you an' the Missus'll have a chance t'meet Mrs. Dr. Alcorn."

Holmes put his bag in one of the bedrooms and descended the stairs with Grammer on his heels. "What'd you say your business was?" Grammer asked.

"I didn't say," Holmes told him, "but in case Mrs. Doctor Alcorn wants to know, I have a patent letter-copying machine company—the ABC Copier Company in Chicago—and I'm here to lease equipment to the Pennsylvania Railroad."

Holmes walked to Pitezel's boardinghouse but he was not there, so he left a message saying where he was staying, but telling him not to let Georgiana see him if he came to the Alcorn Boardinghouse. Then he went to the Broad Street Station and read newspapers until Georgiana's train arrived.

She flew into his arms and they embraced as if not having seen one another for months. She had a valise, a large suitcase and a trunk, so he signaled a redcap to load the luggage on a handcart and get them a carriage to take them to the boardinghouse. They walked behind him, their arms about each other.

"Oh, Henry," she said, eyes overbright, "it's so wonderful to be with you again. I didn't have fun at all, even with Mary Ellen. All I wanted was to be wherever you were. I don't want us ever to be apart again. Ever."

"I've missed you, too, sweetheart," he told her. "I wish we'd never have to be apart anymore. Unfortunately, business is business and I'm afraid there will be times—as short as possible, believe me—when we're not together. But you know what? It looks more and more likely that we're going to Europe. That'll be our real honeymoon."

"Really, Henry! Oh, how wonderful. I can't wait. When?"

"Soon," he told her. "I can't say for sure, but probably before Christmas. Now, first things first. Hungry?"

"Starved!"

"Good. Dinner'll be ready when we get there. And wait'll you meet John Grammer. He looks like a plucked chicken. Come to think of it, he cackles like one, too."

Holmes almost laughed at the surreptitious way Chester Fish slunk into the hotel room. The man was obviously very upset at being here and even the warm and friendly manner in which he shook Fish's hand failed to dispel the doctor's apprehension.

"We can dispense with introductions," Holmes said. "Doctor, this is your subject. He'll answer all your questions and do whatever you wish."

Pitezel shot Holmes an indecipherable glance and then bowed slightly to the doctor but said nothing. Fish took a small notebook and a pencil from his inner pocket.

"We'll get this over as quickly as possible," he said. "Please stand with your back against the wall there. Stand erect, heels against the baseboard."

Pitezel did as directed and Fish marked his height with a tiny pencil mark on the wall, then measured it with a cloth tape he pulled from his pocket.

"Six feet one-quarter inch," he said, jotting down the figure. "What do you weigh?"

"I don't know," Pitezel said. "About one seventy-five, I guess."

"Are you a smoker? If so, how much?"

"I smoke a tin of pipe tobacco about every week. Occasional cigars. Maybe two, three a week."

"You are an alcoholic?"

Pitezel glared at Holmes and made no reply.

"This is no game, sir," Fish said curtly, "and I do not enjoy this any more than you. But a history of alcoholism connotes certain internal changes of which we must be aware. You *are* addicted to alcohol?"

"Yes," Pitezel said in a barely audible voice. "Off and on."

"To what extent? What volume daily?"

"I don't know."

"Make an estimate, please."

"Goddammit, then, a pint, a quart, whatever I can get!"

"You must try to help me. I do not care how much you drink. I only wish to make an educated guess as to what effect it may have had. How much would you say you drink in a twenty-four-hour period, on the average?"

"A pint," Pitezel mumbled. "On the average, I guess about a pint."

"For what length of time? How long has this been going on?"

"I was on the wagon for almost all of 'ninety-two."

"And since then, about a pint a day?"

"I guess."

"Probably moderately sclerotic then," Fish murmured and made another notation. He continued his examination methodically. Eyes, blue. Build, medium. Hair, dark brown. Complexion, light olive. Medium-full mustache, reddish brown. Other than broken nose, no distinguishing marks on face. Pea-sized pedunculated wart on back of neck at collar line. Numerous small inconsequential scars on hands.

"What happened to your thumb?" he asked. The nail was almost black from a hematoma beneath it.

Pitezel held up his hand and looked at it. "Oh, that. I hit it with a hammer. Maybe six weeks ago."

Fish nodded and jotted it down. "Get undressed, please. Completely."

Pitezel flashed a look at Holmes, as if he were about to object, but Holmes motioned him to follow the doctor's order. With poor grace and—amusing to Holmes—a display of embarrassment, Pitezel disrobed until he stood naked. Fish started at his neck and worked his way down, moving slowly around and around the man as he did so. He checked each arm carefully, armpit to wrist, studied the skin of chest and back and sides, lifted Pitezel's flaccid penis and checked his scrotum for rupture, spread his cheeks to check for hemorrhoidal tissue, then continued the examination down each leg to the feet and even checked the soles and between the toes.

"The origin of this cicatrix, please?" he said, studying Pitezel's right leg.

"Huh?" Pitezel said.

"This scar," Fish said, pointing to a slanted, inch-long white mark on the inside of Pitezel's right leg, just below the knee. "What caused it?"

"Fell through a window when I was drunk once, about six years ago," Pitezel replied. "They sewed it up with four, five stitches."

"You may get dressed, sir," Fish said. He looked at Holmes. "Rather good condition, considering the proclivity for alcohol. The actual physical dimensions will be no problem to duplicate. The mustache could be, but it can always be said that was shaved off. The only two points of concern seem to be the cicatrix on the right inner lower leg approximately two inches below the knee and the pedunculated wart on the—"

"What's pedunculated?" Pitezel interrupted suspiciously as he tucked his shirt into his trousers.

"Having the shape and general texture of a cauliflower," Fish said, then continued his comment without pause, "—the pedunculated wart on the nape at the collar line. Those peculiarities are not terribly uncommon, though not usually in conjunction. With judicious disfigurement in some logical manner, these anomalies could be disposed of."

"You can find a suitable subject, then?"

"Our city morgue, to which I have access, has at any given time from two to thirty unidentified cadavers that are, after a proper period, buried in the Potter's Field. A reasonably close associate of mine is night supervisor of that department and can, I am sure, with only moderate difficulty, remove a reasonably fresh corpse of the description required. I am sure he will need from twenty-four to forty-eight hours' notice. He will also have to be paid a reasonable sum to perform this favor."

"How much?" Holmes asked.

"Two hundred dollars," Fish said.

Holmes grunted an assent. "Alert him at once. Here's

one hundred dollars as a down payment, the remainder to be paid when I pick up the cadaver. You can tell him I will bring a trunk in which to transport the subject."

Fish accepted the bills. "I'll tell him. How and where do I notify you when a body becomes available?"

Holmes jotted down the name of H. Howell, care of Alcorn Boardinghouse, 1905 N. Eleventh Street, Philadelphia, and gave it to Fish. "Send a wire here. Just say the merchandise is ready. Sign it 'Trout.' I'll come to pick it up immediately. I must have word from you no later than noon on the last day of this month."

Fish folded the slip of paper Holmes gave him and slid it into his vest pocket. He then pocketed his own note pad and pencil. When he looked up at Holmes again, there was no trace of amity in his expression. "Please do not have any further personal contact with me until I send the wire." He gave Holmes the briefest of nods and left the room without another glance at Pitezel.

The morning was clear and beautiful and despite the promise of grinding August heat later in the afternoon, Holmes felt wonderful. As he was certain she would be, Georgiana was somewhat ill and confined to bed. It eased the necessity of scheduling things to do with her to keep her content. The familiar excitement was building in him again. Everything was coming together perfectly and he walked with jaunty step along Race Street as he headed toward the corner near the Harley Boardinghouse, where he and Pitezel had planned to meet. He hoped Pitezel had not gotten drunk again last night and was still lying in his room sleeping it off, but need not have worried. Ben was waiting for him and they shook hands and walked together toward the office of the real estate broker who was handling the Callowhill Street house. Pitezel was taciturn but Holmes made up for it, animatedly discussing the details of their plan.

"We're on the home stretch with this whole thing, Ben," he said expansively. "We'll be renting the house today and then getting some furniture for it and establishing you there as B. F. Perry. A few more weeks here and you and Carrie will be together again, living in luxury. How are she and the kids doing, anyway? Have you heard?"

"She writes," Ben said. "More'n I do. She's not been

much good lately, Holmes. I don't know what it is. A cold, maybe. Female trouble. Who knows? Wharton's been sick, too. Now Carrie says it looks like Dessie's getting a little peaked."

"Well, I'm sorry to hear that. Georgiana's sort of under the weather herself this morning. Dessie handles the kids okay?"

"Yeah. She rides herd on them pretty well. She's a good girl."

"Yes, she certainly is," Holmes agreed, adding the trite litany, "and she'll make some man a wonderful wife one of these days."

Pitezel changed the subject. "You really think this whole thing's going to work out, Holmes?"

"Absolutely. It's paying attention to detail that counts—considering all the eventualities and being prepared for anything. And planning ahead. Like the insurance, for example. You can't take out a life policy and then just a few weeks later try to pull off something like this. They'd be suspicious immediately. You get the insurance and hold it for a while, pay a few of the premiums and then—" He broke off as Pitezel jolted to a halt with a stricken expression. Holmes turned back to him. "What's the matter?"

"Oh, shit, Holmes, I just remembered. I forgot to pay the insurance premium."

"What!" Holmes almost never lost his temper, but now he exploded with a savagery that frightened Pitezel. "You stupid son of a bitch! God damn you, Pitezel," he gripped his partner's arms and shook him the way an angry parent might shake a naughty child, "you can't be serious! What the hell is wrong with you? Are you crazy? All these months of setting up and you've ruined it by not paying a goddamned premium?"

"Holmes, listen. I . . . I *meant* to do it. I even thought of it on the day when it was due, but I was broke and—"

"Broke? *BROKE?* What the hell are you talking about, broke? Damn it, Ben, I made a point of giving you the money for that premium just two days before it was due. What do you mean, broke?"

"I got to drinking a little. Just a little, that's all." His voice became plaintive, the words blurting from him in a rush. "I wasn't drunk, honest! But then there was a poker game and I . . . son of a bitch, I *lost* it! Then I was afraid to tell you and thought I could make it back and pay it before the grace period was up, but after a while I forgot about it. That's what it was, Holmes, I just plain forgot about it."

Holmes, pale and glaring, was still gripping Pitezel's arms but now something the man had said caused the intense fury to abate and become no more than a cold anger. He dropped his hands but continued to stare at his partner. "You said something about the grace period. How long a grace period?" When Pitezel merely shook his head, Holmes prodded menacingly. "Think, damn you! How long? Is the grace period still in effect?"

"I don't know." Misery nearly choked him. "I don't think so."

"You don't think so, but you don't *know* for sure, do you. Where's the policy?"

"In my bag. In my room."

"Come on, then," Holmes spun him around, "we've got to check on it right now."

They walked as rapidly as they could back to where they had met and Holmes waited on the corner while Pitezel continued to the boardinghouse a few doors farther and disappeared inside. Less that a minute later he emerged with the folded policy in his hand.

"Well?" Holmes asked.

"I haven't looked at it yet. I just grabbed it and brought it out."

Holmes took it from him and unfolded it, running his index finger swiftly down the pages. Abruptly the finger stopped and he read a passage of fine type closely. Then he looked up and his cheeks puffed as he expelled a huge breath. "The grace period ends at midnight, August ninth," he said. "That's today. Come on, we've got to get to the telegraph office."

Within the hour Holmes emerged from the Western Union office and handed Pitezel a yellow copy of the telegraphic money order he had just sent to the Fidelity Mutual Life Association branch office in Chicago, where the policy had been taken out:

GENTLEMEN STOP TAKING ADVANTAGE OF GRACE PERIOD STILL IN EFFECT TO PAY PREMIUM ON MY LIFE INSURANCE STOP THIS IS PAYMENT OF $157.50 SEMIANNUAL PREMIUM DUE ON POLICY NUMBER 044145 IN MY NAME STOP PLEASE CREDIT MY ACCOUNT WITH THIS PAYMENT STOP BENJAMIN F PITEZEL

* * *

"You're such a wonderful reader, Henry," Georgiana said, smiling weakly at Holmes. "You have an expressiveness that just makes the words come alive. I hope you know how much I appreciate your taking so many of your days here to read to me like this. I certainly haven't been very good company for you on this trip, have I?"

"You are always the very best company to me, sweetheart," Holmes said softly. He smiled and lay aside the copy of George du Maurier's new book, *Trilby*, which he'd been reading aloud to her over the past few days. He rose from his chair and squatted beside the sofa, placing a gentle hand on her forehead. "Feeling any better?"

She sighed. "I think so. I'm getting a little hungry, if that's any indication."

"I'd say its a very good one," he told her. "You've had this bug for three weeks now and have hardly been able to keep anything down the whole time. Wouldn't surprise me if you've lost fifteen pounds. Supposing I get Mrs. Dr. Alcorn to fix you some chicken soup? I think it would do you a world of good."

She nodded. "I'd like that, but not just yet. In a little while. I want to talk a little about what you just read to me. That Svengali! Isn't he awful? He—du Maurier, I mean—makes it sound almost possible, doesn't he?"

"You don't think it is?"

"That a person could have powers like Svengali, you mean, and hypnotize people and make them do his bidding?" She shuddered. "No. Absolutely not. People are thinking organisms, Henry. They can't be controlled by someone who just reaches out and takes over their will like that, can they?"

"Of course not," Holmes said mildly. "It's just a story. Want to hear some more of it now, or do you want to eat?"

"I do think I'd like some soup, Henry. You're such a dear, and you work so hard. I feel guilty, lying around for so long."

"You can't help being sick, Georgiana," he told her. "And as for my work, I enjoy it. It's nearly finished and I expect we'll be going home within the next few days. That is, if you're up to traveling."

"Just point me toward the train," she said. "I'm ready. I really am."

There was a gentle tapping on the door and Holmes rose and opened it. Mrs. Dr. Alcorn was there, holding out a yellow envelope. "This wire just came for you, Mr. Howell," she said. She looked past him toward Georgiana as he turned away and opened it. "And how are you feeling today, Mrs. Howell? Any better?"

"Yes," Georgiana replied. "I think I am, thank you."

Holmes refolded the telegram and put it into his pocket. "I have some business I have to attend to immediately," he said. He looked at their landlady. "Do you suppose you might be able to prepare some hot chicken soup for Georgiana? For the first time in much too long, she thinks she might be able to keep it down."

"Of course. Poor dear!" She smiled at Georgiana. "We'll have some hot food in your stomach before you know it, Mrs. Howell." She left.

"She's so nice," Georgiana said as Holmes closed the door, "but I do wish she would call us Howard instead of Howell."

"It's a common mistake," Holmes said. "Now listen, I hate to say it but I may not get back until very late tonight. Why don't you go ahead and read on in *Trilby* while I'm gone? Will you be all right? I'll have Mrs. Dr. Alcorn look in on you."

"I'll be fine," she said. "You go on. I'll read *Trilby* if you insist, but I'd much rather have you read it to me. Go on now. I hope everything goes just fine."

He kissed her, handed her the book, kissed her again and left.

On the way to see Pitezel, who was now ensconced two miles away in the Callowhill Street house, Holmes felt his blood surging as it always did in the final stages of a project. Since that first near-catastrophe involving the life insurance premium, everything had gone along very well. They had gone to see the realtor and Pitezel, using the name B. F. Perry, had rented the place, saying he was going to live upstairs and have his patent office on the ground floor. They immediately had a duplicate key made for Holmes to use.

Across the street from an abandoned Philadelphia & Reading Railroad station, the structure at 1316 Callowhill Street was part of a string of two-story redbrick buildings flush against one another. It was ideally suited to their plans, since the first floor had been made into a sort of storefront. A large front door had two narrow arched glass panes and was two steps up from the sidewalk level. It opened into a foyer where, to the left, a flight of stairs ascended to a two-bedroom second floor and a small attic. Below the steps there was a doorway leading down to a cellar. The entry hall continued back to a door leading to a kitchen and small backyard. To the foyer's right was the large front room, which had a big eight-paned bay window overlooking the street.

Their first task, which helped to give the impression that this was a patent office, had been to move in a box of empty bottles, flasks and tubing, as well as the containers of chemicals Holmes had bought—jugs of benzine, chloroform, naphthalene. They also got the trunk that was to be used to transport the body when it became available. Then, at a secondhand furniture store on Buttonwood Street, they bought under the B. F. Perry name a bed and matting, several chairs, a small desk, a small filing cabinet and an upright shelved cabinet, some lamps and a few other pieces, all of which were delivered the next day.

Immediately upon getting the Callowhill Street office sparsely furnished, Pitezel lettered a big sign of red and black words on a sheet of muslin and hung it inside the bay window. It read:

B. F. PERRY
PATENTS BOUGHT AND SOLD

Nine days ago—August 22—the sign had snagged its first customer. Eugene Smith, a forty-year-old house carpenter and aspiring inventor, was walking on Callowhill between Thirteenth and Broad when he saw the sign and stopped abruptly. He had recently invented a device that he called a saw set sharpener, which, with a minimum of time and effort, could quickly and effectively sharpen a dull handsaw. But having invented it, he had no idea how to go about marketing it or finding an investor to back him. Whoever was operating this place might be able to help him, so Smith had immediately crossed the street and entered the front door.

Pitezel was behind the small desk and came to his feet as Smith entered. "Hello," he said. "I'm B. F. Perry. Can I help you?"

"I hope so," Smith replied.

Pitezel invited him to sit down and they fell to discussing Smith's ingenious device. The carpenter was sure he had come to the right place when Pitezel told him of his own invention of an automatic coal-bin device. "Now, where your invention is concerned," Pitezel told him, "it sounds as if it's very remarkable, but I won't be able to say for sure until I see it. I presume you do have a working model?"

"Oh, sure," Smith said.

"Fine, why don't you bring it in so I can look it over and we'll move ahead from there."

"I'll do that," Smith said and left.

Two days later, on Friday morning, Eugene Smith returned with the device and a couple of dull saws and gave Pitezel a demonstration. When it was finished, he looked at Pitezel with a mixture of shyness and eagerness. "Well, what do you think, Mr. Perry?"

"I think it's possibly a good device, but it seems to me there are a few things you need to change in the model before submitting it. There are certain clumsy aspects, but none that would be difficult to correct."

They entered into a discussion about these faults and were so engaged when Smith broke off as the front door opened and a man wearing a light blue-gray suit and matching derby hat entered. Since Smith was watching the man, he didn't see Perry's reaction, but he did see the stranger make a motion with his head toward the steps and then go up the stairs himself without having spoken.

"Please excuse me," Pitezel said to Smith. "I'll be back in just a few minutes."

He followed the man upstairs and went into the empty bedroom where Holmes was waiting for him. "You should have told me you were coming. I'd've made sure no one was here."

Holmes shrugged. "No matter. Your man down there only saw me for an instant and there's no reason to think he'd put any special significance to it. I came by because I wanted to show you a note I received in the mail from my friend in New York." He handed the brief unsigned letter to Pitezel, who read it quickly:

Unidentified charity patient in city hospital free ward is terminal. Description matches very well. At present rate of deterioration, expiration expected to coincide nicely with your schedule. Remains will be taken to city morgue. Wire will be sent to you immediately thereupon. Trout.

Pitezel had smiled and handed the note back. "Looks like we're in business," he said. "I'd better get back downstairs."

"How soon can you get rid of him?"

"Right away. We were about finished anyway."

"Good. I'll wait till he leaves before I do. No sense pushing our luck."

Pitezel agreed and returned downstairs, where Smith stood up as he approached him. Pitezel had not been gone longer than two minutes, but he apologized. "Sorry to have kept you waiting, Mr. Smith," Pitezel said. "I think we've gone over the main points. I don't see any need in my detaining you any longer. Do you want to take the model with you, or do you have another one at home you can make the improvements on?"

"I have another one in my cellar that I can work on, Mr. Perry. Why don't you just keep this one here for now. I'll make the improvements and bring them back."

"Fine." Pitezel went to the desk and wrote something on a pad. "Here," he said, handing the paper to Smith. "This is a receipt for the model I'm keeping here. I'll be looking forward to seeing you."

Now, on this final day of the month, four days after Smith's last visit, Holmes was approaching the Callowhill building with the telegram just received. He entered the front door and Pitezel, seated at his desk reading a newspaper, came quickly to his feet, his eyes glinting, as Holmes locked the door behind him.

"You've heard!"

Holmes grinned and slapped him jovially on the shoulder as he dug into his pocket and pulled out the telegram. "Listen to this. It'll be music to your ears." He held up the yellow sheet and read aloud: "'H. Howell. Stop. August thirty-first, eighteen ninety-four. Stop. Sir. Stop. Your merchandise is ready. Stop. Pick up soonest. Stop. Trout.' This is it, Ben!"

"I was beginning to think it would never happen," Pitezel said fervently. "You're going right away?"

"Just give me the trunk and I'm off. I'll be back late tonight. With the merchandise. Wait up for me."

It was just 9 P.M. and only a handful of patrons were in the Fritz Richards saloon when Ben Pitezel, sitting alone at his customary rear table, finished his whiskey and signaled to Bill Moebius. The heavyset bartender brought him another, along with the two half-pint bottles he had ordered earlier. Pitezel thanked him and paid a nickel for his whiskey, plus fifty cents for the two half-pints. As soon as Moebius was gone, Pitezel slipped the bottles into his coat pockets and then held up the whiskey glass. "Cheers," he muttered bitterly.

This was the worst day Ben Pitezel could ever remember having, made especially difficult to bear because it had begun with such high expectations. He'd been excited yesterday after Holmes had left for New York City, certain that in only hours this whole miserable scheme could be put to rest. He'd become progressively sorry that he'd even gotten involved in it.

Early in the evening he'd tried to nap, but sleep wouldn't come and so he'd gone back downstairs and sat waiting in the darkened office. It was close to 1 A.M. when the carriage had stopped outside and that's where this miserable day had begun to go wrong. He'd leaped up and lighted the lamp, not even wondering why Holmes had evidently told the driver to wait, but one glimpse at his friend's expression as he entered was enough to quash any flare of jubilation.

"It fell through, Ben," Holmes had told him stiffly. "No body."

Pitezel vaguely remembered sinking into his chair and sitting there stunned, listening with bare comprehension as Holmes elaborated. With as much expectation as Pitezel had been experiencing, he had gone to the morgue with his New York friend and then was dismayed to find, upon viewing the body, that it was all wrong. The height and weight were there, along with the general physical shape, but the head was much rounder, the hands too delicate, the ears much too large. There was a wart on the neck, true, but it was on the side of the neck, lower than Pitezel's and much more prominent, and there was no scar on the leg. The corpse's teeth were small, very even and white, unlike Pitezel's, which were large, misaligned and slightly discolored. Holmes, so he said, had been furious and berated his New York friend, telling him how impossible it would be to attempt to pass that body off as the one it was supposed to represent. And the New York friend had first become furious in his own right and then apologetic, telling Holmes that he couldn't just order up a body that met all the qualifications; if Holmes didn't think it good enough, then he was sorry, but that was all that was available and either he could take it with him or else forget that one and wait for another to become available that would possibly be a closer match. Holmes had refused to take it and then here he was, telling Pitezel to cheer up, that it was a setback but not a disaster; they'd just have to wait a little longer.

Pitezel had hardly realized it when Holmes left and his carriage clip-clopped away in the darkness. There was a portion of a quart of whiskey upstairs and Pitezel had gone to get it and came back down and resumed his place at the desk, as if still waiting. By the time the office was bright with daylight, the whiskey was gone and he had left the house and walked, carrying the empty bottle by the neck. He'd finally pitched the bottle away somewhere but continued walking for hours until, at ten this morning, he had entered this very saloon and drank—slowly but methodically—until noon. The whiskey seemed to have no effect on him. An enormous depression enshrouded him and at length he had walked mechanically back to the patent office and checked his mailbox.

There was a letter from Carrie and for the first time this day his spirits lightened some as he tore it open. On reading it, his depression returned, worse than before. The letter was a litany of tribulations: Carrie was sick and unable to keep any food down; Wharton was sick and was running an extremely high fever; Dessie was sick and unable to take care of the house; the other children—Alice, Nellie and Howard—were taking advantage of everything and running wild; bill collectors were coming to the door; the money Ben left them was almost gone and there were still other bills that needed paying and when was Benny coming home?

Early this afternoon he had returned to the Fritz Richards saloon and drank again, but he found no pleasure in it, no release. He returned to the office and wrote Carrie a letter, telling her he was sick and tired of everything, that nothing had gone right for as long as he could remember and that he was going to come home and forget the whole business here.

Just before 8 P.M. he tapped at the door of the Alcorn Boardinghouse and asked to see Mr. Howell. He was told that the tenant was up in his rooms and to go on up, but Pitezel refused and asked that Howell simply be told there was a visitor downstairs.

Holmes came down and the two went out into the backyard to talk. Pitezel remembered trying not to become emotional, but he had. He was anguished and bitter and, in telling Holmes about Carrie and Dessie and Wharton being sick, he had even broken down and wept, furious with himself that he was doing so but unable to stop.

"What it comes down to, Holmes," he had said, sniffling, when he finally got control of himself, "is that I've had enough of this whole business. I'm going home. Tomorrow. There's a noon train and I intend to be on it."

There had been no sympathy from Holmes at first. "Why do I put up with a drunk like you!" he railed at Pitezel. "Why do I take my time and money and effort to run all these risks? I'll tell you why, dammit. So you and Carrie, for a few days' work on your part, will have ten *thousand* dollars of your own . . . more than you've ever had. And here you are, whining and wailing and ready to give it all up, just because everything hasn't worked out as you wanted it to or as soon as you wanted. What the hell kind of an attitude is that? What the hell kind of thanks is it to me? Jesus, Ben, is that how you really want to treat me? After all we've been through together?"

"But Carrie's sick, Holmes, and Dessie and Wharton, too. I don't have any money to send them."

"So because of that, you'd give it all up?" He was quiet for a space and when he spoke again his voice was softer and filled with a vast sadness. "All right, Ben, if that's what you want, I won't stand in your way." He fumbled in his wallet and handed Pitezel three fifty-dollar bills. "Take this . . . for your family. You should know by now that, no matter what, I would always see to it that Carrie and the kids are taken care off. It's just part of the loyalty I feel for you. Don't ever think I don't know how hard you've worked. I know you have, and I know I've been unfair asking you to give so much of yourself." He placed his hand on Ben's shoulder and looked into his face, his own eyes reflecting burning pinpoints of light from the windows of the house. "I think you should know, though, since I came back this morning without the body, I wired a friend in Chicago who has the same kind of access to cadavers as the one in New York. I won't tell you who he is, Ben. He doesn't want me to, because you know him. The point is, he knows you, too. He knows exactly what you look like and he says there are three unclaimed bodies in the Chicago morgue right now, any one of which could pass for you. He wants an answer from me tomorrow, but even if I say yes, and send him the three hundred dollars he wants, it'll take a day or two to get them here, and I know you want to go home. And, Ben, I understand that, believe me, I do." He squeezed Pitezel's shoulder a final time. "You take care of yourself, friend. I have to get back upstairs to Georgiana. She's still sick. I'll get in touch with you in St. Louis."

Holmes had seemed too distraught to speak more and had turned and started away, but Pitezel had run after him and stopped him, and the words he spoke then still burned in his mind now as he sat in a saloon three doors from his own place on Callowhill Street: "Holmes, I'm sorry. You've been so good to me . . . to us, Carrie and me and the kids. I guess . . . I guess I've just been thinking of myself too much. I want to say I'll help. I owe it to you, I know that. I'm just not sure. Give me tonight. Let me think about it tonight and then come and see me in the morning. Is that okay? Will you do that?"

"Sure, Ben," Holmes had said, but he sounded unconvinced of Pitezel's sincerity. "I'll do that. I'll see you around ten-thirty or eleven." and then he had entered the house and was gone.

And so Pitezel had come back here to the saloon . . . to sit . . . to drink . . . to think . . . and had continued to do so until this moment.

"Why not?" he said aloud.

"What'd you say, Mr. Perry?" asked the bartender, glancing up from his conversation with a customer.

Pitezel didn't answer. He stood up and walked out without a sideways glance, his side pockets weighted down and slightly bulged by the half-pint bottles of whiskey. He walked to the tobacco shop at 1304 Callowhill, next door to the corner. It was 9:30 P.M. now and the proprietor, Alice Pierce, was just closing. She didn't know his name but recognized him and greeted him cheerfully, but he only nodded at her, bought three cigars for a quarter and left without another word.

Mrs. Pierce sniffed as she closed and spoke aloud as she locked the front door. "A man shouldn't go walking around all the time wearing his chin down on his chest."

Outside, Benjamin Pitezel headed directly to his own place at 1316 Callowhill Street.

Georgiana stirred and opened her eyes, blinking against the sunlight streaming into the room. Holmes was just preparing to leave. He was wearing the blue-gray suit she liked so much and she smiled and stretched as he came back to her.

"I fell asleep, didn't I? What time is it?"

"A little after ten o'clock. And if it's a choice," he said, sitting beside her and chuckling, "I'd prefer to think it was the great Svengali who put you to sleep, instead of my reading."

"Oh, it was, it was," she said hastily, trying to keep a straight face. "I kept hearing him say, 'Sleep . . . Sleeeeeep,' so what else could I do?"

He patted her hand. "That's all right. You really do need it. Sleep and Mrs. Dr. Alcorn's chicken soup—best remedies in the world for whatever ails you."

"Ummmm, I'll say. I feel one hundred percent better. That leaves only three hundred percent to go to get me back to feeling normal."

"Think you're up to going home later on today?"

"Is that what we're going to do?"

"I don't know for sure, but it's possible. So, if it won't tire you too much, it might be a good idea to pack up your trunk while I'm gone."

"All right, I can do that. You're off to see the railroad people?"

He grunted an assent as he stood up. Last night when he'd come back to the room after talking with Pitezel he'd found her asleep, but she had awakened as he shut the door and asked him who his visitor had been. He'd told her it was a messenger from the Pennsylvania Railroad Company, requesting that he appear at the residence of one of the line's officials at Nicetown in the morning. She'd been too sleepy last night to question that, but now her brow furrowed.

"Isn't this September second?"

"Yes."

"Well, I thought so. That means it's Sunday. Strange that you'd have a meeting on a Sunday morning."

"Business, I'm afraid," he said, bending over and kissing her, "is no respector of Sunday morning leisure. If they're anxious to close on their contracts for the copiers on a Sunday morning, who am I to object? I have to get moving. See you later."

Outside, Holmes headed directly for 1316 Callowhill Street.

At exactly 3:34 P.M. the door of 1316 Callowhill Street opened very slowly and Holmes leaned out and looked cautiously in both directions. He appeared apprehensive and was disheveled, his hat perched crookedly on his head, suit coat unbuttoned, trousers wrinkled. His tongue flicking out at frequent intervals to lick his lips. He stood there for many seconds, head swiveling back and forth. Still looking out, he stooped and picked up the large bag on the floor behind him and stepped outside, closing but not locking the door. He strode away swiftly, head down. At the corner of Thirteenth he turned right, then left at Carlton, the corner after that. Two more corners and two more turns before he stopped and dropped the bag into a trash container. Within the bag were some beakers, chemicals, rubber tubing, a gallon jug and a variety of other items.

He continued walking without pause until he was finally able to catch a streetcar to the Broad Street Station. Though he'd been sitting for some minutes in the streetcar, he was breathing heavily when he approached the ticket counter.

"When is your next train to Indianapolis?" he asked.

The ticket agent glanced at the clock in a bored manner. "In thirty-two minutes exactly. Track Three at four forty-five."

Holmes shook his head. "Too soon. When's the next one after that?"

The agent sighed and checked his schedule. "At ten twenty-five tonight. Same track."

"Let me have two one-way tickets, please."

Georgiana was shocked at her husband's appearance when he returned to their rooms a few minutes before five o'clock. In streetwear, she had rarely seen him other than impeccably clad. Yet now he entered badly rumpled. Further, he was obviously exhausted, apparently agitated and, initially, distinctly unwilling to talk.

"I'm awfully warm, honey," he told her when she began asking questions. "Let me get cleaned up and changed and then we can talk."

He took off his suit quickly and she noted that his underwear was soaked with perspiration, which seemed odd, since she'd never known him to perspire profusely. His actions were nervous and since, even under the greatest strain, she had never seen him act truly nervous before, she was worried. By the time he finished bathing and getting dressed in a fresh suit, he seemed quite normal again.

"Busy day," he told her, "but a profitable one. Would you believe that idiot had me out playing croquet and lawn tennis in a dress suit? I suppose it was worth it to get an order like that, but I wouldn't want to go through it every day."

"You certainly looked exhausted when you came in," she said hesitantly.

"I didn't just look it. I was! Anyway, it's all finished for now. We're going to catch tonight's 10:25 to Indianapolis. I booked us on the sleeper so we'll have a good rest."

"Couldn't we go tomorrow instead of tonight?" Georgiana looked distressed. "After moving around and getting my trunk packed, I was exhausted, too. Actually, I felt faint for a while. Too much too soon, I think."

"Well," Holmes hedged, "I thought about going in the morning, but the first two trains were booked solid and we wouldn't be able to get away until four forty-five tomorrow afternoon. I really would like to get away before then. You know what? I'll bet more than anything else you're hungry. We'll have a good meal downstairs and after that you'll feel much better, I guarantee it. And when we get to the train, you can stretch out and relax to another chapter or two of *Trilby* so you can find out what happens to our malevolent Svengali."

She was still dubious but smiled and agreed he was probably correct. And later, after dinner with Adella Alcorn and her other boarders at the big table, Georgiana had to admit that she did feel considerably better. She didn't know

quite whether to be amused or angry, however, when a
carriage hired by Henry before he even came home showed
up at nine-thirty to take them and their luggage to the Broad
Street Station. It was evident that no matter what her objection might have been to leaving here tonight, he had decided
they were leaving.

As they rattled and rumbled toward the station, she
looked at him in a puzzled way. "Why was it, Henry," she
asked, "that you lied to Mrs. Alcorn? Why did you tell her
we were going to Harrisburg instead of Indianapolis?"

He chucked her under the chin. "My little detective,"
he said. "Always looking for the hidden meanings. Nothing
mysterious about it at all, though. When my competitors
check at the boardinghouse—as I'm quite sure they will—to
determine where I went, they'll center their activities on
trying to undercut me in Harrisburg. Which will leave me
with a reasonably clear field for making my contacts in
Indianapolis without interference."

She sighed deeply. "I don't know, Henry. To me it just
doesn't really seem worthwhile, always having to be worried
about business enemies this way and having to do honest
work in a clandestine manner. I don't think I could do it."

"You don't have to," he said gently. "That's my job. And I
do it quite well. Which is why we're able to live the way we
do."

Later, the steel wheels clicking on the rails beneath
them with pleasant monotony, Holmes put *Trilby* aside and
smiled down at his peacefully sleeping wife. He stepped to
the luggage rack and brought down his valise and opened it
quietly. The light blue-gray suit, sloppily folded, was to one
side and he slipped his hand inside to the breast pocket and
removed some papers he had forgotten until a short time ago.
They were somewhat crumpled but he smoothed and refolded
them and then dug deeper in the bag and brought out a tin
about the size and shape of a cigar box but with a tiny padlock
on the front. He opened it quietly and lay the papers inside
atop some others. Clicking the little lock shut again, he
replaced the tin inside the valise and the piece of luggage
back up on the rack.

Then he sat down and looked out of the window into the
darkness, but he did not see the lights of the isolated
farmhouses that whizzed past every now and again. What he
saw was the last thing he had seen in a bedroom on the

second floor of 1316 Callowhill Street—the body of a man whose face was burned beyond recognition.

The body of Benjamin F. Pitezel.

Eugene Smith had run the full four blocks to the corner of Buttonwood and Broad and thumped into the Buttonwood Police Station where, out of breath, he managed to gasp out the story of his discovery to Desk Sergeant Patrick Danaher.

"You sure he's dead, Mr. Smith?" Danaher marked the time on his desk log: 9:03 A.M.

"Well, I think so, yes."

"Did you go into the room where he was?"

Smith shook his head. "No, I just saw him from the head of the stairs."

"Then you can't be positive he's dead?"

"Well," Smith squirmed uncomfortably, "Not *actually*, no. But I'm sure of it."

"Expect you're right, but we'll soon find out." The sergeant raised his voice. "Officers Sauer, McKnight and Creed to the desk."

The three uniformed men came toward them, two from one direction, one from the other. One of them—William Sauer—was a paunchy, craggy-faced individual in his late thirties; the other two—Daniel J. McKnight and Philip Creed—eager-appearing young men in their early twenties, either of whom could have been athletes.

"Sauer," Danaher said, pointing his pen at the older officer, "take McKnight and go with Mr. Smith to...." he glanced at his logbook, "... thirteen-sixteen Callowhill. Got a guy on a bedroom floor there. Mr. Smith here thinks he's dead." He jabbed the pen at the younger officer who had approached from the other side of the ready room. "Creed, you go to Scott's Pharmacy, northeast corner of Thirteenth and Vine and ask Dr. William Scott to go to the Callowhill address right away and make a preliminary examination."

Creed left immediately but Officers Sauer and McKnight questioned Smith a little more before leaving. Nevertheless, Sauer and McKnight arrived with Eugene Smith at the Callowhill house just a few moments before Dr. Scott. In fact, as they reached the front door they saw the portly physician hove around the corner onto Callowhill from Thirteenth and so they waited for him. They all went inside and up the stairs together, first Sauer, then Dr. Scott, McKnight and Smith.

"To the left," Smith called from behind as they were ascending.

As they approached the rear bedroom the stench of putrefaction enveloped them and Smith jerked a handkerchief from his pocket and held it over his nostrils, nearly gagging. It was quite clear the man was dead and so Sauer cautioned them not to approach the body until notes were made. He dictated while Officer McKnight scribbled rapidly on his pocket pad.

"Body of middle-aged man lies on its back, head north. Legs extended south toward window, feet turned out naturally. Composed position. Right arm and hand over chest, left arm to side. Face burned, features indistinguishable." He cocked his head toward Smith. "You sure this is the guy you knew as Perry?"

Smith bobbed his head and his voice was muffled behind his handkerchief. "I'm sure of it. Same hair. Same hands. I pay attention to hands. And those clothes. I've seen him wearing them. That's Mr. Perry all right."

"Was he from here? Philadelphia?"

"No. He told me he came from St. Louis. Said he had family there."

"You said B. F. Perry. What's the B.F. stand for?"

"I don't know. He never said."

"All right. We'll get back to more of that later. You ready to go on, Danny?" Officer McKnight grunted an affirmative and Sauer continued: "Head turned right, facing westward toward Broad Street, chin tucked. Generally peaceful position, as if asleep. Clothing not mussed, shirt tucked in trousers."

As the others stood waiting near the door, Sauer walked slowly around the body, continuing his staccato dictation. "Pipe on floor, right of head. Filled with tobacco. Tobacco barely scorched. Pipestem partly under shoulder. Burned-out lucifer match on floor eight-ten inches away. Close to pipe, broken bottle lying on side. Chunks of glass inside bottle." He straightened and looked around the room, continuing in a monotone. "One two three four five six seven eight nine ten bottles, different sizes, on south fireplace mantel. Different fluid level in each. Reddish liquid. Two half-pint whiskey bottles on north mantel. One nearly empty. One unopened.

North fireplace fireboard open about one foot. South fireboard, toward Carlton, closed tight. Window raised about one inch. Shutters bowed, west one farther open than east. Door to hallway open. Door to back room closed." He looked up. "We'll get to the rest of the house later. Your turn in here, Doc. Oh, Danny, mark down no burn on floor, shirt charred over shoulder and right arm. Okay, Doc, go ahead."

The other three men watched with interest as Dr. Scott made a close examination, muttering comments as he jotted notes shorthand. "Face apparently burned. Mustache, right eyebrow and hair of right temple singed. Face discolored, very dark, distorted, swollen, numerous bullae. Mortification. Cutis and cuticle separated, with watery pooling. Tongue swollen, protruding, discolored. Interior mouth unburned. Line of reddish-black fluid issued from mouth has filled grain on floorboard." He raised the head slightly and lowered it, then leaned one hand on the stomach. "Elevation of head and moderate abdominal pressure results in oozing of same."

The two officers watching took the whole thing as routine but Eugene Smith was simultaneously nauseated and fascinated. Oblivious to them, Dr. Scott continued his examination down the body. "Putrefaction of head far advanced over body. Shirt on right shoulder and arm charred, material together but disintegrating at touch. Right axillary, pectoral and biceptal regions burned, continuing down upper side of arm to hand but not underside." He opened shirt and trousers, exposing the undershirt, which he pulled up, and button shorts, which he opened.

"Thoracic and abdominal surfaces well preserved," he murmured. "General posterior lividity. Groin line discolored with commenced putrefaction. Evacuation of bowels and bladder *in situ*." He rose and put away his pad and pencil, briefly sniffed the contents of the bottles on the mantel and then turned back to the others, wiping his hands vigorously on a handkerchief taken from his pocket.

Sauer looked from him to the body, then back to him. "Can you give me an idea how long he's been dead, Doc?"

Scott pursed his lips. "Well, based on no remaining rigor mortis and the extent of dissolution, I'd say somewhere in the vicinity of three days, plus or minus twelve to eighteen hours." He returned his handkerchief to his pocket. "I believe that's about all I can help you with at the moment. I'll write up a report for Ashbridge and I'm sure he'll order an autopsy. You can have the remains taken away at your convenience. At least the location's convenient." Scott's reference was to Samuel Ashbridge, Philadelphia County coroner, and the convenience he referred to lay in the fact that the Philadelphia Morgue was no more than a few hundred yards directly south of this Callowhill Street building, on Wood Street. Scott centered his attention on Officer Sauer. "Anything else before I leave?"

"Actually, yes," Sauer said. "I'd like some comment from you as we analyze the scene here. Something doesn't seem right to me."

Eugene Smith's eyes widened. "You mean *murder*?"

"I didn't say that. I just want to do some speculating on probable cause of death here. Now from what I see, Doctor, superficially it looks as if this guy Perry was holding something in that bottle and struck a match to light his pipe and the stuff in the bottle exploded and killed him."

"Sounds reasonable . . . superficially," Scott said, waiting for Sauer to go on.

"But tell me this, Doc. If this guy got his head blown up like that while he was standing here lighting a pipe, would he fall in a position like this? Christ, it looks like this guy just laid down to take a nap and died. Wouldn't he be sort of . . . I don't know, *crumpled* I guess, if he got knocked down like that?"

"Possibly, Officer," Scott acknowledged, "but not necessarily."

"Okay, then, let's think about those bottles on the mantel. You sniffed 'em. What's the stuff in them smell like to you?"

"I wouldn't want you to take this as a definite statement," Scott said slowly, "but it has some of the olfactory characteristics of benzine and chloroform and maybe a little ammonia. It's hard to say."

"Could it have been some kind of invention he was fooling around with?"

"I think that's altogether possible, since he was a dealer in patents. Assuming, of course, that this is in fact B. F. Perry."

Officer McKnight jumped in. "Is there something you've seen that makes you think it isn't Perry, Dr. Scott?"

"Not at all," the doctor replied hastily. "It's just that we do not yet have a *positive* identification that this was Mr. Perry."

"Hang on a minute. Let me check something here." Sauer stooped and emptied the dead man's pockets. There was a small penknife, $2.60 in change and a wallet. Inside the wallet was $23 in bills, a folded rent receipt for these premises, made out to B. F. Perry and signed by one Walter Shedaker, and an identification card, filled out in ink with the name B. F. Perry and this Callowhill Street address.

"*That* certainly makes it positive it's Mr. Perry," Smith said jubilantly.

Sauer gave him a pitying look. "Couple of other things sort of puzzle me, Doc," he went on. "That broken bottle. Seems to me if the juice inside blew up when he lighted his pipe, there'd be glass blown all over the place. But the bottle's broken almost right in half and the bigger broken pieces are inside the bottom part. What do you make of that?"

"I have to admit," Scott said slowly, "the same thought occurred to me. The nature of the break gives the aspect of the bottle having been taken in hand and crushed against the floor, thereby allowing the pieces to fall inside. Again, however, I think it would require closer study in order to be justified in such a supposition."

"If I could say something?" Smith spoke up. When Sauer made a beckoning motion toward him he continued. "The way Mr. Perry's lying here looks to me like someone might've deliberately put him in that spot and adjusted the shutters just right so that the sun would shine on the body most of the day."

"Which would tend to accelerate decomposition," Dr. Scott added. "Interesting observation, Mr. Smith."

Smith fairly squirmed with pleasure at having offered something of value and his pleasure increased when McKnight bolstered his observation with one of his own.

"Look how the window's open a little bit and so is the fireboard on this north wall fireplace, as if someone wanted a draft to come through and carry the stink up the chimney so no one'd notice it for a long time."

"Except," Sauer said, dashing cold water over the theory, "then why was the door to the hallway open? If someone did it to prevent early discovery, he sure as hell wouldn't've left the door open to let the draft carry the smell through the house."

"I'd have to agree with that," Dr. Scott said.

"You'd rule out foul play then, Doc?" Sauer asked.

"In my opinion, probably. Looks to me, very unofficially, of course, that it was accidental death due to an explosion. Subject to the autopsy, of course."

After the doctor was gone, Officer Sauer sent his partner to the morgue to return with transportation for the corpse. Then, allowing Eugene Smith to accompany him in case the man should recognize something amiss that he himself might overlook, Sauer searched the entire house, attic to cellar, including the tiny backyard and a shed. Everything seemed in order and the only thing that brought a reaction from Smith was when they found his saw set sharpener invention in a downstairs closet with a tag attached to it bearing Smith's name and address. Sauer let the relieved man take it.

It had been late last night when their train arrived at Indianapolis and Holmes immediately had their baggage loaded into a carriage and ordered the driver to take them to the Stubbins House.

"Tired?" he had asked as they rode on a synchrony of clip-clops toward the hotel.

"Mmmmmmm," she breathed, snuggling against him in the darkness, "utterly exhausted. And utterly happy. Even though we've been together these past weeks, it's more like we've been apart, what with my being sick and your business meetings. I've only felt whole again since we got on the train. I guess because no one could come to the door and take you away from me."

Holmes kissed the rim of her ear and then nibbled gently at the lobe. "I'm always with you," he whispered, "even when I'm not. I carry the memory of you along with me in a special pocket of my vest."

She laughed and leaned back to look full into his face, though he was no more than a silhouette as they regularly passed the street lamps. "Now there's romantic garbage if I ever heard it. Do you really have to go tomorrow?"

"I do," he had told her gravely, "but I'll be back fairly soon. And before I leave in the morning I'll get you settled into Morris's place."

So he had. Morris's place was the Morris Boardinghouse on Oakdale Street and it was a pleasant, sprawling house with beautifully appointed rooms; a vast white estate with Southern influence, its multipillared verandah shaded by gigantic oaks. He left his larger suitcase with her there and took only the smaller leather valise.

"I shouldn't be too long in Cincinnati," he told her. "I'll let you know."

"Hurry back," she told him. "You know how I miss you."

He squeezed her hand and left, going directly to the depot where he caught his train. In a short while the conductor came through, pausing at each row to punch tickets, never touching a hand grip, his feet slightly spread and his body automatically adjusting with ballet grace to the erratic swaying of the car.

"Ticket, sir?" He was standing at the row where Holmes sat by himself. He took the ticket Holmes proffered, glanced at it and punched it and then handed it back. He touched three fingers to the bill of his cap. "Enjoy your stay in St. Louis, sir."

As the conductor started away, Holmes stopped him. "Did this train originate in St. Louis this morning?"

"It sure did."

"Any chance you might've picked up a St. Louis paper?"

"Yep. Three or four of 'em left on the seats. Want to see one?"

"Which papers do you have?"

He barked a short laugh. "You don't have any choice. They're all the same. *Globe-Democrat*, Wednesday morning, September fifth. I'll bring you one in a minute."

He continued punching tickets to the end of the car, disappeared for a moment and then returned with a poorly folded newspaper which he handed to Holmes with hardly a pause.

Holmes did not anticipate finding anything in the St. Louis paper this soon, but he scanned the headlines anyway, column after column, page after page. It was almost with physical impact that the story leaped at him from the seventh column at the bottom of page six:

B. F. PERRY'S TRAGIC DEATH

Speculation as to the Causes of a
Former St. Louisan's End at Philadelphia.

Special Dispatch to the Globe-Democrat

PHILADELPHIA, PA., September 4.—With a
blackened face and charred arm, B. F. Perry, aged
about 40 years, who recently came from St. Louis, was
found dead this morning in a second-story back room
at 1316 Callow Hill Street. A broken benzine bottle, a
pipe filled with tobacco and a match which had been
ignited lay on the floor, silent witnesses to his death.

The man died under the most peculiar circumstances, and three theories are advanced as to the
cause of his death. The first is that it was the result
of an accident; the second, that he might have
ended his own life, and, finally, that death might
have been caused by foul play. Circumstances surrounding the case seem to bear out the idea of
accident, the direct cause of death seeming to be an
explosion of benzine or chemical substance.

Perry was a sort of patent broker or merchant.
He moved into the house at 1316 Callow Hill Street
about three weeks ago. The structure is a two and a
half story building, with a store in front. When
Perry went into the house he improvised a counter
and posted two or three signs on the walls. Across
the front window he hung a muslin sign stating that
patents were bought and sold inside. The last time
he was seen alive was Saturday night. Between the
hours of 9 and 10 o'clock on that evening he entered
a saloon in the vicinity of his residence and purchased a pint of whiskey. After leaving the saloon he
went directly to his house. Yesterday morning Eugene
Smith of Rhodes Street, who had business with
Perry, entered the store, but could not find the
proprietor. The door being unlocked, he concluded
that Perry was out, and left, intending to return
again. This morning as Mr. Smith was passing the
place he decided to go in and see Perry. Upon
entering the place he found it deserted. Growing

suspicious, he went upstairs, and in the middle room of the second floor was startled by seeing Perry lying in the center of the floor. Subsequent examination disclosed the man was dead.

Holmes tore out the full page, folded it and put it into his pocket. He was smiling, pleased that the death of the so-called Perry was considered most likely to be an accident. He had planned on seeing Carrie before such a story appeared in the paper, to prepare her. Now, unless he was very lucky, it was too late for that. Well, never mind. He knew he could convince her that Ben was alive and in hiding. The problem now was to decide how, where and when to kill her and the five children. It had to be done very carefully, before she could discover Ben really was dead and either went to the police or tried to force him to pay her her Ben's one-third interest in the Chicago Castle and one-half interest in the Fort Worth Castle.

It was a challenging problem and he was still smiling as he settled back and closed his eyes to cogitate further on the matter.

Carrie Pitezel had spent most of this terrible day in bed.

The malady that had plagued her for weeks still gripped her and she was alarmingly weak from the persistent attacks of diarrhea and vomiting. More than once she had pulled the covers over her head and closed her eyes and prayed that she would never open them again, that she would just die. It had been hard enough when Dessie was able to help her with the other four children, but then Dessie had come down sick, too.

More resilient, of course, Dessie was more able to physically withstand the onslaught, but she was also much less patient with it. She had always enjoyed the robust health of youth and, in being ravaged so terribly with fever, was far less able than Carrie to cope with the fact of her own weakness and the specter of death that she became convinced was hovering close to her. And thus, along with becoming so sick, she had also become less cooperative, almost surly, and a vast self-pity had filled her. Now, at last, she was on the way to recovery and, though still weak, had begun again to assume some of the responsibilities she had abdicated.

Then little Wharton had been stricken and lay in his crib day after day, crying weakly and seemingly teetering at death's threshold. Fortunately, the other three children—Alice, Nellie and Howard—had remained untouched. For the first time in her fifteen years, a full burden of responsibility had fallen upon Alice and she had accepted it with admirable steadiness. At one point—a period lasting a week, when Dessie was at her worst—the whole operation of the household and care of the family had been Alice's and she had handled it well.

Now Dessie was recovering and neither Carrie nor Wharton were so gravely ill as they had been, but all three were very debilitated. In Carrie's case it was worst, due to the smothering depression that blackened her outlook. The money Ben had left with her, which had initially seemed more than merely adequate, had vanished at an alarming rate into the coffers of a succession of doctors who treated them and pharmacists who filled their prescriptions. Added to this were the progressively more discouraging letters from Ben, culminating with the one received on Monday, written by Ben on Saturday afternoon, in which his own depression and self-pity were so dismayingly apparent; the one in which he told her that the grand scheme had fallen through and that he was giving up and coming home.

They had expected him here very soon, maybe even today. Then their whole world had collapsed when they saw that newspaper story this morning: Benny had been killed in an explosion! Carrie had become hysterical and so nearly had Alice, Nellie and Howard. Dessie had held up better and had gone into the bedroom with her mother and tried to console her.

"Mama, listen to me!" she had whispered urgently. "Papa told me before he left that if we heard anything about his death, it wouldn't be true and we weren't to believe it. He said it had something to do with insurance. I don't know what he meant, but he *did* say we shouldn't believe he's dead. That's what he told me, Mama, honest. He's alive!"

Haltingly, choked with emotion, Carrie had told Dessie of the proposed insurance swindle by her father and Holmes; told her of how she had been against it, but Benny had gone ahead anyhow; told her of his growing discouragement with the whole thing. Still Dessie believed he was alive until finally Carrie opened her dresser drawer and took out the

letter received from Ben on Monday. Dessie had read it and
became ashen. She had dropped the letter on the floor and
buried her face in her hands.

"Oh, God, Mama! Papa really *is* dead then, isn't he?"

Carrie had stroked Dessie's head and held her to her
breast and tried to soothe her. "We got to do something,
Dessie," she said and Dessie wailed a muffled agreement, but
neither of them knew what and so they merely sat that way as
the grief engulfed them.

Somehow the day had passed. Carrie remained in bed. Dessie tried to care for everyone else, but mostly they just sat and
stared at nothing for long periods. At intervals, when their eyes met
and they saw their own grief mirrored, they burst into new tears.

Now, at a few minutes after six in the evening, there was a
knock at the door. Dessie opened it and found Holmes standing
there and she broke down again and threw herself into his
arms, repeating in a choked voice, "Oh, Uncle Henry, Papa's
dead. We saw it in the paper. He's dead. He's dead."

He patted her back and gently consoled her and the
others as they clustered around him. His train had arrived an
hour ago and he'd gone directly to Jeptha Howe's office, but
the lawyer was gone for the night, so Holmes had immediately come here. He hugged the children and murmured more
sympathetic words and then finally he asked for their mother.
Dessie led him into the darkening bedroom and he sat
carefully on the side of the bed beside the outstretched
Carrie who lay staring at the ceiling. At a motion from Uncle
Henry, Dessie nodded understandingly and left him there
with her, closing the door quietly after her.

Holmes reached out and took Carrie's hand and squeezed
it with something other than compassion. "Great job, Carrie,"
he whispered. "You've pulled it off beautifully. The children
really believe Ben's gone, don't they?"

"What? What?" She couldn't comprehend and her shoulders shuddered with a residue spasm of her earlier crying.

"The kids," he said, laughing lightly, "they really think
their father's dead. And you've convinced them that you
think he's dead, too. I guess I owe you an apology. I didn't
really think you could pull it off so well."

Abruptly she sat upright, her grip tight on his wrist.
"Henry, what're you saying? Are you telling me Ben's alive?"

"Shhh," he cautioned. "Of course he's alive. What's the
matter with you?" His mouth suddenly fell open in surprise.

"You mean *you* actually thought he was dead, too? Christ, Carrie, we planned all this. You were in on it. You knew what we were going to do. I don't understand this. How the hell could you possibly think he was dead?"

"He's alive? He's *alive*?" She kept her voice low but it quaked with fearful eagerness. "But I got a letter from him. He said—"

"Carrie, for God's sake, where's your brain? I know what he said. He told you he was discouraged and that the whole thing had blown up because we couldn't get a body and he was coming home. That's what he said, wasn't it? Sure it was. And I've got to admit, he really was upset for a while when the first body turned out to be wrong. I guess that's when he wrote to you. But we got another one, Carrie, a derelict who died of a heart attack. You should've seen him. Damned near a spitting image of Ben. They could've been brothers. So we fixed the stiff up, just like we planned." Carrie was listening, enthralled, and he went on without pause. "Hell, it was Ben who poured the stuff on the stiff's face and set it on fire, to make sure no one would see it wasn't him. Everything went off perfectly. God, woman, you ought to be jumping with joy. You and Ben are on your way to being rich!"

She found her voice. "Where is he, Henry? Can I go to him?"

"Of course not," he said, his voice sharpening. "He's in hiding. I don't even know where for sure. Canada, maybe. He's got to stay out of sight. If the insurance detectives got on this thing, first thing they'd do would be to follow you, figuring you'd lead them to wherever he is. So, no, you can't see him, even if I knew where he was. Ben's doing just like we planned—hiding out till the insurance is paid and everything's cooled down. Then he'll get in touch and let me know where you and the kids can join him."

"The children!" she gasped. "We've got to tell them. They think he's dead. They're so upset."

"No. They mustn't know." He was intense. "They'd give it away. They wouldn't mean to, but they would. Just let them keep on thinking he's really dead. It's the best cover we could have."

"But it's dreadful to deceive them like this. So cruel to let them think their own father's dead!"

"As cruel as it would be," Holmes countered sharply, "if we let Ben get caught because we were careless?"

"No," she mumbled, frustrated by her dilemma, "no, we can't do that. But what do we do now?"

"All right, listen carefully. Tomorrow you and I are going

to get you a lawyer to represent you with the insurance company. The original plan was for you to go to Philadelphia and identify the body as Ben's. I hate to say it, Carrie, but not only are you still sick, I just don't think you could be convincing enough. And if you got caught lying, you would be guilty of perjury and could go to prison for that. Dessie's still a minor, so she wouldn't go to jail if she got caught in a lie, but I don't think she'd get caught. She could probably handle it, but we have a problem there because she's been so sick, too. I think it would be risking her health to send her. The next best thing is to let Alice do it, so we'll plan on that. Which brings me to something else. Do you remember when Ben and I talked about that rich lady from Boston, Minnie Williams?"

"No," she frowned, trying to remember, "I don't think so. At least he didn't mention that name." She brightened. "But I remember there was once Ben said something about how maybe one of the girls would have a chance to go East and live in a big country house with a rich lady, who would pay for her to have a good education. Is that the one?"

"That's the one. I'll get in touch with her and see if she still wants to do it. I'm sure she does and it's a great opportunity for Alice. Now here's what we'll do. You tell Alice she's going to have to be the one to go and make the identification and that she's also going to have the opportunity to live in a very rich and fancy way for four or five months. You can even suggest that maybe after she's there for a while, Nellie can join her and have the same opportunity. You continue to be the grieving widow who is beginning to bear up now after the initial shock of loss. I want you to meet me tomorrow morning, nine o'clock, at the Commercial Building. There's a lawyer there named Howe who we're going to hire to help us. Ben knows him very well and approved of this. As soon as I get word from Ben, I'll let you know. He also said to tell you he'll be writing to you in cipher as soon as it's safe." He eyed her critically. "All right, that's it for now. Ben thinks you can do all this and I agreed with him. The question is, do *you* think you can handle all of it just the way Ben wants?"

"I think so," she said, nibbling at her lower lip. "If that's what Benny really wants, then I'll do it."

"Good girl!" Holmes said heartily, standing up. "I'll see you tomorrow morning."

Eight

$\mathcal{L}$aurence G. Fouse—who insisted upon being addressed as L.G.—was variously described by many as irascible, a fuddy-duddy, a tyrant, a kind old man and a wizard. The descriptions were all, each in its own way, accurate. L. G. Fouse was a self-made man who had founded his own company over thirty years before and ruled it with iron determination and considerably more than moderate success. His firm, Fidelity Mutual Life Association, with its home office in Philadelphia, now had branch offices in Cleveland, Detroit, Chicago, St. Louis and Nashville and was still growing, expanding where others had failed because it treated its clients well and did not go out of its way to look for loopholes by which payment of claims could be circumvented. When any claim was made, irrespective of what branch office may have written the policy, it was not only funneled at once to the home office but to the personal attention of L. G. Fouse. When satisfied that all was in order with the paperwork, L.G. gave his stamp of approval for the standard field investigation to be undertaken immediately. And so it was, with both expediency and more than casual care. As soon as it could be determined that there was legitimacy to the claim, it was paid at once and in full.

The telegram dated September 9 had arrived over a week ago at the home office from the St. Louis branch manager and was longer than ordinarily received, due to some peculiar circumstances. The brow of L. G. Fouse had become ridged as he read it.

LOCAL ATTORNEY JEPTHA HOWE HAS APPEARED THIS OFFICE AS REPRESENTATIVE OF CLAIMANT CARRIE A

298

PITEZEL STOP STATES THAT B F PERRY FOUND DEAD IN
PHILADELPHIA ON SEPT 4 AS RESULT OF EXPLOSION AT
1316 CALLOWHILL STREET WAS ACTUALLY B F PITEZEL
INSURED BY US ON POLICY NUMBER 044145 STOP SUG-
GEST INVESTIGATION BEFORE REMAINS LEAVE STOP
GEORGE B STADDEN

L. G. Fouse had the home office files checked at once
and discovered that the firm had indeed insured the Benjamin Fuller Pitezel on the policy number stated, with the
policy having been written at the Chicago office. He thereupon started projects moving in several different directions
simultaneously. Fouse's number one assistant, O. LaForest
Perry, was dispatched to police headquarters and the morgue
to check on the death of the man called B. F. Perry. A
telegram was sent to St. Louis branch manager George
Stadden advising him that his communication was received,
that B. F. Pitezel was insured by them and investigation had
commenced. Another telegram was sent immediately to Edward
H. Cass in Chicago.

Cass, whose official title was cashier at the branch
office of Fidelity Mutual, also doubled as agent, underwrit-
er and claims investigator when occasion demanded, as
it seemed to now. He read the terse wire a second
time:

CLAIM MADE ON BENJ PITEZEL POLICY 044145 WRIT-
TEN YOUR OFFICE NOV 9 93 STOP REPORT RENEWAL
STATUS STOP FOUSE

Cass was certain that he, personally, had not written the
policy, yet the name Pitezel rang a bell. He checked his own
files and discovered that the policy on Benjamin F. Pitezel
had been written in these premises and that he had himself
received and logged the semiannual premium renewal. But
then his eyes widened at the notation he had made on the
record at that time and he hastened to reply to the company
president:

PITEZEL POLICY 044145 WRITTEN IN THIS OFFICE 9
NOV 93 BY AGENT FAY WHO IS NO LONGER WITH
COMPANY STOP SEMIANNUAL PREMIUM RENEWAL RE-
CEIVED BY TELEGRAPHIC MONEY ORDER FROM PHILA-

DELPHIA ON FINAL DAY OF GRACE PERIOD 9 AUG 94
STOP PAYMENT ACCEPTED AND POLICY STILL VALID
STOP AWAIT FURTHER INSTRUCTIONS STOP CASS

The reply from Fouse carried some startling news:

BODY OF MAN CALLED B F PERRY WHO IS SUPPOSED TO
HAVE BEEN B F PITEZEL HAS BEEN BURIED STOP
PROTEST LODGED AND CORONER HAS ISSUED EXHUMA-
TION ORDER STOP EXHUMATION SCHEDULED FOR SEPT
22 STOP URGENT WE HAVE PITEZEL KIN OR CLOSE
FRIEND ON HAND THEN TO POSITIVELY IDENTIFY OR
DISPUTE ALLEGED IDENTIFICATION OF REMAINS STOP
LOCATE SOONEST STOP FOUSE

Since Leon Fay was no longer associated with Fidelity
Mutual, Cass went to his house and questioned him at once.

Fay, referring to his own notes, confirmed that he had
written the policy on Pitezel. The man's wife, Carrie Alice,
was on his notes as sole beneficiary but there was another
notation which Pitezel, at the time, had insisted he take
down. Fay had not included it on the policy: *ICOD ntfy
ffd/H. Holmes, 38 N John St., Wmte.* What it translated
was *In case of death, notify Pitezel family friend, H. Holmes
of 38 North John Street, Wilmette.*

When Cass knocked on the door of that imposing structure in Wilmette, he found himself confronting an attractive,
cultured, gray-eyed woman in her thirties. He handed her
his business card and asked to speak to Mr. Holmes.

"Mr. Holmes is not at home," she replied. "May I help
you? I am Mrs. Holmes."

"Do you know where I could get in touch with Mr.
Holmes?" Cass went on. "You see, our firm has received
word that his friend, Benjamin Pitezel, who is insured by us,
met his end in an unfortunate accident in Philadelphia."

She put neatly manicured fingertips to her lips. "Oh,
my, how awful. I'm so sorry to hear it." She paused, but when
Cass said nothing, she went on. "I'm confused. What has this
to do with my husband?"

Cass shuffled a bit. The woman·was not being uncooperative, but he found it strange that she had evinced no
curiosity over what had caused the death of a man who was
supposedly a close friend of her husband. He found it equally

strange that she should keep him standing at the door instead of inviting him inside. He had the distinct impression she was holding back.

"Since the death was ruled accidental," he went on, "there is no question of the claim being paid *if* the victim was actually Mr. Pitezel. This is what we need to determine and our problem lies in the fact that, when killed, the victim was using a name other than B. F. Pitezel. Also, his features were very badly damaged by the accident, so identification has to be made on other physical characteristics. Since your husband was a longtime friend of Mr. Pitezel's, obviously he could help in this respect."

"Mr. Pitezel's body is being held in Philadelphia, then, pending identification?" Dora queried.

Cass became uncomfortable. "Please forgive my bluntness, ma'am, but it was several days before the body was found. Decomposition had begun and so immediately following the autopsy it was buried. And due to the unusual circumstances of the case, payment of the claim simply cannot be made unless identification is positive."

Dora appeared puzzled. "But how, if the body has been buried, could my husband possibly help make an identification?"

"The point is, Mrs. Holmes, there is to be an exhumation. I realize it's not a pleasant matter to contemplate, but if the body is, in fact, that of Mr. Pitezel, it has to be identified as such before his widow can collect as beneficiary of his life insurance. Unfortunately, she is ill and cannot come to Philadelphia to make the identification herself. And that's why it is requisite that someone who knew Mr. Pitezel very well be on hand."

"I'm sure, Mr. Cass, since it would be of such benefit to Mrs. Pitezel, my husband would agree to assist in any way he could. I'm sorry to say that he is presently on a business trip and moving about considerably. However, I might be able to get word to him to contact you. Would that be of any help?"

"Yes, ma'am, it would."

"Then I will certainly try, Mr. Cass." It was clearly a dismissal.

"Thank you." The Fidelity Mutual agent bowed courteously. "Please accept my sincere apology for having to bother you with this. Good day."

Dora watched him follow the long walk toward the street where he turned right and passed from view. When she stepped inside and closed the door, Henry spun her around and embraced her.

"You did just fine, Dora," he told her.

"Let's hope so," she said, not entirely convinced, the same little thread of concern returning. She first felt it strongly yesterday after he had arrived home and told her about Pitezel's death and what had followed: the visit to Carrie and the children, who had seen the newspaper article and believed Ben had been killed in an explosion; the subsequent meetings, with and without Carrie, at Howe's office to plan strategy; the details that had been mapped out in respect to Howe and Alice going to Philadelphia to make the identification and collect the insurance money; the letter Howe had sent the insurance company, telling them he would arrive in Philadelphia with a family member; learning that Pitezel's body had been buried but would be exhumed for identification; the plan for Holmes to work out some way on his own by which he could also be present in Philadelphia to make sure the identification was accepted as positive; the plan to meet back in St. Louis to divide the insurance money. Dora remained unapproving of what he was doing, again pointing out that this whole scheme lacked the simplicity of others in the past. She reiterated the increase of risk by getting so many people involved. In fact, she persisted, wasn't the whole matter becoming progressively more dangerously involved? But Henry had only laughed and assured her that everything was fine, that it was the very complexity of this present operation that so intrigued him and he fully intended to follow it through to a successful conclusion. Suddenly, with the unexpected but fortuitous arrival of Cass at the house, the knotty problem of getting himself included in the Philadelphia meetings was solved.

Now Holmes grinned in response to her comment. "I can tell you're still worried. Don't be. Everything's going to turn out just fine. I guarantee it." He held out his hand. "All right, give me that card he gave you and I'll be on my way. I've got to get moving. I intend to be there for the exhumation and I'll have to set it up."

"Do you really think that's wise?" she asked. "It's not essential, is it, your being there? Alice Pitezel's going to make the identification, isn't she?"

"Yes. That was originally the plan before the body was buried. Now it's a little touchier. The Fidelity people will be

ar more inclined to accept the identification if two people
agree on it, especially if one is an adult. Remember, Alice is
only fifteen. Who knows what her reaction will be when she
has to look at a decomposed body that's been exhumed? She
might break down altogether and not be able to make the
identification. We've got to be sure."

Dora agreed he was probably correct and then went
upstairs with him to help him pack. Within the hour he was
en route to Indianapolis.

Holmes arrived in the Indiana capital and rejoined
Georgiana in time to take her to dinner. He was light and gay
and pleasantly conversational, with nothing in his demeanor
to indicate that he had been in almost constant movement
since his own departure from St. Louis for Chicago ten days
before. Over the meal he had told her that his business
meetings had gone exceptionally well. "Not only that," he
went on enthusiastically, "I received a telegram today from
the Pennsylvania Railroad people in Philadelphia. Guess what?"
He went on hurriedly. "They want to double their order and
are ready to pay me the full amount in cash, along with the
money still due. Only one little fly in the ointment, so to
speak. They want me to pick it up in person in Philadelphia
right away."

"Oh, Henry," Georgiana cried, "not again! I mean, it's
wonderful that business is going so well for you, but I just
don't think I'm up to another trip there."

"Actually," he admitted, "I wasn't thinking of taking you
on this one. I'd hardly be so cruel, after what you've been
through. I'll be leaving on the noon train tomorrow and while
I'm gone, I want you to just take it easy here. I'll be away a
few days. Rest, read and get plenty of sleep, because when I
get back, we'll be on the verge of beginning our trip to
Germany."

"But I don't have things with me for such a trip," she
protested.

"You will have. There'll be plenty of time for us to go
visit your mother again and you'll have ample opportunity to
pack up a trunk with whatever you want to take along. In
addition, we'll go shopping and get you whatever new outfits
you'll need. You're going to have to plan on being gone for at
least six months, maybe even a year."

Georgiana's eyes glowed. "I can't wait," she breathed. "It's just like a dream come true!"

Once more Holmes checked in at the Alcorn Boarding-house in Philadelphia and waited for his visitor. Exactly at 8 P.M., as prearranged, he showed up. The garrulous John Grammer showed Jeptha Howe up to the room. When the old tenant was not invited to join them, as he had hoped, he stumped downstairs muttering to himself and the two men closed the door and talked for nearly an hour, going over the fine details of their strategy for what lay ahead. At one point during their discussion, Howe paused with his head cocked.

"Is it me," he asked, "or do I keep hearing a funny little scratching sound?"

Holmes laughed and indicated a nearby bureau. "I have company," he said. "There's a mouse in there but whenever I open the drawer, he hides. I'll catch him one of these times."

Howe was not particularly interested. He continued talking, telling Holmes that he and Alice Pitezel had checked into separate rooms in a boardinghouse at the corner of Eleventh and Filbert and that he was planning on seeing Philadelphia's Superintendent of Police, R. J. Linden, first thing in the morning. He laughed at how Linden would be duped into helping them, as a result of the letter of introduction from Howe's senior partner, MacDonald, who asked Linden to provide some insight into the Pitezel case and also an introduction to the officials at Fidelity Mutual, which would add to his standing.

"That's fine," Holmes approved. "Just remember, when we first see one another at the insurance office, probably on Saturday, we act as if we don't know one another. You did bring along a power of attorney from Carrie?"

"Of course," Howe replied.

"Fine," Holmes said. "Now we'll see how good an actor you are."

Shortly before 11 A.M., Fidelity Mutual's assistant to the president, O. LaForest Perry, ushered into L. G. Fouse's office a briefcase-carrying, corpulent, well-dressed young man of about twenty-six and an unusually pretty teen-aged girl in rather seedy clothing. They were introduced to the insurance firm's president as attorney Jeptha Howe of St. Louis and Alice Pitezel, daughter of their policyholder, Benjamin Pitezel. Fouse, aware that this was the young lawyer concerning whom he had just received an introductory letter from Police Chief Linden, shook hands with Howe, nodded to the girl and asked them to sit down. Perry took a seat as well.

"I'm very pleased to meet you, Miss Pitezel," he said, his voice gentle and soothing, "and only regret that it must be under such trying conditions."

"Huh?" Alice said.

"I mean the supposed death of your father."

"Oh, I see."

A faint frown touched Fouse's expression for an instant and was gone. "We will try to make this the least unpleasant for you as possible," he went on. "However much we endeavor to shield you, however, you must steel yourself for tomorrow."

"Steal myself?" Alice misunderstood.

"I mean, Miss Pitezel, you must brace yourself for what will at best be a trying matter for you."

"Uh huh," Alice said.

My God, Fouse thought, she's not only reticent, she's stupid. He retained his smile and turned to Howe. "I received the letter of introduction for you from Bob Linden and will be pleased to do as he says and extend every courtesy possible."

"I appreciate that, Mr. Fouse," Howe said, handing him a document that he had removed from his briefcase and unfolded. "This is the power of attorney granted to me by Mrs. Pitezel. As you know, she is suffering nervous prostration aggravated by a recent illness and simply was not able to make the trip. She has authorized me to act totally in her behalf in this matter."

"I understand," Fouse said, scanning the letter with a practiced eye and then handing it back to Howe. "We have no problem in that direction. Our problem lies in ascertaining the identity of the dead man. We have—" He broke off as one of the firm's executives, Colonel Bosbyshell, showed Henry Holmes into the office and himself withdrew.

Holmes shook hands with both Fouse and Perry—amused, without change of expression, at meeting the latter, since Perry was the man whose surname Pitezel had taken as an alias when he came to Philadelphia—and turned to Howe and Alice. "This child I know," he said. "How are you, Alice dear?

It's good to see you again, though sad under such distressing circumstances."

"Mr. Howe," Fouse said, "this is Mr. Henry Holmes. Mr. Holmes," he turned to face him, "this is Mr. Howe, an attorney from St. Louis who is representing the Pitezel family."

The two men shook hands and exchanged greetings as strangers. Perry drew up a chair for Holmes and they all sat down again. Fouse addressed his next remark to the newcomer.

"I was just explaining to Miss Pitezel and Mr. Howe that our problem here is one of identifying the dead man and whether he was B. F. Perry or B. F. Pitezel or—"

"Excuse me," Howe interjected. "In that respect I have here a number of letters received from Mrs. Pitezel from her husband while he was doing business in Philadelphia under the name of B. F. Perry." He placed a small packet of letters on the desk—letters that had been carefully selected by Holmes and himself from among those Carrie had received from Ben. These were innocuous. Those that had borne incriminating or even questionable remarks had, over Carrie's protests, been burned. "Mr. Pitezel, some time ago," Howe went on, "had gotten into some financial transactions in Indiana that had embarrassed him and made it advisable as a simple expedient to change his name when he came here to do business. You'll find some of that reflected in the letters, along with clear proof that B. F. Pitezel and B. F. Perry were one and the same."

"I see no problem with that," Fouse said, paying no attention to the letters. He leaned back in his chair and laced his fingers over a trim stomach. "Our company has become quite convinced that Perry and Pitezel were the same. We are *not* convinced, however, that the dead man is Pitezel, the man whom we insured."

"What!" The word burst from the astonished Holmes unbidden and he caught himself at once. "I do not wish to impugn this company, sir, but a remark such as that makes it appear as if an effort is being made to grasp at straws to keep from paying off on a life insurance policy."

"Not at all," Fouse said, unruffled by the accusation. "This company has never knowingly reneged on a payment due. But you surely realize we cannot pay any claim willy-nilly without proper investigation. Which is the purpose of this meeting. We need to make a list of all physical marks or peculiarities Mr. Pitezel was known to have had so we can check them against the body that will be exhumed tomorrow. Agreed?"

"That is certainly reasonable,". Holmes admitted and Howe nodded in agreement.

"Wait a minute," Howe suddenly blustered. He pointed at Holmes. "Just who is this man Holmes? Why is he here? What is his purpose?"

"I beg your pardon," Fouse apologized. "I should have made that more clear. Mr. Holmes is a former business acquaintance and close friend of Mr. Pitezel. He had come here at our express invitation to assist in the matter of identity."

"All right," Howe said, mollified. "I guess that's all right."

They set about drawing up a list. Holmes made particular note of the wart on the back of Pitezel's neck that gave him so much trouble when wearing a tight collar. He also mentioned the inch-long scar on the inner side of Pitezel's right leg, just below the knee. Incidentally, he brought out the facts that Pitezel had dark brown hair that was thinning and which he combed in a pompadour to mask his incipient baldness, a reddish brown mustache, large hands that were quite workworn, and large feet. O. LaForest Perry, at a signal from Fouse, wrote all these down. Fouse then turned to Alice.

"What can you add, Miss Pitezel?"

"I don't know."

Once again Fouse frowned. "Well surely there were things about your father that were peculiar only to him that you would recognize."

"Well, sure, he was big. Six foot."

"Unfortunately, many people are. Anything else?"

"He had a busted nose once."

"All right, what else?"

"His teeth."

"His teeth?" Fouse repeated. "What about them?"

"Crooked," Alice said. "All kind of snarldy, but I liked 'em. They went with him just fine. And I'd recognize 'em anywhere."

"Well, that's a step ahead," Fouse said. "It may mean you can be spared looking at any more of the remains than just the teeth. Anything else you can think of?"

Alice poked an index finger into her cheek, thinking, but

finally shook her head. "No. Nothing excep' that wart on his neck that you know about."

"All right, then," Rouse said, "I trust that will give us enough to—"

"Oh, wait!" Alice broke in. "I know something else. He smushed-up his thumb with a hammer a couple'a months ago. The nail was all black when he left home to go to Philadelphia."

"Which thumb, do you remember?"

"'Course I do. The left one."

"Fine. We can check that out, too. I think that finishes our business for now. Good day."

Once again Howe visited Holmes at the Alcorn Boardinghouse. As soon as the door to the room was closed he turned on Holmes in an agitated manner. "It won't go, Holmes. I'll tell you, I'm getting scared. You better get in touch with Pitezel and tell him we're calling this whole business off. *If he's still alive, that is.*"

Holmes looked at him steadily. "Why don't you tell me just what's bothering you, Howe, instead of beating around the bush."

"All right. I saw Fouse again this afternoon and he told me that Eugene Smith—the man who found the body you supposedly planted there in place of Pitezel—is going to be at Potter's Field tomorrow. I stopped by Smith's house and saw him on the way over here. He told me he was in Perry's office when a man came in—evidently you, from what you've said—and he saw you go into a back room—"

"Upstairs," Holmes said mildly, "not a back room."

"All right, upstairs. The point is, he saw you and he's going to be at the exhumation tomorrow. He'll recognize you."

"No he won't," Holmes said. "Pitezel told me about him. Said the man's practically illiterate. And the very fact that he said he saw Pitezel and me go into a back room together shows he doesn't know what he's talking about."

"He does! I don't know whether he said back room or not. But he did see and he says there's no doubt in his mind that the dead man is the one he knew as Perry—in other words, Pitezel. Goddamnit, Holmes, you level with me right now. Is Pitezel dead?"

"No. But you listen to me, Howe. That body was gotten up specifically to match Pitezel and no one who's going to be at the graveyard tomorrow is going to be able to tell any different. Christ Almighty, man, do you think I'd be sticking my neck out if I had the least worry I'd be caught? Now stop acting like such a rabbit and go on back to your hotel. There's nothing to worry about, trust me."

As soon as Howe was gone, Holmes held up his hand horizontally just below his eyes and spread the fingers wide. There was not the slightest tremor, and he grinned.

Howe and Alice were first to arrive at the Fidelity Mutual office in the morning. Holmes arrived a few minutes later and then Eugene Smith. The latter was noticeably uncomfortable in a dark brown suit that still showed the creases from where it had been folded for some considerable length of time before being brought out for today's use. Smith, who had already met O. LaForest Perry and L. G. Fouse in this very office, was introduced: first to Howe, at whom he smiled knowingly as he shook hands; then to Alice Pitezel, to whom he dipped his head and said, "Miss"; finally to "Mr. Holmes of Chicago, who was a close friend of Mr. Pitezel." Smith shook hands firmly with Holmes but evinced no sign of recognition. Holmes, feeling again the exhilaration of danger, caught Howe's eye and winked.

"We'll be leaving here shortly," said Fouse, "but before we do, let's go over this list of identity marks one last time. First, has anyone thought of anything else of any significance since we met here yesterday?"

They glanced at one another but no one responded, so Fouse went on and read through the list handwritten by O. LaForest Perry yesterday but now in typewritten form. When he finished, he looked up over his spectacles. "One final time: any additions from anyone?" Silence. "All right," he said, "these are what we'll go by, then. What we are going to do now is walk over to the coroner's office where we'll meet Dr. Mattern. No," he added, anticipating the remark Eugene Smith was about to make, "I don't mean the morgue. That would be a very long walk. Coroner Ashbridge's office is a few blocks from here at City Hall at Broad and Market. We will be taking streetcars from there out to Potter's Field."

Fouse left the office in charge of Colonel Bosbyshell and

led the way down the stairs, flanked by Perry. Howe and Alice followed and then Holmes and Smith. As they were descending, Smith glanced at Holmes and a puzzled expression came into his face. "You know," he said, "I realize we've just met, but you sure remind me of someone. Any possibility we've met before?"

Holmes's stomach muscles tightened. "I wouldn't know where, unless you've spent some time in Chicago."

"Nope, never been there in my life."

"Then I guess it must be someone else you're thinking of," Holmes said. They had reached the sidewalk by then and, without being too obvious about it, Holmes moved up to join Howe and Alice so they were walking three abreast. After a moment Smith moved past them and joined Fouse and Perry in the front rank. The walk to City Hall was more than merely the few blocks Fouse had casually ascribed to it. Twenty minutes and nine blocks later they arrived at City Hall and went up the broad, creaky, wooden steps to the office of the coroner in the same order they had descended from the insurance office.

The sign on the door said *Dr. Samuel H. Ashbridge, Philadelphia County Coroner,* but it was Dr. William K. Mattern, assistant coroner, who met them, along with two other men. Introductions went around, Fouse first introducing those who had accompanied him here, then introducing Dr. Mattern as the physician who had performed the autopsy on the man whose disinterred body they were soon to view. Mattern was a huge man of about thirty-five with strong features dominated by a great beak of a nose. He was clean shaven and his dense curly hair, reminiscent of pillow padding, made his head appear much larger than it actually was. Though not presently wearing glasses, folded spectacles were visible in his breast pocket. His entire appearance, including the way he moved with a sort of lumbering grace, bestowed upon him a distinctly competent air. When Fouse, introducing him, happened to mention in an offhand manner the ruling of accidental death, Holmes noticed that Mattern's lips tightened. As soon as Fouse was finished, Dr. Mattern introduced his two companions.

"These two gentlemen—Deputy Coroner John Dugan and a colleague of mine, Dr. Ralph Hill—will be accompanying us at my invitation." Dugan was a thin, shy individual who appeared to be wishing he were almost anywhere else than here. Hill was a robust man with fleshy, blue-veined jowls and bright eyes, a man who grinned infectiously at almost anything. Mattern continued: "Both will merely be observers and have been instructed not to offer unsolicited comments or opinions.

"Mr. Fouse has provided me with a copy of the listing of distinctive marks of B. F. Pitezel, which we will look for on the remains of this body that was interred as B. F. Perry. The disinterment was ordered to be undertaken first thing this morning, so the remains will be ready for viewing when we arrive. I must warn you—those of you who may never have witnessed an exhumation—that what we will see and do today will be most unpleasant. I would strongly advise that Miss Pitezel remain out of sight of our activities until requested to approach for specific viewing, at which time the majority of the remains will be draped. There will—I'm afraid I must advise you of this, also—there will be an extremely offensive odor which may be mitigated to some extent, if you wish, by holding a kerchief over your nostrils or plugging them with bits of cloth and taking shallow breaths through the mouth. Should anyone feel an attack of nausea, it would be wise to turn and leave the immediate area until the feeling passes or is relieved through vomiting. We will not linger over this procedure any longer than absolutely necessary. I think we can go now."

The journey to Potter's Field was quite long, involving a ride on one streetcar to its terminus and then transferring to another very nearly to where it also ended. When they reached their destination they alighted from the streetcar and entered the cemetery gate in a cluster. Dr. Mattern led them to the rear of the cemetery grounds where there was a squat brick building and a toolshed separated by a dozen yards. Near the toolshed Mattern stopped them and asked them to wait there for a moment and himself entered the squat building.

"Is that where the body is now?" Fouse asked.

"No." It was Deputy Coroner Dugan answering. "That's the crematory. Dr. Mattern just has to get something in there."

In another minute the physician returned, pulling on a pair of rubber gloves. Two more men were following him and he introduced them to the group. "This," he said, indicating the elder of the two, "is Dr. John Taylor, superintendent of

Potter's Field, and his assistant, who is also his son, John Taylor, Jr. They tell me the remains have been placed on a bench over in the toolshed here. If you'll follow me, please."

They followed him into the shed, where the dirty wooden coffin was resting on a broad wooden table not unlike a picnic table except much lower. They stopped close to it, looking down at the box.

"If it's Ben Pitezel," Holmes abruptly said, his voice loud in the sepulchral quiet, "I'll know it immediately. I've known the man for years."

Dr. Taylor and his son strode to opposite ends of the coffin and gripped the already loosened lid.

"Hold it!" Mattern commanded. He turned to the group. "Perhaps Miss Pitezel would prefer to stand outside?"

"No," Alice said in a tiny voice. "I'll stay."

Mattern shrugged as if he felt that were a mistake and then nodded to the Taylors. They lifted the lid and there was an immediate choked gasping sound from Alice. The body inside the box was clad in checked shirt, blue tie and dull blue trousers. The head had no recognizable face as such; the skin there and on the rest of the body was in a state of advanced decomposition, putrescent and blackened. The stench was sickening. Alice, recognizing the tie and clothing, broke into a ragged crying.

"Deputy Dugan," Mattern said sharply, "please take Miss Pitezel outside and care for her. We'll notify you when we're ready to have you bring her in."

Dugan did not appear to be disappointed at having to miss what was to follow. He put his arm about the girl's shoulders and led her out. Mattern waited until they were gone and then pulled a scalpel from his pocket and placed it on the bench. He lifted and partially turned the head and shoulders of the corpse. Some of the darkened skin at the side of the neck slid, separating from the flesh beneath it and bunched into a roll. Expressionlessly, Mattern looked closely at the neck and then shook his head.

"I see no sign of a wart here. Let me check the right leg for the alleged scar." He pushed up the trouser leg and looked at the leg, though not very closely. No sign of a scar was visible where he was looking at the discolored skin.

"No, no!" Holmes said, moving closer. "You're not looking in quite the right spot. Look right here. More on the inner side of the leg." His pointing finger moved to within an inch or so of the leg, down from the knee and inside.

Mattern nodded and looked closer but still he shook his head. Then Smith startled them all by speaking up. "The skin is loose," he said. "Push it with your thumb and slide it off. If the scar is there, it ought to show up."

Mattern pushed the skin and it slid free in a flap. The underside was not quite so discolored as above and Mattern grunted with sudden interest as he looked more closely. "Mark this down, Dr. Hill, if you will, please." Hill took out a small note pad and pen and wrote as his colleague dictated: "Small cicatrix, approximately one inch long, slightly diagonal, situated approximately two point five inches below the right knee on the interior surface."

"That's it!" Holmes agreed. "Now, check for the wart again on the back of the neck. You've missed it. I'll help you turn the body."

The two men tried to turn the corpse over in the coffin but could not. Even when Taylor and son tried to help by prying underneath with shovels, they were not successful. The corpse started breaking apart and the stench became infinitely worse. Nearly gagging, the two Taylors fell back, but Holmes grasped the large box on the bottom and lifted, turning the box onto its side and causing the remains to slide halfway out onto the table. Mattern gave him a brief, exasperated look, then bent to inspect the neck again. After a moment he shook his head and stepped back. "There's no wart there," he said. He pulled off the gloves and tossed them down on the table. He stepped aside and dipped his hands into a bucket of fresh water off to one side and scrubbed them with the bar of coarse soap resting on the bottom.

Holmes reached into his own breast pocket and pulled out a lancet—a scalpel for fine work, its cutting edge only a quarter-inch long. He snatched up the gloves and put them on as Dr. Mattern stepped back, shaking the excess water from his hands and watching without comment. "If this is Ben Pitezel," Holmes said, "and I'm more convinced than ever that it is, the wart will be right here." He located the spot on the back of the neck where he knew the scar was located and slid the skin back with hard pressure of his thumb. From the underside, the imperfection, about the size of the eraser end of a lead pencil, was clearly visible. With an expertise that surprised Mattern, Holmes cut it free in one fluid movement. He put it on a piece of paper and Mattern stopped to look at it.

"I'd say it is more a mole than a wart," he commented. "Nevertheless, it was where you said it would be."

Holmes was not yet satisfied. He lifted the left hand of the corpse and nearly tore it free as he turned to expose the thumb. "Look here," he said. The nail was far more discolored than the other nails of that hand. Holmes gripped it and with only a small effort, pulled it free of the hand and lay it on the paper next to the wart.

"I take it you're finished, Mr. Holmes," Mattern said. Holmes nodded. Mattern unfolded a large piece of cloth and placed it over the corpse, cutting a four-inch hole over the mouth. He pulled the material apart until the teeth showed to best advantage. Then he looked at Fouse and Perry. "Would you bring Miss Pitezel in here, please? Advise her to take a deep breath and hold it before entering."

Perry strode out and in a moment returned with the girl, Dugan following close behind. Perry led her to the table beside Mattern and then stepped back. "I'm sorry, Miss Pitezel," the physician said gently, "but this final identification is necessary. Please look here and tell me if these are the teeth of your father, Benjamin Pitezel."

The bare teeth gaped through the hole in the cloth, badly misaligned and a distinct cavity in the upper right incisor near the gum line. Alice stared at them, her face drained of color, and then she nodded. "Yes," she whispered, "those are my papa's teeth." She broke into deep sobs and once again Dugan guided her outside.

"Gentlemen," William Mattern said, "there is no doubt in my mind now that this body, buried as B. F. Perry, has been positively identified as Benjamin F. Pitezel." Fouse began slowly nodding and Holmes smiled faintly as Mattern continued: "I will now officially request that Mr. Holmes and Miss Pitezel appear in the coroner's office on Monday morning to sign affidavits attesting to this finding."

"Excuse me," Holmes spoke up, "but my business requires that I leave town just as soon as possible, preferably by noon tomorrow. I realize it will be Sunday, but is it at all possible that these affidavits might be signed tomorrow morning instead of Monday?"

"I'm sure that can be arranged, Mr. Holmes," he said. "I

believe we owe you that much for the time and trouble you have gone to in order to help us. Am I correct in my understanding that the remains of Mr. Pitezel are to be reinterred in Mechanics Cemetery here in Philadelphia?"

Fouse spoke up. "That is correct. Prior arrangements for that were made pending positive identification. The remains will be picked up later today and reburial will be without family members present."

"Very good," Dr. Mattern said. "Mr. Holmes, unless you hear otherwise from us, please present yourself and Miss Pitezel for signing the affidavits at the coroner's office at nine-thirty tomorrow morning."

"We'll be there," Holmes said, turning to leave. He glanced over at Howe and made a barely discernible motion with his head, a motion that subtly told the lawyer to come along.

Only one person besides Howe saw that little movement. Eugene Smith did not see to whom it was directed, but he did see Holmes make it and in that instant he remembered: Holmes was the man in the pale blue-gray suit whom he had seen make an identical motion of his head to the man known as B. F. Perry at 1316 Callowhill Street.

But Eugene Smith was sure he would be laughed at if he said anything about it, so he put the impulse aside and followed the others toward the gate that would let them leave Philadelphia's Potter's Field.

To simplify things, Holmes had Alice stay with him overnight, as his little sister, at the Alcorn Boardinghouse. At 9:30 A.M. on this drizzly Sunday, it was the Philadelphia County coroner himself, Samuel H. Ashbridge, who took their statements in his office at City Hall, while O. LaForest Perry and Jeptha Howe served as witnesses. They had simple statements, quickly executed. Alice's was taken first:

I, Alice Pitezel, live at No. 6343 Michigan Avenue, St. Louis, Mo. I am in my 15th year. Benjamin F. Pitezel was my father. He was 39 years old this year. My mother is living. There are five children. My father came East in July. We learned of his death through the papers. I came on with Mr. Howe to see the body on September 22d. I saw a body at the city burying ground, and fully recognized the body as that of my father by his teeth. I am fully satisfied that it is he.

(SIGNED,)
ALICE PITEZEL

Witnesses,
O. LaF. Perry
Jeptha D. Howe

The statement made by Holmes was almost as brief:

H. H. Holmes
701 63rd Street, Chicago, Ill.

I knew Benjamin F. Pitezel 8 years in Chicago. Had business with him much of that time. More recently he had desk room in our office. I received a communication from E. H. Cass, agent of the Fidelity Co., about Benjamin F. Pitezel. I came to Philadelphia and saw the body on Saturday, September 22d, at the city burial ground. I recollect the mole on the back of the neck, and low growth of hair on the forehead, and general shape of the head and teeth. His daughter had described a scar on the right leg below the knee, front. I found this on the body described by Alice. I have no doubt whatsoever but what it is the body of Benjamin F. Pitezel, who was buried as B. F. Perry. I last saw him in November, 1893, in Chicago. I heard he used an assumed name recently. I never knew him to use any other name but his own. I found him an honest, honorable man in all his dealings.

(SIGNED,)
HARRY H. HOLMES

Witnesses,
O. LaF. Perry
Jeptha D. Howe

Coroner Ashbridge thanked them all for coming and for the statements that had now cleared away this case. No one noticed that Holmes had signed his first name as Harry rather than Henry. Outside the building, Howe made arrangements with Perry to appear at the Fidelity Mutual office tomorrow morning to collect the insurance.

Within two hours, Holmes and Alice were boarding the train bound for Indianapolis. Howe was on hand to see them off and Holmes, after getting Alice settled in her seat, returned to the door of the coach and shook hands with Howe.

"You see," he told the lawyer smugly, "I told you there was nothing to worry about. You collect the money tomorrow. I'll see you in St. Louis."

When he returned to his seat beside Alice, he found the pretty fifteen-year-old crying silently. He put an arm around her and she leaned her head against him. "Come on," he said gently, "no more tears. It's all over now."

"Not really," she told him, sniffling. "I hadn't told you this before, but just before I left home, Mama and Dessa and I sat together in the kitchen and talked. That was when I found out that neither one of them really believed Papa was dead. Dessa said Papa had told her when we got the news he was dead, he really wouldn't be. And Mama told me that when I got here and saw the body that was supposed to be his, even when I saw it wasn't him, I was to say it was." She straightened and looked at Holmes tearfully. "But it *was* Papa. It really was. I recognized him. And now Mama and Dessa will be so sad when I tell them."

"I know, I know," he soothed. But what he knew was that Alice Pitezel would never again see her mother or older sister.

When Jeptha Howe appeared at the offices of Fidelity Mutual Life Association at 9 A.M. Monday to collect the insurance payment on behalf of Carrie Pitezel, he was shown into a comfortable sitting room and asked to wait while the matter was seen to. He took a seat and a few minutes later noticed a tall, serious-looking man he had never seen before entering the office of L. G. Fouse with O. LaForest Perry.

Inside the office, Fouse listened carefully while his firm's chief claims inspector, William E. Gary, spoke earnestly. Gary, a former detective with Pinkerton's National Detective Agency, had been employed by Fidelity Mutual for the past decade. Engaged with other work, he had not been assigned to look into the Pitezel case. Only recently, having completed a different investigation, had he scanned the papers in the Pitezel claim and become interested in the case when he thought he detected some irregularities. On his own he began to make a quiet check of the matter. What he discovered in the police report filed by Philadelphia Police Officer William S. Sauer bothered him.

"Mr. Fouse," he said, "I think you're being hasty in paying off this policy on Benjamin Pitezel. I've looked over the police report and I think there's just as much reason to suspect foul play as there is to accept it as accidental death. What I'm saying is, something stinks about this whole thing."

"Bill," Fouse said, "you really haven't been involved in the case and you can hardly expect to come in here, after the whole thing has been wrapped up to everyone's satisfaction, and start rattling skeletons. B. F. Perry has definitely been identified as Benjamin Pitezel, whose life we insured, and the death has officially been ruled accidental. At this point we have no recourse but to pay up."

"I still think it's a mistake," Gary said doggedly.

"So noted," Fouse told him brusquely.

In the waiting room, Howe saw the tall man leave Fouse's office and a few minutes later Fouse himself emerged and came directly to him.

"Mr. Howe, if you will kindly sign this receipt, I have a check here made out to the order of Mrs. Carrie Pitezel as payment in full of the Benjamin Pitezel life insurance claim. You will note that the sum of two hundred eighty-four dollars and fifteen cents has been deducted from the total amount. This is to defray our expenses in the matters of disinterment of the body at Potter's Field and reinterment at Mechanics Cemetery, plus the travel expense reimbursed to Mr. Holmes."

Howe signed the receipt and accepted the check for $9,715.85, shook Mr. Fouse's hand and thanked him, then left at once for St. Louis, irritated that the check had been made payable to Carrie instead of him as her legal representative, but also grateful that Fouse had not noticed how heavily he had been perspiring.

During the trip back to Indianapolis, Holmes had instilled a delicious sense of adventure and mystery in the rather simple mind of Alice Pitezel. He and her father, he told her, had been involved in a business deal that could bring to the Pitezel family a great deal of money. The fact that her father had been killed in an unfortunate accident did not mean the family still could not collect on the business matter, which had to do with some very important patents. However, Holmes warned, he was telling her this in confidence and it was very important that she not mention anything about it in her letters. If she did, and her letters fell into the wrong hands, they might suddenly find that they had deadly enemies on their trail. These enemies, he went on, would stop at nothing. They would hire professional detectives to trace them and it might result in a very real danger for her mother and Dessie and the other children, as well as herself.

"It's important, too," he added gravely, "that you never refer to me by name in your letters. Instead, use the code four-eighteen-eight. Your mama and Dessie know that means me and they'll understand." Carrie and Dessie didn't know the numbers were the reverse of the combination for the big vault that used to be in his third-floor office in the Castle, but they did know that 4-18-8 was how Ben always referred to him when he wrote to them in cipher.

Alice's eyes had widened as she listened and she had given her promise to do as he said, keenly proud that Uncle Henry was now obviously treating her as an adult and had taken her into his confidence. She didn't understand what all the things meant that he told her about, but their great importance was implicit. It was important, too, that she do exactly as he directed and not become careless, which could endanger her family or the possibility of their getting lots of money.

She had also listened carefully to the reasons he gave for delaying his taking her to live with Minnie Williams. He showed considerable concern over her becoming lonely and so had promised to bring Nellie and Howard to join her here, after which all three of them could go to stay with Miss Williams. That, too, had sounded wonderful and she was thrilled at the exciting turns her life had taken this month and the marvelous things still in store. She was grateful she had gotten to know Uncle Henry so much better on this trip and had been able to see firsthand how concerned he was about her and about her family's welfare. They were so lucky to have him as a friend and she felt a deep affection for him.

It was early evening when their train finally arrived at Indianapolis and Holmes took her directly to the Stubbins House hotel where he registered her in a room of her own under the name of Etta Pitsel. The name change, he whispered conspiratorily, was to throw off anyone who might at this moment be on their trail. She was to stay in the hotel, take her meals there and charge them to her room, while he set about making arrangements to bring Howard and Nellie here.

Alice was no sooner settled in her room than she wrote a letter:

> *Stubbins' European Hotel*
> *One square north of Union Depot on Illinois Street*
> *Indianapolis, Indiana*
>
> SEP. 24, 1894
>
> DEAR ONES AT HOME,
> *I hope you are all well and that you are up. I guess you will not have any trouble in getting the money. 4,18,8 is going to get two of you and fetch you here with me and then I won't be so lonesome at the above address. I am not going to Miss Williams until I see where you are going to live and then see you all again because 4,18,8 is afraid that I will get two lonesome then he will send me on and go to school. I have a pair of shoes now if I could see you I would have a nough to talk to you all day but I cannot very well write it I will see you all before long though don't you worry. This is a cool day. Mr. Perry said if you did not get the insurance all right through the lawyer to rite to Mr. Foust or Mr. Perry. I wish I had a silk dress. I have seen more since I have been away than I ever saw before in my life. I have another picture for your album. I will have to close for this time now so good bye love and kisses and squesses to all.*
>
> YOURS DAUGHTER,
>
> ETTA PITSEL
>
> *P.O. I go by Etta here 4,18,8 told me to Nell you & Howard will come with 4,18,8 & Mama and Dessa later on won't you, as Mama says?*

It was unseasonably cool for Indiana but the Yoke house in Franklin was warm and cozy. Holmes was glad he had given in to the impulse and had taken Georgiana out of the Circle Park Hotel. She'd be happier here. He stood with his back to her now, at the window of their room overlooking the spacious backyard, and spoke without turning around. "I don't really have any choice. I have to go." He turned then and smiled at her apologetically.

The pout she wore may have been exaggerated but it was not entirely without foundation. "You're *always* going away!" she told him. "You say hello with one breath and good-bye with the next. When are we ever going to be able to have a normal husband-wife relationship?"

"Very soon, I assure you," Holmes told her. "Look, Georgiana, I hate it as much as you do, that business always seems to interfere with our being together, but there's really not much help for it. Not at the moment, anyway. I'm doing all I can to get all the business matters wrapped up so we can take our trip to Germany, but it can't be done overnight. Tying up all these loose ends means I have to do a good bit of traveling to the places involved. I can't simply write letters and say, 'Well, take care of things and I'll be back in a year or so,' can I?"

She became contrite. "That's not what I mean, Henry. I know you have your work. It's just that I get so lonely! This time you've brought me to mother's house, at least, but usually I'm all by myself in a hotel room somewhere, far away from anyone I know."

He shrugged helplessly. "Well, all I can say is that things are gradually winding up and within another week or two, maybe even less, we should be on our way. You can get your packing done while I'm gone. But right now there's no help for it. I do have to get back to St. Louis immediately, not only in regard to settling that drugstore matter, but to close the sale of that Fort Worth property to a gentleman who's very anxious to buy."

"You're leaving first thing in the morning?"

"Yes. First thing."

She moved toward him in a slinking manner and linked her fingers behind his neck. "Then," she whispered, smiling seductively, "don't you think we should take advantage of the one night we *do* have, Mr. Howard?"

"I do," he said. He reached down and scooped her up in his arms and started toward the bed. "Indeed I do, Mrs. Howard."

*   *   *

Holmes looked across the office from Jeptha Howe past Marshall MacDonald to Carrie Pitezel and back to Howe again, the veins in his neck swelling in anger.

"That is outrageous!" he exploded. "Thirty-five hundred dollars? We won't give that! A thousand would be excessively generous. Just what the hell kind of a fancy one are you trying to pull here, Howe? Goddammit, man, I've put in all my years of experience in this kind of thing, a full year's thought and worriment on this particular job and damned near all the dirty work. On top of that, I've got this family," he pointed at the woman, "to carry around with me for a month or two until I can get them off to where Pitezel is. I run all the risks and you have none, yet you've got the gall to demand over a third of the insurance payment as your cut?"

Howe's glance flicked to MacDonald and then back to Holmes. "Mac and I have talked it over and figured out what we're entitled to. The figure is thirty-five hundred dollars and we're not going to settle for a cent less. Take it or leave it."

MacDonald, who was leaning against the office wall with one foot crossed over the other, straightened. "Mr. Howard, you're getting emotional. Think about it. Had it not been for my letter recommending Jeptha to Captain Linden of the Philadelphia police and he, as a result, recommending Jeptha to the insurance company, the insurance wouldn't've been paid at all and you and Mrs. Pitezel wouldn't've received a cent."

"Bullshit!" The expletive cracked from Holmes, causing Carrie to flinch in her chair. She looked worried and her eyes rolled back and forth between the speakers. "I brought Howe in on this because it would ease things, but there's no way this fat little shyster was necessary to pull the job."

Howe reddened and started to rise but MacDonald waved him back. "Name-calling will get us nowhere, Howard. You've heard the deal offered. We have the check and you have no choice but to agree. That's it. So what are you going to do about it?"

"I'll tell you what I'll do," Holmes raged. "By God, I'll go to state prison before I'll be browbeaten out of that amount of money! And if I go, you can bet your asses that both of you will go, too."

"Oh, you'll go, all right," MacDonald replied, "but we

won't. You want to know why? Because I'm prepared to send that check back to the insurance company."

"You underestimate me, thinking you can bluff me like that," Holmes said.

"You think so, eh? Howard, you're a fool. I've been dealing with small-time swindlers like you for years. You have no idea what treacherous ground you're on. Jeptha, give me that envelope."

Howe opened his center desk drawer and extracted an unsealed business envelope, stamped and addressed, which he handed with a smirk to MacDonald. The senior lawyer tapped it against the knuckles of one hand for a moment, as if in deliberate effort to build tension. Then he held it up and read off the address box aloud.

"Mr. L. G. Fouse, President, Fidelity Mutual Life Association, nine-fourteen West Walnut, Philadelphia, Pennsylvania." He opened the envelope and unfolded the letter inside. There was a check there as well, which he held up briefly for Holmes to see. It was the insurance check made out to Carrie. MacDonald then read the letter aloud: "'To Mr. L. G. Fouse. Sir: Enclosed please find your check payable to Carrie Pitezel in the amount of nine thousand seven hundred fifteen dollars and eighty-five cents, which we are returning to you in the matter of the life insurance for Benjamin F. Pitezel, Policy Number zero four four one four five. We have learned, to our dismay, that fraud has been involved in this case. The man we were introduced to as Henry Holmes turns out to be a man named Henry Howard, a notorious swindler presently awaiting trial in this city. The body that was supposedly that of Benjamin Pitezel was actually a cadaver substituted in his place. Mr. Pitezel and Mr. Howard, the latter using the alias of Holmes, have worked together in this swindle. We refuse to have anything further to do with a matter involving such illegalities and suggest your firm take immediate steps to prosecute the perpetrators. Please accept our sincere apologies. Sincerely yours, MacDonald and Howe, Attorneys-at-Law.'"

MacDonald enfolded the check in the letter and replaced the letter in its envelope, paying no attention to Carrie, who was sobbing. He ran his tongue across the flap and sealed it, then tossed the missive back on the desk in front of Howe. "Mail it, Jeptha," he said coldly. "Now."

Howe came to his feet and was halfway to the outer door when Holmes said, "Wait." He stopped and looked back as

Holmes continued. "Do you remember those two nights you came to my room at Alcorn's and where I had you sit while we discussed the details of defrauding the insurance company?"

"What about it?"

"Do you remember how you bragged about Marshall MacDonald having friends in high places, such as Police Chief Linden, and how easily they could be duped?"

Howe did not reply, only stared curiously at Holmes as he went on: "Remember asking me about how Ben and I substituted the body and made it look like him? Remember how you said it was one of the slickest swindles you'd ever been part of and that you and I made a good team? Do you remember that strange faint scraping sound you asked about, and I told you there was a mouse in the drawer? Do you remember those things, Howe?"

"I remember," the obese lawyer said. He repeated himself. "What about it?"

"I'm sure," Holmes let his eyes stray to MacDonald and then back to Howe, "that men so worldly-wise as you two gentlemen are certainly familiar with a device called the Edison phonograph, right? Well, I had one of those devices in the bureau drawer right beside where you sat, Howe. That was the so-called mouse you heard. I have a record of every word you spoke. Every single incriminating word."

Howe paled. "Howard," he said bitterly, "you are a miserable son of a bitch!"

Exultation rose in Holmes but he went on without pause, his assumed rage having disappeared and his voice now calm, persuasive. "Tut tut, I see no necessity for us to engage in further petty dispute and threats. We are all reasonable men. So, as it's written in the Bible—Isaiah, isn't it?—'Come now, and let us reason together.' You want thirty-five hundred dollars, which Mrs. Pitezel and I think is too much. We suggest one thousand dollars, which you think is too little. So what do reasonable men do? They compromise, of course. The final offer, gentlemen," his words emerged as cold and hard as chunks of agate, "is twenty-five hundred dollars. And to quote our fat friend here, you really don't have a choice."

It was still well before noon when MacDonald and Howe, frustrated, furious and resigned, accompanied Holmes and Carrie to the Merchants' National Bank a few blocks from their office. Both men were well known and respected at the bank and on their word regarding the check's authenticity, there had been no problem getting it cashed. Carrie, hands shaking badly as she clutched more money than she had ever seen at one time, counted out the $2,500, recounted it and gave it to Howe. The remainder she placed in her bag. Howe grimly counted the money himself, with MacDonald watching closely. The two angry lawyers looked murderously at Holmes but then merely stalked off without any further conversation.

As soon as the men were out of sight, Holmes gripped Carrie's elbow and virtually propelled her from the building, heading for the First National Bank of St. Louis, several blocks distant. As they walked swiftly through the milling Friday morning pedestrian traffic, Carrie managed to gasp out the thought that was on her mind. "What are . . . oh, we're walking so fast! . . . What are you . . . going to do with . . . that Edison phonograph . . . of what Mr. Howe said?"

He laughed so boisterously that passersby turned to look at them curiously. "There is no such record," he told her.

"But . . . the sound. Mr. Howe . . . he admitted he heard it."

"Oh, he heard a sound all right," Holmes said, still elated with his bluff. "It was a spool of black thread I put in the drawer with the trailing end coming right to my hand. It was no trick to pull it without him being aware of it and get the sound." He laughed again and she joined him, her spirits as high as his at finally getting the money. She was acutely aware that by so neatly turning the tables on that pair, he had just saved her a thousand dollars and she felt an increased respect for him.

In the lobby of First National, Holmes steered her toward an unoccupied customers' counter at the rear. He looked around carefully, making sure no one was nearby, and then reached into his pocket and removed a legal paper. She watched him curiously, catching her breath.

"I'll show this to you in a minute," he said. "You remember when Ben and I were in Fort Worth?" She nodded and he continued. "I know when he got back he told you about our deal with the big property there—a fifty-fifty split of everything."

"Yes," she admitted, "that's what he said."

"All right, what did he tell you about the note we took out for sixteen thousand dollars?"

"Well, he said he signed it, but under the name of Benton T. Lyman and that it was coming due in September—September sixteenth, I think he said—but that there was a grace period and I'd have to see to the payment before that grace period was up."

"Right," Holmes said. "We're in the grace period right now, but it's for only two weeks. That means we're just getting in under the deadline. It expires the day after tomorrow. Now, I don't know if he told you or not, but I owed more on it than he did, because I owed him three thousand dollars. So instead of us each having to pay eight thousand dollars on the note, I had to pay eleven thousand dollars and—"

"We had to pay the other five thousand dollars," she broke in. "Yes, I remember. That's what he said. And he told me to be sure to get that payment off to Texas and that you'd help me on that."

"Okay, good. I just wanted to make sure you had everything straight in your own mind that he told you. Now this," he unfolded the paper and showed it to her, "is the note he was talking about." It was the original note that had been made out by R. B. Samuels, that Holmes had told Samuels had been lost. "You can see here where Ben signed it as Benton T. Lyman. And here's the due date—September 16, 1894. I already sent my eleven thousand dollars in when it was due, on the sixteenth, but we've got to get the five thousand dollars off right away that Ben told you had to be sent in."

She clutched the note to her breast. "Another two days," she breathed, "and we could have lost everything. But now we're safe. Oh, Henry, Benny'll be so glad we got it off on time."

"I know it," Holmes said, "but let's not waste any more time. Give me the five thousand cash and the note and I'll have the cashier wire a bank draft to Mr. Samuels. As soon as it is recorded in Texas as having been paid, you and Ben will start receiving large monthly rents from it."

She dug in her bag and carefully counted out $5,000 and gave it to him.

"Wait right here," he told her. He pointed at a grilled window where no one was waiting in line. "I'll go to that counter right there and be back in just a minute with your receipt." He moved to the window and stood at an angle so he could see her from the corner of his eye.

"May I help you, sir?" asked a teller

"Yes, please," Holmes said. He counted out a pile of bills from those Carrie had given him. "I want a cashier's check for four thousand dollars made out to the order of Mr. Frank Blackman. That's B-L-A-C-K-M-A-N."

"All right, sir. One moment please."

While the check was being prepared, Holmes slipped the remaining $1,000 into an inside pocket. In the same movement he withdrew a stamped envelope addressed to Blackman in Chicago. Carrie, he could see, was gazing vapidly around the bank, her gaze only occasionally touching him. He swiftly wrote on the back of a deposit slip: *Frank. $1,000 for Dora, $3,000 for my account, less your commission. HHH* Then, on the back of the $16,000 note, he wrote *$5,000 + $600 received, Account paid in full, Sept. 28th, 1894* and then scribbled an indecipherable scrawl that could pass for a signature. He put the note in his right-hand jacket pocket. The teller returned with the cashier's check and Holmes looked it over carefully and then slipped it into the envelope along with the note to Blackman and sealed it. He slid the envelope back through the grill.

"I'm late for an appointment," he said, "and I'd really appreciate it if you could put this in the bank's outgoing mail box for me."

"Of course, sir."

"Thank you. Good day."

"Good day, sir. Thank *you*."

Holmes sauntered back to Carrie and handed her the note. "You can breathe easier now," he said. "It's all taken care of. Ben will be proud of you."

"Oh," she gripped his arm, "I can't remember when I've been so excited. Uh . . . isn't there supposed to be some sort of a receipt for me, Henry?"

"Oh, sure," he said, reaching into his pocket. "Sorry. Glad you reminded me. Here it is, the original note with the receipt written on the back."

She glanced at it and frowned. "What does this mean, five thousand dollars *plus* six hundred?"

"A penalty for late payment," he said. "It's a standard charge in real estate transactions of fifty dollars daily when you don't pay until you're in the grace period. It was twelve days overdue, so that's six hundred dollars."

"You paid it?"

"Sure, don't worry about it. You can reimburse me when we get back to the house. And speaking of that, we'd better get going. We've got to get Howard and Nellie ready to go to Cincinnati with me, while you and Dessie and Wharton get set to go to Galva."

It was the arrangement Holmes had made with her immediately upon arriving the day before yesterday. The plan made with her husband, he told her, was that he was to take her and the children to be reunited with Ben just as soon as she got the money from the insurance and paid the note. However, he added, Ben was a little nervous about all this and had said that since there was always the possibility that somehow the insurance company had gotten onto the fraud, the safest thing would be not to travel in a group, that detectives would be on the lookout for a woman with five children. Holmes told Carrie he agreed with Ben's reasoning and therefore, since Alice was already staying with this kindly old lady he had hired in Cincinnati and was already enrolled in school there, the most logical thing seemed to be for him to take Nellie and Howard to the same place, enroll them in school there, too, and generally stay out of sight for a while.

At the same time, Holmes had continued, Ben had told him to tell Carrie that she, along with Dessie and Wharton, should go to Galva, Illinois, to visit her parents, the Cannings, as he had promised her she would this year. She was to stay there until Ben felt it was safe and got word to Holmes where he was. Then Holmes could send word to Carrie that the coast was clear for her, Dessie and Wharton to meet him and the three children wherever it was that Ben would direct them to come. From then on they could live a wonderful life of luxury.

Carrie had loved the idea. She'd been disappointed when Alice hadn't come back to St. Louis with Holmes but had been relieved to learn of the nice lady she was staying with in a private home in Cincinnati. Alice, Nell and Howard could have a wonderful time together, without even losing classroom time, and she would be eased of the burden of caring for them. She—with Dessie sharing much of the load of caring for little Wharton—could have a truly relaxing time with her mama and papa in Galva. And at the end of the road was the final wonderful reunion they would all have with Benny, with plenty of money and a good life stretching out in front of them beyond that. It all seemed to be too good to be true.

She wanted to know where Ben had gone and he told her his first stop was Puget Sound in Washington State. After that, he didn't know, nor would he until Ben got in touch with him. That might be in a few weeks or it could be several months, depending upon whether or not there was trouble.

"The main thing, Carrie," he told her, "is that Ben says you have to do exactly as I say in all matters."

When they got back to the Pitezel house, Holmes and Carrie settled their financial matters. She paid him the $600 that he had said he paid as a penalty on the note. She also gave him $100 to go toward Alice, Nellie and Howard's expenses in Cincinnati.

"You've done so much for Benny and me and the children, Henry," she said, her eyes brimming. "And so far as I can see, you're the only one who's not getting anything out of this. You've had to travel to Philadelphia and you've been caring for Alice all along. At least let us pay your expenses."

Holmes lowered his eyes. "That's not necessary, Carrie. It only amounted to about ninety and it's worth it to me to see you and Ben and the children happy. You two have had a rough go of it for a long time. It's about time life handed you some bouquets."

"No," she insisted, "I won't hear of it. We're at least going to pay your expenses. Here is ninety dollars."

"Well, thank you, Carrie. Actually, I was beginning to run a little short of cash. You hang onto the rest of that now. You're going to need it when the time comes for you to start traveling."

He pulled out his watch and looked at it, then snapped it closed and returned it to his pocket. "I have one last business chore I have to do before leaving, so I'd better get at it. Why don't you get the kids' bags packed so they're all ready to leave when I get back in an hour or so?"

"There's not much left to pack," she said. "We've already taken care of almost all of that. But Howard does have a pocket ripped out in his coat, so I could get to work on that for him and sew a new one in."

"Fine," he said. "You do that and I'll be back before long."

Holmes left the house whistling faintly. The day had thus far been a very profitable one for him. Besting Howe and MacDonald at their own game had been sheer delight. He had been expecting they would demand half the $10,000 and their asking for only $3,500 had surprised him. And bluffing another thousand out of them with the Edison phonograph ploy had been wonderful. The fact that Carrie had come out of this whole thing with little to show for it—though she didn't know that yet—perturbed him not at all. He quickly reviewed the insurance payment situation. Fidelity Mutual had deducted that initial $284.15 for exhumation and reburial fees, plus expenses for Holmes. Then there was the $2,500 that went to the lawyers, $5,000 supposedly for the Fort Worth property, plus the $600 in alleged penalties there. Finally, there was the $100 for care of the children and $90 to reimburse him for his expenses, despite the fact he'd already been reimbursed once already. So, out of the $10,000 for her husband's death, Carrie Pitezel had wound up with $1,425.85. Holmes's share had been a hefty $5,790, which was close to what he thought he would get.

Holmes had a feeling he would probably not be coming back to St. Louis for a very long time, if ever. And it was largely because of Jeptha Howe's attempt to blackmail him into submission that he was now en route to enact retaliation in a rather indirect manner.

At the city jail he was permitted to have a visit with his former cellmate, bank robber Marion Hedgepath. They sat on opposite sides of a long counter divided down its center by a heavy, close-meshed iron grillwork. Holmes wasted no time in getting his dig in.

"Your fat lawyer friend," he said, "tried to give me the business today. He won't do that again."

"You mean on that insurance deal in Pennsylvania?" Hedgepath asked.

"That's the one."

"It's done? You pulled it off?" Hedgepath became very animated.

"Yep. Ten thousand bucks insurance money paid over, simple as pie."

"You've brought my five hundred, by God! Hot damn, Howard, you're okay."

"If you want five hundred bucks, Hedgepath, you ask Fat Man for it."

Hedgepath's expression changed. "What're you trying to pull, Howard? You owe me five hundred. You made an agreement, dammit."

Holmes affected a prodigious yawn, enjoying the man's growing discomfort. "What could you hope to spend five hundred dollars on in this place?" he said. "Not much point in giving you money if you can't spend it, is there?" He stood up. "Well, I have to be going. Give my regards to ol' Shyster Jeptha when you see him."

"Howard!" Hedgepath shouted as Holmes began walking away. "Come back here, you bastard. You owe me!"

Holmes continued walking without looking back. The bank robber's furious voice followed him. "Goddamn rotten prick! Pay me my money. Howard! You hear me? *Howard!*"

Even after leaving the room and going far down the long corridor toward the exit, he could still hear the raging convict. "Howard, you son of a bitch, I'll get you for this. You miserable shit, I'll get you! I'll get you!"

Holmes left the jail whistling *"Ta-ra-ra-boom-der-ay."*

Nine

Carrie had packed a trunk with clothes and personal items for Nellie and Howard, along with a few more things for Alice. Pushing Holmes's mild objections aside, she insisted that she and Dessie and Wharton accompany them to the station to see them off, saying this would also give her the opportunity to buy tickets for the trip to Galva on Monday, October 1. While she was busy doing that, the children clustered around her, Holmes moved off by himself to the Western Union office and sent three wires. The first was to Dora in Wilmette:

> DARLING STOP HAVE SENT FRANK ONE THOUSAND TO
> RELAY TO YOU STOP FINAL STEPS ARE IN PROGRESS
> NOW STOP LOVE YOU STOP HENRY

The second wire was to Robert Sweeney, desk clerk of the Stubbins Hotel in Indianapolis:

> MR SWEENEY STOP PLEASE HAVE MY WARD ETTA PITSEL
> ROOM 313 YOUR HOTEL AT UNION DEPOT TO MEET
> ARRIVAL OF ST LOUIS TRAIN AT HALF PAST FIVE STOP
> AM ARRIVING THEN AND WILL MEET YOU TO PAY BILL
> AND SPECIAL CHARGES AND RECEIVE MISS PITSEL STOP
> H HOLMES

The third wire was to Pat Quinlan at the Castle in Chicago. He always let Pat know where to reach him in case of emergency. As usual, this wire was brief and enigmatic to any who should read it other than Quinlan himself:

PAT STOP ATLANTIC H STOP CINCINNATI STOP ALEXAN-
DER COOK STOP ONE STOP PRATT

The deciphering Quinlan would put to it would be that
Holmes would next be at the Atlantic Hotel in Cincinnati
under the name of Alexander Cook for one night. A similar
message would be sent by Holmes to him every time he
moved to a new location.

When he returned to the main hall of the depot,
Holmes saw Carrie with the children at one of the benches
and, after buying tickets for the trip to Cincinnati, rejoined
them there. He gave her what final murmured instructions he could in the presence of the children—reiterating
an order he had given her before, that she was to burn
all letters from him as soon as she finished reading
them—and then boarded the train with Nellie and
Howard.

"You be sure to write me regular now at Grandma and
Grandpa's house in Galva," Carrie called after them. "And
you be good children and do what Uncle Henry tells you,
hear?"

"We will, Mama. 'Bye! 'Bye Dessie. 'Bye Wharton.
'Bye!"

They were still calling farewells as the train started
moving away.

In the twelve days since Marion Hedgepath had been
visited by the man he knew as Henry M. Howard, the anger
within him had festered. He had considered numerous ways
of carrying out his own threat of getting even for the way he
had been bilked out of $500 he felt was rightfully his. The
problem was that in order to get at Howard, he would have to
damage his own attorney, Jeptha Howe, in the process. That
ceased to be a problem yesterday when Howe had visited
him.

"There's just no way I can get you out of here," Howe
had told him through the screen in the visiting room. "As I
told you in the beginning, certain palms might be greased in
order to get you free, but you have not come up with the
money."

"Damn you, Howe," Hedgepath had snarled, "you're my
attorney. If it weren't for me, Howard would never have

gotten in touch with you and cut you in on his deal. Now he's pulled it off and you got your share of the money and I'm left sitting in here with shit all over my face."

Howe had grimaced and made a helpless gesture. "Howard cheated me, too," he said. "I was supposed to get thirty-five hundred dollars and wound up with a thousand less than that."

"Then, by God," Hedgepath said, "use five hundred of that to get me out."

"Sorry, Marion," Howe had said, rising, "but I worked too hard for what I did get. I'm not in this business to give charity. When you get five hundred dollars, get in touch and I'll see what I can do."

Throughout the night Hedgepath had paced his cell and as the first light of dawn crept into his cell he had sat on the edge of his cot and began to write:

St. Louis, Mo.
Weds., Oct. 10th, 1894

Major Lawrence Harrigan
Chief of Police
St. Louis, Missouri

Dear Sir:—

When H. M. Howard was in here some two months ago, he came to me and told me he would like to talk to me, as he had read a great deal of me, etc.; also after we got well acquainted, he told me he had a scheme by which he could make $10,000, and he needed some lawyer who could be trusted, and . . .

Page after page the letter had gone on as Hedgepath described everything he knew about the plan of Henry M. Howard and B. F. Pitezel to defraud the insurance company. And now, his back aching and his fingers cramped, he was finally finishing the lengthy letter.

Please excuse this poor writing as I have written this in a hurry and have to write on a book placed on my knee. This and a lot more I am willing to swear to. I wish you would see the Fidelity Mutual Life Insurance Company and see if they are the ones who have been made the victim of this

*swindle, and if so, tell them to send an agent of the
company to see me if you please.*

YOURS RESP., ETC.,
MARION C. HEDGEPATH

William E. Gary, returning from a Kansas City assignment to the home office in Philadelphia, had managed to
work in a one-day stopover in St. Louis to visit his old friend,
George Stadden. The two men had begun work for Fidelity
Mutual Life Association at the same time some twenty years
ago. They had become fast friends and even when their paths
within the company ultimately diverged—Stadden entering
the executive end of sales and Gary becoming a claims
investigator—they still sought one another out when possible. Now Stadden was the firm's St. Louis branch manager
and Gary was its chief investigator.

When Gary so unexpectedly walked into the branch
office at 520 Olive Street an hour ago, Stadden had shot to his
feet and embraced him in a great hug, thumping his back
with blows that might have floored a smaller man. Gary only
grinned his pleasure and the two had fallen to talking about
old times. Now, sipping coffee, they were still embroiled in
happy yesterdays when a St. Louis uniformed police officer
entered. He spoke with one of the young clerks up front who
nodded and immediately led him back to Stadden's open
office.

"Mr. Stadden," the young man said, "there's a police
officer here who has a letter for you from Chief of Police
Harrigan."

"Come in, come in," Stadden said loudly, directing his
remark to the officer.

The policeman entered, removing his hat. "I'm Officer
Menard," he said, extending an envelope. "The chief asked
me to hand this to you personally, sir, and wait for any reply
you might have." He glanced a bit nervously at Gary and
continued in a faintly apologetic way. "It's . . . I believe it's a
confidential matter dealing with your company."

"Thank you," Stadden said, accepting the envelope and
tearing it open. "However, if it's dealing with the company,
then it's not confidential from this man. This is our company's
chief investigator, William Gary."

As Gary and Officer Menard shook hands, Stadden looked
at the contents of the envelope and his lips pursed in a silent

whistle. He stepped past the two men and closed the office door. The two were watching him curiously.

"Bill," the branch manager said, "whatever plans you had for today, you'd better figure on canceling them. Listen to this: 'Mr. George Stadden, Branch Manager,' et cetera. 'Dear Sir: An inmate of the City Jail, Marion C. Hedgepath, serving a twenty-year sentence for train robbery, has sent me a written statement of some length claiming that your firm has been victimized in a ten-thousand-dollar life insurance swindle. The incident involves the alleged death early in September of a Philadelphia man, formerly of St. Louis, names Benjamin Pitezel who supposedly was accidentally killed while using the alias of B. F. Perry. Hedgepath states that the principal perpetrator of the fraud was his cellmate, Henry M. Howard, presently sought by St. Louis police for jumping bail on an indictment of mortgage fraud. Hedgepath states that Howard laid out the whole plan to him, in which Howard and Pitezel were to substitute a body in the place of Pitezel and then claim the insurance money. A local attorney of some prominence, Jeptha D. Howe, is also implicated by Hedgepath. Undoubtedly Hedgepath hopes to have his sentence mitigated by divulging the scheme, although he claims he wants only vengeance against Howard and Howe for cheating him out of five hundred dollars, which was to be his share of the swindle. There are other details and Hedgepath has agreed to make any further statement necessary. Though without substantiation, he is personally convinced that the dead man actually was Pitezel, who was murdered by Howard. I would suggest that you or some officer of your company return to my office at once with the bearer of this letter. Sincerely yours, Lawrence Harrigan, Major, Chief of Police, City of St. Louis.'"

Stadden looked up at Gary. "Holy shit! How's that for a real bolt out of the blue? You want to take it, Bill?"

He was talking to himself. Gary had snatched the letter from his hand and was already halfway to the front door, Officer Menard hustling to catch up.

L G FOUSE STOP PRESIDENT STOP FIDELITY MUTUAL LIFE INS CO STOP 914 WALNUT ST STOP PHILA PA STOP OCT 14 1894

SIR STOP STRONG CIRCUMSTANTIAL EVIDENCE IN HAND
THAT PITEZEL LIFE CASE WAS FRAUD STOP CONSPIRACY
TO FALSELY IDENTIFY SUBSTITUTE BODY INVOLVES
PITEZEL ALIAS B F PERRY AND H HOWARD WHO MAY BE
H HOLMES STOP ATTORNEY HOWE AND WIFE OF PITEZEL
ALSO INVOLVED STOP SUGGEST IMMEDIATE EFFORTS
BEGIN TO LOCATE HOLMES IN CHICAGO STOP HAVE
OBTAINED SWORN STATEMENT FROM ST LOUIS JAIL
PRISONER M HEDGEPATH DETAILING PLANS OF SWIN-
DLE OUTLINING DETAILS UNKNOWN TO OUTSIDERS STOP
POLICE CHIEF HARRIGAN HERE NOTIFYING CHIEF LIN-
DEN IN PHILA OF POSSIBILITY MURDER COMMITTED HIS
JURISDICTION STOP RETURNING IMMEDIATELY WITH FUR-
THER DETAILS STOP GARY

Receipt of William Gary's telegram from St. Louis caused
a great deal of discussion in the home office of Fidelity
Mutual Life Association. Company officers were inclined to
scoff at the idea that the alleged fraud had been perpetrated,
suspecting that the criminal named Hedgepath was a wily
man who had concocted the story for his own purposes,
which would eventually be made clear.

L. G. Fouse listened to these remarks, wanting to agree
with them, yet harboring a deep and disturbing doubt. As
usual in such circumstances, he called in one of his most
trusted employees, his own personal assistant, O. LaForest
Perry.

"What do you think, Ollie?" he asked. Fouse was the
only person who ever addressed Perry by the diminutive of
his given name.

"I think," Perry said, "we have to bear in mind that Bill
Gary is one of the shrewdest investigators in the business.
We don't know everything he knows and it'll be a while
before we do. In the interim, I think we have to accept his
belief that fraud was committed and start taking steps of our
own at once."

"I agree. I want you to take this wire to Chief Linden
and see if we can get conspiracy warrants issued against
Holmes, Howe, Pitezel and Pitezel's wife. At the same time,
contact Pinkerton's. I want them to put operatives to work on
the case at once. Have them start investigations at the two
locations we're sure of—St. Louis and Chicago—with authori-

zation to follow up wherever the investigation takes them. If and when any of them are located, they are to put them under twenty-four-hour surveillance, but they are not to apprehend them yet. Make sure they understand this. And, Ollie, you start digging right here in Philadelphia."

The more information that had filtered into the home office of Fidelity Mutual Life Association, the more Laurence G. Fouse realized he had been made a fool of by the swindlers Howe, Holmes and Pitezel. His ire became a living thing gnawing at his insides and he silently vowed vengeance against the trio if it took all his money and the rest of his days.

Part of that ire was an admitted anger at himself, to have been so blind to the inconsistencies, to have so easily settled the claim, that he had sloughed off the suspicions of his own chief investigator, William Gary, on the day of the settlement.

The different threads of the investigation had, since Gary discovered the evidence indicating fraud, only underlined the fact that the company had indeed been swindled. The statement by the bank robber, Hedgepath, had nothing in it that could prove that the fraud had been committed and might have been put aside as merely a scheme to get himself out of prison. But there was one comment the convict made, which Gary pointed out when he brought the statement to Philadelphia, that gave credence to what he said. He mentioned that the man he knew as Howard had renewed the life insurance on Pitezel on the final day of the grace period for paying the premium. That was information known by no one except officials of the company and Pitezel himself. So where did Howe and Holmes get this information in order to pass it on to Hedgepath? Gary said Hedgepath had learned this from Howe, who in turn had been told of it by Holmes. But that left the question, how did Holmes know?

Then had come disappointing but no less supportive evidence from the investigators. Gary, sent at once to Wilmette to learn from Myrta Holmes the whereabouts of her husband, found her totally uncooperative, refusing to answer any questions at all, once she knew what Gary wanted. George Stadden in St. Louis reported that Mrs. Pitezel and her children had vanished from there, as had Howe and Holmes. Pinkerton detectives had followed leads to Cincinnati,

Columbus, Indianapolis, Galva, Kingston, and Detroit without turning up anything concrete until Detective Alderman wired from Detroit that the trail seemed to point from there to Toronto, rather than Kingston, as first thought.

Fouse had immediately written a long letter to his old friend, Dr. John Ferguson, medical examiner of the Excelsior Insurance Company of Toronto. In it he detailed the entire case so far as he was able to put it together and asked for Ferguson's help in checking for possible leads in Toronto. Now had come a wire for Fouse from that city and he tore it open eagerly. It was, as he had hoped, from Ferguson:

> FOUSE STOP ON RECEIPT YOUR LETTER PUT OUR MAN HODGINS ON IT STOP FIND MAN MATCHING HOLMES DESCRIPTION AND UNKNOWN WOMAN STAYED AT PALMER HOUSE AS MR AND MRS H HOWELL FROM COLUMBUS STOP DIFFERENT WOMAN ANSWERING PITEZEL WOMAN DESCRIPTION STAYED WITH YOUNGER WOMAN AND SMALL CHILD AT UNION HOUSE REGISTERED AS MRS C A ADAMS AND DAUGHTER FROM COLUMBUS STOP MAN ANSWERING HOLMES DESCRIPTION HAD 2 GIRLS ABOUT 13 AND 15 REGISTERED AT ALBION HOTEL AS ALICE AND NELLIE CANNING OF DETROIT STOP ALL ARE NOW GONE STOP HODGINS SAYS WOMAN AND DAUGHTER CHILD MAY HAVE GONE PRESCOTT ONTARIO WHILE MAN AND WOMAN GONE TO OGDENSBURG NY STOP HODGINS CHECKING FURTHER HERE STOP WILL ADVISE STOP GOOD LUCK STOP FERGUSON

Fouse put the telegram down and sat thinking for several minutes. The identifications were not totally satisfactory, capable of fitting any number of people, but there was some interesting dovetailing and one thing stood out significantly: the two young girls had been registered at the Albion as Alice and Nellie Canning by a man who fit the Holmes description, and Pinkerton agents had already discovered that the parents of Carrie Pitezel, living in Galva, were named Canning.

"Perry!" he called.

O. LaForest Perry entered the office quickly and stood waiting. Fouse looked up at him with a self-satisfied expression. "I think our man Holmes may have tripped himself up. What's the present status of the warrants?"

"Shaky at best, sir. The fraud warrants were issued by the district attorney's office provisionally, with the understanding that we establish reasonable grounds that the crime was committed. We know that it was, but our word alone is not sufficient to maintain the warrant without further proof, at least insofar as extradition from another state is concerned. The statement of a felon presently in the St. Louis jail does not constitute such proof, however damning it might be. I've talked to the D.A. and he says that if Holmes were to be arrested elsewhere in Pennsylvania, we could undoubtedly have him brought to Philadelphia and charged, but even then we could not prevent bond from being set and once that was done he would undoubtedly be bailed out and disappear. So far as extraditing him on the charge if he's arrested in some other state, it can't be done."

"What about the possibility that Holmes and Pitezel killed the dead man whose body was substituted. Or what if Holmes actually killed Pitezel?"

Perry shrugged uncomfortably. "Again, sir, we have problems in that respect. The coroner's office initially ruled it accidental death and that ruling still stands; further, there's no evidence a substitute body was used. The dead man was identified not only by Holmes but by the man's own daughter and the marks of identification were seen on the body by Coroner's Physician Mattern, who accepted them as proof of identity. The identification was then accepted by the coroner's office as legitimate. That holds far more weight than the claims of a felon that a body was substituted. Or even if Pitezel was actually murdered, without solid evidence of foul play we don't have the grounds for having a warrant issued on a charge of murder or even manslaughter."

Holmes stared out the window at the New England hills speeding past. The trees were becoming bare, the intense autumn colors of a few weeks ago now turned into duller russets and browns and the leaves layering themselves in an unbroken blanket on the face of the land.

Why, he wondered, was he doing this? He could just as easily have taken Georgiana directly to Boston instead of planning to meet her train in Concord one week from today. What was to be gained in rekindling embers all but dead? How many years had it been? He shook his head and continued watching from the window, but he saw little of what passed. As usual when riding on a train, he didn't read. He thought. And he planned. And he remembered.

He wondered why, since Toronto, it had become so difficult to review things in their proper perspective, in the cohesive way they had always fallen into place before. This project had dragged on so long. He had *made* it drag on. It was what Dora had questioned and what she had been so concerned about, but he hadn't listened, hadn't heeded the danger signals that had been so clear to her. I've never prolonged anything like this before, he thought, so why now? Why not like always before—the plan made, the deed done, the evidence hidden, the profits made? A neat and orderly tapestry woven skillfully and then put aside. Not this time. This time the loom continued to run and the patterns were becoming mixed, confusing, all but indecipherable. There were frays appearing, loose threads which, if tugged upon, might unravel the whole fabric. The warnings were there, clear enough, and he was finally seeing them himself. It was time to quit this. Time to salvage what was salvageable, time to cut and run. A new life, that's what he needed; a new life in a new land where no clouds hung low over murky horizons. Why not really leave the country? Why not establish a whole new identity free of blemish? When the time was right, he could then send for Dora and Lucy and they could live a life of great luxury wherever they wished, couldn't they? And so the lure he had held out to Georgiana of a trip to Europe was suddenly no longer an elaborate fantasy.

So that answered the question he had posed to himself— why he was making this present trip. Because in the coming days he might very well be making a trip from which he would never return; because being in Vermont, he was close to the place of his birth and the parents and siblings he had left as a youth; because this was most likely the last time he would ever see them. After this brief solo trip to New Hampshire, he would resist the temptation to return to Burlington to view from a distance the devastation caused by the explosion at number 26 Winooska Avenue. No doubt there would be accounts in the newspaper of the unfortunate Mrs. Cook and her grown daughter and little son who were killed. He doubted anyone would have been able to establish that the Cook woman and children were really Carrie Pitezel and Dessie and little Wharton. It would be over and that would end it all. But for him to go back there was stupid and he knew it.

The stay in Ontario's Imperial Hotel in Prescott had been brief for him and Georgiana—less than twenty-four hours. And when they crossed over on the ferry to Ogdensburg, it was with no intention of staying. He had left Georgiana waiting for him in the railroad station while he visited Carrie for an hour at the National Hotel, telling her he was arranging a house for her in another place where at last she would finally be reunited with Ben. In the pattern now well established, he had gone immediately to Burlington, Vermont, with Georgiana and got a room for them at the Burlington House Hotel for one night under the name of G. D. Hale and wife of Columbus, Ohio. The next day he moved her to the Ahern Boardinghouse at 19 George Street as Mr. and Mrs. H. Hall. He left her there in order to "take care of some business," which gave him the opportunity to rent the Winooska Avenue house from W. B. McKillip, giving his own name as J. A. Judson and saying he was renting the place for his widowed sister, Mrs. Alexander E. Cook. All these things were so much easier to accomplish now that he no longer had the burden of Howard, Alice and Nellie.

After not seeing Carrie for over a week, he'd returned and settled her into the new quarters in Burlington, but when Ben hadn't been there as Holmes had promised he would be, she had finally become almost hysterically irate.

"I can't stand this any longer!" she had screamed. "I'm not *going* to stand it any longer. I want to see Ben, do you hear me? I want to see my children! I think you've been lying to me, all along. Nothing ever comes of anything you say. Nothing ever turns out the way you say it will. I'm leaving. I'm going to Indianapolis to look for my babies."

He had anticipated such an eventual blow-up and had prepared for it. He told her that the children were no longer in the Indiana capital, where he'd been assuring her for weeks they were; that, during his absence, he had taken them to Toronto and reunited them with Ben. He said that Alice had become quite a responsible young woman and had even cooked dinner for them all and it had been delicious. He showed her letters in cipher which he said were from Ben and Alice and he had decoded them for her. Alice's was light and airy, telling of her new coat and of how much she liked Toronto and of how well she and Nellie and Howard were doing. Ben's was more sobering, warning her that though the element of danger was now nearly over, they still must wait just a little longer before being reunited. It praised Holmes for his efforts and told Carrie to have patience a little longer.

But this had been happening over and over during these past weeks and Carrie was not so easily mollified this time, continuing to threaten—though with less conviction—to begin searching on her own for Ben and her children. He'd left Carrie then and returned to Georgiana in the Ahern Boardinghouse. That was when he had asked for and gotten the $1,000 he had given Georgiana to hold for him in Indianapolis. He needed it because, at the considerable cost of $300, Holmes had purchased a ten-ounce bottle filled with nitroglycerine and placed it, unknown to Carrie, in a niche beneath the cellar stairs at the Winooska Avenue house. Using extreme care, he had positioned the bottle on a ledge and then stretched black thread, virtually invisible in the dimness, across the opening. When touched, the thread would act as a trigger, dislodging a delicately balanced heavy piece of wood. The wood, crashing into the bottle, would cause an explosion that would demolish the house, blowing Carrie, Dessie and Wharton to oblivion.

To forestall suspicions, Holmes had bought tickets for her and Dessie to Lowell, Massachusetts, for November 19. He had enclosed them in the letter he mailed to her just before stepping on this train. In it he had written:

> Carrie: No more disappointments. Our friend is fairly sure he's in the clear now. You and he are definitely going to be reunited on the 19th. On that day, use the enclosed tickets that will bring you to Lowell. Do not leave the house until then. We don't want any chance encounter to spoil the reunion that's finally here. Now, one other thing, and this is extremely important. Go down into the basement. Under the steps you'll see a bottle filled with a yellow liquid. I put it there temporarily, meaning to hide it elsewhere, but then forgot. It's too visible where it is. Immediately on receipt of this letter, go get it and take it upstairs to the attic and hide it where no one will accidentally see it. I repeat, this is vitally important. Please see to it. I'll be seeing you, with our friend, very soon. 4-18-8.

Also before boarding the train, he had sent a telegram to his parents in Gilmanton, telling them he was at last coming home and when he would arrive. Now, as the train slowed, the conductor passed through the cars crying, "Tilton! Tilton, New Hampshire, next!" His reverie broken, Holmes straightened and gathered up his things.

He expected to see his father and mother—or perhaps a brother or his sister—awaiting in a rig to transport him the final few miles to the old homestead in Gilmanton. He was not at all prepared for the reception he got. As he stepped down onto the platform, a woman's voice called to him from close by.

"Herman! Herman! You really *did* come home at last!"

She had changed considerably in these eleven years since he had seen her last, but he recognized her instantly. It was Clara, his first wife. Beside her stood a gangly boy of fourteen, hanging back shyly as she pulled him forward.

"Herman, this is Teddy. Our son."

The Pinkerton's letter, hand delivered by special courier first thing this morning, stirred a spark of apprehension in L. G. Fouse. He read it through swiftly and now went back and read it again. He sighed and called loudly, "Ollie!"

In a moment O. LaForest Perry entered the office and Fouse looked up at him sourly. "That son of a bitch, Holmes? He's left New Hampshire and gone to Boston and now we've got troubles." He extended the letter to him. "Read this."

His chief assistant read:

> BOSTON, MASS.
> NOVEMBER 15, 1894
>
> L. G. FOUSE, PRESIDENT
> FIDELITY MUTUAL LIFE ASSOC.
> 914 WALNUT STREET
> PHILADELPHIA, PENNA.
>
> SIR:
>   *Please be advised that subject under surveillance, H. H. Holmes, was followed on the train from Tilton, New Hampshire, to Concord where he was rejoined by the woman named Georgiana, who has*

*been traveling with him as his wife. Together they
continued via rail to Boston, in which city he and
the woman are presently registered as Mr. and Mrs.
G. D. Hale at the Simpson Boardinghouse, 712
Marlborough Street, a few blocks off the Boston
Common. Mrs. Pitezel, however, is still tenant with
her older daughter and infant son at 26 Winooska
Avenue, Burlington, Vermont, under alias of Mrs.
A. E. Cook. Since arrival here in Boston, Holmes
has visited a succession of ticket offices for steam-
ship lines. Interviews with personnel at these locations indicates that subject has inquired about state-
room accommodations and fares to England, France
and Germany. It is believed he is ready to book
passage. Do you wish Holmes and the woman with
him apprehended? What about the Pitezel woman?
If apprehension desired, warrants are requisite and
cooperation must be obtained from Boston Deputy
Superintendent of Police O. M. Hanscom. Please
advise at earliest opportunity.*

JOHN CORNISH, SUPT.
PINKERTON'S, BOSTON

"Looks as if our bird is ready to fly, sir," Perry said
grimly, handing the letter back to Fouse. "Are we going to try
to stop him?"

"Damned right, and we're not just going to try! Bill
Gary's still in Chicago?"

"He is."

"All right then, you're going to have to handle this.
What's the status with the warrants?"

"We still have the provisional fraud warrant from the
district attorney's office, but that's useless in matters involving extradition. The coroner's warrant you got from Sam
Ashbridge on a murder charge has been looked over by our
legal department and Colonel Bosbyshell says it is worthless.
Our own Philadelphia police couldn't arrest him on it, much
less Boston's."

"Damn!" Fouse thought a minute and then bellowed,
"Bosbyshell!"

Edward Bosbyshell, with military bearing, appeared at
the doorway very nearly as quickly as Perry had. "You called,
Larry?"

No other employee in the Fidelity offices would ever

have dared address the firm's president in such a manner. He was a distinguished-looking man with a heavy shock of snow white hair and a great walrus mustache, also white. As Fouse's oldest employee, he was one of the rocks upon which the firm was built. He had emerged from the Civil War as a Union Army colonel and joined Fidelity Mutual only a few months after that, but had retained his military title over all these years. It fit him well, without any sense of ostentatiousness. As a liaison man with federal, state and municipal governmental agencies as well as with executives of a wide range of businesses, he had almost no peer. It was even rumored that he was on a first-name basis with President Benjamin Harrison.

"Do you know," Fouse glanced at the last line of the Pinkerton letter, "either John Cornish or O. M. Hanscom?"

"In Boston? Of course. Cornish is Pinkerton's top man there. Been in charge of the Boston office for, oh, eight-ten years. Solid man. Hanscom's assistant chief of the Boston police. Official title's deputy superintendent, but he's assistant chief. Pretty good cop. Came up through the ranks and only implicated in any kind of scandal once, and that time he was cleared. Hadn't been for that, he'd probably be chief today. He'll get there sometime. What's up?"

"How well do you know Hanscom? Enough to get a big favor?"

"Maybe. Depends. Just how big of a big favor?"

"Big enough, I suppose, since it might involve sticking his neck out. Holmes is in Boston, ready to sail for Europe. We've got to nail him. Now."

Bosbyshell pursed his lips and popped them lightly. "Ouch. The warrants we've got—D.A.'s and coroner's—aren't worth a damn. Not here and certainly not there."

"That's the point," Fouse said. "Can we get him to arrest Holmes on an open charge and detain him while we try to get better grounds?"

"Possible. It's toying with false arrest and Hanscom got gunshy on that account years ago, so he might take some convincing. But even if he did go along with it, can we get the grounds he needs?"

Fouse looked gloomy. "I doubt it. We need time, a lot more time, and we don't have it."

Perry spoke up. "What about other warrants? I mean from other states? Mightn't he be wanted somewhere else?"

"That's possible, too," Bosbyshell said. "Consider this. It's a long shot but maybe. If he does have a warrant out against him elsewhere and it's for something worse than defrauding an insurance company, he might elect to come here rather than be sent there."

"All right," Fouse said, leaning back in his chair, "let's try it. We've got to do something." He looked at Bosbyshell. "Get on the telephone and call Hanscom. Lay it on the line. Tell him the bind we're in and not only what we know Holmes has done, but what we *think* he's done. Say we're sending Perry up there to assist in any way possible. Ollie," he turned his glance to Perry, "you leave for Boston now. Go see John Cornish first, then take him along with you to see Hanscom. Hopefully the Colonel will have him softened enough by the time you get there. Maybe you can work out something with him as well for getting the Pitezel woman into custody."

Orinton M. Hanscom looked every bit the police officer he was. A big man, well over six feet tall and pushing 240 pounds, he was nearly bald, perpetually smoked revolting black cigars that were somehow always about two inches long and, bluff and blunt in manner, he virtually oozed professional competence.

Now, looking up from the papers on the desk before him, he gave the two men in his office a wintry smile and shook his head. "I understand your situation, gentlemen," he said. "Colonel Bosbyshell certainly made it clear enough. But you must realize that there is no possibility whatever that I can authorize this police force to go out and arrest a man on warrants as indefinite and poorly drawn as these. Nor will I have this Holmes picked up on an open charge. And the bail-jumping in St. Louis is nonextraditable, as you know. However much I'd like to help, I have no intention of jeopardizing my own career by slapping a man in jail because he might have defrauded an insurance company in another state several months ago. That's insanity."

O. LaForest Perry was not surprised, but he was disappointed. John Cornish, however, was not ready to give up. The chief of the Boston branch office of Pinkerton's National Detective Agency came to his feet. He was of medium height and build, somewhere in his early forties and tended to smile easily. His neat business suit gave him more the aspect of an accountant or lawyer than a detective of considerable skill.

"What about Texas? According to our Fort Worth office, Holmes left there precipitately about a year ago, supposedly with the law on his tail. There may be an outstanding warrant against him there."

Hanscom held out his hands in a helpless gesture and spoke around the stub of a cigar. "Mr. Cornish, what would you have me do? I can't *invent* a warrant and I can't expect Texas to do it either. The wire was sent out over an hour ago. There's been no reply. Which means either there never was a warrant brought out against him there—at least under the name of Holmes—or else they're still digging for it. In either case, we can't—"

He broke off as the young man in shirtsleeves stuck his head in the door. "Chief," he held up a piece of paper, "wire from Fort Worth."

Hanscom beckoned him in and took it. The cigar bounced slightly with the faint movement of his lips as he read. When he looked up he had not changed expression but there was a different quality to his voice. "You're very fortunate, gentlemen." His eyes returned to the sheet and then he looked up again. "There is a valid warrant outstanding for H. Holmes in Fort Worth, Tarrant County, Texas, dated December eighteen ninety-three. We are requested to apprehend and hold for extradition."

Their midmorning stroll, arms linked about each other's waist, had carried them eastward on Boylston Street past Old South Church and prestigious shops that had fascinated Georgiana. They peeked in the door at the interior of the impressive Arlington Street Church and then, on their passage through the Public Garden, stopped briefly on the bridge and watched the ducks on the pond. It was only November 17, so the water was not yet frozen, although a slight skin of ice fringed the shorelines. Weaving their way carefully through the abundant carriage traffic, they crossed Charles Street and chirped at pigeons and squirrels as they crossed Boston Common. When they reached the top of the hill at Beacon Street, they paused on the red brick sidewalk before the State House, craning their necks to look up at the massive dome, its gold leaf brilliant under the midmorning sun.

"Rather impressive, don't you think?" Holmes asked.

"Oh, yes," Georgiana replied. "Have you ever seen it before?"

"A time or two. Getting tired?"

"Little bit," she admitted. "These shoes weren't designed for long walks."

"Oh, I'm sorry," Holmes said quickly. "I should have thought of that. Come on, we'll go back to Simpson's, rest a little and have a bite of lunch and then we can go get our tickets."

"Wonderful!" Georgiana said, eyes aglint with more than just gold-dome reflection. "You know," she continued, as they began walking west on Beacon Street, "this all seems like a dream to me. Small town Indiana girl strolls through one of the world's great capital cities, escorted by a very handsome, very attentive and very lovable man who just happens to be her husband. It just doesn't seem possible. And so much more to come. London. Paris. Berlin. Oh, I'm so happy, Henry."

They were just approaching the corner of Joy Street when two men passed by them from behind and stopped in the middle of the sidewalk directly in front of the broad steps of a publishing house whose name—Little, Brown & Co. —was on a rectangular bronze plaque to the left of the entry. The pair then turned and faced in their direction. Holmes moved to direct Georgiana around them, but one of the men sidestepped in a blocking manner. A third man had moved up behind and stood waiting, alert. The sudden sharp fear that touched Holmes was not reflected in his scowl.

"Do you mind telling me," he said angrily, "why you gentlemen are blocking our path?"

The man in the middle removed his hand from his pocket and flipped open a wallet in which there was a badge. "I am Inspector Glidden, Boston Police Department. This," he indicated the man beside him, "is Mr. John Cornish of Pinkerton's. Detective White is behind you." He returned the wallet to his pocket and brought out a folded paper. "Mr. Holmes, we have a warrant for your arrest. I'm afraid you'll have to come with us."

"Henry," Georgiana gasped, "what is this?"

"On what charge?" Holmes asked, ignoring her.

Inspector Glidden pushed down an impulse to smile. "Horse theft."

Georgiana's mouth opened uncomprehendingly. "*Horse* theft? That's crazy. Henry hasn't stolen a horse. And this is my husband, Henry M. Howard, not Henry Holmes. You've made a mistake. You've got the wrong person." She looked at her husband beseechingly. "Tell them, Henry. You haven't stolen a horse."

"Actually, ma'am," Cornish interjected, "he did. In Texas. Didn't you, Mr. Holmes?"

Holmes patted Georgiana's arm. "It's all a misunderstanding. Nothing to worry about. Come on, we'll go along and get this all cleared up."

They continued down Beacon Hill in strained silence, Georgiana gripping Holmes's right arm so tightly her hands hurt, Inspector Glidden to Holmes's left, Detectives Cornish and White behind. A block beyond Arlington Street they turned south on Berkeley and followed it south six squares to Stuart Street. Police headquarters was located on the southwest corner.

Inside the building they were separated, Georgiana reluctantly moving off with Detective White and a police matron, while Holmes was taken to the office of Deputy Superintendent Hanscom. Holmes jolted to a stop as he recognized one of the two men who had come to their feet.

"Horse theft, eh?" he said, his smile very strained. He threw up his hands in a helpless gesture. "I guess I know what I'm really wanted for."

"That's right, Mr. Holmes," said O. LaForest Perry. "We have a lot of talking to do, don't we?"

Holmes sat quietly by himself in the windowless room to which he had been led. From outward appearances, he was wholly unperturbed by his arrest. Actually, his mind was racing, going over the inconsequential idiocy that had brought him to this situation. That stupid thing in Texas. It was such a joke at the time, occurring only a short while after he and Ben had arrived in Fort Worth under their own names last December. Unexpectedly, Holmes had encountered a rancher named Charley Kinworthy who carried considerable amounts of money. Deciding this to be a challenge of the first order, Holmes had endeavored to separate him from some of it. The plan had nearly worked but, at the last moment, the proposed victim had figured out the swindle and decided Holmes was someone who needed to be shot. As he raced to the house to get his gun, Holmes raced to the hitching post in front of the house and galloped away on Kinworthy's extraordinarily valuable horse. A few days later, after having sold the horse for a piddling amount to a drifter, Holmes discovered to his chagrin that Kinworthy was the brother-in-law of the attorney general of Texas and that he had sworn out a warrant against Holmes for horse theft. That was the funny thing— Henry H. Holmes a horse thief! Only then had he learned how serious a crime horse theft was considered to be in Texas. Men had been hanged for it . . . recently! Men had been sentenced to terms of twenty years to life imprisonment for it . . . recently! And so he and Ben had fled, not terribly perturbed because when they returned to erect the new Castle, he would be using the alias of D. T. Pratt.

It hadn't been that simple. When they'd returned a month later, this time with Georgiana in tow, they soon encountered a related problem that finally convinced Holmes he would be grievously tempting fate to remain in the State of Texas much longer. Once during February, twice in March and twice again in April he had unexpectedly encountered Charley Kinworthy. Through pure luck—or perhaps because he was attuned to the possibility—it was he who saw the rancher first and was therefore able to avoid being seen himself. Ordinary logic dictated that sort of luck would run out. He could, of course, dispose of Kinworthy, but that wouldn't do much good. In addition to a horse theft warrant, he had no doubt there'd be a massive investigation and he'd wind up being sought vigorously for the murder of the brother-in-law of the Texas attorney general. No, the only answer had been for him to junk the Fort Worth plans, make as much money as he could from swindles in a short time and then get out of Texas permanently.

Holmes sighed and looked about him at the four windowless walls. Now that insignificant matter had caught up to him again and he had been given a choice and placed in this room to make his decision: he could either volunteer to return of his own free will to Philadelphia to face a charge of conspiring to defraud an insurance company, or he would be extradited on the existing warrant to Texas to face Lone Star justice.

It wasn't a difficult choice to make, actually. The penalty in Philadelphia on being convicted of conspiracy to commit insurance fraud was a prison sentence of two years. And he was already keenly aware of how Texas treated its horse thieves.

Holmes looked up as the door to his cubicle was unlocked and swung open. Chief Hanscom and Oliver LaForest Perry stood there. It was the police executive who spoke.

"You've decided?"

Holmes nodded. "Philadelphia," he said.

Carrie Pitezel was startled when, a few minutes before noon, someone knocked on the front door of 26 Winooska Avenue. She and Dessie looked at one another, uncertain whether to open the door or not. The knocking came again, more persistently than before, and Carrie went to the door.

"Who's there?" she asked.

A man's voice, low and somewhat muffled, replied. "Mrs. Pitezel? Mr. Holmes sent me. Please open. It's dangerous to be talking through the door."

It had been so long since anyone had addressed her by her real name that Carrie was shocked. But the man's familiarity with her name and Holmes's was reassuring. She opened the door and found a pleasant-appearing man in dark blue overcoat standing there, hat in hands. He smiled and dipped his head.

"Ma'am," he said. "Hope I haven't startled you. Holmes said you might be a little edgy and I was to assure you right off that there was nothing to worry about. May I come in, please?"

She stood back and let him in, shutting the door and turning to him. Dessie stood close by holding Wharton and the man nodded at her.

"You must be Miss Dessie," he said. He looked back at Carrie. "My name's Lane White. I know this is unexpected, but Holmes gave me a letter to give to you and he said you'd understand." He took a sealed envelope from his pocket and gave it to her.

Carrie tore it open wordlessly and immediately recognized the handwriting of Holmes. It was as brief as its content was unexpected:

Boston, Nov. 18, '94

CARRIE:

All's well but there's a shift of plans. The bearer of this is Lane White, an associate of mine. You can trust him. Everything's okay, but forget about going to Lowell on the 19th. Instead, come straight through to Boston with Mr. White. He will escort you and get you and Dessie here safely. You must come with him immediately. 4-18-8.

Had not the code number designating Holmes been on the letter she would have been wary, but now she merely asked White to have a seat while they got ready. It didn't take long, since they were almost completely packed in preparation for the planned trip to Lowell tomorrow. Within the hour they were on a train heading for Boston.

When the train deposited them at the Boston depot, Lane White hired a carriage and gave the driver an address. When they stopped there, Carrie looked with consternation at the building where they had stopped and then at their escort.

"That's right, ma'am," he said, "this is police headquarters and I'm Detective Lane White. You are under arrest as accessory in a conspiracy to defraud. Please come with me."

Talking her elbow, he helped her from the carriage and led her into the building, Dessie following with Wharton. The little boy had begun wailing loudly when he saw both his mother and sister silently crying. They walked down several corridors but Carrie stopped suddenly when her name was called from an office they passed. She saw Holmes leap up from a chair beside a desk in a roomful of men; saw, as well, the man standing behind him who immediately restrained him with a hand on his shoulder, pushing him back into his seat.

"Carrie!" Holmes called again. "Don't worry. You're not in trouble. It's Ben and I who're going to have to suffer for this. You're not to blame."

Holmes was admonished to be quiet and Detective White grasped Carrie's elbow and led her away. He took her to a quiet room with a single window, a table and several chairs.

"You and your daughter have a seat, ma'am," Detective White said, beckoning to a matron to remain with them.

"The chief will be talking with you as soon as he's finished questioning Mr. Holmes."

Carrie watched him shut the door as he left, saw Dessie staring fearfully at her and then saw the heavy iron bars across the window. Her shoulders shook again with renewed sobbing.

Georgiana Howard was in a state of shock. She had been questioned for hours yesterday and today without being given much information in return; questioned as if she were herself a criminal. But the more the questioning had progressed—the more, evidently, Henry had been questioned elsewhere—the more gentle and respectful the questioners had become with her. At length it was the deputy superintendent himself who spoke to her the most reassuringly.

"Miss Yoke," he said, "I know this has—"

"It's Mrs. Howard," she told him, lips tight. "Mrs. Henry Mansfield Howard."

"Uh, yes, well, we'll come back to that in a moment. Indulge me now, if you will. Miss Yoke, this has been difficult for you. I wish to apologize for that, but there was no help for it. We had to ascertain your position in this matter. We are sure now that you yourself have not been involved."

"Just exactly *what* is this so-called matter you keep referring to that I'm not supposed to have been involved in?"

"A matter, Miss Yoke, involving your husband in at least two different criminal activities, possibly more. As you know, last December a warrant was issued in Fort Worth, Texas, for his arrest on a charge of horse theft. He subsequently fled the state to avoid prosecution. Closer to home, he has voluntarily admitted to being involved in a conspiracy to defraud the Fidelity Mutual Insurance Company of Philadelphia out of ten thousand dollars. There could be other charges."

"*Other* charges! My God, what else can you accuse him of?"

Hanscom hesitated and then spoke in a gentler tone. "This will be difficult for you, I'm sure, Miss Yoke, but the man you consider to be your husband is evidently also a bigamist."

The word struck her with the numbing force of a hammer blow. Her lips repeated the word, but without sound.

She felt dizzy and though Hanscom continued talking, only occasional words and phrases were penetrating.

"You see, Miss Yoke, Mr. Holmes, or Mr. Howard, as you know him—and, incidentally, those are both assumed names—he has at least two wives other than yourself that we know of at this point. His name is actually Herman Mudgett and his first wife—his only legal wife—is Mrs. Clara Lovering Mudgett of Tilton, New Hampshire. His own family—parents, brothers and a sister, I mean—reside in Gilmanton, a few miles from Tilton."

"He...he told me..." she was having difficulty speaking "...he had no family."

"Oh, but he does. You'll undoubtedly meet some of them. A brother and the sister are both in the building at this moment and his wife—Clara Mudgett, I mean—should be arriving here very soon. There is another wife, married to him under his identity of Holmes, in the Chicago area; a Mrs. Myrtle Belknap Holmes. He calls her Dora. You will undoubtedly be learning more as time passes. I only wished to stop by and assure you that there are no charges whatever against you and you are free to go whenever you please. Your own personal luggage—which we picked up at Simpson's Boardinghouse, along with his—can be returned to you with the exception of several items we will have to retain."

"Is...is there any chance I might be able to see Henry? Talk to him?"

"I'm afraid not, Miss Yoke. Not yet, at any rate. Perhaps after he's been extradited you can."

"Extradited to where? Texas?"

"No, ma'am. Your husb—uh...Mr. Holmes has made it clear that he is quite fearful of being returned to face the charge against him there. He seems to feel they do not deal kindly with horse thieves in Texas. He said he would rather face the music, as he put it, in Philadelphia on the charge of conspiring to commit insurance fraud. If convicted there he would probably be sent to prison for a couple of years. In Texas he might be facing ten to twenty. Perhaps more. So he's volunteered to return in custody to Philadelphia. To answer your question, I'm sure Philadelphia authorities would eventually let you see him. I'm equally sure they, too, have a good many questions they would like to ask you."

"All right." Her reply was barely audible.

"If you'll excuse me now, I'll have to be getting back to

my office. My sympathies, ma'am, that you have to be going through this."

She was shown to a waiting room and there she met Henry's family: his eldest brother, Fred, who bore only vague resemblance to the man she had married; his older sister, Sophie, who was chunky and matronly; his wife—his *legal* wife—Clara Mudgett. There was a distinct shyness in their conversation at first, an embarrassment, as if each felt guilty of having committed some transgression just in the knowing of the man who was their focal point. Gradually the shyness fell away as they spoke, the confusion and need to know the truth taking precedence. And that was followed, at last, by the hurt and the anger.

Henry, Georgiana discovered, had indeed gone to New Hampshire as he had told her he was going to, but not for the business reasons he gave. He had decided to resume relations with his parents and had sent them a telegram telling them when he would arrive. And they, unaware that he would not also be very desirous of seeing his wife and child—his *child!*, a fourteen-year-old boy—had alerted her of his pending arrival and she had met him at the station. She had taken him to the family homestead in Gilmanton, where his father was postmaster now, and it was there, with Clara and the family gathered around, that he spun his amazing tale.

"He told us everything that happened," Sophie said. "About the accident and all, I mean."

"Accident?"

"Yes, you know—that he'd been in an accident. It was that railroad collision. He told us all about it—out West somewhere, he said, near Denver, Colorado. He told us about the coma he'd been in for so long a while. And then, when he came out of it, he found he was in a hospital and that he had no memory of any previous life."

"That's right," Fred Mudgett put in. "He said he didn't know whether he had family of his own, parents, brothers, sisters, a wife, children, anyone. He didn't even know if he had any friends or a job or even what his occupation was. We thought it was an awful thing to have happened to him, but had heard of things like that happening before."

"That was where you came into the situation," Clara said. "Herman said that he was in the hospital for months and months and that a wonderful woman named Miss Yoke, very rich and full of pity for those who were hurt, used to come in and bring flowers to the patients and read to them. He said she had the sweetest voice he had ever heard and as she read to him and later just talked with him, he had come to know her better and he fell in love with her. He said when he was eventually well enough to leave the hospital, he proposed and Miss Yoke—you, that is—accepted, and you two were married in a church in Denver. He told us that, later on, you saw he was suffering greatly from not being able to remember his past and that through your wealth and the influence of your close friends, you were able to secure the services of one of the foremost surgeons in the world. The doctor operated on him and when he came out of the ether, he found his memory had returned." Clara paused and bit her lip, then shook her head, unable to go on.

Sophie picked up the thread of their combined narrative. "He told us as he lay there with his head all wrapped in bandages, he was horrified when he realized that he was married to Clara and they had a child and what a terrible wrong he had done in marrying this sweet woman—you, I mean—who had been so kind to him in Denver. He said at that point he didn't know what to do but finally decided he wouldn't tell her—you—that you weren't his wife because it would bring you such grief and distress. It was better, he said, that he be the one to bear the suffering and pain in silence, but it had finally become too much and he had to come home at last and take up his old life again."

Georgiana could not stop herself, she had to ask. "Did he," she asked Clara, "when...when you met again this month, did he...did you and he..."

Clara looked at her directly. "Did we become man and wife again? Did we share one another's bed again? Yes! Yes, we did! I'm sorry, Miss Yoke. After all you did, all the expense you went to—to help him regain his health and his memory and all, I mean—after all that, that such an awful shock was in store for—"

"He is a goddamned liar!" Georgiana's bitter words cut Clara off and the three of them stared at her. She looked at each in turn and when she spoke again there was no less bitterness in her voice, but now a sense of resignation, of defeat. "Yes, a liar. I was working in a Chicago store when he came in to make a purchase and we met. He was a Chicago businessman, owner of the ABC Copier Company and involved in real estate. We saw one another for many months and then finally he took me with him to Texas and then to Colorado. He was never in a train wreck, never lost his memory, never was operated on. The only thing he's told you that was the truth is that we were married in a church in Denver. He has another wife, you know. Her name is Dora and she lives near Chicago.'"

"*Another* wife!" Clara was clearly shocked.

Georgiana nodded. "Yes. And maybe more. Who knows?"

"Well, if he lied to us and he lied to you and he lied to that third wife," Fred spoke up, "you can't help wondering who else he's lied to."

"Or," Georgiana added, "what other crimes he's committed."

Deputy Superintendent Orinton M. Hanscom was exasperated and tired, the effects of over forty-eight hours of almost continuous attention to the Holmes case. He had eaten little and slept less and the more he had tried to piece together the pieces of this situation, the more frustrated he had become. It was with a sigh of genuine relief that he shoved aside on his desk the stacks of transcript. They had been prepared by his stenographer, Anne Robbins, and her two assistants, all three of whom had worked at taking down the initial statements in shorthand and then spending the night typing them up. The transcripts were already dog-eared and tattered from excessive handling.

Four other men were in the office, three sitting opposite Hanscom's desk, waiting patiently, while Inspector Glidden stood in relaxed posture by the door, his arms folded across his chest, annoyingly sucking at a bothersome tooth. To the right of the desk, somewhat apart in his seat, was O. LaForest Perry, invited to sit in because of his firm's close involvement with the case. In the two hardback chairs more to the left were the two police officers from Philadelphia who had arrived here several hours ago—Detectives Frank Geyer and Thomas Crawford.

"Gentlemen," Chief Hanscom began, "you've had time to become familiar enough with the circumstances surrounding the arrest of Henry Holmes and Carrie Pitezel. I can't remember a case in recent years that has been more involved, more contradictory. Nor one I will be so delighted to get rid of. I've—" He broke off and waved an index finger in a circle at the officer standing at the door. "Glidden, shut that damned door." Inspector Glidden lifted a hand in acknowledgment and closed it, then leaned against the jamb.

"I've stuck my neck out on this thing," Hanscom continued, "and I don't mind telling you it makes me uncomfortable. We've got a hell of a lot of innuendo and circumstantial crap that makes us believe this Holmes is guilty as hell of a lot of things, ranging anywhere from simple fraud and bigamy all the way up to kidnapping and possible murder. But you know what? The *only* justification we've had for holding the man is a year-old warrant out of Texas on a charge of horse theft. And now I've had my people wire the Texas authorities that we won't be returning him there, which puts me smack into the position of violating the rights of two citizens by holding them without sufficient grounds. And, goddammit, I don't like it a bit! What I should've done, Mr. Perry," he jabbed the two fingers holding his mangled cigar stub at the insurance man, "was to tell you to go fuck a duck when you brought in those papers supposed to be warrants. Warrants my ass! You can tell Bosbyshell when you get back to your office that he'd better not *ever* send me that kind of shit again. And then you two," the two fingers jerked toward the seated detectives, "have the gall to come up here to collect these prisoners and transport them out of the state without any goddamned papers at all. Jesus H. Kee-rist!"

The two Philadelphia detectives stirred uncomfortably but said nothing. Perry chewed at his underlip, also remaining silent. Glidden, wearing the faintest ghost of a smile, seemed to be enjoying this. Chief Hansom, his ire spent, settled back and shoved the soggy and tattered end of the cigar back into his mouth.

"All right," he went on, "now that you know my feelings about this, let's get into the matter. You've talked with Glidden here, with Perry here, with that Pinkerton man, Cornish. Chief Watts gave you what he knew," he rolled his eyes, causing Glidden's faint smile to expand into a grin, "and so now you should be sufficiently confused about everything. You know we had no grounds for getting the Pitezel woman out of Vermont, so Cornish thought up the idea of convincing Holmes it would be in his own best interest to write her a letter telling her to come with the bearer to Boston immediately."

"We've been pretty impressed with everything you and your men have done on this so far, Chief," Crawford said. "We'll tell our own Chief Linden about it when we get back to headquarters."

"You don't know how thrilled that makes me," Hanscom growled. "Maybe he'll write me a citation for my personnel file here." He shook his head and then indicated the stacks of papers on the desk. "We've questioned both Holmes and the Pitezel woman practically nonstop since we got them and here are their statements. Eighty pages of unbelievable garbage. About the only thing we really know for sure at this moment is that in addition to Holmes being a cool customer, he's a clever lying son of a bitch. And she's a scared, stupid, lying bitch. Nevertheless, I've gone over everything and tried to bring it together into some kind of order and here's what I've come up with."

Hanscom leaned forward and picked up a large pad filled with scribbled pencil notations. He looked at it quietly for a moment and when he began to talk again there was a distinct change in his delivery, a crisp, clipped incisiveness that provided subtle insight into why he had risen through the ranks to his present office.

"Henry Holmes is actually Herman Webster Mudgett, originally from Gilmanton, New Hampshire. He's got a whole raft of aliases, but the one he's used most is Holmes, so that's how I'll refer to him. Benjamin Fuller Pitezel also had lots of aliases, including B. F. Perry, but Pitezel is the legitimate one and that's what we'll use. They go into cahoots in Chicago, eight-ten years ago. A year ago they start setting up the swindle. They get a ten-thousand-dollar life policy on Pitezel and plan to substitute a mutilated stiff in place of him and then split the money. Pitezel's wife was in on this part of it. She denies it, but she's lying. Pitezel sets himself up in a fake patent business under the name of Perry in Philly. Holmes makes a deal to get a stiff from the New York morgue. Refuses, incidentally, to implicate whoever helped him there. Holmes says the body was made up to look like Pitezel, disfigured and then left for someone to find. Pitezel—Holmes claims—goes into hiding. Holmes, with this St. Louis shyster, Jeptha Howe, brings Pitezel's middle daughter to Philadelphia. The body's dug up and they find all the marks that show the dead man is really Pitezel, so the insurance is paid. Now, was the dead man really Pitezel, after all? Coroner says yes.

Insurance company says yes. Holmes says no. The wife says she doesn't think so.

"The insurance company," Hanscom shot a quick look at Perry, "pays the death benefit to Howe, who's been authorized by the wife to get it, since she's beneficiary. All three of them—Howe, Holmes and the wife—meet in St. Louis and split the loot, Holmes getting the lion's share. Then they split up the Pitezel family and start running around the country, supposedly to eventually rejoin Pitezel. Holmes and his wife and the Pitezel woman and the two kids with her wind up here in Boston, but somewhere along the way we've lost the Pitezel woman's husband and three of her kids."

Hanscom paused to use three matches in an effort to relight the soggy mass clenched in his teeth. He got one puff from it before it went out, but he didn't notice. "So where are they?" he asked. "That's the problem. The stories the wife and Holmes tell jibe generally, but differ in certain important specifics. When they split up, the wife takes the oldest daughter and the baby boy, Holmes takes the three middle kids, Alice, Nellie and Howard. He boards a train in St. Louis with Howard and Nellie, supposedly to join Alice in Cincinnati. Or is it Indianapolis? Hard to tell. Anyway, it *is* in Indianapolis that he picks up *his* wife, Georgiana Yoke—he married her bigamously under the name of Henry Howard— and he keeps *that* simple soul totally in the dark. Holmes gets word from Pitezel, so he says, alerts Mrs. P. and they all converge in Detroit; but Holmes says he gets wind of someone trailing them so he doesn't let Carrie Pitezel see her husband or the kids he's got. The boy, Howard, has been giving Holmes trouble so Holmes allegedly gives the kid to Pitezel to take with him. Pitezel at this point, according to Holmes, heads for South America by way of San Salvador. They're supposed to keep in contact through coded messages in the *New York Herald* personals column. But Holmes keeps telling the wife she'll be joined by Pitezel any moment.

"They go from Detroit to Toronto, then to Prescott, Ontario, and Ogdensburg, New York, and Burlington, Vermont, and finally Tilton, Gilmanton and Concord in New Hampshire before winding up here, but now the two girls, Alice and Nellie, aren't with them anymore. Where are they? The wife has been thinking they're in Indianapolis all along. Holmes says he took them to Buffalo and turned them over to his secretary, a woman named Minnie Williams, and sent her off to England with them, where he would join them before long. He's supposed to be able to reach her by this same code system in the *New York Herald* personals. This story about giving the two girls to the Williams woman could be true. He did have a secretary by that name in Chicago, but no one seems to know where's she's gone. And the Yoke woman, who says Minnie Williams was a witness at her marriage to Holmes in Denver, verifies that Holmes took her to Niagara Falls and was gone from her for some hours during that time, so he could easily enough have hopped over to Buffalo with the kids and come back. Incidentally," he added, "my recommendation to you two gentlemen, when you get back to Philadelphia and start looking into this matter, is that you concentrate on locating the children and getting their stories. You'll probably come closer to the truth from what they say than anything you'll get from either Holmes or the Pitezel woman—or Pitezel himself, if you ever locate him."

"Now," he said, taking the dead cigar from his mouth and wiping his lips with the back of his hand, "where does that leave you with Holmes? Insurance fraud you've got him on for sure. You can be damned glad he admitted to that and volunteered to go back to Philly with you or I'd've had no choice but to send him to Texas. Even at that, I've knocked hell out of regulations by turning my back on a legitimate warrant and sending him out of state with you," he inclined his head toward the Philadelphia detectives, "so you damned well better nail him good."

He turned a few pages of the note pad and looked up again. "Before I release them to you, a few random items you should note. They're in here," he tapped the pad, "but I'll boil 'em down a little for you. Item: Holmes has a wife in New Hampshire—his legitimate wife—and a fourteen-year-old son by her there, too. He's got this wife, Georgiana Yoke, whom he married in Denver under the Howard name. Then he's got another one he married under the Holmes name. Woman he calls Dora but her name's Myrta Belknap Holmes and he's got her stashed in a big estate-type house in Wilmette, Illinois, a fancy suburb of Chicago. Item: Holmes may have tried to kill the Pitezel woman in Burlington; hid a jarful of stuff under the basement stairs that was supposed to be nitro-glycerin. We wouldn't've known about it except he thought at first one of the things he was being arrested for was because the Burlington house blew up. Said he'd bought the stuff to use it for cracking a safe and hid it at the house, but was afraid she'd moved it and blown herself to hell. Checked it out and found she'd moved it on his instructions, not to the attic as he told her to in a letter, but to another part of the basement, where she hid it. There was an arrangement of threads that should've set the stuff off if she'd bumped 'em, but instead of reaching for the stuff the way he figured she would, she reached in through the open stairs and grabbed the bottle and never touched the threads. Turns out it didn't make any difference anyway. Damned stuff in the bottle turned out to be olive oil, so it looks like Holmes maybe got euchred himself.''

Hanscom turned a page and continued: "Item: We searched the Burlington place and Holmes's rooms here in Boston and found—now this may be important—two tin boxes holding about a half-dozen letters from the Pitezel woman to her kids that were in Holmes's care and twice that many from those kids to her or to their grandparents. They'd been opened, but they'd never been mailed. No postmarks or canceled stamps on any of 'em. There was also some stuff written in a code we couldn't figure out. And a fairly battered copy of a book— *Uncle Tom's Cabin*—was there, too, along with a lady's hanky and a little toy soldier. The cipher might be that *New York Herald* code he talked about. Item: Holmes had a trunk in his room with stuff of his own in it, but that trunk's got a hole just under an inch in diameter right through the top of the lid. We asked him about it and he said it was news to him, that he never even noticed it. Said maybe the railroad did it when they were moving his stuff. But it's a nice neat bored hole. I can't figure that out at all. Anyway, all this stuff— letters, tin boxes, book, luggage, everything pertaining to the case—will be turned over to you.''

As Hanscom turned another page, Detectives Geyer and Crawford looked at one another with expressions that clearly indicated how impressed they were with the information Hanscom had collected in a very short time. They looked back at the deputy chief as he tossed down his pad.

"That about does it. Oh, one final item: Chief Watts tried to pry out of Holmes who the New York contacts were who could get him a stiff. All Holmes would say was that it was a doctor in a very respected position and he didn't want to jeopardize the man needlessly, but he did say this doctor had done this sort of thing for him before, so Holmes and Pitezel may have pulled this same insurance fraud previously."

Hanscom came to his feet, moving with surprising grace for a man of his bulk. "Gentlemen, I believe that concludes our business here. I've signed the releases for you to take the prisoners and whatever of their possessions we have. You may get them and leave at your convenience. I'd like to say it's been a pleasure, but it hasn't been. I'm only thankful you're assuming this headache. I wouldn't wish it on anyone. Not even," he added, an amused glint coming into his eye as he looked at Perry, "on Colonel Bosbyshell."

It came as a surprise to Holmes to find that Georgiana was accompanying the party to Philadelphia. It was only during those few minutes of standing on the platform, waiting to board their train, that he had been able, under the watchful eyes of the Philadelphia detectives a few paces away, to converse with her.

"Why are you going to Philadelphia?" he asked her.

She looked at him a long moment without speaking, feeling the tears welling in her again and determined she was not going to cry. At last she averted her eyes from his and murmured, "They've asked me to come and give a statement."

"Well, I know you're angry with me, but I hope you'll be fair in what you say. I've always treated you well, Georgiana."

"By lying to me?" she flared. "By cheating, stealing and God knows what else? That's treating me well? I suppose you know I talked with your . . ." She broke off, unable to get the word out. "I talked with Clara Mudgett. And your brother and sister."

"I know. I got to talk with them briefly. Georgiana, you have to let me explain something here. A year or so after I left Clara, I petitioned for a divorce. Before it came through, someone told me that she had died, so I never followed up on it. Later on, when I learned she was still alive, I just didn't know how to tell you, so I didn't say anything. But I married you in good faith."

"Like you married this Dora woman in good faith, too? God, I'm sick to death of your lies, Henry. Or Herman." The tears came in spite of her determination and she blubbered as she finished. "I don't have any idea *what* to call you anymore. Except cad. That's the only thing that fits." She turned and stalked away a dozen paces and stopped, her back to him.

"You sure got a way with women," Crawford said, moving up beside him. The detective gave him a pitying look. "No more talking with anyone now, till we get to Philadelphia."

"I'd like to have a few words with Carrie and Dessie," Holmes said.

"No," Crawford told him.

Carrie and Dessie were standing a few feet away with Detective Geyer. Carrie, holding Wharton, looked ghastly, her eyes sunken and haunted, her face pinched with strain. She refused even to look at Holmes. Dessie's eyes were red and swollen and the look she shot at him was full of malevolence.

"Dessie," Holmes called over to her, "you don't have to worry. You and your father and Howard will be together soon. And you'll soon be seeing Alice and Nellie again, too."

"I said for you to shut up!" Crawford said sharply. "I mean it!"

"What about talking to you," Holmes asked. "Is that allowed?"

"On the train. I'll be sitting with you. Not here on the platform. You just be quiet until we're in our seats."

A quarter-hour later, as the train pulled out heading for Philadelphia, Holmes took advantage of the opening Crawford had given him.

"You know," he said, almost cheerfully, "Ben and I really shouldn't have tried to get away with something like this, but what the hell. Ten thousand dollars is awfully tempting."

"'Bout three years of my wages," Crawford agreed. "What'd you do with all that money? Mrs. Pitezel said she gave most of it—'bout six thousand dollars she says—to you. What happened to it all? You sure didn't have that kind of money on you when you were arrested."

"Well, sure, she gave me about that much," Holmes admitted, "but it wasn't mine to keep. Hell, five thousand bucks went to pay off Pitezel's mortgage in Fort Worth. She knows that. Then I had to give Pitezel the money he needed to get to South America with Howard, so that took care of another sixteen hundred. And then when I sent the two girls to England with Minnie, I sewed four hundred dollars cash into Alice's dress so she wouldn't lose it. Hell, damned near all of it went toward the upkeep and convenience of the Pitezels. Although I shouldn't have given Ben anything, the way he bungled the job on that body."

"How do you mean?" Crawford was interested.

"I gave him very specific instructions on how to place the body, how to burn the face and make it look like he was killed in an explosion. So what does he do? He leaves it lying with one hand across the chest like the stiff's died in his sleep, very peacefully. I should've given him the instructions under hypnosis and then he would have followed them correctly."

"Hypnosis?" Crawford questioned. "You can hypnotize people?"

"Sure. I learned it from a doctor out West. How'd you like me to try it out on you?"

"No thanks," Crawford said, edging away somewhat.

Holmes laughed, then sobered and lowered his voice. "A city detective doesn't make a whole lot of money," he said. "How'd you like to make five hundred bucks?"

"How?" Crawford asked.

"You walk with me to the lavatory. When we're out of sight of the others, you let me go and I get off the train my own way. When they ask you what happened, you tell them I hypnotized you. You don't even have to take the money. Tell me where you live and I'll give the money to your wife and no one'll ever know."

Crawford snorted. "I'll know. You're really a crazy bastard, Holmes."

That strange fathomless look came into Holmes's eyes at that and he refused to talk to Crawford any further. When the train arrived in Philadelphia they were met, through prearrangement, by Benjamin Chew, secretary of the Society to Protect Children from Cruelty. Dessie and Wharton, after an emotional farewell with their mother, were placed in his care and he gently took them away. Holmes and Carrie were led immediately to the street for transportation to City Hall. At a newsstand, a five-line headline in the *Philadelphia Inquirer* caught Detective Geyer's eye. He snatched up a copy and gaped at it.

"I don't believe this!" he said. It was a wire service story reprinted in the *Inquirer* from the *Boston Globe*, an exclusive interview of Holmes entitled:

CLEVER FRAUD

NOTORIOUS SWINDLER TELLS
HOW HE GOT $10,000

USED A SUBSTITUTE BODY
TO CLAIM LIFE INSURANCE

"My God, Holmes," Geyer gasped, "Chief Hanscom's going to have a fit. How the hell did you ever pull this off?"

Holmes was grinning. "You'll never know," he said.

"But why? What's to be gained?"

"You'll never know that, either," Holmes replied mysteriously. There was plenty to be gained, but only one other person would know that and it was his only way to get a message through. When she read it in the Chicago paper, Dora would know exactly what to do.

On their arrival at City Hall, Holmes and Carrie were immediately taken to the Identification Room, where photographs were taken of them both by the Detective Service photographer, John Townsend. Then they were taken before District Attorney George Graham and a four-person bill of indictment was drawn up against them. It charged H. H. Holmes, Carrie A. Pitezel, Jeptha D. Howe and Benjamin F. Pitezel with having willfully and fraudulently conspired to cheat and defraud the Fidelity Mutual Life Association of the sum of $10,000, by means of substituting an unidentified body in the place of Benjamin F. Pitezel. Bail was placed at $2,500 each and it was expected that Howe, already in custody in St. Louis, would be extradited to Philadelphia within a few days.

It was expected to take a little longer for Ben Pitezel.

Bella Waugh had for many years been Dora's closest friend. They shared confidences they would never have dreamed sharing with anyone else, even their respective husbands. A dressmaker by profession, Bella didn't know everything there was to know about Dora's activities in respect to Holmes's business, yet over the years she had put together enough pieces of the intriguing puzzle to give her a general picture of what she believed to be a very clever swindling operation. They often skirted the edges of the subject in their conversations and Dora had never denied such involvement. Bella thought it was all a wonderful lark and applauded their genius at being able to carry out their schemes so successfully, stating that she wished she had the courage to try it herself. For all her astuteness, however, she never suspected there was anything beyond mere swindling.

Early this morning Dora had been startled by the frantic knocking on the front door—the large brass knocker being tapped not just in a short series or two but in a steady rapid tattoo that did not cease until she threw open the door. Bella practically stumbled in her haste to come in, a folded newspaper gripped in her hand.

"Bella! What on earth—"

"Dora, shut up! Have you seen this morning's paper?"

"No, not yet." A stirring of alarm touched her. "Why? What's wrong?"

"Look here." She held out the newspaper. "They've caught Henry. He's been arrested."

"Oh, God, when? Where?" She snatched the paper and became pale as she began reading where Bella pointed. "Boston," she whispered. "Philadelphia. Bella," she gripped her friend's hand, "I need you help right now, no questions asked."

"Name it," Bella said grimly. "No questions."

"I want you to come down to the Castle with me and give me a hand."

"Sure. David's not home and the kids are in school, so I'm free. Let's go."

Dora moved quickly to the foot of the stairs and called upward. "Mary!"

"Ma'am?" The nursemaid, apprehensive over the tone in her employer's voice, looked down over the upstairs bannister.

"Mary, I have to leave. I'll be gone most of the day. You take good care of Lucy. If anyone comes to the door, don't talk to them. I mean that! Just say I'm gone for the day and they can call again tomorrow if they care to. Nothing else. Understood?"

"Yes, ma'am. Just as you say."

The two women left the house immediately and went to the station where they caught the first train downtown and then transferred to another which took them to the Englewood Station on Sixty-third. They found Pat Quinlan immediately upon entering the Castle. He looked upset.

"You've seen the paper?" Dora asked.

"I seen it," he replied noncommittally. He looked at Bella with silent question.

"She's all right," Dora told him. "This is my friend. Now listen, we've got a lot to do."

Quinlan listened and then they set to work. There wasn't as much as she had anticipated, but there was enough; within two hours they had emptied the files of all but a scattering of innocuous papers, tossing the bulk of the material helter-skelter into a large trunk. It was nearly filled when they were finished.

Dora took Quinlan off to the side and handed him a twenty-dollar bill. "Pat, I want you to hire a wagon and driver. Get this trunk out of here immediately. I don't care where you take it, just so it's out of here and safe. Get it out of sight as quickly as possible. Then you stay with it. I want it brought up to the Wilmette house by wagon after dark tonight. No shipment by train. And no expressmen. Either hire someone you know and can trust or bring it up yourself."

Quinlan promised he would. Dora and Bella left at once and caught a train back to downtown. While Bella continued to Wilmette, Dora went to Frank Blackman's office, but the broker wasn't there. She left a sealed message with a secretary and then hastened over to Wharton Plummer's office in the Chamber of Commerce Building.

Not unexpectedly, Plummer was aware of Holmes's arrest and sympathetic to her, but she shook her head angrily. "I didn't come here to be mollycoddled," she told him. "You're the lawyer. Give me some legal advice. Right now. There are going to be people coming to the house. Police, maybe. Reporters. What do I tell them?"

"Absolutely nothing," Plummer warned. "Not one word about anything to anybody. You know nothing of your husband's business. He's away most of the time. Beyond that, nothing. You can't be forced to talk if you don't want to, unless they take you into court. Even then it's moot, depending on whether you're his legal wife or not. Evidently he was traveling with one woman who claimed to be his wife and had stopped in New Hampshire to see another who said she was his wife, too. Jesus, what a mess! You didn't know about them, did you?" He peered at her but then shook his head. "Scratch that. I don't want to know. Do *not* go to visit him. Don't write to him. If he writes, don't answer. And remember what I said. Say nothing to anyone. *Nothing!* Period."

"All right," she told him, "I won't. What about Henry? Are you going to represent him?"

"No. It would be damned foolishness for me to get involved in that. I know a good law firm in Philadelphia, though. Legitimate, high priced and very very good. Rotan and Shoemaker. I'll send them a wire and get them on it. Do you guarantee to me to pay their fees, no matter what they are?"

"Yes," she said.

He knew she meant it. "All right. The big thing they've got to do is try to play this whole thing down. Holmes has already confessed, so all they've got to do is get the thing through court as quickly as possible and the case buttoned up so there are no extensive investigations. God forbid anyone starts digging too deep! Go home Dora."

She went home. The evening papers carried a similar story, and an editorial in the *Chicago Herald* infuriated her:

> Chicago has the dubious honor of having a master swindler in her midst. Since the arrest of H. H. Holmes in Boston three days ago on a charge of masterminding a $10,000 swindling plot against a Philadelphia insurance company, over fifty people have called at our own police headquarters to tell sad tales of how they were bilked by Holmes. There is every likelihood that more will surface. Perhaps many more. With his arrest, a remarkable career of fraud and crime is brought to a close. He has evidently worked his schemes over a wide territory, from New York to Texas, but Chicago seems to have been especially favored by this unusual young man. His career stamps him as one of the boldest and shrewdest swindlers in the country. He has left scores of victims in Chicago, where firms and individuals right and left have been swindled out of various sums and goods through all sorts of fantastic methods. Although no Robin Hood, since the profits he made found their way into no one's pockets but his own, nevertheless H. H. Holmes swindled with a dash and vim that must have won the admiration almost of those who lost.

Dora did not sleep this night. She kept vigil in a living room chair positioned so she could watch the street in front; a vigil finally rewarded at 2 A.M. when two men Quinlan had hired pulled their wagon to a stop in front of the Wilmette house. Under her direction they carried the heavy trunk into the house and then down to the basement and placed in on the floor before the furnace. And here Dora sat until the sun was well above the horizon, studying sheet after sheet of the records and thrusting the majority of them through the open furnace door. When at last she finished, what remained was a pile of papers that she stuffed into a briefcase and placed in the hidden safe in their study. And for the first time since Bella had burst through her front door over twenty-four hours before, she felt her strained back muscles begin to relax.

Ten

*T*hat he was faced with being sentenced to two years at the Philadelphia County Prison—more commonly known as Moyamensing—came as a relief to Holmes. It seemed to mean his story of Pitezel's disappearance to South America with Howard was accepted, along with the story of Alice and Nellie having been taken to England by Minnie Williams.

The indictment against him had been presented to the Grand Jury and his plea of guilty had been accepted on the second day of that proceeding. A true bill of indictment was found by the Grand Jury in this preliminary, which meant that when he actually came to court for trial, the maximum two-year sentence would probably be levied.

Both Jeptha Howe and Carrie Pitezel had also taken up a more or less permanent residency at Moyamensing, the former as a result of his sentencing, the latter solely on the instructions of the district attorney. Carrie was frequently visited at the prison in cooperative effort by George Graham and his assistants, as well as William Gary, O. L. Perry and other officials of the Fidelity Mutual firm. Holmes was also visited and requestioned nearly as frequently. The feeling among the investigators grew that though the book may have been temporarily closed on the swindling case, there remained a growing likelihood that not only was the dead man *not* a substitute body for Pitezel, but that the three missing Pitezel children—Howard, Nellie, and Alice—were also no longer alive. If, indeed, the dead man was actually Pitezel, then the conclusion seemed inescapable: Holmes had murdered Benjamin Pitezel. As the *Chicago Inter-Ocean* put it:

... This is the belief not only of the detectives of the Fidelity Insurance Company, which was so cleverly victimized, but of Superintendent of Police Linden and Coroner Ashbridge. The latter said: "I am positive the corpse discovered at 1316 Callowhill Street was B. F. Pitezel. I am not at liberty at present to disclose my reasons for this assertion, but if I were, and pointed them out, you would be convinced, notwithstanding the stories as to the wretched man's expatriation in South America or elsewhere, that he met his death right here in Philadelphia."

The newspapers were delivered to Holmes regularly in his cell, paid for by his attorneys, and with each passing day of reading and analyzing the reports, he realized that the investigation was closing in and it was time to make concerted efforts to protect his flanks. This was his frame of mind as the year slid toward its close. Detective Frank Geyer, at the prison on another matter, passed by Holmes and the prisoner made his decision that instant.

"Mr. Geyer," he said, contrition heavy in his voice, "I have to admit something to you."

Fed up with the continuous lying from Holmes, Geyer was not impressed. "Now what would that be, Holmes? Are you going to tell us that you had your continents mixed up and that you really meant Pitezel had gone to Africa instead of South America?"

Holmes grinned sheepishly. "No. It has to do with what I said about substituting a body in the place of Pitezel in the Callowhill Street house."

This brought Geyer up short. The majority of the interviews to this point had been endeavors to discover the whereabouts of the missing Pitezel children. This was the first time Holmes had voluntarily brought up the matter of the body since his initial confession. "Oh?" he said. "Are you finally going to tell me who provided you with the substitute body?"

"No. There was no substitute body."

Geyer stared at him and Holmes stared back, totally serious. "Do I hear you right?" the detective asked. "You're telling me that there really wasn't a substitute body at all?"

"That's right."

"Then the body had to have been Benjamin Pitezel, just as we've suspected."

"Yes."

Geyer spoke very quietly. "You realize, Holmes, that what you're saying now means that you murdered Pitezel and his three missing children."

"No sir," Holmes said quickly, "that's not what I'm saying. Not at all."

"Then just what in hell *are* you saying, Holmes?"

"I'm saying that Pitezel committed suicide."

Geyer's short laugh was devoid of any trace of humor. He replied with a single word, deliberately spoken: "Bullshit."

"No, truth for a change, not bullshit. I admit I lied before, but I'm not lying now."

Geyer moved past him and leaned against the wall, folding his arms. "Convince me, Holmes, I'm listening."

"All right, then, here it is." He began to walk rapidly in a counterclockwise circle around the cell, his delivery cadenced to his pacing. "It was Sunday morning, the second of September. I was staying at the Alcorn Boardinghouse on North Eleventh Street. I left there about ten in the morning and walked to Tenth Street, got on the streetcar there and went as far as Callowhill. From there I walked the three blocks to Pitezel's place. The night before he'd told me to come by in the morning. I opened the door and walked in, but I didn't see Ben, so I sat down and read the paper. When he hadn't showed up by the time I finished, I looked around the house for him, all through the downstairs rooms and then upstairs, but he wasn't there. That's when I went back downstairs and for the first time noticed a folded piece of paper on the desk. I picked it up and saw it was a note in our cipher code, addressed to me. It said I should look in the cupboard, that there was a bottle in there with a letter in it for me. I went there and found it and tried to shake it out, but it wouldn't come, so I broke the bottle to get it. It was written in cipher, too, and it took me a while to read it. He told me in it that he was tired of life and that he was committing suicide, and that I should take his body and do exactly with it as I had told him to do with the substitute body that we couldn't get. He said I'd find him up in the attic. I ran up there and that's where I found him, dead. He was on his back on the floor with his arm across his chest. He'd placed a cloth over his mouth and nose and on a chair beside him was a gallon bottle of chloroform with a cork in it. He'd shoved a quill through the cork and had connected a rubber tubing to the quill, so the chloroform dripped out onto the cloth. I put my hand on his chest to feel for his heart, then on his neck, but I knew there wasn't any use. He was cold and dead. Rigor mortis had already set in and I couldn't change his position. I dragged him downstairs to the bedroom and put him on the floor. He'd evacuated in his pants when he died, but it was contained in his underwear and not much came free as I moved him, and what did I wiped up. I took a bottle of benzine clothes cleaner and spilled it on his chest till it was empty and then put the bottle next to his body and broke it. Then I lighted it and threw the match down so it looked like an accidental explosion had taken place. I had to do all that. Pitezel was already dead, but if it got known he'd died of suicide, the insurance company wouldn't have paid. I had to make it look like an accident."

Holmes stopped, exhausted by his own recital, and Geyer straightened. "That's it?"

"That's it."

"What happened to the two cipher notes? The one from the desk and the one from the bottle."

"The one from the desk is in the tin lock-box along with the letters. You saw the letters. You must have seen the note."

"I saw that, Holmes," he admitted. "We all did. But we couldn't read the cipher. What about the longer one—the suicide letter?"

"I kept it in the tin box for a while, too, but I didn't want anyone to find it, so I slit open the inside back cover of a book Alice was reading—*Uncle Tom's Cabin*—and put it in there and glued it back together. It's got to still be there."

Geyer was quiet for a little while. "All right, if what you're saying is all true, Holmes, then I have a question: What really happened to the three Pitezel children?"

"The children are . . ." He stopped, then began again. "Minnie Williams has the children. All three of them. In London."

"Where did *you* last see them, Holmes? What'd you do with them?"

"The last I saw Howard Pitezel was in Detroit. It was on the Wednesday before I left for Toronto. Minnie Williams came to the Geis Hotel and took dinner with Howard and me. That's when I gave her Howard and told her to take him to Buffalo. When I went on to Toronto, I took the two girls with me, but finally put them on the train at the Grand Trunk Depot. I rode with them to the first stop—a little station about five miles outside Toronto—and got out there, letting them go on by themselves from there to Niagara Falls. I had wired Minnie to come up from Buffalo and meet them there and then take them back to Buffalo to rejoin Howard. Oh, before leaving Alice, I pinned four hundred dollars inside her dress. From Buffalo, Minnie took them to New York City and then on ship to London. I had asked Minnie to cut Nellie's hair short and dress her as a boy, to avoid suspicion, in case anyone was looking for two girls and a boy. If you go to the shipping offices in New York, you'll find that a woman with a girl and two younger boys sailed for London at that time."

He stopped abruptly and it was a moment before Geyer realized he was finished. Holmes was looking at him expectantly.

"I'll tell you what, Holmes," Geyer said, straightening and walking toward the cell door. He turned and looked back at Holmes balefully. "It's like I said before. Bullshit."

"Wait!" Holmes pleaded. "It's true! I swear it. God-damnit, you've got to believe me."

"I stopped believing you a long time ago, Holmes. Nothing you've said makes me change my mind. You can't open your mouth without lying. Anyway, it doesn't make any difference what I believe. Chief Linden's the one you need to convince. And the D.A., George Graham. Why don't you write to them and tell them you want to make another confession?" He gave a brittle little laugh and walked out, signaling the guard to close the cell doors.

Until recently Detective Frank Geyer had almost never been late to work, not in over twenty years with the Philadelphia Police Department. Yet, since last March his tardiness had become commonplace. Today was another of those occasions. As he walked toward his office this morning his whole aspect was one of dejection. The broad shoulders that were his trademark seemed to have become narrower. He slumped in the very act of walking, diminishing his six-foot height and, unlike the keenly observant man he usually was, paid almost no attention to his surroundings or passersby. The remarkably full mustache, thick and dark and ordinarily neatly trimmed and upturned in sprightly style at the ends, had become shaggy, unkempt, an unfavorable complement to the scruffy two-day growth of beard on the heavy angular jaw. His normal fastidiousness was belied by a badly rumpled suit, but he was unaware of that, uncharacteristically unaware of anything about his appearance. Had he been asked what color suit he was wearing, he would have had to look to answer correctly. His feet placed themselves automatically, one before the other, carrying him steadily and surely, if not rapidly, to the ornate old building that occupied a portion of the four-square-block area that was the heart of this metropolis.

Despite its ostentatious exterior, there was almost nothing of grace or beauty inside Philadelphia's City Hall. This was particularly true of the Detective Service's office in the Police Department's central headquarters. Austere grayed-green walls, peeling, scarred and dirty, were a fitting backdrop to a disarray of battered and cluttered desks. What little morning sunlight was filtering through the never-washed windows and spread itself in ugly speckled rectangles on the wide boards of hardwood flooring, highlighting ancient swirled mop tracks. Dust motes hung as a smoky haze in the weakened sunbeams until someone strode past and transformed them into dervishing wraiths.

One of the largest and most decrepit of the desks was a hulking rolltop with face of latticed oak and a labyrinth of cubbyholes inside to collect and hold documents. The rolltop was almost never closed and some of the papers had taken up such permanent residency in their compartments that they had become yellowed and brittle. The chair behind the desk was equally pitted and bruised from long service, its contoured seat designed to conform to and couch the buttocks of its occupant in far more comfortable manner than the straight-seated hardback chair to its right at the side of the desk. This second chair, for visitors, was not designed to inspire occupants to overstay, encouraging them instead to speak hastily and perhaps with less circumspection than normal conversation would dictate, in order to escape its punishing confines, a facility that had often proved most valuable. The desk and principal chair were Frank Geyer's, steadfast companions for two decades, the latter often occupied for endless hours daily, months on end, yet occasionally vacant for days or even weeks during an especially knotty investigation.

This was not a good day for Geyer, but good days had

been rare of late. Acute grief may ease in time but for the individual suffering under its burden, as Geyer was, it is endless and endlessly debilitating. The occasional days that had come when he had no choice but to be busy had been welcomed by him as diversions from the gnawing ache, but always those times turned out to be no more than momentary diversions. And he knew only too well by now that when the diversion ended, as eventually it did, the grief descended again with far more mental devastation than had it remained constant.

The whole of these past three months had been a nightmarish time for him, initially a period of unparalleled horror that had finally subsided to a pervasive hollow grief. Weighted with this oppressiveness, Geyer at first gave no more than a passing glance to the folded paper in the otherwise solitary clear spot amid the desktop clutter; a paper with his name written across it at an angle. Instead he settled into his chair and, consciously or not, opened the gates to the inevitable rush of memory.

There was no sequence to it, no precedence in respect to chronology or importance, only a montage of occurrence blooming in confused stereoptical imagery: The dual grave. The wake. Martha before and Martha afterward. Esther as an infant, as a toddler, as a bright and insatiably curious girl at puberty's threshold. The fire. The predictably simpering and wholly inadequate eulogy. The trauma of identifying charred remains of wife and daughter in the mid-March sepulchral chill of the city morgue. The barren ache of awakening alone in a bed previously and comfortably occupied by two. And more, much more.

At last his focus on things unseen became focus on the folded note before him. He felt no stirring of premonition, perhaps because he was already suffocating in the mire of vast personal misery. There were those, he knew, who chose to believe that it was—especially for a man in his profession—a divine gift to be able to sense impending fortune or bale. And, within certain limits, he supposed, this was true. Admittedly, more than once an uncommonly strong hunch had led him to solutions that he may not have reached by conventional means, but it always bothered him when that happened. He knew that, assuming several such successes, a distinct danger lay in coming to expect this type of mystical assistance and then beginning to place too much reliance upon it. Besides, his own feeling was that unqualified acceptance of such phenomena presupposed a belief in foreordination, an acceptance of the notion that there existed a destiny toward which every person moved inexorably. Pragmatist that he was, this was a concept that Frank Geyer personally found abhorrent.

So it was without presentiment of any kind that he finally reached out and picked up the note with its simple angled address across the once-folded face:

Detective Frank Geyer

The message inside was both direct and enigmatic:

> JUNE 15, 1895
>
> MR. GEYER
> *District Attorney Graham would appreciate your reporting to him in his office immediately upon reading this. Thank you.*
>> THOS. W. BARLOW
>> SPEC. ASS'T DIST. ATTY.

Though Frank Geyer hadn't been too sure about accepting the assignment he was embarking on today for the district attorney, it was evidently exactly what he needed. For the first time since the fire in March that had stripped him of his home and family, a sense of purpose had been restored in his life. His suit was freshly cleaned and pressed, his thick mustache once again neatly trimmed, an aura of alertness upon him. As he walked toward the depot with his satchel and suitcase, his head was erect and his carriage that of a man infused with strength and determination.

Undoubtedly it was not so much the challenge of the assignment as it was the anger that had changed him, that had allowed him to shake off the deadly inertia that had plagued him for so many weeks. The pain and sense of loss over the death of his wife and daughter was no less within him than it had been, but it was the anger that was stronger now—anger directed against a man who might deliberately bring on another the same kind of suffering that he had himself been undergoing. Not only the same kind of suffering but infinitely worse because seemingly it had been deliberately protracted in an effort to cause the greatest amount of anguish.

That was the way District Attorney Graham had presented it to him in their meeting when he had responded to the written summons eleven days ago.

"I need your help, Mr. Geyer," Graham said without preamble, after they had shaken hands. "I need your mind, your ability, your years of experience."

Already Geyer was shaking his head, uninterested in taking on a project of any kind. Before he could vocalize his refusal, Graham hushed him by gripping his forearm.

"Hear me out, *please*."

Graham was a strong man, noted for his toughness as well as his shrewdness; not the type of man to beg for anything of anyone, yet something in the tone of his voice, in the grip of his hand on Geyer's arm, told the detective that this man was begging now, or at least coming as close to begging as a man of his caliber could. It touched something in Geyer that had not been touched in a long while and he nodded.

"I'll listen," he said.

Graham smiled and began, speaking quietly but with intensity and an orderliness of progression that underlined the analytical quality of his mind. For over two hours he spoke with rarely an interruption from the detective. Aware that Geyer, apart from having helped transport Holmes from Boston to Philadelphia and being first to hear Holmes's revised statement that averred the body had actually been Pitezel's, had had nothing to do with the case, the district attorney brought him up to date on matters concerning Holmes since his arrest in November, seven months ago.

The second official statement by Holmes, Graham then said, dictated in the office of Chief Robert J. Linden on January 2, had rendered invalid the indictment under which he was being held, since that indictment charged Holmes with having *substituted* a body in order to defraud. And so Graham had drawn up a new indictment under which Holmes, not yet tried, was recharged. It accused him of having conspired to defraud the insurance company by *alleging* that Pitezel had died as the result of an accident. Only then was trial scheduled for late in May.

The investigations, meanwhile, had continued without pause, primarily in an effort to answer the question that now was in the minds of the American public from New York to San Francisco. Nor was the Philadelphia County district attorney's office any longer the only agency involved—now there were investigations being made in Chicago, Detroit, Cincinnati, Indianapolis and Toronto by a number of municipal and private investigators, including George T. Johnson, a cousin of Nannie and Minnie Williams, as well as Thomas Capps, a Fort Worth attorney hired by the Williams family in Texas. These investigations had been instigated by Minnie's former guardian, Mossie H. Watt—Mr. Mossie, as she had called him—who had also gotten in touch with District Attorney Graham and urged him, should he encounter her, to have her contact him immediately.

Ever more people were coming forward in Chicago to report missing people who had had contact with Holmes and there was a public clamor for the cellar in the Englewood Castle to be excavated in a search for bodies. Thus far that hadn't happened, since the courts had not yet been provided with evidence enough that foul play had occurred. There was a further problem in that the Castle no longer belonged to Holmes. Despite efforts of Wharton Plummer to block it, the property was sold by court order when the mortgage was not paid. A man named William Rose bought it on February 19 and he, in turn, sold it to a realtor named Peyton Chandler. The building still stood largely as Holmes had left it and Pat Quinlan was still employed there as janitor, but it was questionable how long that would last under the new ownership.

On the first day of his trial under the new indictment, Graham continued, Holmes, against the advice of his attorney, Sam Rotan, entered a plea of not guilty. On the second day, however, with Graham's evidence stacking up solidly against him, Holmes changed his plea to guilty and was promptly sentenced to two years. Due to Rotan's fervent plea to the Court, Holmes was given credit for the time already served, which meant he would be eligible for parole in November, just five months from now.

In a surprise move, Graham had decided to drop all charges against Carrie Pitezel, still being held without trial in Moyamensing Prison, but her release was not to be made until after Geyer, if he so chose, interviewed her to whatever extent he wished. She was grateful and eager to cooperate in any way that might help to bring her three missing children back to her. She had never lost faith that they were still alive . . . somewhere. Graham, on the other hand, became daily more certain that they were dead; yet, if any possibility existed that they were alive, he was determined to trace it to the utmost.

Further interviews were held with Holmes and he persisted unswervingly in his contention that he had turned the children over to Minnie Williams and she had taken them to England. Graham asked Geyer if he were aware that concerted efforts had been made, with the help of Scotland Yard, to locate Minnie Williams and the children in London.

Geyer nodded. "Yes," he said. "Evidently the more detailed information Holmes gave you as to Minnie Williams's whereabouts over there proved to be false?"

"That's correct, so far as we've been able to determine."

Geyer pursed his lips. "It seems to me I heard, too, that if you advertised in a certain way a code in the *New York Herald* personals, Minnie Williams would get in touch with you. Did you do that?"

"We did," Graham said. "To the extent that we had Holmes write out the message and its deciphered form for us. It ran in the paper as he directed but to no avail. We then—"

"Excuse me," Geyer interrupted, "but would it be possible for me to see the sort of cipher that was used and the key to its decoding?"

"Certainly, if you wish. Rather involved at first glance, but once you've got the key, it's easy enough to use. I'll see you get a copy of it. Now, then, when no one answered the ad, we confronted Holmes with this and he had a new story all ready. He said Minnie was afraid to reveal her whereabouts for fear of being charged with homicide. We thought at first he was saying she murdered the children, but that wasn't what he was talking about at all. He said that her younger sister, Nannie, came to stay with them. According to him, he and Nannie started making eyes at each other. Minnie went away somewhere—I think he said Milwaukee— and wasn't to come back for a certain specified time. But he says she came back early and walked in on them, catching them *in flagrante delicto*. He said Minnie and Nannie had a terrible fight and that Minnie picked up a stool and brained Nannie with it and killed her. Then, Holmes says, she begged him to help her dispose of the body. They put it in a trunk, weighted it down with stones and sank it in Lake Michigan.

"The story's longer than that," Graham went on, "and

filled with all sorts of complex details. So much so, in fact, that it just might be true. There are evidently quite a few people right now searching for those sisters and having no luck at all."

Graham shook his head. "I've gone astray," he admitted, "but it was something I think you need to know. I can give you the full details later. Let me get back to what I believe in respect to the disappearance of the Pitezel children. They *may* be alive, but I doubt it. Look at the facts. This man Holmes not only murdered Carrie Pitezel's husband, he separated her from her children and led them on for weeks with promises that they'd all be together again soon.

"Picture it," Graham said, a note of anger in his voice. "Here on the one hand are these children, desperately lonely and homesick, writing pathetic letters to their mother, letters that Holmes said he would mail for them, but never did. Here on the other is the mother, writing letters to them, which Holmes also pocketed. The mother and children must have been amazingly close to each other at times and yet *he never let them know*, Mr. Geyer. He took some kind of twisted pleasure out of their agony. And I feel pretty sure that one by one he killed those children, at the same time convincing their mother they were still alive. And not only them, her husband, too. We can't be positive, but that's what we believe happened. The point is, we've *got* to be sure, one way or another. And that's where you come in. Detective Geyer, I want you to find them—alive or dead. Chief Linden's given full authorization for you to take on this assignment, for however long it takes. I want you to go where you have to go and do whatever you have to do to get us the answers. Because if and when you do, I'm going to see to it that that miserable son of a bitch hangs for murder."

Graham had paused and his voice had become softer when he went on. "I'm aware of your own personal tragedy, Mr. Geyer. I know how it's torn you apart. And I know that, except just at the time of the arrest, you haven't been much involved with this case. But I also know that you're the best damned police officer I've ever known—the only one I could hand a job like this with any hope of getting results. As I said, I need your help. I can't order you to do it and wouldn't, even if I had that power. It's up to you whether or not you'll take the assignment."

Frank Geyer had tried to imagine how he would feel if

right at that moment his own wife and daughter were still alive, desperately trying to contact him but thwarted by a third party, deliberately, maliciously. He imagined Martha and Esther writing him letters and entrusting that third party to mail them to him... and then that person locking those letters away somewhere. That was when his anger had been ignited and continued to grow.

"I'll do it," he'd said simply.

Over the ensuing days he and the district attorney had immersed themselves in a close review of everything even remotely connected to the case. Every interview, every statement, every report was read and studied and discussed. Geyer was provided with a supply of photographs: portraits of Holmes as well as individual photos—some of them school pictures provided by Carrie—of all members of the Pitezel family: Carrie and Ben, Dessie, Alice, Nellie, Howard and even Wharton. Graham arranged a succession of meetings for him: with the officials of Fidelity Mutual; with the officers who were first on the scene of Pitezel's death; with Dr. William Scott, who had performed the postmortem examination; with Dr. William Mattern, who had performed the autopsy; with Holmes himself in his prison cell; and, perhaps most important, with Carrie Pitezel.

Moyamensing Prison had not been a pleasant experience for Carrie. She had aged ten years during these seven months of her incarceration. She was pathetically grateful that at last she was scheduled for release on June 19. During those final three days of her stay, Geyer had interviewed her exhaustively. Their discussions covered everything that might help him in his search and went far beyond merely the period when Holmes had her traveling about the country. He sought to learn all he could about the missing children. What did Alice and Howard and Nellie like? What kind of clothes had they taken with them? Were there any special physical points of identity that might help—marks or scars or deformities? What kind of toys or books or hobbies did they enjoy?

The scarred and scuffed copy of the book Alice Pitezel had been reading, *Uncle Tom's Cabin*, was part of the goods recovered in Holmes's possession when he was arrested and Geyer glanced through it.

"You say Alice took this with her when she left St. Louis?"

Carrie nodded. "But I'm sure she must have finished it. She had only a little bit left to go when she went away."

"I wonder if you'd mind if I borrowed it?" Geyer asked. "I've always heard about what a fuss Harriet Beecher Stowe kicked up, but I've never had a chance to read it."

"You don't have to borrow it, Mr. Geyer," she said. "You're welcome to keep it if you want. I certainly won't be reading it."

"Thank you," he said. "Now, in addition to that list of things she and Nellie and Howard took with them, I'd like you to draw up a list of anything whatsoever you can think of that might help me locate them."

"All right," she said. "As I've already mentioned, Nellie was born with a slight deformity of both feet. It didn't affect her walking so's you'd notice it much, but in her bare feet you could see she was sort of... well...," she hesitated.

"Slightly clubfooted?"

"Yes, I guess that's what they call it."

On and on they went and when they finished with that, Geyer had her tell him, step by step, every detail of the strange odyssey upon which she and her family had been taken by Holmes. And, though she had told the same story numerous times before—to the district attorney, to detectives, to the insurance investigators—she told it again for Geyer. He was certain, as he took voluminous notes, that he was drawing from her things that no one else had yet heard.

When, at last, they were finishing with their discussion, she looked at him almost beseechingly. "Do you believe my little ones are dead, Mr. Geyer?"

Moved, he had put his arm about her shoulders and patted her gently. "I honestly don't know," he said. "Some people, I'm sure, believe they are, but I want you to know that I am embarking on this search under the assumption that they are alive."

"Oh, thank you, thank you!"

Her gratitude was far more than his carefully worded reply called for and he was embarrassed. "At the same time," he added seriously, "you must not get your hopes too high. They've been missing a very long time."

"I know," she said. "Sometimes I've almost accepted the idea that they're dead and then something happens to turn that around. Like the letter I got from Henry. Now I just don't know what to think."

Geyer had nodded, knowing she was referring to the letter she had just received from Holmes, a true copy of which the detective had read in Graham's office. It had been a long rambling letter full of contradictions and outright lies and a strong element of insanity; a letter written in the knowledge that it would be read by authorities before Carrie saw it and therefore filled with subtle and often very clever deceits. In the passages that had evidently raised Carrie's hopes again that the children were alive, Holmes had written:

> ...*I was as careful of the children as if they were my own, and you know me well enough to judge me better than strangers here can do....As to the children, I never will believe, until you tell me so yourself, that you think they are dead or that I did anything to put them out of the way. Knowing me as you do, can you imagine me killing little and innocent children, especially without any motive? ...So far as the children's bodily health is concerned, I feel sure I can say to you they are as well to-day as though with you, also that they will not be turned adrift among strangers....*

"Don't you think, from what Henry said, that the children really *are* alive and well, Mr. Geyer?" she asked fervently.

"I'd like to say yes, Mrs. Pitezel, but I can only say that Mr. Holmes has not established a reputation for telling the truth. In this case, we can only hope this is one of the exceptions."

"Oh, it's *got* to be," she said. "Please God, it's *got* to be. I don't think I could stand it if it's a lie. You do believe he was telling the truth this time, don't you, Mr. Geyer? Don't you?"

The pathetic eagerness tore at him and he nodded, saying, "Maybe," and turned away quickly. How eager would I be, he wondered, if someone held out a chance to me—*any* kind of chance—that Martha and Esther were still alive?

The final days at City Hall Geyer had devoted to deciding how and where to pick up a trail grown so cold. The last known authentic sighting of the children by anyone other than Holmes had occurred only three months short of a year ago—last September 28—when Carrie kissed Nellie and Howard good-bye at the St. Louis Union Station and saw them off to

Cincinnati in the care of Holmes. But no one knew better than he that it was a cold, cold trail.

Now, having arrived at the Pennsylvania Railroad terminal, Geyer went directly to the ticket counter. "Let me have a one-way ticket, please," he told the agent, "to Cincinnati, Ohio."

Frank Geyer ate a hearty breakfast near Union Station in Cincinnati and then went immediately to the office of the superintendent of police, Chief Philip Dietsch, in City Hall. He turned out to be a gray-haired man of blocky medium build and stolid nature.

"Ah, Detective Geyer," Chief Dietsch said, shaking his hand warmly. "Welcome. I read in this morning's paper of your pending arrival in regard to the Holmes case. There's a great deal of interest in it here, as you may know. And we'll be glad to assist you in any way we can."

"In the paper?" Geyer looked at him blankly.

"You didn't know? It's a wire story out of Philadelphia, dated yesterday, so I imagine it's appeared all over the country by now, especially in the cities where you're planning to investigate—here, Detroit, Chicago, wherever. Why don't you tell me about the case and what you need and we'll get started."

Geyer briefed him on the case and then added, "What brings me here in particular is that the last time the Pitezel children were seen—two of them, anyway, Nellie and Howard—they were getting on a train in St. Louis with Holmes to come here and join the third child, Alice, who was supposedly already here. I don't know Cincinnati very well and I'd very much appreciate it if you could assign one of your detectives to work with me in running down some possible leads."

"Absolutely. Hang on a minute." He pressed a button on his desk. "That," he explained, "will bring in someone from our Detective Department."

In a moment a young man stuck his head in. "Yes, sir?"

"Sam, tell Schnooks to step in here right away, will you please?"

"Yes, sir."

A minute or two later a well-built brown-suited man of about thirty entered. He had coarse blond hair, faded blue eyes and a ruddy complexion. A small scar at the right side of his mouth quirked his lips in a lopsided, perpetually sardonic smile.

"Chief?"

"John, shake hands with Detective Frank Geyer from Philadelphia. He's here on special assignment for a few days and I want you to stay with him and help him any way you can. Mr. Geyer, this is Detective John Schnooks."

The two men shook hands and Schnooks cocked an eyebrow. "Geyer? Philly? Sure, you're the one I read about in this morning's paper. Holmes case, right?"

"That's right," Geyer said. He turned to Dietsch and thanked him and then left the office with Schnooks. He showed the Cincinnati detective the pictures he had of Holmes and the three missing children and explained about the man supposedly having been here with them late last September. "What I'd like to suggest we do first," he went on as they left the building, "is to check the hotels that are closest to Union Station and work our way outward from there."

"All right, we'll start with the Union House, right close by the depot."

The desk clerk at the Union House had never seen anyone who resembled the pictures they showed him, nor was there any record in their register of a man and two or three children checking in during the last three days of September. The same was true at the next four hotels checked. But when they entered a cheap hotel called the Atlantic House at 164½ Central Avenue it was another story. During their check at the register at the Atlantic House, Geyer suddenly made an exclamation and put his finger on an entry under the date of Friday, September 28, 1894. *Alexander E. Cook and three children*. Schnooks looked puzzled and Geyer explained.

"When Carrie Pitezel was staying in Burlington, Vermont, the house where she was staying had been rented with her using the name of Mrs. A. E. Cook."

"Ah," Schnooks said. He looked at the clerk. "Can you tell who the clerk was who was on duty when this was entered?"

The clerk studied the book and then grinned. "That was me."

"You remember these people?" He tapped the entry with a stubby index finger.

"Sort of. Man and two girls and a smaller boy, I think."

"Take a look at these pictures. Are they the ones?"

The clerk studied the photos but finally sighed. "I don't know, it's been such a while. I won't say positively this was them, but I think there's a sort of resemblance."

"How long did they stay?" Geyer asked quickly. "Any forwarding address?"

"Just overnight," the clerk said, checking the register again. "They left the next morning. Not many people ever say where they're going to next. These didn't."

Geyer thanked him and they left, the Philadelphia detective feeling buoyed by this early discovery. "Damn, I think we're on the right track," he said. "Let's keep looking."

One by one they checked out the hotels in the vicinity without any luck, then moved to the downtown area and checked there, Schnooks guiding them in a route that involved the least amount of retracing their steps. Nevertheless, it was still a couple of hours later when they reached the corner of Sixth and Vine and entered the Hotel Bristol. The clerk, W. E. Bain, looked at them expectantly as they approached the desk.

"Gentlemen, good morning. May I help you?"

They explained their mission and showed him the pictures and immediately he brightened. "Oh, yes, I remember them. Indeed. Just a moment." He dug out a different ledger and opened it, riffled the pages to the end of September and suddenly nodded. "Here it is: 'A. E. Cook of Cleveland, with three children.' Let's see, they were given Room One-o-three with—"

"Just one room?" Schnooks broke in.

"That's correct, but it's a large room with two beds."

"Mr. Bain," Geyer said, "how is it that you recognized them so quickly from the photographs?"

The clerk colored slightly. "Well, in addition to my having an uncommonly good memory, sir, they stood out because of a problem the man seemed to be having with making the boy behave. Not that he was doing anything terribly bad, so far as I could see, but the man—Mr. Cook, that is—seemed to think so. And then there was the telegram. I have no idea what it said or where it was from, but it seemed to make him, well, anxious. And finally there was the unusual thing about their checking out."

"Oh?" Geyer became alert.

"Yes, sir. Our guests normally check in later in the day—midafternoon to late evening—and check out in the morning, usually fairly early. Now Mr. Cook and the children did just the opposite. They checked in quite early in the morning—that was a Saturday, the twenty-ninth—and checked out well into the afternoon, I'm sure it had to have been after two."

"Were all three of the children with him when he checked out?"

"Actually, sir, none of them were."

"What's that?"

"Let me explain. The next day—Sunday—he took the children out sometime not long after noon, as I recall. I assumed they were going to the zoo, since the two girls were talking about seeing ostriches. Then the man, he came back alone not too much later and checked out. He had one of our porters take their bags to the railroad station. I never did see the children again."

They thanked Bain and strolled back outside, Geyer thoughtful. "It seems obvious, John," he said at last, "that if he came back without the children and checked out, he had to leave them somewhere. That somewhere could have been at a rental house. Carrie Pitezel said Holmes very often preferred to get a rental house in a city he visited instead of staying in a hotel. Let's change our tactics here and visit some of the realty offices."

They did so, stopping in place after place, showing the pictures and describing when they stopped in at 15 East third Street. The clerk at the J. C. Thomas Real Estate Office listened to them and looked at the photos and then nodded.

"Oh, yes," he said. "I distinctly remember the gentleman. I didn't help him myself—Mr. Thomas took care of him—but I do remember him. He came in with a small boy. I can't say for sure it was this boy," he indicated the picture of Howard, "but it was definitely the man."

"We'd like to see your books for that day," Geyer said.

The clerk shook his head. "I'm afraid I can't help there, sir," he said. "They're locked up and Mr. Thomas has the keys."

"Where can we reach him?"

"He's at his home. In Cumminsville. He just moved out there recently and I'm afraid I don't know the address."

Geyer looked at Schnooks and the detective made a motion with his hand. "That's a suburb, about five miles from here. Want to go?"

Geyer said yes and so they got a buggy and drove out. No one in Cumminsville, however, seemed to know who J. C. Thomas was or where he lived, so they returned to the city. By then business hours had ended so Schnooks and Geyer parted, the Cincinnati detective promising to collect Geyer at his hotel first thing tomorrow.

J. C. Thomas was in his office when they arrived there in the morning and he listened to them carefully. "The picture's familiar," he said, "but I'm sure the man didn't say his name was either Cook or Holmes. Let me check the books." He unlocked the files and took out a ledger and found the entry easily. "Hayes. That's the name he gave me. A. C. Hayes. Let's see... He came into this office on Friday, September twenty-eighth, and rented a house at three-o-five Poplar Street for a month, paying fifteen dollars in advance. It was all rather unusual, because he rented the place without even having seen it, after asking just a few questions."

"Questions?" Geyer looked at the realtor with interest. "What kind of questions?"

"Well, he wanted to know whether or not it had a cellar, what kind of heating it had and how much the rent was."

"And you answered what?"

"That it had an unfinished cellar with masonry walls and earth floor, that it had a very nice four-top kitchen stove with lid-lifter, but the only other heat source was a fireplace in the living room, but that there was a good supply of split logs on the back porch. And that the rent was fifteen dollars a month, due on the first and with the first month's rent payable in advance."

"And you say he took it?"

"Yes sir, he did. Oddly enough, he only kept the place a couple of days and then just left the key in the door and disappeared without any further word to us here. However, you might check with Miss Hill—she lives next door—as she mentioned having talked with him."

Miss Hill, who lived at 303 Poplar, one house off Linn Street, was an unattractive, harsh-looking woman with amateurishly dyed hair the color of tarnished brass. She was impressed with the two visitors being detectives and bobbed her head vigorously. "Oh, I remember him, all right," she said. "Him an' that boy. They came here in a wagon on a Saturday mornin', I remember, him an' that boy. Had a couple of coloreds with them that he had carry in a big old iron stove. You know, the big kind like they have in saloons? But the funny thing was, that was the only thing they brought into the house. Next day his man—I forget his name—"

"Hayes? Cook? Holmes?"

She shrugged. "I ain't sure. Cook, maybe, I don't know. Anyway, next day he come by an' said he wasn't stayin' an' if I wanted it, I could have that stove. I sent this friend of mine, Stanley, over an' he got it, but it wasn't worth much an' he wound up selling it."

As they left, Schnooks looked at Geyer. "Now why the hell do you suppose he'd bring a stove in there and then give it away the next day? That doesn't make any sense."

"Why," Geyer countered, more to himself than to Schnooks, "would he rent the house for a month one day and move out the next? Very strange. John, let's get back to headquarters. I think I know where I need to go next."

At City Hall, Geyer thanked Superintendent Dietsch and Detective Schnooks for their help and said he was leaving, but might be coming back again before his investigation was over. He shook hands warmly with the two men and left to check out of his hotel and go to Union Station.

At 5:30 P.M. he was on a train pulling out of Cincinnati toward the northwest. It had taken no great powers of logic for him to determine where he was going next; two of the letters written by the children had been dated on the day after Holmes had checked out of the Hotel Bristol. They had been written from the Hotel English in Indianapolis. That's where Geyer was heading now, not at all disappointed with how things had gone in the Queen City.

On the train, en route to Indianapolis, Frank Geyer reread the copies of the only two letters Carrie Pitezel had received from the missing children. She had received them while she was still in Galva visiting her parents, the Cannings. One was from Alice and the other from Nellie. He read Alice's first:

DEAR MAMA.

We was in Cincinnati yesterday which was Sunday and we got here last night. Nellie is writing to you to, and 4-18-8 said he will write to you to, and he will mail the letters tonight. Howard is a problem to all of us. He's so wild and he never listens and 4-18-8 gets kind of mad at him but he never hits him or nothing like that like papa usta. We went us three over to the Zoological Garden in Cincinnati yesterday and we saw all the different kinds of animals. We saw the ostrich it is about a head taller than I am so you know about how high it is. And the giraffe you have to look up in the sky to see it. I like it lots better here than in Cincinnati. It is such a dirty town Cin. There is a monument right in front of the hotel where we are at and I should judge that it is about 3 times the hight of a 5 story building. I guess I have told you all the news so good bye love to all and kisses. Hope you are all well. Your loving daughter, Alice Pitezel.

The letter from Nellie was even shorter.

Dear Mama, Baby and D.—We are all well here. Mr. 4-18-8 is writing to you too. We are staing in a hotel in Indianapolis it is a pretty nice one we came here last night from C. I like it lots better than in C. It is quite worm here and I have to ware this hevy dress because my close an't ironet. We ate dinner over to the Stibbins Hotel where Alice staid and they knew her to. We are not staing there we are at the English H. We have a room right in front of a monument and I think it was A. Lincolns. Come as soon as you can because I want to see you and baby to. It is an awful nice place where we are staing I dont think you would like it in Cincinnati either but 4-18-8 sais he likes it there. Good bye your dau. Nellie Pitezel.

Geyer had questioned Carrie about the letter from Holmes, which both girls mentioned he was writing to her. Carrie said she had burned it, as he ordered, and that the most important thing about it was that he said he had heard from Ben in code. Ben had told him to let her know he was well. Holmes said Ben had gone on to say that he thought he might have some good words for them in less than two weeks, but not to count on that because things could change quickly. And Ben had reiterated that she was to follow Holmes's directions exactly at all times.

Two hours after leaving Cincinnati, Frank Geyer arrived in the Indiana capital city and checked in at the Spencer House Hotel. It had already been a long day, but he was not yet ready to quit. After gobbling a bit of dinner at the hotel, he went to police headquarters on Alabama Street just south of Washington Street. A desk officer directed him down the hall to the Detective Department. He entered a large room where there were half a dozen men.

"Help you?" A solidly built man in shirtsleeves rose from behind his desk.

The Philadelphia detective identified himself and began to explain his mission, but the man cut him off. "Say no more," he said, offering his hand. "Glad to meet you. Read about you in the papers and wondered when you'd be getting here. I'm George Splann. Captain. I head this department. I'm sure we'll be able to give you all the help you need, but not this evening. In the morning you can see the chief—that's Superintendent Ed Powell—and I'm sure he'll tell me to assign someone to work with—"

He broke off as the door banged open and a uniformed officer rushed in. "Captain Splann," he said, "we've got a report of a man shot and killed at Twenty-fifth and College. The assailant's on foot in the area."

Splann nodded and snatched his coat from a rack, calling several of the other detectives to join him. He looked at Geyer and grinned. "The Saturday-nighters are starting early. Want to tag along?"

"Sure," Geyer said, always interested in seeing how other detectives worked.

They rushed to the scene and found that the man who had been shot was not dead, the bullet having gone through his neck. One of the officers told Splann that Chief Powell was en route to the scene, too. Splann nodded and interviewed a friend of the man who had been shot, then gave the description to several of his detectives and sent them out to search the area. By that time Chief Powell had arrived—a lean, hard-looking man—and Splann introduced them. Geyer quickly explained his business and Powell nodded.

"Tomorrow's Sunday, but that's no problem. Come see me at headquarters first thing in the morning," he said. His words were delivered in the clipped, precise manner of a man well accustomed to giving orders. "I'll detail the best man available to help you and give whatever assistance we can."

As good as his word, Powell, immediately upon Geyer's arrival in the morning, called in a husky, bullet-headed man waiting outside the office.

"Mr. Geyer, this is David Richards, Captain Splann's assistant. He'll help you in any way you want, whatever hours you need him and for as long as you need him. He's not entirely familiar with the case so you'd better brief him on it and then the two of you can get down to business. If you run into any problems, let us know. We'll take care of them."

Geyer and Richards repaired immediately to a private office and spent an hour going over the case. "I didn't stay very long in Cincinnati," Geyer concluded, "because I don't really think it figures too much in this. I don't think that's the case here in Indianapolis. I suspect we're going to have a lot of work to do here."

"We'll get it done," Richards promised. "Do you have a starting point in mind?"

"Yes. The Stubbins House first and then the Hotel English. From there we can be guided by what we've found."

The streets of Indianapolis were fairly deserted on this Sunday morning and the walk to the Stubbins House was pleasant. The hotel register there showed an entry that indicated one Etta Pitsel of St. Louis had checked in on September 24 and left two days later. The hotel manager summoned his chief desk clerk, Robert Sweeney, who had been on duty then. Sweeney remembered it well.

"Very pretty girl, she was." Sweeney said. "Sixteen or seventeen, I suppose. Room Three-twelve. She stayed pretty much to her room until I got the telegram from Mr. Howard."

"Howard?" Geyer asked quickly.

"Telegram?" Richard asked. "What telegram?"

"Well, this gentleman, Mr. Howard, he was the one who checked her in here on the twenty-fourth and—"

"Is this the Mr. Howard?" Geyer showed him the Holmes photograph.

"Yes sir, that's him. That's Mr. Howard, Miss Etta's guardian. And that girl there," he pointed at the picture of Alice Pitezel, "that's Miss Etta Pitsel herself. Anyway, once he checked her in, he left and I didn't see him anymore until four days later when I got this telegram from him in St. Louis. He said he'd be on the train coming through from there to Cincinnati and he wanted me or someone from here to have Miss Etta at the station when the train stopped so he could collect her and take her along with him. So I took her to the station and met the train. He paid me the money due on the bill, plus five dollars extra for my trouble, and took her on the train and that's the last I ever saw them."

So one more piece of the puzzle had been solved. Holmes had been lying to Carrie when he told her in St. Louis that he had left Alice with a kindly old lady in Cincinnati and that she'd been entered into school there. Obviously, Alice had been in Indianapolis all that time and the three children had arrived in Cincinnati together with Holmes.

Pleased with their early progress, Geyer and Richards went next to the downtown area called The Circle and stopped in at the Hotel English. The clerk on duty was Milton Duncan, a trim man of about forty with a pencil-thin mustache. He provided them with the registers for last September and October and stood waiting, faintly nervous. Geyer checked the date of September 30 first, since that was the date Holmes and the children had left the Bristol in Cincinnati. It was there. Three children had been registered under the name Canning, of Galva, Illinois—the name and home of Carrie's parents. They had been given Room 79.

"Did you handle this registry, Mr. Duncan?"

The clerk looked at the book and nodded.

Geyer smiled and brought out the photographs. "Are these the Canning children?"

Duncan looked and nodded again, his Adam's apple bobbing. "They're the ones. Why? What's happened?"

Geyer didn't reply. He showed him the picture of Holmes. "Is this the man who checked them in?"

"I believe it is. I wouldn't want to swear to it in court but, yes, I'd say that's the man."

"And," Geyer glanced at the register again, "they only stayed that one night?"

"That is correct." Duncan put his finger on a small

notation in the entry. "And they checked out at one-ten P.M. the next day, October first."

"Do you have any idea where they went from here?"

"No sir, none at all."

Geyer and Richards left and began checking the other hotels, anticipating early success. They did not get it. At each stop, first the hotel's register would be checked and then the desk clerk would be shown the pictures of the children, but no one else remembered seeing them. Unexpectedly, however, they discovered a curiosity at the fancy Circle Park Hotel that intrigued Geyer. The register showed two sets of entries for Mrs. Georgiana Howard. The first was a check-in on September 18 and check-out on September 24. That, Geyer remembered, was the period during which Holmes was in Philadelphia identifying the exhumed body of Pitezel. The second time she had checked in on September 30 and left on October 4. Geyer spoke with the wife of the manager—a large German woman named Claudia Rhodius—who remembered Georgiana stayed there. She remembered that Georgiana had told her that her husband was a very wealthy man who owned extensive real estate and cattle ranches in Texas and also a lot of property in Berlin, Germany, where they had been planning to go as soon as Mr. Howard had his business matters in order so they could leave.

He found that all very interesting and thought about it the rest of the day as he and Richards continued moving about the city until every hotel had been checked. They had drawn a blank—no one remembered Holmes or the children. In the late afternoon they stood talking in the area of The Circle, Richards promising to come by the Spencer first thing in the morning to collect Geyer and they would decide what to do then. They shook hands and parted, going in different directions. Suddenly Richards jolted to a stop and spun around.

"Frank!"

Geyer stopped and the Indianapolis detective rejoined him, beaming. "I just remembered something—one place we didn't check because we couldn't."

"What do you mean, we couldn't, Dave?"

"Because it's not there anymore. There used to be a hotel called the Circle House on Meridian, just one door off the Circle. See the Circle Park Hotel over there? Where Georgiana Howard had been? Right around the corner."

"What happened to it?"

David Richards shrugged. "Hell, I don't know, they just shut down. Must've been right around the end of the year. I remember the clerk there. Guy by the name of Ackelow. Pretty good contact. Herman Ackelow. Used to buy information from him from time to time."

"Can we find him?"

"I don't know, but we'll sure give it a shot. Let's look at the city directory."

They entered a hotel and checked the big volume but there was no listing for Herman Ackelow. Richards took over. With Geyer in tow, he went to several contacts in succession in the vicinity and finally got lucky. A clerk they had talked to earlier in one of the seedier hotels remembered Ackelow.

"After Circle House shut down I seen him once or twice," the clerk said, "but then he wasn't around no more. Last I heard he was living out in West Indianapolis, I don't know where."

"You know anybody who might?" Richards asked.

"Let me think." His brow furrowed and then abruptly he brightened. "I know, by God! You know Tilly Reisner? He's clerking over at the Cabot."

"The Cabot? That dump just south of the depot?"

"That's the one. He used to be assistant clerk under Ackelow at Circle House. Anybody knows where Herman's at now, he oughta."

Richards shoved a dollar into his pocket in thanks and he and Geyer went at once to the Cabot. Reisner was on duty and he studied the photographs the detectives showed them, but neither recognized them nor knew if they'd stopped at the Circle House, explaining he'd been out of town for a week right about that time.

"What about the register and all the records belonging to the Circle House?" Geyer asked. "What happened to them, do you know?"

"Oh, sure. Bob Everett's got 'em. He was the hotel's lawyer. He's got an office in the Galbraith Building downtown."

"We've got to see those records. Can you meet us at Everett's office at nine tomorrow morning?"

Reisner hesitated and Geyer put two dollar bills down on the desk. They disappeared immediately. "Sure, I'll be there," he promised.

Monday morning at exactly nine, Geyer and Richards

entered the office of Robert R. Everett and found Reisner
already there. He'd told Everett what the detectives wanted
and the attorney had the books all ready for them. As soon as
he checked their credentials, he let them look through them.
The ledgers were so badly kept that they had a hard time
figuring them out and enlisted Reisner's aid.

"Zing!" the clerk said suddenly. "Here it is. On October
first. Ackelow's entry. Checked in on the first, out on the
tenth."

"That settles it," Geyer said. "We have got to see Mr.
Ackelow. Mr. Everett, any idea at all where we can locate
him?"

Everett thought about that and then cleared his throat.
"I don't know that what information I have will be of much
help. It's vague. I heard he moved out to West Indianapolis
and I also heard he had a job running a saloon somewhere,
whether in West Indianapolis or not, I don't know."

Geyer stood up and Richards rose also. "We appreciate
your help. Let's go, Dave."

The streetcar ride out to West Indianapolis did not take
long and the search for Ackelow was not so difficult as
envisioned. In the third saloon checked they found a bartender who knew Ackelow and where he was working. It was only
a few blocks away. They went there at once and found the
former hotel proprietor behind the bar.

"Well, if it isn't Dave Richards," Ackelow said, grinning
as he wiped his hands on his apron and shook hands with the
detective. "Now how the hell did you ever find me out
there?"

"Herman, how are you?" Richards grinned and looked at
him slyly. "We have ways of finding almost anyone we want to
find."

"Evidently," Ackelow said with a grimace. "All right,
you've found me. So tell me why."

"This is Detective Frank Geyer from Philadelphia. He's
here investigating a case involving some people who stayed at
the Circle House when you ran it. Last October. First to
tenth. Three children and a man."

"Here are their pictures," Geyer said, placing them face
up on the bar. He pointed at Alice's picture specifically. "This
one might have been reading a book—blue covered and
pretty well scuffed up."

"Oh, sure," Ackelow said immediately upon seeing them,

"those are the ones. I remember them very well. And the book the older girl was reading. But the man—what was his name . . . ?"

"Holmes?"

"No, that doesn't ring a bell."

"Howard?"

"Yeah, that's it! Howard. The kids' uncle. Now the kids stayed with us, but he didn't. Not too often we had children dropped off as guests and were asked to actually take care of them until they were picked up. But that's what happened. Their uncle, he dropped them off and paid us extra to see to them. Nice kids—the girls anyway. I had my son taking care of them. And Caroline, the chambermaid. The little boy, he was a handful and their uncle, Mr. Howard—this man here," he pointed at the picture of Holmes, "he would tell me what a bad boy the kid was and how he couldn't be made to mind and all. Said he was looking for a farm or private school he could put him into because he didn't want to have to fuss with him anymore. I didn't notice he was so bad, but then I didn't see him all the time, either. My son'd go up to call them for their meals and he'd come down and say he found the girls crying because they were homesick."

"When they finally checked out on October tenth," Geyer asked him, "were all three of the children with Mr. Holmes—the man in the picture here?"

Ackelow shook his head. "I can't recall. I recollect the girls, but I'm not sure of the boy."

"You can't recall whether the boy was with them or not?"

"No, I'd be guessing. I assumed he was, but I can't be positive."

"What about a trunk? Did they have one?"

"Funny you should ask that. Odd thing happened about their trunk that I forgot all about until what you just said reminded me."

Geyer felt his pulse quicken. "What was it?"

"Well, they did have a trunk when they checked in, but the day before they checked out, their uncle came and took it away with him. He was by himself."

A relay suddenly clicked in Geyer's mind. During one of the several interviews he had had with Carrie Pitezel before her release from Moyamensing, she had commented on the fact that the trunk the children had taken with them from St. Louis had disappeared, and that Holmes could probably tell him what happened to it. Later, during one of the numerous interviews he'd had with Holmes, he had asked about the trunk in passing and had written down what Holmes replied, but he couldn't recall right now what that was. He made a mental note to check on it as soon as he got back to his hotel.

"Did the trunk have anything in it?" he asked Ackelow. "I mean, did he act like it was hard to carry, as if it had something in it?"

"No. He had it up on his shoulder and was just sort of balancing it with one hand. If there was anything in it, it couldn't have been very much. I'd guess it was probably empty."

"And that was on the day *before* they checked out?"

"That's right."

"Did you notice whether or not he loaded it into a wagon?"

Ackelow shook his head. "Far as I know he didn't. I watched him go out because it looked like he might have trouble with it at the door and I was going to help him, but he just breezed out and turned and walked past the front windows with it, heading for the Circle."

Geyer thought about this. "One other thing. You mentioned a chambermaid, Caroline. Is she still around? We'd like to talk to her."

"You'd have a tough time talking to Caroline Klausmann. She's German. Doesn't speak English."

Geyer chuckled. "Actually, I'll have no trouble at all. My parents came from Germany. I learned German before I learned English. Where can I find her?"

"It's a long walk. She moved to Chicago. Left here before Circle House closed down. She'd got a job at a German hotel there—the Swiss Hotel, I think she said."

Geyer made a notation on his pad and put it away. "I think that's probably all we need for now." He held out his hand to the man. "I want to thank you, Mr. Ackelow. We appreciate your help. If you think of anything we may have overlooked in regard to these children and Holmes—Mr. Howard, as you knew him—please contact Detective Richards here at police headquarters."

On the way back to downtown Indianapolis, Richards looked at Geyer quizzically. "Evidently you picked up something back there that I missed?"

"Maybe. I'm not sure. Let's get back to the Circle Park Hotel."

When they arrived, Geyer looked up Claudia Rhodius again. "You said before that on the second stay of Mrs. Howard here, she arrived on September thirtieth and checked out on October fourth?"

She rechecked the register. "Well, no, not exactly. She *left* on the fourth, but Mr. Howard, he stayed on until the tenth and he was the one who checked out."

Geyer felt a surge of elation. "Mrs. Rhodius, do you know if Mr. Howard had a trunk when he checked out?"

"No, I'm positive he didn't."

"Why would you be so positive about something like that?"

She erupted in a deep belly laugh. "Because he shipped it away the day *before* he checked out."

"The day before?" Geyer stared at her dumbly.

"Yes. He came down to the desk and asked my husband for a porter to come up and get his trunk and take it over to the baggage platform at the railroad station for him. Said he was sending some things to a friend."

"Where?"

"I'm not sure. Chicago?" She shook her head. "Maybe not. I'm not sure."

"But you *are* sure it was the day before he checked out?"

"Oh, yes, I know it was, because my husband asked him. He said, 'Are you leaving us, Mr. Howard?' or something like that, and Mr. Howard said, 'No, not yet, but soon.' Oh, *that's* it! That's when he said he was sending some things in the trunk to a friend in Chicago. It *was* Chicago."

"Who was the porter?"

"Our colored man, Clevon Jefferson."

"Is Mr. Jefferson around? May I speak to him?"

She lowered her eyes. "I'm afraid not, sir. Clevon took sick and died this past spring."

Geyer blew out a gusty breath. "Mrs. Rhodius, thank you very much. You've been a big help. Good day."

He and Richards left the hotel and went immediately to the Union Station baggage platform. There they ran into a wall. No one among the expressmen, omnibus drivers, porters, redcaps, hackmen and liverymen they questioned had any knowledge whatever of the trunk, either of its destination or even having seen it. The shipping records in the express office showed no trunk shipment anywhere near the time in question that bore any resemblance to the circumstances. Before they left the station Geyer stopped briefly at the ticket counter and checked departure schedules.

"Dave," he said as he rejoined Richards and they headed downtown, "I'll be leaving today."

Richards was surprised. "Really? I thought you'd be here longer."

"Oh, I will be. I'll be coming back, I promise you. But I have to check out a few other things first."

"Okay. Be sure you ask for me when you come back, Frank. I've enjoyed seeing you work. I think you got a lot more than I realize. You're pretty damned good."

"Thanks. You're no novice yourself. And you can bet I'll ask for you."

"Where are you heading from here?"

"I'm not sure yet. Maybe Detroit, maybe Chicago. I have to check on something in my notes."

They went to headquarters where Geyer thanked Chief Powell and Captain Splann and reiterated that he'd probably be back before too long. He shook hands warmly with Dave Richards and left. Ten minutes later he was in his hotel room, paging rapidly through his stack of notebooks. They were scribbled full of the peculiar form of shorthand he had developed for his own use over decades of police work. He found what he wanted quickly—part of his second interview with Holmes.

Q. Carrie Pitezel said the children had a trunk when they left St. Louis with you. Did they?

A. Yes.

Q. What happened to it?

A. I left it in Chicago.

Q. Where?

A. In a hotel where I stayed for a short while.

Q. What hotel?

A. I don't remember the name of it. Not much of a place.

Q. You must remember where it was located, Mr. Holmes.

A. It was on West Madison Street.

Q. Where on West Madison? What number?

A. I don't remember the number, but it was

only about fifty feet from the corner of Ashland Avenue.

Geyer checked out immediately and returned to Union Station. He bought his ticket and had just barely enough time before his train left to send a wire to District Attorney George Graham:

JULY 1 1895 STOP SIR STOP MAKING SATISFACTORY PROGRESS STOP CHILDREN POSITIVELY TRACED IN CINCINNATI AND FROM THERE TO INDIANAPOLIS STOP SUSPECT HOWARD PITEZEL MAY HAVE BEEN KILLED HERE AND BODY SHIPPED AWAY IN TRUNK STOP AM GOING TO CHICAGO IMMEDIATELY STOP GEYER

It was getting on toward evening when Frank Geyer arrived in Chicago and checked into the Imperial Hotel. Having eaten nothing since breakfast, he ate a hearty dinner at a nearby restaurant and then went to police headquarters in City Hall. He was directed to Captain Frederick Stoddenberg in the Detective Division. As soon as he introduced himself, Captain Stoddenberg leaped up and gripped his hand, pumping it enthusiastically and proclaiming his delight at meeting so illustrious a police officer.

Geyer looked at him blankly. "I'm afraid I don't understand," he said.

"Haven't you seen the papers?"

Geyer shook his head. "Afraid I haven't had much time lately to look at newspapers," he said.

"Well, you should have. The whole country's been following your investigation step by step—Philadelphia, Cincinnati, Indianapolis. Now Chicago. Millions of people are holding their breath, waiting for the story that will break when you find the Pitezel children. And the big question, of course, is whether they'll be dead or alive."

"I didn't know," Geyer said slowly, frowning. "I'm not sure I like that."

"Well, we'll do our best to keep the reporters off your tail, Mr. Geyer, but you know how persistent they are, especially with a story like this. I presume you're going to begin investigation here in the morning?"

"I was planning to. I'd appreciate having a detective

assigned to assist me. I don't know a great deal about Chicago, I'm afraid."

"Well, you'll certainly have one," Stoddenberg said. "Why not get a good night's rest and come by in the morning and we'll have it all arranged. Inspector Fitzpatrick's anxious to meet you."

Geyer was unprepared to find himself something of a celebrity. By the time he returned to City Hall in the morning, he learned why. Evidently his search for the Pitezel children on a trail that had been cold for nine months had sparked the admiration and enthusiasm of the press. It was a contagion that admiring but not always accurate reporters spread via their newspaper columns and wire stories to the readership of major cities in the United States and Canada. He was not at all pleased to find that reporters as well as officials of the Chicago Police Department had converged to meet him when word spread of his arrival at City Hall.

Inspector Patrick Fitzpatrick, assistant to the chief of police, shook his hand warmly. "This is quite an investigation you're launched upon, Mr. Geyer. You will, of course, be afforded every courtesy and assistance in our power to provide." He turned to the man standing beside him. "This is Detective Sergeant John C. McGinn. I've assigned him to help you in any way possible."

Embarrassed at the fuss being made over him, Geyer shook the plainclothesman's hand and leaned close to him. "Is there someplace we can talk alone, Sergeant? And can we get away from all these people?"

McGinn winked at him and nodded, murmured a few words to his superior and led Geyer down the hall, dogged by reporters, to a private room. He beckoned him along and they went directly out an opposite door and found themselves alone in another corridor. In moments they had sequestered themselves in a quiet room and enjoyed coffee together while Geyer briefed him on the case to this point. When he was finished, McGinn snorted.

"I was sort of envying you," he said, "heading up an investigation like this. I don't anymore. I don't see how you think you're going to find those poor kids. And now with everybody looking over your shoulder! Jeeze, talk about being put under pressure. I wouldn't change places with you for anything!"

Geyer grinned. "Neither would I. Is there a way for us to get out of here unseen?" he asked.

"Sure, leave it to me. Where do you want to go first?"

"I'd like to see Holmes's lawyer, Wharton Plummer. He's in the Chamber of Commerce Building."

"No sooner said than done. Let's go."

McGinn led him out yet another door and through a series of corridors to a nondescript door on the east side of the building, emptying onto Clark Street. In less than ten minutes they were being shown into the lavish office of Wharton Plummer. The portly lawyer, still holding Geyer's card which the detective had given to the secretary, greeted them with cordial wariness.

"Please, gentlemen," he said, indicating fine overstuffed leather chairs, "be seated. Now, which of you is Detective Geyer?"

"I am. This is Detective Sergeant McGinn."

"Ah, yes, from our Chicago force." He looked back at Geyer. "You, of course, are the officer who is attempting to trace some missing children. A dreary assignment, I should imagine. How may I help you, gentlemen?"

"You are, as I understand it," Geyer said briskly, "Henry Holmes's attorney and friend, is that correct?"

"Well now, that may be putting too much emphasis on the closeness of our association," Plummer hedged. "Mr. Holmes has indeed been a client of mine on occasion in the past, although not for some time now. I have seen to the legal paperwork in a number of matters for him, primarily real estate."

"In my last interview with Mr. Holmes before I left Philadelphia," Geyer said levelly, watching Plummer closely, "he told me that during the time he was traveling with the three children, he came to Chicago and stayed at a hotel on West Madison Street. He said he contacted you and that you came to the hotel and met him, then dined with him and the Pitezel children in the hotel that evening."

A faint sheen of perspiration appeared on Plummer's cheeks. "I cannot remember exactly when I had my last meeting with Mr. Holmes," he said. "He came to town and he did contact me and we did meet for dinner. But that meeting was on the North Side, not the West Side, and on Division Street, not Madison. We ate at a restaurant, not a hotel, and it was lunch, not dinner. At no time, then or any other time, did I meet the the Pitezel children. I did meet their father on one or two occasions, but I was never in his home and never met his family."

"Isn't it strange, then," Geyer said, "that they should have named their latest son Wharton? Mr. Holmes says the boy was named after you."

"Mr. Geyer, Wharton is not an uncommon name. That the Pitezels would have named a son after me is patently ridiculous. I do not mean to appear disloyal to a client, Mr. Geyer, but isn't it common knowledge at this point that Mr. Holmes is a pathological liar? If he were not, would you be presently embarked upon this search of yours?" He came to his feet and moved to the door. "I'm sorry you've wasted your time in coming here, gentlemen, but it has indeed been a waste of time, and I'm afraid that time is my most precious commodity. Unless there's something else specific—based neither on innuendo nor hearsay—you'll have to forgive me."

McGinn shot a look at Geyer, who nodded and rose. They walked to the door and started out, but Geyer paused and looked directly into Plummer's eyes. "It would be presumptuous of me to give advice to a lawyer . . . but I'll risk it. Watch your flanks, Mr. Plummer—they're becoming dangerously exposed."

On the sidewalk outside the building, McGinn chuckled. "Did you see his face after that final remark of yours? You sure scared the shit out of him. He was lying, wasn't he?"

"About not seeing the children? About where he last met with Holmes? No, as a matter of fact, I'm pretty sure he was telling the truth."

"Then why'd he turn white? How come he—"

"*I* may not know what he's got to hide, Sergeant, but *he* does."

McGinn looked at him speculatively and then hooted with laughter. "I think," he said, when he finally caught his breath, "I could get to like you a lot. All right, where now?"

"The Swiss Hotel, wherever that is."

"Not too far. Come on."

The Swiss Hotel was on Wells Street between Ohio and Ontario streets. They found Caroline Klausmann without difficulty and Geyer, speaking with easy fluency in German, explained his quest. She was a middle-aged women with frizzy blond hair who kept saying "Ja, ja," each time he paused. When he showed her the pictures of the children she grasped them and held them to her ample bosom and her eyes filled with tears. In rapid German she talked about how the children, while staying at the Circle House in Indianapolis, filled their days with drawing pictures and reading and often simply standing at the window, looking outward and crying.

"I could not talk to them and they could not talk to me," she told Geyer, "but because they were there alone, I thought that they were orphaned children and that the reason they were crying was over the recent death of their mama and papa. I was so sorry that I could not speak English so I could have comforted them more."

Geyer showed her the picture of the missing trunk. "Do you recognize this trunk?" he asked.

"Ja, ja. That is the trunk they had with them in their room."

She did not, however, recognize the picture of Holmes, but that was because no one had visited the children during those times when she was in the room with them. Geyer thanked her and left and he and McGinn went to West Madison Street and Ashland Avenue and looked for the hotel where Holmes had said he left the trunk. There was no hotel but they did find a boardinghouse in about the location he had described, operated by a hard-eyed woman who identified herself as Miss Jennie Irons.

Her manner was hostile as soon as she learned her two visitors were police detectives, but she softened when Geyer explained that the nature of their business had nothing to do with anything she may have done. She looked at the photos and denied ever having seen the children, but, interestingly enough, she picked out Holmes as a man she knew as Harry Gordon, who had stayed in her place over a year ago with a woman. From the description she gave, Geyer was reasonably sure the woman she was referring to was the elusive Minnie Williams. Miss Irons said she knew nothing of a trunk, however, and denied ever having seen the one in the photo.

Their next stop was the Holmes Castle at Sixty-third and Wallace. Geyer located and interviewed Patrick Quinlan about Holmes and the missing children, trying to give Quinlan the impression that he knew a great deal more than he actually did. The Irishman was surly and uncooperative, answering in monosyllables and offering little. He admitted knowing the

Pitezel children but said he'd had no personal contact with them or Holmes for a couple of years.

"If that body found in Philadelphia really was Pitezel and Holmes murdered him and murdered the children, too," Quinlan declared righteously, "why, he damned well ought to be hung for it and, by God, I'll be willing to spring the trap to do it!"

Quinlan was disinclined to discuss Minnie Williams and gave nothing away about her except for referring to her several times as Holmes's wife. But when Geyer tried to pin him down in regard to Holmes's having married her, the janitor became evasive. Geyer had had experience with people who would give virtually no information and Quinlan was of such a cut.

"There's a man," he told McGinn after they left the Castle, "who knows a great deal. He's not very big and he doesn't look very strong, but I'd be willing to bet you couldn't get a damned thing out of him no matter what you did."

By the end of the day Geyer had come to the conclusion that his Chicago visit was becoming a wasted effort. Holmes was undoubtedly guilty of a number of things here, but not in the direction Geyer was searching. He doubted very much that Holmes had come anywhere near Chicago with the children after leaving Indianapolis.

Geyer had not decided whether he would follow his inclination and return to Indianapolis or go to Detroit, which was where Carrie said Holmes and the children had gone after leaving Indianapolis. The decision was made for him when, on returning to his hotel, he found a wire awaiting him from District Attorney Graham. It neatly undermined the theory he had been developed that Howard Pitezel had been killed in Indianapolis and the body shipped elsewhere. The wire read:

DET GEYER STOP FRANK ALDERMAN GEN MGR FIDELITY
MUTUAL IN DETROIT HAS PROOF HOLMES AND HOWARD
PITEZEL TOGETHER MID OCT IN DETROIT STOP HOLMES
RENTED HOUSE THERE STOP GRAHAM

He checked out of his hotel immediately and went directly to the depot where he purchased his ticket and boarded the train for Detroit. As soon as it began moving he opened his valise and became absorbed in reviewing some of the papers he had brought with him. He was particularly interested in the time period when Holmes and the children were winding down their stay in Indianapolis, hoping to find some clue as to the whereabouts of Howard at that time. Three of the unmailed letters found in Holmes's possession when he was arrested had been written during this period and Geyer studied his true copies of them now with a new perspective. The first had been written by Nellie:

OCTOBER 6TH

DEAR MAMA, GRANDMA AND GRANDPA:—

We are all well here. It is a little warmer today. There is so many buggies go by that you can't hear yourself think. I first wrote you a letter with a crystal pen, but I made some mistakes and then I am in a hustle because 4-18-8 has to go at 3 o'clock I don't know where. It is all glass so I hafto be careful or else it will break, it was only 5 cents. We hafto get up early if we get brekfast. We have awful good dinners pie fruit and sometimes cake at supper and this aint half. They are all men that eat at the tables we do not eat with them we have a room to ourselves. They are dutch but they can cook awful nice. Their is more bicycles go by here in one day than goes by in a month in St Louis. I saw 2 great bit ostriges alive and we felt of their feathers and they are awful smooth½ they are black with white tails they are as big as a horse. Why have buffaloes got big rings in their noses for I want Grandma and Grandpa to write to me. Is the baby well and does he like coco I want you all to write why dont you write mama. I will close for this time goodby write

YOURS TRULY,
NELLIE

Alice eyes hurt so she wont write this time.

The second letter, written the following day, was from Alice:

OCT. 7TH SUN. MORNING

DEAR MAMA.

We are all well except I have a bad cold. I have

read so much in the Uncle Toms Cabin book that I could not see to write yesterday when Nell did. I am wearing my new dress today because it is warmer today. Nell and Howard and I have all got a crystal pen all made of glass five cents a piece and I am writing with it now. I expect Grandma and Grandpa was awful glad to see you. The hotel we are staying at faces right on a big bulvard and there is more safties and buggies passing than a little bit and how I wish I had a safty. Last sunday we was at the Zoological Garden in Cincinnati, O. And I expect this Sunday will pass away slower than I dont know what and Howard is too dirty to be seen out on the street to-day. Why dont you write to me. I have not got a letter from you since I have been away and it will be three weeks day after tomorrow. It is raining out now quite hard. Nell is drawing now. The hotel is just a block from Washington street and that is where all the big stores are. There is a shoe store there And there has been a man painting every day this week. They give these genuwine oil paintings away with ever $1.00 purchase of shoes with small extra charge for frames. You cant get the pictures with out the frames though I wish I could get one you don't know how pretty they are. We go there every day and watch him paint. He can paint a picture in 1½ minutes aint that quick. Nell keeps jarring the stand so I can hardly write. I made half a dozen mistakes on the other side because she made me. This letter is for you all because I cant write to so many of you I guess I have told you all the news so good bye love to all and kisses

> YOUR LOVING DAUGHTER
> ALICE PITEZEL

P.O. write soon. Howard got a box of colors and took one out and lost box and all contents.

The final letter was also written by Alice.

TEUSDY, OCT 9TH

DEAR MAMA

Howard wont mind me at all. He wanted a

*book and I got life of Gen. Sheridan and it is awful
nice but now he dont read it at all hardly. 4-18-8
told him to stay in the next morning that he wanted
him and would come and get him and take him out
and he would not stay in at all he was out when
4-18-8 came and was he ever madd. We have each of
us Nell and me written 2 or 3 letters to you and I
guess you will begin to get them now Hope you will
all keep well*

*(later) I have just finished Uncle Tom's Cabin
and it is a nice book but I don't believe anybody
could be so cruel as that to other people so much. I
wish I could see you all. This is another warmer
day. The son of the man downstairs at he desk
said we pay $12,00 a week for our room and
board and I think that is pretty cheap for the
good meals we have Yesterday we had mashed
potatoes, grapes, chicken glass of milk each, ice
cream each a big sauss dish full awful good too,
lemon pie, cake dont you think that is pretty
good. They are Germans. I guess I will have to
close so good bye, love to all and kisses. Write
soon keep well. Yours truley*

ALICE PITEZEL

Two points in the letters were of particular interest to
Geyer. Howard was obviously alive and well on October 7,
because Alice mentioned in her postscript that he had lost a
box of colored crayons. Two days later, however, she wrote
that Howard was not on hand when Holmes wished him to
be, so that Holmes could "come and get him and take him
out"—a phraseology that had the effect of causing Geyer's
scalp to prickle. And then she had added that Holmes was
very angry. Was he angry enough to kill the boy? For that
matter did he even *need* to be angry to kill him? Was it
possible that this was the last day of Howard's life? No,
evidently not, since District Attorney Graham's wire said the
Fidelity Mutual executive in Detroit had proof that Howard
was there with Holmes in mid-October.

"I'll be most interested in seeing Mr. Alderman's proof
when I get there," Geyer murmured aloud. He put the letters
back into the valise and leaned back and closed his eyes. But
he was most definitely not sleeping.

Eleven

T he officer assigned by Police Chief Cecil Starkweather to aid Frank Geyer in Detroit was Herb Tuttle, a pipe-smoker with dark bushy hair and mustache and clothing that bore a marked similarity to an unmade bed. He was alleged to be one of Detroit's best and most experienced detectives, the sharpness of his mind belying the rumpled exterior.

Together they stopped in the Michigan branch office of Fidelity Mutual and met its overenthusiastic general manager, Frank Alderman. The insurance executive boasted of the great work he had done in tracing Holmes in Chicago and Detroit and discovering that the Pitezel boy, Howard, was with him. But it took only a few minutes of questioning by Geyer to discover that his "tracing" of Holmes in Chicago consisted of nothing more than having paid a brief visit to the Castle and questioned Pat Quinlan with marked inconclusiveness. As for his claim of "proof" that Howard was with Holmes in Detroit, what he had was nothing more than a hearsay report Alderman had gleaned from the realtor who had rented a house to Holmes. It took some fancy maneuvering to discourage Alderman from accompanying them when they went to see the realtor in his office at 60 E. Monroe Street, facing onto Cadillac Square.

The outer office had a number of people in it and they were directed to a tall, well-dressed gentleman speaking with a secretary. Geyer, with Tuttle directly behind him, approached Frederick Boninghausen and handed him his card. "Would it be possible for us to speak privately somewhere?" he asked.

The realtor led them to his private office, showed them to seats and served them coffee from a heavy white-speckled blue enameled pot on a small stove. Then he sat behind his own desk and looked at them inquiringly.

"Mr. Boninghausen," Geyer said, setting his cup aside and pulling out the photographs, "have you ever seen this man before?" He handed him one of the pictures.

"Oh, certainly," Boninghausen said immediately. "That's Mr. Hollis—Melvin Hollis—the man to whom I rented a house on Forest Avenue last October."

"What date in October sir?" asked Tuttle quickly.

Boninghausen opened a desk drawer and took out a ledger. He flipped the pages and found what he was looking for. "October thirteenth."

"Under what circumstances?" Geyer asked.

"Well, he came into this office—I was working alone that day—and said he was desirous of renting a house for his sister. He said she was a widow with three children. What he was looking for was a place that was out a little way, yet with easy enough access to transportation into the center of town."

"And you had such a place?"

"Yes. I was not only the agent for it, but I owned a half interest in the house."

"Where is it located?"

"At two-four-one East Forest Avenue, just a couple of blocks off Woodward, where the streetcar passes. The house is between Bush and Beaubien Streets. He said it sounded like what he wanted and went to see it."

"You gave him the key?"

"No. The keys were at McAllister's Drug Store on Forest, not far from the house. I told him he could pick them up there." He paused.

"Then what?" Tuttle prompted.

"Oh. Well, a couple of hours later he came back and said it was exactly what his sister wanted and he asked what the rent was. I told him twenty dollars a month and he said his sister wasn't due to arrive for three or four days and how would it be if he left five dollars as a deposit and then came in when she got here and paid six months' rent in advance."

"You accepted that?"

"Yes, I thought that was just fine."

Geyer handed him three more pictures. "Do you recognize any of these children, Mr. Boninghausen?"

The realtor studied them and then sighed and shook his

head apologetically. "I don't really know. Actually, I don't pay much attention to children, as a rule."

"Mr. Alderman, whom I understand talked with you, said you told him that this man had a small boy with him when he rented the place."

"I don't know that I told Mr. Alderman positively that Mr. Hollis had a boy with him."

"Did he or didn't he?"

"Well, he *may* have. So many people come in and out all the time and after a while they sort of all run together. I just didn't pay that much attention, but it seems to me that, yes, he did have a boy with him. While Mr. Alderman was here, another prospective client came in and—"

"What was his name?" Tuttle interrupted.

"Moore. John Moore. Anyway, he was here while Mr. Alderman and I were talking and when I asked him about it—"

"How would he know anything about it?" Tuttle interrupted again. "You said you were alone in the office when this Hollis was here."

"I said I was *working* alone. Two or three people— customers—had come in and gone out while Mr. Hollis and I were conversing. Mr. Moore was one of those who came in."

"All right, go on."

"Well, he—Mr. Moore, that is—came in again while Mr. Alderman and I were talking and I asked him if he was here on the day that Mr. Hollis rented the house and he said he thought he was; and I asked him if he remembered if Mr. Hollis had a little boy with him and he said he was pretty sure he did have."

"Where might we find this Mr. Moore now?" Geyer asked.

"Well, when Mr. Hollis never came back to put down the rent for his sister, I eventually wound up renting that place to Mr. Moore. He's there now."

Geyer looked at Tuttle and grinned. "Sometimes we *do* get lucky." He looked back at the realtor. "I presume you wouldn't mind if we went out and took a look at the house?"

"Well, that's up to Mr. Moore, since he's the tenant now. I'm sure he wouldn't mind, and I certainly don't."

"Thank you for your help, Mr. Boninghausen. We may be dropping in to see you again."

Outside, Geyer and Tuttle discussed what they'd do

next. "I know Carrie Pitezel stayed at the Geis Hotel," Geyer said, "so we'll save that for later. I'd like to check the registers of some of the hotels around the depot, so let's start there."

At the first few hotels they found nothing, but their luck improved when they entered the New Western and spoke with its proprietor, P. W. Cotter, at the front desk. He listened to them and then let them see the register for last October. They found what they were looking for under the date of the twelfth. At close to midnight on that day, two girls had been brought to the hotel by a man they addressed as their uncle. He had registered them as Etta and Nellie Canning of St. Louis and they had been given Room 5.

"Take a look at these photographs, Mr. Cotter," Geyer said. "Are these the two girls you're referring to?"

Cotter bent close to them and squinted. "They're the ones," he said, straightening.

"Is this the man who brought them here?"

Cotter examined the Holmes photo and nodded. "That's him."

"How long did they stay?"

"Just overnight. That man called for 'em the next day and took 'em away. I never saw 'em again after that."

"There was a little boy with them, too?"

"Nope, just the two girls."

Geyer felt the familiar gripping in his stomach. No little boy. No Howard. "Did they have a trunk with them?" he asked.

"All they had was a couple satchels. No trunk."

Geyer unconsciously chewed at his mustache. Holmes had been here. The two girls had been here. But no Howard and no trunk. More than ever he was becoming convinced that the two were connected. Find Howard and he would find the trunk; find the trunk and he would find Howard— perhaps *inside* the trunk.

They had learned all they could for the time being from Cotter, so Geyer and Tuttle thanked him and left. "Holmes didn't stay with the girls here," Tuttle pointed out. "So where did he stay?"

"That's what we're going to find out. Knowing his expensive tastes, let's check some of the better places."

They found the entry they were looking for on the register of the Normandie Hotel, signed on October 12 as *G. Howell and wife, Adrian*. It was no trick any longer for Geyer to recognize Holmes's handwriting. The clerk said he had been on duty that night and Geyer showed him the photos of Holmes and Georgiana.

"That's definitely the woman," he said. "I think it's the man, too, but I can't be sure. They checked out the following day."

Geyer decided it was time to go out to the house on Forest Avenue and talk to Mr. Moore. He turned out to be a chubby little man with florid face and good nature. He welcomed them into the house and told them if they wished to look around the place, they should feel free to do so. They examined every foot of earth in the yard and cellar and found none of it disturbed until they checked behind the steps leading into the cellar from upstairs. There, deep in shadows and unnoticed heretofore was a hole—four feet long, three feet wide and three-and-a-half feet deep.

"Grave?" Tuttle asked.

Geyer grunted noncommittally. "Possibly. But, if so, why wasn't it used? It doesn't make any sense. Come on, we've found enough. Let's get out of here."

To add one more brick to the foundation of proof being constructed, they stopped at the nearby drugstore and talked with Dr. McAllister, the pharmacist, who had been keeper of the keys. He recognized the picture of Holmes at once as the man who had gotten the keys from him.

The two detectives returned to police headquarters and reviewed their findings thus far. They still had to determine not only where the two girls had gone after leaving the New Western Hotel, but where Holmes and Georgiana had gone after checking out of the Normandie. Geyer felt a nagging certainty that he had overlooked something of importance in the children's letters that had been found in Holmes's tin box; something that would help; something that hadn't really registered in his mind as being important prior to now. He got his valise and brought out the copies. The letter written by Alice on October 14 had some drawings in it, including one with the notation in Alice's hand, *Copied from Uncle Tom's Cabin*. At the bottom of one page of the drawings was a notation: *All these pictures were drawn at No. 91 Congress Street, Detroit, Michigan*.

Tuttle looked at his new friend admiringly and shook his head. "You don't forget much, do you?"

"I try not to," Geyer laughed. "Lead on, MacDuff." He

spoke lightly but he still felt there was something more in the correspondence he was missing—a piece of the puzzle still hidden from him.

The 91 Congress Street address turned out to be the Lucinda Burns Boardinghouse and Mrs. Burns, a pleasant, shapeless widow of about forty, a former schoolteacher, immediately identified the pictures as the two girls who had stayed with her for six days beginning October 13.

"A gentleman came here the morning of the thirteenth," she said, "and said he wanted to lodge his two nieces. He paid a week's rent in advance and went away, but came back later with the girls and introduced them to me as Miss Annie and Miss Amy. I never did get their last names. He seemed concerned about them because they were young and innocent and asked me to keep an eye on them and not let them go wandering around the city on their own."

"When they left here on the nineteenth, was it with him? And did they say where they were going?"

"No, they didn't leave with him. Actually, the day before they left he stopped by and said a carriage would come around for them in the morning and that they were going home to St. Louis. And that's what happened. I mean, the carriage came for them and they left and I never did see him or them again."

A further search of hotels failed to turn up any record of Holmes and Georgiana after they checked out of the Normandie and finally Tuttle made a suggestion. "If he put the girls in a boardinghouse, why not the same thing for him and the woman?"

Geyer thought that a pretty good idea, especially since Holmes and Georgiana were known to have stayed in boardinghouses at Burlington and Boston. The two detectives immediately began checking out the numerous boardinghouses throughout the city. Time after time they knocked or rang doorbells, showed the pictures, told an abbreviated version of what they wanted and met with failure. On the second day of such checking they entered the May Ralston Boardinghouse at 54 Park Place. The avenue was shaded by large beautiful trees and was a semicircular thoroughfare of stately old homes—some of them now exclusive boardinghouses—overlooking the lovely vista of Grand Circle Park.

"Oh, my!" said Mrs. Ralston when she saw the pictures. "It's Mr. and Mrs. Holmes!"

"They used the name Holmes?" Tuttle murmured.

"Getting bold," Geyer remarked. "Can you tell us about their stay here with you, Mrs. Ralston?"

"Well, they were awfully nice folk. Mr. Holmes paid a week's rent in advance, but they left after only four or five days. I guess that's the way it is with theater people, always on the move."

"They were theater people?" Geyer asked.

"Oh, my, yes! Wonderful people. So polished and nice. The other boarders and I were all disappointed when they left so suddenly."

"Exactly when was it they left, Mrs. Ralston?"

"Well, I remember it very clearly because it was my husband's birthday, may he rest in peace. He's been gone ten years now, but his birthday is still always sort of a special day for me."

"And when was that?" Tuttle asked. "What date, I mean?"

"October eighteenth, it was. Very unexpected—their leaving, I mean—because as soon as they got that telegram, they were gone. We all decided it was because they'd gotten a new booking somewhere for their show."

"You don't know who the telegram was from?" Geyer asked. "Or *where* it came from?" Damn, how he'd like to see that telegram!

"No," she replied, "I'm afraid not."

"Any possibility Mr. and Mrs. Holmes might have mentioned where they were going?"

"Well, as a matter of fact he did, if I can just bring it to mind." She thought for a moment. "Yes," she said suddenly, "I'm sure it was in Canada somewhere, but I'm not sure where. I seem to recollect he said Kingston."

"Mrs. Ralston, do you recognize any of the luggage in these photos?" Geyer handed them to her.

"Yes, this one—the canvas-covered trunk. That was the one Mrs. Holmes was using while she was here."

"But not this smaller one?" It was the picture of Howard's trunk.

"No," she said at once. "No, I never saw that one before."

They bade her good-day and, at Geyer's suggestion, went directly to the Geis Hotel, where Carrie had told him she had stayed with Dessie and Wharton. The identification was quickly made through the photographs and the register showed that Holmes had signed them in as Mrs. C. A. Adams and daughter of Chicago. Their arrival was late evening on the thirteenth and they had checked out on the morning of the eighteenth, supposedly returning to Chicago. While here, they stayed in Room 33. The housekeeper, Minnie Mulholland, was summoned and she not only recognized their pictures but also that of their two trunks—one large and flat-topped, the other small. Neither was Howard's trunk.

"That poor woman!" Miss Mulholland exclaimed. "You never seen a woman so bowed down with the world's troubles as she was. Scared an' anxious an' shakin' like a leaf all the time, she was. Ever I seen anyone teeterin' on the brink an' ready for a shove, she was it. An' that room she had, Number Thirty-three, was way at the back with a window that didn't have no view at all. An' she never went out nor nothin'. I guess it was driving her kind of crazy. I felt so sorry for her. So after while I let her come to my room—it's up front— during daytimes, whilst I was workin', so's could sit in my rocker an' watch out the window. An' that poor soul, she sat there hour after hour after hour, lookin' an' lookin', like as if she was waitin' for someone who she knew would never come, but she had to sit there hopin' an' prayin' anyway. 'Twas pitiful, it was."

Geyer was not sure why it should have, but a picture had risen up in his own mind and it all but overpowered him—a picture of his own Martha and Esther waiting for him . . . somewhere. "Thank you," he mumbled. "Thank you for your help." He turned and left the building hurriedly, a perplexed Tuttle at his heels.

"What was that all about?" the Detroit detective asked.

"That despicable unfeeling son of a bitch!"

"Who? What the hell are you talking about, Frank?"

"That bastard Holmes, that's who! Can you believe he has this poor Pitezel woman sitting cooped up here, scared out of her wits, not knowing whether her children are alive or dead, sitting in a window, waiting and watching. And here are those very children she's aching for, cooped up *three god-damned blocks away*—and the kids themselves are out of their minds with fright and worry and wonder over why their mama doesn't even write to them. And here's this son of a bitch Holmes standing back, stealing the letters they write and watching the anguish on both sides and getting a big laugh out of it all. Jesus God!"

They walked in silence for half a block and then Geyer spoke abruptly. "I'm finished here. For now, anyway. I'll be taking the train out tonight."

"Where to, Frank?"

Geyer considered this. Holmes and Georgiana had told Mrs. Ralston they were heading for Kingston, Ontario. Holmes and the girls had told Mrs. Burns they were heading for St. Louis. Carrie had told Miss Mulholland they were heading for Chicago. But all of them—Holmes, Georgiana and Carrie— in their statements in Philadelphia, had agreed on where they had gone from Detroit, and what they had agreed on was an entirely different destination.

"Toronto," Geyer replied.

It was Frank Geyer's custom—in addition to sending occasional telegrams—to write a report each Sunday afternoon to District Attorney Graham detailing his activities of the preceding week. This Sunday was no different and, though he detested paperwork, it served two very useful purposes—keeping Graham apprised of his progress, and serving to let his own wandering thoughts gel and perhaps point new directions. The reports he sent to Chief Linden were more formal and less filled with his own speculations.

He now tossed aside the newspaper he'd been reading on his bed, got to his feet and stretched prodigiously, then went to the little desk near the window and sat down. For half an hour he went over the notes he had taken this past week, gleaning from his shorthand a virtual total recall of events and conversations. Then he put them aside and bent to the task of writing his third such report.

> ROSSIN HOUSE, TORONTO
> ONTARIO, CANADA
> SUN. A.M., JULY 14TH, 1895

HON. GEORGE S. GRAHAM
DISTRICT ATTORNEY, PHILADELPHIA COUNTY
CITY HALL, PHILADELPHIA, PENNA.

DEAR SIR:

> *Although work is progressing well, I regret to say I do not yet see an end in sight to the investigation. Once during this week we thought sure we had*

come to the end of the particular trail, but all too soon that prospect took flight. As you know, when I completed the Detroit portion of the investigation last week, I was distressed more than ever at the terrible treatment Holmes gave to those who were apparently closest to him. The great anger I felt then for the man has tempered somewhat over these intervening days, but I fear my antipathy is so deep-rooted I will never become entirely free of it. This, I know, is not a good frame of mine for an investigator, but the very knowledge that it exists should help me to keep it from swaying me unduly and coloring judgment that needs to be impartial.

Immediately after finishing last week's report, I posted it to you and then packed my bags. I took a bite of dinner at the hotel and caught the late evening train out of Detroit for Toronto. It is a slow run, made slower by the necessity of passing through Customs upon entering Canada. There are also several extended stops en route, the most lengthy of which was at Hamilton, Ontario.

I arrived in Toronto at 9:30 A.M. I am not a stranger to this city, police work having brought me here on a number of occasions in the past. Thus, when I arrived at the station I had the cabman take me directly to this place, the Rossin House, where I have stayed before. I breakfasted and then took a short rest to relax from the long and tiresome ride, after which I gathered up my bundle of papers and photographs and proceeded to the police headquarters.

On entering the Detective Department, I met an old friend, Detective Sergeant Alfred Cuddy. After greeting him and shaking hands with all the boys whom I had met before, I was taken into the office of the kind, affable and courteous Inspector Stark, to whom I told the oft-repeated story. He listened to me very attentively, and then took me into the room of Chief Constable Grassett, whom I had not the pleasure of meeting before. To him I presented my letter of introduction from the superintendent of police of Philadelphia, and recounted to him the object of my errand. The chief assured me that his department would do everything in their power to assist me, and sent a messenger for Inspector Stark to come into the room. He instructed the Inspector to detail a man to work with me as long as he was needed. Thanking the chief for his courtesy and attention, I returned with the Inspector to the Detective Department, where my old friend Cuddy was assigned to help me out in Toronto. This suited me very well, for I knew Cuddy to be an energetic fellow and not afraid of work, and willing to keep on until every clue had been run out, and the investigation either a success or a failure. Into a private room we went, and I narrated the entire story to Cuddy, so that he would know what he was doing.

Proceeding as I did before, I thought it wise to examine the registers in the hotels around the Grand Trunk Depot, and we first wended our way to the Walker House and asked permission to see the register of 1894. We were informed that it had been packed away in the storeroom, but if it was important they would send a bell boy to get it. We told the clerk we would consider it a great favor if he would do so, and in a few minutes we had the register in our possession. Turning over the leaves until we came to October 18th, we found that "G. Howell and wife, Columbus," had registered for supper that day and left after dinner on the 20th, occupying room No. 14.

Our next visit was to the Union House. There the same request was made and complied with, and on the 18th of October we found the name of "Mrs. C. A. Adams and daughter, Columbus." Having located Holmes and Mrs. Pitezel, the next thing to do was to locate the girls, so we continued our search among the hotels, until we reached the Albion, and upon examining the register there found the names of "Alice and Nellie Canning, Detroit." This registry was made October 19th and had evidently been written by one of the girls.

The photographs of the girls were then shown to Mr. Herbert Jones, the chief clerk of the hotel, who positively identified them as the pictures of the children who were brought to the hotel by their porter, George Dennis, on Friday evening, October 19th. Mr. Jones also informed us that on the morning following their arrival, a gentleman called to see them and was there on almost every succeeding day during their stay at the hotel, with the exception of Sunday. The picture of Holmes was shown Mr. Jones. He recognized it as the man who called at the hotel for the children in the morning of the days they stopped at the hotel. He said this man took the children away with him for the day, but they usually returned alone in the evening for supper. On the morning of the 25th of October, this same man called as usual at the hotel, paid the children's board bill, took them away with him, and that is the last time they were seen by him or any one in the hotel.

Holmes having left the Walker House on the afternoon of October 20th, and knowing that he was in Toronto as late as the 25th, I determined to discover where he had registered and remained in another hotel—so I continued my search until we arrived at the Palmer House, and there, under the date of October 21st, we found him registered under the name of "H. Howell and wife, Columbus," room No. 32.

Mr. Graham, so thoroughly convinced was I that Holmes had rented a house in Toronto, Ontario, that after hearing Mr. Jones's story, I wrote in my report to the Superintendent of Police in Philadelphia, dated at Toronto, July 9th, 1895, the following: "It is my impression that Holmes rented a house in Toronto the same as he did in Cincinnati, Ohio, and Detroit, Michigan, and that on the 25th of October he murdered the girls and disposed of their bodies by either burying them in the cellar, or some convenient place, or burning them in the heater. I intend to go to all the real estate agents and see if they can recollect having rented a house about that time to a man who only occupied it for a few days, and who represented that he wanted it for a widowed sister."

Inspired by my belief that perseverance and energy would bring forth good result, I determined to get a Toronto directory and prepare a list of real *estate agents, and interview each and every one of them. So, on Wednesday morning, July 10th, I went to police headquarters, where I met Cuddy and suggested my idea to him. It was a big task, yet it had to be done, so in we started upon the directory— Cuddy reading off the names while I copied them. It took some time to prepare the list, and when finished we started, first going to those who were in the business portion of the city. It took considerable time to impress each agent with the importance of making a careful search for us, and before we knew it, night was upon us and the real estate offices were closed. Seriously meditating as to the best method to pursue to arouse the citizens of Toronto, I then determined to meet the newspapermen, give them my views of the case and explained to them my theories, so that the matter would be brought before the public, and the story of the disappearance of the children read in every household in the city.*

That night I was besieged by a number of reporters who called at my room in the Rossin House. I gave them the whole story, and told them I was prepared to let them have the photographs of Holmes and the children, and would esteem it a favor if they would publish them. I also requested them to call the attention of real estate agents and private renters to the matter, so that if any person had rented a house under such circumstances as I described, I would be glad to have them communicate with me.

The next morning every newspaper published in Toronto devoted several columns to the story of the disappearance of the children, and requested all good citizens to forward any information they might have to Police Headquarters, or to me at the Rossin House.

Thursday morning, July 11th, Detective Sergeant Cuddy and I continued our search among the real estate agents. We found a majority of them prepared to meet us, for they had read the morning papers and our task was thus facilitated very much. In the afternoon, we decided to visit several suburban towns, known as Mimico and North and South

Parkdale, so away we went singing the same old story to each and every agent we came across. However, we kept fighting on, hoping against hope, with no word or sign of encouragement. Another day went by and there was not the slightest clue to give us a grain of comfort. On our return to Police Headquarters, we received word that a man giving the name of Holmes had rented a house on the outskirts of the city—a house that stood in the middle of a field, and was surrounded by a board fence six feet high. This house was situated at Perth and Bloor Streets. We wanted nothing more, and away we journeyed. We found the house situated as already described, and occupied by an aged couple with a son about twenty years old. After introducing ourselves as officers, we ascertained from the old gentleman that they had only lived there a few months, and did not know who occupied the house the previous October. We explained to them our suspicions and said that we believed that Holmes had murdered the children, and had buried them somewhere under the house. "That accounts for that pile of loose dirt under the main building," said the old man. "Get a shovel" was Cuddy's suggestion, so the old man led the way to show us how we could get under the house, while the young man went in search of a shovel. He soon returned, and taking off our coats, we crawled into a small hole and were soon underneath the floor of the main building. The floor was not more than two feet above the earth, and it did not take us long to discover what the old gentleman meant by the pile of loose dirt. As it was getting dark, we requested that some light be furnished. The boy crawled out from under the floor and in a short time we had several coal oil lamps burning and commenced digging, feeling positive that we would unearth the children. A hole was dug about four feet square, when it was decided to give it up for the night and return the next morning.

Friday morning, July 12th, I called at Police Headquarters and met Cuddy, and proposed to him that we go and see the agent who rented the house at Perth and Bloor, and see if he could identify the *photograph of Holmes as the man who had rented the house. The agent was not a very early riser, consequently our patience was taxed in waiting for him. However, when he came and looked at the picture, he said that it was not the man. Again we were disappointed, and the balance of the day was spent at the Grand Trunk Depot, in trying to ascertain if there had been any half tickets sold on the morning of the 25th of October from Toronto to Suspension Bridge. The ticket agent treated us very courteously, and examined his records and found that on that day, there had been only one whole ticket sold for Niagara Falls, or Suspension Bridge. In answer to a question, whether a conductor would take a whole ticket for two children, he said he would, so we were unable to say positively that Holmes had not sent the girls to the Suspension Bridge to meet Minnie Williams, as he claimed to have done—he going as far as Parkdale.*

We then endeavored to learn through the freight office, what amount of baggage was shipped to Prescott, Canada, on the night of the 25th of October and the morning of the 26th. We learned that two pieces had been sent there on the night of the 25th, and one piece on the morning of the 26th. This corresponded with the amount of baggage carried by Holmes and Mrs. Pitezel, and convinced me that Prescott was the place they had gone to, and in the event of not meeting with success in Toronto, I determined that Prescott would be my next stopping place. As Holmes had left the Walker House on the afternoon of October 20th, and his whereabouts from that time until the afternoon of the 21st not being known, I was impressed with the belief that he had taken his wife to Niagara Falls.

Yesterday morning, July 13th, I concluded that I would go there and see if I could locate them, and if so, ascertain whether they had the children with them. Taking the boat to Lewistown, and from there the trolley cars, I arrived at Niagara Falls (Canada side) about 11 A.M., and began a search among the hotels, and in a short time my labor was rewarded by locating them at King's Imperial Hotel, where

*they arrived on the afternoon of the 20th, and left
on the afternoon of the 21st. There were no children
with them, and they had evidently gone there simply
to view the Falls.*

*I returned to Toronto and visited a number of
newspaper offices for the purpose of examining their
files, and made a list of private renters who advertised their houses to rent, as I intend to call upon
every one of them in person. Mr. Graham, I am so
positive that Holmes has disposed of the children in
Toronto, that I cannot think of leaving, until I have
made a more extended search. Last evening I met
with Cuddy for dinner, and over that we discussed
our plans for Monday morning.*

*That, then, is where we stand at this moment. I
am smitten at times with waves of disappointment,
as well dejection at not having located the objects of
this search. Yet I do not let such disappointments
and dejections prey upon me and soon they are
passed away and I am once again filled with the
hope that a new day will bring the culmination we
seek.*

*Should anything of more than ordinary signifi-
cance occur between now and next week at this
time, I will wire you immediately. Otherwise, I will
write you another report next Sunday. Until then, I
remain, sir,*

MOST RESPECTFULLY,
FRANK P. GEYER

When Detective Frank Geyer entered police headquarters on Monday, he had with him the list he had drawn up
late Saturday afternoon at the newspaper offices. It was quite
long. Over fifty private renters had advertised their house to
rent in the classified section of the papers last October and
these individuals were scattered all over the city.

Alf Cuddy made an exaggerated gulp when he saw the
list. "To think," he mourned, affecting an injured air, "I
actually *volunteered* to help in this thing. Next time I hear
you're coming, Frank, I'm going to put in for a vacation."

Geyer laughed. "Now, Alf, don't be that way. You know
it's not going to take more than two or three months to check
them out."

Cuddy groaned, then grinned. "Let's get at it. Oh, by the way, here's something else to check out while we're at it. Some old man, late seventies, came in yesterday afternoon and talked to the duty officer. Said he saw the stories in the newspapers and thinks he might have seen Holmes and the girls. More'n likely just wants a little limelight for himself and it'll turn out to be just one more blind lead. Anyway, the duty officer gave me this to give to you." He extended a slip of paper to Geyer. "It's the old man's name and address."

Geyer glanced at the note and saw the man's name was Thomas Ryves. Suddenly he became more alert. Cuddy watched curiously as he began paging rapidly through his list of renters and then jabbed his finger to one entry with an exclamation. "Alf, look here. This note from Ryves gives his address as eighteen St. Vincent Street. Now listen to this." He read aloud the address he was holding his finger to on the list. "'Mrs. Frank Nudel, fifty-four Henry Street: house to rent October twentieth at sixteen St. Vincent Street.'"

"Nudel?" Cuddy said. "I know Frank Nudel. He works over in the Education Department."

Cuddy was missing the point and Geyer shook his head. "The addresses, Alf," he said excitedly. "Look at them. The rental house was at sixteen St. Vincent. This Ryves man lives at eighteen St. Vincent!"

"Well, what do you know," Cuddy murmured, his own pulse quickening. "I guess that's our priority this morning. But I've got a suggestion. The last time we dug half the night and then when we checked with the agent, it was the wrong description. Let's not make the same mistake twice. I vote we go see Nudel first. We don't even have to go out to Henry Street. His office is only a block or so from here."

Geyer agreed and a few minutes later they were talking with Frank Nudel at the Toronto Education Department.

"Sure," Nudel told them when Cuddy finished explaining what they wanted. "My wife owns that sixteen St. Vincent house. And she did rent it to a man last October. He paid her a month's rent, but only stayed a week. She rented it later to someone else."

They thanked Nudel and left. The St. Vincent Street house was closer than Nudel's, so they decided to stop first at number eighteen and talk with Ryves. He turned out to be an alert old Scotsman with pure white hair, who instantly

invited them in when they identified themselves. The first
thing Geyer did was to show him the three important pictures.

"This could be the man," he said, indicating the picture
of Holmes, "but I'm not really positive. But I think this girl
here," he pointed at the picture of Nellie Pitezel, "is the one
I saw a couple of times. I never did get a good look at the
older girl," he touched the photo of Alice, "so I don't know
whether that's her or not."

"What did the man you saw tell you about his renting
this place?" Geyer asked.

"Only that he was renting it for his widowed sister, who
was over in Hamilton just then. Said he expected her in a few
days."

Geyer and Cuddy exchanged significant glances.

"Did he bring any kind of furnishings in?" Geyer asked.

"Anything unusual about his actions while he was here?"
Cuddy asked at the same time.

"Not much furniture that I saw," the old Scotsman
replied. "There was an old bed and a mattress. Oh, yes, a big
trunk, too. When he left, I saw he was taking the trunk
along, but he didn't have the bed or mattress." He shifted his
glance to Cuddy. "I didn't see him do anything particularly
unusual, except for borrowing my spade."

"Your spade!" The two detectives said it simultaneously.

Ryves was taken a little aback. "Why, yes. He borrowed
it because he said he wanted to dig a hole in the cellar for his
sister to store potatoes in."

"Mr. Ryves," Geyer said, "is anyone living next door
now?"

"Yes. Family name of Armbrust. Jim Armbrust, he's a
baker, I believe. His wife's name is Agnes. She's home most
of the time except Monday mornings when she goes to
market. That's where she is right now, but she's usually gone
only an hour or two, so she ought to be back pretty soon."

Geyer nodded. "All right. We're going to go see Mrs.
Nudel and then we'll be back. Will you be here?"

"I will."

"Fine. We'll see you again soon. Come on, Alf."

It was Mrs. Nudel's daughter who answered when they
rang the bell at 54 Henry Street. Cuddy recognized her and
smiled. "Morning, Charlotte," he said. "This is a friend of
mine, Frank Geyer. Is your mother home?"

"Yes, she is."

"Could you tell her," Geyer spoke up, "that we'd like to see her at once. It's very important."

"Of course. Please, come in." She showed them into the parlor, asked them to be seated and said she'd be right back. In a minute or so she returned with her mother. Without giving them much of a chance to say anything, Geyer handed her the photograph of Holmes.

"Have you ever seen this man before?"

The two women looked at it and in unison agreed they had. "It's Mr. Howard," Mrs. Nudel elaborated. "The man who rented my house on St. Vincent Street. The one who paid rent for a whole month but only stayed a few days."

"Did he tell you why he wanted it?" Cuddy asked.

"Yes. He said it was for his widowed sister who would be coming on from Detroit in a few days."

Geyer quickly explained why they were asking their questions and the two women were shocked, especially when he told them he thought the two girls might be buried in the cellar. "I'm sure you won't mind, Mrs. Nudel," he concluded, "if we go back out there right now to check."

"No," she said. "No, of course not. Just tell Mrs. Armbrust I said it was all right."

They left immediately and returned to Ryves's house and borrowed his spade. He told them he'd been watching and Mrs. Armbrust had returned shortly after they left to see Mrs. Nudel, but he hadn't spoken to her. "I'll introduce you to her if you want," he added.

He led them to the house and the door was opened by a prematurely gray middle-aged woman. When she learned what they wanted she led them at once to the kitchen and pulled back the piece of linoleum covering the trapdoor. Geyer lifted the lid.

"Not very deep," he said, "but dark. Would you happen to have a lamp or two you might let us borrow, Mrs. Armbrust?"

She said she had and brought them to him. Geyer and Cuddy took off their coats and descended into the cellar with the lighted lamps. A cursory inspection disclosed a few boards and building debris, but no real indication that any digging had been done. They used the space to test the earth at intervals and found it very hard until they got to the southwest corner. Tossing some boards and other debris aside, they jabbed at the ground with the spade and found it was softer there. At once they began to dig and within moments a disgusting stench assailed their nostrils. They continued digging grimly and at a depth of about three feet they uncovered what appeared to be the bone of a human arm.

"That's it," Geyer said. There was no exultation in his voice, only a heaviness. He tossed a few shovelfuls of dirt back into the hole, covering over what little of the remains they'd exposed, in order to help keep down the stench. Then they returned to the kitchen.

"How do you want to handle it?" Cuddy asked.

"I think first of all we'd better tell Inspector Stark and have him tell us what undertaker we should get to bring out the bodies."

Cuddy agreed and they asked Mrs. Armbrust if she had a telephone. She did not, but she said there was one in the telegraph office on Yonge Street a few blocks away. They went there at once and Cuddy placed the call.

"Inspector? Alf Cuddy here. We found the bodies of the girls.... Yes sir.... Absolutely.... Who?... Just a minute, I'll find out." He put a hand over the mouthpiece of the box phone on the wall, lowered the receiver from his ear and turned to Geyer. "Stark says there's a Toronto reporter in his office right now. Any objection to letting him know?"

"They went out of their way to help us. I'd say it's okay, sure."

Cuddy spoke into the telephone again. "He says it's all right, sir.... Yes sir, all I can, but there's not much yet. We left as soon as we found them to call and let you know. They're buried in the cellar at sixteen St. Vincent Street.... No, rental tenants. Name of Armbrust. The owner's Frank Nudel's wife. You know Frank, I think.... Yes sir.... Education Department. His wife rented the place to Holmes last October. He stayed a few days, killed the girls and buried them and left.... No, sir. Just enough to determine the remains were human. The smell's pretty bad. We covered it a little bit to hold it down when we left to call you. Geyer wants to know what undertaker we should have come and collect the remains.... Humphrey?... Yes sir, I know where.... You will?... Right, sir. We'll be there.... Thank you, sir.... Yes, sir, I'll tell him.... Yes, sir.... All right, Inspector. Good-bye."

He hung up the telephone and turned to Geyer, grinning widely. "Damn, he's more excited than we are. And you should've heard that reporter in the background. We're going to have them at the house in droves. Stark said he'll contact A. J. Johnston—he's our coroner—and get him over there right away. In the meanwhile, he said for us to go to B. D. Humphrey's place, just a block from here—he's the undertaker—and tell him what we want him to do. Oh, and Frank, he said to pass on his congratulations to you on one hell of a fine job of investigative work. He's damned impressed."

Geyer was pleased, but he was all business now. "Let's go over to see Humphrey and then get back to the house. I don't want reporters running all over the place without us there."

At the Humphrey Undertaker Parlor on Yonge Street, only half a block from the telegraph office, they quickly briefed Bernard Humphrey on the situation and the fact that Inspector Stark had authorized his exhumation of the bodies. "You'd better bring several pairs of rubber gloves," Geyer added. "The bodies are in such a state of decay it'll be impossible to lift them out of the hole without them."

Humphrey, a man of about thirty, wisely brought along a heavy smock and put it on over his clothes before getting into the hole to help Geyer and Cuddy. They worked quietly and grimly, sickened by the stench as they uncovered the remains of the two girls, head to feet, one atop the other. The top one had a long braid attached to the scalp. In many places there was still a good bit of decayed flesh adhering to the bones and as they were making preparations to lift the remains out of the hole, a messenger was sent to the funeral parlor to have two coffins sent to them. They spread a rubberized sheet and attempted to lift the body that was on top—Nellie's—but so advanced was the decomposition that the weight of the braided hair pulled the scalp off her head. They placed the remains on the sheet, along with the hair, and wrapped the sheet around it, then carried it upstairs. Johnston, the coroner, had arrived, as well as a score or more of reporters, photographers and sketch artists. Their clamor was augmented by crowds that had been attracted. By this time the wagon from the funeral parlor had also arrived with the coffins and they placed the sheet containing its grisly weight inside one of them and returned to the cellar.

The removal of Alice's remains was accomplished in the same manner and they were placed in the second coffin. By this time perhaps a hundred onlookers were crowded in front of the building in a great semicircle that stretched clear across St. Vincent Street. Congratulations were called to the detectives from all sides and there was a hubbub of voices, many expressing horror at the discoveries.

Geyer and Cuddy were finished here for the time being and they parted, Cuddy returning to headquarters to write his report, Geyer planning to do the same at the Rossin House, but first returning to the telegraph office. The wire he sent to Graham was one that he had begun to wonder if he would ever send:

GEORGE S GRAHAM STOP DISTRICT ATTORNEY STOP CITY HALL STOP PHILA PENNA STOP 2:45 P.M. JULY 15 1985 STOP

SIR STOP SUCCESS STOP BODIES OF ALICE AND NELLIE PITEZEL FOUND BURIED IN CELLAR OF HOUSE IN TORONTO STOP PRELIMINARY INQUEST WILL BE HELD SOONEST STOP FINAL INQUEST PENDS ARRIVAL CARRIE PITEZEL TO IDENTIFY REMAINS STOP PLEASE CONTACT HER WITH INSTRUCTIONS TO COME HERE SOONEST STOP WILL MEET HER TRAIN IF SHE NOTIFIES ME OF ARRIVAL STOP GEYER

"I'm takin' a hell of a risk bringing this morning's paper to you," the Moyamensing guard said. "I could lose my job."

"You bring me a newspaper every morning, as arranged for by my lawyer," Holmes said. "Why should this morning be different from any other?" He did not look terribly well. Not only had he lost weight, but he seemed to have lost the inclination to keep himself looking neat and presentable. As with other prisoners who could afford to do so, he had from the beginning elected to wear and care for his own clothes, rather than wear the drab garb supplied by the prison. Now, however, his black suit was soiled and rumpled and he looked shabby.

"I don't know and I don't care," the guard whispered. "All I know is that the D.A. sent word here yesterday you weren't to be allowed to see any more newspapers until he had an interview with you this morning. This is going to cost you extra."

"An interview this morning?" It was the first Holmes had heard anything of it. He glanced at the guard. "You'll get extra. Now get out of here."

As soon as the guard was gone he walked to the other side of the cell where the light was better next to the window. He opened the paper and the headline struck him with almost physical impact:

BODIES OF MISSING GIRLS FOUND

Toronto Cellar Yields Pathetic Corpses
After Determined Search by Detective Geyer

SWINDLER HOLMES IS MURDERER

Mother of Alice and Nellie Pitezel Is
En route to Toronto to Identify Remains

Holmes's legs very nearly caved in beneath him. His reaching hand grasped the back of the chair and he lowered himself into it, heart pounding with brutal impact in his chest, his breath catching in his throat. The article was a wire story out of Toronto and he started to read it but could not finish. The print blurred in his vision and he buried his face in his hands, the paper falling to the floor. For several minutes he sat this way and then he straightened. He laid out a fresh shirt and suit of clothes and ran water into his small basin to cleanse himself and shave. He had to look presentable when summoned to the district attorney's office.

As he made his physical preparations, his mind raced, adjusting itself to a new story to meet the unexpectedly changed situation.

George Graham was furious.

"If I find out who supplied Holmes with that newspaper this morning," he growled to Tom Barlow, his special assistant, "he'll be the sorriest individual there ever was. Damn! I really wanted to spring this on him by surprise. Do you know he was all cleaned up and in a fresh suit and waiting for Genteen and Alexander when they got there? And what was his reaction?" He mimicked what Detective Genteen and Court Officer Alexander told him Holmes had said. "'Oh, this is rough. It's eleven o'clock now and lunch is served in an hour. If I go, I'll miss my meal.' That cool bastard!" His face was suffused with the anger and it was only with difficulty that he composed himself. He motioned with his head for his special assistant to follow him into the room where Holmes, under guard, was waiting. In no mood for amenities, he was brusque in the extreme.

"Holmes, I won't ask you who smuggled that newspaper in to you this morning. We'll find out soon enough. What I want to know is why you killed and buried those Pitezel children in Toronto."

"I?" Holmes said with an aggrieved tone. "Mr. Graham, I'm surprised at you. You're grasping at straws. I had nothing whatever to do with their deaths, if, in fact, they really are dead."

"Then suppose you clarify for me how you could have taken the girls from Toronto, as you said you did, to Niagara Falls, turned them over to Minnie Williams, as you said you did, and yet now their bodies turn up buried in a cellar in Toronto."

"Mr. Graham," Holmes answered politely, wholly unruffled, "I can only tell you, in light of this discovery, what I surmise must have happened. You remember I have mentioned this rascal Hatch, who sometimes did business with me? You remember that I had Mrs. Pitezel in Toronto at the same time as the girls and didn't let her know they were there? There was a good reason for that. We thought about sending her along to Europe with Minnie and the children, but she'd been in an extremely anxious state of mind and wasn't getting any better. We believed she would jeopardize everything in her frame of mind, so we decided it was better she be left in the dark."

"We, Holmes? We, who?"

"Minnie, Hatch and myself."

"This Hatch you talk about—he was in on this from the beginning?"

"Of course he was. That's what I've been telling you for weeks. Anyway, Hatch was in Toronto with me at the time we decided to send Nellie and Alice on to Niagara Falls, where Minnie and Howard were. It had been getting harder and harder to keep Carrie from finding out the girls were there. I took the girls to the railroad station and Hatch was there by prearrangement. When I was about to get off the train, Hatch suggested he accompany the girls a few stations farther so that there would not be any mistakes about their tickets. Nellie and Alice were traveling on half-fares, and I wanted to be sure they got along on one whole ticket, which the conductor had taken up when I left the train. So Hatch went along with the children, and he can tell where they are to be found if anybody can. All I can fathom out of this is that somehow hatch found out about the thousand dollars I'd pinned in Alice's dress..."—Graham shot a meaningful glance at Barlow, since this was the first time Holmes had ever mentioned $1,000 pinned into Alice's dress—"...and the four hundred I'd pinned in Nellie's, and in order to get it he had to kill them. Then he probably threatened Minnie with death, too, if she didn't go over to England and send me word that they'd arrived over there all right. Beyond that, I don't know a thing. I never harmed a hair on the heads of those children. Hatch and Minnie—they're the key to this whole business. Find them and you'll have all the answers. And you can question me all you want beyond this, but I'm not going to add another word. I'm sick and tired of this whole thing. Now, if you'll have me taken back to my cell, please? I prefer the company of my roommates there—two spiders and a mouse."

A muscle in Graham's jaw twitched, but he motioned Genteen and Alexander to take Holmes away.

Back in his cell following the interview with Graham, Holmes immediately wrote to Dora. The letter, he knew, would be read by prison officials and then no doubt relayed to Graham's office to be checked again there for any secret message or code. And, indeed, there was a very definite code in it, but he had no fear it would be detected.

> MOYAMENSING COUNTY PRISON
> JULY 16, 1895
>
> DEAR DORA:
>   You undoubtedly have no desire to hear from me, yet I feel compelled to write to ask forgiveness for the shame I've brought to your life. As you no doubt know by now, they have found the bodies of the Pitezel girls and are blaming their deaths on me, though I had nothing to do with it. I doubt that you have any great concern about me now, but I'm

sending this just in case you are wondering what to do now with that part of me that has been left behind.

You may wish I hadn't written but don't worry, because I will never again write to you. I know you well enough to realize you still feel a certain amount of concern, even though you no longer love me. That such a dreadful thing was done to those poor children I cannot believe. Were I truly guilty of this monstrosity, I would not think ill of them if they hanged me immediately, without a trial.

Feel free to do anything you wish with the house, since it's now yours. Any personal possessions of mine that are still there you can merely discard or place in the hands of needy people.

All letters written by inmates of this place are censored by the authorities for incriminating comments, but who would incriminate himself? It is more than enough that I and my loved ones have been subjected to the humiliation of all this, and everything about my whole life seems pointless now. I guess my biggest concern is that, where I am concerned, you will burn with hatred for the rest of your life. I only hope you will not think your world is ruined because of my crimes, for people are fundamentally good and will understand your plight and nothing is really lost to you, no matter what problems you may envision.

I did not wish to bring you heartache and though you must feel unkindly toward me, there is still one small favor that I would ask of you. Can you possibly find it in your heart to momentarily put aside all enmity toward me long enough to write and send your forgiveness? I don't think you can appreciate how imperative, how very imperative! *it is in my present state to at least know this much.*

Give my love to our darling daughter Lucy and please try not to think too badly of me. I have not done all the terrible things they are attributing to me.

YOUR HUSBAND
H. H. HOLMES

The letter from Henry arrived in the morning's mail on July 20 and Dora Holmes grimaced as she removed it from her mailbox. Though the envelope was sealed, it was obvious that it had been opened and reclosed. She returned into the house and locked the door. Lucy was close to her legs, and Dora called to the maid to come get her and take her upstairs. When they were gone, she took the letter into the study and opened it carefully. As she unfolded the pages she saw immediately that it was a coded letter. The clue to this was that in the salutation, Holmes had greeted her as *Dear Dora* instead of *Dear Myrta* as he ordinarily did. With that clue alerting her to the fact that there was a secret message contained, she studied the letter carefully.

The deciphering was easy enough if one knew what to do. The first and last paragraphs in the body of the letter were to be ignored. Beginning with the second paragraph and continuing to the end of the next to the last paragraph, the process was as follows: the last word of the first sentence was to be circled; then the next-to-last word in the second sentence; the third from the last in the third sentence and so on through the remainder of the pertinent paragraphs with this progression. When finally all were circled, the order of the selected words was reversed and that was the coded message. In this case the hidden words read:

> Imperative! *All is lost. Burn everything incriminating in house immediately. I love you.*

The fireplaces in the Wilmette house were kept busy the remainder of the day as Dora fed into the flames every scrap of material that might be construed as incriminating, including every piece of material that had been brought from the Castle to the house.

Financially secure for the rest of her life, Dora Belknap Holmes knew she was now finished forever with involvement in any illegalities. She knew also, with sudden certainty, that she would never again see the man who had been her husband.

"Alf, just saying thanks seems awfully inadequate after all you've done to help me. Maybe someday, somehow, I'll be able to repay the favor. I hope so."

Cuddy grinned and gripped Geyer's outstretched hand. "You'd've done exactly the same, Frank, if our positions had been reversed. You know that. Hell, it was great working with you. We make a pretty damned good team, if I do say so myself."

"We do at that, don't we? I won't forget it, Alf. Thanks."

The handshake turned into a warm embrace as the two men hugged one another. When they stepped apart the conductor was calling "Boaaaarrrd!" and Geyer stepped up into the train. He stood in the doorway as the train began to move, raised a hand in final farewell to his friend and moved inside the train, not looking forward at all to this ride.

Carrie Pitezel was already seated in the car, cloaked in a contagious mantle of misery; just being in her presence was deadly depressing. It reminded Geyer far too painfully of his own depression of these past months. Yet, he knew he would sit with her without complaint, doing all he could to ease the burden that these past few days had been for her.

She sat midway in the coach, on the right-hand side, her gaze sliding across the cityscape of Toronto, unseeing, uncaring. She seemed unaware of him when he prepared to sit beside her, she spoke without turning, her voice flat and dull.

"Mr. Geyer, would you mind a very great deal if I sat alone on this ride? I don't have any more words left in me right now. I don't have anything." She turned then and looked at him, her face etched in lines of grief. She bit her lower lip and then reached out and touched his hand. "I just would like it if I could be left to myself. Please?"

"I wouldn't think of disturbing you if you wish to be alone, Mrs. Pitezel." He glanced around and saw that the first seat at the front left of the car was unoccupied. "I'll be up toward the front of the car on the other side if you need me," he added, but she was no longer listening.

He reached up and brought down his valise from the luggage rack, leaving his large suitcase next to her luggage. He was feeling a little guilty at the lift in his spirits at not having to sit with her, and not merely because of the depressiveness of it. This was Sunday, his day for writing the weekly report to District Attorney Graham. If he sat with her, it would have meant hours of tiring riding and then having to spend hours beyond that in writing the report when he finally got to his hotel.

Now, all but giddy at his reprieve, he raised the flap table and sat down. From his case he removed his notebooks, bedraggled with the wear of heavy use, and settled back to review this past week's very eventful occurrences. In moments he was even less aware of the train's passage through the Ontario countryside than was Carrie Pitezel.

At last, with Toronto twenty miles behind, he shoved the notebooks aside and began to write his report:

JULY 21, 1895

MR. GEORGE S. GRAHAM
DIST. ATT'Y., PHILADELPHIA COUNTY
CITY HALL, PHILADELPHIA, PENNA.

DEAR MR. GRAHAM:

I will open this week's report with an apology for any difficulty you may have reading what I will write. I am at this moment aboard the Canadian Pacific train, taking advantage of the hours stretching out like the miles before me. The car sways and rocks and bumps at the whim of those who wielded tong and hammer to build this road and I can only trust that their way was smooth and their minds at peace so that my written lines will not stray too far from the parallel.

By our telegram messages of last Monday and the brief letter I wrote you that night, you have already been apprised of the events of that fateful day of discovery. Now I shall pick up the thread of account on the following morning, Tuesday, July 16th.

I met Detective Sergeant Cuddy at headquarters and we set off to find the tenant who had succeeded Holmes in the St. Vincent Street house. We sought out Mrs. Nudel once more and learned from her that she had rented it, a month after Holmes's departure, to a family named MacDonald. Unfortunately, the MacDonalds had stayed only a short while and then moved away, to where, no one seemed to know. But then, due largely to Cuddy's tenacious searching and questioning among mer-

chants and postal carriers, their present whereabouts was pinpointed to No. 17 Russell Street.
Cuddy and I called there and explained to Mrs.
MacDonald the object of our visit. At first she said
all she had found at the St. Vincent Street house on
moving in was an old bedstead and mattress.
Discovering that she had a 16-year-old son, Willis,
who was not at home just then, and knowing the
curiosity of youth, I requested that she send him to
see us at police headquarters as soon as he arrived
home and for him to bring along anything he had
found at the St. Vincent Street house. The remainder of the day was taken up with interviews with
reporters who flocked to us in seemingly never-
ending droves, flashing their stories across the country. It was through them that we learned that
Chicago authorities, at last fully convinced that
Holmes was more than merely a swindler, had ordered that his strange Castle be searched and its
cellar floor unearthed in a search for bodies, since
any number of missing persons there are believed to
have wound up as his victims. That may be only the
familiar sort of hysteria one encounters at such
times or it may be true, but that is neither here nor
there insofar as our present investigation is concerned. We had found the missing girls, but for the
disappearance of their brother, Howard, there was
no answer.

While we were at the MacDonald house, Coroner A. J. Johnston, a very kindly man, called up a
Coroner's Jury for the inquest, which he announced
would be held at the morgue at half past seven
o'clock. He sent me a message requesting my presence there. This was only to be a preliminary inquest to view the bodies. As soon as we had all
presented ourselves and the Jury was sworn, Dr.
Johnston sent for the morgue superintendent, who
announced everything was ready. Dr. Johnston thereupon sent the jurors into the dead house to examine
the bodies. Their visit was very limited, I assure
you, as none could long bear the offensive stench of
the decomposed remains. Dr. Johnston then adjourned

the inquest until the next evening, the 17th, when the jury would meet at Police Court, City Hall.

Very early Wednesday morning the MacDonald lad showed up at headquarters, bringing with him a little wooden egg which, when parted in the middle, allowed a toy snake to spring out. He told us he had discovered it in a small leather purse in one of the upstairs closets. I immediately referred to the list of items Mrs. Pitezel had supplied me with of clothing, toys, books and the like that the children had with them so far as she knew. Thereon, to my elated surprise, I found a description of just such an egg, making it a strong link in the chain of identification. Another link of the chain was forged by Mrs. Armbrust. As you know now, the children's bodies were found in a nude condition (as well as the feet of the younger girl, Nellie, being missing) and part of our inquiry dealt with the manner in which their clothing had been disposed of. A part of a waist and a piece of ribbon were found in the grave with the children, but the important discovery was made by Mrs. Armbrust shortly after she had moved into the St. Vincent Street house. She said she had seen some rags and straw hanging down from the chimney in the front room fireplace. She pulled them down and found part of a gray striped waist, a piece of brownish-red woolen garment and a section of blue cloth. In a woodbox she had discovered a pair of girl's button boots and one odd boot, along with other bits of clothing. All these things she had thrown away, but each matched the description of clothing on the list earlier supplied by Mrs. Pitezel.

Because Mr. Ryves had mentioned the trunk Holmes had brought with him and then took away, we thought there might have been the possibility that he had brought the body of Howard to the house in it from Detroit and had also buried him in the cellar. We hired a crew of men and had them dig up every inch of the cellar, but nothing further was found.

It is my personal belief, based on what we found in the house, that Holmes, in killing the girls, somehow enticed them to climb into the large trunk

*that was in his possession when he was arrested—
the one with the circular hole bored through the top
lid. Perhaps he told them someone was approaching
the house to do them harm and that they should
hide in the trunk. Whatever the case, I deduce that
he managed to get them into this trunk and latched
the lid and then, utilizing a length of rubber hose,
attached one end to the gas jet on the wall and put
the other end into the trunk through the hole on
top. He then turned on the gas and asphyxiated
them, after which he disrobed and buried them,
having first cut off Nellie's distinctive feet to help
confound possible identification.*

*The finding of the bodies, as I have said,
caused great excitement in Toronto and if the good
people of the city had been furnished with an opportunity, I'm sure they would have made short
shrift of Holmes. The press now follows us everywhere we go, as do hoards of sightseers.*

*I received your notification that you had wired
Mrs. Pitezel at the home of her friends where she
was staying in Chicago and asked her to come to
Toronto to meet me and, if possible, to identify the
remains as her children. Also your later wire that
she would inform me of her expected arrival time
here so I could meet her. (I was also pleased to learn
that you had wired Miss Georgiana Yoke, invoking
her promise to come to Philadelphia to testify if the
bodies of the children be found, and especially
pleased to learn that she had wired back that she
was on her way to you. Perhaps now we shall find
some answers that have eluded us.)*

*At the continuing inquest on Wednesday eve-
ning, I informed the coroner that Mrs. Pitezel would
be coming, but probably not until the following day.
I'm afraid I was encouraged to monopolize that
Wednesday evening session of the inquest and was
on the stand for two hours and a half reciting, as
much for the reporters as for the Jury, the story of
Holmes and the insurance swindle and the disappearance and finding of the children. A few other
witnesses were briefly heard and then the meeting
was adjourned to await the arrival of Mrs. Pitezel.*

On Thursday morning I received a wire from Mrs. Pitezel informing me that she had left Chicago and was on her way to Toronto. Unfortunately, she neglected to inform me the hour when her train was to arrive. I found it necessary, therefore, to be on hand to greet every incoming train during the day, none of which bore Mrs. Pitezel. I finally left in the early evening to take some dinner and get word to Dr. Johnston that he would have to postpone the evening's inquest until the next evening, since Mrs. Pitezel had not yet arrived. When I returned to the Grand Trunk Depot, at 7:30 P.M., I found the station a mob of people awaiting her arrival. Apparently everyone in Toronto but I knew when she was due in. The reason for this, as I later ascertained, was that Chicago reporters had been dogging her with great persistence up to the time when she had boarded her train and left for Toronto, at which time the papers wired their correspondents in Toronto of the arrival time and the news spread quickly.

Only a short time after my return to the station her train arrived and I observed her getting off the car. Immediately the crowd pressed around her and the reporters began firing questions at her. She declined to answer questions or make a statement. She was dressed all in black and of mournful countenance. I discovered that several ladies on the train had tried to engage her in conversation to cheer her up, but to no avail. One of the passengers told me she had cried all the way from Chicago and now, pressed by the crowd and reporters, she cried all the more bitterly. When one of the reporters shouted the question, "Do you think Holmes is the murderer of your daughters?", she became all but hysterical. I had a most difficult task making my way through the crowd to meet her, but quickly as possible I placed her in a carriage I had hired and took her to the Rossin House, where I had made arrangements to have her placed under medical care in the room opposite my own. When we entered, still followed by crowds, I left word that she was not to be disturbed.

She was in an absolutely prostrated condition

when we reached her room and a kindly chamber-maid applied restoratives. In a short time she had revived sufficiently to talk to me and amid tears and groans she said, "Oh, Mr. Geyer, is it true that you have found my Alice and Nellie buried in a cellar?"

I did all I could to calm her, but it was necessary to tell her that she must prepare for the worst. She promised she would try to bear up with it and would do the best she could. I then told her gently as I could that I found the children, but I did not describe to her their horrible condition, nor under what circumstances they were discovered. I did not stay with her long, leaving her to rest, with several of the hotel's ladies charged with seeing to her needs and comfort.

On Friday morning, July 19, I knocked at Mrs. Pitezel's door and found that she had improved, feeling somewhat rested even though she had not slept well. She told me Chicago was in a frenzy and that full pages of the newspapers were being devoted to story after story about the Holmes case. I was much bothered by the fact that Holmes was already tried and convicted as a murderer in the press there and even a newspaper as respected and normally restrained as the Chicago Tribune was referring to Holmes as the arch-fiend! I told her I would go out and make arrangements for taking her to the morgue during the day to look at the children. I then left and was joined by Detective Sergeant Cuddy at headquarters, after which we called at Coroner Johnston's house. He told us he hoped to have the bodies so arranged that we could bring the mother to look at them at four o'clock in the afternoon.

The Armbrust family was given leave to return to their home and they did, but they stayed only a short while and by evening had left again, the reason being that despite efforts to fumigate the house, the stench of the dead bodies found there is so bad they cannot stand it.

Cuddy and I then returned to the Rossin House, where we took every care possible to prepare Mrs. Pitezel for the awful ordeal that lay ahead of her. I was especially sensible of what she would have to go *through, since only so recently I had undergone the similar horror of having to identify the terrible remains of my own wife and daughter. As I had been instructed to do by Coroner Johnston, I told her that it would be absolutely impossible for her to view anything but Alice's teeth and hair and only the hair of Nellie. This had such a paralyzing effect upon her that she almost fainted. Knowing what was ahead, I prepared for the worst.*

At 4 P.M. we had a carriage at the Rossin House and I informed her we were ready to proceed to the morgue. In a few minutes she was ready and, after supplying ourselves with brandy and smelling salts, we started for the morgue. A fairly large crowd of reporters had gathered outside the door and they pressed eagerly upon us on our arrival. Mrs. Pitezel was seated in a waiting room while I went into the dead house to see that everything was in readiness before conducting her in. I found that Coroner Johnston, along with his physician, Dr. John Cavan, and several assistants, had removed the putrid flesh from the skull of Alice. The teeth had been nicely cleaned and the bodies covered with canvas. The head of Alice was covered with paper and a hole sufficiently large had been cut in it so that Mrs. Pitezel could see the teeth. The hair of both children had been carefully washed and laid on the canvas sheet which was covering Alice. The coroner said we could now bring Mrs. Pitezel in.

I entered the waiting room and told her we were now ready. With Cuddy on one side and I on the other, we entered and led her up to the slab upon which was lying all that remained of poor Alice. In an instant she recognized the teeth and hair of her daughter, Alice, pointing to a peculiarity in the upper front row of teeth. Then turning to me she asked, "Where is Nellie?" About this time she noticed the long dark plait of hair belonging to Nellie lying in the canvas. She could stand it no longer, and the shrieks of that poor forlorn creature are still ringing in my ears. Tears were trickling down the cheeks of strong men who stood about us. The sufferings of the stricken mother were beyond description. We gently led her out of the room and into the carriage. She returned to the Rossin House completely overcome with grief and despair, having one fainting spell after another. The ladies in the hotel visited and expressed kind sympathy to her in her bereavement and this seemed to ease her mind.

At 7 P.M. I received word from Coroner Johnston that, if it were possible, he would like to have Mrs. Pitezel attend the inquest that evening and give her testimony. While I did not feel she was in a fit condition to leave the hotel, I communicated to her what Dr. Johnston had said, and she said she thought she would be able to go and get through with it. At 7:30 P.M. I called a carriage and we started for the City Hall, where I gave Mrs. Pitezel in charge of a matron and then went into the court room and informed Coroner Johnston that she was ready to testify. Testimony was then being given by the 16-year-old Willis MacDonald, in which both the purse was identified as having belonged to one of the girls and the toy snake as having belonged to Howard Pitezel. They asked us to bring her in and Detective Sergeant Cuddy and I brought her in and placed her on a seat beside the coroner. In a few moments, after taking the necessary oath, she began her story. For two hours and a half this poor woman was kept on the stand and prodded with all kinds of questions. So weak did she become that at times her voice became inaudible and several times we feared she would totally collapse. Finally the Crown's Assistant Attorney thought he had heard enough and consented to allow her to leave the stand. She returned to the matron's room and was scarcely there when she became hysterical and her shrieks for Alice and Nellie and Howard could have been heard a block away. Several doctors present at the inquest immediately prescribed for her and, after working with her about an hour, we got her in condition to move her to the hotel. The matron at City Hall was a professional nurse and volunteered to accompany Mrs. Pitezel to the hotel and remain with her during the night, if she desired it. I was only too willing to have her join us and render the poor woman all the assistance and sympathy possible. I sent for a carriage and we returned to the hotel, where Mrs. Pitezel spent a terrible night.

The inquest had revealed to everyone's surprise with what apparent ease Holmes had murdered the two little girls in the very center of the city of Toronto without arousing the least suspicion of a single person there. It startles one to realize how such a hideous crime could be committed and detection avoided. Surely if the investigation and search for the children had not been made by the Philadelphia authorities, these murders would never have been discovered and Mrs. Pitezel would have gone to her grave without knowing whether her children were alive or dead. This was the one consolation she had in the very darkest hour of her life: she knew the fate of her unfortunate daughters—the mystery of their disappearance had been solved and the only remaining problem was the discovery of her little son, Howard. She could not believe he was dead and clung fondly to the hope that he would ultimately be found alive.

Yesterday was not so traumatic as the days before, but it was nevertheless a very sad day. In the afternoon, Cuddy and I placed Mrs. Pitezel between us on the seat of an enclosed carriage and we followed the hearse carrying the two coffins containing the remains of Alice and Nellie Pitezel. It led us to the two small graves that had been newly dug at St. James Cemetery. Mrs. Pitezel was barely up to the ordeal, after the previous events, but she nevertheless insisted on going. To prevent crowds, no advance public notice of the funeral had been given—expenses for which were borne by Toronto authorities—and so the three of us were the only mourners at the short burial service given at graveside by the Reverend W. F. Wilson of Trinity Methodist Church. It was a sad scene.

Now it is Sunday again and I am near the end of this lengthy report. Mrs. Pitezel is on the train with me and I was prepared to sit with her. and console her on the journey as best I could, but she spared me this endeavor by saying that she needed to be alone. She is taking the train all the way to Chicago, where she will again stay several days with her friends, Mr. and Mrs. Eugene Hayward of 6046 S. Sangamon Street, before she continues to her parents' home in Galva, Illinois. As for me, I will be leaving this train at Detroit, to resume once more the search that I hope will eventually lead me to the discovery of Howard Pitezel.

Again, should anything of special consequence occur, I shall send you a wire at once. Otherwise, you may expect to hear from me again in the weekly report I will write for you next Sunday. Until then, I remain, Sir,

MOST RESPECTFULLY YOURS,
FRANK P. GEYER

"If you feel that way, George," Tom Barlow said reasonably, "why don't you just hold off giving the press a statement. No one says you have to."

Graham shook his head and turned away from his special assistant and stood looking out the window at a small flock of pigeons circling over the trees in the park area surrounding City Hall. "I can't do that," he said. "A public servant can keep his actions and plans quiet only so long and then the clamor of public outcry forces him to make a statement. Normally I don't mind doing that. I've always had good relations with the press. This time it's a little different. I want this man Holmes. I want to convict him. I want to see him hang. We know he's a murderer. We know he killed the Pitezel girls. He probably killed the Pitezel boy. According to the papers out of Chicago, it looks like he might have made a business out of killing people. They're already screaming in their headlines that he's killed ten or twenty or maybe a hundred people, but so far it's only talk. Where's the proof? How in the name of God can a man have committed so many crimes as Holmes appears to have done and left so goddamned little evidence? Now the reporters are waiting for me to go out there and tell them that I'm charging him with murder."

"We know he killed Benjamin Pitezel here in Philadelphia," Barlow pointed out.

"No, Tom, we don't *know* that. We suspect it. All the evidence we have points to it, but we don't have hard proof."

"What about just letting Toronto have him? Or Chicago? Or Fort Worth? They all want to try him, and they've all got good grounds."

The district attorney spun away from the window, his nostrils flaring, brows pinched together. "Because *I* want to nail him. That son of a bitch came into my jurisdiction and cold-bloodedly murdered a man who just happened to be his friend, and I intend for the people of this city and state to know that you can't get away with murder in Philadelphia. Yet, here we are with the man in custody and the only crime we can *prove* he's committed here is defrauding an insurance company. The last I heard, that wasn't a hanging offense."

"Well, *are* we going to slap the murder charge on him?"

Graham flung out an arm in a helpless gesture. "I don't know. I just don't know. I'm working toward that end but it's touchy."

"What about Pugh?" Barlow asked. Marshall Pugh was Philadelphia's city engineer at the Bureau of Surveys.

"I sent him the order. He's doing a scale plan of all three floors of the Callowhill Street house. We've got witnesses waiting in the wings here, but either what they can attest to is circumstancial at best or they're reluctant—Georgiana Yoke, for example. She's come here as she said she would, but when I asked her what side she'd take if and when this case came to court, she looked me right in the eye and said, 'I will tell a plain story and it will be favorable to my husband.' Christ! The guy's setting her up to murder her so he can get her property and she's still so damned loyal she'll protect him if she can. If we charge him, we're going to have to have more than we've got right now, because it'll be a fight. His attorney—Shoemaker, not Rotan—told me flat out that Holmes will never confess to murder."

Graham fell silent and walked to his desk. Barlow waited a respectful moment more before speaking. "I understand you heard from the Toronto authorities today."

Graham nodded and picked up a slip of paper from his desk. "From Coroner Johnston. He says since the deformed feet of Nellie were missing and the only positive identification of her was the braided hair, which was shaky identification at best, they went for a verdict on the death of Alice Pitezel only. His jury was out for only fifteen minutes and came in with this." He glanced at the paper and read: "'That Alice Pitezel came to her death on or about the twenty-fifth day of October, at the city of Toronto, and that H. H. Holmes, alias Mudgett, alias Howell, alias Howard, did, on or about the day last aforesaid, unlawfully, willfully, and with malice aforethought, kill and murder her, the said Alice Pitezel, contrary to the peace of our sovereign lady the Queen, her crown and dignity.' Johnston says he immediately issued an arrest warrant for Holmes on the charge of first degree murder."

"But you don't want him extradited to Canada?"

"No, nor anywhere else, if there's any chance at all we can nail him."

There came a tapping on the door. It opened and Graham's secretary leaned in. "The natives are getting restless," she reminded. "Can I tell them how much longer"

"Right now," Graham said. "Come on, Tom, we can't put it off anymore."

A few minutes later they were facing a roomful of reporters. Graham waited for the undercurrent of voices to die away and then began speaking in a well-modulated voice, firmly but without passion. "The time has come," he said, "when it is proper for me to make to the public a full statement of the present condition of this Holmes case." He then went on to encapsulate the history of the investigation, from the first clue that insurance fraud had been perpetrated, through the suspected murder of his partner, Benjamin Pitezel, and then the subsequent murders of the Pitezel girls in Toronto. In conclusion he said, "In view of these discoveries, the reasonableness of the theory that Holmes killed Pitezel at thirteen-sixteen Callowhill Street in this city becomes apparent, and whether the prisoner, who is securely held in our county prison, shall be tried for the murder of Pitezel in this jurisdiction or be taken to Toronto to be tried there for the murder of the two little girls there, remains to be determined. It will depend on circumstances."

"That's not really much of an answer, Mr. Graham," one of the reporters called out. "Are you or aren't you going to try him for murder here?"

Graham's reply carried a little heat with it. "I think I've been making it quite clear. I wish to say it is my desire to have Holmes tried for murder. *Where* he is tried on that charge is not the matter of importance. What is important is that the jurisdiction in which he is charged should be the jurisdiction with the best case to present against him. It is important that a clear case of murder be made out against him, from which there will be no probability of escape."

"You'd send him to Canada then," another reporter asked, "if it came to that?"

"If it shall appear that this conviction can be readily secured at Toronto, I will arrange for his being sent there for trial and withdraw all objections to the removal."

A reporter near the back of the room spoke up. "What about Chicago, sir? The papers are claiming they're finding bones in stoves in that so-called Castle of his there, along with pieces of skeletons in his basement. What about trying him there instead of sending him out of the country?"

"So far as I have been able to determine in my years as prosecutor," Graham replied, "newspaper stories have never been construed as proof of a crime in a court of law. And God forbid that they ever are."

In Chicago during these past ten days since Detective Geyer's discovery of the bodies of the Pitezel girls, Holmes was the topic of the majority of discussions and monopolized the headlines. And the more that was spoken and printed, the more speculation there was as to just how far his crimes had carried him. Past history of minor crimes was dredged up and every unsolved disappearance was suddenly being laid at his feet as one more of his murders. And, though proof in most was still sorely lacking, the accusations were largely true.

As soon as the major story began breaking, Wharton Plummer took his family and left Chicago for an extended vacation in Pennsylvania, "somewhere in the Pocono Mountains," it was said.

Pat Quinlan and his wife, Ella, suddenly became very difficult for reporters to find for interviews, and rumor had it that when they surfaced, they would be immediately detained by police for close questioning. Surface they did, in a few more days, and immediately they were taken into custody and subject to intensive "sweatbox" questioning. Day after day the questions were pounded at them; day after day the Quinlans professed to know nothing of any of Holmes's clandestine activities ... and most certainly they had never engaged in any themselves.

What appeared to be rib bones were found in a stove in Holmes's apartment in the Castle, and a variety of other items were being discovered as well, not only in stoves but in nooks and crannies of the building and buried in the cellar: several pearl dress buttons, shoe hooks, pieces of clothing, assorted bone fragments, part of a gold watch chain, a charred shoe, a partially melted metallic handle from a lady's handbag, partially filled bottles of suspicious fluids such as chloroform, carbolic acid, ether and benzine, the remains of some tintypes, charred cloth sticking inside a stove, an ink bottle that allegedly belonged to Minnie Williams, some hair, allegedly human, caught in a stovepipe hole, and a variety of other questionable items. A barrel with extra-heavy hoops was discovered to contain acid. A dissecting table was discovered, badly bloodstained, along with a variety of surgical knives. At least a couple of skeletons, the bones disarticulated, were found in a box under the bench. A tank was found containing a fluid with fumes so noxious that chemists who analyzed it reported it would almost instantly kill any human who breathed its vapors. The great Warner Process furnace, with its glass-bending gas jets, caused a stir of grisly speculation, but whatever had been burned in it in the past was unidentifiable. Each discovery spurred on the investigators prowling through the Castle and the workmen spot-digging by lantern light in the gloomy depths of the cellar.

Carrie Pitezel, staying with the Woodwards of Sangamon Street not far from the Castle, was hounded by reporters who had an uncanny knack for asking questions deliberately geared to shock or upset her. When, during one of the early press conferences she had agreed to, one of the reporters had asked, "Did the bodies of your daughters smell very bad?" she had gone into hysterics and was still teetering on the brink of a breakdown.

Chicago detectives in charge of the Holmes investigation were mystified by the discovery, in Holmes's Castle apartment, of a bankbook in the name of Lucy Burbank, showing she was a heavy depositor, putting money into the bank nearly every day, with individual deposits as high as $300 being made. The problem was, no one had any idea who

Lucy Burbank was and speculation was rampant that she was one more of Holmes's victims.

One of the more prominently played-up disappearances was that of Julia Conner and her daughter, Pearl. The skeleton of a child was unearthed in the cellar by police workman Pat McGovern, its skull and leg bones missing, buried two and a half feet deep in a bed of quicklime, wrapped in a black cape or coat with long fringe, and thought possibly to have been Pearl. There was evidence strong enough, in fact, for Chicago authorities to swear out a warrant for Holmes's arrest on a charge of murdering Julia, the warrant to be held and used against him should he be released or exonerated in Philadelphia. Suspicion surrounded the disappearance of Emeline Cigrand. And then, of course, there were the missing Williams sisters, Minnie and Nannie.

E. F. Laughlin, inspector for the Chicago Department of Buildings, roamed aghast through the Castle and then wrote, in part, in his report:

> ... The structural parts of the inside are all weak and dangerous, built of the poorest and weakest kind of material. A combination bay window and winding stairway on Wallace Street side, starting at second story joist and projecting three feet from building line, is breaking away from the building and is dangerous. All dividing partitions between flats are combustible ... several parts weakened by fire and not properly repaired ... uneven settlement of foundations, upward of four inches in a span of twenty feet ... first floor stores are the only habitable parts of the building; the rest should be condemned. The sanitary condition of the building is horrible. ...

In Wilmette, Myrta Holmes continued refusing to be interviewed by newspaper reporters. But neighbors complained that large shipments of furniture and other goods were being carted away from the house at night by her brother, John Belknap, and demanded a search be made. And a search was made, but nothing incriminating was found, and if goods had been shipped away, the police were unable to trace them.

Joseph Owens, handyman in the Holmes Castle, was picked up and subjected to intensive questioning. He told police of secret rooms and chambers and trapdoors in the Castle and of heavy trunks brought to and taken away from the building, usually at night. An enterprising reporter located Ned Conner in the drugstore he now owned in Assumption, Illinois, and got a brief interview, during which Conner said, "If I should divulge all I know about Holmes, I think he would feel the hangman's rope about his neck." Three hours after the reporter left, Conner sold his store and disappeared.

Barney Zeigle, arrested for swindling in Chicago, told of Holmes's having tried to hire him to burn down the Castle at Sixty-third and Wallace and, not liking the quoted price, had done the job himself and muffed it. And a prisoner in Arkansas State Penitentiary, John Allen, alias A. E. Bond, Hiram Caldwell and Mascot, claimed he was also the mysterious Edward Hatch that Holmes spoke of and that he would, if granted immunity from prosecution and freedom from his present incarceration, tell everything about Holmes.

And then, five men working in the basement were seriously injured when they broke through a wall into a hidden tank. There was a great gush of noxious gases and, within moments, a terrific explosion.

Following a long period of investigation into the Emeline Cigrand disappearance, Chicago Police Chief John C. Badenoch made his first public statement to the press in respect to the Holmes case. At the front door of City Hall he said: "I wouldn't be surprised if we found the bones of ten or fifteen persons in the basement of Holmes Castle. The deeper we go into this case, the more horrible it becomes. Every hour brings forth some new and startling phase of Holmes's black career, and he is undoubtedly the greatest criminal that ever lived. It is almost impossible to understand how he carried on his dark deeds without having been detected long before his arrest in Philadelphia. He is certainly the king of criminals."

Not to be outdone, even Chicago Mayor Swift got into the act. "If Holmes is guilty of all that is charged against him," he intoned, "he is a fiend incarnate."

Twelve

A penetrating enervation had settled over Frank Geyer. It was as much mental as physical. He felt sapped, drained, frustrated by the days that had stretched into interminable weeks of following lead after lead into ultimate dead-ends. For the first time since his search had begun eight weeks ago, his optimism faltered and he faced the likelihood that he would never locate Howard Pitezel, either alive or whatever remained of him.

He had been so buoyed with his Toronto success that on reaching Detroit he was sure that he was on the final leg of his search. On his way from the railroad station to the Cadillac Hotel late that Sunday afternoon, he put thoughts of the Pitezel girls in the background—that part of the investigation was now finished—and concentrated only on where to focus his search for the boy. Just because the girls had been killed, he could not rule out the possibility that Howard was still alive. Holmes had been known to threaten he would place the boy in an institution or bind him out as a farm worker. Had he really done so? Wouldn't it have been much easier and safer than killing him and then having to dispose of the body? And yet, problems of body disposal had not provided any noticeable deterrent to Holmes in the past.

He was still mulling the problem when he entered the Cadillac. He mailed the thick letter report to George Graham and then checked in. As soon as his bags were safely in the room, he walked immediately to police headquarters. As he entered the Detective Department, a voice boomed at him and he turned to see Detective Tuttle approaching with hand outstretched.

"Geyer! Geyer, you canny old fart, you *did* it, didn't you? You really found 'em. Goddlemighty, the papers've been full of it. Congratulations!" Tuttle wrung his hand and thumped him on the back, as excited as if the triumph were his own. "What a fantastic piece of detective work. You've got to tell me about it, every last detail."

"Thanks, Herb," the Philadelphia detective grinned. "I'll be glad to tell you about it, but first I'd like to see Superintendent Starkweather."

"Starkweather! You jest. Hey, it's after five o'clock." He glanced up at the wall clock. "Quarter after, to be exact. The brass doesn't hang around here for even a minute after quitting time. He'll be here at nine in the morning. For now, you're stuck with me and, by God, I'm buying you the best damn steak dinner you've had this side of Pittsburgh. And while we're stuffing our faces, you can stuff my ears. Christ, I can't wait to hear how you did it."

So, over steak dinner—which was good, but hardly the best—Geyer told the Detroit detective all the details of what had occurred since he left here, with Tuttle continually prodding and poking with questions of his own. By the time dinner was finished, Geyer felt his eyes getting very heavy. It had been a long day and he wanted to have a good night's sleep for a strong start in the morning, so he bade Tuttle good night and promised to see him in the morning.

He did, too, but only briefly. Headquarters was electric with the excitement of his arrival, thanks to Tuttle. His hand was shaken and his back slapped a dozen times or more before the grinning Detroit detective deposited him at Chief Starkweather's office. Then it was Starkweather's turn to offer congratulations and probe for details of the successful investigation in Toronto. It was all becoming very tiresome now to Geyer, and his account was greatly abbreviated.

"And now," the chief said, when Geyer finished, "no doubt, you're back with your nose to the grindstone, looking for the missing boy?"

"Yes sir. As before, I'd very much appreciate your cooperation and the loan of one of your men."

"You have every bit of our cooperation and I'm sure Detective Tuttle would be proud to work with you again. That all right with you?"

"Certainly." Actually, Geyer would have liked the chance to work with someone else but had no desire to make Tuttle feel slighted. The man was a dependable detective, if not inspired.

An hour later, he and Tuttle called together on Frank Alderman again. The Michigan manager for Fidelity Mutual was pleased to see him and said that the home office in Philadelphia was abuzz with praise for the work he had done. Geyer thanked him almost curtly and then got down to business.

"Mr. Alderman, I'm still trying to locate the Pitezel boy. I've dropped by only to see whether you may have learned anything else in regard to the boy from the realtor, Mr. Boninghausen. You may recall that he was not all that certain, when we questioned him, about whether Holmes had a boy with him or not."

"No," Alderman said slowly, "I've not heard anything else on that. But didn't he say Mr. Moore, the one who rented the Forest Avenue house, had seen him?"

"That's what he said, but I don't believe Mr. Moore was any too sure. At any rate, I have to pin this down and I thought you might want to go with me when I call on them again."

Alderman accompanied them, but the results were disappointing. Boninghausen waffled even more than the first time, saying he had no absolutely positive recollection of a boy being there. Moore, at 241 East Forest Avenue, also backed off considerably. "I never was *positive* that there had been a boy with Holmes," he said. "Several people with children were in Mr. Boninghausen's office that day I went in and at the time I *thought* one of them, a small boy, was with Holmes, but I wouldn't swear to that at all. It's just an impression I had."

With Moore's permission Geyer and Tuttle made one more thorough search of the entire premises, including a small barn, outhouse and the yard. When they finished, Geyer made a negative sound. "I think we can say for sure that if the boy had been here and was killed on these premises, he was not buried. The only other way he could have been disposed of was by being burned in the big furnace, and there is no trace of anything like that, either."

They thanked Mr. Moore for his help and left. When they reached downtown again, Alderman bade them goodbye and returned to his office, while Geyer and Tuttle went to the Wabash Railroad depot. They attempted to learn the number of half-tickets that had arrived from Chicago at 11:15 P.M. last October 12, but were given the disheartening news that the canceled tickets had all been destroyed.

"Let's go get a bite to eat and talk this out," Geyer suggested. "There's something about this whole business that's been nagging at me since the last time I was here and I can't quite put my finger on it. Maybe if I go over it aloud, we can figure it out."

They went to a small restaurant and ate, though Geyer had no idea what it was he was chewing and swallowing as he talked. Tuttle scarcely said a word, listening intently to what Geyer was saying.

"All right, here's how it stacks up right now," Geyer began. "Holmes arrives here in Detroit on the evening of October twelve. He sends the girls—and Howard, too?... we don't know that—into the station and tells them to wait for him there. Then he rejoins Georgiana, who has no idea the children are with him, and takes her to the hotel. He leaves Georgiana there right away and returns to the station and takes the children to the New Western Hotel. He registers them there as Etta and Nellie Canning. But what about Howard? Where did he put him, *if* the boy was with him? The next day he moves the girls to the Burns Boardinghouse on Congress... but, again, only the girls. No Howard. At that place Alice writes to her grandparents. She encloses drawings she did, one of which she titled 'Uncle Tom's Cabin,' after an illustration in the book she's been reading. The very one that I've been carting around and reading. She gives the letter to Holmes to mail, but he keeps it himself. In the letter she complains about not having warmer clothing, which Holmes doesn't buy her because he knows it would be a waste of money since he's going to be killing her soon. In fact, he was right then digging the grave out in the cellar at Forest Avenue. The girls' mother and sister were only blocks away, and neither group knew the other was there. So what happens? Why doesn't he carry out the murder here? Because he gets word—no doubt a telegram—from someone, probably in Chicago, who warns him he's got detectives on his trail. So they all leave for Toronto. And there's never been any indication whatever that Howard was with them in toronto. So where was he?"

Tuttle finished the sip of coffee he was taking and set

down his cup. "You say you got that letter from Holmes? The one Alice wrote where she enclosed the drawings?"

"Yes. He had it when we arrested him."

"Well, didn't she mention Nellie or Howard in it?"

Geyer looked at him for a long moment without replying and then nodded slowly. "Yes, she mentioned that she and Nell have colds and that it's so cold out that all she and Nellie can do is stay inside and draw. And she says 'Howard is not with us now.' I thought she was talking about Howard not with them there, at the Burns Boardinghouse. But, dammit, Tuttle, I think she meant he was not with them in Detroit at all, that he had never even come there with them. It's the only thing that fits. If he was with them when they arrived, where did he disappear to between the time they got off the train and the time they checked in at the New Western? Holmes couldn't have had time to dispose of him then. Hell, he was running to get Georgiana checked into one hotel and the girls checked into another. That's it, by damn! Howard wasn't with them at all. Howard never even *got* to Detroit. Holmes had to have gotten rid of him somehow, somewhere else. And there's only one place that could've been. Tuttle," he ended jubilantly, "lead me to the nearest telegraph office."

The wire he had sent to Graham—a duplicate of which he sent to Chief Linden—was succinct:

SIR STOP AM CONVINCED HOWARD NEVER REACHED DETROIT STOP AM LEAVING FOR INDIANAPOLIS IMMEDIATELY STOP GEYER

By early afternoon Geyer was on the train to Indianapolis. A long delay held him up at Peru, Indiana, however, and the train did not arrive in the Indiana capital until the next morning, July 24. He registered again at the Spencer House and went at once to see Superintendent of Police Ed Powell. As in Detroit, the personnel at police headquarters were greatly excited over Geyer's return. He now had great celebrity status and the genuine admiration of his fellow officers. Powell, as Starkweather had in Detroit, agreed to provide whatever help he needed in the continuing investigation, fascinated by Geyer's deduction that Howard's disappearance had occurred in this city. He assigned Detective Dave Richards to help Geyer again, and the Philadelphia detective wasted no time in laying out his plan.

"I want a city directory," he said, after they'd finished their greetings, "and I want to make a list of absolutely every real estate agent here—not only in the city proper, but in the surrounding vicinity. We're going to interview these people one by one until we find someone who rented a house last October to a man who wanted it for his widowed sister."

"Widowed sister?" Richard asked.

"That's his story. He used it in Detroit. He used it in Toronto. He used it in Burlington. And I'm damned sure he used it here, too."

It was the beginning of a lot of very tedious work. Once the list was finished, they had begun checking the realtors. Day after day they went from realtor to realtor and day after day they met no success. At least here he was known and his search a matter of common knowledge. The Indianapolis newspapers had published all the wire stories of the Toronto discoveries and now that Geyer was back in Indianapolis, his presence was heralded in headlines and reporters frequently asked for interviews and dogged their steps. Story after story appeared in the Indianapolis papers and, before long, Geyer was sure every person in Indianapolis who could read was anxious to help and remaining watchful for the missing boy. It was not all to the good. People began making stories up for the momentary place it would give them on stage. Dozens upon dozens of people called at the Spencer House with tips and suggestions. At first there had only been scattered reports of mysterious people renting houses last fall, but quickly they had become a torrent, and Geyer and Richards became exhausted merely checking out every report, all of which ended in cul-de-sacs.

The days turned into a week, with no positive results at all. Geyer's initial optimism had now reversed itself and he began to think Holmes was more clever than he had given him credit for being. Once again Geyer went out to West Indianapolis and checked with Herman Ackelow, the former proprietor of the Circle House. Was Howard with the girls when they left, or had he gone away first? Ackelow was unable to supply the answer.

The telegram came on August 1:

DET FRANK GEYER STOP SPENCER HOUSE HOTEL STOP
INDIANAPOLIS IND STOP

MR GEYER STOP PLEASE GO TO CHICAGO AT ONCE TO
INTERVIEW POLICE STOP SKELETAL REMAINS OF CHILD
FOUND IN HOLMES CASTLE STOP MAY BE HOWARD STOP
GRAHAM

Geyer left Indianapolis the same evening and arrived in
Chicago the next morning. He checked into the Sherman
House Hotel and then had an immediate conference with
Chief Badenoch and Inspector Fitzpatrick, lasting several
hours. It needn't have taken so long. When all the dross was
cleared away, it became obvious that not only were the bones
those of a child considerably smaller than Howard, they were
those of a child who had died at least a couple of years ago.

Disgusted, Geyer returned to his hotel room, not sure
what he would do next. A bellhop brought a telegram to his
room and he tore it open quickly. It was another from
Graham:

MR GEYER STOP WHEN YOU ARE CLEAR IN CHICAGO
PLEASE RETURN TO PHILADELPHIA FOR CONSULTATION
STOP GRAHAM

He checked out without even sleeping in the room and
caught the very next Pennsylvania Limited. At 4:30 P.M. the
following day, August 3, he strode into Graham's office. It was
a Saturday, but he expected the district attorney would be
there. He was. So, too, was Barlow. Both men leaped up and
greeted him enthusiastically.

"What did you do, Mr. Geyer," Graham chuckled, "grow
wings? I can't believe you got here so quickly."

"I couldn't wait," Geyer replied. He grinned. "Besides,
it saved me the price of a telegram. Chicago fell through. The
bones might've been a child Holmes killed, but it wasn't
Howard. Too small and dead two or three years, maybe
more."

"Too bad," Barlow put in, "but we have faith you'll find
Howard when you get back to Indianapolis."

Geyer could hardly believe his ears. "You may have
more faith in me than I have at this point. I've checked out
practically every realtor there, not only in the city proper but
in the outlying towns as well."

"We know," Barlow said. He squeezed Geyer's shoulder.
"You've done an incredible job, but you're not done yet and

you won't be able to rest until you are. You know that . . . and so do we."

Graham agreed. "Frank—you don't mind if I call you Frank, do you? And, unless we're in court, you call me George."

"And me Tom," Barlow put in.

"Frank," Graham began again, "you have a great ability in what you do. Almost unbelievable skill and patience. We couldn't possibly have chosen a better man. I truly believe that no other detective could have traced those girls down as you did. And you're going to do the same with Howard. I know it."

"Well, I'll certainly continue to try, if that's what you want . . . George." He felt uncomfortable addressing the district attorney so familiarly.

"We want. And you will. I have no doubt of it. No, I'll rephrase that. You'll find him if anyone can. And if you don't, then he's lost forever. _That's_ what I believe. Now, you go home and get some well-deserved rest over this weekend. Be back here at nine o'clock Monday morning and we'll discuss further plans for your searching Indianapolis and vicinity. And if you're not successful there, then in the railroad junction towns between Cincinnati, Indianapolis, Chicago and Detroit."

Geyer had to admit it, the weekend was a welcome respite. He slept most of the time, occasionally reading a few pages in Alice Pitezel's copy of _Uncle Tom's Cabin_. It was good, for a change, not to be thinking every moment of his next move in the Holmes case. And for the first time since the tragedy that had so disrupted his own life, he was able to remember Martha and Esther without thinking of them at the morgue, remembering instead the joy of the years they had shared. The gap in his life that their departure from it had left would always be there, but gradually the razor-sharp edges were becoming blunted and thinking of them was accompanied more with pleasure than with pain. And somehow he knew that this was as Martha would have had it be.

Both Graham and Barlow were in the district attorney's office when he got there at precisely 9 A.M. on Monday. So too was Laurence Fouse, president of Fidelity Mutual, and his chief investigator, William Gary. Geyer had met Fouse once before but not Gary, though he'd heard of him. He liked the man's looks and was gratified at the hearty handshake when they were introduced.

The five of them discussed the case to this point, and Barlow filled in the gaps from the Philadelphia end. He and Graham had had several meetings with Holmes since the discovery of the bodies, questioning him extensively—always with one of his attorneys present—and hoping something he would inadvertently say would give them a new lead. There was nothing of the kind. Barlow told him of Holmes's latest version of his disposal of the children, that he had turned them over to the nebulous Hatch and it was no doubt Hatch who had killed them in Toronto to get the money Holmes had allegedly pinned inside their dresses.

"So what it amounts to, Frank," Graham said when Barlow finished, "is that you've given us a lot more than we've given you. Now we want you to give us even more. We know you're scheduled for meetings all day tomorrow with Chief Linden and others, but he has reconfirmed that you're still ours if we need you, as well we do. Are you up to heading for Indianapolis on Wednesday and digging in again?"

"Yes. I'm ready."

"Excellent! And this time you won't be doing the majority of it all yourself. Mr. Fouse here has agreed that Bill Gary should accompany you, if that suits you."

Geyer smiled. "I couldn't be more pleased." He winked at Gary. "I think we'll make a great team."

Instead of going directly to Indianapolis on August 7 as initially planned, Geyer and Gary took the evening train out of Philadelphia for Chicago and questioned Quinlan when they got there. The Holmes Castle janitor disavowed any knowledge that would help them in their search. Geyer quickly decided they were not going to find what they wanted in Chicago and suggested to Gary that they head back toward Indianapolis, checking some railroad towns en route where Holmes conceivably could have stopped to dispose of Howard.

"Lead on," Gary said. "Wither thou goest..."

They went first to Logansport, Indiana, and split up, checking out the hotels and boardinghouses as well as real estate agents. The work went much faster with two of them doing it. They were not at all surprised when they failed to turn up evidence of Holmes and Howard. In succession they stopped at Peru, Indiana, Adrian, Michigan, and then Montpelier, Ohio. Everywhere the story was the same. Finally Geyer sent a wire to Graham:

MR GRAHAM STOP GARY AND I ARE RETURNING TO
INDIANAPOLIS TO RESUME INVESTIGATION THERE STOP
I STILL FEEL THAT IS WHERE WE WILL FIND THE
ANSWER IF THERE IS ONE STOP WE WILL REMAIN
THERE UNTIL WE FIND HOWARD OR YOU ORDER US
HOME STOP GEYER

As Geyer had before, they set themselves up at the Spencer House and began checking out the final list of realtors he had not been able to contact before. There was still a dishearteningly large list of them. The Indianapolis police remained as patient and helpful as they had been from the very beginning. Still, day by day, despite the police help and the announcements published by the Indianapolis newspapers of the renewal of the search, the rejuvenated confidence that had suffused the two men when they left Philadelphia together was eroding.

"Do you really think we're getting anywhere with this, Frank?" Gary asked tiredly one evening as they were dining at the Stubbins House.

Geyer paused before replying. His own voice was hardly any less discouraged than Gary's. "I can't shake the belief that Howard was killed right in this Indianapolis area," he said. "But I'll have to say this, Bill. I'm puzzled and annoyed and getting damned frustrated. What in the hell happened to that boy? He can't have vanished into thin air. Somewhere there's an answer."

No element of excitement remained in their quest. It had become merely a succession of boring days, visiting realtor after realtor, introducing themselves in the same way, waiting tiredly for that same shake of the head or shrug or blank look. Little broke that tedium. Once they received word that after more than two weeks of intensive questioning by Chicago police, the Quinlans had been released. A peculiar footnote to that story was that on the very next day, the Holmes Castle was destroyed by fire.

A pervasive frustration gnawed at Geyer and more than once he was ready to wire Philadelphia and tell Graham they were giving up. Yet, somehow he couldn't bring himself to do that. And so plodding day after plodding day they continued to check every realtor they had previously not checked within the city limits and then, town by town, every realtor in the communities within fifteen miles of the city. Gradually the list dwindled, and when they returned exhausted to their hotel on Monday, August 26, they had followed up on over nine hundred individual possibilities and had drawn a blank on each. They were very nearly at the end of the line. There was only one town left to check.

After they finished dinner and retired to their room, Geyer wrote a letter to Graham. The tone of discouragement ran all through it and he concluded his final paragraph by writing:

> . . . *Only one town remains to be checked. Tomorrow we will both go to Irvington to check there, but with almost no hope left. After Irvington, I scarcely know where we shall go.*

There were lowering clouds in the morning, gray and gloomy, matching the mood of Geyer and Gary as they boarded the trolley car and took it to the little village of Irvington, six miles from downtown Indianapolis. As they neared their destination, Gary raised his voice in a question to the motorman.

"Do you know where the hotels are located in Irvington?"

"In Irvington?" The motorman barked a short laugh. "Mister, Irvington's too small to have a hotel. It doesn't even have a boardinghouse, so far as I know."

That seemed to clinch the matter. When, a few minutes later, the streetcar stopped in Irvington, the two men alighted and looked around. The town was a pretty little place with stately oaks and maples, but it did not have a population of more than four or five hundred. On the main street—Union Avenue—there were a number of small shops.

"Look," Gary said, pointing. Less than fifty yards ahead was a small sign in front of a house. It said *G. Brown—Real Estate*.

"Well," Geyer said, "it's a starting place, I guess."

They entered and found the front room had been converted into an office with a counter and some maps were tacked to the walls. A gentle-faced man behind the counter looked up and smiled over his spectacles at them.

"Good morning, gentlemen. I'm Gerald Brown. May I help you?"

Geyer set his bundle of papers and photographs on the counter. He began untying it to remove a photo of Holmes to show him, as he had done nearly a thousand times already in the Indianapolis area. And he responded the way he had so many times before. "I am Detective Frank Geyer and this is Detective William Gary. We're from Philadelphia and we're here investigating a police matter. Would you by any chance know of a house that was rented in Irvington last autumn to a man who said he wanted it for his widowed sister? He would have stayed for only a short while." He handed Brown the photo.

"Why, yes," the old man said, "I remember that. It was in October." He squinted at the picture and nodded. "Yep, this looks like him."

Geyer and Gary stared at one another, stunned. The days and weeks of travel and toil and frustration. The hundreds upon hundreds of real estate offices and hotels and boardinghouses they had checked. The unknown scores of individual renters they had checked from advertisements in last October's papers. And now, in this one glorious, wonderful, triumphant moment, just as they were on the edge of defeat, they had won!

"Tell us about your renting it to him," Geyer said, surprised that he was even able to talk.

"Actually, I didn't handle the renting of this house, but I did have the keys. One day in the early part of October— maybe the fifth or sixth—this man," he tapped the photo, "came into this office and without a hello or a by your leave said, 'I want the key for the Dr. Thompson house.' I remember the man very well because I sure didn't like his manners. I felt he should've had more respect for my gray hairs."

"I agree," Gary said. He couldn't seem to stop grinning. "Then it was Dr. Thompson who rented the house to him?"

"Yep."

"Would you know where we could find Dr. Thompson now?"

"I do. If you like, I'll take you over there right now. I

don't think anyone's going to be beating the doors down for real estate before I get back."

He led the way outside and the two detectives followed him, still beside themselves with elation at their turn of fortune at last. Brown led them directly into the doctor's office about a block from his own.

"Morning, Ted," he said to the middle-aged man sitting at a desk. "These two gentlemen are from Philadelphia. They're detectives."

Dr. Ted Thompson came to his feet and shook hands with them both. "Gentlemen. You've come a long way from Philadelphia. How can I be of service?"

"We're looking for a boy who disappeared last fall, Dr. Thompson," Gary said. "He was with a man and we understand from Mr. Brown here that the man he was with rented a house from you here in Irvington."

"This is his picture," Geyer said, handing him the Holmes photo.

"Yes, that's him all right," Dr. Thompson said. "He rented my cottage a few blocks from here for his sister. Said her name was Mrs. A. E. Cook. But he didn't have a little boy with him when he rented it. In fact, I never saw a boy with him. However, I have a young man working for me, Elvet Moorman, who must have seen the boy if he was here. I keep a cow in the barn over at the cottage and Elvet goes over there twice every day, morning and evening, to milk her. He's out in the field over here. Let me call him and see if he can help."

He stepped outside and around to the side of the house, then cupped his mouth and hallooed for the youth out in the field. The young man looked their way and Dr. Thompson waved him in, calling, "Come here, Elvet."

The youth trotted to them and was introduced to the detectives. Geyer showed him first the picture of Holmes, then the photograph of Howard and he nodded vigorously. "Yep, that's them all right."

Now any lingering doubt was swept away. Geyer and Gary were eager to begin searching the place and Dr. Thompson led the way, Brown and Moorman bringing up the rear. The house, a story-and-a-half white clapboard cottage, was in the eastern part of the little town, directly across the street from the Methodist Church and a couple hundred yards north of the Pennsylvania Railroad tracks.

The first thing they checked was the cellar. It had an earth floor, primarily rock-hard clay. It was immediately apparent that there had been no digging done in that floor, so they went outside. A small porch had a latticework from floor to ground. Geyer peered through the latticework and saw something unusual.

"How can I get under there?" he asked Dr. Thompson.

"Just pull the steps away," the doctor answered. "They're not attached."

Geyer and Gary pulled the steps away, exposing an opening, and Geyer crawled in. A moment later he emerged with what had attracted his attention. In the light of day it turned out to be a piece of a trunk which had been repaired with a two-inch-wide strip of blue calico pasted along the seam. The figure on the calico was a small white flower. Geyer handed the section of trunk to Gary and crawled back into the opening. Far to the rear it seemed to him that the ground had been disturbed, and he asked if there were a shovel available. Dr. Thompson sent Elvet running to the barn to get it. In a moment he was back.

Geyer dug rapidly and deeply but encountered nothing. He decided to cease that activity for now and come back to it later if need be. The group then went out to the barn. There they found some items of furniture and a forty-two-inch-high coal stove with the brand name *Peninsular Oak* in raised letters on the iron front. It had a diameter of about twenty-two inches and the entire top worked on a pivot principal.

Word had spread through the special grapevine common to small towns, and scores of people were gathering to watch. Geyer and Gary continued inspecting the premises, paying particular attention to the ground and digging wherever it seemed the least bit soft. None of the test diggings revealed a thing. By the time they finished with this, the crowd had grown to several hundred people—a large percentage of the town's total population—and people were now interfering with the search.

Geyer announced that he was going to suspend his and Gary's searching for the day and go back into Indianapolis to dispatch some telegrams. He told Dr. Thompson that they were staying at the Spencer House and then he and Gary immediately took a streetcar back to town. They went directly to the telegraph office and Geyer sent his first wire:

CARRIE PITEZEL STOP GALVA ILLINOIS STOP 1:15 P.M.
AUG 27 1895

DID MISSING TRUNK HAVE STRIP OF BLUE CALICO WITH
WHITE FIGURE OVER BOTTOM SEAM STOP ANSWER IM-
MEDIATELY STOP WILL WAIT STOP FRANK GEYER

The minutes ticked away with excruciating slowness, but
then the sound of a rapid-fire metallic clattering indicated a
message coming in. Fast as it was, it was not transcribed fast
enough to suit them. They snatched the sheet from the
telegrapher and read it eagerly.

DET FRANK GEYER STOP YES STOP TRUNK HAD BLUE
CALICO STRIP WITH WHITE FIGURE ON BOTTOM STOP
ADVISE STOP CARRIE A PITEZEL

Find the trunk and you find Howard. Geyer was reminded of his own thoughts during the investigation in Detroit.

The telephone in the telegraph office rang while the two
detectives were pounding each other's back. The telegraph
clerk answered it and then turned to the men. "Detective
Geyer, it's for you."

Surprised, Geyer went to the wall phone and accepted
the phone with thanks. "Hello? Geyer here."

"Detective Geyer? This is Brown over at the *News* and
it's imperative you come over here right away. Can you do
that?"

"I can," Geyer said. "What's it about?"

"Just get over here fast. You'll find out." He hung up.

Geyer replaced the receiver and turned to the telegraph
clerk. "Can you please tell me where the *News* offices are
located?"

"Sure, just around the corner in the next block." He
gave him directions and Geyer thanked him and raced out,
beckoning Gary to follow. They trotted all the way to the
Indianapolis Evening News building and found the city editor, Bill Brown, waiting for them. Introductions were brief.

"You're supposed to stay here," Brown said. "Dr.
Thompson's partner, Dr. Barnhart, is on his way here from
Irvington right now. He has something of vital importance to

tell you. Now suppose *you* tell *me* what the hell all this
excitement is."

"Provisionally only. Nothing for print yet. I'll let you
know when it is, agreed?"

"Agreed."

"All right. It looks like we've discovered where Howard
Pitezel was killed. Out in Irvington."

"Holy shit!" Brown's mouth dropped open and he stared.
Then he snatched up a pad and began to interview the
detectives. "I know, I know," he said impatiently when Geyer
started to object. "I'm not printing anything yet, dammit! I'm
just getting ready. Talk. Tell me about it."

Brown had almost the whole story down when Dr.
Barnhart, a thick-waisted man of about forty, entered in a
lather. He was carrying a small package. They moved into
Brown's office and Dr. Barnhart opened it and showed the
contents. "These," he said, pointing to several pieces of
charred bone, "are portions of a femur and the skull of a child
between eight and twelve years old." The section of skull
showed the natural sutures plainly.

"You found them!" Geyer cried. "Where, man?"

"I didn't," the doctor said. "After you and Mr. Gary left,
Dr. Thompson and I continued the search. We had a couple
of boys with us—Walter Jenny and Oscar Kettenbach. One of
them, I forget who, suggested they go play detective together. They went into the cellar where that partial cement floor
is, where the chimney rises from. In the chimney block there's
a pipehole about three and a half feet above the floor.
Jenny—I think it was Jenny, yes, Jenny—put his arm into the
opening and pulled out a handful of ashes. One of these
pieces of bone was in it. Then they ran and got Ted and me
and we saw immediately what it was. We went back and the
boys got another handful out and the piece of skull was in
that one. We told them to quit then and I caught the
streetcar to town while Ted went to make the phone call."

"We weren't planning to come back today," Geyer said,
"but you couldn't keep us away now. Let's go!"

By the time they returned, Dr. Barnhart and a handful of
reporters and photographers in tow, it was getting toward
evening and virtually all of the town's population had gathered.
There was a subdued carnival air about them, an interesting
paradox of excitement and yet sobriety over the incredible
discovery of a hideous crime having been committed in their

tiny community. But the crowds, in the yard, barn and house, did indeed present a problem and Geyer had no choice but to ask the marshall of police, who was present, to clear all the sight-seers from the house. He did so and then only Geyer, Gary, the two doctors and several reporters were allowed to come in.

They went to the cellar and, with a hammer and chisel someone had provided, Geyer began dismantling the lower part of the chimney. An old screen from the house was used to sift the ashes and soot pulled from the chimney. In this manner he recovered almost a complete loose set of teeth as well as a segment of jawbone. These he handed over to a dentist who had arrived, Dr. John Quincy Bryam.

"Oh ho, what's this?" Geyer muttered as he delved into the bottom of the chimney. He extracted a large bulk of charred fleshy material. When sliced open, it was discovered to be a combination of liver, spleen and stomach baked into a hard mass. This material was given into the hands of Dr. Barnhart for his inspection and care.

There were also some iron pieces found in the chimney that turned out to be pieces of the trunk as well as a crocheting needle, some buttons and a little scarf pin. Satisfied that they had probably found all they were going to find of Howard Pitezel, Geyer called a halt to the search. Preparing to return to the city, the group was halted by the arrival of a man with another bit of news.

"My name is Klevitts," he said. "Steve Klevitts. I run the grocery about a mile from here. Last October a man came in and left a boy's overcoat with me. He said he had given a lift to a boy who had asked him to drop the coat off at my store, that he would pick it up the next day. He never showed up, though. I still have that coat in a box over at the store. Anyway, that's what happened."

"Was this the man who brought it in?" Geyer asked, showing him the picture of Holmes.

"Yes, sir, by golly, he's the one!"

One more link in the chain.

Even though it was fairly late in the evening, they returned to City Hall, having been informed by a messenger that Chief Powell was waiting for them. And so he was. The chief not only shook the hands of Geyer and Gary, he embraced them both in an uninhibited rush of enthusiasm.

"You are a credit to the profession of law enforcement,"

he said. "An example to men in the business as well as to young men with their sights set on such a career. I intend writing to your superiors with the highest praise I can generate."

"Thank you, Chief Powell," Geyer said. "I have to admit, we were getting pretty discouraged and were on the verge of calling it quits."

"But you didn't," Powell pointed out, "and that's what counts. Go back to your hotel now and get a good night's rest. Tomorrow morning I'd like you to get together first thing with the county coroner, Dr. Castor. He'll set up the inquest."

"We'll be there, sir," Gary told him. "Good night."

They left and went directly to the telegraph office where Geyer sent the telegram he had so deeply longed to be able to send:

> MR GRAHAM STOP REMAINS OF HOWARD PITEZEL FOUND STOP PRELIMINARY INQUEST TOMORROW STOP WILL ADVISE CARRIE PITEZEL TO COME HERE SOONEST STOP WE ARE TIRED BUT VERY GRATIFIED STOP MORE LATER STOP GEYER

Gary sent a similar telegram to Fouse and then the two detectives returned to the Spencer House. They ate quickly and then collapsed into their beds. Frank Geyer enjoyed the best night's sleep he had had for two months.

Or maybe since before the fire last March.

"I'm surprised you're going to write it," William Gary said. "After all, you'll be seeing him in a little over an hour."

Frank Geyer chuckled. "I wouldn't miss writing this one," he said. "All through this investigation I've looked forward to that last report I'd have to write to the district attorney, and it's finally come. I'll be savoring every word."

Gary slouched in his seat and turned his head to watch the passing scenery outside the window of their railroad car. "Your choice," he said. "Me, I'm just going to sort of wallow here in a dopey daze and enjoy not thinking about anything for a while."

"Bill, you're going to be an old man before your time."

The little barb had no effect, so Geyer smiled and busied

himself getting set up to write. And when he began in a few minutes, it was with firm sure strokes.

Pennsylvania R.R. Coach
Somewhere in Central Penna.
Sunday, Sept. 1st, 1895

Hon. George S. Graham
District Attorney, Phila. County
City Hall, Philadelphia, Penna.

DEAR MR. GRAHAM:

I'm pleased to say this will not only be a short Sunday report, it will be the last one. And I won't even have to mail it. I'll be placing it in your hand personally, since you said you're meeting our train and you and Mr. Barlow will be taking us to dinner. I'm looking forward to that.

Enough telegrams have passed between us over the past several days for you to be aware generally of what happened up to the point where the remains of Howard Pitezel were found in the ashes of the chimney in the Thompson cottage in Irvington.

The day following those discoveries at the Irvington house, the Marion County sheriff asked us to appear before the Grand Jury and we did so, one final time reciting our whole story of the Holmes-Pitezel matter leading us to this discovery of the remains in Irvington.

An inquest was held by the coroner, Dr. Hiram H. Castor, and once again Mrs. Pitezel had to be summoned to a very sad scene. As you know, she had been hoping to the last that her son had been placed in some institution or in the care of some person in a secluded part of the country, perhaps on a farm. It will be remembered that Holmes declared that to be his purpose to Mr. Herman Ackelow, proprietor of the Circle House, and Mrs. Pitezel always clung to the hope that Howard would ultimately be found alive. The Irvington revelation came to her, therefore, with all the force of a dreadful shock. It was a great tax on her strength to have to leave Galva again and make another sad journey, this time to Irvington.

She first identified the overcoat found at the grocer's as Howard's. She had repaired it in a number of places and sewed a new pocket into it and had no difficulty proving the identification. The piece of trunk was easily recognized because of the strip of calico which her father had pasted along the bottom. A little spinning top and a tin man, which Holmes had bought for Howard at the World's Fair and which I found in the Irvington house after further investigation, were also identified by her; she had placed them in the trunk herself at the time of the departure of Holmes with Nellie and Howard from St. Louis. A small scarf-pin and a pair of shoes she also identified as Howard's, and a crochet needle that had belonged to her daughter Alice. These had all been found in the Irvington house.

The 17-year-old lad, Elvet Moorman, testified that he went over to the house one afternoon early in October of 1894 and saw a transfer wagon with furniture unloading, and a man and a boy assisting in transferring the articles to the house. Later in the afternoon of the same day he went over to milk a cow that was kept in the barn, connected with the house. While he was milking, the man who was with the boy came to him and asked him to assist him in putting up a stove, which he did. Moorman asked the man when he did not make a gas connection (for natural gas) and use a gas stove, and the man said he did not think gas was healthy for children. A photograph of Holmes was shown the witness and he identified it as the man whom he had assisted in putting up the stove. He also said that the photograph of Howard Pitezel shown him was the boy he had seen with Holmes and who was present when the stove was put up. He also said that after Holmes and the boy disappeared, he had examined the house and found a lot of corn rubbish on the floor that seemed to indicate that a fire had been made with corn cobs.

Dr. Bryam, a dentist, identified the teeth and portion of the jaw as those of a child between the ages of eight and eleven years, and Dr. Barnhart declared the bones found to be portions of a skele-

ton of a child between the ages of seven and ten years. The large portion of charred remains found contained the liver, the stomach and portions of the intestines.

Albert Schiffling testified that he keeps a repair shop at No. 48 Virginia Avenue, Indianapolis. On the 3rd of October, a man, whom he identified as Holmes, came into his shop accompanied by a small boy. Holmes had two cases of surgical instruments, which he wanted sharpened. He returned for the instruments on October 8th, paid for the repairs and took them away. Other testimony and identifications of Holmes and Howard were heard, but all in corroboration of the evidence which I have briefly stated. Dr. Bryam, the dentist, very cleverly and skillfully mounted the teeth on wax jaws, which exhibited their character and their age most admirably, and Doctors Barnhart and Thompson made a very exhaustive and scientific report of the contents of the chimney which had been found. The Coroner's Jury had no difficulty in finding that little Howard Pitezel had come to his death at the hands of H. H. Holmes.

The work of William Gary and I being done, we visited the City Hall and thanked Superintendent Powell and his assistants for their kind and courteous treatment during our stay in Indianapolis. In fact, we were grateful to everybody, for we had received from all citizens the most generous and unselfish aid in the performance of our task.

So, with our job successfully completed, I close this final report with sincere thanks to you and Mr. Barlow, for your support of me in this investigation and for your unshakable faith that it would come to a successful conclusion. If I may be of further service to you in the future, I would consider it to be an honor and a pleasure. And with that, Sir, I remain,

MOST RESPECTFULLY YOURS,
FRANK P. GEYER

Geyer folded the report and slipped it into an envelope, across the face of which he wrote *District Attorney George S.*

Graham, and placed it into an inner breast pocket of his coat. Across from him William Gary was asleep and faintly snoring. Geyer smiled and opened his smaller bag and brought out the book he had been reading at rather infrequent intervals during the investigation, *Uncle Tom's Cabin*—the copy given to him by Carrie Pitezel that had belonged to Alice. The fact that he'd had precious little time to read was evidence in that he was still less than halfway through it. He settled back with it now, for the first time with nothing else on his mind to distract him from it.

Twenty minutes later their train pulled into the station at Philadelphia and both Graham and Barlow were on hand to greet them, along with a crowd of reporters and other people. Geyer and Gary were immediately ringed by people shouting congratulations and asking questions.

Gary leaned close to Geyer and murmured sardonically, "Hail! The conquering heroes!"

It took long minutes for them to extricate themselves and get into a carriage with the district attorney and his special assistant. And when they settled themselves in their seats in one of the city's finer restaurants, George Graham lifted his glass and proposed a toast.

"To a pair of the finest investigators this tired old world has ever produced."

They drank and then it was Barlow who added a toast of his own. "To the successful prosecution of H. H. Holmes."

Again they drank and then Geyer looked at the district attorney questioningly. Graham set his glass down and touched his napkin to his lips. He smiled and nodded.

"Yesterday I filed a charge of first-degree murder against Herman W. Mudgett, alias H. H. Holmes, in the death of Benjamin Fuller Pitezel."

Holmes was incensed that he should be brought from Moyamensing to the Court of Oyer and Terminer in this van loaded with common criminals. They were such a beastly, uncouth lot—assaulters, petty thieves and such. He held himself aloof from them as much as possible as they lurched through the Philadelphia streets and was slightly mollified when he was separated from the other prisoners upon reaching their destination. They were taken to the common "cage" to await their turn; Holmes was taken to a special cell that had been reserved just for him.

Ten months in prison had not served him well. He bore a telltale prison pallor and was much thinner, the finely tailored double-breasted black suit that had once fit him so well now hanging loosely on his frame and his shirt collar several sizes too big. He had trimmed his muttonchops and now had a dark beard cut to a point. But the most significant changes were not those of appearance so much as attitude. The jauntiness of his step was missing, the erect carriage and arrogant lift of the head. Now he tended to shuffle just a little and hunch forward as he walked.

He sat alone in the cell for perhaps an hour and then was escorted to the courtroom by two guards. The place was filled with spectators and lawyers, and he walked across the front of the room, looking neither left nor right, and took his place in the dock. He sat down, head bent, paying no attention to his lawyers, William A. Shoemaker and Samuel P. Rotan, who sat close by.

"The prisoner will rise," intoned the clerk.

Holmes rose and leaned on the front rail of his enclosure. His knuckles were white from the force of his grip on the rail and his lips parted slightly as he looked directly at the clerk.

"Herman W. Mudgett, alias H. H. Holmes, you are here arraigned on a charge of murder in the first degree, in that you did, on September second, eighteen ninety-four, in the City of Philadelphia, Pennsylvania, willfully, purposely and with malice aforethought, kill and murder and take the life of Benjamin Fuller Pitezel." The clerk paused a moment and then added, "How say you Herman W. Mudgett, alias H. H. Holmes? Guilty or not guilty?"

"I'm not guilty, sir," Holmes said, his voice hardly audible.

"How will you be tried?"

Holmes seemed puzzled at what to answer until Sam Rotan leaned close and whispered to him. Then he replied, no louder than before, "By God and my countrymen."

"May God send you a safe deliverance," replied the clerk automatically.

District Attorney George Graham came to his feet. "If it please Your Honor, it is the desire of the Commonwealth in this matter before the Court that a trial date be set at a time remote enough to allow ample opportunity for the accused and his counsel to prepare for the contest that will decide his guilt or innocence."

"Five weeks should be ample enough opportunity," responded the Court. "Trial is herewith set to begin on Monday, October twenty-eighth, and both sides are given notice to be fully prepared and present themselves in court on that date."

The first-degree murder trial of Herman W. Mudgett, alias H. H. Holmes, began at 10 A.M., October 28, 1895. The gallery of Philadelphia's Criminal Court, which could seat five hundred spectators, accommodated only a small portion of the unbelievable crowd that had gathered for what was to be one of the most spectacular trials in the history of American criminal jurisprudence.

For all the crowds it attracted, for all the fanfare it generated, for all the sensational news stories it spawned—locally as well as those relayed by wire service through the United States and much of the world—the trial was thoroughly anticlimactic.

It plodded and dragged and not even the fact that at one point Holmes fired his attorneys and undertook his own defense, or that later he reinstated them to carry on for him, added luster to it; and not even the tear-ridden testimony of Carrie Pitezel could imbue it with more than mediocre pathos. Dozens of witnesses testified, forging link after link in the chain of evidence placing Holmes in various situations conjunctive to Benjamin F. Pitezel prior and subsequent to the man's death, yet none of this testimony proved he killed Pitezel. In addition to the witnesses assembled locally, thirty-five others had presented themselves, subpoenaed by District Attorney George Graham and brought at considerable effort and great cost from as far away as Detroit, Cincinnati, Chicago, Fort Worth, Burlington, Indianapolis, Boston and Toronto. And then Graham and Thomas Barlow and especially Frank Geyer were devastated when all testimony of these witnesses relating to the deaths of Alice, Nellie and Howard Pitezel was declared inadmissible by Judge J. Michael Arnold, who ruled: "The prisoner is now on trial for the killing of Benjamin F. Pitezel in the City of Philadelphia, and that is the case—*and the only case*—to be tried here. Evidence of

he subsequent killing of these children elsewhere will *not* be
dmitted."

For Geyer, sitting in the witness chair when the ruling
vas made, it was as if he had been punched in the stomach.
'he weeks of investigation, the endless agonizing days of
earching into every possible lead, the finding of the bodies
gainst what had initially appeared to be insurmountable
dds—all that was now ruled inadmissible in this court.

The testimony of Dr. William Scott and Dr. William
Mattern established beyond dispute that Benjamin F. Pitezel
ad died as a result of chloroform poisoning through inhala-
ion. And the most important testimony of all—that given by
Dr. Henry Leffman, esteemed professor of analytical chemis-
ry and toxicology—addressed itself to the extremely perti-
ent issue of whether Benjamin Pitezel was murdered or
ommitted suicide.

"Professor Leffman," District Attorney Graham said,
are you familiar with the effects and use of chloroform?"

Leffman adjusted his wire-rimmed spectacles and cleared
is throat gently, as if preparing himself for a classroom
ecture. "I have seen chloroform administered a great many
imes in the course of my attendance in college and I have
dministered it a great many times to small animals. I have
ever seen a death from chloroform in my experience."

"What are the immediate effects of the inhalation of
hloroform?"

"The first effect is some excitement and stimulation,
vhich varies a great deal in different individuals, and also
aries with regard to the administrator. Expert operators can
dminister chloroform so as to produce very little distur-
ance. It is not exactly a spasmodic condition. It is, rather,
ne of intoxicating excitement, which is soon followed by a
ondition of relaxation and insensibility."

"Is there," Graham asked, "any struggle before insensi-
ility takes place?"

"There very often is a struggle by the patient being
pparently not exactly aware of the character of the struggle.
t is, rather, an involuntary struggle. Or, at least, a semicon-
cious condition."

"An effect of nature, is it not, to resist the effect?"

Leffman bobbed his head. "To resist the effects. It is
robably connected with the direct intoxicating effect of the
drug."

District Attorney Graham bored in. "The description given us in this case by those who found the body describe i as being found lying upon the back with one arm place thus," he demonstrated, "across the body—the right arm— and the left arm close to the side. The feet stretched out heels together in a composed condition, lying on the back. want to ask you whether or not it is possible for a man t administer chloroform to himself and then compose himsel into such a position as that."

"I think not."

"Why?"

"No one is aware of the time when consciousness ceases Judging from my own experience, I have been four time under the influence of anesthetic. There is a condition o confusion before true insensibility comes on and it would be I think, impossible for anyone to arrange the body in perfectly composed condition like that by a person's own act It would not, I think, be a natural position in which the bod would come by a person administering chloroform to himse without the assistance of anyone else."

"Taking the history of this case as I have given it to you," Graham concluded, "could you say whether or not, in you opinion as an expert, the chloroform in this case was self administered or administered by a second person?"

The professor shook his head. "I should say that such a amount of chloroform as necessary to produce death coul *not* have been self-administered under those conditions."

It seemed that settled the matter, but in cross-examination Holmes probed the matter of self-administration of chloro form more specifically. "If," he said, "adding to the condition which the district attorney has already stated to you, th chloroform, instead of passing into the mouth directly from the tube, had passed from a bottle through a tube into a larg towel covering the entire face of the man, and where th rubber tubing is constricted so that the chloroform woul pass out very slowly, do you think that the condition woul necessarily preclude a possibility of being self-administered?"

"If a large towel were fastened around the face," Leffma said carefully, "with a mechanical arrangement for placing th tube for delivering the liquid, I would expect that uncon sciousness might come on without the assistance of a secon person."

"Let me rephrase, Dr. Leffman. It is possible for

person to administer chloroform to himself by inhalation, that would result in death, is it not?"

"Yes, sir, it is possible. It has occurred."

"Thank you, Doctor. That is all."

And the only real surprise of the trial came just after the prosecution rested its case. With everyone then poised to hear what sort of case the defense would put on, the defense, without calling one witness, rested its case as well.

"Is the prosecution ready to sum up?"

"Ready, Your Honor," Graham said. He took a position before the jury box and began to speak, his words issuing in the familiar roll of oratorical delivery he had used in the summation of scores of cases before this. With undeniable persuasiveness—sometimes thundering his remarks, sometimes offering them with a strong sense of appeal to reason—he built his case against Holmes. It was a very strong case, carefully constructed to miss no aspect of evidence that would be of benefit to his thesis. All the disjointed bits and pieces of overlapping testimony that had been offered in this trial were suddenly fitted together in a framework admirably free of redundancy and powerful in its clear and perfectly organized reconstruction of the crime of murder charged against Holmes. At times he quoted witnesses verbatim from the recorded testimony; most often he relied on the carefully gathered evidence and his own impressive deductions to hammer home his nails of accusation into the coffin of condemnation. And finally, at the close of his long delivery, he addressed the jurymen in a manner which gave each the strong impression he was being spoken to directly and personally.

"Now this strange trial is drawing rapidly to a close," he said. "It has been dramatic in its incidents, but these incidents have nothing to do with the case. The fact that this man," his arm shot out and pointing finger impaled Holmes in the dock, "appears without counsel and then *with* counsel has nothing to do with the question of his guilt or innocence. The simple question is, has the Commonwealth of Pennsylvania, as it is bound to do, made out its case beyond a fair and reasonable doubt, as I have endeavored to point out to you? If you believe it has, then your duty is to find a verdict of murder in the first degree against this man. I ask you to face your duty and acquit yourselves like men. There are no two standards of judgment. There are no two standards of reaching a result. Your minds must operate simply and only as honest men, because you are sworn as jurors. You are given no higher powers of discrimination, but you are asked simply to acquit yourselves as in the everyday affairs of life. If this testimony convinces you of his guilt, you must say so. If it convinces you of his innocence, honestly, then you should say that. But I say to you, in the sure knowledge of the evidence here presented, that there can be but one conclusion in your decision—that the man is guilty in the manner in which he stands indicted of this crime.

"I thank you for your patience and earnest attention. I have been talking to you for nearly two hours and a half—much longer than I expected. And, although uninteresting and rather prosaic and full of detail, you have given me your earnest attention from beginning to end. I ask you to give it to the end. With your verdict, whatever it may be, I will be satisfied, as all good men ought to be."

As he turned and walked back to the prosecutor's table, a din began to arise from the spectators, but it broke off instantly at the sharp triple rap of the gavel.

"Probably no one in this courtroom," defense counsel Samuel Rotan began his summation, leaning against the rail of the now-vacant witness box, "feels the weight of responsibility to such extent as I do at this present time. You, gentlemen—each of you—has a much greater responsibility than have I. You are picked out from among the citizens of this county and put here in the jury box to decide whether a man's life shall be taken. The law says that this is the penalty, and your function is to decide whether this case is a case of murder or whether this man is guiltless.

"Gentlemen of the jury, unfortunately I was not here at the time this jury was impaneled, but I have watched you carefully from day to day and, while I did not see you go into the jury box, yet I feel that each and every one of you is a man who can decide the case upon the testimony given from this stand." He slapped his hand to the rail of the witness box. "That each and every one of you can throw aside all prejudice. If you do *not* do this, gentlemen of the jury, you violate the oath which you took when you went into that box. If you are affected by the prejudice and by the poison which got into the public mind before this case came to trial, and if you allow that to influence you and keep you away from your duty and your oaths, gentlemen, you do a wrong—you do a wrong which probably can never be repaired. I, gentlemen of the jury, assume—and I do so with confidence—that you were unprejudiced when you came into the box, and that you are willing to try this case by the evidence...and the evidence only."

From this starting gate of oratory, he launched himself into an attack on the prosecution's case and a reexamination of the evidence presented over these past five days. He made no effort to deny that his client was guilty of defrauding an insurance company and had probably been guilty of the same thing before. He described in minute detail how Holmes came to the Callowhill Street house and found that his friend, who had been so despondent the evening before, had in fact killed himself by stretching out on the attic floor with a towel over his face and allowing chloroform to drip repeatedly on the cloth at a speed just fast enough to render him at first unconscious and then kill him. Since the insurance would not pay in the event of suicide, Rotan went on, Pitezel beseeched Holmes in a cipher note—unfortunately lost and therefore not entered into evidence—to dispose of the evidence of suicide and make his death appear to be accidental, and this was what Holmes endeavored to do. Stronger and higher he constructed his argument for suicide, citing the decedent's conspiracy with Holmes, to which both Pitezel's wife and eldest daughter were in varying degrees privy. He cited the ridiculousness of a man such as Holmes, sauntering out of his room on a Sunday morning and going casually to the abode of his friend, who was larger and stronger by far, and doing him in.

As Graham had done to his own advantage, Rotan occasionally quoted from the trial record certain testimony given in evidence that went far to preclude the possibility of murder and enhance the probability of suicide. He asked the jurors to bear in mind the powerful testimony of the Commonwealth's own star witness, Dr. Henry Leffman, in which it was stated that an individual could commit—and individuals successfully *had* committed—suicide through the inhalation of chloroform. He then reconstructed in telling manner a reasonable version of the suicide.

What was Holmes's inducement to make Mrs. Pitezel

travel with him the way he did? It was, Rotan said, simply an effort to keep viable in her the belief that Benjamin Pitezel was alive so that she would not break with him and perhaps, in her grief or anger, purposely or accidentally, reveal to authorities the nature of the hoax gone wrong. Why did Holmes elect to go to Philadelphia rather than to Texas when arrested? It was, Rotan said, because the crime he had committed in Philadelphia was *less* severe than the one in Texas. He went back over the death scene and built his case for the suicide. He made a strong case for Holmes's not having committed murder in so stupid a manner and he hammered home the idea that the district attorney had presented his summation in a masterly manner and they must not allow themselves to be swayed by his use of words and his power of rhetoric; that they must base their judgment on the *evidence* that was presented, not on words.

"I now let this case go to you," he concluded, "with a great deal of confidence; so much confidence that we have not put on a defense. We feel the Commonwealth has failed in removing the reasonable doubt, and that we could safely rely upon this case going to you and your rendering a verdict of not guilty. This poor man has endured suffering long and undoubtedly will suffer—if not here, in other places—for a long while, and I simply say that we hope and fully expect you will render a verdict of acquittal."

Rotan's summation ended at 4:30 P.M. and had run just over two hours. There was a sense of relieved tension when he finished, a general releasing of breaths that resulted in a pervading sigh and the shuffling of many feet as he returned to the defense table. Holmes nodded as he approached and leaned over the rail of the dock to shake his hand in appreciation, but neither man smiled.

Judge J. Michael Arnold tapped his gavel and immediately set about giving his charge to the jury. His talk lasted for over an hour, as he reviewed the case for the twelve good men and true in the jury box, but its crux was in its conclusion.

"Consider this defendant's case calmly, considerately and patiently," he said, "and render such a verdict as approves itself to your conscience on the evidence in the case. You must bring your minds to the one question—the one case on trial before you—the case of the charge against this defendant of the murder of Benjamin F. Pitezel on September second, eighteen ninety-four, and say from the evidence in the case whether he is guilty or not guilty of the offense charged. You *must* decide it upon the evidence and the evidence *only*! I have no doubt that if you do all that, if you will adhere to the evidence, you will have no trouble in reaching a righteous verdict.

"If, after considering the testimony, you are unable to come to the conclusion that he is guilty—that there is some doubt about it—and you hesitate, or, in other words, you are not fairly satisfied by the evidence of his guilt—he is entitled to the benefit of the doubt and should be acquitted for that reason. Likewise, if there is no doubt in your mind, but if upon a consideration of the entire evidence, you are firmly convinced of his guilt, that it is a case of murder as charged and he is guilty of the offense, you should say so. If you believe the death was willful, deliberate murder, with intent to take life, you must say he is guilty of murder... and murder in the first degree. That is law. That is reason. That is justice."

At 5:40 P.M. the twelve jurors, under escort of a team of court officers, filed from the box and out of the courtroom to the jury room to engage in their deliberations. Holmes was smiling faintly as he was taken back to his cell in the building, but those closest to him saw that his hands were trembling.

Again Judge Arnold rapped his gavel to quell the courtroom buzz. As order was restored, he spoke briefly. "I will remain in this building until midnight, if necessary. If the jury has not reached its verdict by that time, I will leave here and return to court at ten o'clock tomorrow morning. This court now stands in temporary recess."

A babble of voices broke out as he rose and disappeared into his chambers. The spectators knew it could be a considerable while before the jury returned, yet not a seat was vacated. There was a "feel" that a verdict would be reached quickly.

Precisely three hours later the word swept through the crowd that the jury was coming in. District Attorney George Graham and his special assistant, Thomas Barlow, entered and moved directly to their table. The loud command came—"All rise!"—and Judge J. Michael Arnold entered and sat at the bench. The spectators sat down and then the jury filed in, expressions unreadable, and took their seats in the jury box. A heavy silence filled the room and then the side door opened and the defendant was led in and escorted to the dock. He did not sit down, but stood facing the bench, his hands clasped behind his back. His only sign of nervousness was occasionally licking lips that persisted in going dry.

"Jurors," the clerk of the court said loudly, "look upon the prisoner. Prisoner, look upon the jurors. How say you, gentlemen of the jury? Do you find the prisoner at the bar, Herman W. Mudgett, alias H. H. Holmes, guilty of the murder of Benjamin F. Pitezel, or not guilty?"

Linford L. Biles, foreman of the jury, rose. He was a tall, well-dressed man who was chief payroll clerk of the Atlantic Oil Company. He cleared his throat faintly and then spoke in a firm, clear voice.

"Guilty of murder in the first degree."

Sam Rotan entered Holmes's cell at exactly 8 A.M. on May 7, 1896.

Holmes, clad in an ill-fitting black suit having a cutaway coat, was sitting at his little desk, busily writing, and he smiled brightly at his attorney.

"You look all right," Rotan said, shaking hands with him. "A lot better than you looked last night. Been up long?"

"Shows what a good night's sleep'll do for you," Holmes said. "I never slept better. Got up at six. This is the shank of the day, Sam. Have a seat."

Rotan sat down on the edge of the cot and cocked his head slightly as he studied his client. "Are you nervous?"

"Do I look nervous?" He stretched out his arm and held his hand in front of the lawyer's face. There was no sign of a tremble.

"Not at all," Rotan said, smiling. "I don't think I could hold up that well if I were in your position." He paused and then spoke more seriously. "I want you to know how sorry I am. We tried everything we could."

"I know that," Holmes said briskly, "and you don't need to apologize. No one could have done more. Look, Sam, don't feel so bad. I read the initial appeal you and Shoemaker submitted and it couldn't have been presented any better. So what happened? They rejected it and said I had to hang. Then I read your appeal last month to Governor Hastings and

I don't see how he was able to deny clemency. But he did. There was nothing more you could do, Sam. Their minds are made up and I've accepted that now."

"It didn't help your cause any when you sold that confession," Rotan reminded.

"We needed the money, so why not? As I say, 'their minds were made up anyway."

They were referring to the incident of a month ago when Hall Caine, a representative of the William Randolph Hearst Corporation, visited Holmes in this Moyamensing Prison cell and offered him $10,000 for an exclusive confession. He'd given it—a fanciful and gruesome narration of his life in which he admitted to killing twenty-seven people and filled in all the gory details. Included in the list were Minnie and Nannie Williams, Julia and Pearl Conner, Emeline Cigrand, Wade Warner and Bob Leacock, among many others. Often the revelations involved disappearances not heretofore attributed to Holmes. The Hearst people loved it and dutifully paid the agreed-upon fee to Rotan. There was a lot in it that was true, and the fact that it was also packed with information that was patently—and provably—false had not discouraged the syndicate in the least. The lengthy "Holmes Confession," as it was headlined, was published in newspapers all over the country.

"Well," Holmes said after a moment, "we've still got a little time left, so we better get busy with it."

"Just about everything's been taken care of, so far as I know."

"The vultures are gathering, I take it?"

Rotan became glum. "Already. Twenty or thirty out there when I came in and more coming all the time."

"They've been waiting for this," Holmes said. He shrugged. "Why deprive them? Is Geyer going to be here?"

"Yes."

"Good man. Brilliant. Hell of a detective. I couldn't believe it when he backtracked me like that and put everything together. Hell of a detective," he repeated, chuckling ruefully. "Do you know, he visited me a few weeks ago. Said he wanted me to tell him the truth—'For once in your life, Holmes, just this once, between you and me only, please,' is what he said to me."

"Truth about what?"

"About the number of people I have killed."

Rotan hesitated. "Did you tell him?"

"I told him that as near as I could remember, I had killed one hundred and thirty-three people."

Rotan's mouth opened. At last some words came, dry and scratchy. "And was that the truth?"

Holmes grinned. "Are you sure you really want to know, Sam?"

The lawyer thought about it and then shook his head. "No. No, I don't."

Holmes released a strange little giggle uncharacteristic of him. After a moment he spoke again. "Have you heard anything more on possible corpse-snatching?"

"A man came into my office yesterday," Rotan said, his eyes glinting angrily. "Offered me five thousand dollars if I could deliver your body to him. I threw the son of a bitch out of the office. Bodily."

Holmes reached out and put his hand on Rotan's arm. "Thanks," he said. "I want no one to get my body, either by buying it or stealing it. You've arranged for the cement?"

"All taken care of," Rotan told him. "O'Rourke's handling the funeral and he knows exactly what to do. The burial plot's all ready in Holy Cross Cemetery. Did you get to see a priest?"

"Two of them. P. J. Dailey and Henry McPake. Church of the Annunciation. They came while I was eating breakfast." He laughed as he remembered. "Couldn't believe I had such an appetite on my execution day. They're going to chant some mumbo-jumbo as I walk those last steps. Incidentally, I've asked that you be allowed to walk up to the gallows with me. They hemmed and hawed a little but finally said okay. I hope you don't mind. I'd like you close by, Sam." His eyes abruptly became overbright and he turned and indicated a stack of envelopes and documents on one side of the desk. "These letters and things I've written are for you to take care of. Mail the letters. The rest are self-explanatory."

"As good as done," Rotan told him.

A silence fell between them. At last it was Rotan who broke it. "I wish," he said, "I had had more to give you in my summation—that I had been more forceful, more convincing. I thought I was, but I look back and see that I fell through."

"No," Holmes said. "I don't think anyone could have made an argument for me that would have helped. Their minds were made up before they ever left the courtroom."

Rotan looked at him sharply, wondering if he knew. He tried to think of something to say, but Holmes spoke first.

"Did you think I wouldn't hear about it?" he asked bitterly. "You can't keep something like that a secret. One minute! Christ, Sam, *one minute!* That's all it took that goddamned jury to find me guilty. On a voice vote! And then they sat in that fucking jury room for three hours for appearance's sake—*appearance's!*—so they would give the impression of having deliberated like proper Philadelphians should. So you see, no matter what you or anyone else might have said, it would have made no difference at all. They had the noose on my neck from the moment they became a jury."

They fell silent again for a short while and then, at Holmes's suggestion, began tying up loose ends as best they could. And then the time had run out and, with Prison Superintendent Perkins and Philadelphia County Sheriff Clement leading the way, Holmes was taken to the black-painted Moyamensing Prison gallows. It was exactly 10 A.M. The white-robed, crucifix-holding priests, Fathers P. J. Dailey and Henry McPake, walked up the thirteen steps on either side of him, chanting the *Miserere*, while Sam Rotan and Assistant Prison Superintendent Paul Richardson were close behind. Fifty-one tickets of admission to the execution had been distributed to selected people by Sheriff Clement but, to his intense irritation, the number present was nearly double that, due to prison inspectors and guards bringing their own unauthorized friends. Among those in attendance, though not close together, were the president of Fidelity Mutual, L. G. Fouse, and Detective Frank P. Geyer.

"If you have any final words to say," Sheriff Clement told Holmes, "you may say them now."

Holmes stepped to the front of the scaffolding platform and placed his hands on the low rail. He looked down at the body of spectators arced on the grounds before the gallows. When he spoke, his voice was without quaver and clearly audible to all in attendance.

"Gentlemen, I have very few words to say. In fact, I would make no remarks at this time were it not for the feeling that if I did not speak, it would imply that I acquiesced in my execution. I only wish to say that the extent of the wrongdoing I am guilty of, in taking human life, is the killing of two women. They died by my hands as the results of criminal operations. I also wish to state, so that no chance of misunderstanding may exist hereafter, that I am not guilty of taking the lives of any of the Pitezel family, either the three children or their father, Benjamin F. Pitezel, for whose death I am now to be hanged. I have never committed murder. That is all I have to say."

He turned and placed a hand on Rotan's shoulder and smiled at him. He enfolded him in a strong embrace and murmured, "Goodbye, Sam. You've done all you could."

Rotan could make no reply. As soon as Holmes released him, he turned and clattered down the stairs. Holmes watched him go and then, at the bidding of the priests, kneeled and prayed. He came to his feet, then shook hands with Fathers Dailey and McPake. As they stepped aside he buttoned his coat and then nodded to the prison officials standing to one side. Richardson stepped forward self-consciously, pulled Holmes's hands behind him and handcuffed them there. Clement and Perkins descended from the scaffolding as this was being done.

All that remained was to pull the black cloth hood and then the noose over Holmes's head, but Richardson became very nervous and fumbled. Holmes smiled at him and spoke with a note of irony. "Take your time about it. You know, I'm in no hurry."

Detective Frank P. Geyer stood toward the rear of the crowd assembled to watch the execution of Holmes. The coolness of the prisoner as he delivered his last words had struck him hard. He thought bitterly of the bodies of the Pitezel girls that he had discovered in their shallow grave and the pitiable remains of Howard Pitezel found in the ashes. And he thought of his own daughter, Esther, and of Martha. His stomach twisted and he wished he could be the one to pull the trap.

He wanted to yell at the man: You couldn't even tell the truth right at the end, could you? Why not, Holmes? Why keep up the charade? What possible difference does it make now?

Holmes's smile—the faintly smirking smile—just as the hood was drawn over his head! Geyer gritted his teeth. How it galled him, that smile. He wished the man had trembled, that he had wept and wailed, that he had begged for mercy or cursed his executioner or society. But he had merely smiled and Geyer knew he would never forget it. A thought struck him and with it his anger vanished: Maybe the smile had been a good thing after all, because now the doubts that had assailed Geyer so terribly these past months were suddenly gone. Now he knew—*knew!*—that what he himself had done was right. Not just, perhaps, and certainly not legal, but *right*. So... very... right.

He watched as Paul Richardson finished adjusting the black hood over Holmes's face and head and then the heavy hemp noose; watched as Richardson snugged it to the side of the condemned man's neck; watched as Richardson stepped back and pulled a white handkerchief from his breast pocket and held it aloft; watched as the cloth fluttered from Richardson's hand.

It was 10:12 A.M.

The trapdoor upon which Holmes stood opened in the center and he plummeted through amidst the clatter. The rope jerked him up short, snapped his head sharply to the left and caused his legs to flail wildly for an instant. The hooded man's torso heaved and his hands clenched and unclenched twice. One leg lifted slightly for an instant and then fell back. The figure became still and the swaying and turning quickly slowed.

Geyer continued to watch, paying no attention to the sound of revulsion that came from some of the spectators, ignoring the two who collapsed in faints and the two others who had turned and bent over and were retching disgustingly. He watched the two attending physicians—Doctors Clarkson Sharp and Benjamin F. Butcher—approach the swinging figure and feel for the pulse. A three-step platform was brought and in turn they mounted it and pressed their ears to the chest for the telltale thud of a lingering heartbeat. They took their time and checked over and again and put their heads together to confer and then checked one final time. One of them—Dr. Butcher—glanced at his watch and then stepped apart and faced toward the prison officials.

"At ten twenty-seven A.M., May seventh, eighteen hundred and ninety-six, we do hereby pronounce and declare Herman W. Mudgett, alias H. H. Holmes, to be dead."

Superintendent Perkins ordered that the body remain hanging by the neck for another fifteen minutes before being taken down. When this time had passed, a flatbed wagon was brought into place beneath the hanging man and he was lowered into it. The noose had sunk deeply into the flesh but Superintendent Perkins, who ordered it and the hood removed, would not allow it to be cut. There was considerable difficulty involved in loosening it, but the job was finally done. The face was grossly distorted. The doctors made another examination and announced that the neck was broken.

Through all of this, Geyer watched.

He was still watching when, shortly before noon, the undertaker's wagon was admitted to the prison yard through the Reed Street gate and the body of Holmes was transferred to it. In large gold letters in a semicircle on the side of the enclosed death van were the words *J. J. O'Rourke Funeral Home*. The corpse was stretched out in a plain pine box and then driven out through the same gate that had been entered. Geyer strode to his waiting carriage and followed. At Tenth and Tasker streets, the van turned into the driveway at the O'Rourke establishment and pulled around in back. Geyer stopped his carriage and alighted and followed them.

A heavier-duty wagon was there with a larger box on it. Five barrels of cement and sand were ready. The waiting team of men, at O'Rourke's direction, mixed the material into concrete and poured a ten-inch layer in the bottom of the larger box. They let it take a set for ten or fifteen minutes and then Holmes's body was lifted from the smaller box and placed atop the layer of fresh concrete. A square of cloth was placed over the dead man's face and another layer of concrete was poured over him, covering him completely, and more added until the box was all but filled and there was no blemish on the concrete surface. The lid was carefully nailed in place and then the journey begun, southwestward along the Delaware River Road and finally, over three hours later, just after crossing the county line into Delaware County, the final destination was reached—Holy Cross Cemetery.

All this way, Frank Geyer followed them.

An oversized grave excavation—ten feet deep, eight feet long and five feet wide—had been prepared and was waiting. The six workmen who had ridden the coffin wagon had considerable difficulty sliding the enormously heavy box to the wagon's edge and letting it thump to the ground. Once on the ground, however, they were unable to budge it farther and the grave was still six or seven feet away. They tugged and shoved and succeeded only in breaking off the rope handles. Help was sent for and seven more husky men arrived. The thirteen men put their shoulders to it and strained mightily. Inch by excruciating inch the box ground a path on the earth until at last it teetered at the edge and was tipped into the hole, landing on one end and turning completely over so that the embedded corpse was face down. There was no way to turn it right side up. No one even suggested trying. Tomorrow the grave would be filled from the adjacent mound of earth from which two shovels projected.

It was late in the day now. The sun had set and a chill little breeze sprang up in the oncoming dusk. The workers went their way and finally no one was left except one man standing quietly at the lip of the grave.

Detective Frank P. Geyer.

He reached into the side pocket of his coat and removed a badly worn, blue-covered copy of a book: Harriet Beecher Stowe's *Uncle Tom's Cabin*. He opened it to the back cover and lifted the inner lining flap that he had slit open so long ago, on that first train ride from Philadelphia to Cincinnati. As Holmes had said they were, three folded letter sheets filled with writing were concealed there. The pages, still there, had been studied by him over many hours and now he knew would be the final time. It was an extensive letter, seemingly incomprehensible at first, since it was written all in cipher. But beneath each of the lines, in a smaller hand, it had been deciphered. The smaller hand was Geyer's. He had cracked the code by utilizing the key for the coded advertisement that Holmes had written for District Attorney Graham to place in the *New York Herald* as a supposed message to Minnie Williams. Even with this key to the code, it had taken long hours of difficult work for Geyer to decode the numbers and letters and write them out. He had done it mostly in hotel rooms and railroad cars. And when he had it all decoded and written out, he had been stunned at its message. And though it was evidence of the greatest importance—evidence that would have reversed the verdict ultimately handed down—he had withheld it; the only time in his life he had deliberately committed a felony.

He read the letter again now, the words still visible enough in the growing twilight.

Sptbr. 1–'94

HOLMES:

Its nearly midnight and I havent slept for two days and Im very tired of all this. Nothing has gone right for us on this whole thing and now we didnt get the stiff that was promised and that ruins everything. I knew you were only trying to get me back on the track earlier tonight and I thank you but its no good. This afternoon after getting the letter from Carrie and her telling me how bad things were for them I sent her a little letter telling her we were bust here and I was coming home. I meant it when I wrote that but I have changed my mind. My coming home wouldnt do nobody any good and it would be more of the same all over again. You know I been sick for a long time and its getting worse. And the drinking too. So I thought it all over and decided that I didnt want to go on with any of this anymore. I mean anything, not just the insurance thing here which was a good idea and it would be a shame to lose it all just because we couldnt get a body that looked like mine. Well old friend now we have got one. Mine. When you read this I will be dead a few hours already because Im killing myself as soon as I finish this. You will find me up in the attic. Now its up to you to do with my body what you told me to do with the stiff we were supposed to get, so nobody thinks it was suicide. Just fix me up like we talked about so it looks like an accident so the insurance will get paid to Carrie. I havent done a whole lot of good for her and the kids up to now so this is the one thing I can do that will help them all out of a tight spot. You got to make sure nobody ever sees this letter but you. Even Carrie has got to believe it was an accident killed me. You take care of Carrie and my children Holmes. We been through a lot together over the years and you owe this to me. Make sure they are taken care of good as I would have if this whole thing had gone through the way we planned it.

Goodbye Holmes.

BEN

Geyer refolded the sheets and replaced them in the back flap. He closed the book and looked at the scruffy front cover. The words that Alice had written in her undelivered letter upon finishing the book came back to him now:

I have just finished Uncle Tom's Cabin and it is a nice book but I don't believe anybody could be so cruel as that to other people so much.

The book had traveled a long way. Far enough. He tossed it into the grave and it landed with a plop on the wooden upward-facing bottom of the concrete-filled coffin. He stepped to the mound of earth and pulled out one of the shovels sticking in the dirt. It took five shovelfuls of dirt tossed atop the book before no edges of the volume remained visible. Satisfied, he stuck the shovel back into the dirt pile.

And then Detective Frank P. Geyer turned and walked away.

Author's Note

*I*n this present day we have all become uncomfortably familiar with the terrible phenomenon known as the serial murderer. As opposed to a mass murderer, who kills a number of people at the same time, the serial murderer is a person who kills a great many people—occasionally numbering in the hundreds—over a span of many weeks or months, sometimes years. And, unlike the mass murderer—who is usually almost immediately caught or killed or takes his own life—the serial murder plans his killings with uncanny ability and an incredible knack for escaping detection.

Henry Lee Lucas, Ted Bundy, David "Son of Sam" Berkowitz, John Wayne Gacy and Juan Corona represent a few of our present-day convicted serial murders. But while the term "serial murderer" is relatively new, the *fact* of serial murders is not. William Burke and William Hare were serial murders who were caught and finally executed for their crimes in 1829. Jack the Ripper was a serial murderer of the 1890s who was never caught.

Herman W. Mudgett, alias H. H. Holmes, was such a serial murderer—perhaps among the worst. In various confessions and statements he admitted from twenty-seven to one hundred thirty-three murders, although the actual total was probably over one hundred fifty and may have topped two hundred. This novel is based on his life and incredible career. In order to provide the narrative flow requisite of a novel, certain liberties have been taken with dialogue and various incidents. Nevertheless, the basic elements of this story are true and the people mentioned are, in large measure, real people who lived the roles in which they are depicted. Many of the more grisly atrocities committed by Herman W. Mudgett, alias H. H. Holmes, have been omitted or modified, simply because they are well beyond the limits of palatability and to have chronicled them would have served no purpose beyond that of sensationalism.

So abundantly documented was the Holmes Case, as it came to be known, that it would have taken approximately six books of the size of this one to report faithfully every aspect known and recorded. Even though his defense attorneys presented no case of their own to counteract that of the Commonwealth, the trial transcript totals 589 single-spaced typewritten pages. Newspaper and magazine accounts were easily twice that voluminous and a number of books written about the turn of the century told the Mudgett/Holmes story from a variety of viewpoints. A close study of the evidence of the case indicates that, ironically, for all the many murders he committed, Mudgett/Holmes was finally convicted and executed for the murder of a man who actually committed suicide.

What motivates the serial murderer? Society still cannot answer that question. Perhaps it never will. Yet perhaps, as present-day research projects into the subject mature and increase our understanding as well as point out behavioral patterns and possible causes, we may learn how to prevent one of the most dread and least understood of mankind's maladies.

—ALLAN W. ECKERT

Everglades, Florida

ABOUT THE AUTHOR

ALLAN W. ECKERT, recently awarded an Honorary Doctorate in Humane Letters, Bowling Green State University, Ohio, is a historian, naturalist and playwright who has written twenty-nine books, including the highly acclaimed *Winning of America* series and his new children's fantasy series, *The Mesmerian Animals*. A five-time Pulitzer Prize nominee, he has also written over two hundred *Wild Kingdom* television scripts. He has received many awards for his writing, including a Newbery Honor Book award for *Incident at Hawk's Hill*, the Friends of American Writers award for *Wild Season*, and the Ohioana Book Award for *The Frontiersmen*. He has also received an Emmy Award for television writing.

TRUTH IS ALL TOO OFTEN
STRANGER THAN FICTION

These investigations into the world of true crimes prove just that point.

BANTAM
SHOP·AT·HOME
C·A·T·A·L·O·G

Special Offer
Buy a Bantam Book
for only 50¢.

Now you can have an up-to-date listing of Bantam's hundreds of titles plus take advantage of our unique and exciting bonus book offer. A special offer which gives you the opportunity to purchase a Bantam book for only 50¢. Here's how!

By ordering any five books at the regular price per order, you can also choose any other single book listed (up to a $4.95 value) for just 50¢. Some restrictions do apply, but for further details why not send for Bantam's listing of titles today!

Just send us your name and address and we will send you a catalog!